외투기업의 No.1 노무법인
KangNam Labor Law Firm

Practical Manual
on Labor Law (11/20)

Labor Inspection Manual

근로감독 매뉴얼

Dr. Bongsoo Jung
Labor Attorney / Ph.D. in Law
공인노무사/법학박사 **정 봉 수**

Taewook Ahn
Labor Consultant
전문위원 **안 태 욱**

- Labor Law Practical Manuals
① *Work Force Restructuring*
② *Foreign Employment and Immigration*
③ *Lawful Dismissal*
④ *Labor Union*
⑤ *Wage*
⑥ *Working Hours, Holidays and Leave*
⑦ *Irregular Employment and 'Employee' Status*
⑧ *Employment Contract*
⑨ *Industrial Accident Compensation*
⑩ *Preventing Workplace & Sexual Harassment*
⑪ *Labor Inspection Preparation*
⑫ *Rules of Employment*

실무자를 위한 노동법 실무 매뉴얼 시리즈
① 구조조정 매뉴얼
② 외국인 고용과 비자 매뉴얼
③ 해고 매뉴얼
④ 노동조합 매뉴얼
⑤ 임금 매뉴얼
⑥ 근로시간, 휴일, 휴가 매뉴얼
⑦ 비정규직과 근로자성 판단 매뉴얼
⑧ 근로계약 매뉴얼
⑨ 산재보상 매뉴얼
⑩ 직장 내 괴롭힘과 성희롱 예방 매뉴얼
⑪ 근로감독 준비 매뉴얼
⑫ 취업규칙 매뉴얼

강남노무법인

Preface

On June 24, 2024, a fire broke out at the 'Aricel' battery manufacturing plant, resulting in the deaths of 23 people, 18 of whom were temporary foreign workers. Foreigners are not permitted to engage in temporary or dispatched work. At the time, out of approximately 100 workers on-site, around 50 were illegally employed foreigners. This illegal employment practice often only comes to light and is corrected when major accidents occur. The previous Moon Jae-in administration hired around 1,000 labor inspectors to conduct regular labor inspections. However, the current government has refrained from regular inspections, leading to the spread of illegal foreign dispatches and temporary work. To prevent illegal labor law violations like those seen in the Aricel tragedy, proactive labor inspections are essential.

The urgent need to create this 'Labor Inspection Manual' arose from experiencing the importance of labor inspections first-hand during the Aricel disaster. This manual consists of three chapters. Chapter 1 presents actual labor inspection cases, explaining the process of inspections and the subsequent actions required. Chapter 2 details the 'Self-Diagnosis Checklist for Compliance with Labor Relations Laws' published annually by the Ministry of Employment and Labor. Chapter 3 provides background knowledge and related cases for a comprehensive understanding of 16 different areas of labor inspection. The appendix includes instructions on how to use the labor inspection checklist available in the mobile app provided by KangNam Labor Law Firm.

It is hoped that this 'Labor Inspection Manual' will serve not only as a preparation guide for labor inspections in workplaces but also as a basic manual for companies to check their compliance with labor laws. In particular, it aims to be a guideline to prevent accidents that may occur in workplaces and to create a safe working environment.

In the publication of this book, my co-author, Legal Team Leader Tae-uk Ahn, diligently compiled and organized labor-related materials, and his advice on legal interpretations greatly enhanced the completeness of this book. I also extend my gratitude to Young-chul Jung for his editorial and publishing efforts, allowing this book to come to light. Special thanks to my long-time friend and English proofreader, Dave Crofton.

August 10, 2024
Bongsoo Jung, Taewook Ahn
Labor Attorney, PhD in Law

머리말

 2024년 6월 24일 배터리 제조업체 '아리셀' 공장에서 화재가 발생하여 23명이 사망했는데, 그 중 18명이 일용직 외국인이었다. 외국인은 용역이나 파견근무를 할 수 없다. 당시 사업장에 100여명 근무자 중 50여명이 불법적으로 사용 중인 외국인이었다고 한다. 이렇게 불법적으로 외국인을 사용하는 것이 현장에서 큰 사고가 터졌을 때에야 확인되어 시정조치를 하고 있다. 지난 문재인 정부는 근로감독관 1000여명을 뽑아서 근로감독을 주기적으로 실시하였다. 그러나 현 정부는 정기적인 근로감독을 자제하고 있어 이렇게 불법적인 외국인 파견이나 용역 사용이 확산되고 있다. 앞으로 아리셀 참사와 같은 노동법 위반의 불법적인 행태를 예방하기 위해서는 사전 예방 근로감독이 필수적이라고 생각한다.

 이번 '근로감독 매뉴얼'을 서둘러서 만들게 된 이유가 아리셀 참사를 경험하면서 근로감독의 중요성을 실감했기 때문이다. 이번 근로감독 매뉴얼은 3개의 장으로 구성하고 있다. 제1장은 실제 근로감독 사례를 제시하여 근로감독이 이루어지는 내용과 관련 후속조치를 어떻게 해야 하는지를 설명하였다. 제2장은 고용노동부가 매년 발간하고 있는 근로감독의 '노동관계법 준수 자기진단표'의 내용을 설명하였다. 제3장은 근로감독 16개의 분야에 대해 충분한 이해를 할 수 있도록 관련된 배경 지식과 관련 사례를 제시하였다. 그리고 부록에서 강남노무법인의 모바일 앱에서 제공하고 있는 근로감독 체크리스트 사용방법을 설명하였다.

 이 '근로감독 매뉴얼'이 사업장에 근로감독 준비 매뉴얼 역할뿐만 아니라 회사가 노동관계법령 준수 여부를 확인하고 법령준수의 기본 매뉴얼이 되기를 바란다. 특히, '근로감독 매뉴얼'은 사업장에서 발생할 수 있는 사고를 미연에 방지하고 안전한 사업장을 만드는 지침서로서 활용되기를 바란다.

 본서 출간에 있어 공동 집필자로서 안태욱 법무팀장님은 노무관련 자료를 모아서 잘 정리해주었고, 특히 법적인 해석 부분에 대해 조언을 많이 해주셔서 이 책의 완성도를 높여주었다. 또한 이 책이 빛을 볼 수 있도록 편집과 출판을 해주신 정영철 사장님께 감사드린다. 특히 나의 오랜 친구이자 영문교정을 맡고 있는 Dave Crofton에게도 감사드린다.

2024년 8월 10일

정봉수, 안태욱

Contents

Chapter 1. Labor Inspections

Section 1. Cases Related to Labor Inspections ·················· 5
    <Case-1> Labor Inspection and Company Follow-up Measures ············ 5
    <Case-2> Labor Inspection over Unpaid Wages for Temporary Workers ······· 9
Section 2. Regulations Basis for Labor Inspection by Labor Inspectors ···· 17

Chapter 2. Labor Inspection Checklist

1. Written Statement of Working Conditions ·················· 25
2. Preservation of Employee Registers and Contract Documents ············ 28
3. Payment of Various Money and Goods such as Wages ·················· 29
4. Violation of limits on working hours and overtime ·················· 35
5. Granting recess hours ·················· 38
6. Paid holidays ·················· 39
7. Annual paid leave ·················· 41
8. Children and Maternity Protection ·················· 44
9. Rules of Employment ·················· 51
10. Payment of retirement benefits ·················· 55
11. Prevention of workplace harassment ·················· 59
12. Observation of minimum wage ·················· 61
13. Prevention of sexual harassment in the workplace ·················· 63

차 례

제1장 근로감독

제1절 근로감독 관련 사례 ·· 5
    <사례 1> 일반기업 근로 감독 ·· 5
    <사례 2> 비정규직 임금체불 진정에 따른 근로감독 ········ 9
제2절 근로감독관의 근로감독 근거 규정 ···························· 17

제2장 근로감독 체크리스트

1. 근로조건 서면명시 ·· 25
2. 근로자 명부 및 계약서류 보존 ······································ 28
3. 임금 등 각종 금품 지급 ·· 29
4. 근로시간 및 연장근로 한도 위반 ·································· 35
5. 휴게시간 부여 ·· 38
6. 유급휴일 부여 ·· 39
7. 연차유급휴가 부여 ·· 41
8. 모성보호와 연소자 ·· 44
9. 취업규칙 ··· 51
10 퇴직급여 지급 ·· 55
11. 직장 내 괴롭힘 예방 ·· 59
12. 최저임금 준수 ·· 61
13. 직장 내 성희롱 예방 ·· 63

14. Prohibition of Sex Discrimination in Employment 66

15. Prohibition of discrimination against non-regular workers 70

16. Establishment of labor-management council 74

Chapter 3. Explanations of Labor Inspections

Section 1. Written Statement of Working Conditions 81

Section 2. Preservation of Employee Registers and Contract Documents 89

Section 3. Payment of Various Money and Goods such as Wages 90

Section 4. Violation of limits on working hours and overtime 114

Section 5. Granting recess hours 122

Section 6. Paid holidays 129

Section 7. Annual paid leave 134

Section 8. Children and Maternity Protection 147

Section 9. Rules of Employment 161

Section 10. Payment of retirement benefits 181

Section 11. Prevention of workplace harassment 194

Section 12. Observation of minimum wage 204

Section 13. Prevention of sexual harassment in the workplace 212

Section 14. Prohibition of Sex Discrimination in Employment 223

Section 15. Prohibition of discrimination against non-regular workers 230

Section 16. Establishment of labor-management council 238

⟨Appendix⟩

Introduction to the 'Labor Inspection Checklist' in the 'Labor Law App' 250

14. 고용상 성차별 금지 ·· 66

15. 비정규직 차별 금지 ·· 70

16. 노사협의회 설치 ·· 74

제3장 근로감독 체크리스트 설명자료

제1절 근로계약 작성 ·· 81

제2절 근로자 명부 및 계약서류 보존 ·· 89

제3절 임금 ·· 90

제4절 근로시간 계산의 원칙 ··· 114

제5절 휴게시간과 근로시간 설계 ··· 122

제6절 약정휴일 및 약정휴가 ··· 129

제7절 연차유급휴가 ·· 134

제8절 모성보호와 연소자 ·· 147

제9절 취업규칙 ·· 161

제10절 퇴직급여 지급 ·· 181

제11절 직장 내 괴롭힘 예방 ··· 194

제12절 최저임금법 ·· 204

제13절 직장 내 성희롱 예방 ··· 212

제14절 균등처우의 판단기준과 관련사례 ······································ 223

제15절 비정규직 근로자에 대한 차별시정제도 ···························· 230

제16절 노사협의회 설치와 운영 ·· 238

〈부록〉

'노동법 앱'의 '근로감독 체크리스트 소개 ································ 250

Chapter 1 Labor Inspections

Section 1. Cases Related to Labor Inspections
⟨Case - 1⟩ Labor Inspection and Company Follow-up Measures
⟨Case - 2⟩ Labor Inspection over Unpaid Wages for Temporary Workers

Section 2. Regulations Basis for Labor Inspection by Labor Inspectors

제1장 근로감독

제1절 근로감독 관련 사례

〈사례 1〉 일반기업 근로 감독

〈사례 2〉 비정규직 임금체불 진정에 따른 근로감독

제2절 근로감독관의 근로감독 근거 규정

Section 1. Cases Related to Labor Inspections

Section 1-1: Labor Inspection and Company Follow-up Measures[1]

1. Summary

A labor inspector informed a company (hereinafter called "Company T") located in Seoul on October 17, 2019 of his plans to audit the company. He visited the workplace 3 days later on October 20 to learn whether the company was following appropriate labor standards. While inspecting the company Rules of Employment and payroll documents, the labor inspector noticed many problems: unpaid overtime allowance and compensation for unused annual leave, incorrect calculation of average wages for severance pay, some violations of the Rules of Employment, no Labor-Management Council, and no education on sexual harassment prevention. On November 17, the labor inspector sent a correction order to Company T regarding the above Labor Standards violations.

The company hired a labor attorney to implement the correction order. This labor attorney recalculated overtime allowance, etc., considering the company's characteristics as an IT business and the working situations of the dispatch employees. He also assisted the company in meeting the correction deadline by adding supplements to the Rules of Employment, establishing a Labor-Management Council, and correcting the average wage calculations for employees who had left the company to make up for the inadequate severance payments. As use of annual leave and overtime was too ambiguous to calculate, employees' written explanations on actual use were considered in recalculation. When the company calculated unpaid wages in accordance with the correction order, the total amount to be paid came out to about ₩60 million, but this was adjusted by confirming with the employees (through written statements) whether the leave had actually not been used, and whether the recorded overtime had been done. After all this, the company and the labor inspector agreed that the total amount not paid was about ₩2 million. Company T finished carrying out its correction order by paying the confirmed unpaid wages to the appropriate employees. What follows is a detailed explanation of how the company was able to avoid unnecessary costs and meet the labor inspector's requirements.

---

[1] This case was represented by Labor Attorney Bongsoo Jung at KangNam Labor Law Firm. (November 2019)

제1절 근로감독 관련 사례

제1-1절 일반기업의 근로감독과 사업주의 조치내용[1]

1. 개요

　근로감독관은 2019. 10. 17. 서울에 위치한 한 회사(이하, "T회사"라 함)에 사업장 방문 점검을 한다고 통보한 후, 실제로 2019. 10. 20 사업장을 방문하여 근로기준 준수여부를 점검하였다. 근로감독관은 회사의 취업규칙과 급여대장 등의 서류를 점검하면서, 연장근로수당 및 연차휴가미사용수당 미지급, 퇴직금 평균임금 산정 오류, 취업규칙 일부 수정사항, 노사협의회 규정미비 및 성희롱예방교육 미실 등의 사항을 지적하였다. 근로감독관은 2019. 11. 7. 시정지시서를 회사에 발송하여 근로기준 위반사항에 대해 시정을 요구하였다.
　회사는 근로감독의 시정지시를 이행하기 위해 외부전문가인 공인노무사에게 이 지적사항에 대한 보완을 의뢰하였다. 이에 이 사건을 담당한 노무사는 IT업종의 특징과 파견근로자들의 속성을 가지고 연장근로수당 등을 재산정하였다. 시정기간 내에 미비한 취업규칙, 노사협의회 규정 등을 보완하였고, 퇴직자에 대한 잘못 산정한 평균임금을 제대로 산정하여 그 차액을 지급하였다. 그리고 사용내역이 불명확한 연차휴가나 연장근로 수당에 대해서는 근로자의 확인서를 받아 대체하였다. 근로감독관이 시정지시 한 내용에 따라 계산을 한 결과 미지급 임금이 약 6000만 원으로 집계되었다. 그러나 근로자들의 실질적 휴가사용 및 연장근로 내역 확인을 통해서 미지급 임금이 재조정되었고, 근로감독관과 함께 최종적으로 미지급된 임금은 200만 원이라는 데에 대해 결론을 내리게 되었다. 이에 사용자는 확정된 미지급 임금을 해당 근로자들에게 지급함으로써 근로감독관의 지적 내용을 시정할 수 있었다.
　이하에서는 근로감독관 시정지시 내용과 회사의 조치상항에 대해 구체적으로 살펴본다.

---

[1] 강남노무법인 정봉수 노무사가 T 회사를 대리하여 처리한 사건 (2019년 11월)

Section 1. Cases Related to Labor Inspections

2. Violations of the Labor Standard

When visiting Company T and inspecting the working conditions on October 20, 2019, the labor inspector noticed the violations listed above (unpaid allowance for unused annual leave, incorrect calculation of overtime allowance and average wages, etc.). The company received a correction order for the following items on November 17, 2019.

Related LSA Articles	Correction Order
1. Article 17 of the Labor Standards Act	The company shall stipulate details regarding annual leave (according to Article 60 of the LSA) additionally in the employment contract, and then submit a copy to the Labor Office.
2. Article 56 of the LSA	The company shall pay the additional amount by recalculating overtime allowances for 30 employees including Kim 00, and then submit evidence of its payment.
3. Article 36 of the LSA	The company shall pay the additional amount of severance pay for 9 resigned employees including Lee 00, by correcting average wage calculations, and then submit evidence of its payment.
4. Article 60 of the LSA	The company shall pay compensation for annual leave unused in 2018 to 28 employees including Park 00, and then submit evidence of its payment.
5. Article 94 of the LSA	The company shall revise its Rules of Employment by updating the details on maternity leave so that they are in accordance with Article 74 of the Labor Standards Act, and report to the Labor Office.
6. Article 4 of the LMC Act	The company shall establish a Labor Management Council and report its operational rules to the Labor Office.

2. 회사의 근로기준 위반내용

근로감독관은 2019.10.20. T 회사를 방문하여 근로기준에 대해 점검한 결과 연차휴가수당 미지급, 연장근로수당 계산 오류, 평균임금산정 오류 등을 지적하였다. 2019.11.7.에 근로감독관은 아래의 7가지 사항에 대해 시정지시를 내렸다.

위반 법조항	시 정 지 시 내 용
1. 근로기준법 제17조	근로계약서상 근로기준법 제60조에 따른 연차유급휴가 부여 사항을 추가로 기재하여 그 사본을 제출하시기 바랍니다.
2. 근로기준법 제56조	김○○ 등 30명에 대한 연장근로수당 차액분을 지급하고 그 결과를 제출하여 주시기 바랍니다.
3. 근로기준법 제36조	퇴직자 이○○ 등 9명에 대한 평균임금 산정 착오에 따른 퇴직금 차액을 지급하고 그 결과를 제출하시기 바랍니다.
4. 근로기준법 제60조	박 ○○ 등 28명에 대한 2018년도 연차휴가미사용에 대한 수당을 지급하고 그 결과를 제출하시기 바랍니다.
5. 근로기준법 제94조	취업규칙 중 임산부 보호 조항에 대하여 근로기준법 제74조에 따른 임산부 보호 규정에 맞게 변경하여 취업규칙을 변경신고 하시기 바랍니다.
6. 근로자참여 및 협력증진에 관한 법률 제4조	노사협의회를 설치하고 그 협의회 규정을 신고하시기 바랍니다.

Section 1. Cases Related to Labor Inspections

| 7. Article 13 of the Equal Employ. Act | The company shall set up training on preventing sexual harassment at work during 2019, and then submit evidence that this has been done. |

The labor inspector audited [Company T's] working conditions on Oct 20, 2019, confirmed the existence of labor standard violations and issues the correction orders above. The company shall post this correction order on the notice board where employees can see easily, and then give to the Labor Office, by November 25, 2019, documents verifying that these corrections have been carried out.

3. Correction of the Violations

(1) Categorization of Company T's business

Company T is a software developer (Business Rules Engine: BRE) composed of project teams. When a client requests development of its system, Company T sends the project team members to the client's office and sets up the system there. The company has a total of 48 employees: 15 engaged in management and administration at the company office, and 33 software engineers assigned to client projects. These 33 engineers were not required to attend company meetings or to otherwise report, except as specifically requested, such as at year-end meetings etc. Although annual salaries are relatively higher than that of its competitors, the company paid a fixed allowance of ₩60,000 for any overtime claim for work done during the weekend and not under the employer's supervision and control. This was recorded in the payroll files, and was the particular cause of most of the violations.

(2) Details on Company T's correction of each violation

1) **Article 17 of the LSA (Absence of an article in the employment contract related to annual leave)**

   The company included details regarding the use of annual leave in the employment contract, and then submitted one copy of the revised employment contract.

2) **Article 56 of the LSA (Recalculation of annual leave allowance and holiday work allowance)**

   The contractual working hours are 8 hours per day, 40 hours per week, with

7. 남녀고용평등법제13조	2019년도 직장내 성희롱 예방교육을 실시하고 그 결과를 제출하시기 바랍니다.

2019.10.20. 실시한 근로조건 자율개선 지원사업장 확인점검 결과 지적된 근로기준법 위반 사항에 대하여 위와 같이 시정 지시하니, 이 시정지시서를 근로자가 잘 볼 수 있는 장소에 게시하시고, 시정 결과와 게시 사실에 대한 증빙자료를 첨부하여 2019.11.25 까지 보고하시기 바랍니다.

3. 회사의 업무형태와 사업주의 조치사항

(1) 회사의 업무 형태

T 회사는 소프트웨어 개발 회사로 외부업체가 시스템 구축을 요청 받으면, 프로젝트 팀이 구성되고 당해 팀에 소속된 근로자는 외부업체에 상주하면서 근로를 제공한다. 직원은 48명이고 그 중 관리 및 행정을 담당하는 15명을 제외한 33명이 개발자들로 송년회, 기타 회사에서 특별히 열리는 회의 등에 참석하기 위해 본사에 오는 경우를 제외하고는, 본사로 출퇴근 하여야 하거나 보고를 하여야 하는 등의 의무가 없었다. 연봉수준이 동종업계에 비하여 높음에도 불구하고, 관리감독하에 있지 않은 연장근로시간에 대하여 급여대장에 특근수당이라는 항목을 넣어 일괄적으로 1일 6만 원으로 산정하여 지급한 점이 이번 점검에서 문제로 드러났다.

(2) 각 시정항목별 사업주의 조치 내용

1) 근로기준법 제17조 (연차휴가 부여 내용 누락)

회사는 근로계약서에 연차휴가 사용에 관한 내용을 추가하여 재작성하였고, 그 한 부를 시정내용에 제출하였다.

2) 근로기준법 제56조 (연장근로수당 및 휴일근무수당 재정산)

T회사는 소정근로시간이 1일 8시간과 1주 40시간으로 정하고 있으며, 매일 2시간 씩 고정연장근로 수당을 지급하고 있다. 문제는 기본 연봉에 포함되지 않은 토요 휴무나 주휴일 근로에 대해 근로자가 근로한 날짜와

Section 1. Cases Related to Labor Inspections

the fixed overtime allowance paid for two hours each working day. The important point was that the company paid a fixed amount of ₩60,000 per day for overtime on Saturdays and Sundays, upon receiving email from the employees that they had worked those days. This was done as the work was outside of Company T premises, and verification was difficult any other way. The labor inspector requested that the company pay an additional allowance for actual working hours, calculated according to the standard found in the Labor Standards Act.

The company received written statements from the engineers to confirm and recalculate actual overtime and holiday working hours, as it could not independently confirm their actual working hours on Saturdays and Sundays. The company paid an additional amount to those who worked more overtime hours than what was covered by the fixed overtime allowance of ₩60,000 per day.

3) **Article 36 of the LSA (Inadequate severance pay due to incorrect calculation of average wages)**

When calculating average wages for severance pay, the company included only basic pay and bonuses, excluding overtime and other allowances. The company recalculated average wages and paid the amounts owed (approximately ₩600,000).

4) **Article 60 of the LSA (Inadequate compensation for unused annual leave)**

Each project team manager scheduled team members' leave at his/her own discretion, and provided 10 days or more leave in the middle of a project or at the end as necessary, after obtaining verbal approval from the company to do so. As the leave application form was not used, it was impossible to track and record the number of leave days used.

Compensation was not paid for unused annual leave because no record was kept of used leave. Company T confirmed the number of used leave days through written statements of all dispatched engineers and paid an allowance for only the number of days of unused leave confirmed by their statements. The company submitted to the Labor Office verification that it paid allowance and that recorded leaves were confirmed with employee statements.

5) **Article 94 of the LSA (Absence of articles in company Rules of Employment protecting pregnant employees)**

The company added missing items on premature or stillborn birth into the

시간을 적어내면 1일 6만 원으로 연장근로수당을 지급하였다는 점이다. 연장근로가 외부업체에서 이루어지는 것이므로, 사업주는 근로자가 적어낸 근로한 날짜와 시간은 전적으로 근로자들의 신청서에 의거하여 정액으로 지급하였는데, 이와 관련하여 연장근로시간에 대한 근로기준법상의 계산을 요구받았다.

T회사는 외부업체에서 근무하는 직원들에게 연장근로 내역에 대해 자필로 받아 실제로 근무한 것에 대해 재산정하였다. T회사가 외부업체에서 근무하고 있는 개발자들의 토요휴무 또는 일요일 근무를 확인 할 구체적인 방법이 없기 때문에, 해당 근로자들이 실제 근로를 하였는지의 여부에 대한 확인서를 작성하고 실제로 근로를 한 자들에 대해서는 법정 산정된 연장근로수당에서 이미 지급하였던 연장근로수당(1일 6만 원)을 제외한 나머지를 지급하였다.

3) 근로기준법 제36조 (평균임금 산정 착오로 인한 퇴직금 차액)
급여담당자가 퇴직금 계산을 위한 평균임금 산정시 기본급과 보너스만으로 하였고, 연장근로수당과 각종 수당을 누락하였다. 이로 인하여 퇴직금 계산에 착오로 발생된 미 지급된 퇴직금을 모두 지급하였다.(약 60만 원)

4) 근로기준법 제60조 (미사용 연차휴가 수당으로 미지급)
외주업체에 파견된 팀원들의 리더가 재량으로 휴가를 결정하며, 보통 프로젝트를 하는 중간에 휴식이 필요하거나 프로젝트가 끝나는 경우 개발자들에게 10일 이상의 휴가가 부여되며, 팀 리더는 회사에 구두보고 승인을 득하여 사용하였다. 휴가 사용시 휴가신청서를 제출하지 않았기 때문에 휴가일수 추적이 불가능하였다.

이 미사용 연차휴가수당의 미지급 문제는 휴가 기록 등 관리가 철저하지 않아 발생된 것이므로, 실제 근로자들이 지난해에 사용하였던 연차휴가 일수를 서면으로 작성하게 하여 실제로 미사용 휴가 잔여일 수에 대해서만 수당으로 지급하였다. 이 부분에 있어 수당지급 내역과 근로자들이 자필로 작성한 휴가 사용자필 확인서를 제출하였다.

5) 근로기준법 제94조 (임산부 보호규정 법 변경 내용 누락)
취업규칙에 임산부의 조산, 사산 휴가 내용이 누락되어 이를 추가하여

maternity leave section in the Rules of Employment, and submitted it to the Labor Office with evidence of the fact that the company received majority agreement from the employees on the revised rules. A copy of its report was included in its submission.

6) **Article 4 of the Act on the Promotion of Worker Participation and Cooperation (No Operational Rules for a Labor-Management Council)**
Employers who ordinarily employ 30 workers or more shall establish a Labor-Management Council and report its operational rules to the Labor Office, something the company had not done. A Labor-Management Council was accordingly established, and its rules of operation were submitted to the Labor Office.

7) **Article 13 of the Equal Employment Act (no training on prevention of sexual harassment at work)**
Training to prevent sexual harassment at work shall be done once a year in workplaces where ten employees or more are working. Company T carried out some training with audiovisual material (CD) distributed by the Labor Office, and submitted a document with attendee signatures.

Section 1-2. Labor Inspection over Unpaid Wages for Temporary Workers

Ⅰ. Introduction

I would like to introduce a recent case regarding claims for unpaid wages against a local council and how it was handled. Since 2016, the local council has been hiring 30 audit assistants for 40 days each year to assist with administrative audits. These assistants worked for KRW 100,000 per day, 5 days a week and 8 hours a day.

An audit assistant sought to claim the weekly holiday allowance and annual paid leave, neither of which had been given, but the local council explained that the assistant would not be regarded as a worker because he was hired for a commissioned position only during the administrative audit period. In response, the audit assistant filed a complaint with the Labor Office on December 9, 2022, stating that the local council owed him unpaid wages. During investigation by the Labor Office on December 28, the local council argued that audit assistants were not workers because they were used for commissioned work only during the

취업규칙을 보완하였고, 근로자들의 과반수이상의 의견을 첨부하여 관할 노동사무소에 신고하였다. 그리고 그 결과를 시정보고서에 첨부하였다.

6) 근로자참여 및 협력증진에 관한 법률 제4조 (노사협의회 규정 미신고)

상시 근로자 30인 이상을 사용하는 사용자는 노사협의회를 설립하고, 그 노사협의회 규정을 신고하도록 되어 있었으나, 회사에서는 아직 노사협의회가 설치되어 있지 않았다. 이에 회사는 노사협의회를 구성하고 관련 규정을 작성하여 노동부에 신고하였다.

7) 남녀고용평등법 제13조 (성희롱 예방교육 미실시)

직장 내 성희롱 예방교육은 10인 이상 근로자를 사용하는 사업장은 의무적으로 1년 1회 이상 실시하도록 되어 있다. 이에 IT회사는 노동부에서 제공된 성희롱 예방교육 CD를 활용하여 교육을 실시하였고, 교육참가자들의 서명이 적힌 교육일지를 시정보고에 첨부하였다.

제1-2절 비정규직 임금체불 진정에 따른 근로감독
(지방의회 일급직 사무보조자의 임금체불)

I. 사실관계

최근 모 지방의회에서 발생한 임금체불 사건과 그 처리과정에 대해서 소개하고자 한다. 의회는 행정감사 수행을 위해 2016년부터 매년 30여명 사무보조인을 40여일간 채용하고 있다. 근로조건은 일급 10만 원이고, 주 5일과 하루 8시간 근무하는 조건이었다.

한 사무보조인은 의회에 대하여 '주휴수당' 미지급과 '연차유급휴가' 미지급 부분에 대해 이의를 제기하였으나, 의회는 행정감사 기간 동안만 '위촉직'으로 채용하고 있기 때문에 근로자로 볼 수 없다고 설명하면서 요구한 금품을 지급하지 않았다. 이에 사무보조인은 2022년 12월 9일, 노동청에 의회가 임금체불을 하였다는 내용으로 진정을 제기하였다. 의회 담당자는 12월 28일 노동청 조사 시 지방조례에 따라 행정감사 기간 동안만 업무지원을 받기 위해

Section 1. Cases Related to Labor Inspections

administrative audit period in accordance with local ordinances. However, the Labor Office ordered the local council to pay KRW 800,000 in unpaid weekly holiday allowance and unused annual paid leave allowance since the complainant was a worker. The local council paid the amount ordered by the Labor Office. However, the complainant requested criminal punishment whether the delayed wages were paid or not. On February 17, 2023, the labor inspector visited the local council and conducted a labor inspection. The labor inspector pointed out 6 violations of the Labor Standards Act during the inspection, and ordered the payment of unpaid wages amounting to KRW 96 million, by March 7, 2023.

Herein, I would like to review the six violations pointed out by the labor inspectors during the inspection, and look carefully into three major disputed issues that came up: (1) the details on unpaid wages, (2) the retroactive scope of unpaid wages, and (3) criminal penalties against the local council.

II. Details of the Corrective Orders from the Labor Inspection

On February 17, 2023, the labor inspector visited the local council and conducted a labor inspection on the tasks of administrative assistants, and issued corrective orders for six items.

1. Violation of the Labor Standards Act, Article 17, Paragraph 2 (Duty to Create a Written Employment Contract)

(1) Corrective order: Labor contracts shall be issued to workers and include specifications on major working conditions such as wages, contractual working hours, weekly holidays, and annual paid leave. However, since the working conditions of 133 audit assistants, including the complainant, were not specified in writing and issued to the assistants, evidence (copies of employment contracts, etc.) that this has been done must be submitted.

(2) Follow-up actions and basis: The local council acknowledged its failure to create and issue appropriate labor contracts and agreed to do so in the future. The assistants were, in fact, temporary workers to assist during specific periods of administrative audit, but, notwithstanding this, the employer shall preserve a register of workers and important documents concerning labor contracts for three years, as prescribed by Presidential Decree. These important documents related to labor contracts are: 1. Labor contracts, 2. Wage ledgers, 3. Documents on wage determination, payment method and basis for wage

사무보조인들을 위촉직으로 채용하였기 때문에 근로자가 아니라고 주장하였다. 그러나 노동청은 진정인이 근로자에 해당되기 때문에 미지급된 주휴수당과 월차수당 80만 원 지급을 지시하였다. 의회는 노동청에서 제시한 금액을 모두 지급하였다. 그러나 진정인은 의회에 대해 임금체불 지급여부와 상관없이 형사처벌을 요구하였다. 이에 근로감독관은 2023년 2월 17일 지방의회를 방문하여 근로감독을 실시하였고 사업장 근로감독을 통해 근로기준법 위반사항 6가지(아래 본문 참조)를 지적하고, 2023년 3월 7일 까지 미지급 수당 9600만 원의 지급을 명하였다.

이번 호에는 노동청 근로감독관이 근로감독을 통해 지적한 6가지 구체적 내용에 대한 판단과 주요 쟁점이 되었던 (i) 임금체불에 대한 내용, (ii) 임금체불에 대한 소급 범위, 그리고 (iii) 지방의회에 대한 형사 처벌과 관련된 내용에 대해 구체적으로 살펴보고자 한다.

II. 시정지시 내용과 이해

2023년 2월 17일 근로감독관은 지방의회를 방문하여 행정보조 업무들에 대하여 근로감독을 실시하였고, 다음 6가지에 대해 시정지시를 하였다.

1. 근로기준법 제17조 제2항 위반 (서면작성의무)

(1) **시정지시**: 근로계약을 체결할 때에 근로자에게 임금, 소정근로시간, 주휴일, 연차유급휴가 등 주요 근로조건을 명시하여 교부하여야 한다. 그러나 진정인 등 사무보조자 133명의 근로조건을 서면으로 명시하여 교부하지 않았으므로 이를 이행하고 증빙자료(근로계약서 사본 등)를 제출하여야 한다.

(2) **조치내용과 관련 근거**: 의회는 근로계약서 미작성을 인정하고 앞으로 시정을 약속하였다. 사실상 한시적으로 의회의 행정감사를 위해 고용된 근로자들이었고, 모두 퇴사하였다. 그럼에도 불구하고 사용자는 근로자명부와 대통령령으로 정하는 근로계약에 관한 중요한 서류를 3년간

Section 1. Cases Related to Labor Inspections

calculation, 4. Documents on employment, dismissal and termination of employment relations, 5. Documents about leaves, etc. The three-year retention period for these important documents begins with the date of termination of the employment relationship. If the labor contract is not made in writing, the employer is subject to a fine of up to KRW 5 million.[2] In addition, if an employee requests a certificate verifying the period of employment, type of work, position and wages, and other necessary matters even after the worker resigns, the employer shall immediately provide such certificate with the actual facts thereon. Persons who can claim a certificate of employment shall be workers who have continuously worked for 30 days or more. Requests for such certificates can be made by the worker up to 3 years after resignation.[3]

2. Violation of the Labor Standards Act, Article 36 (Settlement of Payment)

(1) Corrective order: The employer shall pay all money and valuables including wages within 14 days from the date of the termination of employment relations, unless there is an agreement otherwise between the parties regarding an extension of the payment period. However, the local council failed to pay a total of KRW 96.1 million to its audit assistants: weekly holiday allowances of KRW 82.2 million (132 persons) and annual paid leave allowance of KRW 10.9 million (109 persons). Proof of payment must be submitted to the Labor Office (e.g. receipt of deposit or payment confirmation).

(2) Follow-up actions and basis: Considering the statute of limitations for overdue wages, the local council paid weekly holiday allowances and annual paid leave allowances to audit assistants who had worked during the past five years. If a worker dies or employment relations are terminated, the employer shall pay wages, compensation, and all other money and goods within 14 days from the occurrence of the reason for payment. However, it is specified that in special circumstances, the period may be extended by agreement between the parties. If money and other valuables are not paid within 14 days after the termination of employment relations, the employer will be subject to imprisonment for up to 3 years or a fine of up to KRW 30 million.[4]

---

[2] Labor Standards Act, Article 42 (Retention of Contract Documents) and the Enforcement Decree, Article 22 (Subsidized Documents, etc.) and Article 114 (Penalty)
[3] Labor Standards Act, Article 39 (Certificate of Use) and the Enforcement Decree, Article 19 (Requests for Certificate of Employment)
[4] Labor Standards Act, Article 36 of the (Settlement of Payment) and Article 109 (Punishment)

보존해야 한다. 대통령령으로 정하는 근로계약에 관한 중요한 서류는 1. 근로계약서, 2. 임금대장, 3. 임금의 결정, 지급방법과 임금계산의 기초에 관한 서류, 4. 고용, 해고, 퇴직에 관한 서류, 5. 휴가에 관한 서류 등이다. 이러한 근로계약에 관한 중요한 서류보존기간은 근로관계가 끝난 날로부터 기산하여 3년이다. 근로계약서를 미작성한 경우 사용자는 500만원 이하의 벌금에 처해진다.[2] 그리고 사용자는 근로자가 퇴직한 후라도 사용 기간, 업무 종류, 지위와 임금, 그 밖에 필요한 사항에 관한 증명서를 청구하면 사실대로 적은 증명서를 즉시 내주어야 한다. 사용증명서를 청구할 수 있는 자는 계속하여 30일 이상 근무한 근로자로 하되, 청구할 수 있는 기한은 퇴직 후 3년 이내로 한다.[3]

2. 근로기준법 제36조 위반 (금품 청산)

(1) **시정지시**: 사용자는 당사자 사이에 지급기일 연장에 관한 합의가 없는 한 퇴직일로부터 14일 이내에 임금 등 일체의 금품을 지급하여야 하나, 사무보조인에게는 주휴수당 82,200,000원 (132명) 및 연차유급휴가 미사용 수당 10,900,000원 (109명) 총합 96,100,000원을 지급하지 않았으므로 이를 지급하고 증빙자료 (입금증 또는 지급확인서 등)를 제출하여야 한다.

(2) **조치내용과 관련 근거**: 의회는 임금체불의 공소시효를 고려하여 최근 5년간 활동한 사무보조인에 대한 주휴수당과 연차유급휴가 수당을 지급하였다. 사용자는 근로자가 사망 또는 퇴직한 경우에는 그 지급 사유가 발생한 때부터 14일 이내에 임금, 보상금, 그 밖의 모든 금품을 지급하여야 한다. 다만, 특별한 사정이 있을 경우에는 당사자 사이의 합의에 의하여 기일을 연장할 수 있다고 명시하고 있다. 퇴직 후 14일 이내에 임금 등 금품을 미지급한 경우, 사용자는 3년이하의 징역 또는 3천만원 이하의 벌금에 처해진다.[4]

---

[2] 근로기준법 제42조 (계약 서류의 보존) 와 시행령 제22조(보조 대상 서류 등), 제114조 (벌칙)
[3] 근로기준법 제39조 (사용증명서)와 시행령 제19조 (사용증명서의 청구)
[4] 근로기준법 제36조 (금품청산)와 제109조 (벌칙)

Section 1. Cases Related to Labor Inspections

3. Violation of the Labor Standards Act, Article 48, Paragraph 2 (Pay Slips)

(1) Corrective order: When paying wages, the employer shall issue to the worker a wage statement in writing with matters as prescribed by Presidential Decree, such as the composition of wages, method of calculation, details of deductions, etc. and submit proof (copy of pay slips) to the Labor Office.

(2) Follow-up actions and basis: The local council acknowledged that it had failed to issue pay slips and agreed to correct the situation. The employer must issue wage statements to workers when paying them. This regulation applies even to workplaces with fewer than 5 employees, even if only one part-time worker is employed. In addition to a statement of the total amount, information related to the method of calculating wages must be written so that workers can confirm that they have been paid fairly in accordance with the amount of time they worked and the conditions given in the initial contract with the employer. If the employer fails to issue such a wage statement, an administrative fine of up to KRW 5 million won shall be imposed.[5]

4. Violation of the Labor Standards Act, Article 60, Paragraph 2 (Annual Paid Leave)

(1) Corrective order: The employer did not grant annual paid leave to 109 audit assistants, despite the requirement that it grant one day of paid leave for every one month of work to workers who have worked continuously for less than one year. Verification materials must be submitted to the Labor Office.

(2) Follow-up actions and basis: The local council paid annual paid leave allowances to audit assistants who had worked during the past five years in accordance with the statute of limitations for unpaid wages. An employer shall grant one day of paid leave for every month of work to a worker who has worked continuously for less than one year. If such annual paid leave is not granted, the unused leave shall be compensated in money. If the annual paid leave allowance is not paid, the employer shall be subject to imprisonment for up to two years or a fine of up to KRW 20 million.[6]

---

[5] Labor Standards Act, Article 48, paragraph 2 (Pay Slips) and Article 116 (Administrative Fines)

3. 근로기준법 제48조 제2항 위반 (임금명세서)

(1) **시정지시**: 사용자는 임금을 지급하는 때에는 근로자에게 임금의 구성항목, 계산방법, 공제 내역 등 대통령령으로 정하는 사항을 적은 임금명세서를 서면으로 교부하여야 하나, 임금명세서를 교부하지 않았으므로 이를 시정하고 증빙자료 (임금명세서 사본)를 제출하여야 한다.

(2) **조치내용과 관련근거**: 의회는 임금명세서 미교부를 인정하고 시정을 약속했다. 사용자는 근로자에게 임금을 지급하는 때에 근로자에게 반드시 임금명세서를 교부하여야 한다. 해당 규정은 5인 미만 사업장의 경우에도 적용되므로 아르바이트 한 명 만을 고용하고 있다 하더라도 임금명세서를 교부하여야 한다. 근로자들이 사용자와 처음에 계약한 대로 일한 만큼 급여가 지급되었는지 확인할 수 있도록 총액 뿐만 아니라 급여의 계산 방식 등과 관련한 정보를 적도록 하고 있다. 사용자가 임금명세서를 교부하지 않은 경우에는 500만 원 이하의 과태료에 처해진다.[5]

4. 근로기준법 제60조 제2항 위반 (연차유급휴가)

(1) **시정지시**: 사용자는 계속하여 근로한 기간이 1년 미만인 근로자에게 1개월 개근 시 1일의 유급휴가를 주어야 함에도 불구하고 사무보조인 109명에게 연차유급휴가를 부여하지 아니하였으므로 이를 시정하고 증빙자료를 제출하기 바란다.

(2) **조치내용과 관련근거**: 의회는 임금체불의 공소시효에 해당하는 최근 5년 동안 활동한 사무보조인들의 연차유급휴가 수당을 지급하였다. 사용자는 계속하여 근로한 기간이 1년 미만인 근로자에게 1개월 개근 시 1일의 유급휴가를 주어야 한다. 이러한 연차유급휴가를 부여하지 못한 경우에는 그 미사용 휴가에 대해 금전으로 보상하여야 한다. 연차유급휴가 수당을 미지급한 경우 사용자는 2년이하의 징역 또는 2천만 이하의 벌금에 처해진다.[6]

---

[5] 근로기준법 제48조 (임금명세서) 제2항, 제116조 (과태료)

Section 1. Cases Related to Labor Inspections

5. Violation of the Labor Standards Act, Article 70, Paragraph 1 (Restrictions on Night Work and Holiday Work)

(1) Corrective order: When a female worker aged 18 or older is required to work at night or on holidays, worker consent shall be obtained, but this was not done. Evidence needs to be submitted to the Labor Office that such consent was obtained.

(2) Follow-up actions and basis: The local council promised to thoroughly implement this requirement with employment of new workers. Female workers aged 18 or older may be allowed to work at night and on holidays with their prior consent. Violation of this is punishable with imprisonment for up to two years or a fine of up to KRW 20 million.[7]

6. Violation of the Minimum Wage Act, Article 11 (Duty to Inform)

(1) Corrective order: The employer shall post the minimum wage in a place where the workers of the business can easily see it, or widely publicize it to workers in other appropriate ways, as prescribed by Presidential Decree. Since the minimum wage notice obligation has been violated, correct the matter and submit verification evidence (posted photos, etc.).

(2) Follow-up actions and basis: The local council posted the required information in a notice on its website. Employers have a duty to notify workers of the minimum wage by posting it in a place where workers can easily see it or by other appropriate means. Matters to be posted include
① the minimum wage of workers subject to application,
② wages that are not included in the minimum wage,
③ scope of workers excluded from application of the minimum wage in the business in accordance with the law,
④ the effective period of the minimum wage. Violation of this duty to

---

[6] Labor Standards Act, Article 2 and 5 (Annual Paid Leave) and Article 110 (Punishment)
[7] Labor Standards Act, Article 70 (Restrictions on Night and Holiday Work) and Article 110 (Punishment)

5. 근로기준법 제70조 제1항 위반 (야간근로와 휴일근로의 제한)

(1) **시정지시**: 18세 이상의 여성을 야간근로 및 휴일근로를 시킬 경우 근로자의 동의를 받아야 하나 이를 이행하지 아니하였으므로, 여성근로자에 대하여 야간근로 및 휴일근로에 대한 동의를 받고, 증빙자료를 제출하기 바란다.

(2) **조치내용과 관련근거**: 의회는 해당사항에 대해 철저한 이행을 약속하였다. 18세 이상의 여성근로자에 대하여는 그 근로자의 동의를 받아 야간 및 휴일에도 근로하게 할 수 있다. 이를 위반한 경우 2년 이하의 징역 또는 2천만 원 이하의 벌금에 처해진다.[7)]

6. 최저임금법 제11조 위반 (주지 의무)

(1) **시정지시**: 최저임금의 적용을 받는 사용자는 '대통령'으로 정하는 바에 따라 해당 최저임금을 그 사업의 그 사업의 근로자가 쉽게 볼 수 있는 장소에 게시하거나 그 외의 적당한 방법으로 근로자에게 널리 알려야 함에도 불구하고 최저임금 주지의무를 위반하였으므로 이를 이행하고 증빙자료 (게시 사진 등)를 제출하기 바란다.

(2) **조치내용과 관련근거**: 의회는 홈페이지 공지사항에 해당사항을 게시하였다. 사용자는 최저임금에 관한 사항을 근로자가 쉽게 볼 수 있는 장소에 게시하거나, 그 외 적당한 방법으로 알려야 할 주지의무가 있다. 특히, "게시되어야 할 사항"으로
① 적용을 받는 근로자의 최저임금액,
② 최저임금에 산입하지 아니하는 임금,
③ 법에 따라 해당 사업에서 최저임금의 적용을 제외할 근로자의 범위,
④ 최저임금의 효력발생 연월일 이 있다. 주지의무 위반은 100만 원

---

6) 근로기준법 제60조 (연차 유급휴가) 제2항과 제5항. 제110조 (벌칙)
7) 근로기준법 제70조 (야간근로와 휴일근로의 제한), 제110조(벌칙)

inform is punishable with a fine of not more than KRW 1 million.[8]

III. Major Issues Disputed on during the Labor Inspection

1. Details on unpaid wages

(1) Related details: An audit assistant who worked from October 11, 2022 to December 2 (39 days) submitted a claim to the Labor Office for unpaid weekly holiday allowance and annual paid leave allowance. The local council attended an investigation hearing of the Labor Office on December 28, 2022 and submitted to an investigation, and agreed the day after the investigation to pay KRW 800,000 for weekly holiday and annual paid leave allowances. On February 17, 2023, the labor inspector visited the local council and conducted a labor inspection on the employment relationship with audit assistants. The labor inspector found that the local council had not paid weekly holiday allowance or unused annual paid leave allowance during employment of its audit assistants. The Labor Office directed the local council to retroactively pay unpaid wages to all audit assistants employed during the last five years.

(2) Judgment: If a worker hired for hourly or daily wage continues to work, an additional weekly holiday allowance shall be paid. If wages are calculated on a monthly basis, the weekly holiday allowance shall be included in the monthly wage. A related precedent states that the hourly or daily wage system does not include weekly holiday pay, which is a statutory allowance under Article 55 of the Labor Standards Act (LSA), paid even if the employees do not actually work on such paid holidays. Therefore, if a worker on the hourly or daily wage system receives a fixed allowance paid for a certain period of time exceeding one month, he or she can claim the difference between the weekly holiday pay calculated based on the newly calculated hourly wage and the previously paid fixed allowance, and this is not a duplicated pay for the weekly holiday pay."[9]

2. Retroactive payment of unpaid wages

---

[8] Minimum Wage Act, Article 11 (Duty to Inform) and Article 31 (Administrative Fine)
[9] Supreme Court ruling on Jan. 28, 2010, 2009da74144; see also Supreme Court ruling on Aug. 20, 2014, 2014da6275

이하의 과태료에 처해진다.[8]

Ⅲ. 근로감독의 내용 중 주요 쟁점

1. 임금체불에 대한 쟁점 내용

(1) **사실관계**: 2022년 10월 11일~12월 2일 까지(39일)을 근무한 사무보조자 1명이 의회가 주휴수당과 연차유급휴가 수당을 지급하지 않았다고 하여 노동청에 진정을 제기하였다. 의회는 2022년 12월 28일 노동청에 출석하여 조사를 받았고, 해당 의회는 조사받은 다음날 주휴수당과 연차수당 80만 원을 지급하였다. 노동청의 근로감독관은 2023년 2월 17일 해당 의회를 방문하여 사무보조인 고용관계에 대해 근로감독을 실시하였다. 근로감독관은 의회가 사무보조인들을 사용하면서 주휴수당과 연차유급휴가의 미사용 수당을 지급하지 않았다는 사실을 확인하였다. 노동청은 의회에 대하여 공소시효에 해당되는 지난 5년 동안 고용했던 사무보조원 전체에 대해 소급하여 미지급한 수당을 지급하도록 지시하였다.

(2) **관련판례**: 시급, 일급으로 고용된 근로자가 계속해서 근무하는 경우에는 주휴수당을 별도로 추가하여 지급하여야 하고, 월급으로 계산된 임금의 경우에는 주휴수당이 월 급여에 포함되어 있다. 관련 판례는 "시급제 또는 일급제는 근로기준법 제55조에 따라 부여되는 유급휴일에 실제로 근무를 하지 않더라도 근무를 한 것으로 간주하여 지급되는 법정수당인 주휴수당이 포함되어 있지 않다. 따라서 시급제 또는 일급제 근로자가 1개월을 초과하는 일정기간마다 지급되는 고정수당을 받았다면 새로이 산정한 시간급 통상임금을 기준으로 계산한 주휴수당액과의 차액을 청구할 수 있고, 이를 주휴수당의 중복 청구라고 할 수 없다."고 판시하고 있다.[9]

2. 임금체불에 대한 소급 범위

---

[8] 최저임금법 제11조 (주지의무), 제31조(과태료)
[9] 대법원 2010.1.28. 선고 2009다74144 판결, 대법원 2014.8.20. 선고 2014다6275 판결 참조

Section 1. Cases Related to Labor Inspections

(1) **Related details:** The labor inspector conducted an on-site audit on February 17, and on February 21, 2023, directed the local council to pay an amount equivalent to KRW 96.1 million, calculated as unpaid weekly holiday allowances of KRW 85.2 million (for 132 persons) and unused annual paid leave allowances of KRW 10.9 million (for 109 persons over the past 5 years between 2018 and 2022.

(2) **Judgment:** "Extinctive prescription" refers to expiration of the period during which an employee with the right to receive compensation may exercise a claim against the employer in the event of a delay in the payment of wages or severance pay. The extinctive prescription for prosecution refers to expiration of the period when prosecution can occur for violating labor law, such as delaying the payment of wages, and begins either on the date the violation occurred or the date a continuing violation ends.

The period before the extinctive prescription kicks in for prosecution of violation of labor-related acts in terms of delayed payment of wages was extended from 3 years to 5 years in 2007. The period before the extinctive prescription for prosecution kicks in shall be deemed to have started 14 days from the date the wages should have been paid or the date the violations terminate.[10] According to Article 49 of the LSA, the extinctive prescription for a wage bond kicks in after 3 years. However, since the extinctive prescription for prosecution is now 5 years, prosecution for delayed payment of wages will continue to be possible.[11] Thus, an employee may file a claim for unpaid wages for a period of 5 years.

3. Criminal punishment for late payment of wages

(1) **Related content:** On December 9, 2022, one audit assistant filed a complaint with the Labor Office that wages were overdue. On December 28, the local council was investigated by the Labor Office, and the next day, it paid KRW 800,000 in unpaid weekly holiday pay and unused annual paid leave. However, the petitioner requested criminal punishment for violation of the LSA, regardless of whether the unpaid wages were paid.

(2) **Judgment:** Late payment of wages is subject to criminal punishment. Workers who have received unpaid wage want their employer to be punished. However,

---

[10] Criminal Procedure Act, Article 249, Paragraph 1, Item 5 (Duration of Criminal Prescription) and Article 252 (Starting Time for Statute of Limitations)
[11] Ministry of Employment and Labor Guide, "Guide on Handling Unpaid Wages," 2016, pp. 31-32.

(1) **사실관계**: 노동청은 2023년 2월 17일에 현장조사를 실시하였고, 2월 21일 지난 5년간 2018년부터 2022년 사이 미지급한 주휴수당 85,200,000원(132명)과 연차유급휴가 미사용 수당 10,900,000원(109명) 총합 96,100,000원의 지급을 지시하였다.

(2) **관련판례**: 소멸시효는 돈 받을 권리가 있는 근로자가 사용자를 상대로 임금이나 퇴직금의 체불이 있는 경우에 청구권을 행사할 수 있는 기간을 말한다. 이에 대해 공소시효는 임금체불 등 노동법 위반 사용자를 법 위반 행위가 있는 날 또는 법 위반행위가 계속되는 경우 종료일로부터 형벌권을 행사할 수 있는 기간을 말한다.

임금체불로 인한 노동관계법령 위반 범죄의 공소시효 기간은 2007년에 기존 3년에서 5년으로 연장되었다. 공소시효 기산점은 "범죄행위가 종료된 때부터 임금지급일 또는 퇴직일로부터 14일이 경과한 때"까지를 말한다.[10] 이에 반해 임금채권의 소멸시효는 3년이다(근기법 제49조). 임금채권의 소멸시효 3년이 완성되었다 하더라도 공소시효가 아직 남아 있기 때문에 임금체불사업주에 대해 형사처벌이 가능하다.[11] 따라서 공소시효를 근거로 하여 근로자는 체불된 임금에 대해 5년간 청구가 가능하다.

3. 임금체불에 대한 형사처벌

(1) **사실관계**: 2022년 12월 9일 사무보조인 1인은 임금체불이 되었다고 노동청에 진정을 제기하였다. 12월 28일 의회의 담당자가 노동청의 조사를 받았고, 그 다음날 주휴수당과 연차유급휴가 미사용 수당 80만 원 지급을 완료하였다. 그러나 진정인은 체불임금 수령과는 별개로 근로기준법 위반에 대해 의회의 형사처벌을 요구하였다.

(2) **관련판례**: 임금체불은 형사처벌의 대상이 된다. 임금체불금을 지급받은 근로자가 사용자의 처벌을 원하고 있다. 그러나 검찰은 임금체불을 한

---

[10] 형사소송법 제249조(공소시효의 기간) 제1항 제5호, 제252조(시효의 기산점)
[11] 고용노동부 근로기준정책과, 「체불사건 업무처리 요령」, 2016. 31-32면.

prosecutors did not prosecute the local council as the employer responsible for the late payment of wages. The reason for this is that the local council's violation of the obligation to pay weekly holiday allowance and unused annual leave allowance was not intentional. A related precedent states, If there are grounds to dispute the existence of the obligation to pay wages and severance pay, it should be seen that there is a considerable reason why the employer did not pay the wages and severance pay. It is difficult to reason that the employer intentionally committed the crime of violating Article 36 of the Labor Standards Act (Settlement of Payment). Whether there are grounds for dispute regarding the existence and scope of the obligation to pay wages and severance pay depends on the reason for the employer's refusal to pay and the basis for the payment obligation, and the organization and scale of the company operated by the employer. Also, all matters such as business purpose, and the existence and scope of payment obligations, such as other wages, should be judged in light of the general circumstances at the time of the dispute. Even if the employer's civil liability for payment is recognized retroactively, it should not be immediately concluded that the employer's violation of Article 36 of the Labor Standards Act is recognized intentionally.[12]

Ⅳ. Opinion

This case is a good example of the characteristics of labor law. Labor law violations do not end with correction of a single person's violation. Through this example of unpaid wages for daily wage workers, the following characteristics of labor law can be understood.

First, even if an administrative agency temporarily hires a commissioned worker, if that worker provides work under the management supervision of the employer and receives wages, employee status is recognized.

Second, a notice of violation of the LSA is applied to all workers in the same category, and unpaid wages can be claimed retroactively for 5 years, which is the statute of limitations for criminal punishment.

Thirdly, even if a violation regarding wages occurs, if there was no intentional violation of the law and there exists a legitimate reason for not paying the wages in question, criminal punishment may be avoided.

---

[12] Supreme Court ruling on June 28, 2007, 2007do1539.

사용자인 의회에 대해 기소하지 않았다. 그 이유는 피진정인인 의회가 임금체불 위반에 대한 고의성이 없다고 판단하였다. 관련 판례는 "임금과 퇴직금 지급의무의 존재에 관하여 다툴 만한 근거가 있는 것이라면 사용자가 그 임금과 퇴직금을 지급하지 아니한 데에는 상당한 이유가 있다고 보아야 할 것이다. 사용자에게 근로기준법 제36조 (금품청산)의 위반죄에 고의가 있었다고 인정하기 어렵고, 임금 및 퇴직금 지급의무의 존부 및 범위에 관하여 다툴 만한 근거 여부는 사용자의 지급거절 이유와 그 지급의무의 근거, 그리고 사용자가 운영하는 회사의 조직과 규모, 사업 목적 등 제반 사항, 기타 임금 등 지급의무의 존부 및 범위에 관한 다툼 당시의 제반 정황에 비추어 판단하여야 한다. 사후적으로 사용자의 민사상 지급책임이 인정된다고 하여 곧바로 사용자에 대한 근로기준법 제36조의 위반에 대해 고의가 인정된다고 단정해서는 안 된다."고 판시하고 있다.[12]

Ⅳ. 의견

이번 지방의회의 한시적인 일급 위탁직의 임금체불 사건은 노동법의 특징을 잘 설명해 준 사례다. 노동법 위반은 단 한 사람의 위반에 대한 시정으로 끝나지 않는다. 이번 지방의회의 일급직 근로자의 임금체불 사례를 통해서 다음과 같은 노동법의 특징을 이해할 수 있다.

첫째, 행정기관에서 위촉직으로 일시적으로 채용하였다고 하더라도 사용자의 관리 감독 하에서 근로를 제공하고 임금을 받았다고 한다면 근로자 신분이 된다.
둘째, 근로기준법의 위반에 대한 지적은 동종 근로자 전체에 적용되고, 공소시효 기간인 5년 동안 소급하여 미지급된 임금을 청구할 수 있다.
셋째로, 임금체불의 위반행위가 발생하였다고 하더라도 법위반의 고의성이 없었고, 지급하지 않았던 이유가 별도로 있었던 경우에는 형사처벌을 면할 수 있다는 사실이다.

---

12) 대법원 2007.6.28 선고 2007도1539 판결

Section 2. Regulations Basis for Labor Inspection by Labor Inspectors

To ensure standards for working conditions, a labor inspector can visit any workplace, inspect it, and request to see books and documents, as well as interview both employer and employees. Employers or employees shall, without delay, report on the matters required, or shall present themselves to the Labor Office if the labor inspector requests it in relation to enforcement of the Labor Standards Act.

The Labor Standards Act

Article 101 (Supervisory Authorities) ① The Ministry of Employment and Labor and its subordinate offices shall have a labor inspector to ensure the standards of the conditions of labor.

Article 102 (Authority of Labor Inspectors) ① A labor inspector has the authority to inspect a workplace, dormitory and other annexed buildings, to request presentation of books and documents, and to question both employer and workers.

Article 13 (Duty to Report and Attend) An employer or worker shall, without delay, report on matters required, or shall present himself, if the Minister of Labor, the Labor Relations Commission under the Labor Relations Commission under the Labor Relations Commission Act or a Labor Inspector requests him or her to do so in relation to the enforcement of this Act.

---

1. Inspection of workplaces

Labor Inspectors Regulation, Article 11 (Definition of Workplace Inspection)

In this directive, workplace labor inspection refers to a series of processes where an inspector conducts on-site investigations of workplaces, dormitories, and other auxiliary buildings to ensure compliance with labor condition standards, checks for violations of labor-related laws, and takes corrective actions, administrative measures, or judicial actions against any violations.

제2절 근로감독관의 근로감독 근거 규정

 근로감독관은 근로기준이 제대로 준수되는지 확인하기 위해 사업장을 방문하여 점검할 수 있고 장부와 서류를 제출을 요구할 수 있으며 사용자와 근로자에 대해 심문을 할 수 있다. 그리고 사용자 또는 근로자는 근로기준법 시행에 관하여 근로감독관의 요구가 있으면 지체 없이 필요한 사항에 대해서 보고하거나 출석하여야 한다.

근로기준법
제101조 [감독기관] ① 근로조건의 기준을 확보하기 위하여 고용노동부와 그 소속 기관에 근로감독관을 둔다.
제102조 [감독관의 권한] ① 근로감독관은 사업장, 기숙사, 그 밖의 부속 건물에 임검하고 장부와 서류의 제출을 요구할 수 있으며 사용자와 근로자에 대하여 심문할 수 있다.
제13조 [보고, 출석의 의무] 사용자 또는 근로자는 이 법의 시행에 관하여 고용노동부장관, 노동위원회법에 따른 노동위원회 또는 근로감독관의 요구가 있으면 지체없이 필요한 사항에 대해서 보고하거나 출석하여야 한다.

---

1. 사업장 감독

근로감독관 집무규정 제11조 (사업장 감독의 정의)
 이 훈령에서 사업장 근로감독이란 감독관이 근로조건의 기준을 확보하기 위하여 사업장, 기숙사 그 밖의 부속건물을 현장조사하여 노동관계법령 위반 여부를 점검하고 법 위반사항을 시정하도록 하거나 행정처분 또는 사법처리하는 일련의 과정을 말한다.

Section 2. Regulations Basis for Labor Inspection by Labor Inspectors

Labor Inspectors Regulation, Article 12 (Types of Workplace Inspections)

The types of workplace inspections are as follows:

1. Regular Inspection: Labor inspections conducted according to the comprehensive (detailed) implementation plan for workplace labor inspections outlined in Article 13.

2. Occasional Inspection: Labor inspections conducted with a separate plan for workplaces or industries that meet any of the following criteria, after the comprehensive (detailed) implementation plan for workplace labor inspections has been finalized and could not be included in the regular inspection plan.
   a. Workplaces deemed to have a potential for violating labor-related laws based on trends, reports, media coverage, etc.
   b. Workplaces recognized as needing inspection due to the receipt of labor inspection petitions.
   c. Workplaces where the possibility of violating labor-related laws for a significant number of workers is identified during the handling of reported cases according to Chapter 3.
   d. Workplaces or industries that fall under any of the above criteria, or similar reasons, where a local office establishes its own plan, or when the head office notifies of an occasional inspection plan.

3. Special Inspection: Labor inspections conducted to investigate violations of labor-related laws in workplaces that meet any of the following criteria:
   a. Workplaces where serious violations of labor-related laws, collective agreements, work rules, or employment contracts have caused or are likely to cause labor disputes.
   b. Workplaces with significant violations of labor-related laws, such as habitual or intentional wage arrears, illegal dispatch, discriminatory treatment of non-regular workers, verbal abuse, physical violence, and workplace sexual harassment or bullying, resulting in multiple victims or a high likelihood of occurrence, making inspections necessary and

근로감독관 집무규정 제12조 (사업장 감독의 종류)

사업장감독의 종류는 다음 각 호와 같다.

1. 정기감독: 제13조의 사업장근로감독종합(세부)시행계획에 따라 실시하는 근로감독

2. 수시감독: 사업장근로감독종합(세부)시행계획이 확정된 이후 정기감독계획에 반영하지 못한 사항 중 다음 각 목의 어느 하나에 해당하는 사업장 또는 업종을 대상으로 별도의 계획을 수립하여 실시하는 근로감독

    가. 동향, 제보, 언론보도 등을 통하여 노동관계법령 위반 가능성이 있다고 판단되는 사업장

    나. 근로감독 청원 등이 접수되어 사업장 감독이 필요하다고 인정되는 사업장

    다. 제3장에 따른 신고사건을 처리하는 과정에서 해당 사업장의 다수의 근로자에 대한 노동관계법령 위반의 가능성이 있다고 판단되는 사업장

    라. 위 각 목의 어느 하나에 해당하거나 그에 준하는 사유가 있는 사업장 또는 업종에 대하여 지방관서에서 자체 계획을 수립하거나, 본부에서 수시감독 계획을 통보한 경우

3. 특별감독: 다음 각 목의 어느 하나에 해당하는 사업장에 대하여 노동관계법령 위반사실을 수사하기 위해 실시하는 근로감독

    가. 노동관계법령·단체협약·취업규칙 및 근로계약 등을 위반하는 중대한 행위로 인하여 노사분규가 발생하였거나 발생 우려가 큰 사업장

    나. 상습·고의적 체불, 불법파견, 비정규직에 대한 차별적 처우, 폭언·폭행 및 직장 내 성희롱·괴롭힘 등 노동관계법령을 위반하는 중대한 행위로 다수의 피해자가 발생하거나 발생 우려가

Section 2. Regulations Basis for Labor Inspection by Labor Inspectors

> often reported in the media.
> c. Workplaces where the head office has notified of a special inspection plan due to concerns about any of the above criteria or similar reasons.
>
> 4. Re-inspection: Labor inspections conducted on workplaces that have undergone any of the inspections described in items 1 to 3 within the past three years and have received new complaints of violations of labor-related laws.

2. Scope of Workplace Inspections

> **Labor Inspectors Regulation, Article 14 (Scope of Workplace Inspections)**
> ① As a principle, workplace inspections shall be conducted comprehensively covering all matters related to labor-related laws according to the inspection checklist. However, the scope may be separately defined in the comprehensive inspection plan or may vary depending on the purpose of the workplace inspection.
> ② Regular and occasional inspections, as specified in Article 12, shall cover matters related to labor-related laws that occurred within one year prior to the inspection date, and special inspections shall cover those that occurred within three years prior to the inspection date. However, if there are reasonable grounds to believe that violations of labor-related laws have been repeated or have occurred before that period, the inspection scope may be extended to include violations not subject to the statute of limitations as of the inspection completion date.
> ③ If it is determined during the workplace inspection that there are violations of labor-related laws in businesses related to the inspected workplace through subcontracting or labor dispatch contracts, inspections may also be conducted on the relevant subcontractors, primary contractors, labor dispatch companies, or user companies of dispatched workers.

> 있어 언론에 보도되는 등 감독 필요성이 상당한 사업장
> 다. 위 각 목의 어느 하나에 해당하거나 그에 준하는 사유가 발생할 우려가 있는 사업장에 대하여 본부에서 특별감독계획을 통보한 경우
>
> 4. 재감독: 최근 3년 이내에 제1호부터 제3호까지의 어느 하나에 해당하는 사업장감독을 받은 이후 노동관계법령 위반에 따른 신고사건이 접수된 사업장에 대하여 실시하는 근로감독

2. 사업장감독의 범위

> **근로감독관 집무규정 제14조 (사업장감독의 범위)**
> ① 사업장감독은 감독점검표에 따라 노동관계법령 관련 사항 전반에 걸쳐 종합적으로 실시함을 원칙으로 한다. 다만, 감독종합계획에서 그 범위를 따로 정하거나 사업장감독의 목적에 따라 달리 정할 수 있다.
> ② 제12조에 따른 사업장감독 중 정기·수시감독은 실시일 전 1년간, 특별감독은 실시일 전 3년간 해당 사업장에서 이루어진 노동관계법령 관련 사항을 대상으로 한다. 다만, 노동관계법령 위반 행위가 그 이전부터 반복되거나 그 이전에 법 위반 행위가 있었다고 판단할 만한 상당한 이유가 있는 경우에는 점검 종료일 현재 공소시효가 완료되지 아니한 법 위반사항까지 감독대상을 확대할 수 있다.
> ③ 사업장감독 과정에서 해당 사업장과 도급계약 또는 근로자파견계약 등의 관계에 있는 사업장에서 노동관계법령 위반 사실이 있다고 판단되는 경우에는 해당 도급업체·수급업체·근로자파견업체·파견근로자 사용업체 등에 대해서도 사업장 감독을 실시할 수 있다.

Section 2. Regulations Basis for Labor Inspection by Labor Inspectors

3. Inspection Follow-Up (Article 21)

Labor Inspectors Regulation, Article 21 (Inspection Follow-Up)
① An inspector shall handle confirmed violations identified during workplace inspections in accordance with the standards for handling violations. However, in any of the following cases, the inspector must immediately initiate criminal charges or impose fines. If separate handling standards are communicated by the head office considering the violations and necessary actions, those standards shall be followed:
   1. If, upon reviewing whether the violation of major labor conditions was intentional or due to gross negligence, it is determined that the violation was intentional or due to gross negligence, or if it caused significant public concern, necessitating immediate criminal charges or imposition of a fine.
   2. If violations are identified as a result of special inspections as stipulated in Article 12, Paragraph 3.
   3. If, within three years from the date of inspection, the same violations as per the standards for handling violations in labor inspections are repeated.
   4. If an employer who received support for autonomous improvement of labor conditions falsely reports the inspection results.
   5. If violations identified through occasional inspections as per Article 12, Paragraph 2, are deemed to be the primary purpose of the inspection.
   6. If, as a result of re-inspection as per Article 12, Paragraph 4, violations are found that were the same as those identified in the immediate preceding workplace inspection or the complaints received after the immediate preceding workplace inspection.

② The inspector shall, immediately after reporting the inspection results in accordance with Article 20, issue a correction order to the employer specifying the violated legal provisions, details of the correction instructions, and the correction period. The inspector shall also guide the employer to post the correction order in a place where employees can easily see it and to submit supporting evidence.

③ The correction order referred to in Paragraph 2 shall be issued after

3. 감독결과 조치 (제21조)

근로감독관 집무규정 제21조 (감독결과 조치)
① 감독관은 사업장감독 결과 확인된 위법사항에 대하여는 위반사항 조치기준에 따라 처리하되, 다음 각 호의 어느 하나에 해당하는 경우에는 즉시 범죄인지 또는 과태료 부과 조치를 하여야 한다. 다만, 본부에서 위반사항과 조치해야 할 내용 등을 고려하여 별도의 조치기준이 통보된 경우에는 이에 따른다.
 1. 주요 근로조건 위반에 대해 고의 또는 중과실 여부 등을 검토한 결과, 고의 또는 중과실로 주요 근로조건을 위반하였거나, 사회적 물의를 일으켜 즉시 범죄인지 또는 과태료 부과가 필요하다고 판단되는 경우
 2. 제12조제3호에 따른 특별감독 결과 위법사항을 확인한 경우
 3. 감독실시일 기준 최근 3년간 근로감독결과 위반사항 조치기준의 동일한 사항을 다시 위반한 경우
 4. 근로조건 자율개선 지원을 받은 사용자가 점검결과를 허위로 보고한 경우
 5. 제12조제2호의 수시감독을 통해 확인한 위법 사항이 감독의 주된 목적에 해당한다고 판단되는 경우
 6. 제12조제4호의 재감독 결과 재감독 직전에 실시한 사업장감독에서 위반한 사항 또는 직전에 실시한 사업장감독 이후에 접수된 신고사건과 동일한 사항을 위반한 경우
② 감독관은 제20조에 따른 감독결과 보고 즉시 시정지시서에 위반 법 조항, 시정지시 내용, 시정기한 등을 구체적으로 적시하여 사용자에게 발부하여야 하며, 사용자로 하여금 시정지시서를 사업장의 근로자들이 잘 볼 수 있는 장소에 게시하고, 이에 대한 증빙자료를 제출하도록 지도하여야 한다.
③ 제2항의 시정지시서는 근로감독행정 정보시스템을 통해 과장의

Section 2. Regulations Basis for Labor Inspection by Labor Inspectors

obtaining the approval of the department head through the labor inspection administration information system.

④ If the employer requests an extension of the correction period specified in the correction order in Paragraph 2 due to unavoidable reasons, the inspector may extend the correction period within the scope of the initial correction period, notwithstanding the handling standards.

⑤ The request referred to in Paragraph 4 must be made within the period specified in the correction order in Paragraph 2.

⑥ If two or more violations with different correction periods are ordered for the same workplace, the confirmation of correction shall be done separately for each case. However, the correction result report can be replaced by a single report based on the case with the longest correction period.

⑦ If, during the workplace inspection process, it is confirmed that a construction company has subcontracted work to a person who is not a construction contractor under Article 2, Paragraph 7 of the Construction Industry Basic Act by violating Articles 16, 25, or 29 of the same Act, the relevant facts shall be notified to the administrative agency responsible for the construction company's registration.

결재를 받아 발부하여야 한다.
④ 감독관은 사용자가 부득이한 사유로 제2항의 시정지시서에서 정한 기한 내에 시정하지 못하여 시정기한 연장을 요청한 때에는 조치기준에도 불구하고 1차 시정기간의 범위에서 시정기간을 연장할 수 있다.
⑤ 제4항의 요청은 제2항 시정지시서에 정한 기간내에 하여야 한다.
⑥ 동일 사업장에 시정기간을 달리하는 2건 이상의 법위반 사항을 동시에 시정지시한 경우, 시정여부의 확인은 사안별로 하여야 한다. 다만, 시정결과보고는 시정기간이 가장 긴 사안을 기준으로 1회의 보고로 갈음할 수 있다.
⑦ 사업장감독을 진행하는 과정에서 건설회사가 「건설산업기본법」 제16조, 제25조 및 제29조 등을 위반하여 동법 제2조제7호에 따른 건설업자가 아닌 자에게 하도급한 사실을 확인한 경우에는 관련 사실을 해당 건설회사의 건설업 등록 행정기관에 통보하여야 한다.

Chapter 2 Labor Inspection Checklist

1. Written Statement of Working Conditions
2. Preservation of Employee Registers and Contract Documents
3. Payment of Various Money and Goods such as Wages
4. Violation of limits on working hours and overtime
5. Granting recess hours
6. Paid holidays
7. Annual paid leave
8. Children and Maternity Protection
9. Rules of Employment
10. Payment of retirement benefits
11. Prevention of workplace harassment
12. Observation of minimum wage
13. Prevention of sexual harassment in the workplace
14. Prohibition of Sex Discrimination in Employment
15. Prohibition of discrimination against non-regular workers
16. Establishment of labor-management council

제2장 근로감독 체크리스트

1. 근로조건 서면명시
2. 근로자 명부 및 계약서류 보존
3. 임금 등 각종 금품 지급
4. 근로시간 및 연장근로 한도 위반
5. 휴게시간 부여
6. 유급휴일 부여
7. 연차유급휴가 부여
8. 모성보호와 연소자
9. 취업규칙
10 퇴직급여 지급
11. 직장 내 괴롭힘 예방
12. 최저임금 준수
13. 직장 내 성희롱 예방
14. 고용상 성차별 금지
15. 비정규직 차별 금지
16. 노사협의회 설치

Chapter 2: Labor Inspection Checklist

The "Labor Inspection Checklist" is based on the "Labor Management Guidebook" and the "Self-Diagnosis Checklist for Compliance with Labor Relations Laws," published annually by the Ministry of Employment and Labor.[13] When a labor inspector visits a workplace for an inspection, they conduct detailed inspections using specific questions across 16 key areas. This chapter provides specific questions related to these 16 areas of labor inspection, along with the corresponding legal standards. Employers can use the questions and explanations in the "Labor Inspection Checklist" to assess their company's compliance with labor relations laws.

It is crucial for employers to periodically conduct self-diagnoses to ensure that their company is complying with labor relations laws, has the necessary documentation as required by these laws, and is implementing the relevant procedures. Regular verification is essential because compliance with labor relations laws can lapse due to various circumstances, even if the company was previously in compliance. In particular, when using internal subcontracting or external services, the legality of such practices is evaluated based on the actual labor relations at the time of assessment. Initially, subcontracting or external services might not pose any legal issues, but active labor management by the company could undermine the independence of these services, leading to the employer being held accountable as the de facto employer. Therefore, to prevent such situations, employers should regularly conduct labor inspections to evaluate and ensure compliance with labor relations laws.

Given that the content of labor inspections involves assessing compliance with labor-related laws, it is often challenging for internal staff to maintain objectivity and expertise. Hence, it is advisable for employers to engage the support of labor attorneys, who are experts in labor relations laws, to conduct realistic labor inspections and address any deficiencies.

---

[13] Ministry of Employment and Labor, "Labor Management Guidebook," "Self-Diagnosis Checklist for Compliance with Labor Relations Laws," 2024

제2장 근로감독 체크리스트

'근로감독 체크리스트'는 고용노동부가 매년 발간하고 있는 '노무관리 가이드북'과 '노동관계법 준수 자가진단표'를 바탕으로 작성되었다.[13] 근로감독관이 사업장에 방문하여 근로감독을 할 경우에, 근로감독관은 아래의 16개 분야에 세부질문을 가지고 현장점검을 하면서 근로감독을 실시한다. 이 장은 근로감독관의 근로감독 내용인 16개 분야의 구체적인 질문과 그 질문에 관한 노동법적 기준을 설명하고 있다. 사업주는 '근로감독 체크리스트' 질문과 그 해설을 통해 회사가 얼마나 노동관계법을 준수하고 있는지 확인할 수 있다.

사업주는 회사가 실제로 노동관계법을 준수하고 있는지, 노동관계법령에 따른 각종 서류를 구비하고 있는지, 그리고 관련 절차를 실행하고 있는지 여부를 주기적으로 자가진단을 해보는 것이 중요하다. 그 이유는 노동관계법령의 준수 여부는 계속해서 확인하지 않으면, 기존의 준수 여부와 상관없이 여러 사정으로 노동법을 위반하는 사례가 종종 발생하기 때문이다. 특히, 사내 하도급이나 외부용역을 사용하고 있는 경우에 그 적법 여부는 평가 당시의 실질적 근로관계를 토대로 판단하고 있다. 처음에는 하도급이나 외부용역이 법위반의 소지가 없었지만, 회사의 적극적 노무관리는 오히려 하도급이나 외부용역에 대한 독립성을 잃게 하여 사업주가 실질적인 사용자로서의 책임을 지는 경우가 발생할 수 있다. 따라서 사업주는 이러한 상황을 예방하기 위해서 주기적인 근로감독을 실시하여 사업장의 노동관계법 준수 여부에 대해 주기적으로 평가해야 할 것이다.

근로감독의 내용은 회사의 노동관련법령의 준수 여부를 평가하는 것이기 때문에 회사의 담당자들이 담당하기에는 객관성이나 전문성이 부족한 경우가 많다. 따라서 사업주는 노동관계법 전문가인 공인노무사의 지원을 받아 회사의 노동관련법령의 준수 여부에 대해 실전과 같은 근로감독을 실시하고 부족한 부분을 개선하는 것이 필요하다고 본다.

---

[13] 고용노동부, "노무관리 가이드북", "노동관계법 준수 자가진단표", 2024.

Chapter 2: Labor Inspection Checklist

<Contents of the Evaluation of Compliance with Labor Relations Laws>

1. Written Statement of Working Conditions
1-1. Written statement of working conditions
1-2. Written statement of working conditions for fixed-term and part-time workers

2. Preservation of Employee Registers and Contract Documents
2-1. Preservation of contract documents
2-2. Payroll

3. Payment of Various Money and Goods such as Wages
3-1. Settlement of payments
3-2. Payment of wages
3-3. Pay slips
3-4. Wage payment for subcontracting
3-5. Shutdown allowance
3-6. Extended, night and holiday work

4. Violation of Limits on Working Hours and Overtime
4-1. Working hours
4-2. Restrictions on overtime work

5. Granting recess hours

6. Paid Holidays

7. Annual Paid Leave

8. Protection of Maternity and Children
8-1. Night and holiday work for minors and women
8-2. Overtime work for women soon after childbirth
8-3. Protection of pregnant women
8-4. Paternity leave
8-5. Childcare leave
8-6. Reduction of working hours during childcare period

9. Rules of Employment
9-1. Creation of and reporting rules of employment
9-2. Changes to rules of employment
9-3. Compliance with laws and collective agreements

10. Payment of Retirement Benefits
10-1. Payment of severance pay
10-2. Payment of defined benefit (DB) retirement pension
10.3 Payment of defined contribution (DC) retirement pension
10-4. Payment of SME Retirement Pension Fund System Benefits

11. Preventing Workplace Harassment

12. Observing Minimum Wage
12-1. Effect of minimum wage
12-2. Obligation to notify workers of minimum wage

13. Preventing Sexual Harassment in the Workplace
13-1. Prohibiting sexual harassment in the workplace
13-2. Preventing sexual harassment in the workplace

14. Prohibiting Gender Discrimination in Employment

15. Prohibiting Discrimination against Non-regular Workers

16. Establishing a Labor-Management Council
16-1. Establishing a labor-management council
16-2. Labor-management council meetings

⟨노동관계법 준수여부 평가 내용⟩

1. 근로조건 서면명시
1-1. 근로조건 서면명시
1-2. 기간제 및 단시간 근로자의 근로조건 서면명시

2. 근로자 명부 및 계약서류 보존
2-1. 계약서류 보존
2-2. 임금대장

3. 임금 등 각종 금품 지급
3-1. 금품청산
3-2. 임금지급
3-3. 임금명세서
3-4. 도급사업에 대한 임금지급
3-5. 휴업수당
3-6. 연장, 야간 및 휴일근로

4. 근로시간 및 연장근로 한도 위반
4-1. 근로시간
4-2. 연장근로의 제한

5. 휴게시간 부여

6. 유급휴일 부여

7. 연차유급휴가 부여

8. 연소자와 모성보호
8-1 연소자 및 여성의 야간 및 휴일근로
8-2 산후여성 근로자의 시간외근로
8-3 임산부의 보호
8-4 배우자 출산휴가
8-5 육아휴직
8-6 육아기 근로시간 단축

9. 취업규칙
9-1 취업규칙 작성·신고
9-2 취업규칙 변경
9-3 법령 단체협약의 준수

10 퇴직급여 지급
10-1 퇴직금 지급
10-2 확정급여형퇴직연금(DB) 급여 지급
10-3 확정기여형퇴직연금(DC) 급여 지급
10-4 중소기업 퇴직연금기금제도 급여 지급

11. 직장 내 괴롭힘 예방

12. 최저임금 준수
12-1 최저임금 효력
12-2 최저임금 주지의무

13. 직장 내 성희롱 예방
13-1. 직장 내 성희롱 금지
13-2. 직장 내 성희롱 예방

14. 고용상 성차별 금지

15. 비정규직 차별 금지

16. 노사협의회 설치
16-1. 노사협의회 설치
16-2 노사협의회 회의

Chapter 2: Labor Inspection Checklist

1. Written Statement of Working Conditions

1-1 Written statement of working conditions

1-1-1 Have you drawn up employment contracts for all relevant workers?

An employment contract clearly stipulates core working conditions such as wages and working hours between the worker and the employer. Important working conditions in Article 17 of the Labor Standards Act must be specified in writing in the labor contract.

In this case, important working conditions are:

1. Wage components, calculation method, payment method,
2. Contracted working hours,
3. Weekly holidays, and
4. Annual paid leave.

The above four items must be specified in writing, and an employment contract must be given to the worker.

(Penalty) Article 114 of the Labor Standards Act, a fine of up to 5 million won

1-1-2 Are all important working conditions (wages, working hours, holidays, vacations, etc.) written in the employment contracts?

Labor Standards Act Article 17 Paragraph 1 sentence 1

The important working conditions in the question are:

1. Wage components, calculation method, payment method,
2. Contracted working hours,
3. Weekly holidays,
4. Annual paid leave.

The above four items correspond to the objects to be specified in writing that the employer must write down in the labor contract when signing the labor contract, and all of them must be written and delivered to the worker.

(Penalty) Article 114 of the Labor Standards Act, a fine of up to 5 million won

1-1-3 If important working conditions have changed, have you rewritten and issued a new employment contract?

1. 근로조건 서면명시

1-1 근로조건 서면명시

1-1-1 근로계약서를 작성하였습니까?

근로계약서란 근로자와 사용자 간 임금, 근로시간 등 핵심 근로조건을 명확히 정하는 것으로, 근로기준법 제17조의 중요 근로조건은 근로계약서에 서면 명시하여 작성되어야 합니다.

이 때, 중요 근로조건이란

1. 임금의 구성항목, 계산방법, 지급방법,
2. 소정근로시간,
3. 주휴일,
4. 연차유급휴가입니다.

위의 4가지 항목은 반드시 서면으로 명시하고, 근로계약서를 근로자에게 주어야 합니다.

(벌칙) 근로기준법 제114조 500만 원 이하의 벌금

1-1-2 근로계약서에는 중요 근로조건 (임금, 근로시간, 휴일, 휴가 등)을 모두 기재하였습니까?

근로기준법 제17조 제1항 1문

질문의 중요 근로조건이란

1. 임금의 구성항목, 계산방법, 지급방법,
2. 소정근로시간,
3. 주휴일,
4. 연차유급휴가입니다.

위의 4가지 항목은 사용자가 근로계약 체결 시 근로계약서에 기재하여야 할 서면 명시대상에 해당하며 모두 기재하여 근로자에게 교부하여야 합니다.

(벌칙) 근로기준법 제114조 500만 원 이하의 벌금

1-1-3 중요 근로조건이 변경된 경우, 근로계약서를 다시 작성하여 교부하였습니까?

Labor Standards Act Article 17 Paragraph 1 sentence 2

Even if important working conditions are changed after the labor contract is concluded, the employer is obligated to rewrite and deliver them to the worker as well.

(Penalty) Article 114 of the Labor Standards Act, a fine of up to 5 million won

1-1-4 Is one copy issued to each worker in writing and one copy kept at the workplace?

Main text of Article 17 (2) of the Labor Standards Act

When signing a labor contract, the employer must prepare two copies of the labor contract, give one copy to the worker, and keep one copy at the workplace.

(Penalty) Article 114 of the Labor Standards Act, a fine of up to 5 million won

1-1-5 Have the wages, working hours, holidays and vacations stipulated in the labor contract changed due to changes in the collective agreement or rules of employment after the labor contract was concluded? If a worker requested a labor contract with the changes specified, was the labor contract reissued?

Proviso to Article 17 (2) of the Labor Standards Act

After signing a labor contract, important working conditions may be changed by written agreement with the worker, changes in collective agreements or employment rules, or by law.

3 reasons (changed by written agreement with the employee representative, changed by employment rules or collective agreement, changed by statute), and if there is a request from the worker, there is a change in the important working conditions of the worker's employment contract It must be reissued to the worker.

(Penalty) Article 114 of the Labor Standards Act, a fine of up to 5 million won

1-2 Written statement of working conditions for fixed-term and part-time workers

1-2-1 Have you written and issued employment contracts for each fixed-term and part-time worker?

Article 17 of the Act on the Protection of Fixed-Term and Part-Time Workers (the Fixed-term Workers Act)

When concluding a labor contract with a fixed-term or part-time worker (when hiring a worker), the employer must prepare an employment contract.

(Fine for negligence) Fine for negligence up to 5 million won under Article 24 of the Fixed-term Workers Act

근로기준법 제17조 제1항 2문
중요 근로조건이 근로계약 체결 후 변경되는 경우에도 사용자는 마찬가지로 근로자에게 이를 다시 작성하여 교부할 의무가 발생합니다.
(벌칙) 근로기준법 제114조 500만 원 이하의 벌금

1-1-4 1부는 근로자에게 서면으로 교부하고, 1부는 사업장에 보관하고 있습니까?

근로기준법 제17조 제2항 본문
사용자는 근로계약 체결 시에 근로계약서를 2부 작성하여 1부는 근로자에게 주고, 1부는 사업장에 보관하고 있어야 합니다.
(벌칙) 근로기준법 제114조 500만 원 이하의 벌금

1-1-5 근로계약 체결 후 단체협약 또는 취업규칙이 변경되어 근로계약서 상의 임금, 근로시간, 휴일 및 휴가가 변경되었습니까? 변경된 사항이 명시된 근로계약서를 근로자가 요구한 경우, 근로계약서를 재교부하였습니까?

근로기준법 제17조 제2항 단서
근로계약 체결 후 중요 근로조건은 근로자와의 서면 합의, 단체협약 또는 취업규칙의 변경, 법령에 의하여 변경될 수 있습니다.
3가지 사유(근로자대표와의 서면합의에 의하여 변경된 경우, 취업규칙 또는 단체협약에 의하여 변경된 경우, 법령에 의하여 변경된 경우)에 해당하며 근로자의 요구가 있다면 근로자의 근로계약상 중요 근로조건이 변경된 경우 근로자에게 재교부하여야 합니다.
(벌칙) 근로기준법 제114조 500만 원 이하의 벌금

1-2 기간제 및 단시간 근로자의 근로조건 서면명시

1-2-1 기간제 또는 단시간 근로자 채용시 근로계약서를 작성하였습니까?

기간제 및 단시간근로자 보호 등에 관한 법률(이하 기간제법) 제17조
사용자는 기간제, 단시간 근로자와 근로계약을 체결할 때(근로자를 채용할 때) 근로계약서를 작성하여야 합니다.
(과태료) 기간제법 제24조 500만 원 이하의 과태료

Chapter 2: Labor Inspection Checklist

1-2-2 Are all the essential items listed in the employment contract?

Article 17 of the Fixed-term Workers Act

When an employer concludes a labor contract with a fixed-term or part-time worker, all required items (term of labor contract, working hours and breaks, wages, holidays and vacations, place of employment and work, working days and working hours) in each subparagraph must be entered. The employment contract must be specified in writing and delivered.

(Fine for negligence) Fine for negligence up to 5 million won under Article 24 of the Fixed-term Workers Act

1-2-3 Do employment contracts for part-time workers include the working days and working hours per working day?

Article 17 of the Fixed-term Workers Act

According to Article 17 Subparagraph 6 of the Fixed-term Workers Act, part-time workers must additionally specify in writing working days and working hours per working day in addition to the contents of the labor contract for general workers.

(Fine for negligence) Fine for negligence up to 5 million won under Article 24 of the Fixed-term Workers Act

1-2-4 If the worker requested re-issuance of the labor contract due to a change in working hours by agreement between the parties, did you draw up a new contract with the changes therein and reissue it?

Article 17 of the Fixed-term Workers Act

The employer may change the working hours by agreement with the worker, and in this case, if the worker requests a reissue of the labor contract, the changed content must be rewritten and issued.

(Fine for negligence) Fine for negligence up to 5 million won under Article 24 of the Fixed-term Workers Act

1-2-5 Is one copy issued to each worker in writing and one copy kept at the workplace?

Article 17 of the Labor Standards Act

In the case of an employment contract, one copy must be given to the worker in writing and one copy must be kept at the workplace.

(Fine for negligence) Fine for negligence up to 5 million won under Article 24 of the Fixed-term Workers Act

1-2-2 근로계약서에는 필수 기재사항이 모두 기재되어 있습니까?

기간제법 제17조

사용자는 기간제, 단시간 근로자와 근로계약을 체결하는 경우 각 호의 필수 기재사항(근로계약기간, 근로시간 및 휴게, 임금, 휴일 및 휴가, 취업의 장소 및 종사업무, 근로일 및 근로시간)이 모두 기재된 근로계약을 서면 명시하여 교부하여야 합니다.

(과태료) 기간제법 제24조 500만 원 이하의 과태료

1-2-3 단시간근로자의 근로계약서 작성시 근로일 및 근로일별 근로시간을 기재하였습니까?

기간제법 제17조

단시간 근로자는 기간제법 제17조 제6호에 따르면 일반 근로자의 근로계약 내용 외에 근로일 및 근로일별 근로시간을 추가로 서면 명시하여야 합니다.

(과태료) 기간제법 제24조 500만 원 이하의 과태료

1-2-4 양 당사자간 합의로 근로시간이 변경되어 근로자가 근로계약서 재교부를 요구한 경우 이를 다시 작성하여 교부하였습니까?

기간제법 제17조

사용자는 근로자와의 합의에 따라 근로시간을 변경할 수 있으며 이 경우 근로자가 근로계약서 재교부를 요구한 경우 변경된 내용에 대하여 다시 작성하여 교부하여야 합니다.

(과태료) 기간제법 제24조 500만 원 이하의 과태료

1-2-5 1부는 근로자에게 서면으로 교부하고, 1부는 사업장에 보관하고 있습니까?

근로기준법 제17조

근로계약서의 경우, 1부는 근로자에게 서면으로 교부하고, 1부는 사업장에 보관하여야 합니다.

(과태료) 기간제법 제24조 500만 원 이하의 과태료

Chapter 2: Labor Inspection Checklist

1-2-6 Are you preparing and issuing an employment contract for daily workers who sign an employment contract on a daily basis?

Article 17 of the Fixed-term Workers Act

Even in the case of daily workers, since they are workers with a fixed period, Article 17 of the Fixed-Term Contract Act applies, and a written labor contract must be written and issued.

(Penalty) Article 114 of the Labor Standards Act, a fine of up to 5 million won

2. Preservation of Employee Registers and Contract Documents

2-1 Preservation of contract documents

2-1-1 Do you keep documents related to labor contracts, such as employee registers, labor contracts,

Article 42 of the Labor Standards Act

In accordance with Article 42 of the Labor Standards Act, employers are required to preserve documents related to labor contracts, such as worker lists, labor contracts, payroll books, and written agreements, for three years.

(Fine for negligence) Article 116 of the Labor Standards Act: Fine for negligence up to 5 million won

2-2 Payroll

2-2-1 Do you prepare a wage ledger every time you pay wages?

Article 48 of the Labor Standards Act

According to Article 48 of the Labor Standards Act, employers must prepare a wage ledger whenever wages are paid.

(Fine for negligence) Article 116 of the Labor Standards Act: Fine for negligence up to 5 million won

2-2-2 Are all items stipulated by law written in the wage ledger?

Article 27 (1) of the Enforcement Decree of the Labor Standards Act

The wage ledger includes information that can identify the worker, such as name, date of birth, and employee number, date of employment, work performed, matters that are the basis for calculating wages and family allowances, number of days worked, number of working hours, overtime, night work, or holidays. In the case of work, the number of hours, basic

1-2-6 1일 단위의 근로계약을 체결하는 일용직 근로자에게도 근로계약 체결시 근로계약서를 작성하여 교부하고 있습니까?

기간제법 제17조

일용직 근로자의 경우에도 기간의 정함이 있는 근로자에 해당하기에 기간제법 제17조가 적용되고 반드시 근로계약서를 서면으로 작성하고 근로계약서를 교부하여야 합니다.

(벌칙) 근로기준법 제114조 500만 원 이하의 벌금

2. 근로자 명부 및 계약서류 보존

2-1 계약서류 보존

2-1-1 근로자명부, 근로계약서, 임금대장, 서면합의서 등 근로계약에 관한 서류를 보존하고 있습니까?

근로기준법 제42조

근로기준법 제42조에 따라 사용자는 근로자명부, 근로계약서, 임금대장, 서면합의서 등 근로계약에 관한 서류를 3년간 보존해야 합니다.

(과태료) 근로기준법 제116조 500만 원 이하의 과태료

2-2 임금대장

2-2-1 임금을 지급할 때마다 임금대장을 작성하고 있습니까?

근로기준법 제48조

근로기준법 제48조에 따라 사용자는 임금을 지급할 때마다 임금대장을 작성하여야 합니다.

(과태료) 근로기준법 제116조 500만 원 이하의 과태료

2-2-2 임금대장에는 법에서 규정한 사항을 모두 기재하고 있습니까?

근로기준법 시행령 제27조 제1항

임금대장에는 '성명, 생년월일, 사원번호 등 근로자를 특정할 수 있는 정보, 고용 연월일, 종사하는 업무, 임금 및 가족수당의 계산기초가 되는 사항, 근로일수, 근로시간수, 연장근로, 야간근로 또는 휴일근로를

wage, allowance, amount of other wages by detail (if there is wages paid in a currency other than currency, the name and quantity of the wages, and the total evaluation amount), part of the wages in accordance with laws or collective agreements should be included in the amount (health insurance premium, national pension, employment insurance premium, income tax, etc.).

(Fine for negligence) Article 116 of the Labor Standards Act: Fine for negligence up to 5 million won

3. Payment of Various Money and Goods such as Wages

3-1 Settlement of payments

3-1-1 If a worker dies or retires, are wages, compensation, and all other money and valuables paid within 14 days?

Article 36 of the Labor Standards Act

In case of death or retirement, wages, compensation, and all other money and valuables must be paid within 14 days from the occurrence of the reason for the payment. However, in special circumstances, the period may be extended by agreement between the employer and the worker.

(Penalty) Article 109: Imprisonment for up to 3 years or a fine of up to 30 million won

3-1-2 Have you paid all the money and valuables that were supposed to be paid to the workers, including business expenses in addition to wages and severance pay?

All money and valuables include not only compensation for the work provided by the worker, but also money and valuables to be paid by the employer based on the labor relationship.

(Penalty) Article 109: Imprisonment for up to 3 years or a fine of up to 30 million won

3-1-3 In the event of special circumstances, the payment date can be extended by agreement between the parties within 14 days from the date of retirement/resignation. If applicable, have you reached an agreement on this?

Exceptionally, in special circumstances, the payment date can be extended by agreement between the parties. In this case, the agreement between the parties must be made within 14 days from the date of occurrence of the reason for payment.

시킨 경우에는 그 시간 수, 기본급, 수당, 그 밖의 임금의 내역별 금액(통화 이외의 것으로 지급된 임금이 있는 경우에는 그 품명 및 수량과 평가총액), 법령 또는 단체협약에 따라 임금의 일부를 공제한 경우에는 그 금액(건강보험료, 국민연금, 고용보험료, 소득세 등)'이 포함되어야 합니다.
(과태료) 근로기준법 제116조 500만 원 이하의 과태료

3. 임금 등 각종 금품 지급

3-1 금품청산

3-1-1 근로자가 사망 또는 퇴직한 경우 14일 이내에 임금, 보상금, 그 밖의 일체의 금품을 지급하고 있습니까?

근로기준법 제36조

사망 또는 퇴직한 경우 그 지급 사유가 발생한 때부터 14일 이내에 임금, 보상금, 그 밖에 일체의 금품을 지급하여야 합니다. 다만, 특별한 사정이 있을 경우에는 사용자와 근로자 사이의 합의에 의하여 기일을 연장할 수 있습니다.

(벌칙) 제109조 3년 이하의 징역 또는 3천만 원 이하의 벌금

3-1-2 임금, 퇴직금뿐만 아니라 업무상 지출경비 등 근로자에게 지급하기로 한 일체의 금품을 지급하였습니까?

일체의 금품이란 근로자가 제공한 근로에 대한 대가뿐 아니라 근로관계에 기초하여 사용자가 지급해야 할 금품이라면 모두 포함됩니다.

(벌칙) 제109조 3년 이하의 징역 또는 3천만 원 이하의 벌금

3-1-3 특별한 사정이 있는 경우, 퇴직일로부터 14일 이내에 당사자간 합의로 지급기일을 연장할 수 있는데 이에 대한 합의를 했습니까?

예외적으로 특별한 사정이 있는 경우에는 당사자간 합의로 지급기일을 연장할 수 있는데, 이 경우 당사자간 합의는 지급사유 발생일로부터 14일 이내에 해야 합니다.

(Penalty) Article 109: Imprisonment for up to 3 years or a fine of up to 30 million won

3-1-4 If the payment was delayed due to an agreement with the involved parties, was interest paid for the delayed period?

Article 17 of the Enforcement Decree of the Labor Standards Act

In principle, unpaid wages and severance pay must be paid, including delay interest (20% per annum) for the number of delayed days until the payment date. However, delay interest does not apply if the cause of Article 18 of the same Enforcement Decree, such as the commencement of corporate rehabilitation procedures or a decision to declare bankruptcy, etc.

(Penalty) Article 109: Imprisonment for up to 3 years or a fine of up to 30 million won

3-2 Payment of wages

3-2-1 Are wages paid to workers in Korean currency?

Article 43 of the Labor Standards Act

Wages must be paid in convertible currency under the Korean Bank Act, except where the law or collective agreement stipulates that wages be paid in other ways.

However, in cases stipulated by the collective agreement, part of the wages may be paid in kind, stocks, or commodity exchange vouchers only to union members.

(Penalty) Article 109: Imprisonment for up to 3 years or a fine of up to 30 million won

3-2-2 Are wages paid directly to workers?

Article 43 of the Labor Standards Act

Wages must be paid directly to workers.

It is also not permitted to pay wages to workers' parents or legal representatives.

It is possible for workers to deposit money into a bank account at a designated bank and withdraw it on payday.

(Penalty) Article 109: Imprisonment for up to 3 years or a fine of up to 30 million won

(벌칙) 제109조 3년 이하의 징역 또는 3천만 원 이하의 벌금

3-1-4 당사자와의 합의로 지급이 지연된 경우 지연된 기간만큼의 지연이자도 지급하였습니까?

근로기준법 시행령 제17조

원칙적으로 미지급된 임금 및 퇴직금 등에 대하여 지급하는 날까지 지연일수에 대한 지연이자(연20%)를 포함하여 지급하여야 합니다.

다만, 회생절차개시, 파산선고의 결정이 있는 경우 등 동 시행령 제18조의 사유에 해당하면 지연이자는 적용되지 않습니다.

(벌칙) 제109조 3년 이하의 징역 또는 3천만 원 이하의 벌금

3-2 임금지급

3-2-1 근로자에게 임금을 통화로 지급하고 있습니까?

근로기준법 제43조

임금은 법령이나 단체협약에 다른 방식으로 지급하기로 정한 경우를 제외하고는 강제통용력이 있는 「한국은행법」에 의한 화폐로 지급해야 합니다.

다만, 단체협약으로 정한 경우에는 조합원에 한하여 임금의 일부를 현물, 주식, 상품교환권 등으로 지급할 수 있습니다.

(벌칙) 제109조 3년 이하의 징역 또는 3천만 원 이하의 벌금

3-2-2 임금을 근로자에게 직접 지급하고 있습니까?

근로기준법 제43조

임금은 근로자에게 직접 지급해야 합니다.

근로자의 친권자나 법정대리인에게 임금을 지급하는 것도 허용되지 않습니다.

근로자가 지정한 은행의 은행예금 계좌에 입금하여 임금지급일에 인출할 수 있도록 하는 것은 가능합니다.

(벌칙) 제109조 3년 이하의 징역 또는 3천만 원 이하의 벌금

3-2-3 Are wages paid in full without unauthorized deductions?

Article 43 of the Labor Standards Act

Part of wages cannot be deducted from wages, except when there are special provisions in laws or collective agreements, and the full amount must be paid to workers.

Therefore, deductions are possible when there are legal grounds (income tax, local tax, four major insurances) and when collective agreements stipulate deductions for labor union fees and welfare facility usage fees.

However, in principle, wage deduction based on the provisions of the employment rules or the contents of the labor contract is not permitted.

On the other hand, since wages must be paid in full to the worker, even if the employer has a claim for damages from the worker, the full wage must be paid without the worker's consent.

However, when wages are overpaid due to a calculation error, wages can be offset, but even in this case, the timing of offset is reasonable enough to be seen as an adjustment to the wages paid in excess, and the amount and method of offset are disclosed to the worker. It must be a case where there is no fear of harming the lives of workers by giving advance notice.

(Penalty) Article 109 Imprisonment for up to 3 years or a fine of up to 30 million won

3-2-4 Are wages paid on a fixed date at least once a month?

the Labor Standards Act Article 43

Wages must be paid on a fixed date at least once a month.

Employment rules must specify the wage payment period, and even if a worker joins the company midway through the month, part of the wage must be paid on the first wage payment day following the month of joining.

(Penalty) Article 109 Imprisonment for up to 3 years or a fine of up to 30 million won

3-3 Pay slips

3-3-1 Are pay slips issued each time wages are paid?

Article 48 Paragraph 2 of the Labor Standards Act

When paying wages, the employer must issue a wage statement that includes the statutory details to the worker. (Applied to all workplaces with at least

3-2-3 임금을 임의로 공제하지 않고 전액 지급하고 있습니까?

근로기준법 제43조

임금은 법령이나 단체협약에 특별한 규정이 있을 때를 제외하고는 임금의 일부를 공제할 수 없고 전액을 근로자에게 지급해야 합니다.

따라서, 법령에 근거가 있는 경우(소득세, 지방세, 4대 보험)와 단체협약에 노동조합비, 복리후생시설 이용비 등에 관한 공제를 규정하고 있는 경우에는 공제가 가능합니다.

그러나, 취업규칙의 규정이나 근로계약 내용을 근거로 한 임금공제는 원칙적으로 허용되지 않습니다.

한편, 임금은 근로자에게 전액 지급되어야 하므로 사용자가 근로자에게 손해배상을 청구할 일이 있다 하더라도 근로자의 동의가 없다면 임금 전액을 지급해야 합니다.

다만, 계산의 착오로 임금이 초과 지급되었을 때에는 임금을 상계할 수 있으나, 이 경우도 상계하는 시기가 초과 지급한 임금에 대한 조정으로 볼 수 있을 만큼 가까워 합리성이 있고, 상계 금액과 방법을 근로자에게 예고하여 근로자 생활을 해할 염려가 없는 경우이어야 합니다.

(벌칙) 제109조 3년 이하의 징역 또는 3천만 원 이하의 벌금

3-2-4 매월 1회 이상 일정한 기일을 정하여 임금을 지급하고 있습니까?

근로기준법 제43조

임금은 매월 1회 이상 일정한 날짜를 정하여 지급해야 합니다.

취업규칙에는 반드시 임금지급 시기를 명시하여야 하며, 월도중에 근로자가 입사해도 입사한 달에 도래하는 첫 임금 지급일에 임금 일부가 지급되어야 합니다.

(벌칙) 제109조 3년 이하의 징역 또는 3천만 원 이하의 벌금

3-3 임금명세서

3-3-1 임금을 지급할 때마다 임금명세서를 교부하고 있습니까?

근로기준법 제48조 제2항

사용자는 임금을 지급할 때 근로자에게 법정 기재사항이 포함된 임금

one full-time worker)

(Fine for negligence) Article 116 Fine for negligence up to 5 million won

3-3-2 Are all items stipulated by law written on the pay slip?

Article 48 Paragraph 2 of the Labor Standards Act

The pay slip is a written statement (including electronic documents pursuant to Article 1, Article 2 of the 「Framework Act on Electronic Documents and Electronic Commerce」) stating matters prescribed by the Presidential Decree, such as the composition of wages, calculation method, details of cases in which a part of wages are deducted pursuant to the proviso of Article 43 (1) of the Labor Standards Act.

(Fine for negligence) Article 116 Fine for negligence up to 5 million won

3-4 Wage payment for subcontracting

3-4-1 Are wages paid to subcontract workers up to date (direct upper or higher level contractors)?

Article 44 of the Labor Standards Act

In the case where a project is carried out under a subcontract, if the wages of workers hired by a subcontractor are in arrears due to reasons attributable to the immediate upper-level contractor, the immediate upper-level contractor shall be jointly and severally responsible for the payment of wages with the subcontractor.

If the immediate upper-level contractor pays wages in arrears to workers hired by the sub-contractor, the immediate upper-level contractor may exercise the right to indemnity against the sub-contractor.

With the revision of the Labor Standards Act, this provision applies even if a contract has been made once, so it is also applied in case of non-payment of wages to workers hired by the contractor due to reasons attributable to the contractor.

(Penalty) Article 109 Imprisonment for up to 3 years or a fine of up to 30 million won

3-5 Shutdown allowance

3-5-1 Has the company ever shut down for reasons attributable to the employer? Were the workers paid at least 70% of their average wage during the period of suspension?

Article 46 of the Labor Standards Act

'Suspension' refers to a case in which a worker tries to provide work but is

명세서를 교부하여야 합니다. (상시근로자 1인 이상 사업장 전체 적용)
(과태표) 제116조 500만 원 이하의 과태료

3-3-2 임금명세서에 법에서 규정한 사항을 모두 기재하고 있습니까?

근로기준법 제48조 제2항

임금명세서는 임금의 구성항목, 계산방법, 제43조 제1항 단서조항에 따라 임금의 일부를 공제한 경우의 내역 등 대통령령으로 정하는 사항을 기재한 서면(「전자문서 및 전자거래 기본법」 제2조 제1호에 따른 전자문서를 포함)으로 교부하여야 합니다.

(과태료) 제116조 500만 원 이하의 과태료

3-4 도급사업에 대한 임금지급

3-4-1 우리 사업장(직상수급인 또는 상위수급인)의 귀책사유에 의해 하수급인 소속 근로자에 대한 임금체불이 발생하지 않았습니까?

근로기준법 제44조

사업이 도급계약으로 이루어지는 경우 직상 수급인의 귀책사유로 하수급인에게 고용된 근로자의 임금이 체불된 경우에는 직상 수급인은 그 하수급인과 연대하여 임금지급의 책임을 집니다.

직상 수급인이 하수급인이 고용한 근로자에게 체불 임금을 지급한 경우에는 직상 수급인은 하수급인에게 구상권을 행사할 수 있습니다.

근로기준법 개정으로 도급이 한 차례 이뤄진 경우에도 이 규정이 적용되므로 도급인의 귀책사유로 수급인에게 고용된 근로자에 대한 임금체불이 발생한 경우에도 적용됩니다.

(벌칙) 제109조 3년 이하의 징역 또는 3천만 원 이하의 벌금

3-5 휴업수당

3-5-1 사용자 귀책사유로 휴업한 적이 있습니까? 휴업기간동안 평균임금의 70% 이상을 지급하였습니까?

근로기준법 제46조

'휴업'이란 근로자가 근로를 제공하려 하지만 그 의사에 반하여 근로

unable to provide work against his or her will, or the employer refuses to accept the work.

In the case of suspension of business due to reasons attributable to the employer, the employer must pay workers an allowance of at least 70/100 of the average wage during the period of suspension.

However, if the amount equivalent to 70/100 of the average wage exceeds the ordinary wage, the ordinary wage may be paid as a suspension allowance.

In addition to intention and negligence, management failures that occur within the scope of the employer's power are regarded as causes attributable to the employer, but force majeure such as natural disasters or wars, and other circumstances outside the company that do not fall within the scope of the employer's power are not considered to be attributable to the employer. not.

Penalty (Article 109) Imprisonment for up to 3 years or a fine of up to 30 million won

3-5-2 Do you know the concept of average wage?

Average wages means the amount obtained by dividing the total amount of wages paid to the worker for the three months preceding the date on which the reason for calculating them occurred by the total number of days in that period.

3-5-3 If employment adjustment is unavoidable due to a business crisis, are you prepared to take advantage of the Employment Retention Subsidy Program that provides support for maintaining employment through business suspensions, etc.?

The 'Employment Maintenance Subsidy System' is a system to prevent workers from losing their jobs by providing support to employers who are forced to adjust their employment due to business crises such as declines in sales and production, and take measures to maintain employment, such as temporary shutdowns or layoffs.

3-6 Extended, night and holiday work

3-6-1 Are you familiar with the concept of extended/night/holiday work?

'Overtime work' refers to work that exceeds the statutory working hours, 'night work' refers to work provided from 10:00 pm to 6:00 am, and 'holiday work' refers to work performed on a holiday.

3-6-2 Are additional wages paid for extended/night/holiday work?

제공이 불가능하거나, 사용자에 의하여 노무수령이 거부된 경우를 의미합니다.

사용자의 귀책사유로 휴업하는 경우 사용자는 휴업기간 동안 근로자에게 평균임금의 100분의 70 이상의 수당을 지급하여야 합니다.

다만, 평균임금의 100분의 70에 해당하는 금액이 통상임금을 초과하는 경우에는 통상임금을 휴업수당으로 지급할 수 있습니다.

고의, 과실 이외에도 사용자의 세력범위 내에서 생긴 경영상 장애까지 사용자의 귀책사유로 보지만, 천재지변이나 전쟁 등과 같은 불가항력, 그 밖에 사용자의 세력범위에 속하지 않는 기업 외적인 사정은 사용자의 귀책사유로 보지 않습니다.

(벌칙) 제109조 3년 이하의 징역 또는 3천만 원 이하의 벌금

3-5-2 평균임금의 개념을 알고 있습니까?

'평균임금'이란 이를 산정하여야 할 사유가 발생한 날 이전 3월간 그 근로자에 대해 지급된 임금의 총액을 그 기간의 총일수로 나눈 금액을 말합니다.

3-5-3 경영상 위기로 고용조정이 불가피한 경우 휴업 등으로 고용을 유지할 경우 지원받을 수 있는 고용유지지원금제도를 알고 있습니까?

매출액, 생산량 감소 등 경영상 위기로 고용조정이 불가피하게 된 사업주가 휴업, 휴직 등 고용유지조치를 실시하는 경우 이를 지원함으로써 근로자의 실직을 예방하기 위한 제도로 '고용유지지원금제도'가 있습니다.

3-6 연장, 야간 및 휴일근로

3-6-1 연장·야간·휴일근로의 개념에 대해 알고 있습니까?

'연장근로'란 법정근로시간을 초과한 근로를, '야간근로'는 오후 10시부터 오전 6시까지 제공하는 근로를 말하며, '휴일근로'는 휴무일에 근무한 경우를 말합니다.

3-6-2 연장·야간·휴일근로에 따른 가산임금을 지급하고 있습니까?

For the three types of work, 1) overtime/night/holiday work allowances as compensation for the workers themselves, and

2) All additional allowances for overtime/nighttime/holiday must be paid.

(Penalty) Article 109 Imprisonment for up to 3 years or a fine of up to 30 million won

3-6-3 Do you know how to calculate additional wages for extended/night/holiday work?

In principle, for the three types of work,

1) labor allowance (100%) for working hours exceeding the contractual work and

2) additional allowance (50%) must be paid.

On the other hand, when working on paid holidays,

1) holiday work allowance,

2) additional holiday work allowance, and

3) holiday allowance (e.g., weekly holiday pay) must be paid.

In addition, holiday work additional allowances must be paid by adding 50% of the regular wage for up to 8 hours, and 100% of the regular wage for hours exceeding 8 hours.

Penalty (Article 109) Imprisonment for up to 3 years or a fine of up to 30 million won

3-6-4 Are part-time workers (part-timers) paid overtime pay if they work in excess of the contractual working hours, even if it is less than 8 hours a day?

In the case of short-time work, 50% or more of the ordinary wage must be added to pay for working hours that exceed the prescribed working hours, even within the statutory working hours (40 hours per week and 8 hours per day).

(Penalty) Article 109: Imprisonment for up to 3 years or a fine of up to 30 million won

3-6-5 If a young worker who works 7 hours a day works over 7 hours, is overtime pay paid for the excess hours?

For minor workers, the statutory working hours are 7 hours per day and 35 hours per week. If these are exceeded, both overtime and overtime pay must be paid.

(Penalty) Article 109: Imprisonment for up to 3 years or a fine of up to 30 million won

3가지 근로에 대하여는 1) 근로자체에 대한 대가인 연장/야간/휴일 근로수당과 2) 그에 대한 가산수당인 연장/야간/휴일 가산수당을 모두 지급해야 합니다.

(벌칙) 제109조 3년 이하의 징역 또는 3천만 원 이하의 벌금

3-6-3 연장·야간·휴일근로에 따른 가산임금 산정방법을 알고 있습니까?

3가지 근로에 대하여는 원칙적으로
1) 근로자체에 대한 근로수당(100%)과
2) 그에 대한 가산수당(50%)을 지급해야 합니다.

한편, 유급휴일에 근무한 경우에는
1) 근로의 대가인 휴일 근로수당과,
2) 휴일근로 가산수당,
3) 휴일수당(예: 주휴수당)이 모두 지급되어야 합니다.

또한, 휴일근로 가산수당은 8시간까지는 통상임금의 50%를, 8시간 초과한 시간은 통상임금의 100%를 가산하여 지급해야 합니다.

(벌칙) 제109조 3년 이하의 징역 또는 3천만 원 이하의 벌금

3-6-4 단시간근로자(아르바이트생)에게는 1일 8시간이 되지 않더라도 소정근로시간을 초과하여 근무하면 연장근로수당을 지급하고 있습니까?

단시간 근로의 경우 법정근로시간(1주 40시간과 1일 8시간) 이내라도 소정근로시간을 초과한 근로시간에 대해서는 통상임금의 50% 이상을 가산하여 지급해야 합니다.

(벌칙) 제109조 3년 이하의 징역 또는 3천만 원 이하의 벌금

3-6-5 1일 7시간 근무하는 연소근로자가 7시간을 초과하여 근무할 경우, 초과하는 시간에 대해 연장근로수당을 지급하고 있습니까?

연소근로자의 경우는 1일 7시간, 1주 35시간이 법정근로시간이므로 이를 초과하는 경우 연장근로에 해당하여 연장근로수당과 가산근로수당을 모두 지급하여야 합니다.

(벌칙) 제109조 3년 이하의 징역 또는 3천만 원 이하의 벌금

3-6-6 Is 100% of the regular wage paid additionally for holiday work exceeding 8 hours?

Holiday work must be paid at 50% of the regular wage for up to 8 hours, and 100% of the regular wage for hours exceeding 8 hours.

(Penalty) Article 109: Imprisonment for up to 3 years or a fine of up to 30 million won

3-6-7 Are additional allowances paid to supervisory and intermittent workers for night work?

In the case of those who engage in surveillance/intermittent work and whose employer has obtained approval from the Minister of Employment and Labor, they are not subject to working hours, but additional allowances for night work are applicable and must be paid.

(Penalty) Article 109: Imprisonment for up to 3 years or a fine of up to 30 million won

4. Violation of Limits on Working Hours and Overtime

4-1 Working hours

4-1-1 Do you know what statutory working hours, prescribed working hours, overtime working hours, night working hours, and holiday working hours are?

'Legal working hours' refers to the standard working hours stipulated by law, and regular workers are 8 hours per day and 40 hours per week. (7 hours a day, 35 hours a week for young workers under the age of 18, 6 hours a day, 34 hours a week for workers engaged in harmful or hazardous work, etc.)

'Prescribed working hours' refers to the working hours set between the worker and the employer within the statutory working hours.

'Overtime working hours' refers to working hours provided in excess of the statutory working hours, and 'night working hours' refers to working hours provided from 10:00 pm to 6:00 am.

'Holiday working hours' refers to working hours on weekly holidays, Labor Day, public office holidays and substitute holidays, and days designated as labor-management holidays under collective agreements or employment rules.

3-6-6 8시간을 초과한 휴일근로에 대하여 통상임금의 100퍼센트를 추가로 지급하고 있습니까?

휴일근로 가산수당은 8시간까지는 통상임금의 50%를, 8시간 초과한 시간은 통상임금의 100%를 가산하여 지급해야 합니다.
(벌칙) 제109조 3년 이하의 징역 또는 3천만 원 이하의 벌금

3-6-7 감시·단속적 근로종사자가 야간근로를 하는 경우 가산수당을 지급하고 있습니까?

감시.단속적 근로에 종사하는 자로 사용자가 고용노동부 장관의 승인을 받은 자의 경우에는 근로시간의 적용을 받지는 않으나 야간근로 가산수당은 적용을 받으므로 이를 지급하여야 합니다.
(벌칙) 제109조 3년 이하의 징역 또는 3천만 원 이하의 벌금

4. 근로시간 및 연장근로 한도 위반

4-1 근로시간

4-1-1 법정근로시간, 소정근로시간, 연장근로시간, 야간근로시간, 휴일근로시간이 각각 어떤 내용인지 알고 있습니까?

'법정근로시간'이란 법에서 정한 기준 근로시간을 말하며, 통상근로자는 1일 8시간, 1주 40시간이며, 다만 법에서는 근로자의 연령 또는 작업 성질에 따라 법정근로시간을 달리 정하고 있습니다. (18세 미만인 연소근로자의 경우에는 1일 7시간, 1주 35시간, 유해 . 위험작업 종사 근로자의 경우에는 1일 6시간, 1주 34시간 등)
'소정근로시간'이란 법정근로시간 내에서 근로자와 사용자 사이에 정한 근로시간을 의미합니다.
'연장근로시간'이란 법정근로시간을 초과하여 제공한 근로시간을, '야간근로시간'은 오후 10시부터 오전 6시까지의 시간에 제공한 근로시간을 말합니다.
'휴일근로시간'은 주휴일, 근로자의 날, 관공서 공휴일 및 대체 공휴일, 단체협약이나 취업규칙 등에 의하여 노사간 휴일로 정한 날의 근로시간을 말합니다.

4-1-2 Do you know that waiting time under the supervision of the employer is working time?

Article 50 Paragraph 3 of the Labor Standards Act

Waiting time, etc. under the direction and supervision of the employer is working time, not break time, so the employer must pay wages for that time.

(Penalty) Article 110: Imprisonment for up to two years or a fine of up to 20 million won

4-1-3 Are you complying with the statutory working hours?

'Legal working hours' refers to the standard working hours stipulated by law, and regular workers are 8 hours a day and 40 hours a week, and overtime is possible up to 12 hours a week by agreement between the parties concerned.

However, the law stipulates different statutory working hours depending on the age of the worker or the nature of the work. (7 hours a day, 35 hours a week for young workers under the age of 18, 6 hours a day, 34 hours a week for workers engaged in harmful or hazardous work, etc.)

(Penalty) Article 110: Imprisonment for up to two years or a fine of up to 20 million won

4-2 Restrictions on overtime work

4-2-1 Do you know the exact criteria for calculating overtime hours?

Article 53 of the Labor Standards Act

'Extended working hours' refers to working hours that exceed the legal working hours of 8 hours per day and 40 hours per week based on actual working hours.

In the case of part-time workers, this refers to working hours provided in excess of the prescribed working hours.

4-2-2 Do you agree with the workers to work overtime?

Article 53 of the Labor Standards Act

By agreement between the parties, the statutory working hours (8 hours per day, 40 hours per week) can be extended up to 12 hours per week, but workers who do not agree to overtime cannot be forced.

4-1-2 사용자의 지휘감독 아래 있는 대기시간은 근로시간임을 알고 있습니까?

근로기준법 제50조 제3항

사용자의 지휘·감독 아래에 있는 대기시간 등은 휴게시간이 아닌 근로시간이므로 사용자는 해당 시간에 대하여 임금을 지급하여야 합니다.

(벌칙) 제110조 2년 이하의 징역 또는 2천만 원 이하의 벌금

4-1-3 법정근로시간을 준수하고 있습니까?

'법정근로시간'이란 법에서 정한 기준 근로시간을 말하며, 통상근로자는 1일 8시간, 1주 40시간이며, 당사자간의 합의로 주12시간을 한도로 연장근로가 가능합니다.

다만 법에서는 근로자의 연령 또는 작업 성질에 따라 법정근로시간을 달리 정하고 있습니다. (18세 미만인 연소근로자의 경우에는 1일 7시간, 1주 35시간, 유해·위험작업 종사 근로자의 경우에는 1일 6시간, 1주 34시간 등)

(벌칙) 제110조 2년 이하의 징역 또는 2천만 원 이하의 벌금

4-2 연장근로의 제한

4-2-1 연장근로시간을 산정하는 기준을 정확히 알고 있습니까?

근로기준법 제53조

'연장근로시간'이란 실 근로시간을 기준으로 법정근로시간인 1일 8시간, 1주 40시간을 초과하는 근로시간을 의미합니다.

단시간 근로자의 경우에는 소정근로시간을 초과하여 제공한 근로시간을 말합니다.

4-2-2 근로자와 합의하고 연장근로를 시킵니까?

근로기준법 제53조

당사자간에 합의하면 법정근로시간(1일 8시간, 1주 40시간)을 1주 간에 12시간을 한도로 연장할 수 있으나 연장근로에 동의하지 않는 근로자에게 강제할 수는 없습니다.

합의는 원칙적으로는 사용자와 근로자 간의 개별적 합의를 의미하는데

Agreement, in principle, means an individual agreement between the employer and the worker. According to the precedent, it is not necessary to do it every time overtime work is done, and it is possible to make an agreement in advance through an employment contract, etc.

It is possible to set it by collective agreement, but it should not deprive or limit individual workers' right to agree on overtime work.

(Penalty) Article 110: Imprisonment for up to two years or a fine of up to 20 million won

4-2-3 Do you restrict overtime work to 12 hours a week for each relevant worker?

Article 53, Article 59 of the Labor Standards Act

By agreement between the parties, the statutory working hours (8 hours per day, 40 hours per week) can be extended by up to 12 hours per week, so in principle, the maximum working hours per week is limited to 52 hours.

In the case of the following industries, overtime work in excess of 12 hours per week is permitted upon written agreement with the employee representative.

1) Land transportation and pipeline transportation (excluding route buses)
2) Water transportation
3) Air transport business
4) Other transport-related service businesses
5) health industry

However, in this case, 11 hours of continuous rest time must be granted after the end of the working day until the start of the next working day.

(Penalty) Article 110: Imprisonment for up to two years or a fine of up to 20 million won

4-2-4 Are you aware of flexible work arrangements that can be used?

Article 51, 52 of the Labor Standards Act

The 'flexible working hour system' is a work system that allows flexible working hours, such as the flexible and selective working hour system and the discretionary working hour system.

The 'flexible working hour system' means that the average working hours for a certain period are set within the legal standard working hours (40 hours per week) by shortening the working hours on other working days and

판례에 의하면 연장근로를 할 때마다 할 필요는 없고 근로계약 등으로 미리 약정하는 것도 가능합니다.

단체협약으로 정하는 것도 가능하지만 개별근로자의 연장근로 합의권을 박탈하거나 제한하여서는 아니됩니다.

(벌칙) 제110조 2년 이하의 징역 또는 2천만 원 이하의 벌금

4-2-3 1주 연장근로를 최대 12시간까지만 시키고 있습니까?

근로기준법 제53조, 제59조

당사자간에 합의하면 법정근로시간(1일 8시간, 1주 40시간)을 1주 간에 12시간을 한도로 연장할 수 있으므로 원칙적으로 1주 최대 근로 가능 시간은 52시간으로 제한됩니다.

다음 업종의 경우에는 근로자대표와 서면합의를 하면 1주 12시간을 초과한 연장근로가 가능합니다.

1) 육상운송 및 파이프라인 운송업(노선버스 제외)
2) 수상운송업
3) 항공운송업
4) 기타 운송관련 서비스업
5) 보건업

다만, 이 경우에는 근로일 종료 후 다음 근로일 개시 전까지 11시간의 연속 휴식시간을 부여하여야 합니다.

(벌칙) 제110조 2년 이하의 징역 또는 2천만 원 이하의 벌금

4-2-4 활용가능한 유연근무제를 알고 있습니까?

근로기준법 제51조, 제52조

'유연근로제'란 근무시간을 탄력적으로 운용할 수 있는 근무제도로서 탄력적.선택적 근로시간제, 재량 근로시간제 등이 있습니다.

'탄력적 근로시간제'란 어떤 근로일이나 어떤 주의 주당 근로시간을 연장시키는 대신 다른 근로일, 다른 주의 근로시간을 단축시킴으로써, 일정 기간의 평균 근로시간을 법정기준근로시간(1주 40시간) 내로 맞추는 제도를 말합니다. 따라서, 특정일에 8시간, 특정주에 40시간을

weeks instead of extending the working hours per week on one working day or week. Therefore, workers are not obliged to receive overtime pay even if they exceed 8 hours on a specific day and 40 hours on a specific week.

However, as the requirements differ depending on the period, 1) the flexible working hour system within 2 weeks can be introduced by introducing the system and changing working hours in the rules of employment, but 2) in the case of the flexible working hour system within 3 months and between 3 months and 6 months a written agreement with the employee representative is required.

The 'selective working hour system' refers to a system in which only the total working hours of the settlement period within one month are set, and the start and end times of the working hours are left to the employee's decision within the standard working hours of 40 hours per week on average. A written agreement with the worker representative is required.

In addition to the flexible and selective working hour system, the flexible working hour system includes the deemed working hour system, in which the calculation of working hours for hours worked outside the workplace is agreed upon, and the discretionary working hour system, which leaves the means of performing work and time allocation to the discretion of workers.

5. Granting Recess Hours

5-0-1 Are breaks of 30 minutes or more given for each 4-hour block of working hours?

Article 54 of the Labor Standards Act
The break time must be 30 minutes or longer for 4-hour working hours and 1 hour or longer for 8-hour working hours.
(Penalty) Article 110: Imprisonment for up to two years or a fine of up to 20 million won

5-0-2 Do workers who work 8 working hours receive a 1 hour break or more during the course of the 8 hours?

Article 54 of the Labor Standards Act
The break time must be 30 minutes or longer for 4-hour working hours and 1 hour or longer for 8-hour working hours.
(Penalty) Article 110: Imprisonment for up to two years or a fine of up to 20 million won

초과하더라도 연장근로가산수당을 지급할 의무가 없습니다.

다만, 기간에 따라 요건을 달리하는 바, 1) 2주 이내 탄력적 근로시간제는 취업규칙의 작성 및 변경으로 도입 가능하지만, 2) 3개월 이내 및 3개월 초과 6개월 이내의 탄력적 근로시간제의 경우에는 근로자대표와의 서면 합의가 필요합니다.

'선택적 근로시간제'란 1개월 이내의 정산기간의 총 근로시간만을 정하고 기준근로시간인 주 평균 40시간의 범위에서 근로시간의 시작 및 종료 시각을 근로자의 결정이 맡기는 제도를 말하며, 취업규칙에 대상이 되는 근로자 집단을 규정하여야 하며, 근로자대표와의 서면 합의를 요건으로 합니다.

유연근로제에는 탄력적·선택적 근로시간제 외에도 사업장 밖에서 근무하는 시간에 대한 근로시간 산정을 합의로 정하는 간주 근로시간제와 업무의 수행수단 및 시간배분 등을 근로자 재량에 맡기는 재량 근로시간 제도가 있습니다.

5. 휴게시간 부여

5-0-1 근로시간이 4시간인 경우 30분 이상의 휴게시간을 부여하고 있습니까?

근로기준법 제54조

휴게시간은 근로시간이 4시간인 경우에는 30분 이상, 8시간인 경우에는 1시간 이상을 부여해야 하는데, 일시에 부여해도 되고 분할하여 부여해도 됩니다.

(벌칙) 제110조 2년 이하의 징역 또는 2천만 원 이하의 벌금

5-0-2 근로시간이 8시간인 경우 1시간 이상의 휴게시간을 부여하고 있습니까?

근로기준법 제54조

휴게시간은 근로시간이 4시간인 경우에는 30분 이상, 8시간인 경우에는 1시간 이상을 부여해야 하는데, 일시에 부여해도 되고 분할하여 부여해도 됩니다.

(벌칙) 제110조 2년 이하의 징역 또는 2천만 원 이하의 벌금

5-0-3 Are breaks granted during working hours?

Article 54 of the Labor Standards Act

Breaks must be granted 'during working hours'. It is a violation of the Labor Standards Act to grant breaks before work starts or after work ends, rather than during working hours. For example, it is a violation of the law to grant a rest period of 30 minutes after an 8-hour work day ends.

(Penalty) Article 110: Imprisonment for up to two years or a fine of up to 20 million won

5-0-4 Can workers freely use their break times?

Article 54 of the Labor Standards Act

During break time, workers can use it freely, away from the employer's command and supervision, so going out must be guaranteed.

However, it is allowed to go out of the workplace, but restrictions to maintain minimum order (going out report system, etc.) are possible.

(Penalty) Article 110: Imprisonment for up to two years or a fine of up to 20 million won

5-0-5 Do you count individual breaks taken while waiting as working hours?

Article 54, 50 of the Labor Standards Act

Waiting for work is not a break time. In other words, occasional visitor reception and telephone reception duties are recognized as working hours as they violate the principle of free use of break time.

(Penalty) Article 110: Imprisonment for up to two years or a fine of up to 20 million won

6. Paid Holidays

6-0-1 Are your workers given an average of one or more paid holidays (weekly holidays) per week when they complete the prescribed working days for a week?

Article 55 of the Labor Standards Act

An average of one day per week must be granted as a paid holiday for workers who have completed the prescribed working days during the week.

5-0-3 휴게시간을 근로시간 도중에 부여하고 있습니까?

근로기준법 제54조

휴게시간은 '근로시간 도중에' 부여하여야 합니다. 휴게시간을 근로시간 도중이 아닌 업무의 시작 전 또는 업무가 끝난 후에 부여하는 것은 근로기준법 위반에 해당합니다. 예를 들면 1일 8시간 근로가 종료된 후 나머지 30분의 휴게시간을 부여하는 경우 법 위반에 해당합니다.

(벌칙) 제110조 2년 이하의 징역 또는 2천만 원 이하의 벌금

5-0-4 근로자는 휴게시간을 자유롭게 이용할 수 있습니까?

근로기준법 제54조

휴게시간은 근로자가 사용자의 지휘 . 감독에서 벗어나 자유로이 이용할 수 있으므로 외출도 보장되어야 합니다.

다만 사업장 밖으로 나갈 수 있도록 하되, 최소한의 질서유지를 위한 제한(외출신고제 등)은 가능합니다.

(벌칙) 제110조 2년 이하의 징역 또는 2천만 원 이하의 벌금

5-0-5 대기하면서 틈틈이 쉬는 개인휴식을 근로시간으로 간주하고 있습니까?

근로기준법 제54조, 50조

업무를 위한 대기는 휴게시간이 아닙니다. 즉 간혹 있는 방문객 응접, 전화 수신업무를 맡기는 등은 휴게시간 자유이용의 원칙에 어긋나므로 근로시간으로 인정됩니다.

(벌칙) 제110조 2년 이하의 징역 또는 2천만 원 이하의 벌금

6. 유급휴일 부여

6-0-1 근로자가 1주 동안의 소정근로일을 개근한 경우, 1주 평균 1회 이상의 휴일(주휴일)을 유급으로 주고 있습니까?

근로기준법 제55조

1 주 동안 소정근로일을 개근한 근로자에게는 1주 평균 1일 이상을 유급으로 휴일로 부여하여야 하며, 주중에 결근한 경우에는 '무급'으로

The weekly holiday does not have to be Sunday, but other days can be specified in the employment contract or employment rules. This is because one week means seven days including holidays, so one week does not necessarily have to be from Sunday to Saturday on the lunar calendar.

(Penalty) Article 110: Imprisonment for up to two years or a fine of up to 20 million won

6-0-2 Are you properly calculating your workers' weekly holiday pay?

How to Calculate Weekly Holiday Allowance

Weekend pay = number of contracted working hours per day x hourly wage

Even if the working hours of the business place exceed the statutory working hours, the weekly holiday pay should be paid in accordance with the statutory working hours.

For example, even if you work 9 hours a day and 45 hours a week, you only have to pay the statutory working hours of 8 hours.

(Penalty) Article 110: Imprisonment for up to two years or a fine of up to 20 million won

6-0-3 Are weekly holidays paid for part-time workers who work more than 15 hours a week?

Article 63 of the Labor Standards Act

Exceptions to the weekly holiday application include 1) those whose weekly working hours are less than 15 hours, and 2) those excluded from the application of Article 63 of the Labor Standards Act.

6-0-4 From January 2022, workplaces with at least 5 employees are to treat Labor Day and public office holidays as paid holidays. Is your business in compliance with this requirement?

Articles 55 and 63 of the Labor Standards Act, and Articles 2 and 3 of the Regulations on Holidays in Public Offices

Types of holidays include contracted holidays, which both parties decide autonomously, and legal holidays stipulated by law. Legal holidays include weekly holidays, Labor Day, weekly holidays, public office holidays, and substitute holidays.

Weekly holidays are applied to workers whose prescribed working hours are 15 hours or more per week at all workplaces with one or more employees, and there are exceptions under Article 18 of the Labor Standards Act.

휴일을 부여하면 됩니다.

주휴일은 반드시 일요일일 필요는 없으나, 근로계약 또는 취업규칙에 다른 요일을 특정하여야 합니다. 1주는 휴일을 포함한 7일을 의미하므로 1주를 반드시 월력상의 일요일부터 토요일로 해야 하는 것은 아니기 때문입니다.

(벌칙) 제110조 2년 이하의 징역 또는 2천만 원 이하의 벌금

6-0-2 주휴수당의 산정방법을 알고 있습니까?

주휴수당 산정방법

주휴수당 = 1일 소정근로시간 수 x 시간급 임금

사업장의 근로시간이 법정근로시간을 초과하는 경우에도 주휴수당은 법정근로시간에 해당하는 임금을 지급하면 됩니다.

예를 들어 1일 9시간, 1주 45시간을 근무하더라도, 주휴수당은 법정근로시간인 8시간 분만 지급하면 되는 것입니다.

(벌칙) 제110조 2년 이하의 징역 또는 2천만 원 이하의 벌금

6-0-3 1주 15시간 이상 근무하는 단시간 근로자에게도 주휴수당을 지급하고 있습니까?

근로기준법 제63조

주휴일 적용의 예외 근로자로는 1) 1주 소정근로시간이 15시간 미만인 자와 2) 근로기준법 제63조의 적용 제외 근로자가 있습니다.

6-0-4 근로자의 날(모든 사업장), 관공서 공휴일을 대체공휴일('22.1월부터 5인 이상 사업장)을 유급휴일로 부여하고 있습니까?

근로기준법 제55조, 제63조, 관공서의 공휴일에 관한 규정 제2조 및 제3조

휴일의 종류에는 노사 양 당사자가 자율적으로 결정하는 약정휴일과 법에서 정하는 법정휴일이 있으며, 법정휴일에는 주휴일, 근로자의 날, 주휴일, 관공서공휴일 및 대체공휴일이 있습니다.

주휴일은 1인 이상 모든 사업장에서 소정근로시간이 주15시간 이상인 근로자에 적용되며 근로기준법 제18조에 의한 예외 업무가 있습니다.

Labor Day is applied to all workers at all workplaces with one or more employees, and there is no separate industry excluded from application.

Government holidays and substitute holidays are applied to workers whose prescribed working hours are 15 hours or more per week at workplaces with 5 or more employees.

(Penalty) Article 110: Imprisonment for up to two years or a fine of up to 20 million won

7. Annual Paid Leave

7-0-1 Do you grant annual paid leave?

Article 60 of the Labor Standards Act

The regulations on annual paid leave apply to all workers who work at workplaces with 5 or more full-time workers.

Workers not covered include:
1) workers at workplaces with 4 or fewer full-time workers, and
2) so-called short-time workers whose prescribed working hours are less than 15 hours a week.

(Penalty) Article 110: Imprisonment for up to two years or a fine of up to 20 million won

7-0-2 Are 15 days of annual paid leave granted to workers who show up for at least 80% of their contractual working hours for one year?

Article 60 of the Labor Standards Act

15 days of annual paid leave must be given to workers who have worked for 80% or more for one year, and paid leave with 1 day added for every 2 years of continuous service exceeding the first year to workers who have worked continuously for 3 years or more It must be given, and it is limited to 25 days.

For example, 15 days in the 2nd and 3rd years beyond 1 year, 16 days in the 4th and 5th years, 17 days in the 6th and 7th years, and the maximum of 25 days after the 20th year should be given.

(Penalty) Article 110: Imprisonment for up to two years or a fine of up to 20 million won

7-0-3 Are additional vacations granted to workers who have worked continuously for 3 years or more?

근로자의 날은 1인 이상 모든 사업장의 모든 근로자에게 적용되며 적용제외 업종은 별도로 없습니다.
관공서 공휴일 및 대체공휴일은 5인 이상 사업장에서 소정근로시간이 주 15시간 이상인 근로자에게 적용됩니다.
(벌칙) 제110조 2년 이하의 징역 또는 2천만 원 이하의 벌금

7. 연차유급휴가 부여

7-0-1 연차유급휴가를 부여하고 있습니까?

근로기준법 제60조

연차유급휴가에 대한 규정은 상시근로자 5인 이상 사업장에 근무하는 모든 근로자에게 적용됩니다.

적용이 되지 않은 근로자로는 1) 상시근로자 4인 이하 사업장 소속 근로자와 2) 소정근로시간이 1주 15시간 미만인 이른바 '초단시간 근로자'가 있습니다.

(벌칙) 제110조 2년 이하의 징역 또는 2천만 원 이하의 벌금

7-0-2 1년간 80퍼센트 이상 출근한 근로자에게 15일의 연차유급휴가를 부여하고 있습니까?

근로기준법 제60조

1년간 80% 이상 출근한 근로자에게 15일의 연차유급휴가를 주어야 하며, 3년 이상 계속하여 근로한 근로자에게 최초 1년을 초과하는 계속근로 연수 매 2년에 대해 1일을 가산한 유급휴가를 주어야 하고, 최대 25일을 한도로 합니다.

예를 들면 1년을 초과한 2년차와 3년차에는 15일, 4년차와 5년차에는 16일, 6년차와 7년 차에는 17일의 휴가가 발생하며 20년차 이후에는 최대인 25일의 휴가를 주어야 합니다.

(벌칙) 제110조 2년 이하의 징역 또는 2천만 원 이하의 벌금

7-0-3 3년 이상 계속하여 근로한 근로자에게는 가산휴가를 부여하고 있습니까?

Article 60 of the Labor Standards Act

15 days of annual paid leave must be given to workers who have worked for 80% or more for one year, and paid leave with 1 day added for every 2 years of continuous service exceeding the first year to workers who have worked continuously for 3 years or more It must be given, and it is limited to 25 days.

(Penalty) Article 110: Imprisonment for up to two years or a fine of up to 20 million won

7-0-4 Are workers in their first year of employment granted 1 day of paid leave for every 1 month of attendance?

Article 60 of the Labor Standards Act

Up to 11 days of paid leave are granted for each full month of attendance until less than one year after joining the company (first year). If the attendance rate for the first year after joining the company is 80% or higher, in the second year, as a rule, a total of 15 days of paid annual leave must be granted.

(Penalty) Article 110: Imprisonment for up to two years or a fine of up to 20 million won

7-0-5 Is annual paid leave granted to workers who have returned to work after child care leave?

Article 60 of the Labor Standards Act

The childcare leave period is considered as work, and the attendance rate is calculated to calculate the number of vacation days. In other words, even if an employee did not go to work for the total number of prescribed working days during childcare leave for one year, the number of days of annual paid leave must be calculated by considering the entire period as attendance.

(Penalty) Article 110: Imprisonment for up to two years or a fine of up to 20 million won

7-0-6 Can workers freely use their annual paid leave?

Article 60 of the Labor Standards Act

In principle, employers must allow workers to freely use them at the time they wish to use them if they request paid leave.

However, the employer may change the period of use if giving leave at the time requested by the worker has a great impediment to business operation.

근로기준법 제60조

1년간 80% 이상 출근한 근로자에게 15일의 연차유급휴가를 주어야 하며, 3년 이상 계속하여 근로한 근로자에게 최초 1년을 초과하는 계속근로 연수 매 2년에 대해 1일을 가산한 유급휴가를 주어야 하고, 최대 25일을 한도로 합니다.

(벌칙) 제110조 2년 이하의 징역 또는 2천만 원 이하의 벌금

7-0-4 입사 1년차인 근로자에게도 1개월 개근시 1일의 유급휴가를 부여하고 있습니까?

근로기준법 제60조

입사 후 1년 미만(1년차)까지는 1개월 개근 시 1일씩 유급휴가가 최대 11일 발생합니다. 입사 후 1년간의 출근율이 80% 이상인 경우 2년차에는 원칙대로 총 15일의 연차유급휴가를 주어야 합니다.

(벌칙) 제110조 2년 이하의 징역 또는 2천만 원 이하의 벌금

7-0-5 육아휴직 후 복직한 근로자에게도 연차유급휴가를 부여하고 있습니까?

근로기준법 제60조

육아휴직기간은 출근한 것으로 간주하여 출근율을 계산하여 휴가일수를 산정합니다. 즉 1년 동안 육아휴직을 사용하여 총 소정근로일을 출근하지 아니하였다 하더라도 해당 기간을 모두 출근한 것으로 보고 연차유급휴가 일수를 산정하여야 합니다.

(벌칙) 제110조 2년 이하의 징역 또는 2천만 원 이하의 벌금

7-0-6 연차유급휴가를 근로자가 자유롭게 사용할 수 있습니까?

근로기준법 제60조

원칙적으로 사용자는 근로자가 유급휴가를 청구하면 사용을 희망한 시기에 자유롭게 사용할 수 있도록 허용해야 합니다.

다만, 근로자가 청구한 시기에 휴가를 주는 것이 사업운영에 막대한 지장이 있는 경우 사용자는 사용시기를 변경할 수 있습니다.

판례에 의하면 근로자가 연차휴가 사용시기를 정하여 청구한 경우

According to a precedent, even if a worker sets the timing for using annual leave and uses it without the employer's approval, it cannot be treated as absenteeism unless the employer exercises the right to change the timing.

It is a violation of the Labor Standards Act to refuse a request for annual paid leave simply because of a heavy workload or busy hands.

(Penalty) Article 110: Imprisonment for up to two years or a fine of up to 20 million won

7-0-7 Do you avoid preventing workers from using their annual paid leave at their desired time simply because they are busy with work?

Article 60 of the Labor Standards Act

In principle, employers must allow workers to freely use them at the time they wish to use them if they request paid leave.

However, the employer may change the period of use if giving leave at the time requested by the worker has a great impediment to business operation.

According to a precedent, even if a worker sets the timing for using annual leave and uses it without the employer's approval, it cannot be treated as absenteeism unless the employer exercises the right to change the timing.

It is a violation of the Labor Standards Act to refuse a request for annual paid leave simply because of a heavy workload or busy hands.

(Penalty) Article 110: Imprisonment for up to two years or a fine of up to 20 million won

7-0-8 Are you paying workers an allowance for their unused annual paid leave?

Article 60 of the Labor Standards Act

Annual paid leave is available for one year from the date of occurrence.

If all or part of the vacation is not used, the employer must pay unused vacation days equal to the number of unused vacation days as compensation for the vacation.

According to a precedent, unused annual paid leave allowance should be calculated based on ordinary wages, unless otherwise stipulated in the employment rules.

Unless otherwise specified, the payment date must be paid on the first regular wage payment date after the expiration of the one-year period for annual leave.

(Penalty) Article 110: Imprisonment for up to two years or a fine of up to

사용자의 승인 없이 사용했다 하더라도 사용자가 시기변경권을 행사하지 않는 한 이를 당연히 결근으로 처리할 수는 없습니다.

단순히 업무량이 많다 거나 일손이 바쁘다는 이유로 연차유급휴가 사용청구를 거부하는 것은 근로기준법 위반에 해당합니다.

(벌칙) 제110조 2년 이하의 징역 또는 2천만 원 이하의 벌금

7-0-7 단순히 업무가 바쁘다는 이유로 근로자가 청구한 시기에 연차유급휴가를 사용하지 못하게 하고 있지는 않습니까?

근로기준법 제60조

원칙적으로 사용자는 근로자가 유급휴가를 청구하면 사용을 희망한 시기에 자유롭게 사용할 수 있도록 허용해야 합니다.

다만, 근로자가 청구한 시기에 휴가를 주는 것이 사업운영에 막대한 지장이 있는 경우 사용자는 사용시기를 변경할 수 있습니다.

판례에 의하면 근로자가 연차휴가 사용시기를 정하여 청구한 경우 사용자의 승인 없이 사용했다 하더라도 사용자가 시기변경권을 행사하지 않는 한 이를 당연히 결근으로 처리할 수는 없습니다.

단순히 업무량이 많다 거나 일손이 바쁘다는 이유로 연차유급휴가 사용청구를 거부하는 것은 근로기준법 위반에 해당합니다.

(벌칙) 제110조 2년 이하의 징역 또는 2천만 원 이하의 벌금

7-0-8 연차유급휴가를 미사용할 경우 수당으로 지급합니까?

근로기준법 제60조

연차유급휴가는 발생일로부터 1년간 사용 가능합니다.

휴가의 전부 또는 일부를 사용하지 않은 경우 사용자는 그 휴가에 대한 보상으로 사용하지 않은 휴가 일수만큼 미사용수당을 지급하여야 하며, 지급하지 않을 경우 임금체불에 해당됩니다.

판례에 의하면 연차유급휴가 미사용수당은 취업규칙에 달리 정함이 없는 한 통상임금을 기초로 하여 산정하여야 합니다.

지급일은 특별한 정함이 없는 한 연차휴가를 실시할 수 있는 1년의 기간이 만료된 후 최초의 임금정기지급일에 지급해야 합니다.

20 million won

7-0-9 Are unused annual paid leave allowances paid to workers whose contract period is 1 year?

Article 60 of the Labor Standards Act

Annual paid leave is available for one year from the date of occurrence. However, in the case of workers who have worked continuously for less than one year, it can be used for the first year.

Even in the case of a worker whose contract period is one year, if all or part of the vacation is not used, the employer must pay an unused allowance equal to the number of unused vacation days as compensation for the vacation.

(Penalty) Article 110: Imprisonment for up to two years or a fine of up to 20 million won

8. Children and Protection of Maternity

8-1 Night and holiday work for minors and women

8-1-1 When a female worker works at night (between 10:00 pm and 6:00 am the next day) or on a holiday, do you get her explicit consent beforehand?

Article 70 of the Labor Standards Act

The Labor Standards Act prohibits, in principle, night work (from 10:00 pm to 6:00 am) and holiday work for pregnant women and young workers under the age of 18. You can work even on holidays.

(Penalty) Article 110: Imprisonment for up to two years or a fine of up to 20 million won

8-1-2 Do you avoid having pregnant female workers or workers under the age of 18 work at night or on holidays?

Article 70 of the Labor Standards Act

In the case of pregnant female workers and workers under the age of 18, 1) only when nighttime or holiday work is unavoidable, 2) there must be an explicit request (in the case of a pregnant woman) or consent from the party concerned, and 3) an employee representative and 4) After obtaining

(벌칙) 제110조 2년 이하의 징역 또는 2천만 원 이하의 벌금

7-0-9 계약기간이 1년인 근로자에게도 연차유급휴가 미사용수당을 지급합니까?
근로기준법 제60조

연차유급휴가는 발생일로부터 1년간 사용 가능합니다. 다만, 계속근로 1년 미만인 근로자의 경우는 최초 1년간 사용 가능합니다.

계약기간이 1년인 근로자의 경우에도 휴가의 전부 또는 일부를 사용하지 않았다면 사용자는 그 휴가에 대한 보상으로 사용하지 않은 휴가 일수만큼 미사용수당을 지급하여야 하며 이를 지급하지 않는다면 임금체불에 해당됩니다.

(벌칙) 제110조 2년 이하의 징역 또는 2천만 원 이하의 벌금

8. 모성보호와 연소자

8-1 여성의 야간 및 휴일근로

8-1-1 여성근로자가 야간근로(오후10시부터 다음날 오전 6시 사이의 근로) 및 휴일근로를 할 경우 여성근로자의 명시적인 동의를 받았습니까?
근로기준법 제70조

근로기준법은 임산부와 18세 미만의 연소근로자에 대해서는 원칙적으로 야간근로(오후 10시부터 오전 6시까지) 및 휴일근로를 금지하고 있으나, 18세 이상의 여성근로자에 대하여는 그 근로자의 동의를 받아 야간 및 휴일에도 근로하게 할 수 있습니다.

(벌칙) 제110조 2년 이하의 징역 또는 2천만 원 이하의 벌금

8-1-2 임신한 여성근로자나 18세 미만 근로자가 야간 또는 휴일근로를 하고 있나요?
근로기준법 제70조

임신한 여성근로자와 18세 미만의 근로자의 경우에는 1) 야간 또는 휴일근로가 불가피한 경우에 한하여, 2) 당사자의 명시적 청구(임신한 여성의 경우) 또는 동의가 있어야 하며, 3) 근로자대표와의 협의를 거쳐, 4) 고용

approval from the Minister of Employment and Labor, workers may be allowed to work at night or on holidays.

Examples of cases in which nighttime or holiday work is unavoidable include the implementation of the shift system, public services essential to daily life such as transportation and broadcasting, and temporary increases in order volume.

(Penalty) Article 110: Imprisonment for up to two years or a fine of up to 20 million won

(Penalty) Article 114 A fine of up to 5 million won in case of violation of sincere consultation with the worker representative

8-2 Overtime work for women soon after childbirth

8-2-1 Are female workers exempted from overtime work for one year after childbirth, miscarriage or stillbirth?

Article 71 of the Labor Standards Act

Even female workers can, in principle, be allowed to work overtime up to 12 hours a week by agreement between the parties.

However, female workers who have not passed 1 year after giving birth cannot be forced to work overtime in excess of 2 hours per day, 6 hours per week, and 150 hours per year. Even if there is an agreement between the parties or a collective agreement stipulates otherwise, the time within the limit set by law cannot be exceeded.

Female workers who have miscarriage or stillbirth are also included in postpartum female workers.

(Penalty) Article 110: Imprisonment for up to two years or a fine of up to 20 million won

8-3 Protection of pregnant women

8-3-1 Are pregnant women given at least 90 days of maternity leave (120 days if pregnant with more than one child at a time)?

Article 74 of the Labor Standards Act

For pregnant female workers, leave before and after childbirth can be used without the employee's application process, so if the worker is pregnant and has given birth, even if she expresses her intention to give up maternity leave, if the company does not grant leave before and after childbirth, it is a violation of the Labor Standards Act.

노동부장관의 인가를 받아야 야간 또는 휴일에 근로하게 할 수 있습니다. 야간 또는 휴일근로가 불가피한 경우의 예로는 교대제 실시, 운송·방송 등 일상생활에 필수적인 공익사업, 일시적 주문량 증가 등이 해당됩니다.

(벌칙) 제110조 2년 이하의 징역 또는 2천만 원 이하의 벌금
(벌칙) 제114조 근로자대표와의 성실한 협의 위반시는 500만 원 이하의 벌금

8-2 산후여성 근로자의 시간외근로

8-2-1 여성근로자가 출산 또는 유사산한 경우 1년간 시간외근로 시간을 제한하고 있습니까?

근로기준법 제71조

여성근로자의 경우에도 원칙적으로 당사자간 합의로 1주 12시간 한도로 연장근로를 하게 할 수 있습니다.

그러나 산후 1년이 지나지 아니한 여성근로자에게는 1일 2시간, 1주 6시간, 1년 150시간을 초과한 연장근로를 시킬 수 없습니다. 당사자간 합의가 있거나 단체협약에서 다른 규정을 두더라도 법에서 정한 한도 내의 시간을 초과할 수 없습니다.

유산, 사산한 여성근로자도 산후 여성근로자에 포함되며, 산후 1년의 기산점인 출산일(유.사산일)로부터 1년을 의미합니다.

(벌칙) 제110조 2년 이하의 징역 또는 2천만 원 이하의 벌금

8-3 임산부의 보호

8-3-1 임신한 여성 근로자에 대하여 출산전후휴가 90일(한 번에 둘 이상 자녀를 임신한 경우에는 120일) 이상을 부여하였습니까?

근로기준법 제74조

임신중인 여성근로자에 대하여 출산전후휴가는 근로자의 신청절차 없이 사용할 수 있는 것이므로 근로자가 임신과 출산을 했다면 휴가를 포기하는 의사를 밝히더라도 출산전후휴가를 부여하지 않으면 근로기준법 위반에 해당합니다

The leave period is 90 days (120 days when pregnant with two or more children), including holidays and days off, and leave must be granted for at least 45 days after childbirth (60 days for multiple births).

(Penalty) Article 110: Imprisonment for up to two years or a fine of up to 20 million won

8-3-2 Are female workers who have given birth granted leave of at least 45 days (60 days if pregnant with more than one child at a time) after the date of childbirth?

Article 74 of the Labor Standards Act

For pregnant female workers, leave before and after childbirth can be used without the employee's application process, so if the worker is pregnant and has given birth, even if she expresses her intention to give up leave, if she does not grant leave before and after childbirth, it is a violation of the Labor Standards Act.

The leave period is 90 days (120 days when pregnant with two or more children), including holidays and days off, and leave must be granted for at least 45 days after childbirth (60 days for multiple births).

1) In case of single birth: 44 days or less before childbirth + 1 day after childbirth + 45 days or more after childbirth
2) In case of multiple births: 59 days or less before childbirth + 1 day after childbirth + 60 days or more after childbirth

(Penalty) Article 110: Imprisonment for up to two years or a fine of up to 20 million won

8-3-3 Is maternity leave granted to workers after they experience a miscarriage and stillbirth?

Article 74 of the Labor Standards Act

Workers who have had a miscarriage or stillbirth must also be granted maternity leave before and after childbirth.

However, in the case of artificial termination of pregnancy, leave for miscarriage or stillbirth is not guaranteed unless it is for reasons stipulated in the 「Maternal and Child Health Act」.

1) In case the person or spouse has a eugenic or genetic mental disorder or physical disease as prescribed by the Presidential Decree
2) In case the person or spouse has a contagious disease as prescribed by the Presidential Decree
3) In case of pregnancy due to rape or quasi-rape

휴가기간은 90일(둘이상의 자녀를 임신한 경우 120일)이며 휴일, 휴무일을 포함하여 계산하고 반드시 출산 후에 45일(다태아 60일) 이상이 되도록 휴가를 부여해야 합니다.
(벌칙) 제110조 2년 이하의 징역 또는 2천만 원 이하의 벌금

8-3-2 출산한 여성 근로자에게 출산일 이후로 45일(한 번에 둘 이상의 자녀를 임신한 경우에는 60일)이상의 휴가를 부여하였습니까?

근로기준법 제74조

임신중인 여성근로자에 대하여 출산전후휴가는 근로자의 신청절차 없이 사용할 수 있는 것이므로 근로자가 임신과 출산을 했다면 휴가를 포기하는 의사를 밝히더라도 출산전후휴가를 부여하지 않으면 근로기준법 위반에 해당합니다

휴가기간은 90일(둘이상의 자녀를 임신한 경우 120일)이며 휴일, 휴무일을 포함하여 계산하고 반드시 출산 후에 45일(다태아 60일) 이상이 되도록 휴가를 부여해야 합니다.

1) 단태아인 경우 : 출산 전 44일 이하 + 출산일 1일 + 출산 후 45일 이상
2) 다태아인 경우 : 출산 전 59일 이하 + 출산일 1일 + 출산 후 60일 이상

(벌칙) 제110조 2년 이하의 징역 또는 2천만 원 이하의 벌금

8-3-3 유.사산 근로자에게도 출산전후휴가를 부여하고 있습니까?

근로기준법 제74조

유.사산한 근로자에게도 출산전후휴가를 부여하여야 합니다.

다만, 인공적으로 임신중절한 경우「모자보건법」에서 규정하고 있는 사유에 의한 것이 아니라면 유.사산 휴가를 보장하지는 않습니다.

1) 본인이나 배우자가 대통령령으로 정하는 우생학적 또는 유전학적 정신장애나 신체질환이 있는 경우
2) 본인이나 배우자가 대통령령으로 정하는 전염성 질환이 있는 경우
3) 강간 또는 준강간에 의하여 임신된 경우

4) In case of pregnancy between blood relatives or relatives who cannot legally marry
5) In case the continuation of pregnancy seriously harms or is likely to harm the mother's health for health and medical reasons

(Penalty) Article 110: Imprisonment for up to two years or a fine of up to 20 million won

8-3-4 Are reduced working hours allowed for female workers during the first 12 weeks of pregnancy and from the 36th week of pregnancy?

Article 74 of the Labor Standards Act

During the first 60 days of leave before and after childbirth (75 days for multiple births), the employer must pay the worker a wage equivalent to the normal wage, and the wage must be paid for the first 60 days of leave for miscarriage or stillbirth.

However, for companies subject to preferential support, the government provides maternity leave benefits of up to KRW 2 million for the first 60 days of maternity leave, and the employer must pay the portion of the ordinary wage that exceeds the government subsidy.

(Penalty) Article 110: Imprisonment for up to two years or a fine of up to 20 million won

8-3-5 If a pregnant female worker applies for a change in the start and end times of work while maintaining the prescribed working hours per day, is it allowed?

Article 74 of the Labor Standards Act

If a female worker within 12 weeks or after 36 weeks of pregnancy applies for a reduction in working hours of 2 hours per day, the employer must allow it.

However, workers whose daily working hours are less than 8 hours may be allowed to reduce working hours so that the daily working hours are 6 hours.

There are no restrictions on how to delay coming to work or leaving work early.

Also, the worker's wages must not be reduced on the grounds of reduced working hours.

(Fine for negligence) Article 116 Fine for negligence not exceeding 5 million won

4) 법률상 혼인할 수 없는 혈족 또는 인척 간에 임신된 경우
5) 임신의 지속이 보건의학적 이유로 모체의 건강을 심각하게 해치고 있거나 해칠 우려가 있는 경우

(벌칙) 제110조 2년 이하의 징역 또는 2천만 원 이하의 벌금

8-3-4 임신 12주 이내, 36주 이후에 있는 여성근로자가 요구하는 경우 단축근로를 허용했습니까?

근로기준법 제74조

사용자는 출산전후휴가의 최초 60일(다태아 75일)동안 근로자에게 통상임금에 해당하는 임금을 지급하여야 하며, 유.사산 휴가기간도 최초 60일까지는 임금을 지급하여야 합니다.

다만 우선지원대상 기업의 경우 정부가 출산전후휴가의 최초 60일 동안 최대 200만 원까지 출산전후휴가급여를 지원하는데, 통상임금 중 정부지원금을 초과하는 부분은 사업주가 지급해야 합니다.

(벌칙) 제110조 2년 이하의 징역 또는 2천만 원 이하의 벌금

8-3-5 임신 중인 여성근로자가 1일 소정근로시간을 유지하면서 업무의 시작 및 종료 시간의 변경을 신청하는 경우 허용했습니까?

근로기준법 제74조

사용자는 임신 후 12주 이내 또는 36주 이후에 있는 여성근로자가 1일 2시간의 근로시간 단축을 신청하는 경우 이를 허용하여야 합니다.

다만 1일 근로시간이 8시간 미만인 근로자는 1일 근로시간이 6시간이 되도록 근로시간 단축을 허용하면 됩니다.

출근을 늦추거나 퇴근을 일찍 하는 등 방식은 제한이 없으나, 원칙적으로 근로근로자가 신청하는 방식으로 허용하여야 하며, 사용자가 일방적으로 단축방법을 강제할 수는 없습니다.

또한 근로시간 단축을 이유로 해당 근로자의 임금을 삭감하여서는 아니 됩니다.

(과태료) 제116조 500만 원 이하의 과태료

8-3-6 Are pregnant female workers prohibited from working overtime?

Article 74 of the Labor Standards Act

If a pregnant female worker applies for a change in the start and end times of work while maintaining the prescribed working hours per day, this must be allowed.

However, it may not be permitted if it causes a significant impediment to normal business operations, or if changing the start and end times of work violates laws and regulations related to the safety and health of pregnant female workers.

(Fine for negligence) Article 116 Fine not exceeding 5 million won

8-3-7 Have pregnant female workers been switched to easier types of work if requested?

Article 74 of the Labor Standards Act

An employer must switch to an easy type of work if there is a request from a pregnant female worker.

(Penalty) Article 110: Imprisonment for up to two years or a fine of up to 20 million won

8-3-8 Have you returned workers coming back from maternity leave to the same job or a job that pays the same level of wages?

Article 74 of the Labor Standards Act

Employers must return female workers who have returned from maternity leave to the same job or a job that pays equivalent wages.

(Penalty) Article 114 Fine of up to 5 million won

8-4 Paternity leave

8-4-1 Is paternity leave granted when an employee's spouse gives birth?

Article 18-2 of the Equal Employment Act

Employers must grant 10 days of leave when a worker requests leave for the reason of his spouse's giving birth, and in this case, the used leave period must be paid.

(Fine for negligence) Article 39 Fine for negligence up to 5 million won

8-3-6 임신 중인 여성 근로자에게 시간외근로를 금지시켰습니까?

근로기준법 제74조

임신 중인 여성근로자가 1일 소정근로시간을 유지하면서 업무의 시작 및 종료 시각의 변경을 신청하는 경우 이를 허용해야 합니다.

다만 정상적인 사업 운영에 중대한 지장을 초래하는 경우, 업무의 시작 및 종료시각을 변경하게 되면 임신 중인 여성근로자의 안전과 건강에 관한 관계 법령을 위반하게 되는 경우에는 허용하지 않을 수 있습니다.

(과태료) 제116조 500만 원 이하의 과태료

8-3-7 임신 중인 여성 근로자가 요구하는 경우 쉬운 종류의 근로로 전환하도록 했습니까?

근로기준법 제74조

사용자는 임신 중인 여성근로자의 요구가 있는 경우에는 쉬운 종류의 근로로 전환하여야 합니다.

(벌칙) 제110조 2년 이하의 징역 또는 2천만 원 이하의 벌금

8-3-8 출산전후휴가를 종료하고 돌아온 근로자에게 동일한 직무 또는 동등한 수준의 임금을 지급하는 직무로 복귀시켰습니까?

근로기준법 제74조

사업주는 출산전후휴가를 종료하고 돌아온 여성근로자에게 동일한 업무 또는 동등한 수준의 임금을 지급하는 직무에 복귀시켜야 합니다.

(벌칙) 제114조 500만 원 이하의 벌금

8-4 배우자 출산휴가

8-4-1 직원의 배우자가 출산한 경우 배우자 출산휴가를 부여하고 있습니까?

남녀고용평등법 제18조의 2

사업주는 근로자가 배우자의 출산을 이유로 휴가를 청구하는 경우에 10일의 휴가를 주어야 하며, 이 경우 사용한 휴가기간은 유급으로 하여야 합니다.

(과태료) 제39조 500만 원 이하의 과태료

8-4-2 Is split use of spousal paternity leave permitted?

Article 18-2 of the Equal Employment Act

Employees can share their paternity leave limited to once during the period of 90 days from the date of childbirth.

An employee cannot claim maternity leave after 90 days from the date of childbirth.

(Penalty) Article 37 Imprisonment for up to 3 years or a fine of up to 30 million won

8-5 Childcare leave

8-5-1 Is childcare leave granted to pregnant female workers and workers raising children under the age of 8 or in the 2nd grade of elementary school when they apply for it?

Article 19 of the Equal Employment Act

The employer protects the motherhood of the pregnant female worker, or the child under the age of 8 or elementary school

If you apply for childcare leave to raise a child in the second grade or younger, this should be allowed.

(Penalty) Article 37 Imprisonment for up to 3 years or a fine of up to 30 million won

8-5-2 Is childcare leave allowed for male workers, fixed-term workers, and dispatched workers?

Article 19 of the Equal Employment Act

Parental leave should also be granted to male workers, fixed-term workers, and dispatched workers.

However, the period of childcare leave for fixed-term workers and dispatched workers is not included in the period of use under the Fixed-Term Act or the period of dispatch under the Dispatch Act.

(Penalty) Article 37 A fine not exceeding 5 million won

8-5-3 Are workers who have taken childcare leave protected from dismissal or other unfavorable treatment for taking the childcare leave?

Article 19 of the Equal Employment Act

8-4-2 배우자 출산휴가의 분할 사용을 허용하고 있습니까?

남녀고용평등법 제18조의 2

근로자는 배우자 출산휴가를 출산일로부터 90일 이내 기간 중 1회에 한정하여 나누어 사용할 수 있습니다.

근로자는 출산한 날로부터 90일이 지나면 출산휴가를 청구할 수 없다.

(벌칙) 제37조 3년이하의 징역 또는 3천만 원 이하의 벌금

8-5 육아휴직

8-5-1 임신 중인 여성 근로자, 만 8세 이하 또는 초등학교 2학년 이하의 자녀를 양육하는 근로자가 육아휴직을 신청할 경우 육아휴직을 부여하고 있습니까?

남녀고용평등법 제19조

사업주는 임신 중인 여성근로자가 모성을 보호하거나 만 8세이하 또는 초등학교 2학년 이하의 자녀를 양육하기 위하여 '육아휴직을 신청하는 경우에는 이를 허용하여야 합니다.

(벌칙) 제37조 3년이하의 징역 또는 3천만 원 이하의 벌금

8-5-2 남성근로자, 기간제근로자, 파견근로자에게도 육아휴직을 허용하고 있습니까?

남녀고용평등법 제19조

남성근로자, 기간제근로자, 파견근로자에게도 육아휴직을 부여하여야 합니다.

다만 기간제근로자 및 파견근로자의 육아휴직 기간은 기간제법상 사용기간 또는 파견법상 파견기간에 포함되지 않습니다.

(벌칙) 제37조 500천만 원 이하의 벌금

8-5-3 육아휴직을 이유로 근로자에게 해고나 그 밖의 불리한 처우를 하지는 않았습니까?

남녀고용평등법 제19조

해고의 사유와 관계없이 육아휴직 기간에는 해고를 할 수 없습니다.

Regardless of the reason for dismissal, dismissal cannot occur during childcare leave.

Dismissal, leave of absence, suspension, transfer of placement, wage reduction, etc., for the reason of childcare leave are not permitted to cause economic, mental, or living disadvantages to workers.

(Penalty) Article 37 Imprisonment for up to 3 years or a fine of up to 30 million won

8-5-4 When returning to work after childcare leave, are workers given the same or similar tasks as before the leave?

Article 19 of the Equal Employment Act

After childcare leave is over, the employer must return to the same job or job that pays the same level of wages as before the leave.

(Penalty) Article 37 fine of up to 5 million won

8-5-5 Do you include childcare leave in the service period of the applicable worker?

Article 19 of the Equal Employment Act

The period of childcare leave must be included in the service period, which is the basis for calculating severance pay and adding annual leave.

(Penalty) Article 37 fine of up to 5 million won

8-6 Reduction of working hours during childcare period

8-6-1 If a worker applies for reduced working hours in lieu of childcare leave, is it permitted?

Article 19-2 of the Equal Employment Act

Employers must allow workers to apply for reduced working hours in order to raise children under the age of 8 or in the second grade of elementary school. However, it may not be permitted in cases prescribed by Presidential Decree, such as when it is impossible to hire substitute personnel or when it causes a significant impediment to normal business operations.

The reduction in working hours during the childcare period is limited to one year, but up to two years is possible since the unused period of childcare leave (up to one year) can be added.

(Penalty) Article 37 Imprisonment for up to 3 years or a fine of up to 30 million won

육아휴직을 이유로 해고, 휴직, 정직, 배치전환, 감봉 등 근로자에게 경제, 정신, 생활상의 불이익을 주는 처우를 할 수 없습니다.
(벌칙) 제37조 3년이하의 징역 또는 3천만 원 이하의 벌금

8-5-4 육아휴직 후 복직시 해당 근로자에게 휴직전과 동일 또는 유사 업무를 부여하고 있습니까?

남녀고용평등법 제19조

사업주는 육아휴직을 마친 후에는 휴직 전과 같은 업무 또는 같은 수준의 임금을 지급하는 직무에 복귀시켜야 합니다.
(벌칙) 제37조 500만 원 이하의 벌금

8-5-5 육아휴직기간을 근속기간에 포함시키고 있습니까?

남녀고용평등법 제19조

육아휴직 기간은 퇴직금 산정, 연차휴가 가산 등의 기초가 되는 근속기간에 포함시켜야 합니다.
(벌칙) 제37조 500만 원 이하의 벌금

8-6 육아기 근로시간 단축

8-6-1 근로자가 육아휴직 대신 근로시간 단축을 신청한 경우 이를 허용하고 있습니까?

남녀고용평등법 제19조의 2

사업주는 근로자가 만 8세 이하 또는 초등학교 2학년 이하의 자녀를 양육하기 위하여 근로시간의 단축을 신청하는 경우에 이를 허용하여야 합니다.

다만 대체인력 채용이 불가능한 경우, 정상적인 사업 운영에 중대한 지장을 초래하는 경우 등 대통령령으로 정하는 경우에는 허용하지 않을 수 있습니다.

육아기 근로시간 단축은 1년 이내로 하되, 육아휴직(최대 1년) 미사용 기간을 합산할 수 있으므로 최대 2년까지 가능합니다.
(벌칙) 제37조 3년이하의 징역 또는 3천만 원 이하의 벌금

8-6-2 Are workers protected from unfavorable treatment for having reduced working hours during the childcare period?

Article 19-2 of the Equal Employment Act

Employers must allow workers to apply for reduced working hours in order to raise children under the age of 8 or in the second grade of elementary school.

Dismissal, leave of absence, suspension, transfer of placement, wage reduction, etc., for the reason of reduced working hours during the childcare period, cannot be treated that puts workers at a disadvantage in economic, mental, and daily life.

(Penalty) Article 37 Imprisonment for up to 3 years or a fine of up to 30 million won

8-6-3 Are workers protected from having to work overtime during reduced working hours due to a childcare period?

Article 19-2 of the Equal Employment Act

Employers cannot demand overtime work from workers who are taking advantage of reduced working hours during the childcare period.

However, if the worker explicitly requests it, the employer may allow overtime work within the limit of 12 hours per week.

(Penalty) Article 37 Imprisonment for up to 3 years or a fine of up to 30 million won

9. Rules of Employment

9-1 Creation and reporting of employment rules

9-1-1 If your workplace employs 10 or more full-time workers, do you have employment rules at your workplace?

Article 93 of the Labor Standards Act

Employers who regularly employ 10 or more workers must prepare employment rules for certain matters and report them to the Minister of Employment and Labor. Changes to the rules of employment must also be reported.

(Penalty) Article 116 Fine for negligence not exceeding 5 million won

8-6-2 육아기 근로시간 단축을 이유로 근로자에게 불리한 처우를 하지 않습니까?

남녀고용평등법 제19조의 2

사업주는 근로자가 만 8세 이하 또는 초등학교 2학년 이하의 자녀를 양육하기 위하여 근로시간의 단축을 신청하는 경우에 이를 허용하여야 합니다.

육아기 근로시간 단축을 이유로 해고, 휴직, 정직, 배치전환, 감봉 등 근로자에게 경제, 정신, 생활상의 불이익을 주는 처우를 할 수 없습니다.

(벌칙) 제37조 3년이하의 징역 또는 3천만 원 이하의 벌금

8-6-3 육아기 근로시간 단축 중 근로자에게 연장근로를 시키고 있지는 않습니까?

남녀고용평등법 제19조의 2

사업주는 육아기 근로시간 단축을 활용 중인 근로자에게는 연장근로를 요구할 수 없습니다.

다만 근로자가 명시적으로 청구하는 경우에는 사업주는 주 12시간의 범위내에서 연장근로를 시킬 수 있습니다.

(벌칙) 제37조 3년이하의 징역 또는 3천만 원 이하의 벌금

9. 취업규칙

9-1 취업규칙 작성·신고

9-1-1 귀 사업장이 상시근로자 10인 이상이라면 사업장에서 취업규칙을 작성하고 있습니까?

근로기준법 제93조

상시 10명 이상의 근로자를 사용하는 사용자는 일정한 사항에 관한 취업규칙을 작성하여 고용노동부장관에게 신고하여야 합니다. 취업규칙을 변경하는 경우에도 이를 신고하여야 합니다.

(벌칙) 제116조 500만 원 이하의 과태료

9-1-2 Are all legal items written in the rules of employment?

Article 93 of the Labor Standards Act

Matters that must be written in the rules of employment

1. Matters pertaining to the beginning and ending time of work, recess hours, holidays, leaves, and shifts;
2. Matters pertaining to the determination, calculation and payment method of wages, the period for which wages are calculated, the period for paying wages, and pay raises;
3. Matters pertaining to the methods of calculation and payment of family allowances;
4. Matters pertaining to retirement;
5. Matters pertaining to retirement benefits set under Article 4 of the Act on the Guarantee of Employees' Retirement Benefits, bonuses, and minimum wages;
6. Matters pertaining to the burden of employees' meal allowances, expenses of operational tools or necessities and so forth;
7. Matters pertaining to educational facilities for employees;
8. Matters pertaining to the protection of employees' maternity and work family balance assistance, such as leaves before and after childbirth and child-care leaves;
9. Matters pertaining to safety and health;
9-2. Matters pertaining to the improvement of a workplace environment according to characteristics of employees, such as sex, ages, or physical conditions;
10. Matters pertaining to assistance with respect to occupational and non-occupational accidents;
11. Matters pertaining to the prevention of workplace harassment and the measures to be taken in cases of occurrence of workplace harassment;
12. Matters pertaining to award and punishment;
13. Other matters applicable to all employees within the business or workplace concerned.

(Fine for negligence) Article 116 Fine not exceeding 5 million won

9-1-3 Have the revised laws and regulations been reflected in the rules of employment?

Article 93 of the Labor Standards Act

With the recent revision of the 「Labor Standards Act」, matters related to the prevention of 'workplace bullying' and measures to be taken when it occurs must be included in the employment rules.

In addition to the 「Labor Standards Act」, the 「Equal Employment Act」

9-1-2 취업규칙에 법적 기재사항이 모두 기재되어 있습니까?

근로기준법 제93조

취업규칙에 반드시 기재해야 할 사항

1. 업무의 시작과 종료 시각, 휴게시간, 휴일, 휴가 및 교대근로에 관한 사항
2. 임금의 결정.계산.지급방법, 임금의 산정기간.지급시기 및 승급에 관한 사항
3. 가족수당의 계산.지급방법에 관한 사항
4. 퇴직에 관한 사항
5. 「근로자퇴직급여 보장법」 제4조에 따라 설정된 퇴직급여, 상여 및 최저임금에 관한 사항
6. 근로자의 식비, 작업 용품 등의 부담에 관한 사항
7. 근로자를 위한 교육시설에 관한 사항
8. 출산전후휴가 . 육아휴직 등 근로자의 모성보호 및 일·가정 양립 지원에 관한 사항
9. 안전과 보건에 관한 사항

9의2. 근로자의 성별.연령 또는 신체적 조건 등의 특성에 따른 사업장 환경의 개선에 관한 사항

10. 업무상과 업무 외의 재해부조에 관한 사항
11. 직장 내 괴롭힘의 예방 및 발생 시 조치 등에 관한 사항
12. 표창과 제재에 관한 사항
13. 그 밖에 해당 사업 또는 사업장의 근로자 전체에 적용될 사항

(과태료) 제116조 500만 원 이하의 과태료

9-1-3 취업규칙에 개정법령을 반영하였습니까?

근로기준법 제93조

최근 「근로기준법」 개정으로 '직장 내 괴롭힘'의 예방 및 발생 시 조치 등에 관한 사항을 취업규칙에 포함해야 합니다.

「근로기준법」 외에도 「남녀고용평등법」에서는 직장 내 성희롱 예방 및 금지를 위하여 성희롱 예방지침을 마련하여 근로자가 볼 수 있도록 게시하도록 정하고 있습니다. 대부분의 사업장에서는 취업규칙에 이 내용을

stipulates that sexual harassment prevention guidelines be prepared and posted so that workers can view them in order to prevent and prohibit sexual harassment in the workplace. Most workplaces include this in their employment rules.

(Fine for negligence) Article 116 Fine not exceeding 5 million won

9-1-4 Did you listen to the opinions of the worker group after drafting the rules of employment?

Article 93 of the Labor Standards Act

When drafting or changing the rules of employment, in principle, a labor union organized by the majority of workers or, if there is no such union, the opinion of the majority of workers must be heard.

Listening means that labor and management exchange opinions and consult, and do not have to reach an agreement.

(Fine for negligence) Article 116 Fine not exceeding 5 million won

9-1-5 Did you report the written rules of employment to the Ministry of Employment and Labor?

Form No. 15 of the Enforcement Rules of the Labor Relations Act

The employer must fill out a report on the rules of employment and report it to the competent office of Ministry of Employment and Labor, attaching documents proving that the opinions of the rules of employment, the labor union of majority of workers, or the opinion of the majority of workers have been heard.

If the employer does not report the rules of employment, a fine is imposed.

(Fine for negligence) Article 116 Fine not exceeding 5 million won

9-2 Changes to rules of employment

9-2-1 When changing other regulations that are similar to rules of employment in nature, do you go through the appropriate procedures and report those changes?

Article 94 of the Labor Standards Act

Regardless of the name or form, if the content is about working conditions or service rules, it falls under employment rules. Therefore, if the changed regulations have the nature of employment rules, you must go through the statutory change procedure.

1. Working conditions: Conditions set in relation to wages, working hours,

포함시키고 있습니다.
(과태료) 제116조 500만 원 이하의 과태료

9-1-4 취업규칙 작성 후 근로자 집단의 의견을 청취하였습니까?

근로기준법 제93조

취업규칙을 작성 또는 변경할 때에는 원칙적으로 근로자의 과반수로 조직된 노동조합, 그러한 노동조합이 없는 경우에는 근로자 과반수의 의견을 들어야 합니다.

의견청취는 노사가 의견을 교환하고 협의하는 것을 의미하며 합의에 도달하여야만 하는 것은 아닙니다.

(과태료) 제116조 500만 원 이하의 과태료

9-1-5 작성된 취업규칙을 고용노동부에 신고했습니까?

근로기준법 시행규칙 별지 제15호 서식

사용자는 취업규칙 신고서를 작성하여 취업규칙, 근로자 과반수 노동조합 또는 근로자 과반수의 의견을 청취하였음을 증명하는 서면을 첨부하여 관할 고용노동부에 신고하여야 합니다.

사용자가 취업규칙을 신고하지 않은 경우 과태료가 부과되지만, 판례에 의하면 취업규칙을 신고하지 아니한 경우에도 취업규칙이 직원들에게 알려진 이상 효력은 인정됩니다.

(과태료) 제116조 500만 원 이하의 과태료

9-2 취업규칙 변경

9-2-1 취업규칙의 성격을 가지는 다른 규정도 변경할 때 절차를 거치고 신고했습니까?

근로기준법 제94조

명칭이나 형식에 관계없이 내용이 근로조건이나 복무규율에 관한 것이면 취업규칙에 해당합니다. 따라서 변경한 규정이 취업규칙의 성격을 가지고 있다면 법정 변경절차를 거쳐야 합니다.

1. 근로조건: 근로관계에서 임금, 근로시간, 해고, 그 밖에 근로자의 대우에

dismissal, and other treatment of workers in labor relations
2. Service rules: Rules on work order that workers must abide by in the process of providing work and sanctions in case of violation

(Penalty) Article 114 Fine of up to 5 million won

9-2-2 When changing the rules of employment, do you listen to opinions or obtain consent from the labor union or the employee representative of a majority of workers?

Article 94 of the Labor Standards Act

Work rule change process step 1: hearing or consent

When changing the rules of employment unfavorably to workers, the consent of a majority of workers or a labor union organized by a majority of workers must be obtained, and opinions must be heard if the change is not unfavorable.

Regarding 'consent', the precedent states that if there is a labor union organized by a majority of workers, if the union representative agrees and signs, the union is deemed to have agreed, and it is not necessary to obtain the consent of a majority of the union members.

If there is no union organized by the majority of workers, 1) the employer explains the contents of the rules of employment and the reason for the revision, 2) after the worker group reviews and exchanges opinions without intervention or interference by the employer, and 3) with the consent of a majority of workers. At this time, the method of circulating the changes to the employment rules and the consent form without sufficient explanation from the employer and the process of exchanging opinions among the worker group, or requiring individual signatures, is regarded as not going through the consent process.

(Penalty) Article 114 Fine of up to 5 million won

9-2-3 Did you report existing changes to your rules of employment?

Form No. 15 of the Enforcement Rules of the Labor Relations Act

Step 2 of changing procedure in the rules of employment: Report to the local employment and labor office

The employer must fill out the reporting form of Employment Rules and report it to the Ministry of Employment and Labor, attaching documents proving that the changes in the employment rules, the labor union of the majority of

관하여 정한 조건
2. 복무규율: 근로자가 근로를 제공하는 과정에서 지켜야 할 작업질서에 관한 규칙과 이를 위반한 경우의 제재

(벌칙) 제114조 500만 원 이하의 벌금

9-2-2 취업규칙을 변경할 때 근로자 과반수 노동조합 또는 근로자 집단으로부터의 의견을 청취하거나 동의를 받았습니까?

근로기준법 제94조

취업규칙 변경 절차 1단계: 의견청취 또는 동의

취업규칙을 근로자에게 불리하게 변경할 때에는 근로자 과반수로 조직된 노동조합이나 근로자 과반수의 동의를 얻어야 하고, 불리하게 변경하는 것이 아닌 경우에는 의견을 청취해야 합니다.

'동의'와 관련하여 판례는 근로자 과반수로 조직된 노동조합이 있는 경우에는 노동조합 대표자가 동의하여 서명하면 노동조합이 동의한 것으로 보며 조합원 과반수의 동의를 받아야 하는 것은 아니라고 합니다.

근로자 과반수로 조직된 노조가 없는 경우에는

1) 사용자는 취업규칙의 내용, 개정이유를 설명하고,
2) 사용자의 개입이나 간섭이 없는 상태에서 근로자 집단이 검토하고 의견을 교환하는 과정을 거친 후에
3) 근로자 과반수의 동의를 받아야 합니다. 이 때 사용자의 충분한 설명과 근로자 집단의 의견 교환 과정을 생략한 채 취업규칙 변경 내용과 동의서를 회람하거나, 개별적으로 서명하게 하는 방식은 동의 절차를 거치지 않은 것으로 봅니다.

(벌칙) 제114조 500만 원 이하의 벌금

9-2-3 변경한 취업규칙을 신고했습니까?

근로기준법 시행규칙 별지 제15호 서식

취업규칙 변경 절차 2단계: 관할 지방고용노동청에 신고

사용자는 취업규칙 신고서를 작성하여 취업규칙 변경 내용, 근로자 과반수 노동조합 또는 근로자 과반수의 의견을 청취하였음을 증명하는

workers, or the opinions of the majority of workers that have been heard.

(Fine for negligence) Article 116. Fine not exceeding 5 million won

9-3 Compliance with laws and collective agreements

9-3-1 Are there any parts of the rules of employment that are inconsistent with the law?

Article 96 of the Labor Standards Act

Employment rules, which are company regulations, must not violate laws such as the Labor Standards Act. Any part of the employment rules that is inconsistent with the law has no effect.

9-3-2 Are there any parts of the rules of employment that are inconsistent with the collective agreement?

Article 96 of the Labor Standards Act

As with laws and regulations, the contents of employment rules should not be disadvantageous compared to the standards set forth in collective agreements or regulations closely related to them.

9-3-3 Did you comply with all Ministry of Employment and Labor orders to change the rules of employment?

Article 96 of the Labor Standards Act

If an ineffective employment rule is left unattended, there is a risk that it will be applied to workers who are not familiar with the circumstances. To prevent this, the Minister of Employment and Labor may order changes to the employment rule that are inconsistent with the law or collective agreement.

Employers who violate the order of the Minister of Employment and Labor will be punished with a fine of up to 5 million won.

(Penalty) Article 114. Fine of up to 5 million won

10. Payment of Retirement Benefits

10-1 Payment of severance pay

10-1-1 Do you calculate your workers' severance pay based on their average wages?

Article 9 of the Employee Retirement Benefit Security Act (Retirement Benefit Act)

Severance pay should be calculated based on average wages. The retirement

서면을 첨부하여 관할 고용노동부에 신고하여야 합니다.
(과태료) 제116조 500만 원 이하의 과태료

9-3 법령 . 단체협약의 준수
9-3-1 취업규칙이 법령에 어긋나는 부분은 없습니까?
근로기준법 제96조

회사의 규정인 취업규칙은 근로기준법 등 법령에 어긋나서는 안됩니다. 취업규칙의 내용 중 법령에 어긋나는 부분은 효력이 없습니다.

9-3-2 취업규칙이 단체협약과 어긋나는 부분은 없습니까?
근로기준법 제96조

취업규칙의 내용은 법령과 마찬가지로 단체협약에서 정한 기준이나 이와 밀접하게 관련 있는 규정에 비해 불이익해서는 아니됩니다.

9-3-3 고용노동부의 취업규칙 변경명령을 이행하였습니까?
근로기준법 제96조

효력이 없는 취업규칙을 그대로 방치할 경우, 사정을 잘 모르는 근로자들에게 그대로 적용될 위험성이 있으므로 이를 방지하기 위하여 고용노동부장관은 법령이나 단체협약에 어긋나는 취업규칙의 변경을 명령할 수 있습니다.

고용노동부장관의 명령을 위반한 사용자는 500만 원 이하 벌금의 벌칙을 받게 됩니다.
(벌칙) 제114조 500만 원 이하의 벌금

10. 퇴직급여 지급

10-1 퇴직금 지급
10-1-1 평균임금을 기준으로 퇴직금을 계산하였습니까?
근로자퇴직급여보장법(이하 퇴직급여법) 제9조

퇴직금은 평균임금을 기준으로 계산되어야 합니다. 퇴직금제도란 근로자

pay system is in accordance with the Employee Retirement Benefit Security Act, and refers to a system in which an average wage equivalent to 30 days or more is paid in a lump sum to workers per year of continuous service.

10-1-2 Do you calculate severance pay including non-taxable items?

Even if it falls under non-taxable items, money and goods paid by the employer to workers in exchange for work, which are continuously/regularly paid to workers and for which the employer is obligated to pay them by collective agreements/employment rules/labor contracts/labor practices, etc., are wages. When calculating severance pay, it should be included in the average wage.

10-1-3 Do you pay severance pay within 14 days of the date the reason for payment occurs?

Article 9 of the Retirement Benefit Act
Retirement pay must be paid in whole or in part within 14 days from the date of retirement of the worker.
(Penalty) Article 44 of the Retirement Benefit Act: Imprisonment for up to 3 years or a fine of up to 30 million won

10-1-4 Is severance pay paid separately from wages?

Article 9 of the Retirement Benefit Act
Severance pay must be paid separately from wages. This is because, in principle, the right to receive severance pay arises after retirement. However, exceptions are recognized in case of legitimate interim settlement.
(Penalty) Article 44 Imprisonment for up to 3 years or a fine of up to 30 million won

10-1-5 When the 4 major insurances were registered later, is severance pay paid for all consecutive working periods other than the period covered by the 4 major insurances?

Retirement Benefit Act Article 8 Paragraph 1
Regardless of whether or not the 4 major insurances have been registered, if the employee's continuous service period exceeds one year, severance pay for the entire period must be paid. Period of continuous employment refers to the period of continuous employment, from the day the worker joined the company to the day he or she retired (the period from the conclusion of the employment contract to the termination of the employment contract).

퇴직급여 보장법에 따른 것으로, 계속근로기간 1년에 대하여 30일분 이상의 평균임금을 근로자에게 일시금으로 지급하는 제도를 의미합니다.

10-1-2 비과세 항목을 포함하여 퇴직금을 계산하였습니까?

비과세 항목에 해당하더라도 사용자가 근로의 대가로 근로자에게 지급하는 금품으로서, 근로자에게 계속적/정기적으로 지급되고 단체협약/취업규칙/근로계약/노동관행 등에 의해 사용자에게 그 지급의무가 지워져 있는 것은 임금으로서 퇴직금 산정 시 평균임금에 산입되어야 합니다.

10-1-3 퇴직금을 지급 사유 발생일로부터 14일 이내에 지급했습니까?

퇴직급여법 제9조

퇴직금은 근로자가 퇴직한 날로부터 14일 이내에 퇴직급여액의 전부 또는 일부를 지급하여야 합니다.

(벌칙) 제44조 3년 이하의 징역 또는 3천만 원 이하의 벌금

10-1-4 퇴직금을 임금과 별도로 지급하고 있습니까?

퇴직급여법 제9조

퇴직금은 임금과는 별도로 지급되어야 합니다. 퇴직금은 원칙적으로 퇴직한 이후에 그 권리가 발생하기 때문입니다. 다만, 적법한 중간정산의 경우 예외가 인정됩니다.

(벌칙) 퇴직급여법 제44조 3년 이하의 징역 또는 3천만 원 이하의 벌금

10-1-5 4대보험에 가입한 기간 이외의 모든 계속근로기간에 대해 퇴직금을 지급합니까?

퇴직급여법 제8조 제1항

4대보험에 가입했는지 여부와 상관없이 근로자의 계속근로기간이 1년을 넘었다면 전 기간에 대한 퇴직금을 지급하여야 합니다. 계속근로기간이란 계속하여 근로를 제공한 기간으로서 근로자가 입사한 날부터 퇴직한 날까지의 기간(근로계약을 체결하여 해지될 때까지의 기간)을 의미함

10-2 Payment of defined benefit (DB) retirement pension

10-2-1 Are you paying at least the minimum reserve as of the end of each business year?

Article 16 Paragraph 1 of the Retirement Benefit Act

Employers must accumulate more than the minimum reserve at the end of each business year to secure the ability to pay retirement benefits.

10-2-2 Do you require the retirement pension provider to pay retirement benefits within 14 days from the date the reason for payment occurred?

Article 17 Paragraph 2 of the Retirement Benefit Act

The employer must have the retirement pension provider pay all or part of the retirement benefit within 14 days of the employee's retirement.

(Penalty) Article 44 Imprisonment for up to 3 years or a fine of up to 30 million won

10-2-3 If the salary level paid by the retirement pension provider is insufficient, do you pay the insufficient amount within 14 days?

Article 17 Paragraph 3 of the Retirement Benefit Act

If the level of wages paid by the retirement pension provider is insufficient, the employer must pay the amount that is insufficient within 14 days from the date of occurrence of the reason for payment of retirement pay if the level of wages equivalent to the average wage for 30 days per year of continuous service is insufficient. must be paid to the account of the IRP system designated by

(Penalty) Article 44 Imprisonment for up to 3 years or a fine of up to 30 million won

10-3 Payment of defined contribution (DC) retirement pension

10-3-1 Are contributions equivalent to 1/12 or more of the total annual wages paid?

Article 20 Paragraph 1 of the Retirement Benefit Act

An employer who has established a defined contribution retirement pension plan must pay contributions equivalent to at least 1/12 of the total annual wages in cash to the account of the subscriber's defined contribution retirement pension plan.

10-2 확정급여형퇴직연금(DB)급여 지급

10-2-1 매 사업연도 말 기준 최소 적립금을 납입했습니까?

퇴직급여법 제16조 제1항

사용자는 퇴직급여 지급 능력을 확보하기 위하여 매 사업연도 말 최소 적립금 이상을 적립하여야 합니다.

10-2-2 퇴직급여를 지급사유 발생일로부터 14일 이내에 퇴직연금사업자로 하여금 지급하도록 하였습니까?

퇴직급여법 제17조 제2항

사용자는 퇴직연금사업자로 하여금 근로자가 퇴직한 날로부터 14일 이내에 퇴직급여액의 전부 또는 일부를 지급하도록 하여야 합니다.
(벌칙) 제44조 3년 이하의 징역 또는 3천만 원 이하의 벌금

10-2-3 퇴직연금사업자가 지급한 급여수준이 부족한 경우 14일 이내에 그 부족한 금액을 지급하였습니까?

퇴직급여법 제17조 제3항

퇴직연금사업자가 지급한 급여수준이 부족한 경우, 사용자는 계속근로기간 1년에 대하여 30일분 평균임금에 상당하는 급여수준에 미치지 못하는 경우 퇴직금 지급 사유가 발생한 날부터 14일 이내에 그 부족한 금액을 해당 가입자가 지정한 IRP제도의 계정으로 지급하여야 합니다.
(벌칙) 제44조 3년 이하의 징역 또는 3천만 원 이하의 벌금

10-3 확정기여형퇴직연금(DC) 급여 지급

10-3-1 연간 임금총액의 12분의 1 이상에 해당하는 부담금을 납입하고 있습니까?

퇴직급여법 제20조 제1항

확정기여형퇴직연금제도를 설정한 사용자는 연간 임금총액의 12분의 1 이상에 해당하는 부담금을 현금으로 가입자의 확정기여형퇴직연금제도 계정에 납입하여야 합니다.

10-3-2 When a reason for payment occurs, if the contribution to the subscriber is unpaid, do you pay the contribution and delayed-payment interest within 14 days from the date the reason for payment of the pension occurs?

Retirement Benefit Act Article 20 Paragraph 5

It must be paid within 14 days from the date the worker resigns (the date of occurrence of the reason for payment of severance pay), and if there is an unpaid contribution, an annual interest rate of 20% for the number of delayed days from the next day to the payment date must be paid. The payment date may be extended by agreement of the parties, but the employer is still obliged to pay interest on delay unless it falls under any reason for exclusion from application of delayed interest.

(Penalty) Article 44 of the Retirement Benefit Act Imprisonment for up to 3 years or a fine of up to 30 million won

10-4 Payment of SME Retirement Pension Fund System Benefits

10-4-1 Are contributions equivalent to 1/12 or more of the total annual wages paid?

Retirement Benefit Act Article 23-7 Paragraph 1

Employers must regularly pay at least 1/12 of the subscriber's total annual wages in cash to the subscriber's small business retirement pension fund account at least once a year.

(Penalty) Article 44 Imprisonment for up to 3 years or a fine of up to 30 million won

10-4-2 When a reason for payment occurs, if the contribution to the subscriber is unpaid, do you pay the contribution and delayed-payment interest within 14 days from the date the reason for payment of the benefit occurs?

Article 23-7 Paragraph 2 of the Retirement Benefit Act

In the case of non-payment of contributions to subscribers when a reason for payment of severance pay occurs, the contributions and delayed interest must be paid to the fund system employer contribution account of the subscriber within 14 days from the date of occurrence of the reason. However, in special circumstances, the payment date may be extended by agreement of the parties. However, even in this case, the delayed interest for the number of delayed days must be paid from the next day to the day the contribution is paid.

(Penalty) Article 44 Imprisonment for up to 3 years or a fine of up to 30 million won

10-3-2 지급사유가 발생한 때에 그 가입자에 대한 부담금이 미납된 경우, 사유 발생일로부터 14일 이내에 부담금과 지연이자를 지급했습니까?

퇴직급여법 제20조 제5항

근로자가 퇴직한 날(퇴직금 지급사유 발생일)로부터 14일 이내에 지급하여야 하고, 미납부담금이 있다면 그 다음날부터 지급하는 날까지의 지연 일수에 대하여 연 20%의 지연이자를 지급하여야 합니다. 당사자의 합의에 따라 지급기일은 연장할 수 있지만, 지연이자 적용제외 사유에 해당하지 않는 한 사용자는 여전히 지연이자를 지급할 의무가 있습니다.

(벌칙) 제44조 3년이하의 징역 또는 3천만 원 이하의 벌금

10-4 중소기업퇴직연금기금제도 급여 지급

10-4-1 연간 임금총액의 12분의 1 이상에 해당하는 부담금을 납입하고 있습니까?

퇴직급여법 제23조의7 제1항

사용자는 매년 1회 이상 정기적으로 가입자의 연간 임금총액의 12분의 1 이상에 해당하는 부담금을 현금으로 가입자의 중소기업퇴직연금기금제도 계정에 납입하여야 합니다.

(벌칙) 퇴직급여법 제44조 3년이하의 징역 또는 3천만 원 이하의 벌금

10-4-2 지급사유가 발생한 때에 그 가입자에 대한 부담금이 미납된 경우, 사유 발생일로부터 14일 이내에 부담금과 지연이자를 지급했습니까?

퇴직급여법 제23조의7 제2항

퇴직금 지급사유 발생시 가입자에 대한 부담금 미납의 경우, 사유 발생일부터 14일 이내에 부담금과 지연이자를 해당 가입자의 기금제도사용자부담금계정에 납입하여야야 합니다. 다만, 특별한 사정이 있는 경우 당사자의 합의에 따라 납입 기일을 연장할 수 있습니다. 그러나 이러한 경우에도 그 다음날부터 부담금을 납입한 날까지 지연일수에 대한 지연이자를 납입하여야 합니다.

(벌칙) 제44조 3년이하의 징역 또는 3천만 원 이하의 벌금

11. Preventing Workplace Harassment

11-0-1 Have you made yourself aware of the meaning of bullying in the workplace?

Labor Standards Act Article 76-2

Workplace harassment is prohibited by Article 76-2 of the Labor Standards Act. An employer or worker takes advantage of superiority in position or relationship at work to inflict physical or mental pain on other workers beyond the scope appropriate for work or damage the work environment. It means doing something aggravating.

The conditions for harassment in the workplace are:

1. Using superiority in position or relationship at work,
2. Behavior that exceeds the scope appropriate for work,
3. Giving physical or mental pain or worsening the working environment, three requirements must be met.

(Penalty) Article 109, Article 116, paragraphs 1 and 2

11-0-2 Do the rules of employment include efforts to prevent workplace harassment and measures to handle it when it occurs?

Article 76-3 of the Labor Standards Act

The employer must include rules for preventing and responding to workplace harassment in order to protect workers from workplace harassment, etc. in the rules of employment.

Items to be included include

1. Prohibited acts of bullying in the workplace,
2. Preventive activities such as workplace bullying prevention education,
3. Counseling for grievances,
4. Case handling procedures,
5. Measures to protect victims,
6. Sanctions against perpetrators,
7. Measures to prevent recurrence,
8. Efforts to prevent secondary harm, such as leakage of secrets, etc.

11. 직장 내 괴롭힘 예방

11-0-1 직장 내 괴롭힘의 의미를 제대로 알고 있습니까?

근로기준법 제76조의2

직장 내 괴롭힘이란 근로기준법 제76조의2에 의하여 금지되고 있는 것으로, 사용자 또는 근로자가 직장에서의 지위 또는 관계 등의 우위를 이용하여 업무상 적정범위를 넘어 다른 근로자에게 신체적 . 정신적 고통을 주거나 근무환경을 악화시키는 행위를 하는 것을 의미합니다.

직장 내 괴롭힘의 성립요건으로는

1. 직장에서의 지위 또는 관계 등의 우위를 이용할 것,
2. 업무상 적정 범위를 넘는 행위일 것,
3. 신체적 . 정신적 고통을 주거나 근무환경을 악화시켰을 것으로, 크게 3가지 요건이 충족되어야 합니다.

(벌칙) 제109조, 제116조 제1항 내지 2항

11-0-2 취업규칙 등에 직장 내 괴롭힘 예방 및 발생 시 조치 등에 관한 사항이 포함되어 있습니까?

근로기준법 제76조의3

사용자는 취업규칙 등에 직장 내 괴롭힘으로부터 근로자를 보호하기 위하여 이를 예방.대응하기 위한 규정이 포함되어 있어야 합니다.

기재되어야 할 사항으로는

1. 금지되는 직장 내 괴롭힘 행위,
2. 직장 내 괴롭힘 예방교육 등 예방 활동,
3. 고충상담,
4. 사건처리절차,
5. 피해자 보호조치,
6. 가해자 제재,
7. 재발방지대책 등,
8. 비밀누설 등 2차 가해 방지 노력 등이 있습니다.

11-0-3 If there is a report of bullying at work, do you take action in accordance with the principles stipulated by law?

Article 76-3 (2) of the Labor Standards Act

When a employer receives a report or becomes aware of the occurrence of bullying in the workplace, the employer must conduct an objective investigation without delay to confirm the fact with the person concerned. At this time, the organization in charge of carrying out the procedure can be determined according to the size and characteristics of the business site, but in the case of a formal investigation procedure, considering fairness and professionalism, it is possible to consider organizing an investigation committee or entrusting an external agency.

(Fine for negligence) Article 116 Fine not exceeding 5 million won

11-0-4 If bullying at work has occurred, do you protect the alleged victim and handle the alleged perpetrator appropriately?

Article 76-3 (4) to (5) of the Labor Standards Act

When it is confirmed that bullying has occurred in the workplace, the employer must protect the victimized worker and take action against the perpetrator. In this case, measures include change of workplace, change of placement, paid leave, etc. upon request of the victimized worker. In addition, before taking necessary measures, such as disciplinary action or change of workplace, against the harasser, the victim's opinion on the measures must be heard.

(Fine for negligence) Article 116 Fine not exceeding 5 million won

11-0-5 Do you treat the alleged victim of bullying at work or the worker who reported it unfavorably?

Article 76-3 (6) of the Labor Standards Act

Employers must not give disadvantageous treatment (dismissal, etc.) to workers who have been victims of workplace harassment or who have reported it. Regardless of whether or not it constitutes workplace harassment, unfavorable treatment of the reporter is prohibited. Therefore, even if the report is not workplace harassment as a result of the investigation, unfavorable treatment cannot be given to the reporter.

Representative examples of disadvantageous treatment are:

11-0-3 직장 내 괴롭힘에 대한 신고가 있을 경우 법에서 정한 원칙에 따라 조치를 취하고 있습니까?

근로기준법 제76조의3 제2항

사용자는 신고를 접수하거나 직장 내 괴롭힘 발생 사실을 인지한 경우 지체 없이 당사자 등을 대상으로 그 사실 확인을 위하여 객관적으로 조사를 실시하여야 합니다. 이때 절차를 수행할 담당기구를 어떻게 구성할 것인지는 사업장의 규모, 특성에 맞게 결정할 수 있으나, 정식 조사 절차의 경우 공정성과 전문성 등을 고려할 때 조사위원회 구성이나 외부기관 위탁을 고려해볼 수 있습니다.

(과태료) 제116조 500만원 이하의 과태료

11-0-4 직장 내 괴롭힘이 있었을 때 피해근로자를 보호하고 행위자에게 조치를 취했습니까?

근로기준법 제76조의3 제4항 내지 제5항

사용자는 직장 내 괴롭힘 발생 사실이 확인된 때에는 피해근로자를 보호하고 행위자에게 조치를 취해야 합니다. 이 때, 조치로는 피해근로자가 요청하는 경우 근무장소의 변경, 배치전환, 유급휴가 등이 있습니다. 또한, 괴롭힘 행위자에 대하여 징계, 근무장소의 변경 등 필요한 조치를 하기 전에는 그 조치에 대하에 피해 근로자의 의견을 들어야 합니다.

(과태료) 제116조 500만원 이하의 과태료

11-0-5 직장 내 괴롭힘의 피해 근로자나 이를 신고한 근로자에게 불리한 처우를 하였습니까?

근로기준법 제76조의3 제6항

직장 내 괴롭힘의 피해 근로자나 이를 신고한 근로자에게 사용자는 불리한 처우(해고 등)를 하여서는 아니됩니다. 직장 내 괴롭힘에 해당하는지와 관계없이 신고자에 대하여 불리한 처우는 금지되기 때문에, 조사결과 직장 내 괴롭힘이 아니어도 신고자에게 불리한 처우를 할 수는 없습니다.

불리한 처우의 대표적인 사례로는

1. Disadvantageous measures equivalent to loss of status, such as dismissal, dismissal, and dismissal;
2. Unjust personnel measures such as disciplinary action, demotion, suspension, salary reduction, and restriction on promotion;
3. Job refusal and job reassignment.
4. Discrimination in performance evaluation or peer evaluation or discrimination in payment of wages or bonuses,
5. Restriction on training opportunities for developing and improving vocational skills,
6. Bullying, acts that cause mental and physical damage, such as assault or abusive language, or acts that neglect the occurrence of such acts, and
7. Other disadvantageous treatment against the will of the worker who made the report and the victim, etc.

(Penalty) Article 109 Imprisonment for up to 3 years or a fine of up to 30 million won

11-0-6 Are you making efforts to prevent secondary harms, such as by maintaining confidentiality of all information learned in the process of investigating a report of workplace harassment?

Article 76-3 (7) of the Labor Standards Act

In accordance with Article 76-3, Paragraph 7 of the Labor Standards Act, employers must make efforts to prevent secondary harm, such as those involved in workplace harassment investigations not to disclose confidential information about it to others. As a way to prevent secondary harm, there are ways to keep the identity of all involved, including the victim, thoroughly confidential, who participated in the case handling process.

(Fine for negligence) Article 116 Fine not exceeding 5 million won

12. Observing Minimum Wage

12-1 Effect of minimum wage

12-1-1 Are your workers paid at least the minimum wage?

Minimum Wage Act Article 6 Paragraph 1

According to Article 6, Paragraph 1 of the Minimum Wage Act, employers must pay wages higher than the minimum wage to workers. In a labor

1. 파면, 해임, 해고 등 신분 상실에 해당하는 불이익 조치,
2. 징계, 강등, 정직, 감봉, 승진 제한 등 부당한 인사조치,
3. 직무 미부여, 직무 재배치, 그 밖에 본인의 의사에 반하는 인사조치,
4. 성과평가 또는 동료평가 등에서 차별이나 그에 따른 임금 또는 상여금 등의 차별 지급,
5. 직업능력 개발 및 향상을 위한 교육훈련 기회의 제한,
6. 집단 따돌림, 폭행 또는 폭언 등 정신적 신체적 손상을 가져오는 행위를 하거나 그 행위의 발생을 방치하는 행위,
7. 그 밖에 신고를 한 근로자 및 피해 근로자 등의 의사에 반하는 불리한 처우 등이 있습니다.

(벌칙) 제109조 3년 이하의 징역 또는 3천만 원 이하의 벌금

11-0-6 직장 내 괴롭힘 조사과정에서 알게 된 비밀을 누설하지 않도록 하는 등 2차 가해 방지를 위한 노력을 하고 있습니까?

근로기준법 제76조의3 제7항

근로기준법 제76조의3 제7항에 따라 직장 내 괴롭힘 조사에 관여한 사람은 이에 대한 비밀을 다른 이들에게 누설하여서는 아니되는 등 사용자는 2차 가해 방지에 대한 노력을 하여야 합니다. 2차 가해 방지를 위한 방안으로는 사건 처리 과정에서 참여한 사람들, 즉 피해자를 포함한 모든 관련자 신원에 대하여 철저한 비밀유지를 하는 방법 등이 있습니다.

(과태료) 제116조 500만원 이하의 과태료

12. 최저임금 준수

12-1 최저임금 효력

12-1-1 근로자에게 최저임금 이상의 임금을 지급하고 있습니까?

최저임금법 제6조 제1항

최저임금법 제6조 제1항에 따라 사용자는 근로자에게 최저임금 이상의 임금을 지급하여야 합니다. 최저임금에 미치지 않는 금액을 받기로 한 근로계약은 금액에 대한 부분은 무효로 보며, 최저임금액과 동일한

contract in which an amount less than the minimum wage is agreed to, the portion of the amount is considered invalid, and the wage equal to the minimum wage is deemed to be paid.

(Penalty) Imprisonment for not more than 3 years or a fine of not more than 20 million won, imprisonment and a fine may be imposed concurrently

12-1-2 Are new workers who have begun their 3-month probation paid at least minimum wage?

Minimum Wage Act Article 5 Paragraph 2

If 3 months have passed since the start of probation, after 3 months, you must pay at least the minimum wage even if you are probationary (trial or intern). Therefore, if a labor contract is concluded for one year or more, 90% of the minimum wage can be paid for three months from the start of probation as a period during which the minimum wage reduction can be applied. However, the minimum wage must be guaranteed for the following period.

(Penalty) Imprisonment for not more than 3 years or a fine of not more than 20 million won, imprisonment and a fine may be imposed concurrently

12-1-3 Are workers engaged in simple labor jobs paid 100% of the minimum wage even during their probationary period?

Proviso to Article 5 (2) of the Minimum Wage Act

In the case of workers engaged in simple labor jobs, it is impossible to reduce the minimum wage. Therefore, even during the probationary period, all minimum wages of 100% must be paid.

(Penalty) Imprisonment for not more than 3 years or a fine of not more than 20 million won, imprisonment and a fine may be imposed concurrently

12-2 Obligation to notify workers of minimum wage

12-2-1 Are matters concerning the minimum wage posted in a place where workers can easily see them, or are the workers notified in other appropriate ways?

Article 11 of the Minimum Wage Act

Employers have an obligation to notify workers of minimum wage by posting it in a place where workers can easily see it or by other appropriate

임금을 지급하기로 한 것으로 봅니다.
(벌칙) 제28조 3년 이하의 징역 또는 2천만 원 이하의 벌금, 징역과 벌금 병과 가능

12-1-2 수습을 시작한지 3개월이 지난 근로자에게 최저임금 이상의 임금을 지급하고 있습니까?

최저임금법 제5조 제2항

수습시작 후 3개월이 지났다면, 3개월 이후부터는 수습(시용 또는 인턴)이라도 적어도 최저임금 이상의 임금을 지급해야 합니다. 따라서, 1년 이상의 근로계약을 체결하는 경우 수습 시작일로부터 3개월 동안은 최저임금 감액적용 가능 기간으로 최저임금의 90%를 지급할 수 있습니다. 그러나 이 후의 기간동안 최저임금은 보장되어야 합니다.
(벌칙) 제28조 3년 이하의 징역 또는 2천만 원 이하의 벌금, 징역과 벌금 병과 가능

12-1-3 단순노무직에 종사하는 근로자에게는 수습기간이더라도 최저임금 100%를 지급하고 있습니까?

최저임금법 제5조 제2항 단서

단순노무직에 종사하는 근로자의 경우에는 최저임금 감액이 불가능합니다. 따라서 수습기간이라도 최저임금 100%를 모두 지급하여야 합니다.
(벌칙) 제28조 3년 이하의 징역 또는 2천만 원 이하의 벌금, 징역과 벌금 병과 가능

12-2 최저임금 주지의무

12-2-1 최저임금에 관한 사항을 근로자가 쉽게 볼 수 있는 장소에 게시하거나 그 외 적당한 방법으로 알리고 있습니까?

최저임금법 제11조

사용자는 최저임금에 관한 사항을 근로자가 쉽게 볼 수 있는 장소에 게시하거나, 그 외 적당한 방법으로 알려야 할 주지의무가 있습니다. 특히, 게시되어야 할 사항으로는,

means. In particular, matters to be posted include:
1. The minimum wage of workers subject to application,
2. Wages not included in the minimum wage,
3. Scope of workers excluded from the application of the minimum wage in the business in accordance with the law,
4. There is the effective date of the minimum wage.

(Fine) Minimum Wage Act Article 31 Fine for negligence up to KRW 1 million

13. Preventing Sexual Harassment in the Workplace

13-1 Prohibiting sexual harassment in the workplace
13-1-1 Do you know the criteria for defining sexual harassment in the workplace?

Equal Employment Opportunities Act

Article 2 Subparagraph 2 of the Equal Employment Opportunity Act defines what sexual harassment in the workplace is. Accordingly, there can be five major criteria for determining sexual harassment in the workplace.

1. You must use your position in the workplace or be related to your job. However, even if it does not occur within the work place or within the work place (in a car on a business trip, at a work-related dinner party, picnic place, a situation where you were called out for business discussions and met outside), the victim may be victimized by sexual language or behavior that occurred in such circumstances. If you feel sexually humiliated or disgusted, this is sexual harassment in the workplace.

2. It must be an act the victim does not want. This refers to language or behavior that contains sexual connotations that the other party does not want. Not only when the other party expressly expresses their intention to reject, but also when they passively or implicitly refuse 2. If the perpetrator is in a high-ranking position or has strong authority, such as determining the victim's working conditions, the victim has not explicitly expressed his or her intention to refuse) is also an act that the victim does not want.

3. It must be sexually explicit or otherwise. Sexual speech and behavior can be established even once, and sexual speech and other requests have

1. 적용을 받는 근로자의 최저임금액,
2. 최저임금에 산입하지 아니하는 임금,
3. 법에 따라 해당 사업에서 최저임금의 적용을 제외할 근로자의 범위,
4. 최저임금의 효력발생 연월일 이 있습니다.
(과태료) 최저임금법 제31조 100만 원 이하의 과태료

13. 직장 내 성희롱 예방

13-1 직장 내 성희롱 금지
13-1-1 직장 내 성희롱 판단기준을 알고 있습니까?

남녀고용평등과 일 가정 양립 지원에 관한 법률(이하 남녀고용평등법) 남녀고용평등법 제2조 제2호은 직장 내 성희롱이 무엇인지 정의하고 있습니다. 이에, 직장 내 성희롱의 판단기준으로는 크게 5가지가 있을 수 있습니다.

1. 직장 내 지위를 이용하거나, 업무와의 관련성이 있어야 합니다. 그러나, 근무시간 내, 근무장소에서 발생한 것이 아니더라도(출장 중인 차안, 업무와 관련이 있는 회식장소, 야유회장소, 업무협의를 위해 불러내어 밖에서 만난 상황), 이와 같은 상황에서 발생한 성적 언동 등으로 피해자가 성적 굴욕감이나 혐오감을 느꼈다면 이는 직장 내 성희롱에 해당합니다.

2. 피해자가 원하지 않는 행위이어야 합니다. 이는 상대방이 원하지 않는 성적의미가 내포된 언어나 행위를 의미합니다. 상대방이 명시적으로 거부의사를 표현한 경우 뿐 아니라, 소극적 묵시적으로 거부하는 경우(예를 들어 1. 피해자가 사회경험이 부족하여 직장 내 성희롱 상황에서 어떻게 대처해야 하는지 몰라 적극적으로 거부하지 못한 경우, 2. 행위자가 고위 직급이거나, 피해자의 근로조건을 결정하는 등 강력한 권한을 가지고 있어서 피해자가 명시적으로 거부의사를 표현하지 못한 경우 등)도 피해자가 원하지 않는 행위에 해당됩니다

3. 성적 언동 또는 그 밖의 요구이어야 합니다. 성적 언동이 단 1회뿐이라도 성립하며, 성적 언동이나 그 밖의 요구는 성적인(sexual)의

sexual connotations. For example, 1. Calling a female employee Ajumma, 2. Behavior that demeans women, such as talking only to female employees, 3. Behavior that enforces stereotyped gender roles, such as running errands for coffee only to female employees, etc. there is

4. It is irrelevant whether the actor intended to commit sexual harassment or not, and whether sexual harassment in the workplace is established. In other words, whether the victim felt unpleasant becomes an important criterion for judgment.
5. Since sexual humiliation or disgust is a subjective emotion, it can be felt differently for each individual, so the reasonable victim's perspective and gender sensitivity are also the criteria for judgment. In this regard, our Supreme Court should examine and judge based on whether it was to the extent that one could feel "sexual humiliation or disgust" in the "position of an average person in the same position as the victim", not the general and average person in our society. I saw it do.

13-1-2 Are you familiar with the concept of sexual harassment in the workplace?

Equal Employment Opportunity Act Article 2 Subparagraph 2

In Article 2, Subparagraph 2 of the Equal Employment Opportunity Act, sexual harassment in the workplace is defined as when an employer, superior, or worker makes use of his/her position in the workplace or makes other workers feel sexually humiliated or disgusted by sexual words and actions, or It is defined as giving disadvantages in working conditions and employment for reasons of not complying with other requests.

The types of sexual harassment in the workplace can be broadly classified into 1. Physical acts (eg, physical contact regardless of the other person's intention, touching a specific body part, etc.), 2. Verbal acts (such as making lewd jokes or sexual harassment of women). 3. Visual acts (posting or showing obscene pictures, pictures, graffiti, etc., intentionally exposing or touching certain body parts) etc.), and 4. Other acts (all acts that are recognized as causing sexual humiliation or disgust under socially accepted norms).

미가 내포된 경우를 의미합니다. 예를 들어, 1. 여성직원을 아줌마라고 부르는 경우, 2. 여성직원에게만 반말을 하는 등 여성을 비하하는 행동, 3. 여성직원에게만 커피 심부름을 시키는 등 고정관념적 성역할을 강요하는 행동 등이 있습니다.

4. 행위자가 성희롱을 하려고 했는지 의도와, 직장 내 성희롱의 성립 여부는 무관합니다. 즉, 피해자가 불쾌감을 느꼈는지 여부가 중요한 판단기준이 됩니다.
5. 성적 굴욕감 또는 혐오감은 주관적 감정이므로 개인마다 다르게 느껴질 수 있기 때문에, 합리적인 피해자의 관점과 성인지 감수성 또한 판단기준이 됩니다. 이와 관련하여 우리 대법원은 우리 사회의 일반적이고 평균적인 사람이 아니라, 피해자와 같은 처지에 있는 평균적인 사람의 입장에서 성적 굴욕감이나 혐오감을 느낄 수 있는 정도였는지를 기준으로 심리, 판단하여야 한다고 보았습니다.

13-1-2 직장 내 성희롱의 개념에 대해 정확히 알고 있습니까?

남녀고용평등법 제2조 제2호

남녀고용평등법 제2조 제2호에서는 직장 내 성희롱을 '사업주, 상급자 또는 근로자가 직장 내의 지위를 이용하거나 업무와 관련하여 다른 근로자에게 성적 언동 등으로 성적 굴욕감 또는 혐오감을 느끼게 하거나 성적 언동 또는 그 밖의 요구 등에 따르지 아니하였다는 이유로 근로조건 및 고용에서 불이익을 주는 것'으로 정의하고 있습니다.

직장 내 성희롱의 종류는 크게

1. 육체적 행위(예) 상대방의 의사와 상관없이 신체적을 접촉, 특정 신체부위를 만지는 행위 등),
2. 언어적 행위(음란한 농담을 하거나, 여성의 성과 관련된 물리적 현상과 관련하여 성적인 비유나 함의, 행위를 묘사하는 행위 등),
3. 시각적 행위(음란한 사진, 그림, 낙서 등을 게시하거나 보여주는 행위, 자신의 특정 신체부위를 고의적으로 노출하거나 만지는 행위 등),
4. 기타 행위(사회통념상 성적 굴욕감 또는 혐오감을 느끼게 하는 것으로 인정되는 모든 행위)로 분류될 수 있습니다.

13-1-3 Do you know what to do in the event that sexual harassment occurs at work?

Article 14 Paragraphs 4 through 7 of the Equal Employment Opportunity Act
In accordance with Article 14 of the Equal Employment Opportunity Act, employers are obliged to take appropriate measures in case of sexual harassment in the workplace. At this time, within the scope of not going against the will of the injured worker, it is possible to change the place of work, change the placement, order paid leave, etc. In principle, these measures need to be approached in a way that helps the victim to live a healthy working life again, and it is desirable to take measures to prevent recurrence of the perpetrators and improve the overall organizational culture and system to prevent similar incidents from recurring. . When a case of sexual harassment in the workplace is received, it must be dealt with promptly, but at the consultation stage, the victim's intention regarding the direction of problem resolution must be confirmed and respected. And care must be taken to ensure that additional damage is not caused to the victim during the investigation process.
(Fine) Article 39 fine of up to 5 million won

13-2 Preventing sexual harassment in the workplace

13-2-1 Do you conduct sexual harassment prevention training at work once a year?

Equal Employment for Men and Women Act Article 13 Paragraph 1
According to Article 13, Paragraph 1 of the Equal Employment Opportunity Act, employers must conduct annual training to prevent sexual harassment in the workplace (hereinafter referred to as sexual harassment prevention training).
For specific training-related content, it must be conducted at least once every year from January 1st to December 31st, and training targets include employers and all workers. Education must be conducted by calculating the appropriate number of people, and in the case of education methods, both in-house/consignment/cyber education are possible. However, in the case of a business that employs less than 10 workers on a regular basis, or a workplace where both the owner and workers are of one gender, circulating and distributing education may be acceptable. The person in charge of training can also invite external lecturers such as business owners, human resource managers, business managers, and related persons. The contents of training include
1. Laws related to sexual harassment in the workplace,

13-1-3 직장 내 성희롱이 발생했을 경우 어떻게 조치하여야 하는지 알고 있습니까?

남녀고용평등법 제14조 제4항 내지 7항

남녀고용평등법 제14조에 따라 사용자는 직장 내 성희롱 발생 시 이에 대하여 적절한 조치를 할 의무를 부담합니다. 이때, 피해근로자의 의사에 반하지 않는 범위 내에서 근무장소의 변경, 배치전환, 유급휴가 명령 등을 할 수 있습니다. 이러한 조치는 원칙적으로 피해자가 다시 건강한 직장생활을 할 수 있도록 돕는 방향으로 접근할 필요가 있으며, 유사한 사건이 반복되지 않도록 행위자에 대한 재발방지 조치, 전반적인 조직문화 및 제도의 개선 등도 병행하는 것이 바람직합니다. 직장 내 성희롱 사건 접수 시부터 신속하게 처리하되 상담 단계에서 문제 해결 방향에 대한 피해자의 의사를 확인하여 존중해야 합니다. 그리고 조사과정에서 피해자에게 추가적인 피해가 발생하지 않도록 주의가 필요합니다.

(과태료) 제39조 500만 원 이하의 과태료

13-2 직장 내 성희롱 예방

13-2-1 연 1회 직장 내 성희롱 예방교육을 실시하고 있습니까?

남녀고용평등법 제13조 제1항

남녀고용평등법 제13조 제1항에 따르면 사업주는 직장 내 성희롱의 예방을 위한 교육(이하 성희롱 예방 교육)을 매년 실시하여야 합니다. 구체적인 교육관련 내용으로는, 매년 1월 1일부터 12월 31일까지 1회 이상 실시되어야 하며, 교육대상은 사업주 및 모든 근로자가 포함됩니다. 적정인원을 산정하여 교육이 이루어져야 하며, 교육방법의 경우 자체/위탁/사이버 교육 모두 가능하지만, 일반적으로 교재 회람/게시판에의 자료게재 및 배포 등의 방식으로는 교육이 인정되지 않습니다. 다만, 상시 10명 미만의 근로자를 고용하는 사업, 사업주 및 근로자 모두가 한 가지 성별로 구성된 사업장의 경우 회람, 배포 방식의 교육이 인정될 수 있습니다. 교육진행 담당자는 사업주, 인사책임자, 업무 담당자 및 관련자 등 외부 전문강사를 초빙하는 것도 가능합니다. 교육내용에는
1. 직장 내 성희롱 관련 법령,

2. Procedures and measures for handling sexual harassment in the workplace,
3. Grievance counseling and relief procedures for victims of sexual harassment in the workplace,
4. Sanctions such as disciplinary actions against those who engage in sexual harassment in the workplace,
5. There are other matters necessary to prevent sexual harassment in the workplace.

(Fine) Article 39 Fine for negligence up to 5 million won

13-2-2 Do the employer as well as the workers participate in the training?

In the case of sexual harassment prevention education in the workplace, the target of education is not limited to workers (including full-time, fixed-term, part-time, dispatched, and part-time workers), but also includes employers. We conduct sexual harassment prevention education, and employers often do not attend because they mistakenly believe that they are not subject to sexual harassment prevention education. However, employers must also take it. Therefore, business owners must also participate in sexual harassment prevention training.

13-2-3 Are educational materials on preventing sexual harassment always posted or kept in a place where workers can freely read them?

Gender Equal Employment Act Article 13 Paragraph 3

According to Article 13, Paragraph 3 of the Equal Employment Opportunity Act, the contents of sexual harassment prevention education in the workplace must be posted or equipped at all times in a place where workers can freely read and inform the workers. Materials and textbooks containing the contents of sexual harassment prevention training are manuals, video training materials, or similar materials produced, disseminated, or certified by the Ministry of Employment and Labor.

(Fine for negligence) Article 39 Fine for negligence not exceeding 5 million won

14. Prohibiting Gender Discrimination in Employment

14-0-1 When recruiting or hiring workers, do you avoid discriminating on grounds such as gender, religion, marital status, family status, pregnancy or childbirth without reasonable grounds?

Equal Employment Opportunities Act Article 7 Paragraph 1

Employers must not discriminate between male and female workers in all

2. 직장 내 성희롱 발생시 처리절차와 조치기준,
3. 직장 내 성희롱 피해근로자의 고충상담 및 구제절차,
4. 직장 내 성희롱 행위자에 대한 징계 등 제재조치,
5. 그 밖의 직장 내 성희롱 예방에 필요한 사항이 있습니다.
(과태료) 제39조 500만 원 이하의 과태료

13-2-2 근로자뿐 아니라 사업주도 해당 교육에 참여하였습니까?

직장 내 성희롱 예방교육의 경우, 교육대상은 단지 근로자(정규직, 기간제, 단시간, 파견, 아르바이트 근로자 모두 포함)에 한정되는 것이 아니라 사업주도 포함됩니다. 성희롱 예방교육을 실시하며 사용자는 자신이 성희롱 예방교육 대상이 아니라고 착각하여 수강하지 않는 경우가 종종 있으나, 사용자도 반드시 수강하여야 합니다. 따라서 사업주도 성희롱 예방교육에 참여하여야 합니다.

13-2-3 성희롱 예방교육자료를 근로자가 자유롭게 열람할 수 있는 장소에 항상 게시하거나 갖추어 두고 있습니까?

남녀고용평등법 제13조 제3항

남녀고용평등법 제13조 제3항에 따르면 근로자가 자유롭게 열람할 수 있는 장소에 직장 내 성희롱 예방교육의 내용을 항상 게시하거나 갖추어 두어, 근로자에게 알려야 합니다. 성희롱 예방교육의 내용을 담은 자료, 교재는 고용노동부가 제작, 보급하거나 인증한 매뉴얼, 동영상 교육자료 또는 이에 준하는 자료입니다.
(과태료) 제39조 500만 원 이하의 과태료

14. 고용상 성차별 금지

14-0-1 근로자를 모집 또는 채용할 때 성별, 혼인, 가족 안에서의 지위, 임신 또는 출산 등의 사유로 합리적인 이유 없이 차별한 사실이 있습니까?

남녀고용평등법 제7조 제1항

사업주는 고용상 전 영역에서 남녀근로자를 차별하여서는 아니되며,

areas of employment, and discrimination here means different conditions when recruiting or hiring without reasonable grounds due to gender, marriage, family status, pregnancy or childbirth, etc. It means the case of taking other adverse measures. In particular, in relation to 'recruitment and hiring', even if the employer applies the same conditions for hiring or working, the number of men or women who can meet the conditions is significantly smaller than that of the other gender, resulting in disadvantageous results for a particular gender. Discrimination also falls under discrimination.

However, the following cases do not constitute discrimination.
1. In cases where a specific gender is unavoidably required in light of the nature of the job,
2. In cases where measures are taken to protect female workers such as pregnancy, childbirth, and lactation,
3. Active employment improvement measures in accordance with this Act or other laws If it falls under any of the three cases of doing so, it does not constitute discrimination.

In addition, if there are other reasonable reasons for discrimination and unfavorable treatment is justified, discrimination does not exist.

(Penalty) Article 37 A fine of up to 5 million won

14-0-2 When recruiting or hiring workers, do you avoid presenting or implying that physical conditions (appearance, height, weight, etc.) or specific marital status are preferred that are not necessary for the performance of the job?

Equal Employment Opportunities for Men and Women Act Article 7 Paragraph 2

In accordance with Article 7, Paragraph 2 of the Equal Employment Opportunity Act, when recruiting and hiring workers, employers shall not present or demand conditions that are not necessary for the performance of their duties, such as physical conditions such as appearance, height, and weight, and unmarried conditions. .

Representative cases of recognized discrimination in recruitment and hiring are as follows.
1. In cases where recruitment and employment opportunities are not given to specific genders (Example: only male employees are recruited),
2. Recruitment is done by dividing men and women by job type or job, or by allocating the number of people expected to be hired according to gender. Restricting employment opportunities for a specific gender in a job (Example: '? male in sales'),
3. Recruiting or hiring a specific sex for a lower rank or position than other

여기서 "차별"이란 성별, 혼인, 가족 안에서의 지위, 임신 또는 출산 등의 사유로 합리적인 이유 없이 모집 또는 채용할 때 그 조건을 다르게 하거나, 그 밖의 불리한 조치를 하는 경우를 의미합니다. 특히 '모집 및 채용'과 관련하여, 사업주가 채용조건이나 근로조건은 동일하게 적용하더라도 그 조건을 충족할 수 있는 남성 또는 여성이 다른 한 성(性)에 비하여 현저히 적고 그에 따라 특정 성에게 불리한 결과를 초래하며 그 조건이 정당한 것임을 증명할 수 없는 경우도 "차별"에 해당합니다.

다만, 다음의 경우에 해당하는 경우에는 차별에 해당하지 않습니다.
1. 직무의 성격에 비추어 특정 성이 불가피하게 요구되는 되는 경우,
2. 여성 근로자의 임신·출산·수유 등 모성보호를 위한 조치를 하는 경우,
3. 이 법 또는 다른 법률에 따라 적극적 고용개선조치를 하는 경우의 3가지 경우에 해당한다면 이는 차별에 해당하지 아니합니다.

또한, 그 밖에도 차별을 할 합리적인 이유가 존재하여 불리한 대우가 정당화되는 경우에는 차별이 성립하지 아니합니다.
(벌칙) 제37조 500만 원 이하의 벌금

14-0-2 근로자를 모집채용할 때 그 직무의 수행에 필요하지 아니한 용모·키·체중 등의 신체적 조건, 미혼 조건을 제시하거나 요구한 사실이 있습니까?

남녀고용평등법 제7조 제2항

남녀고용평등법 제7조 제2항에 따라 사업주는 근로자를 모집·채용할 때 그 직무의 수행에 필요하지 아니한 용모·키·체중 등의 신체적 조건, 미혼 조건 등의 조건을 제시하거나 요구하여서는 아니됩니다.

모집·채용 시 차별이 인정된 대표적인 사례는 다음과 같습니다.
1. 특정 성에게 모집·채용의 기회를 주지 않는 경우(예) 남자사원만 모집),
2. 직종·직무별로 남녀를 분리하여 모집하거나, 성별에 따라 채용예정 인원을 배정하여 둠으로써 특정 직종·직무에 특정 성의 채용 기회를 제한하는 경우(예) '판매직 남자 ○명'),
3. 학력·경력 등이 같거나 비슷함에도 특정 성을 다른 성에 비해 낮은

genders, even though the education and experience are the same or similar (Example)) 'Class 5 office worker: male with a high school diploma, Level 6 office worker: female with a high school graduation'),

4. When hiring a specific gender without reasonable grounds, requesting separate documents, etc.
5. Even though both men and women have the same or similar qualifications
6. When the recruitment age for a specific occupation is differentiated by gender without a reasonable reason,
7. Specific In the case of imposing physical conditions such as appearance that are not necessary for the performance of duties or conditions such as marital status only on sex.

(Penalty) Article 37 A fine of up to 5 million won

14-0-3 Do you pay equal wages to male and female workers for work of equal value within the same business?

Equal Employment Opportunity Act Article 8 Paragraph 1

Employers must pay the same level of wages to male and female workers for labor with the same value within the same business. Paying different levels of wages on the basis of sex constitutes wage discrimination.

Representative examples of recognized wage discrimination include:

1. In the case of paying a low wage to a specific gender by applying a daily wage uniformly set according to gender,
2. In the payment of various allowances such as family allowances, education allowances, commuting allowances, and kimchi-making allowances included in the category of wages, gender
3. In case of discrimination in wages by applying different criteria according to gender in basic pay, calculation of grade level, and raise in salary, etc.
4. Women on the grounds that female workers spend more money for maternity protection, etc.
5. In the case of adding a salary level to military service personnel, the extent of the addition exceeds the period of military service, or if the additional salary level is applied to men who have been exempted from military service or have not completed the military service, and pays wages,

직급 또는 직위에 모집 . 채용하는 경우(예) '사무직 5급: 고졸 남자, 사무직 6급: 고졸 여자'),
4. 채용 시 특정 성에게만 합리적인 이유 없이 별도의 구비서류 등을 요구하는 경우,
5. 남녀가 같거나 비슷한 자격을 갖추고 있음에도 불구하고 특정 성을 다른 성보다 불리한 고용 형태로 채용하는 경우(예) '남자는 정규직, 여자는 임시직' 등),
6. 특정 직종의 모집 연령을 합리적인 이유 없이 성별로 차이를 두는 경우,
7. 특정 성에게만 직무수행에 필요하지 않은 용모 등 신체적 조건이나 결혼 여부 등의 조건을 부과하는 경우.

(벌칙) 제37조 500만원 이하의 벌금

14-0-3 동일 사업 내의 동일 가치 노동에 대하여 남녀 근로자에게 동일한 임금을 지급하고 있습니까?

남녀고용평등법 제8조 제1항

사업주는 동일한 사업 내의 동일한 가치를 가진 노동에 대하여는 남녀 근로자를 불문하고 동일한 수준의 임금을 지급하여야 합니다. 성별을 이유로 다른 수준의 임금을 지급하는 것은 임금 차별에 해당합니다.

임금 차별이 있었다고 인정된 대표적인 사례는 다음과 같습니다.

1. 성별에 따라 일률적으로 책정된 일당을 적용하여 특정 성에게 낮은 임금을 지급하는 경우,
2. 임금의 범주에 포함되는 가족수당 · 교육수당 · 통근수당 · 김장수당 등 각종 수당을 지급함에 있어 성을 이유로 차별하는 경우,
3. 기본급 . 호봉산정 . 승급 등에 있어서 성별에 따라 그 기준을 달리 적용함으로써 임금을 차별하는 경우,
4. 모성보호 등을 위하여 여성 근로자들에게 더 많은 비용이 지출된다는 이유로 여성의 임금을 낮게 책정하는 경우,
5. 군 복무자에 대하여 호봉을 가산하는 경우에 있어 그 가산의 정도가 군복무 기간을 상회하거나, 병역면제자 또는 미필자인 남성에게도 호봉 가산을 적용하여 임금을 지급하는 경우,

6. When wages for occupations with a majority of a specific gender are set lower than for other occupations without reasonable grounds.

14-0-4 Have you been able to completely avoid discriminating, without reasonable justification, on the grounds of gender, religion, marital status, family status, pregnancy or childbirth, etc. in welfare items (beyond wages), education/placement/promotion, retirement/retirement, and dismissal?

Articles 9 through 11 of the Equal Employment Opportunity Act

Employers shall not discriminate without reasonable grounds on grounds such as gender, marriage, status in the family, pregnancy or childbirth, etc. in welfare benefits, education/placement/promotion of workers, retirement age/retirement and dismissal.

Representative examples of discrimination in education, placement, and promotion are as follows.

1. In the case of organizing and operating a curriculum separately according to gender without a reasonable reason, or changing the contents of education;

2. This also applies if it has resulted in disadvantageous results for a particular gender. However, this excludes cases where there is evidence from the business owner regarding job relevance and legitimacy.

3. In the case of hiring a person with the same or similar educational background and qualifications, assigning a specific gender to the main job and the other gender to an auxiliary job against the applicant's will. In cases where job transfer is restricted or excluded between the majority of occupations (rows) and occupational groups, except for cases where the employer proves job relevance and legitimacy.

5. In case a specific sex is given the opportunity to promote, but relatively unfavorable conditions and procedures are applied to make it difficult to promote

6. When a particular sex is treated unfavorably as a result of taking longer than other sexes to reach the rank.

The following are representative cases where discrimination in retirement, resignation, and dismissal is recognized:

6. 특정 성이 대다수인 직종의 임금을 합리적인 이유 없이 다른 직종보다 낮게 정하여 지급하는 경우.

14-0-4 임금 외의 복리후생항목, 교육배치승진, 정년퇴직 및 해고에서 성별, 혼인, 가족 안에서의 지위, 임신 또는 출산 등의 사유로 합리적인 이유 없이 차별한 사실이 있습니까?

남녀고용평등법 제9조 내지 제11조

사업주는 복리후생, 근로자의 교육 . 배치 . 승진, 정년 . 퇴직 및 해고에서 성별, 혼인, 가족 안에서의 지위, 임신 또는 출산 등의 사유로 합리적인 이유 없는 차별을 하여서는 아니됩니다.

교육 . 배치 . 승진상 차별이 인정된 대표적인 사례는 다음과 같습니다.

1. 합리적인 이유 없이 성별에 따라 교육과정을 분리하여 편성 · 운영하거나 교육내용을 달리하는 경우,
2. 각종 교육대상자 선정 기준을 특정 직무 또는 직급으로 한정하여 교육대상자에 포함되는 특정 성의 비율이 현저히 낮고, 그로 인하여 특정 성에게 불이익한 결과를 초래한 경우 또한 이에 해당됩니다. 다만, 직무 관련성, 정당성 등에 대한 사업주의 입증이 있는 경우는 제외합니다.
3. 같거나 비슷한 학력 . 자격으로 채용한 후 특정 성은 주요 업무에 배치하고 다른 성은 본인의 의사에 반하여 보조업무로 배치하는 경우,
4. 특정 성이 대다수인 직종(렬) . 직군과 다른 성이 대다수인 직종(렬) · 직군 상호간에 전직을 제한하거나 배제하는 경우이나 다만 직무 관련성, 정당성 등에 대한 사업주의 입증이 있는 경우는 제외합니다.
5. 특정 성에게 승진 기회는 부여하고 있지만, 상대적으로 불리한 조건, 절차들을 적용하여 승진을 어렵게 만드는 경우,
6. 특정 성(姓)의 직급(위)을 다른 성에 비해 더 많은 단계로 세분화하여 일정 직급에의 도달까지 다른 성보다 장기간 소요되게 함으로써 결과적으로 특정성을 불리하게 대우하는 경우.

정년 · 퇴직 · 해고에 있어 차별이 인정된 대표적인 사례는 다음과

1. When different retirement ages are set for men and women in the same or similar job categories or positions.
2. When the retirement age for men and women is set lower without reasonable justification in job categories or positions predominantly occupied by a particular gender, compared to other job categories or positions.
3. When employees are dismissed due to marriage, pregnancy, childcare, or because both spouses work at the same company.
4. When an employee is dismissed by treating one gender unfavorably compared to the other in terms of disciplinary reasons, disciplinary levels, or procedures.

(Penalty)
1. Discrimination in Retirement Age, Retirement, and Dismissal - Article 37 Paragraph 1 of the Equal Employment Opportunity Act Imprisonment for up to 5 years or a fine of up to 30 million won
2. Discrimination in welfare items other than wages- Article 37, Paragraph 4, Subparagraph 2 of the Equal Employment Opportunity Act, fine of up to KRW 4 million
3. Discrimination in education, placement, and promotion- Article 37, Paragraph 4, Subparagraph 3 of the Equal Employment Opportunity Act, fine of up to 5 million won

14-0-5 Have you entered into an employment contract that presupposes marriage, pregnancy, or childbirth of a female worker as a reason for retirement?
Equal Employment Opportunity Act Article 11 Paragraph 2
An employer shall not enter into a labor contract that presupposes a female worker's marriage, pregnancy, or childbirth as a reason for retirement.
(Penalty) Article 37 Imprisonment for up to 5 years or a fine of up to 30 million won

15. Prohibiting Discrimination against Non-regular Workers

5-0-1 Do you avoid discriminating against workers of a using employer who perform the same or similar work simply because they are dispatched workers?
Act on the Protection of Dispatched Workers (hereinafter the Dispatch Act) Article 21 Paragraph 1
According to Article 21, Paragraph 1 of the Dispatch Act, dispatching employers and using employers must not discriminate against dispatched

같습니다.
1. 동일 . 유사한 직종 . 직급에서 남녀 정년을 달리 정한 경우,
2. 특정 성이 다수를 차지하는 직종 . 직급에서 남녀 정년을 합리적인 이유 없이 다른 직종 . 직급 등보다 낮게 정하는 경우,
3. 혼인, 임신, 육아 등을 이유로 하거나 부부가 같은 직장에 근무한다는 이유로 특정 성의 근로자를 해고하는 경우,
4. 징계사유, 징계수준, 절차 등에 있어 특정 성을 다른 성에 비하여 불리하게 대우해 해고하는 경우.
(벌칙)
1. 정년 . 퇴직 . 해고에서의 차별- 남녀고용평등법 제37조 제1항 5년 이하의 징역 또는 3천만 원 이하의 벌금
2. 임금 외의 복리후생항목에서의 차별- 남녀고용평등법 제37조 제4항 제2호 400만 원 이하의 벌금
3. 교육 · 배치 · 승진에서의 차별- 남녀고용평등법 제37조 제4항 제3호 500만 원 이하의 벌금

14-0-5 여성 근로자의 혼인, 임신 또는 출산을 퇴직사유로 예정하는 근로계약을 체결한 사실이 있습니까?

남녀고용평등법 제11조 제2항
사업주는 여성 근로자의 혼인, 임신 또는 출산을 퇴직 사유로 예정하는 근로계약을 체결하여서는 아니됩니다.
(벌칙) 제37조 5년 이하의 징역 또는 3천만 원 이하의 벌금

15. 비정규직 차별 금지

15-0-1 파견근로자임을 이유로 사용사업주의 동종 또는 유사한 업무를 수행하는 근로자에 비하여 합리적 이유없이 차별적 처우를 하고 있습니까?

파견근로자 보호 등에 관한 법률(이하 파견법) 제21조 제1항
파견법 제 21조 제1항에 따르면, 파견사업주와 사용사업주는 파견근로자라는 이유로 사용사업주의 사업 내의 동종 유사한 업무를 수행하는

workers compared to workers performing the same or similar work within the business of the using employer because they are dispatched workers. In this case, dispatched worker refers to a worker hired by an employer who runs a worker dispatch project and dispatched to the workplace to work.

As for the criteria for determining what same/similar work is,

1. Whether or not it is the same/similar work should be judged based on the work actually performed by the worker, not the work stipulated in employment rules or labor contracts. In this regard,
2. Even if the duties do not completely match each other and there are some differences in the scope, responsibility and authority of the duties, etc., if there is no essential difference in the content of the main duties, it is regarded as the same or similar duties unless there are special circumstances.

In this case, discriminatory treatment means:

1. wages in accordance with the Labor Standards Act,
2. regular bonuses such as regular bonuses and holiday bonuses,
3. bonuses based on business performance,
4. other reasonable reasons in terms of working conditions and welfare benefits, etc. It means to treat unfavorably without.

At this time, even if there was unfavorable treatment, it is not immediately recognized as discriminatory treatment. If there is a reasonable reason for unfavorable treatment means the case where the need to treat non-regular workers differently than comparable workers is recognized, and the method and degree of such treatment are appropriate (if the necessity is not recognized, the method and degree If it is not appropriate, it corresponds to the case where there is no reasonable reason).

(Fine for negligence)

1. A fine of not more than 100 million won is imposed on those who fail to comply with the corrective order confirmed in Article 46, Paragraph 1 of the Dispatch Act without justifiable reasons.
2. A fine of up to 5 million won is imposed on those who fail to comply with the request for submission of the implementation status of the Minister of Employment and Labor, Article 46, Paragraph 4 of the Dispatch Act, without justifiable reasons.

15-0-2 Do you avoid discriminating against workers who are engaged in the same or similar work and have contracts with an indefinite period simply because

근로자에 비하여 파견근로자에게 차별적 처우를 하여서는 아니됩니다. 이때, 파견근로자란 근로자파견사업을 하는 사업주에게 고용된 근로자로서 사업장에 파견되어 근무하는 근로자를 의미합니다.

동종 유사한 업무가 무엇인지와 관하여 판단기준으로는

1. 동종·유사한 업무인지 여부는 취업규칙이나 근로계약에서 정한 업무가 아니라 근로자가 실제 수행한 업무를 기준으로 판단하여야 하며, 우리 대법원은 이와 관련하여
2. 업무가 서로 완전히 일치하지 않고 업무의 범위나 책임과 권한 등에서 다소 차이가 있더라도 주된 업무의 내용에 본질적인 차이가 없다면, 특별한 사정이 없는 한 동종 또는 유사한 업무라고 보고 있습니다.

이때 차별적 처우란

1. 근로기준법에 따른 임금,
2. 정기상여금, 명절상여금 등 정기적으로 지급되는 상여금,
3. 경영성과에 따른 성과금
4. 그 밖에 근로조건 및 복리후생 등에 관한 사항에서 합리적인 이유 없이 불리하게 처우하는 것'을 말합니다.

이때, 불리한 처우가 있었다고 하여 곧바로 차별적인 처우로 인정되는 것은 아닙니다. 불리한 처우에 합리적 이유가 있는 경우란, 비정규직 근로자를 비교대상 근로자에 비하여 다르게 처우할 필요성이 인정되고, 또한 그 방법, 정도도 적정한 경우를 의미합니다(필요성이 인정되지 않거나, 그 방법, 정도가 적정하지 아니하다면 합리적인 이유가 없는 경우에 해당합니다).

(과태료)

1. 파견법 제46조 제1항 확정된 시정명령을 정당한 이유 없이 이행하지 아니한 자에게는 1억원 이하의 과태료
2. 파견법 제46조 제4항 고용노동부장관의 이행상황 제출요구를 정당한 이유 없이 따르지 아니한 자에게는 500만 원 이하의 과태료

15-0-2 기간제근로자임을 이유로 동종 또는 유사한 업무에 종사하는 기간의 정함이 없는 근로계약을 체결한 근로자에 비하여 차별적 처우를 하고

they are fixed-term workers?

Article 8 Paragraph 1 of the Act on the Protection of Fixed-Term and Part-Time Workers (hereinafter referred to as the Fixed-Term Act)

According to Article 8, Paragraph 1 of the Fixed-Term Employment Act, an employer shall not discriminate against workers who are engaged in the same or similar work in the business or place of business who have entered into a labor contract with an indefinite period on the grounds that they are fixed-term workers. In this case, fixed-term workers means workers who are engaged in the same or similar work for an unspecified period.

As for the criteria for determining what same/similar work is,

1. Whether or not it is the same/similar work should be judged based on the work actually performed by the worker, not the work stipulated in employment rules or labor contracts. In this regard,
2. Even if the duties do not completely match each other and there are some differences in the scope, responsibility and authority of the duties, etc., if there is no essential difference in the content of the main duties, it is regarded as the same or similar duties unless there are special circumstances.

In this case, discriminatory treatment means:

1. wages in accordance with the Labor Standards Act,
2. regular bonuses such as regular bonuses and holiday bonuses,
3. bonuses based on business performance,
4. other reasonable reasons in terms of working conditions and welfare benefits, etc. It means to treat unfavorably without.

At this time, even if there was unfavorable treatment, it is not immediately recognized as discriminatory treatment. If there is a reasonable reason for unfavorable treatment means the case where the need to treat non-regular workers differently than comparable workers is recognized, and the method and degree of such treatment are appropriate (if the necessity is not recognized, the method and degree If it is not appropriate, it corresponds to the case where there is no reasonable reason).

(Fine for negligence)

1. A fine of not more than KRW 100 million is imposed on those who fail to comply with the corrective order confirmed in Article 24, Paragraph 1 of the Fixed-term Manufacturing Act without justifiable reasons.

있습니까?

기간제 및 단시간근로자 보호 등에 관한 법률(이하 기간제법) 제8조 제1항

기간제법 제8조 제1항에 따르면 사용자는 기간제 근로자임을 이유로 당해 사업 또는 사업장에서 동종 또는 유사한 업무에 종사하는 기간의 정함이 없는 근로계약을 체결한 근로자에 비하여 차별적 처우를 하여서는 아니됩니다. 이때 기간제 근로자란, 동종 또는 유사한 업무에 종사하는 기간을 정하지 아니한 근로자를 의미합니다.

동종·유사한 업무가 무엇인지와 관하여 판단기준으로는

1. 동종·유사한 업무인지 여부는 취업규칙이나 근로계약에서 정한 업무가 아니라 근로자가 실제 수행한 업무를 기준으로 판단하여야 하며, 우리 대법원은 이와 관련하여
2. 업무가 서로 완전히 일치하지 않고 업무의 범위나 책임과 권한 등에서 다소 차이가 있더라도 주된 업무의 내용에 본질적인 차이가 없다면, 특별한 사정이 없는 한 동종 또는 유사한 업무라고 보고 있습니다.

이때 차별적 처우란

1. 근로기준법에 따른 임금,
2. 정기상여금, 명절상여금 등 정기적으로 지급되는 상여금,
3. 경영성과에 따른 성과금
4. 그 밖에 근로조건 및 복리후생 등에 관한 사항에서 합리적인 이유 없이 불리하게 처우하는 것'을 말합니다.

이때, 불리한 처우가 있었다고 하여 곧바로 차별적인 처우로 인정되는 것은 아닙니다. 불리한 처우에 합리적 이유가 있는 경우란, 비정규직 근로자를 비교대상 근로자에 비하여 다르게 처우할 필요성이 인정되고, 또한 그 방법, 정도도 적정한 경우를 의미합니다(필요성이 인정되지 않거나, 그 방법, 정도가 적정하지 아니하다면 합리적인 이유가 없는 경우에 해당합니다).

(과태료)

1. 기간제법 제24조 제1항 확정된 시정명령을 정당한 이유 없이 이행하지 아니한 자에게는 1억원 이하의 과태료

2. A fine of not more than 5 million won is imposed on those who fail to comply with the request of the Minister of Employment and Labor to submit the implementation status of Article 24, Paragraph 2 of the Fixed-term Act without justifiable reasons.

15-0-3 Are part-time workers treated the same as regular workers engaged in the same or similar work?

Term Production Act Article 8 Paragraph 2

According to Article 8, Paragraph 2 of the Fixed-Term Act, an employer shall not discriminate against workers who have entered into an employment contract with an indefinite period of time to engage in the same or similar work in the business or workplace, on the grounds that they are part-time workers. In this case, part-time worker means a worker whose contracted working hours are shorter than other regular workers engaged in the same type of work at the workplace.

As for the criteria for determining what same/similar work is,

1. Whether or not it is the same/similar work should be judged based on the work actually performed by the worker, not the work stipulated in employment rules or labor contracts. In this regard,
2. Even if the duties do not completely match each other and there are some differences in the scope, responsibility and authority of the duties, etc., if there is no essential difference in the content of the main duties, it is regarded as the same or similar duties unless there are special circumstances.

In this case, discriminatory treatment means:

1. wages in accordance with the Labor Standards Act,
2. regular bonuses such as regular bonuses and holiday bonuses,
3. bonuses based on business performance,
4. other reasonable reasons in terms of working conditions and welfare benefits, etc. It means to treat unfavorably without.

At this time, even if there was unfavorable treatment, it is not immediately recognized as discriminatory treatment. If there is a reasonable reason for unfavorable treatment means the case where the need to treat non-regular workers differently than comparable workers is recognized, and the method and degree of such treatment are appropriate (if the necessity is not recognized, the method and degree If it is not appropriate, it corresponds to the case where there is no reasonable reason).

2. 기간제법 제24조 제2항 고용노동부장관의 이행상황 제출요구를 정당한 이유 없이 따르지 아니한 자에게는 500만 원 이하의 과태료

15-0-3 단시간근로자임을 이유로 동종 또는 유사한 업무에 종사하는 통상근로자에 비하여 차별적 처우를 하고 있습니까?

기간제법 제8조 제2항

기간제법 제 8조 제2항에 따르면 사용자는 단시간 근로자임을 이유로 당해 사업 또는 사업장에서 동종 또는 유사한 업무에 종사하는 기간의 정함이 없는 근로계약을 체결한 근로자에 비하여 차별적 처우를 하여서는 아니됩니다. 이때 단시간 근로자란, 사업장에서 같은 종류의 업무에 종사하는 다른 통상 근로자에 비하여 소정근로시간이 짧은 근로자를 의미합니다.

동종 유사한 업무가 무엇인지와 관하여 판단기준으로는

1. 동종·유사한 업무인지 여부는 취업규칙이나 근로계약에서 정한 업무가 아니라 근로자가 실제 수행한 업무를 기준으로 판단하여야 하며, 우리 대법원은 이와 관련하여
2. 업무가 서로 완전히 일치하지 않고 업무의 범위나 책임과 권한 등에서 다소 차이가 있더라도 주된 업무의 내용에 본질적인 차이가 없다면, 특별한 사정이 없는 한 동종 또는 유사한 업무라고 보고 있습니다.

이때 차별적 처우란

1. 근로기준법에 따른 임금,
2. 정기상여금, 명절상여금 등 정기적으로 지급되는 상여금,
3. 경영성과에 따른 성과금
4. 그 밖에 근로조건 및 복리후생 등에 관한 사항에서 합리적인 이유 없이 불리하게 처우하는 것'을 말합니다.

이때, 불리한 처우가 있었다고 하여 곧바로 차별적인 처우로 인정되는 것은 아닙니다. 불리한 처우에 합리적 이유가 있는 경우란, 비정규직 근로자를 비교대상 근로자에 비하여 다르게 처우할 필요성이 인정되고, 또한 그 방법, 정도도 적정한 경우를 의미합니다(필요성이 인정되지 않거나, 그 방법, 정도가 적정하지 아니하다면 합리적인 이유가 없는 경우에 해당

(Fine for negligence)
1. A fine of not more than KRW 100 million is imposed on those who fail to comply with the corrective order confirmed in Article 24, Paragraph 1 of the Fixed-term Manufacturing Act without justifiable reasons.
2. A fine of not more than 5 million won is imposed on those who fail to comply with the request of the Minister of Employment and Labor to submit the performance status of Article 24, Paragraph 2 of the Fixed-term Act without justifiable reasons.

16. Establishing a Labor-Management Council

16-1 Establishing a Labor-Management Council

16-1-1 If you have 30 or more full-time workers, have you established a labor-management council?

Act on the Promotion of Worker Participation and Cooperation (hereinafter Worker Participation Act) Article 4 Paragraph 1
According to Article 4, Paragraph 1 of the Employee Participation Act, in the case of businesses or workplaces that regularly employ 30 or more workers, a labor-management council must be established at each business or workplace that has the right to decide on working conditions. Therefore, if there are 30 or more full-time workers, a labor-management council must be established in the workplace.
At this time, the persons excluded from the number of full-time workers include:
1. Those who do not have the status of workers, such as CEOs or executives,
2. Those who are providing work at the workplace, such as dispatch or contract work, but do not have a direct labor relationship. We have manpower.
(Penalty) In the case of refusing or obstructing the establishment of the labor-management council under Article 30, Subparagraph 1 of the Employee Participation Act without justifiable grounds, a fine of up to 10 million won

16-1-2 If yes, has the labor-management council been established in accordance with the procedures stipulated by law?

Articles 6 through 19 of the Employee Participation Act
According to the Employee Participation Act, the establishment of the labor-management council is largely divided into five stages and is as follows.
1. Announcement on the establishment of the Labor-Management Council: This is because it is desirable for the employer to actively share opinions with workers and prepare for the establishment of the Labor-Management Council jointly, as it cannot be properly implemented without consensus

합니다).

(과태료)

1. 기간제법 제24조 제1항 확정된 시정명령을 정당한 이유 없이 이행하지 아니한 자에게는 1억원 이하의 과태료
2. 기간제법 제24조 제2항 고용노동부장관의 이행상황 제출요구를 정당한 이유 없이 따르지 아니한 자에게는 500만 원 이하의 과태료

16. 노사협의회 설치

16-1 노사협의회 설치

16-1-1 상시근로자가 30명 이상이고 노사협의회를 설치하였습니까?

근로자참여 및 협력증진에 관한 법률(이하 근로자참여법) 제4조 제1항
근로자참여법 제4조 제1항에 따르면, 상시 30명 이상의 근로자를 사용하는 사업이나 사업장의 경우 근로조건에 대한 결정권이 있는 사업이나 사업장 단위로 노사협의회를 설치하여야 합니다. 따라서, 상시 근로자가 30명 이상이라면 사업장에 노사협의회를 설치하여야 합니다.

이때, 상시근로자수에서 제외되는 인원으로는 대표적으로

1. 대표이사나 임원 등 완전히 근로자의 지위를 갖지 않는 대상,
2. 파견, 도급 등 당해 사업장에서 근로를 제공하고 있으나 직접적인 근로관계가 없는 인력이 있습니다.

(벌칙) 근로자참여법 제30조 제1호 노사협의회 설치를 정당한 사유 없이 거부하거나 방해하는 경우 1천만 원 이하의 벌금

16-1-2 노사협의회를 법에서 정한 절차에 따라 설치하였습니까?

근로자참여법 제6조 내지 제19조
근로자참여법에 따르면 노사협의회 설치는 크게 5단계로 이루어지며 다음과 같습니다.

1. 노사협의회 설치 관련 공고: 이는 노사협의회 설치의 필요성에 대하여 노사간 공감 없이는 제대로 이루어질 수 없기 때문에 사용자가 적극적으로 근로자들과 의견을 나누고 노사공동으로 노사협의회 설치를 준비

between labor and management on the need for the establishment of the Labor-Management Council.

The contents of the announcement include (1) the contents of the law related to the labor-management council, (2) the necessity of the labor-management council, (3) the status and vision of the labor-management council in the company, and (4) the role of the labor-management council members. .

2. Formation of the Preparatory Committee for Establishment of the Labor-Management Council: Before forming the members of the Labor-Management Council and preparing regulations, etc., it is desirable to form a 'Preparatory Committee for Establishment' to clarify the roles, etc.

Through the 'Installation Preparatory Committee', tasks such as (1) setting the vision of the labor-management council and collecting employees' opinions, (2) preparing for the formation of council members, and (3) preparing council regulations can be carried out. Through this, the direction of operation of the labor-management council, the number of members of the labor-management council, the selection method, and operation policies can be determined so that the labor-management council can effectively participate and share information. Based on these discussions, the labor-management council regulations (draft) can be drawn up.

3. Appointment or election of members of the labor-management council: The labor-management council must consist of an equal number of 3 or more and 10 or less workers and employers.

The election of the employer member can be the representative of the business or business site and the person commissioned by the representative. In principle, a specific individual is appointed, but it is also possible to appoint a position (e.g., head of personnel and labor department, head of production department, etc.).

The procedure for electing workers' representatives differs depending on whether there is a labor union organized with a majority of each worker, and the procedure is as follows.

(1) When there is no trade union organized by the majority of workers
  1) Candidacy: You can run for office after receiving recommendations from 10 or more workers.
  2) Election: Elected through direct, secret, and anonymous voting by workers.
  3) Confirmation of Elected Persons: Elected workers' representatives are determined in the order of the majority of votes.

(2) Where there is a trade union organized by a majority of workers

The process of candidacy, election, and confirmation of the winner is carried out by the representative of the labor union and a person commissioned by the labor union.

4. Enactment of labor-management council regulations: When the council

하는 것이 바람직하기 때문입니다.

공고 내용 으로는, (1) 노사협의회와 관련한 법령상의 내용, (2) 노사협의회의 필요성, (3) 당해 회사에서 노사협의회의 지위와 비전, (4) 노사협의회 위원들의 역할 등이 있습니다.

2. 노사협의회 설치 준비위원회 구성: 노사협의회의 위원을 구성하고 규정 등을 작성하기 전에, 역할 등을 명확히 하기 위하여 '설치 준비위원회'를 구성하는 것이 바람직합니다.

'설치 준비위원회'를 통하여 (1) 노사협의회의 비전 설정 및 종업원의 의견수렴, (2) 협의회위원 구성준비작업, (3) 협의회 규정 마련 등의 작업이 진행될 수 있습니다. 이를 통하여 노사협의회가 실효성 있는 참여 및 정보공유의 장이 될 수 있도록 그 운영방향, 노사협의회 위원수, 선출방법, 운영방침 등을 정할 수 있습니다. 이와 같이 논의한 내용을 바탕으로 노사협의회 규정(안)을 작성할 수 있습니다.

3. 노사협의회 위원의 위촉 또는 선출: 노사협의회는 근로자위원과 사용자위원 각 3명 이상 10명 이하 동수로 구성되어야 합니다.

사용자위원의 선출은 사업 또는 사업장의 대표자와 대표자가 위촉하는 자로 선출될 수 있으며, 특정 개인을 위촉하는 것이 원칙이지만 직명위촉(예: 인사노무부장, 생산부장 등)을 하는 것도 가능합니다.

근로자위원의 선출은 각 근로자 과반수로 조직된 노동조합이 있는지 여부에 따라 그 절차가 상이하며, 아래와 같습니다.

(1) 근로자 과반수로 조직된 노동조합이 없는 경우
 1) 입후보: 근로자 10인 이상의 추천을 받아 입후보하게 됩니다.
 2) 선거: 근로자의 직접, 비밀, 무기명 투표를 통하여 선출됩니다.
 3) 당선자 확정: 다수 득표자 순으로 근로자위원 당선자를 확정합니다.

(2) 근로자 과반수로 조직된 노동조합이 있는 경우
 노동조합의 대표자와 노동조합이 위촉하는 자로 입후보, 선거 및 당선자 확정의 절차가 진행되게 됩니다.

4. 노사협의회 규정 제정: 협의회 위원이 구성되면 노사협의회를 개최하여, 향후 노사협의회 운영에 대한 기본방향을 설정하는 협의를 진행하고, 설치준비위원회에서 마련한 노사협의회 규정(안)을 수정한 후

members are formed, a labor-management council meeting is held to discuss the basic direction for future labor-management council operation, and the labor-management council regulations (draft) prepared by the establishment preparation committee are revised and enacted. do.

5. Report to the Ministry of Employment and Labor: Within 15 days after the establishment of the labor-management council (enactment of the council regulations), the labor-management council regulations must be reported to the head of the competent local employment and labor office.
(Fine for negligence) Article 33 In case of failure to submit the provisions of the Employee Participation Act, a fine of up to 2 million won is imposed.

16-1-3 Have workers democratically elected worker representatives?

Employee Participation Act Article 6 Paragraphs 2 and 3

Since workers' members must be elected in a democratic manner, Article 6, paragraphs 2 and 3 of the Workers' Participation Act stipulate that workers' members must be elected by direct, secret and anonymous ballot with the participation of a majority of workers. However, according to the proviso of Article 6, Paragraph 2 of the Workers' Participation Act, it is stipulated that if it is unavoidable due to the specificity of a business or workplace, it is possible to elect worker members through indirect elections. However, in this case, the workers (member electors) who will elect the worker members in proportion to the number of workers in each work department are directly, secretly and anonymously voted, and the majority of the elected member-electors direct, secretly and anonymously vote to select the worker members. should be elected.

Workers' representatives must be elected in a democratic manner and through an autonomous selection process. Therefore, if 1. an employer unilaterally appoints a worker member or 2. intervenes in the election of a worker member, the Ministry of Employment and Labor may request correction in accordance with Article 11 of the Worker Participation Act.

(Penalty) Article 31 If an employer fails to comply with a corrective order without justifiable reasons, a fine of up to 5 million won

16-1-4 Do the labor-management council regulations include all the contents stipulated by the law?

According to Article 18, Paragraph 1 of the Employee Participation Act, once the labor-management council enacts or changes regulations on its organization and operation (hereinafter Council Regulations), it is notified to the Minister of Employment and Labor within 15 days from the date of establishment of the

제정합니다.

5. 고용노동부 신고: 노사협의회 설치(협의회규정 제정) 후 15일 이내에 노사협의회 규정을 관할 지방고용노동관서의 장에게 신고하여야 합니다.

(과태료) 제33조 협의회규정 제출하지 아니한 때에는 200만 원 이하의 과태료

16-1-3 근로자들이 근로자위원을 민주적 방식으로 선출하도록 했습니까?

근로자참여법 제6조 제2항 내지 제3항

근로자위원은 민주적인 방식으로 선출되어야 하기 때문에, 근로자참여법 제6조 제2항 내지 제3항에 따르면, 근로자위원은 근로자 과반수가 참여하여 직접, 비밀, 무기명 투표로 선출하여야 한다고 규정되어 있습니다. 다만, 근로자참여법 제6조 제2항 단서에 따르면 사업 또는 사업장의 특수성으로 인하여 부득이한 경우에는 간접선거에 의한 근로자위원 선출도 가능하다고 규정하고 있습니다. 그러나 이러한 경우에는 작업부서별로 근로자 수에 비례하여 근로자위원을 선출할 근로자(위원선거인)을 직접, 비밀, 무기명투표에 의하여 선출하고, 선출된 위원선거인 과반수의 직접, 비밀, 무기명투표에 의하여 근로자위원을 선출해야 합니다.

근로자위원은 민주적인 방식으로, 자율적인 선출절차를 통하여 선출되어야 합니다. 따라서, 1. 사용자가 일방적으로 근로자위원을 위촉하거나, 2. 근로자위원 선출에 개입하는 경우 이에 대하여 근로자참여법 제11조에 따라 고용노동부가 시정을 요구할 수 있습니다.

(벌칙) 제31조 사용자가 정당한 사유없이 시정명령을 이행하지 아니하는 경우 500만 원 이하의 벌금

16-1-4 노사협의회 규정에 법에서 정한 내용을 모두 포함하였습니까?

근로자참여법 제18조

근로자참여법 제18조 제1항에 따르면, 노사협의회는 그 조직과 운영에 관한 규정(이하 협의회규정)을 제정또는 변경하고 나면 노사협의회를 설치한 날부터 15일 이내에 고용노동부장관에게 이를 제출하여야 하며,

labor-management council. According to Article 18, Paragraph 2 of the Workers' Participation Act, regulations are stipulated by the Enforcement Decree.

Article 5 of the Enforcement Decree of the Employee Participation Act stipulates the required items that must be included in the council regulations as follows.

1. Number of members of the labor-management council,
2. Matters concerning the procedure for electing workers' members and registration of candidates,
3. Matters concerning the qualifications of employer members,
4. Matters concerning the hours deemed to be worked by members of the labor-management council,
5. Matters concerning the labor-management council
6. Matters concerning the method and procedure for voluntary arbitration under Article 25 of the Employee Participation Act,
7. Matters concerning the number of grievance handling members and grievance handling

(Fine for negligence) In case of failure to submit the provisions of Article 33, Paragraph 1 of the Employee Participation Act, a fine of up to 2 million won is imposed.

16-1-5 Have you enacted labor-management council regulations and reported them to the Ministry of Employment and Labor?

Employee Participation Act Article 18 Paragraph 1

According to Article 18, Paragraph 1 of the Employee Participation Act, the labor-management council must report the regulations of the labor-management council to the head of the competent local employment and labor office within 15 days of enactment of the council regulations (establishment of the council). If this is violated, fines will be imposed.

(Fine for negligence) Article 33 In case of failure to submit the provisions of the Employee Participation Act, a fine for negligence of up to 2 million won is imposed.

16-2 Labor-management council meetings

16-2-1 Are labor-management council meetings held at least every 3 months?

Employee Participation Act Article 12 Paragraph 1

According to Article 12, Paragraph 1 of the Employee Participation Act, the labor-management council must be held regularly every three months. This means that it is mandatory to hold at least once every quarter. In addition to holding regular meetings, Article 12, Paragraph 2 of the Employee

근로자참여법 제18조 제2항에 따르면 규정사항은 시행령으로 정한다고 규정합니다.

근로자참여법 시행령 제5조에서는 협의회규정에 들어가야 하는 필수기재사항을 다음과 같이 정하고 있습니다.

1. 노사협의회 위원수,
2. 근로자위원의 선출절차와 후보등록에 관한 사항,
3. 사용자위원의 자격에 관한 사항,
4. 노사협의회 위원이 근로한 것으로 보는 시간에 관한 사항,
5. 노사협의회의 회의소집, 회기, 그 밖의 노사협의회 운영에 관한 사항,
6. 근로자참여법 제25조의 규정에 의한 임의중재의 방법, 절차 등에 관한 사항,
7. 고충처리위원수 및 고충처리에 관한 사항

(과태료) 근로자참여법 제33조 제1항 협의회규정 제출하지 아니한 때에는 200만 원 이하의 과태료 부과

16-1-5 노사협의회 규정을 제정하여 고용노동부에 신고하였습니까?

근로자참여법 제18조 제1항

근로자참여법 제18조 제1항에 따르면, 노사협의회는 협의회규정 제정(협의회 설치) 후 15일 이내에 노사협의회 규정을 관할 지방고용노동관서의 장에게 신고하여야 합니다. 만약 이를 위반하는 경우, 과태료가 부과됩니다.

(과태료) 근로자참여법 제33조 제1항 협의회규정 제출하지 아니한 때에는 200만 원 이하의 과태료

16-2 노사협의회 회의

16-2-1 노사협의회 회의를 3개월마다 개최하였습니까?

근로자참여법 제12조 제1항

근로자참여법 제12조 제1항에 따르면 노사협의회는 3개월마다 정기적으로 개최되어야 합니다. 이는 적어도 분기마다 한번은 의무적으로 개최해야 함을 의미합니다. 또한 정기협의회 개최와 별도로, 근로자참여법 제12조 제2항에 따르면 필요시 임시회의를 개최할 수 있다고

Participation Act stipulates that temporary meetings can be held when necessary. In the case of an extraordinary meeting, it can be held at the request of a member representing both labor and management.
(Penalty) Article 32　a fine of up to 3 million won

16-2-2 Have you implemented the matters decided during labor-management council meetings?

Article 24 of the Employee Participation Act

According to Article 24 of the Employee Participation Act, workers and employers must faithfully implement the matters decided by the council.

Labor-management council decisions refer to matters related to workers' education and training and competency development plans, worker welfare facilities and funds, and labor-management joint organizations, which the employer and worker members have the duty to resolve at the council, and report matters It is a concept distinct from agreements and agreements. It is stipulated in detail in Article 21 of the Employee Participation Act and is as follows.

1. Establishment of basic plans for education and training and competency development of workers
2. Installation and management of welfare facilities
3. Establishment of the in-house labor welfare fund
4. Matters not resolved by the Grievance Handling Committee
5. Establishment of various joint labor-management committees
   (Penalty) Article 30 Fine of up to 10 million won

16-2-3 If you have 30 or more full-time workers, have you appointed a grievance handling member to the committee?

Article 26 of the Employee Participation Act

According to Article 26 of the Workers Participation Act, every business or workplace must have a grievance handling committee to listen to and handle grievances of workers. However, there is no exceptional obligation for businesses or workplaces that employ less than 30 full-time workers.

Difficulty refers to dissatisfaction and unstable conditions experienced by workers in their work life caused by individual complaints about the working environment or working conditions of workers, other workers' personalities, psychological conditions, and personal problems.

The Grievance Handling Committee consists of no more than 3 members, and the term of office is 3 years. If the workplace has a labor-management council, the labor-management council appoints a grievance handling

규정하고 있습니다. 임시회의의 경우, 노사 일방의 대표위원이 소집을 요구하여 개최할 수 있습니다.
(벌칙) 제32조 300만 원 이하의 벌금

16-2-2 노사협의회에서 의결된 사항을 이행하였습니까?

근로자참여법 제24조

근로자참여법 제24조에 의하면 근로자와 사용자는 협의회에서 의결된 사항을 성실하게 이행하여야 합니다.

노사협의회 의결 사항은 근로자들의 교육훈련 및 능력개발계획, 근로자 복지시설 기금, 노사 공동기구와 관련된 사항으로 사용자위원과 근로자 위원이 협의회에서 의결할 의무를 가지고 있는 사항들을 의미하며, 보고사항 및 협의사항과는 구별되는 개념입니다. 근로자참여법 제21조에 자세히 규정되어 있으며 다음과 같습니다.

1. 근로자의 교육훈련 및 능력개발 기본계획의 수립
2. 복지시설의 설치와 관리
3. 사내근로복지기금의 설치
4. 고충처리위원회에서 의결되지 아니한 사항
5. 각종 노사공동위원회의 설치

(벌칙) 제30조 1천만 원 이하의 벌금

16-2-3 상시근로자가 30명 이상이고 고충처리위원을 선임하였습니까?

근로자참여법 제26조

근로자참여법 제26조에 따르면, 모든 사업 또는 사업장에는 근로자의 고충을 청취하고 이를 처리하기 위하여 고충처리위원을 두어야 합니다. 다만, 상시 30명 미만의 근로자를 사용하는 사업이나 사업장의 경우 예외적으로 의무가 없습니다.

고충이란, 근로자의 근로환경이나 근로조건에 관한 개별적인 불만, 기타 근로자의 성격, 심리적 상태, 개인적 문제 등이 원인이 되어 직장생활에서 근로자가 겪게 되는 불만족 및 불안정 상태를 말합니다.

고충처리위원은 3명 이내의 위원으로 구성되며 임기는 3년입니다. 사업장에

committee member from among its members. At this time, there are things to consider, and they are as follows.

1. A grievance handling committee member must be formed to effectively deal with workers' grievances. For example, in the case of workplaces with many female workers, it is also desirable to appoint one member of the grievance handling committee to handle grievances specific to women.
2. Workers who have grievances can report their grievances verbally or in writing to the grievance handling committee member, and the grievance handling committee member must prepare a ledger for grievance reception and handling, which must be kept for one year.

(Penalty) Article 32 of the Employee Participation Act, a fine of up to 2 million won

노사협의회가 설치된 경우라면, 노사협의회가 그 위원 중에서 고충처리위원을 선임합니다. 이때, 고려해야할 사항이 있으며 다음과 같습니다.

1. 근로자의 고충을 효과적으로 처리할 수 있도록 고충처리위원을 구성해야 합니다. 예를 들어, 여성 근로자가 많은 사업장의 경우, 여성에 특유한 고충 발생을 처리하기 위하여 고충처리위원 중 1명을 여성으로 위촉하는 것도 바람직합니다.
2. 고충이 있는 근로자는 고충처리위원에게 구두 또는 서면으로 고충을 신고할 수 있고, 고충처리위원은 고충 접수 처리에 관한 대장을 작성해야 하며, 이는 1년간 보관되어야 합니다.

(벌칙) 근로자참여법 제32조 200만 원 이하의 벌금

Chapter 3 Explanations of Labor Inspections

Section 1. **Written Statement of Working Conditions**
Section 2. **Preservation of Employee Registers and Contract Documents**
Section 3. **Payment of Various Money and Goods such as Wages**
Section 4. **Violation of limits on working hours and overtime**
Section 5. **Granting recess hours**
Section 6. **Paid holidays**
Section 7. **Annual paid leave**
Section 8. **Children and Maternity Protection**
Section 9. **Rules of Employment**
Section 10. **Payment of retirement benefits**
Section 11. **Prevention of workplace harassment**
Section 12. **Observation of minimum wage**
Section 13. **Prevention of sexual harassment in the workplace**
Section 14. **Prohibition of Sex Discrimination in Employment**
Section 15. **Prohibition of discrimination against non-regular workers**
Section 16. **Establishment of labor-management council**

제3장 근로감독 체크리스트 설명자료

제1절 근로계약 작성
제2절 근로자 명부 및 계약서류 보존
제3절 임금
제4절 근로시간 계산의 원칙
제5절 휴게시간과 근로시간 설계
제6절 약정휴일 및 약정휴가
제7절 연차유급휴가
제8절 모성보호와 연소자
제9절 취업규칙
제10절 퇴직급여 지급
제11절 직장 내 괴롭힘 예방
제12절 최저임금법
제13절 직장 내 성희롱 예방
제14절 균등처우의 판단기준과 관련사례
제15절 비정규직 근로자에 대한 차별시정제도
제16절 노사협의회 설치와 운영

Section 1. Items to be Considered When Writing an Employment Contract

Ⅰ. Introduction

When an employer hires someone, the first thing that must be done is to create an employment contract, which outlines the responsibilities of both parties to the contract─the worker provides work to the employer and the employer pays wages in return (Article 2 of the Labor Standards Act, or LSA).[14] Preparing a written employment contract is to clarify working conditions between workers and employers, and to prevent disputes. The employer is obligated to prepare one, and failure to do so can result in a fine of not more than 5 million won for each worker who does not have a written contract. In labor disputes, the burden of proof is on the employer. I will outline the essential items in an employment contract, with these items examined through standard employment contracts for each employment type.

Ⅱ. Required Information to be Stipulated in a Written Employment Contract

1. Items required to protect workers

Article 17 of the Labor Standards Act requires employers to specify certain items in employment contracts and hand them out to new hires to sign. It should be issued again when changes are made. Such items include (1) wages, (2) contractual working hours, (3) holidays under Article 55, (4) annual paid leave under Article 60, and (4) matters concerning the place of employment and the work expected. When entering into an employment contract with a worker under the age of 18, a parental consent form must be attached (Article 66 of the LSA).

When entering into an employment contract with a fixed-term or part-time worker, the following essential items must be specified in writing: (1) Matters concerning the period of the work contract, (2) Matters on working hours and

---

[14] Ha, Kaprae,「The Labor Standards Act」33rd Ed., Jongang Economy, 2020, p. 127.

제1절 근로계약 작성

Ⅰ. 문제의 소재

사용자가 근로자를 채용할 경우 제일 먼저 해야 할 일은 근로계약서의 작성이다. 근로계약은 근로자가 사용자에게 근로를 제공하고 사용자는 그 대가로 임금을 지급하는 쌍방의 의무를 가진 계약이다(근기법 제2조).[14] 근로계약을 서면으로 작성하는 것은 근로조건을 근로자와 사용자가 명확히 하자는 것이고, 차후 분쟁이 발생할 것을 예방하기 위함이다. 그러한 취지에서 근로계약의 서면 작성은 사용자의 의무사항이고, 이를 위반할 경우 사용자에게 미작성 근로계약 건당 500만 원 이하의 벌금(과태료)를 부과한다. 노동분쟁에 있어 입증책임은 사용자가 지기 때문에 사용자 스스로를 보호하기 위해서도 근로계약의 서면 작성은 반드시 필요하다. 이에, 다음에서 근로계약서의 필수 기재사항을 설명하고, 각 고용형태별 실제 표준 근로계약서와 각각의 유의사항에 대해서도 살펴보고자 한다.

Ⅱ. 근로계약 작성시 필수기재사항

1. 근로자 보호를 위해 필요한 기재사항

근로기준법 제17조를 살펴보면 사용자가 근로계약서를 서면으로 작성하면서 필수 기재사항을 명시하고 동일 서류를 근로자에게도 교부해야 한다고 명시하고 있다. 이를 변경할 때에도 동일하게 교부해야 한다. 작성해야 할 조건은 (1) 임금, (2) 소정근로시간, (3) 제55조에 따른 휴일, (4) 제60조에 따른 연차유급휴가, (4) 취업의 장소와 종사하여야 할 업무에 관한 사항 등이다. 18세 미만인 근로자와 근로계약을 체결하는 경우에는 친권자의 동의서를 반드시 첨부해야 한다(근기법 제66조).

기간제근로자나 단시간근로자와 근로계약을 체결하는 때에는 다음과 같은 필수 기재사항을 서면으로 명시하고 교부해야 한다. (1) 근로계약기간에 관한

---
[14] 하갑례, 「근로기준법」 제33판, 중앙경제, 2020, 127면.

breaks, (3) Matters on the composition of wages and methods of calculation and payment, (4) Matters on holidays and leave, and (5) the place of employment and the work expected. In particular, (6) working days and working hours per working day are only required for part-time workers (Article 17 of the Fixed-Term and Part-time Employment Act).

2. Items to protect employers

Employment contracts should be drawn up based on mutual agreement between labor and management and on equal terms, but in reality, since the employer selects and hires the most desirable worker from a number of applicants, the employment contract is concluded with the working conditions dictated by the employer. Since the employer decides the details of the contract from a superior position, the Labor Standards Act places restrictions on contract details.

Despite these restrictions, employers can take steps to protect themselves and take actions, such as dismissal, with unqualified or poor workers. First, workers unsuitable for the job can be dismissed within the probation period, which is usually set at 3 months, but can be extended if necessary. Workers on probation may be dismissed without prior notice, unless the probationary period exceeds three months, then a notice of dismissal must be made 30 days before dismissal.

Second, if it is difficult to evaluate whether a worker is eligible for work through the probation period, a one-year fixed-term working condition can be set together with the probation period. Third, it is necessary to obtain a pledge to comply with the service regulations (security), and prepare grounds for disciplinary action for workers who violate them. Fourth is related to employees' personal information, which, in general, employers can use in personnel management, but only upon gaining the employee's consent for areas not already permitted by law. Essentially, a letter of consent signed by the employee is necessary before using that employee's personal information.

3. Employment Contract Forms and Related Explanations

With the five standard employment contracts proposed by the Ministry of

사항, (2) 근로시간·휴게에 관한 사항, (3) 임금의 구성항목·계산방법과 지불방법에 관한 사항, (4) 휴일·휴가에 관한 사항과 (5) 취업의 장소와 종사하여야 할 업무에 관한 사항이다. 특히, (6) 근로일과 근로일별 근로시간은 단시간근로자에만 해당된다(기간제법 제17조).

2. 사용자 보호를 위해 필요한 기재사항

근로계약은 노사가 대등하고 동등한 입장에서 작성되어져야 하지만, 실제는 사용자가 다수의 지원자 중에 가장 바람직한 근로자를 선발하여 고용하기 때문에 사용자가 제시한 근로조건 위주로 근로계약이 체결된다. 사용자가 사회적 강자의 입장에서 계약 내용을 결정하기 때문에 근로기준법은 근로계약 작성시 일정 제한을 두고 있다.

이러한 제한 조치에도 불구하고, 사용자는 스스로 보호할 수 있는 조항을 두어 부적격한 근로자나 불성실한 근로자에 대해 해고 등의 필요한 조치를 할 수 있다. 그 조항은 다음과 같다. 첫째, 수습기간을 정하여 업무에 적합하지 않은 근로자를 수습기간 내에 해고할 수 있다. 수습기간은 보통 3개월로 정해지지만, 필요시 연장할 수 있다. 이 경우 최초 3개월 내의 수습근로자에게는 사전예고 없이 해고할 수 있으나, 3개월 초과하여 수습기간을 둔 경우에는 해고 30일 전에 해고예고를 하여야 한다.

둘째, 수습기간을 통해 근로자의 업무 적격여부를 평가하기 어려운 경우에는 수습기간과 함께 1년의 기간제 근로조건을 설정할 수 있다. 셋째, 복무규정 (보안) 준수 서약서를 받아서, 근로자가 복무규정 위반시 징계할 수 있도록 근거를 마련해야 한다. 넷째, 개인 정보 사용동의서이다. 일반적으로 사용자는 고용된 근로자의 개인정보를 인사관리 목적상 사용할 수 있지만, 인사업무상 법령과 관련 없는 업무에는 사용할 수 없기 때문에 미리 개인정보 사용동의서를 받아 두어야 한다.

3. 근로계약서 서식 및 관련 설명

고용노동부에서 제시한 다섯 가지의 표준 근로계약서를 가지고 각 타입별로

Chapter3-1. Items to be Considered When Writing an Employment Contract

Employment and Labor, I would like to review each characteristic in detail.

(1) Indefinite term employment contract

---

1. Work commencement date: _____ Month / Day / Year
2. Working place:
3. Details of work:
4. Contractual working hours: from_____ to ____ (break time: from_____ to____)
5. Working days/holidays: _____ working days every week / weekly holidays: every____day
6. Wage
   - Monthly (day, hour) wage: KRW_____
   - Other benefits (subsidies, etc.): Yes (), No ()
     KRW _____, KRW _____
   - Wage payment date: _____ day of every month (every week or every day) (if payment date falls on a holiday, payment will be made one day prior to the holiday)
   - Payment method: Issued directly to the worker (), direct deposit to the employee's bank account ()
7. Annual paid leave
   - Annual paid leave is granted in accordance with the Labor Standards Act.
8. Subscribed social insurances (check the relevant boxes)
   ☐ Employment insurance ☐ Industrial accident compensation insurance
   ☐ National pension ☐ Health insurance
9. Duty to faithfully perform employment contracts, employment rules, etc.
   - Employers and workers must each observe and faithfully implement employment contracts, employment rules, and collective agreements.
10. Other: Matters not specified in this contract are subject to the rules of employment and labor laws.

<Related explanation>
1) Work commencement date: The date on which the employment contract is

자세히 검토해보고자 한다.

(1) 무기계약 근로계약서

---

1. 근로개시일 :   년   월   일부터
2. 근무 장소 :
3. 업무 내용 :
4. 소정근로시간 : ___시 __분부터 ___시___분까지
    (휴게시간 : ___시 __분 ~ ___시___분)
5. 근무일/휴일 : 매주___일(또는 매일단위) 근무, 주휴일 매주   요일
6. 임 금
    - 월(일, 시간)급 : _____원
    - 기타급여(제수당 등) : 있음 (   ), 없음 (   )
      ._____원, _____원
    - 임금지급일 : 매월(매주 또는 매일)   일(휴일의 경우는 전일 지급)
    - 지급방법 : 근로자에게 직접지급(   ), 근로자 명의 예금통장에 입금(   )
7. 연차유급휴가
    - 연차유급휴가는 근로기준법에서 정하는 바에 따라 부여함
8. 사회보험 적용여부(해당란에 체크)
    □ 고용보험   □ 산재보험   □ 국민연금   □ 건강보험
9. 근로계약, 취업규칙 등의 성실한 이행의무
    - 사업주와 근로자는 각자가 근로계약, 취업규칙, 단체협약을 지키고 성실하게 이행하여야 함
10. 기타 - 이 계약에 정함이 없는 사항은 취업규칙과 근로기준법령에 의함

<관련 설명>
1) 근로개시일 : 근로계약이 체결된 날과 근로개시일을 다르게 설정할 수

concluded and the date of commencement of work may be different. The period between the date the employment contract is concluded and the date of commencement of work is called the successful candidate period. Once the employment contract has been concluded, the employer cannot terminate it without justifiable reason.[15] Therefore, it is advisable to set a probation period if at all possible to verify whether a new hire is indeed able to do the work. The probationary period can be from 1 to 6 months, and whether or not the worker is to be employed longer is determined within that period. When dismissing a worker on probation, an objective evaluation should be used, and there should be at least two evaluators. A probationary employee's competence should be assessed not through a one-time apprenticeship evaluation, but through additional intermediate apprenticeship evaluations.

2) Work place and 3) Job description: The head office, the workplace of the relevant worker, and the job description (such as personnel and general affairs) must be clarified. If needed, state that the workplace and job description may change if necessary.

4) Contractual working hours refer to the hours set by an employer within the legal working hours. The limit is generally 40 hours per week and 8 hours per day, while overtime is limited to a maximum of 12 hours per week in excess of the legal working hours (Article 53 of the LSA). These limitations are intended to ensure workers have the right to pursue health and happiness.

5) Working days and holidays: Working days are generally set from Monday to Friday, but can differ depending on the type of business. For weekly holidays, a paid holiday of at least one day a week must be given to each worker who has completed the contractual working days for one week (Article 54 of the LSA). Therefore, one or more paid holidays can be given on the day(s) specified by the employer.

6) Wage: Wages must be at least equal to the minimum wage. The wage specified in the employment contract is ordinary wage, which is the basis for calculating various additional wages. Wages must be paid in full to workers directly in currency. Here, deposits to the worker's bank accounts are also considered direct payment in currency. In addition, wages must be paid at least once a month on a fixed date (Article 43 of the LSA). The inclusive wage system refers to a wage system that does not calculate basic wages in advance for a

---

[15] Lim, Jongryul, 「Labor Law」 18th Ed., Parkyoungsa, 2020, p. 405; Seoul Appellate Court ruling on April 28, 2000: 99na41468.

있다. 근로계약 체결일과 근로개시일 사이를 채용내정이라고 하며, 사용자는 일단 근로계약이 체결되었기 때문에 정당한 사유 없이 근로계약을 해지할 수 없다.[15] 이러한 문제를 해결하기 위해 가급적 수습기간을 두어 신입 근로자의 업무 적격여부를 판단하는 것이 바람직하다. 수습기간은 1개월에서 6개월까지 정하고, 그 기간 내 정식 고용여부를 결정한다. 수습근로자를 해고할 경우에는 객관적인 수습평가서를 사용하고, 가급적 1인 평가가 아닌 2인 이상이거나, 일회성이 아닌 중간 수습평가를 통해 수습근로자의 업무 적격 판단에 신중을 기한다.

2) 근무장소와 (3) 업무내용 : 해당 근로자의 근무장소는 본사, 업무내용은 인사총무 등과 같이 명확히 정해야 하지만, 필요시 인사권 행사를 위해 단, 회사의 사정 및 업무상 필요에 따라 직원의 근무 장소와 업무내용은 변경 될 수 있다라고 기술해 둘 필요가 있다.

4) 소정근로시간은 법정근로시간 내에서 근로자와 사용자가 일하기로 정한 시간을 말한다. 여기서 법정근로시간이라고 하면 일반적으로 1주 40시간, 1일 8시간을 말한다. 연장근로는 법정근로시간을 초과하여 최대 1주 12시간까지로 제한하고 있다(근기법 제53조). 소정근로시간은 근로자의 무리한 근로를 제한하여 근로자의 건강과 행복추구권을 보장하고 사용자의 권리남용을 방지하기 위한 것이다.

5) 근무일과 휴일 : 근무일은 월요일부터 금요일로 정하는게 일반적이지만, 업종에 따라 달리 정할 수 있다. 또한 주휴일의 경우에도 1주 동안의 소정근로일을 개근한 자에게 1일 이상의 유급휴일을 주어야 한다(근기법 제54조). 따라서 사용자가 지정한 날에 1일 이상의 유급휴일을 부여하면 된다.

6) 임금 : 임금은 최저임금 이상을 지급하여야 한다. 근로계약에 정해진 임금이 곧 통상임금으로 각종 가산임금 계산의 기초가 된다. 임금은 통화로 직접 근로자에게 그 전액을 지급하여야 한다. 여기서 통장으로 입금하는 경우도 직접지급으로 간주된다. 그리고 임금은 매월 1회 이상 일정한 날짜를 정하여 지급하여야 한다(근기법 제43조). 포괄임금제는 소정근로시간에 대한 기본임금을 미리 산정하지 않고, 법정근로시간과

---

[15] 임종률, 「노동법」 제18판, 박영사, 2020, 405면; 서울고등법원 2000.4.28 선고 99나41468 판결.

given working time, but rather stipulates that daily or monthly wages shall include the total amount of statutory working hours plus additional working hours.[16] Since the LSA stipulates that basic wages and contractual working hours shall be defined in the employment contract, the inclusive wage system is effectively in violation of that Act.

7) Annual paid leave: It is stipulated that annual leave is used in accordance with the employment rules and the Labor Standards Act.

8) Whether or not social insurances are subscribed to: In principle, the employed workers are automatically subscribed to the four social insurances. However, exceptions exist: those aged 60 or over do not need to subscribe to the national pension while those 65 or over do not need to subscribe to employment insurance. In addition, those under the age of 18 do not contribute to the national pension. For foreign workers, subscription to employment insurance is voluntary. Part-time workers with remarkably few working hours (those with an average of less than 15 hours in 4 weeks) are covered only by industrial accident insurance, but not the other three.

9) Other items to be entered: It is desirable to stipulate that items not listed in the employment contract are subject to the rules of employment.

(2) Fixed-term employment contract

---
1. Employment contract period: From _____ (year/month/day) to _____(year/month/day)

This is the same as the general standard employment contract, but includes a contracted period of employment.

(3) Employment contract for minors

---
8. Certificate of family relations and parental consent form
   - Whether a certificate of family relations has been submitted:_____
   - Whether parental or guardian consent is provided:_____
---

[16] Lee, Seunggil, A Study on Judicial Principles and Benefits of the Inclusive Wage System, 「Labor Law Studies Collection」 29th Ed., Korean Comparative Labor Law Study Association, Dec. 2012, p. 575.

추가 연장근로시간에 대한 제수당을 합한 금액을 월급여액이나 일일분 임금으로 정해 근로자에게 지급하기로 하는 임금제도를 말한다.[16] 근로기준법상 근로계약 작성시 필수 기재사항인 기본임금과 소정근로시간을 정하도록 명시되어 있는 점을 볼 때, 포괄임금제는 사실상 근로기준법을 위반하는 임금지급제도라고 할 수 있다.

7) 연차유급휴가 : 취업규칙과 근로기준법에 따라 연차휴가를 사용한다고 명시한다.

8) 사회보험 적용여부 : 입사한 근로자는 원칙상 4대보험에 자동 가입된다. 다만, 예외적으로 국민연금은 60세, 고용보험은 65세 이상은 해당되지 않는다. 특히, 18세 미만자는 국민연금 당연가입 대상에 해당되지 않는다. 외국인근로자의 경우에는 고용보험 임의 가입대상에 해당된다. 근로시간이 현저히 짧은 단시간 근로자 (4주 평균 15시간 미만자)는 산재보험만 해당되고, 나머지 사회보험은 적용되지 않는다.

9) 기타 기재사항 : 근로계약서에 기재되지 않은 사항은 취업규칙에 따른다고 명시한다.

(2) 기간제 근로계약서

```
1. 근로계약기간 :      년   월    일부터      년   월   일까지
```

기간제 근로자의 경우에는 일반 표준근로계약서와 동일하지만, 기간의 정함이 있는 부분만 달리 적용된다.

(3) 연소자 근로계약서

```
8. 가족관계증명서 및 동의서
   - 가족관계기록사항에 관한 증명서 제출 여부 : _____
   - 친권자 또는 후견인의 동의서 구비 여부 : _____
```

---

[16] 이승길, "포괄임금제의 법리와 효용성에 관한 연구", 「노동법논총」 제29호, 한국비교노동법학회, 2013.12. 575면.

Chapter3-1. Items to be Considered When Writing an Employment Contract

Under the Labor Standards Act, minors are those under the age of 18, while under the Civil Act, minors are those under the age of 19. Juristic acts of minors require parental consent. Therefore, employment contracts for minors must be accompanied by written parental consent. The parents/guardians retain the right to terminate the employment contract of the minor under their care (Articles 66 and 67 of the LSA). Except for these two differences, juristic acts under labor law are the same as those for workers who have reached the age of majority.

(4) Employment contract for daily workers

---

1. **Employment contract period:** From_____(year/month/day) to _____(year/month/day)
※ If the employment contract period is not specified, only the work commencement date is entered.
6. **Wage**
   - Monthly (daily, hourly) wage: KRW____ (circle the relevant time unit)
   - Other allowances (overtime, night, holiday work, etc.): KRW _____ (describe in detail)
     · Overtime allowance: KRW _____ (____hours per month)
     · Night work allowance: KRW _____ (____hours per month)
     · Holiday work allowance: KRW _____ (____hours per month)
   - Wage payment date: _____(day) of every month/week or every day (if the payment date falls on a holiday, payment will be made one day prior to the holiday)
   - Payment method: Direct payment to the worker (   ), deposit to the worker's bank account (   )

Daily workers are employed on a daily basis or work for a remarkably short period. Therefore, the date of commencement of the employment contract or the duration of the employment contract must be specified.

In terms of wages, hourly wage, daily wage, monthly wage, etc. must be specified, as must additional allowances for overtime, night work, and holiday work.

(5) Employment contract for part-time workers

근로기준법상 연소자는 18세 미만자이고, 민법상 미성년자는 만19세 미만자이다. 미성년자의 법률행위는 친권자의 동의를 요구하고 있다. 따라서 연소자의 근로계약은 친권자의 동의서를 첨부해야 하고, 친권자는 미성년자의 근로계약을 해지할 수 있다. (근기법 제66조, 제67조). 위의 2가지 외에는 모두 노동법상 법률행위는 일반근로자와 동일하게 적용된다.

(4) 일용근로자 근로계약서

```
1. 근로계약기간 :      년   월   일부터     년   월   일까지
   ※ 근로계약기간을 정하지 않는 경우에는 "근로개시일"만 기재
6. 임 금
   - 월(일, 시간)급 : _____원
     (해당사항에 ○표)
   - 기타 제수당(시간외 · 야간 · 휴일근로수당 등): _____원
     (내역별 기재)
     • 시간외 근로수당: _____원(월 _____시간분)
     • 야  간 근로수당: _____원(월 _____시간분)
     • 휴  일 근로수당: _____원(월 _____시간분)
   - 임금지급일 : 매월(매주 또는 매일) _____일
     (휴일의 경우는 전일 지급)
   - 지급방법 : 근로자에게 직접지급(    ),
     근로자 명의 예금통장에 입금(    )
```

일용근로자의 특징은 일일 단위로 고용을 하거나 현저히 짧은 기간을 근로한다. 따라서 근로계약 개시일이나 근로계약 기간을 명시하여야 한다.
 임금부분에 있어서도 시급, 일급, 월급 등을 명시하여야 하고, 시간외 근로, 야간근로, 휴일근로 등에 대한 가산수당도 명시하여야 한다.

(5) 단시간근로자 근로계약서

4. Working days and working hours per working day

	Mon	Tues	Wed	Thurs	Fri	Sat
Working hours	__HRS	__HRS	__HRS	__HRS	__HRS	__HRS
Start	__H/M	__H/M	__H/M	__H/M	__H/M	__H/M
Finish	__H/M	__H/M	__H/M	__H/M	__H/M	__H/M
Break	__H/M ~ __H/M	__H/M ~ __H/M	__H/M ~ __H/M	__H/M ~ __H/M	__H/M ~ __H/M	__H/M ~ __H/M

○ Holiday: Every _____ (day of the week)

5. Wage

- Hourly (daily, monthly) wage: KRW _____ circle the relevant time unit)
- Additional wage rate for overtime:___%
- Wage payment date: _____(cardinal day) of every month (or every week/day) (if payment date falls on a holiday, payment will be made one day prior to the holiday)
- Payment method: Direct payment to the worker (), or deposit to the employee's bank account (   )

1) This contract type stipulates working days and working hours per working day to be included in the written description for part-time workers.

2) The contractual working hours of part-time workers must be specified. This shall be within the limit of 12 hours, in addition to the one-week contractual working hours of part-time workers, even for overtime. That is, extended hours for part-time workers are judged based on contractual working hours rather than legal standard working hours (Article 6 of the Fixed-Term and Part-time Employment Act). If the worker works for more than the time specified in the contract, an additional wage of 50% or more of the ordinary wage will be paid even if the hours remain within the legal working hours.

4. 근로일 및 근로일별 근로시간

	( ) 요일	( ) 요일	( ) 요일	( ) 요일	( ) 요일	( ) 요일
근로시간	시간	시간	시간	시간	시간	시간
시 업	시 분	시 분	시 분	시 분	시 분	시 분
종 업	시 분	시 분	시 분	시 분	시 분	시 분
휴게 시간	시 분~ 시 분	시 분~ 시 분	시 분~ 시 분	시 분~ 시 분	시 분~ 시 분	시 분~ 시 분

○ 주휴일 : 매주___요일

5. 임 금

- 시간(일, 월)급 : _____원(해당사항에 ○표)
- 상여금 : 있음 (   ) _____원, 없음 (   )
- 초과근로에 대한 가산임금률: _____%
- 임금지급일 : 매월(매주 또는 매일) ____일(휴일의 경우는 전일 지급)
- 지급방법 : 근로자에게 직접지급(   ), 근로자 명의 예금통장에 입금(   )

1) 단시간근로자의 서면 기재 내용으로 근로일 및 근로일별 근로시간을 규정하고 하고 있다.
2) 단시간근로자의 소정근로시간을 명시해야 한다. 이는 단시간근로자의 연장근로도 단시간근로자의1주 소정근로시간에 가산하여 12시간 한도 내에서 인정된다. 즉, 단시간근로자의 연장근로는 법정근로시간이 아닌 소정근로시간을 기준으로 판단한다(기간제법 제6조). 단시간근로자와 사용자 사이에 근로하기로 정한 시간을 초과하여 근로하면 법정 근로시간 이내라도 통상임금의 100분의 50%이상의 가산임금 지급한다.

III. Details Not to Include in Employment Contracts

The Labor Standards Act specifies invalid details in employment contracts. These include:

(1) Working conditions that do not meet the standards of the Labor Standards Act, with such invalid section(s) to be judged as in accordance with the Labor Standards Act (Article 15);

(2) If any of the working conditions set forth in an employment contract is found to be inconsistent with actual conditions, the worker concerned shall be entitled to claim damages from the employer resulting from breach of the working conditions (Article 19);

(3) Employers shall not prescribe penalties or damages for failure to fulfill the employment contract (Article 20);

(4) No employer shall offset wages against an advance or other credits given in advance on the condition of a worker's labor (Article 21); and

(5) No employer shall enter into a contract with a worker, in addition to a labor contract, which stipulates compulsory savings or the management of savings (Article 22).

IV. Conclusion

When an employer hires someone, an employment contract must be the first thing given. If the details of the employment contract do not match the rules of employment, the rules of employment shall apply (Article 97 of the LSA). If the employer changes the rules of employment unfavorably to workers, the details of the employment contract shall take precedence in accordance with the principle of preferential working conditions, unless the employment contract is also modified. Therefore, the employer must re-issue the contract with the new working conditions specified. It is important to keep in mind that changes to the rules of employment will not take effect until this is done.

Ⅲ. 기재해서는 안 되는 근로계약 내용

사용자가 근로계약서에 기재하면 안 되는 내용은 다음과 같이 근로기준법에 명시되어 있다.
(1) 우선 근로기준법의 기준에 미치지 못하는 근로조건을 정한 근로계약은 무효이고, 그 무효가 된 부분은 근로기준법에 따른다(제15조).
(2) 근로계약에 명시된 근로조건이 사실과 다를 경우에는 사용자가 근로조건 위반을 원인으로 근로자에게 손해배상을 해야 한다(제19조).
(3) 사용자가 근로계약 불이행에 대한 위약금 또는 손해배상액을 예정하는 근로계약을 체결할 수 없다(제20조).
(4) 전차금이나 그 밖에 근로할 것을 조건으로 하는 전대채권과 임금을 상계하는 계약을 체결하지 못한다(제21조).
(5) 사용자는 근로계약에 덧붙여 강제 저축과 또는 저축금의 관리를 규정하는 계약을 체결하지 못한다(제22조).

Ⅳ. 결론

사용자가 근로자를 고용하게 되면 가장 먼저 해야 할 일이 근로계약서의 작성이다. 근로계약의 내용이 취업규칙에 미치지 못하면 취업규칙이 우선 적용되지만(근기법 제97조), 근로계약의 내용이 취업규칙 보다 유리하면 유리한 근로계약의 내용이 적용된다. 사용자가 취업규칙의 내용을 근로자에게 불리하게 변경한 경우, 근로계약을 수정하지 않는 이상 근로조건의 유리한 조건 우선의 원칙에 따라 근로계약의 내용이 먼저 적용되기 때문이다. 따라서 사용자는 근로계약서 작성시 필수 기재사항 뿐만 아니라 일반 근로조건에 있어서도 근로조건이 변경된 경우 변경된 근로조건을 반영하여 근로계약서를 새로 교부하여야 하고, 근로조건에 불리한 변경이 있을 경우에는 해당 근로자의 근로계약서를 필히 변경하여야 새롭게 변경된 근로계약이 효력을 가진다는 사실을 명심하여야 할 것이다.

Section 2: Employee Register and Contract Document Retention

I. Employee Register

Employers are required to maintain an employee register for each workplace and promptly update any changes. This regulation applies to all workplaces with one or more employees. However, it is not mandatory to maintain an employee register for daily workers whose employment period is less than 30 days (Article 41 of the LSA). The employee register must include the following information:

1. Name
2. Gender
3. Date of birth
4. Address
5. Employment history
6. Type of work performed
7. Date of employment or renewal, contract period (if specified), and other employment-related details
8. Date and reason for termination, resignation, or death
9. Other necessary information

II. Retention of Employment Contract Documents

Employers must retain important documents related to the employee register and employment contracts for three years (Article 42 of the LSA). The retention period begins from the date the employee is terminated, resigns, or dies. However, wage ledgers must be retained for three years from the wage payment date. Additionally, employers are obligated to provide a certificate containing factual details about the employee's period of employment, type of work, position, and wages upon the employee's request, even after resignation. Such employment certificates must be issued within three years after the employee's resignation if requested and must only include the information specified by the employee (Article 39 of the LSA). The documents to be retained include:

1. Employment contracts

제2절 근로자 명부 및 계약서류 보존

I. 근로자 명부

사용자는 각 사업장 별로 근로자 명부를 작성하고, 그 변경사항을 지체없이 정정해야 한다. 이 규정은 1인 이상 사용하는 모든 사업장에 해당된다. 다만, 사용기간이 30일 미만인 일용근로자에 대해서는 근로자 명부를 작성하지 아니할 수 있다 (근기법 제41조). 근로자 명부의 기재 사항은 다음과 같다.
1. 성명
2. 성(性)별
3. 생년월일
4. 주소
5. 이력(履歷)
6. 종사하는 업무의 종류
7. 고용 또는 고용갱신 연월일, 계약기간을 정한 경우에는 그 기간, 그 밖의 고용에 관한 사항
8. 해고, 퇴직 또는 사망한 경우에는 그 연월일과 사유
9. 그 밖에 필요한 사항

II. 근로계약 서류의 보존

사용자는 근로자 명부와 근로계약에 관한 중요한 서류를 3년간 보존하여야 한다 (근기법 제42조). 서류 기간의 보존은 근로자가 해고되거나 퇴직한 날, 또는 사망한 날로부터 기산한다. 다만, 임금대장은 그 해당 임금 지급일로부터 3년간 보존해야 한다. 또한 사용자는 근로자가 퇴직한 후라도 사용 기간, 업무 종류, 지위와 임금, 그 밖에 필요한 사항에 관한 증명서를 청구하면 사실대로 적은 증명서를 즉시 내주어야 한다. 다만, 사용증명서는 근로자가 퇴직한 후 3년 이내에는 근로자의 청구가 있는 경우에는 사용증명서를 발급해야 하고, 근로자가 요구한 사항만 적어야 한다 (근기법 제39조).
1. 근로계약서

2. Wage ledgers
3. Documents related to the determination and payment methods of wages, and the basis for wage calculation
4. Documents related to employment, termination, and resignation
5. Documents related to promotions and demotions
6. Documents related to leave
7. [Deleted]
8. Agreements under Article 51 (flexible working hours), Article 52 (selective working hours), Article 53 (special extended working hours), Article 55 (substitute holidays), Article 57 (compensatory leave), Article 58 (discretionary working hours), Article 59 (exceptional working hours), and written agreements under Article 62
9. Documents related to the certification of minors as per Article 66.

Section 3. Wages

Section 3-1. Preventing Unpaid Wages and the Small Amount Insolvency Payment Claim System

Ⅰ. Preventive Measures for Delayed Payment of Wages

Providing work not meant to be on a voluntary basis and not receiving wages is slave labor. Thus, delaying payment of wages is a serious offense and subject to imprisonment for up to three years or a fine of up to 30 million won.[17] Delayed payment of wages is punishable for each violation towards individual workers, so if the employer delays payment of wages to a large number of workers, that employer will face heavy penalties. Despite these strong penalties, it is not easy to settle problems related to unpaid wages. Even if a worker who was not paid complains to the local Employment Labor Office (hereinafter referred to as Labor Office), and the Labor Office confirms that the wages remain unpaid and the employer is punished, the worker still has to take separate legal action to receive the unpaid wages. If the employer does not have any property, the employer can

---
[17] The Labor Standards Act (LSA): Article 109 (paragraph 1).

2. 임금대장
3. 임금의 결정·지급방법과 임금계산의 기초에 관한 서류
4. 고용·해고·퇴직에 관한 서류
5. 승급·감급에 관한 서류
6. 휴가에 관한 서류.
7. 삭제.
8. 법 제51조에 의한 탄력적 근로시간제 합의서, 제52조에 의한 선택적 근로시간제 합의서, 제53조에 의한 특별연장근로 합의서, 제55조의 휴일근로대체 합의서, 제57조에 의한 보상휴가제 합의서, 제58조에 의한 재량 근로시간제 합의서, 제59조에 의한 특례 근로시간 합의서, 제62조에 따른 서면 합의 서류,
9. 법 제66조에 따른 연소자의 증명에 관한 서류.

제3절 임금

제3-1절 임금체불예방

Ⅰ. 임금체불의 예방조치

근로를 제공하고 임금을 받지 못하는 것은 노예노동에 해당된다. 따라서 임금체불은 중대범죄에 해당하므로 3년 이하의 징역 또는 3천만 이하의 벌금을 처벌받는다.[17] 이 벌칙과 벌금은 체불된 근로자 개인에 해당되므로 다수의 근로자에게 임금을 체불하게 되면 가중처벌을 받는다. 이러한 강력한 처벌조항에도 불구하고 임금체불을 해결하는 방법은 쉽지가 않다. 체불된 근로자가 지방고용노동관서(이하 '노동청')에 진정하여 임금체불확인을 받고 사용자를 형사처벌하더라도 사용자가 임금을 지급하지 않는 경우에는 근로자는 별도의 민사소송을 통해서만 체불된 임금을 받을 수 있다. 사업주가 재산이 없는 경우 임금채권보장기금의 체당금제도를 통해서 최우선변제 임금을 일정한

---
[17] 근로기준법 제109조 제1항.

receive a certain amount of money for the most preferential wages from the Wage Bond Guarantee Fund. Receiving unpaid wages through civil litigation and the Insolvency Payment Claim System is a complex process and takes a long time, which is not helpful in practical terms.

To resolve these problems, a new payment solution has been proposed in addition to legal preventive measures. A high rate of 20% interest is placed on employers to facilitate their payment of delayed wages. This is to preclude employers avoiding punishment if they do not pay the unpaid wages until they are prosecuted.

II. High interest levied

The Labor Standards Act:Article 37 (Late Payment Interest on Unpaid Wages)

① An employer who fails to pay all or part of the wages or benefits (only those paid in a lump sum) pursuant to Article 36 or subparagraph 5 of Article 2 of the Employee Retirement Benefit Security Act, respectively, within fourteen days from the day when the cause for payment occurs, shall pay late payment interest for the number of days from the date following expiry of the fourteen day period until the payment is made, at a rate up to 40/100 and as prescribed by Presidential Decree in consideration of financial conditions, including the late payment interest rate applicable among banks under the Banking Act.

② If an employer delays payment of wages due to a natural disaster, armed conflicts or other reasons prescribed by Presidential Decree, the provisions of paragraph (1) shall not apply to the period during which such reasons continue to exist.

In order to prevent delayed payment of wages and early liquidation of unpaid wages, the Labor Standards Act was amended in 2005 to create a "Late Payment Interest System for unpaid wages." If an employer fails to pay all or part of wages and retirement benefits owed within 14 days of the required date of payment, the

한도 내에서 지급받을 수 있다. 이러한 민사소송과 체당금제도를 통해 체불임금을 받는 것은 복잡한 과정과 오랜 시간이 소요되므로 실질적인 도움은 되지 않는다.

이러한 임금체불을 해결하기 위해 법적인 예방조치와 함께 새로운 임금체불 해결책이 제시되고 있다. 그 예방책으로 체불된 임금의 지급을 촉진하기 위해 연 20%의 고율의 지연이자제도와 사업주가 체불된 임금을 지급하면 형사처벌을 면해주는 반의사불벌죄가 있다.

Ⅱ. 지연이자제도

> 근로기준법 제37조(미지급 임금에 대한 지연이자)
> ① 사용자는 제36조에 따라 지급하여야 하는 임금 및 「근로자퇴직급여보장법」제2조제5호에 따른 급여(일시금만 해당된다)의 전부 또는 일부를 그 지급 사유가 발생한 날부터 14일 이내에 지급하지 아니한 경우 그 다음 날부터 지급하는 날까지의 지연 일수에 대하여 연 100분의 40 이내의 범위에서 「은행법」에 따른 은행이 적용하는 연체금리 등 경제 여건을 고려하여 대통령령으로 정하는 이율(연 20%)에 따른 지연이자를 지급하여야 한다.
> ② 제1항은 사용자가 천재·사변, 그 밖에 대통령령으로 정하는 사유에 따라 임금 지급을 지연하는 경우 그 사유가 존속하는 기간에 대하여는 적용하지 아니한다.

임금체불의 예방 및 체불임금의 조기청산을 유도하기 위하여 2005년 근로기준법 개정을 통해 '미지급임금에 대한 지연이자 지급제도'가 마련되었다. 사용자는 임금 및 퇴직 급여의 전부 또는 일부를 그 지급사유가 발생한 날로부터 14일 이내에 지급하지 아니하는 경우 그 다음날부터 지급하는 날까지의 지연일수에 대하여 대통령령이 정하는 이율(현행 연20%)에 따른 지연이자를 지급하여야 한다. 지연이자제도는 사용자가 불가피한 사정없이 의도적으로 임금을 체불하는 것을 막기 위해 고율의 이자를 부가하는 제도로 사용자가

employer shall pay the late payment interest rate prescribed by Presidential Decree (currently 20% per year) for the number of days payment was delayed, starting from the day following the required date of payment. This high interest rate helps to prevent an employer from intentionally paying back wages only when he/she is forced to, and without consequences. If an employer delays payment of wages due to a natural disaster, armed conflict or other reasons such as legal or actual bankruptcy, this provision shall not apply to the period during which such reasons continue to exist.

The late payment interest system levies a much higher rate of interest (20% annually) than the statutory interest of 6% a year, as a way to induce quick payment. However, if the employers do not have any money or assets to effect payment, there is no way to protect the affected workers' rights, no matter how high the interest rate.[18] The reasons why 20% annual interest payment is not used well on unpaid wages is as follows.

First, there is no penalty for failing to pay the late payment interest, unless the worker takes the employer to civil court.[19]

Second, workers tend to agree to withdraw their complaints if they simply receive their unpaid wages.

Third, the Labor Inspector only considers whether the unpaid wages have been paid when determining punishment, and not the interest for delaying payment, since there are no items related to delayed payment interest in the Official Document on Details of Unpaid Wages.

Delayed payment interest is only considered in civil lawsuits for unpaid wages, meaning there is very limited effectiveness in preventing wage payment delays.

Ⅲ. No-punishment offenses against one's intention

The Labor Standards Act: Article 109 (Penal Provisions)
① Any person who violates the provisions of Article 36, 43 (Payment of

---

[18] Park, Keun-hoo et al., Ministry of Employment and Labor, A Study on Expansion of the Wage Bond Guarantee System, December 23, 2016, p. 17.
[19] Ha, Kap-rae, 「The Labor Standards Act」 32nd ed., 2019, p. 296.

천재지변, 법률상 또는 사실상 도산 등으로 임금을 지급할 수 없는 경우에는 적용이 면제된다.

지연이자제도는 체불사업주로 하여금 법정이자(상법 연6%)보다 높은 연 20%의 이율을 부담하게 하여 신속한 체불청산을 유도하기 위하여 도입되었으나, 체불사업주가 사실상 무자력자가 되어 근로자가 임금채권 자체를 지급받지 못할 경우에는 임금에 대하여 아무리 높은 이율의 이자가 붙더라도 근로자의 권리보장에 실질적인 기여를 하지 못한다는 근본적인 한계점이 있다.[18] 체불임금에 대한 연 20%의 지연이자 지급이 현실적으로 강제되지 않고 있는 이유는

첫째, 지연이자를 지급하지 않은데 대한 벌칙규정이 없고, 근로자의 민사상 청구권만 인정되기 때문이다.[19]

둘째, 근로자들이 체불임금만 받으면 진정 또는 고소사건 취하해주려는 경향이 있기 때문이다.

셋째, 노동청이 사법처리 단계에서도 처벌수위 결정시 체불임금 원금 지급 여부만 고려될 뿐 지연이자 지급여부까지는 고려되지 않는다는 점이 작용하고 있기 때문이다.

특히, 체불금품확인원에 기재되는 '체불임금등 내역'에도 따로 지연이자에 관한 항목이 마련되어 있지 않아 현재 체불 진정사건 조사과정에서 체불금액에 대한 지연이자 조사가 별도로 이루어지기 어려운 상황이다. 따라서 지연이자 적용은 임금체불 민사소송에서만 활용되고 있기 때문에 사실상 임금체불을 예방하는데 한계가 있다.

Ⅲ. 반의사불벌죄 제도

근로기준법 제109조(벌칙)
① 제36조(퇴직후 14일 이내 임금지급), 제43조(임금지급의 원칙),

---

18) 박근후 외 4명, 고용노동부 용역자료, 임금채권보장제도 확대방안 연구, 2016.12.23. 17면.
19) 하갑례, 「근로기준법」 제32판, 2019, 296면.

> Wages), 44 (Payment of Wages in Subcontract Businesses), 44-2 (Joint Responsibility for Paying Wages in the Construction Industry), 46 (Allowances during Business Suspension), or 56 (Extended Work, Night Work and Holiday Work) shall be punished by imprisonment of up to three years or by a fine not exceeding thirty million won.
> ② Prosecution against a person who violates the provisions of Article 36, 43, 44, 44-2, 46 or 56 shall not take place against the clearly expressed wishes of the victim.

No-punishment offenses against one's intention is a system where imprisonment of up to three years or a fine of up to 30 million won is imposed on employers who have delayed payment of wages in principle, but the Ministry of Employment and Labor (MOEL) does not prosecute if it is against the clearly expressed wishes of the related worker(s). Employers were forced to solve voluntary liquidation of unpaid wages through agreement with workers by paying unpaid wages instead of suffering criminal penalties. However, if a large number of workers whose wages remain unpaid, the employer shall be deemed to have committed the same offense against each unpaid worker.[20] Accordingly, in order to avoid penalties according to the no-punishment offenses system, written consent from all unpaid workers must be obtained.[21]

IV. Conclusion

As a way to rectifying the problem for some workers of their wages remaining unpaid, there is a delayed payment interest system and no-punishment offenses against workers' intention that can be used within the legal framework. The delayed payment interest system involves levying an additional 20% in annual interest to the amount of unpaid wages, which should be described with delayed payment interest at the Labor Office's issuance of an Unpaid Wage Confirmation Certificate. In cases of no-punishment offenses against workers' intention, criminal penalties are imposed on employers in the form of fines (rather than imprisonment), which can equal up to 20% of the total unpaid wages. Korea should introduce punitive fines as is done in the United States, charging fines several times higher than the actual unpaid wages, and promote the perception that work without wages is slave labor.

---

[20] Supreme Court ruling on April 14, 94da1724.
[21] Labor Inspector's practical guide, Ministry of Employment and Labor, Handling of Unpaid Wages, 2016, p. 33.

> 제44조(도급사업의 임금지급), 제44조의2(건설업의 임금지급 연대책임), 제46조(휴업수당) 또는 제56조(가산임금)를 위반한 자는 3년 이하의 징역 또는 3천만 원 이하의 벌금에 처한다.
> ② 제36조, 제43조, 제44조, 제44조의2, 제46조 또는 제56조를 위반한 자에 대하여는 피해자의 명시적인 의사와 다르게 공소를 제기할 수 없다.

반의사불벌죄는 임금지급을 지체한 사용자에 대하여 원칙적으로 3년 이하의 징역 또는 3000만 원 이하의 벌금을 처하도록 하되, 해당 근로자가 처벌을 원하지 않는 경우에는 공소를 제기할 수 없도록 하는 제도이다. 사용자가 형사처벌을 받지 않는 대신에 체불된 임금을 지급함으로써 근로자와의 합의를 통한 자율적인 임금체불청산을 강제하기 위하여 도입되었다. 다만, 임금체불이 다수인 경우 그 범죄가 단일한 것이라고 인정하기 어려울 때에는 지급을 받을 수 없었던 근로자 각자에 대하여 같은 범죄가 있다고 인정하여야 한다.[20] 따라 반의사불벌죄에 의거하여 처벌을 면하려면 체불된 개별 근로자들의 전원 서면 동의를 얻어야 한다.[21]

Ⅳ. 의견

근로자의 임금체불 문제를 해결하기 위한 방법으로 법적 테두리 내에서 활용할 수 있는 제도로는 지연이자제도와 반의사불벌죄 제도가 있다. 이를 개선하기 위해서는 노동청의 임금체불확인서 발행단계에서 지연이자 연 20%를 반드시 포함하여 체불임금액을 산정하여야 할 것이다. 또한 반의사불벌죄의 형사처벌도 대부분 벌금형을 부과하는 방식으로 하고 있고, 벌금도 체불금의 20% 이내에서 부과하고 있다. 우리나라도 미국과 같이 징벌적 벌금을 과하여 실제 체불된 임금보다 몇 배의 벌금을 과하도록 하여 임금체불이 노예노동이라는 인식을 확산시켜야 할 것이다.

---

[20] 대법원 1995.4.14. 선고 94도1724 판결
[21] 고용노동부 근로감독관 실무지침서, 체불사건 업무처리요령, 2016, 33면.

Chapter3-3. Wages

Section 3-2 The Principle of Complete Payment of Wages & Exceptions

I. Introduction

Company A gives a 20 percent discount to its employees when they buy company products, up to a maximum of KRW 2 million per year. Only employees and their direct family members living together may receive this discount when they purchase products. However, it was confirmed that one employee violated this company regulation, so the company issued a written warning and deducted, with the employee's agreement, KRW 500,000 from his salary: the amount involved in the violation. This type of situation has occurred frequently in business, and deals directly with whether a company can recover claimed damages by deducting employee wages.

As the wages paid in return for work provided directly support the employee's ability to sustain him or herself, deducting wages to pay for claims is strictly regulated. Article 43 (Payment of Wages) of the Labor Standards Act stipulates, (1) Payment of wages shall be made in full to workers; however, if otherwise stipulated by special provisions of laws or decrees or a collective agreement, wages may be partially deducted or may be paid by other means than cash. Other provisions that deal with this subject include Article 20 (Prohibition of Predetermination of Nonobservance)[22], Article 21 (Prohibition of Offsetting Wages against Advances)[23], Article 22 (Prohibition of Compulsory Saving)[24], and Article 95 (Limitation on Punitive Provisions)[25]. Despite the principle of complete payment, there are a few exceptions. Some legitimate reasons for deductions include: ① deductions allowed by law or decrees (court rulings); ② deductions allowed by the collective agreement; ③ deductions made to correct miscalculation of wages.[26] Also, even though an exception for wage claims has the employee's consent, this needs to be handled in a strictly regulated manner. Here I would like to take a substantial look into exceptions to complete payment of wages.

II. The Principle of Complete Payment & Exceptions

---

[22] Article 20 (Prohibition of Predetermination of Nonobservance): No employer shall enter into a contract by which a penalty or indemnity for possible damages incurred from breach of a labor contract is predetermined.

[23] Article 21 (Prohibition of Offsetting Wages against Advances): No employer shall offset wages against an advance or other credits given in advance on the condition of worker's labor.

[24] Article 22 (Prohibition of Compulsory Saving): (1) No employer shall enter into a contract with a worker, in addition to a labor contract, which stipulates compulsory savings or the management of savings.

[25] Article 95 (Limitation on Punitive Provisions): If a punitive reduction in wages for a worker is stipulated in the rules of employment, the amount of reduction for each infraction shall not exceed half of one day's average wages, and the total amount of reduction shall not exceed one-tenth of the total amount of wages during each period of wage payment.

[26] Jongyul Lim, 『Labor Law』, 14th Edition, 2016, Parkyoungsa, pg. 417.

제3-2절 임금 전액지급의 원칙과 예외

I. 문제의 소재

A 회사는 자사제품에 대해 직원에게 연간 200만 원 한도 내에서 20%을 할인해주고 있다. 그 수혜대상은 직원본인과 동거 직계가족에 한한다. 한 직원이 이 규정을 위반하여 회사의 물품을 구입한 것이 확인되어 회사는 해당 근로자에게 서면경고를 하면서, 본인의 동의를 얻어 급여에서 부당이익금 50만 원을 공제하였다. 이와 같은 사례는 일반적으로 많이 발생하는 사례로서 임금채권과 손해배상 채권을 상계할 수 있는 지 여부에 대한 문제와 밀접한 관련이 있다.

근로의 대가로 받는 임금은 근로자의 생존권 보장에 직결되기 때문에 임금에서 채권의 공제를 엄격히 제한하고 있다. 근로기준법 제43조 제1항에서 임금은 전액을 지급하여야 하며, 임금의 일부 공제는 법령 또는 단체협약에 특별한 규정이 있는 경우에 한한다고 명시하고 있다. 그 밖에도 '위약 예정의 금지',[22] '전차금 상계의 금지',[23] '강제저축의 금지',[24] '제재 규정(감급)의 제한'[25] 등의 명시적 규정이 있다. 또한 임금 전액지급을 원칙으로 하면서 최소한의 예외를 두고 있다. 임금 공제가 합법적으로 가능한 것으로는 ① 법령(법원의 판결문), ② 단체협약, ③ 임금착오 지급에 의한 공제가 있다.[26] 다만, 임금채권에 대해 근로자의 동의를 전제로 전액지급의 예외, 즉 상계에 대한 예외를 인정하지만 엄격히 규제하고 있다. 이러한 전액지급의 예외에 대해 살펴보고자 한다.

II. 전액지급의 원칙과 예외

---

[22] 제20조 (위약 예정의 금지) 사용자는 근로계약 불이행에 대한 위약금 또는 손해배상액을 예정하는 계약을 체결하지 못한다.
[23] 제21조 (전차금 상계의 금지) 사용자는 전차금이나 그 밖에 근로할 것을 조건으로 하는 전대(前貸)채권과 임금을 상계하지 못한다.
[24] 제22조 (강제 저금의 금지) ① 사용자는 근로계약에 덧붙여 강제 저축 또는 저축금의 관리를 규정하는 계약을 체결하지 못한다.
[25] 제95조 (제재 규정의 제한) 취업규칙에서 근로자에 대하여 감급(減給)의 제재를 정할 경우에 그 감액은 1회의 금액이 평균임금의 1일 분의 2분의 1을, 총액이 1임금지급기의 임금 총액의 10분의 1을 초과하지 못한다.
[26] 김형배, 『노동법』제24판, 박영사, 2015년, 364면; 임종률, 『노동법』, 제14판, 박영사, 2016, 417면.

Chapter3-3. Wages

1. The principle of complete payment

The purpose of complete payment of wages is designed to protect employees and provide stability in their earning of a living by means of prohibiting employers from unilaterally deducting wages and requiring the complete payment of wages. Some exceptions exist, but these are strictly regulated in special provisions of laws or decrees or in collective agreements.[27] The courts have ruled, In cases where an employer reduces personnel and at the same time unilaterally cuts bonuses, if the employees continue to work without any particular claims, this deduction of wages still amounts to a unilateral decision by the employer and the employees' rights to claim these unilaterally-reduced bonuses shall not be considered waived.[28]

2. Exceptions

(1) Deductions allowed by law and decree

Laws and decrees which allow deductions are limited to income tax law, social security insurance laws, and other stipulated laws. In addition, a court decision to allow seizure of wages can be implemented by seizing one-half of wages exceeding the minimum cost of living (KRW 1.5 million)[29]

A particularly remarkable judicial ruling was recently made which ruled that deductions can be made from monthly wages, but not from severance pay or retirement pension. Since Article 7 (Protection of Right to Receive Benefits) of the Employee Retirement Benefit Security Act (ERBSA) stipulates that the right to receive benefits under a retirement pension plan shall neither be transferred to others nor offered as collateral, such provision prohibiting transferring the retirement benefits as collateral is part of statutory law. Accordingly, a court ruling to allow seizure of benefits under a retirement pension plan is null and void, and a third-party debtor can refuse the payment, by quoting the above, from an employee's benefits, even if ordered by a court. On the other hand, Article 246 (Claims Subject to Prohibition of Seizure) of the Civil Execution Act (CEA) regulates that an amount equivalent to a maximum of 1/2 of wages, retirement pension or other wage claims of similar nature can be deducted. Since Article 7 (Protection of Right to Receive Benefits) of the ERBSA and Article 246 (Claims Subject to Prohibition of

---

[27] Article 109 (Penal Provisions): (1) Persons who violate the provisions of Article 43 shall be punished by imprisonment of up to three years or by a fine not exceeding twenty million won.

[28] Supreme Court on June 11, 1999, 98 Da 22185

[29] Supreme Court on March 16, 1994, 94 Ma 1882; Civil Execution Act: Article 246 (Claims Subject to Prohibition of Seizure) (1) None of the following claims shall be seized: 4. Amount equivalent to 1/2 of wages, pension, salary, bonus, retirement pension, or other wage claims of similar nature: Provided, that where the amount falls short of the amount prescribed by Presidential Decree in consideration of the minimum cost of living under the National Basic Living Security Act or exceeds the amount prescribed by Presidential Decree in consideration of the cost of living for a standard family, such amount (1.5 million won) prescribed by Presidential Decree shall apply respectively;

1. 전액지급의 원칙

　임금 전액지급의 취지는 사용자가 일방적으로 임금을 공제하는 것을 금지하여 근로자에게 임금 전액을 확실하게 지급받게 함으로써 근로자의 경제생활을 위협하는 일이 없도록 그 보호를 도모하려는 데 있다. 임금의 전액지불에 대한 예외는 법령이나 단체협약으로 가능하다고 명시하여 엄격하게 제한하고 있다.[27] 법원은 경영위기로 인하여 인원을 감축하면서 상여금을 일방적으로 삭감하고 이에 대해 근로자들이 별다른 이의 없이 근무하고 있는 경우에도 이는 사용자의 일방적인 임금삭감으로 근로자가 상여금 청구권을 포기하였다고 볼 수 없다.고 판시하고 있다.[28]

2. 전액지급원칙의 예외

(1) 법령에 의한 예외

　법령에 의해 공제가 인정되는 경우는 소득세법, 4대보험징수법 등으로 명시된 경우에 한해서 가능하다. 또한 채권자가 법원에서 임금채권에 대한 압류 판결을 받은 경우에는 월 지급되는 임금에 한해서 최저생계비 150만 원을 초과하는 임금의 2분의 1 상당액을 압류할 수 있다.[29]

　특히 주목해야 할 최근 판례는 임금채권 압류는 월임금에서는 가능하지만, 퇴직금이나 퇴직연금에 대해서는 압류할 수 없다고 명확히 판결하고 있다. 근로자퇴직급여보장법 제7조에서 퇴직연금제도의 급여를 받을 권리에 대하여 양도를 금지하고 있으므로 위 양도금지 규정은 강행법규에 해당한다고 볼 것이다. 따라서 퇴직연금제도의 급여를 받을 권리에 대한 압류명령은 실체법상 무효이고, 제3채무자는 그 압류채권의 추심금 청구에 대하여 위 무효를 들어 지급을 거절할 수 있다. 한편 민사집행법은 제246조 제1항 제4호에서 퇴직연금 그 밖에 이와 비슷한 성질을 가진 급여채권은 그 1/2에 해당하는 금액만 압류하지 못하는 것으로 규정하고 있으나, 이는 위 퇴직급여법상의 양도금지

---

[27] 제109조 (벌칙) (1) 43조를 위반한 자는 3년 이하의 징역 또는 2천만 원 이하의 벌금에 처한다.
[28] 대법원 1999. 06. 11. 선고 98다 22185 판결
[29] 대법원 1994. 3. 16. 선고 94마1822판결; 민사집행법 제246조(압류금지채권) 제1항 제4호에서 급료.연금.봉급.상여금.퇴직연금, 그 밖에 이와 비슷한 성질을 가진 급여채권의 2분의 1에 해당하는 금액. 다만 단서에서 근로자의 급여 중 최저생계비(4인 가족 기준 150만 원)에 해당하는 금액의 압류금지

Seizure) of the CEA are affected by the relationship between general law and special law, it is translated that all benefits under retirement pensions shall not be transferred as collateral.[30] This means that because the ERBSA is a special law, it takes precedence over the CEA, which is a general law.

(2) Deductions allowed by a collective agreement

Deductions of union dues (or dues checkoff) are typical deductions allowed by a collective agreement. In cases where the labor union requests that the company deduct 10 times the usual monthly union dues (such as KRW 500,000 from each union member towards preparations for a strike), the company will need to decide whether to cooperate or not. For its part, the Ministry of Employment and Labor (MOEL) expressed its official opinion that if the labor union decides to raise funds to prepare for a strike by means of a legitimate decision-making process such as by resolution at a general meeting of all union members (or union representatives), the company shall cooperate by deducting the special union fees from employee monthly wages even though there is no individual consent to do so.[31] This means that, according to MOEL, it would be considered unfair labor practice for an employer to refuse to deduct the amount requested by the labor union to prepare for a strike.

(3) Deductions to correct miscalculation of wages

In cases where an employer overpaid an employee by mistake, equivalent deductions from wages would be to correct the miscalculation, making it possible to adjust wages or severance pay, regardless of the principle of complete payment of wages. Provided, even in this case, the courts have ruled that the amount of retirement benefits deducted to retrieve overpaid wages shall be a maximum of 1/2 of the retirement benefits.[32]

III. Criteria for Judgment & Related Cases Regarding Other Deductions

1. Criteria for judgment

The principle of complete payment of wages strictly regulates, in accordance with Article 43 of the Labor Standards Act, related judicial rulings and MOEL

---

[30] Supreme Court on January 23, 2014, 2013 Da 71180
[31] Labor Ministry Guideline: June 6, 2004, Labor Union 1501
[32] Supreme Court on May 20, 2010, 2007 Da 90760

규정과의 사이에서 일반법과 특별법의 관계에 있으므로, 퇴직급여법상의 퇴직연금채권은 그 전액에 관하여 압류가 금지된다고 보아야 한다.[30]

(2) 단체협약에 의한 공제

단체협약에 의한 공제는 조합비 공제(check-off)가 대표적인 내용이다. 이와 관련하여 노동조합에서 매월 공제되는 조합원 조합비의 10배에 상당하는 조합원 1인당 50만 원의 쟁의기금의 공제를 요구하는 경우에 회사는 이에 대해 협조해야 하는 문제가 있다. 이에 대해 고용노동부는 개인의 동의가 없더라도 노동조합의 적법한 결의 절차[조합원의 총회(대의원)의 의결이나 노조 규약상 관련이 있는 경우]를 통해 결정한 쟁의기금에 대해서도 조합비 공제로서 공제해주어야 하며, 이 경우에 조합원 개별 동의가 필요하지 않다는 입장이다.[31] 즉, 사용자가 노동조합이 회사를 상대로 투쟁하기 위한 조합비 특별공제를 거부하는 경우에는 부당노동행위에 해당된다고 볼 수 있다.

(3) 임금계산 착오지급에 의한 공제

사용자가 임금계산의 착오 등으로 인하여 임금이 초과로 지급된 경우에는 급여계산상의 문제이므로 임금전액지급 원칙과 상관없이 급여나 퇴직금에서 정산이 가능하다. 다만, 이 경우에도 법원은 사용자가 근로자에게 부당이득 반환채권을 자동채권으로 하여 근로자의 퇴직금채권을 상계하는 것은 퇴직금채권의 2분의 1을 초과하는 부분에 해당하는 금액에 관하여만 허용된다고 보고 있다.[32]

Ⅲ. 기타 공제(상계)의 가능 여부에 대한 판단기준 및 관련 사례

1. 판단기준

근로자의 임금이 사용자가 가지는 근로자의 불법행위를 원인으로 하는 채권과 상계(공제)가 가능한지에 대해 근로기준법 제43조 제1항의 임금의

---

[30] 대법원 2014. 1. 23. 선고 2013다71180 판결
[31] 고용노동부 행정해석: 2004. 6. 5. 노동조합과-1501
[32] 대법원 2010.5.20. 선고 2007다90760 전원합의체 판결

Guidelines an employer from deducting an employee's wages to cover damage claims against the employee.[33] This is because such a deduction is determined unilaterally by the employer.

Regarding the justification for this, judicial ruling has stipulated the following criteria for judgment: It is prohibited for an employer to unilaterally deduct an employee's wages to cover claims against the employee by the employer, but in cases where the employer deducts or replaces the employee's wages after obtaining the employee's consent, as this consent can be regarded as the employee voluntarily agreeing to this deduction, this would not be a violation of Article 43 of the Labor Standards Act. Provided, in view of considering the purpose of the principle of complete payment of wages, determination of whether the employee actually voluntarily agreed to this deduction shall be strictly and carefully made.[34]

2. Related cases

(1) Reimbursement of training expenses

In cases where an employer assigns an employee overseas and subsidizes all training expenses for the employee to attend a training program, and that employee does not serve the compulsory employment period after completing the training, the employer can legitimately require the employee to reimburse part or all of the training expenses covered by the company. Accordingly, a training regulation that exempts an employee from the duty of reimbursement if that employee serves the compulsory employment period after completing the commissioned overseas training is not equivalent to a contract by which a penalty or indemnity is predetermined for damages incurred from a breach of the labor contract. Neither does such a training regulation violate Article 7 of the LSA (Prohibition of Forced Labor: No employer shall force a worker to work against his own free will through any means which unlawfully restrict mental or physical freedom) nor Article 21 (Prohibition of Offsetting Wages against Advances: No employer shall offset wages against an advance or other credits given in advance on the condition of a worker's labor).[35]

(2) Deductions from bonuses

Sometimes an employer reduces or does not pay bonuses, with labor union

---

[33] Supreme Court on September 28, 1976, 73 Da 1768
[34] Supreme Court on October 23, 2001, 2001 Da 25184
[35] Supreme Court on February 25, 1992, 91 Da 26232 (Korean Air)

전액지급 원칙과 판례와 행정해석에서도 이를 금지하고 있다.[33] 이것은 상계(공제)라는 것이 사용자의 일방적인 의사표시에 의해서 행해지기 때문이다.
  이에 대해 상계의 가능여부에 대한 판단기준을 판례[34]는 다음과 같이 판시하고 있다. 사용자가 근로자에 대하여 가지는 채권을 가지고 일방적으로 근로자의 임금채권을 상계(공제)하는 것은 금지된다고 할 것이지만, 사용자가 근로자의 동의를 얻어 근로자의 임금채권에 대하여 공제(상계)하는 경우에 그 동의가 근로자의 자유로운 의사에 터잡아 이루어진 것이라고 인정할 만한 합리적인 이유가 객관적으로 존재하는 때에는 근로기준법 제43조 제1항 본문에 위반하지 아니한다고 보아야 할 것이다. 다만 임금 전액지급의 원칙의 취지에 비추어 볼 때 그 동의가 근로자의 자유로운 의사에 기한 것이라는 판단은 엄격하고 신중하게 이루어져야 한다.라고 판시하고 있다.

2. 관련사례

(1) 연수비 상환의 경우
  기업체에서 비용을 부담 지출하여 직원을 해외에 파견하여 위탁교육을 시키고 이를 이수한 직원이 교육 수료일자로부터 일정한 의무재직기간 이상 근무하지 아니할 때에는 「기업체가 부담한 해당 교육비용의 전부 또는 일부를 상환하도록 할 수 있다. 따라서 해외 위탁교육을 받은 후 의무재직기간 동안 근무하는 경우에는 이를 면제하기로 한 기업체의 교육훈련규정」은 근로기준법 제20조에서 금지된 위약금 또는 손해배상예정의 약정은 아니다. 근로기준법 제7조가 금지하는 사용자가 정신 또는 신체상의 자유를 부당하게 구속하는 수단으로써 근로자의 자유의사에 반하는 근로를 강요하는 것이거나 같은 법 제21조가 금지하는 전차금 기타 근로할 것을 조건으로 하는 전대채권과 임금을 상계하기로 하는 내용의 것이 아니라고 볼 수 있다.[35]

(2) 상여금의 삭감
  기업의 경영상 어려움을 타개하기 위해서 노동조합과 합의를 통해서 상여금을

---
33) 대법원 1976. 9. 28. 선고 75다1768 판결
34) 대법원 2001. 10. 23. 선고 2001다25184 판결
35) 대법원 1992. 2. 25. 선고 91다26232 판결(대한항공)

consent, in the process of coping with the company's business difficulties. The MOEL has released guidelines for two different cases: bonuses already incurred and bonuses expected to be incurred. In cases where the employer intends to deduct from bonuses already incurred, which were paid in return for employee labor service, this is null and void even with labor union agreement or revision of company rules. In such cases, individual employee consent must be received. However, the employer reducing or deducting from bonuses expected in the near future is possible through revision of the collective agreement with labor union consent, or revision of the company rules after obtaining the consent from the labor union or the majority of employees. In such cases, receiving individual employee consent is not necessary.[36]

The courts have made rulings that align with this guideline. The wages (including bonuses) or severance benefits already incurred are considered the employee's private property, so unless the labor union receives individual employee agreement, it is not possible to deduct or delay those payments through a collective agreement. Accordingly, a collective agreement cannot require employees to reimburse payments already received, unless there is agreement from each individual employee.[37]

(3) Housing loans from the company

In cases where an employee resigns before he/she has reimbursed the company for a housing loan received from the company, if the employer deducts all unpaid debt in a lump sum from the severance benefits, this may be considered a violation of the principle of complete payment of wages. However, the courts have ruled in favor of lump sum deductions from severance benefits for the following reason: Since the collective agreement is the agreement to determine items occurring in labor and management relations, it can be a real expression of the intentions of both parties. It can also be admitted that the individual employee's voluntary decision and agreement make it possible to deduct wages instead of entering a formal claim for repayment of debts owed to the company by that employee. In view of these points, if the collective agreement was made justifiably and contains items permitting the requirement to reimburse unpaid loans, such a collective agreement does not violate the principle of complete payment of wages.[38]

---

[36] Ministry of Employment & Labor Guidelines: April 15, 1999, LSA 68207-587
[37] Supreme Court on January 28, 2010, 2009 Da 76317

삭감하거나 반납하는 경우가 있다. 이에 대해 고용노동부는 이미 발생한 근로에 대한 상여금과 앞으로 발생할 상여금을 구분하여 판단하고 있다. 이미 발생한 근로의 대가로서의 상여금을 삭감(반납)하는 경우에는 노동조합과의 합의 또는 회사규정의 개정만으로는 무효이고, 개별 근로자들의 동의가 있어야 한다. 그러나 앞으로의 근로조건으로서의 상여금을 삭감(하향조정)하는 경우에는 노동조합과의 합의를 거쳐 단체협약을 개정하거나 회사규정을 노조 또는 근로자 과반수의 동의를 얻어 변경하는 것으로 가능하며, 개별 근로자들의 동의는 필요하지 않다.[36]

법원에서도 동일하게 판단하고 있다. 이미 지급청구권이 발생한 임금(상여금 포함)이나 퇴직금은 근로자의 사적 재산영역으로 옮겨져 근로자의 처분에 맡겨진 것이어서, 노동조합이 근로자들로부터 개별적인 동의를 받지 않는 이상 사용자와 사이의 단체협약만으로 이에 대한 포기나 지급유예와 같은 처분행위를 할 수 없으므로, 단체협약으로 근로자에게 이미 지급한 임금을 반환하도록 하는 것은 그에 관하여 근로자들의 개별적인 동의가 없는 한 효력이 없다.[37]

(3) 주택자금 등 대출금의 경우

회사가 주택자금을 근로자에게 대여해주고, 일정액을 급여에서 상환하다가 중도에 퇴직하는 경우에는 사용자가 퇴직금에서 주택자금 미상환된 전체금액에 대해 공제하는 경우에 전액지급의 원칙에 위배되는지에 대한 문제가 있을 수 있다. 이에 대해 판례는 단체협약은 노동조합이 사용자 또는 사용자 단체와 근로조건 기타 노사관계에서 발생하는 사항에 관하여 체결하는 협정으로서 체결과정에 있어서도 그 진정성과 명확성이 담보되어 있다는 점과, 개별 근로자의 자유로운 의사에 터잡아 이루어진 동의가 있는 경우 사용자는 근로자에 대한 자동채권과 근로자의 임금채권을 상계할 수 있다는 점 등에 비추어 볼 때, 적법하게 체결된 단체협약이 사용자의 근로자에 대한 대출 원리금 등 채권 등을 공제할 수 있도록 규정하고 있도록 한 단체협약이 임금 전액지급 원칙에 위배되어 무효라고 볼 수 없다.라고 판시하면서 퇴직금에서 주택자금 대출금 공제를 인정하고 있다.[38]

---

[36] 고용노동부 행정해석: 1999. 4. 15. 근기 68207-587
[37] 대법원 2010. 1. 28. 선고 2009다76317 판결
[38] 대법원 2003. 6. 27. 선고 2003다7623 판결

IV. Conclusion

As in the cases given above, companies frequently deduct or require reimbursement for claims of illegal acts or other damages. Strictly speaking, this is a violation of the principle of complete payment of wages, which by law prevents the reduction of wages for general claims (debts) that an employee owes to his or her employer. Accordingly, if an employer deducts wages unilaterally to cover these claims, this deduction is invalid and makes the employer subject to punishment for violating the Labor Standards Act.

Section 3-3. Procedures for Wage Adjustments (Increases, Reductions, Freezes, Returns) and Related Cases

I. Introduction

Labor and management together can freely determine and adjust wages through labor contracts, employment rules, and collective agreements. So far, wage adjustment has been used to mean wage increase as wages have been increased every year due to inflation. However, as the coronavirus epidemic over the past year has caused enormous damage to all industries, many companies have overcome difficulties through other forms of wage adjustment, such as wage cuts, freezes, and returns. An employer unilaterally cutting wages has no effect. Reductions, freezes, or wage returns are unfavorable changes to working conditions, so legal procedures must be adhered to by the labor and management before taking such steps.

Wage cuts refer to reducing wages lower than existing levels for the same job and require collective consent of the affected workers. Wage freezes have the same effect as wage reductions when annual wage increases or service allowances are currently in place, and therefore require collective consent. However, deciding to keep the same wage as before without increasing wages does not require collective consent. Regarding wage returns, since wages are accrued in return for work

---

[38] Supreme Court on June 27, 2003, 2003 Da 7623

Ⅳ. 결론

앞에서 인용한 사례와 같이 일상적으로 근로자의 불법행위에 대한 배상채권이나 기타 손해배상 채권 등 에 대한 공제(변제)가 빈번하게 일어나고 있다. 하지만 이는 임금 지급의 전액지급 원칙을 위반하는 것이다. 임금 전액지급 원칙은 사용자가 가지는 근로자에게 가지는 일반채권을 일방적으로 임금채권에서 공제(상계)하는 것을 방지하기 위한 강행규정이기 때문이다. 따라서 사용자의 편의를 위해 사용자가 근로자에게 가지는 채권을 일방적으로 급여에서 공제하는 경우에 그 행위는 무효이고 근로기준법 위반으로 처벌의 대상이 될 수 있다는 것을 명심하여야 할 것이다.

제3-3절 임금조정 (인상, 삭감, 동결, 반납) 절차와 관련사례

Ⅰ. 문제의 소재

임금은 노사가 근로계약, 취업규칙, 단체협약을 통해 자유로운 의사로 결정하고, 조정할 수 있다. 지금까지 임금조정을 임금인상이라는 용어로 사용한 것은 물가인상으로 매년 임금이 인상되어 왔기 때문일 것이다. 그러나 지난 1년 동안 코로나 바이러스의 유행으로 전 산업에 막대한 피해를 줌으로써 많은 회사들이 임금 삭감, 동결, 반납과 같은 임금조정을 통해 노사가 어려움을 다같이 이겨내고 있다. 근로조건의 핵심인 임금은 노사가 협의하여 자유로이 결정하는 것으로 회사가 일방적으로 삭감하면 이는 무효가 된다. 임금인상이 아닌 임금의 삭감, 동결, 반납은 근로자에게 불리한 변경조건 이기에 노사의 적법한 절차를 거쳐야 한다.

임금삭감은 동일한 업무에 대해 기존 임금을 낮추는 것으로 대상 근로자의 집단 동의를 필요로 한다. 임금동결은 매년 호봉승급이나 근속수당의 임금인상 요인이 있는 경우에는 임금 삭감과 같은 효력이 있으므로 집단 동의를 필요로 한다. 그러나 호봉승급 없이 기존 임금과 동일하게 지급하는 경우에는 집단 동의가 필요 없다. 임금반납의 경우에는 기왕의 근로에 대한 대가로 발생한

already performed, those wages belong to individual workers, so the employer must obtain the consent of that individual worker. If the company deducts wages based only on collective consent, not individual consent, those deducted wages will be considered unpaid wages. The table below provides a brief summary of wage reductions, freezes and returns. In the next sections, I will review the related principles and related labor cases in detail.[39]

<Comparison of Wage Reductions, Freezes and Returns>

	Wage Reductions/Freezes	Wage returns
Target wage	Future wage	Wages already accrued
Method of implementation	Collective consent	Individual worker consent
Scope of effectiveness	All workers in same category	Individual workers with consent
Base wages for calculation of average wages	Wages paid after reduction or freeze	Wages paid before return

II. Wage Increases and Wage Reductions

Wage increases are decided through collective bargaining if there is a labor union. Wages have generally been raised every year through collective bargaining between labor and management, and if negotiations do not result in wage increases, the labor union increases the pressure through strikes. Employers generally increase their workers' wages to the minimum extent acceptable to the labor union. Wages can also be reduced through collective bargaining if the economy is bad or the company is in trouble. In this case, if the union consists of a majority of the workers concerned, non-union members are also affected by the wage adjustment concluded by the labor union due to the general binding force of the workplace (Article 35 of the Labor Union Act). In workplaces without a labor union, wage increases are determined unilaterally by the company within an appropriate range through changes to the employment rules or labor contract. However, since wage reductions are regarded as an unfavorable change working conditions, an agreement

---

[39] Ha, Gap-Rae, 「Labor Law」, 33rd ed., Joongang Economy, 2020, pp. 311-316; Labor Ministry Guidelines: Labor Standards Division-797, Mar. 26, 2009.

임금이므로 이는 개별근로자에게 귀속되어 있기 때문에 개별 근로자들의 동의를 받아야 한다.

개별동의가 아닌 집단 동의만 받고 임금을 공제하면 임금체불이 된다. 관련 내용은 아래 표와 같이 정리될 수 있으며, 실제 사례에 적용되는 원칙과 그 사례에 대해 구체적으로 살펴보고자 한다.[39]

<임금 삭감/동결과 반납 비교>

구 분	임금삭감/동결	임금반납
임금조정대상	장래의 임금	이미 발생한 임금
시행 방법	집단적 동의	개별 근로자 동의
효력 범위	동종 전체 근로자	동의한 개별 근로자
평균임금 기준	삭감/동결된 임금	반납하기 전 임금

Ⅱ. 임금인상 및 임금삭감

임금인상은 노동조합이 있는 경우 집단적 교섭을 통해 이루어진다. 노사협상을 통해 매년 임금을 인상해 왔고, 원만하게 인상되지 않는 경우 노동조합은 파업을 통해 협상력을 높여 임금인상을 한다. 사용자는 노동조합의 임금인상 요구에 수용가능한 만큼 임금인상을 하게 된다. 노동조합과 교섭을 통해 경기가 좋지 않거나 회사가 어려움에 처한 경우에는 임금삭감도 가능하다. 노동조합이 당해 사업장의 과반수로 구성되어 있는 경우에는 비조합원도 사업장 단위의 일반적 구속력(노동조합법 제35조)에 의해 임금인상이나 삭감도 당해 노동조합이 체결한 임금조정안을 적용 받는다. 노동조합이 없는 사업장의 경우에는 임금인상은 취업규칙이나 근로계약을 변경하는 방법으로 회사가 적정한 범위에서 일방적으로 결정한다. 다만, 임금삭감은 불이익한 근로조건으로의 변경이므로 노사간 협상을 통한 합의가 필요하다.

임금삭감은 종전보다 장래 일정시점 이후로 임금을 낮추어 지급하는 것이다. 기본급이나 각종 수당을 축소 또는 폐지하면서 임금지급 총액을 낮추게 된다.

---

[39] 하갑례, 「노동법」, 33판, 중앙경제, 2020, 311-316면. 행정해석: 근로기준과-797, 2009.3.26 참조

between labor and management is necessary.

Wage reductions refer to a lower wage than before being paid at a certain point in the future. The total wages paid is lowered by reducing or abolishing the basic wage and/or various allowances, with the process carried out in a manner decided in collective decision-making. If there is a majority union, this is done through a collective agreement, but if there is no majority union, it is necessary to go through the procedures required to make unfavorable changes to the employment rules. Even if labor and management have agreed, wages cannot be reduced below the minimum wage level, and additional rates or legal allowances (such as overtime/night/holiday work allowances, weekly holiday allowance, annual paid allowance, etc.) are not subject to reductions, in accordance with the Labor Standards Act.[40] Also, the reduced wage is not included in the calculation of average wage. Wage reductions are judged differently for each case. Here are some of these individual cases.

(1) Even if individual workers agree on a wage reduction, this cannot replace collective consent. Wage reductions involve paying less in the future for the same work that is currently provided, which makes them an unfavorable change to working conditions. In order for consent to a reduction in wages obtained from individual workers to be considered valid, the collective agreement must be changed according to required procedures.[41]

(2) In order to overcome a management crisis, a company significantly reduced its workforce and unilaterally stopped paying bonuses to workers who were retained. The fact that workers who were retained have continued to work without objection to the unilateral cessation of bonuses, does not mean that those workers have given up their right to claim future bonuses.[42]

(3) In accordance with the general binding force of Article 35 of the Labor Union Act, the effect of an agreement on wage reductions with a majority labor union also extends to non-union workers in the same kind of job in a workplace. However, if a separate contract for wages is signed for each worker, such as an annual salary contract, the individual worker's consent for a wage reduction is also required.[43] On the other hand, if the number of workers who were in the labor union at the time of the labor-management agreement on wage reduction did not reach a majority of the workers, the general binding force of Article 35 of the Labor Union Act cannot be granted.[44]

---

[40] Ministry Guidelines: Labor Standards Team-797, Mar. 26, 2009.
[41] Incheon District Court ruling on June 25, 2010: 2009 gahop 14735.
[42] Supreme Court ruling on June 11, 1999: 98da22185.
[43] Labor Ministry Guidelines: Industrial Relations Team-1112, Nov. 18, 2008.

임금삭감 절차는 집단적 의사결정 방식에 의해 이루어진다. 과반수의 노동조합이 있는 경우에는 단체협약을 통해서 이루어지지만, 과반수 노동조합이 없는 경우에는 취업규칙 불이익 변경절차를 거쳐야 한다. 노사가 합의하였다고 하더라도 최저임금 수준 이하로 삭감할 수 없고, 근로기준법에서 정한 할증률이나 지급의무를 규정하고 있는 법정수당 (연장/야간/휴일근로수당, 주휴수당, 연차수당 등)은 감액대상으로 할 수 없다.[40] 또한 삭감된 임금은 평균임금 산정시 포함되지 않는다. 임금삭감과 관련된 사례는 사안별로 달리 판단되며, 개별 사례는 다음과 같다.

(1) 임금삭감에 개별 근로자들이 동의하였다고 하더라도 이를 집단적 동의로 대체할 수 없다. 임금삭감은 장래 일정시점 이후부터 현재와 동일한 내용의 근로제공에 대하여 종전보다 임금을 낮추어서 지급하는 것으로, 이는 근로조건의 불이익변경에 해당한다. 단체협약에서 정한 임금의 삭감에 대한 근로자들의 동의가 유효하기 위하여는 단체협약 변경 절차를 거쳐야 한다.[41]

(2) 회사가 경영 위기 상황을 극복하기 위하여 직원을 대폭 감축하면서 회사에 잔류한 직원들에 대하여 일방적으로 상여금 지급을 중지하였고, 회사에 잔류한 근로자들이 그와 같은 조치에 관하여 별다른 이의 없이 근무하여 왔다는 사정만으로는 근로자들이 장래에 발생할 상여금청구권을 포기하였다고 볼 수 없다.[42]

(3) 단체협약은 노동조합법 제35조의 일반적 구속력에 따라 과반수로 구성된 노동조합과의 임금 삭감에 대한 합의의 효력은 동종의 비조합원 근로자에게도 미친다. 다만 연봉계약과 같이 근로자 개인별로 임금에 관한 별도의 계약을 체결했다면 임금삭감에 대한 개별 근로자의 동의도 필요하다.[43] 한편, 임금삭감에 대한 노사합의 당시 노동조합에 가입한 근로자 수가 근로자의 과반수에 이르지 못하였던 경우에는 노동조합법 제35조의 일반적 구속력을 부여할 수 없으므로 노동조합원이 아닌 근로자에게는 단체협약 변경의 효력이 미치지 않는다.[44]

---

[40] 행정해석: 근로기준과-797, 2009.3.26
[41] 인천지방법원 2010.6.25. 선고 2009가합14735 판결.
[42] 대법원 1999. 6. 11. 선고 98다22185 판결
[43] 노사관계법제과-1112, 2008.11.18
[44] 대법원 2005.5.12. 선고 2003다52456 판결.

(4) In changing the shift work system, reducing the shift from 4 groups/3 shifts to 3 groups/3 shifts is an unfavorable change for workers. Conversely, if the increase is from 3 groups/3 shifts to 4 groups/3 shifts, unless the contractual working hours are shortened or wages are reduced, it is not regarded as a disadvantageous change to working conditions, even though related wages or allowances are reduced due to the reduction in overtime work.[45]

(5) A change in the pay system can also lead to a reduction in wages. In cases where the amount of wages decreases from a reduction in the proportion of basic salary and an increase in the proportion of performance salary, the court considers it as a disadvantageous change in working conditions even though only some employees' wages decrease while the wages of most employees increase.[46]

(6) If the wage peak system is introduced within the statutory retirement age, it is a disadvantageous change in working conditions because it results in a reduction in wages for workers at that time.[47] In this case, if there is a labor union organized by a majority of workers, the consent of that labor union is required. Here, a union organized by a majority of workers refers to a union organized by a majority of all workers who are subject to the existing employment rules, regardless of the scope of union membership.[48]

Ⅲ. Wage Freezes

Freezing wages refers to keeping wages the same for future work as was paid for past work of the same type. In cases where a company regularly increases regular wage, ceasing or additionally restricting this regular increase in wage is an unfavorable change to working conditions. The company can freeze wages through amendment of the collective agreement or following the procedures for changing the employment rules disadvantageously. However, it is not a disadvantageous change to working conditions if wages are frozen when there is no regular salary increase.

(1) If the personnel regulations stipulate that regular increases occur on January 1st and July 1st of each year, and if the annual increase in salary has been carried out regularly and uniformly, this is considered to be a habitual wage

---

[44] Supreme Court ruling on May 12, 2005: 2003da 52456.
[45] Labor Ministry Guidelines: Labor Standards Team 68207-1732, Nov. 4, 1994.
[46] Supreme Court ruling on June 28, 2912: 2010da 17468.
[47] Suwon District Court ruling on June 23, 2017: 2016gadan 115485.
[48] Supreme Court ruling on February 29, 2008: 2007da 85997.

(4) 교대제를 변경함에 있어, 4조3교대를 3조3교대조로 근무조를 줄이는 것은 근로자에게 불리한 조건으로의 변경이다. 반대로 3조3교대에서 4조3교대로 근무조를 늘린다면, 소정근로시간이 단축되어 임금이 삭감되지 않는 한 연장근로 시간이 줄어들게 되므로 관련 임금이나 수당이 줄더라도 이를 불이익변경으로 보지 않는다.[45]

(5) 급여체계의 변경도 임금 삭감이 될 수 있다. 기본연봉의 비중을 줄이고 성과연봉의 비중을 높여 확정적으로 확보되었던 임금액수가 줄어드는 경우, 법원은 대다수 직원들의 임금이 증가하더라도 일부 직원들의 임금만이 감소하는 경우 불이익 변경으로 보고 있다.[46]

(6) 법정정년 이내에서 임금피크제를 도입하는 경우 해당 시점의 근로자들의 임금삭감을 가져오기 때문에 근로조건의 불이익 변경에 해당된다.[47] 만일 근로자의 과반수로 조직된 노동조합이 있는 경우에는 노동조합의 동의를 필요로 한다. 여기서 과반수로 조직된 노동조합이란 기존의 취업규칙의 적용을 받고 있던 근로자 중 조합원 자격 유무를 불문한 전체 근로자의 과반수로 조직된 노동조합을 의미한다.[48]

Ⅲ. 임금동결

임금동결은 동일한 내용의 근로제공에 대해 종전과 같은 임금을 지급하는 것을 말한다. 임금인상을 하지 않더라도 정기호봉승급이 있는 회사에서 승급을 제한하는 경우에는 근로조건의 불이익 변경으로 단체협약의 수정이나 취업규칙의 불이익 변경을 통해서 임금동결을 할 수 있다. 그러나 정기호봉승급이 없는 경우 임금을 동결하더라도 이는 근로조건의 불이익한 변경이 아니다.

(1) 인사규정에서 정기승급을 매년 1월 1일과 7월 1일에 실시하고 정기·일률적으로 호봉승급을 하여 왔다면 이는 임금지급과 관련하여 관행이 성립된 것으로 본다. 이 경우 근로자 집단적 의사결정방식에 의한 적법 절차를 거치지 아니하고 사용자가 일방적으로 정기승급을 동결하였다면

---

[45] 행정해석: 근로기준과 68207-1732, 1994.11.4.
[46] 대법원 2012.6.28. 선고 2010다17468 판결.
[47] 수원지방법원 안양지원 2017.6.23. 선고 2016가단115485 판결.
[48] 대법원 2008.2.29. 선고 2007다85997 판결.

practice. In this case, if the employer unilaterally freezes the regular increase without engaging with workers in the collective decision-making method, is the courts have deemed that the amount of regular increase that remains unpaid by the regular payment date each month as unpaid wages.[49]

(2) A certain school had financial difficulties, and the principal explained the situation to teachers at a school affairs meeting, suggested that the basic salary increase for general school teachers be frozen that year. The teachers present did not object at the time to this. However, this lack of objection at the meeting with the teachers cannot be considered the same as obtaining collective consent.[50]

Ⅳ. Wage Returns

Wage returns refer to the return of wage bonds (wages, bonuses, etc.) already incurred for previous work based on the free-will consent of the individual worker. Due to the waiver of the right to claim wages that occurred legally, wages can only be returned through due process. Since a unilaterally-determined wage deduction by the employer violates the principle of paying full wages, individual workers' written consent is required.[51] However, even in this case, any waiver of the right to claim severance pay is invalid because it violates the Labor Standards Act.[52]

For procedures to be deemed reasonable, individual workers' consent is required. Since the return of wages is effective only if it is the individual workers' voluntary decision, individual workers must recognize the purpose of wage returns and sign a return consent form in their own name.[53] While the court holds that it is desirable to obtain consent for each individual worker when returning wages, it is also possible to obtain individual consent by having workers sign a name list of workers if the company has sufficiently explained the difficult situation to the workers.[54] An agreement to return wages in the collective agreement has no effect. This is because the return of wages involves wages that already belong to

---

[49] Labor Ministry Guideline: Wage 68200-649, December 5, 2000
[50] Supreme Court ruling on June 9, 2005: 2005do 1089.
[51] Article 43 of the Labor Standards Act (Wage Payment) and Supreme Court ruling June 11, 1996: 98da22185 Waiver of wage claims is recognized as a clear expression of the employee's intention.
[52] Supreme Court ruling July 26, 2002: 2000da27671.
[53] Labor Ministry Guidelines: Labor Standards Team 68207-843, Dec. 13, 1999.
[54] Supreme Court ruling on Sep. 29, 2000: 99da67536.

각 근로자별 정기승급이 이루어지는 달의 임금 정기지급일에 정기승급으로 인하여 가산되는 임금이 전액 지급되지 아니한 것으로 본다.[49]

(2) 학교가 재정적 어려움에 시달리던 중 피고인은 신학기 교무회의에서 교사들에게 사정을 설명하고 올해에는 호봉인상은 하되 일반학교 교사들의 본봉을 기준으로 하는 기본급(본봉) 인상은 동결하자고 제의하였고, 그 자리에 참석한 교사들은 이에 대하여 아무런 이의를 제기하지 아니하였다. 이와 같이 사용자인 피고인이 참석한 상태에서 기본급의 동결을 제의하여 이에 대한 교사들의 의견을 묻는 방식으로 회의가 진행되었고 이에 대해 교사들이 이의를 제기하지 아니하였다고 하여 근로자들의 동의가 있었다고 볼 수는 없다.[50]

Ⅳ. 임금반납

임금반납은 기왕의 근로에 의해 이미 발생된 임금채권(임금, 상여금 등)을 개별근로자의 자유의사에 따른 동의를 바탕으로 반납하는 것을 말한다. 적법하게 발생한 임금청구권의 포기로써 적법 절차를 통해서만 임금반납은 가능하다. 사용자의 일방적 임금공제는 임금의 전액 부지급원칙을 위반하기 때문에 개별 근로자의 서면동의가 필요하다.[51] 특히, 퇴직금 청구권의 포기는 근로기준법 위반이 되어 무효이다.[52]

합당한 절차를 밟기 위해서는 개별 근로자의 동의서가 필요하다. 임금반납은 개별 근로자의 자유의사에 기초할 때만 유효하므로 반드시 개별 근로자들이 임금 반납의 취지를 인식하고 반납동의서를 개별 명의로 작성해야 한다.[53] 다만, 법원은 임금반납 시 개별 근로자 각각의 동의서를 받는 것이 바람직하나 회사가 어려운 사정을 근로자에게 충분히 설명했다면 회람 형식으로 동의 여부를 표시하도록 하는 방식을 취하는 것도 가능하다는 입장이다.[54] 단체

---

[49] 행정해석, 임금 68200-649, 2000.12.5
[50] 대법원 2005.6.9. 선고 2005도1089 판결.
[51] 근로기준법 제43조(임금지급 원칙)과 대법원 1996.6.11. 선고 98다22185 판결: 근로자의 명백한 의사표시로서 임금채권포기는 인정된다.
[52] 대법원 2002.7.26 선고 2000다27671 판결.
[53] 행정해석, 근기68207-843, 1999.12.13.
[54] 대법원 2000.9.29. 선고 99다67536 판결.

individual workers, and the union cannot be forced to abandon individual member property rights. Wages returned by workers come from the workers' income and are returned voluntarily, and the employer is not obligated to return them again to the worker.[55] Returned wages are included in the calculation of average wages as they are wage bonds that were given to the employee and then returned to the employer by the employee.[56] Examples of cases where a return of wages was not recognized:

(1) To waive unpaid wages for which individual workers have the right to claim payment due to the arrival of the payment period, a collective agreement with the labor union is not enough for the workers to be deemed to have agreed to waive the unpaid wages. It can only be done to the extent that the company has received individual and explicit consent from the workers in advance to waive their right to the unpaid wages. Even if a labor union agrees to give up some worker wages in the collective agreement or through labor-management consultations, this has no effect on labor union members who have not individually consented.[57]

(2) Even if wages and bonuses are returned in accordance with a revised collective agreement, if a worker does not individually consent to the return of wages and bonuses incurred by his/her previous work, that worker shall not have their wages returned. If the workers who did not agree to the return of wages and bonuses later resigned after those wages/bonuses were deducted without their individual consent, those returned wages will be considered unpaid wages.[58]

(3) Daegu 00 Company gave a donation to help Daegu citizens suffering from the corona pandemic in April 2020 by resolution of its labor-management council. It then informed the employees of the council's decision, and deducted KRW 10,000 from each individual. In response, the new labor union filed a complaint with the Daegu Labor Office for violation of Article 43 (Wage Payment) of the Labor Standards Act as these wages were deducted without the individual consent of the workers. The company then requested individual consent from all the workers, but only 50% agreed, so the deducted wages had to be returned to those workers who did not submit individual consent forms.[59]

---

[55] Seoul District Court ruling on Apr. 16, 2003: 2002na 20291.
[56] Supreme Court ruling on Apr. 10, 2001: 99da39531.
[57] Jeonju District Court ruling on Apr. 26, 2000: 99na5708.
[58] Labor Ministry Guidelines: Unemployment 68430-84, Oct. 21, 1999.

협약에 의한 임금반납 합의는 효력이 없다. 임금반납은 이미 조합원 개인에게 귀속된 임금에 대한 것이므로 노동조합이 조합원 개인 재산권을 포기하도록 할 수 없기 때문이다. 근로자가 반납한 임금은 근로자의 소득으로 귀속되었다가 자진 반납한 것으로써 사용자는 반환할 의무가 없다.[55] 다만, 반납된 임금도 평균임금 산정에 포함된다. 반납된 임금은 일단 근로자의 소득으로 귀속되었다가 반납한 임금채권이기에 평균임금 산정에 포함해야 한다.[56] 임금반납으로 효력을 인정받지 못하는 사례는 다음과 같다.

(1) 지급시기가 도래하여 개개의 근로자에게 지급청구권이 발생한 체불임금의 포기에 대해서는 회사가 노동조합과의 단체협약으로 체불임금 포기를 수용한 것만으로는 부족하고 각 근로자로부터 사전에 개별적이고 명시적인 포기권한을 받은 한도에서만 할 수 있다고 할 것이다. 이러한 포기권한 없이 노동조합이 단체협약이나 노사협의 등 집단합의 방식에 따라 근로자의 임금을 사전 또는 사후에 포기하더라도 조합원인 근로자에게는 아무런 효력이 미치지 않는다.[57]

(2) 개정된 단체협약에 의하여 임금과 상여금을 반납하였다고 하더라도 기왕의 근로에 의하여 발생한 임금과 상여금 반납에 대해 당해 근로자가 개별적으로 동의하지 않은 경우 당해 근로자에 대해서는 적용할 수 없다. 이직한 근로자들이 임금과 상여금 반납에 동의하지 않았다면, 기왕의 근로에 의하여 발생한 임금이 체불된 것으로 볼 수 있다.[58]

(3) 대구○○회사는 2020년 4월 코로나 역병으로 인해 고통받는 대구시민 돕기 성금을 납부하기로 노사협의회에서 결정하고, 직원들에게 통보한 후 개인별로 10,000원을 공제하여 기부하였다. 이에 대해 최근에 생긴 신설노동조합은 근로자들의 개별동의 없이 임금을 공제하였기 때문에 이는 근로기준법 제43조(임금지급원칙)을 위반하였다고 회사를 대구노동청에 고소하였다. 회사는 이에 대해 개별근로자들의 동의를 요청하였으나 50% 정도 밖에 동의하지 않아 개별동의서를 제출하지 않은 근로자들에게는 공제된 임금을 반환하여야만 했다.[59]

---

[55] 서울지방법원 2003.4.16. 선고 2002나20291 판결.
[56] 대법원 2001.4.10. 선고 99다39531 판결.
[57] 전주지방법원 2000.4.26. 선고 99나5708 판결.
[58] 행정해석: 실업 68430-84, 1999.10.21.
[59] 대구노동청은 행정해석 (근기68207-843, 1999.12.13.)과 같이 위법한 임금반납으로 판단함.

Chapter3-3. Wages

(4) If each worker agrees to return the allowance for unused annual leave that has occurred, it cannot be considered a violation of the law if the employer does not pay an allowance within the agreed range for unused annual leave. However, if the return of unused annual leave allowance agreed upon by the worker also applies to leave that will occur in the future, procedures must be followed that allow a collective agreement or the employment rules to be changed disadvantageously.[60]

V. Conclusion

To overcome difficulties due to the COVID-19 pandemic, company management is increasingly working with labor to have wages returned or have them reduced or frozen. In such cases, it is necessary to understand and prepare in advance because the legal outcomes vary. The return of bonuses or other allowances is to return the wages vested to the worker for previous work and requires written consent from the individual worker. If the company handles a wage return through the labor union, the problem of delayed payment of wages arises. Wage reductions mean less in wages in the future, so even if management comes to an agreement with individual workers, wage cuts are invalid unless procedures are followed to make a disadvantageous change to the employment rules or collective agreement. Therefore, for wages to be reduced, employment rules and collective agreements must be changed through collective consent rather than individual worker consent. And in particular, according to the principle of favorable conditions, unexpected problems may arise, so it is necessary to change both the labor contract and the employment rules to prevent future disputes.

Section 3-4. Obligation to Issue Pay Slips

Article 48 of the Labor Standards Act was amended November 19, 2021, requiring that employers (companies) issue pay slips to employees when paying wages. This regulation also applies to workplaces with fewer than five employees,

---

[59] Daegu Labor Office decided this deduction was illegal. Related Labor Ministry Guidelines: Labor Standards-68207-843, Dec. 13, 1999.
[60] Labor Ministry Guidelines: Labor Standards 684207-871, Mar. 23, 2000.

(4) 근로자 각자가 기발생한 미사용 연차휴가에 대한 수당을 반납하는데 동의하였다면 당해 근로자에게 동의한 범위내에서 미사용 연차휴가에 대한 수당을 지급하지 않더라도 이를 법 위반이라 볼 수는 없다. 그러나 근로자가 동의한 미사용연차휴가 반납이 향후 발생할 휴가에도 해당될 경우에는 단체협약이나 취업규칙의 불이익 변경 절차를 거쳐야 한다.[60]

V. 결론

코로나 대유행으로 회사의 어려움을 노사가 함께 타개하기 위하여 회사에서는 임금을 반납하거나 삭감하거나 동결하는 일이 많아지고 있다. 이 경우 사안별로 법률적인 판단이 달라지기 때문에 이에 대한 사전 이해와 준비가 필요하다. 상여금이나 기타수당의 반납은 기왕의 근로에 대해 근로자에게 귀속된 임금을 반환하는 것으로 개별근로자의 서면동의를 필요로 한다. 집단적 동의로 진행하게 되면 임금체불의 문제가 발생한다. 임금삭감은 미래에 발생할 임금을 삭감하는 것이므로 개별근로자와 동의하더라도 취업규칙의 불이익 변경이나 단체협약을 변경하지 않으면 임금삭감의 효력을 가질 수 없다. 따라서 임금삭감을 할 경우에는 반드시 개별근로자들의 동의가 아니라 집단적 동의를 통해 취업규칙과 단체협약을 모두 변경해야 한다. 특히 유리한 조건우선의 원칙에 따라 예상하지 못한 문제가 발생할 수 있으므로 근로계약과 취업규칙을 모두 변경해야 차후 발생할 수 있는 분쟁을 사전에 예방할 수 있다.

제3-4절 임금명세서 교부의무

2021년 11월 19일부터 근로기준법 제48조가 개정되어, 사용자(회사)는 근로자에게 임금을 지급하는 때에 근로자에게 반드시 임금명세서를 교부하여야 한다. 해당 규정은 5인 미만 사업장의 경우에도 적용되므로 아르바이트 1명

---

[60] 행정해석: 근기 684207-871, 2000.3.23.

meaning that even one part-time worker must receive a pay slip (pay stub). In order to ensure that employees have been paid as much as they actually worked, and also as originally contracted with the employer, employers are required to write down information on how they calculate the wage as well as the total amount.The following items need to be stated in the pay slip:

1. Information that can identify the relevant employee, such as the employee's name, date of birth, and employee ID number;
2. Date wages are being paid;
3. Total amount paid;
4. Items of Wage Structure: The basic salary, all allowances separately, bonuses (including performance-based) separately, and other wage items (if wages are paid by means of valuable goods other than money, the name, quantity, and total assessed value of the goods must be itemized);
5. Calculation of the items of Wage Structure: Methods for calculating the amount of each wage item (including the working hours for any overtime duty, night duty, or holiday duty), if the amount of each wage item changes according to the number of working days, working hours, etc.;
6. Details of deductions, including the amount of each deduction and the total amount of deductions, under the proviso of Article 43 (1) of the Act in cases of partial deduction of wages.

A wage statement can be provided not only in written form but also as an electronic document. In this context, an "electronic document" refers to information that is created, converted, transmitted, received, or stored in electronic form by an information processing system (as defined in Article 2, Paragraph 1 of the Framework Act on Electronic Documents and Transactions). Typical examples include emails and mobile phone text messages. Therefore, wage statements can be delivered not only via written documents but also through emails or text messages.

An employer who violates this obligation to issue a pay slip may be subject to a fine of not more than KRW 5 million (Article 116 (2) of the Labor Standards Act). Attached Table 7 of the Enforcement Decree of the Labor Standards Act sets the standard for imposing fines for violations of the obligation to issue pay slips. The fines are imposed on the employer for each worker, so care must be taken.

만을 고용하고 있다고 하더라도 급여명세서(임금명세서)는 교부하여야 한다. 근로자들이 사용자와 처음에 계약한 대로 일한 만큼 급여가 지급되었는지 확인할 수 있도록 총액뿐만 아니라 급여의 계산 방식 등과 관련한 정보를 적도록 하고 있다. 임금명세서에 기재해야할 내용은 다음과 같다.

1. 근로자를 특정할 수 있는 정보 : 성명, 생년월일, 사원번호 등 정보를 기재해야 한다. 성명만으로도 근로자를 특정할 수 있다면 성명만 기재하는 것도 가능하다. 다만 사업장 내 동명이인이 존재하는 경우에는 성명 이외에도 생년월일 등 기재해야 한다.
2. 임금 지급일 : 근로계약서 등에서 근로자에게 임금을 지급하기로 정한 날 즉, 임금지급일을 기재해야 한다.
3. 임금 총액 : 근로소득세 등 세금을 공제하기 이전 임금 총액을 기재하여야 하며, 공제 후 실지급액을 함께 기재하는 것이 바람직하다.
4. 임금의 구성항목별 금액 : 기본급, 연장근로수당 및 각종 수당 등 임금을 구성하는 항목과 그 금액을 기재해야 한다.
5. 임금의 구성항목별 계산 방법 : 기재한 임금 구성항목과 그 금액이 어떻게 산출되었는지에 관한 계산식 또는 계산방법을 기재해야 한다.
6. 공제항목별 금액 및 총액 등 공제내역 : 근로소득세, 사회보험료 근로자 부담분 등 임금총액에서 공제항목과 공제항목별 금액을 모두 기재해야 한다. 다만, 공제와 관련된 계산방법은 기재하지 않을 수 있다.

임금명세서는 서면 뿐만 아니라 전자문서로 교부할 수 있다. 이 때, '전자문서'란 정보처리시스템에 의하여 전자적 형태로 작성, 변환되거나 송신·수신 또는 저장된 정보를 의미하는데(전자문서 및 전자거래 기본법 제2조제1호), 대표적으로 이메일과 휴대전화 문자메시지가 이에 해당한다. 따라서, 서면으로 된 문서 뿐만 아니라 이메일 또는 문자메시지 등으로도 임금명세서를 교부하는 것이 가능한다. 임금명세서 교부 의무를 위반한 사용자에게는 500만원 이하의 과태료가 부과될 수 있다(근로기준법 제116조제2항). 근로기준법 시행령 별표 7에서는 임금명세서 지급과 관련한 법률 위반행위 및 횟수에 따른 과태료 부과기준을 두고 있으며, 근로자 1인 각각을 기준으로 과태료를 부과하도록 하고 있으므로 주의를 기울여야 한다.

Chapter3-3. Wages

Section 3-5. Corona Virus Infections and Shut-down Allowances

I. Introduction

The spread of coronavirus infections has severely hampered business activity. All areas where an infected person has been are temporarily closed and infected individuals are quarantined. The Seoul Lotte Department Store was closed for a period of time, and the Gwangju Post Office was temporarily closed and then reopened. There are reports that Samsung Electronics in Gumi, North Gyungsang province might be temporarily closed. When a workplace is shut down and closed, it is difficult for the workers to survive, so the Labor Standards Act guarantees a wage of 70% on average as a shut-down allowance in case of closure for reasons attributable to the employer. It is possible to reduce a shut-down allowance if there is a huge disruption to the operation of the business to the point where the employer cannot continue to operate. In addition, the Civil Act states that if a worker is suspended due to the intention or negligence of an employer, the full wage shall be paid (Article 538), but if the business is closed through no fault of the employer, the shut-down allowance shall not be paid (Article 537). Payments can be divided into: (i) 100% pay, (ii) payment of shut-down allowances, (iii) reduction of shut-down allowances, and (iv) unpaid leave.

Here, I would like to explain the legal stipulations of shut-down allowances in accordance with the spread of coronavirus infections and to examine related cases in detail.

II. Spread of Coronavirus Infection and Companies' Countermeasures

1. The spread of coronavirus infections

Coronavirus infection is a respiratory infection caused by a new type of coronavirus that has spread worldwide since first being discovered in Wuhan, China in December 2019. It is spread when it penetrates an infected person's saliva, respiratory tract, or the mucous membranes of the eyes, nose, or mouth. After infection, the incubation period is 2-14 days (estimated), followed by a fever (above 37.5 degrees), respiratory symptoms such as coughing and difficulty breathing, and pneumonia.[61] On January 31, 2020, the Ministry of Employment and

제3-5절 코로나바이러스의 감염 확산과 휴업수당

Ⅰ. 문제의 소재

코로나바이러스 감염증이 확산되고 있어 기업활동에 상당한 지장을 주고 있다. 확진자가 지나간 동선이 모두 일시적으로 폐쇄되고 감염된 개인들이 격리되고 있다. 서울 롯데백화점 본점이 일정기간 폐쇄되었고, 광주우체국 집중국이 일시적으로 폐쇄되었다가 재개장 되기도 하였다. 경북 구미의 삼성전자도 확진자가 나와 공장을 일시적으로 폐쇄한다는 보도가 나오고 있다. 사업장이 폐쇄되고 공장가동을 중단하게 되면 거기서 근무하는 근로자의 생계가 어려워지기 때문에 근로기준법에서는 사용자의 귀책사유로 휴업하는 경우, 평균임금의 70%를 급여로 보장하고 있다. 또한, 사업주 입장에서도 사업 지속이 불가능할 정도로 기업운영에 막대한 지장이 있는 경우 휴업수당을 감액하는 것도 가능하다. 민법에서는 사용자의 고의 과실로 인하여 근로자가 휴업하는 경우 임금 전액을 지급해야 하고(제538조), 사용자의 귀책사유가 없이 휴업하는 경우에는 휴업수당을 지급하지 않아도 된다고 기술하고 있다 (제537조). 즉, (i) 임금 100% 지급, (ii) 휴업수당 지급, (iii) 휴업수당 감액, (iv) 무급 휴업을 하는 경우로 구분해 볼 수 있다.

이번 호에서는 코로나바이러스 감염 확산에 따른 휴업수당의 법적기준을 이해하고, 관련된 사례에 대해 구체적으로 살펴 보고자 한다.

Ⅱ. 코로나바이러스 감염의 확산과 기업의 대응방안

1. 코로나바이러스 감염의 확산

코로나바이러스 감염은 2019년 12월 중국 우한에서 처음 발생한 뒤 전 세계로 확산된, 새로운 유형의 바이러스에 의한 호흡기 감염질환이다. 감염자의 침이 호흡기나 눈, 코, 입의 점막으로 침투될 때 전염된다. 감염되면 2~14일(추정)의 잠복기를 거친 뒤 발열(37.5도 이상) 및 기침이나 호흡곤란 등 호흡기 증상, 폐렴이 주된 증상으로 나타난다.[61] 2020년 1월 31일 발표된 고용노동부의

Labor applied Class 1 Infectious Disease Syndrome to coronaviruses in its Workplace Guidelines for the Prevention from Spread of Coronavirus Infections. According to Article 2 (Definition) of the Infectious Disease Control and Prevention Act (IDPA), Class 1 Infectious Diseases have a high mortality rate or a high risk of group outbreaks, so they should be reported immediately and require high-level quarantine, such as special isolation wards. Therefore, infected patients with first-degree infection should be hospitalized by an infectious disease management institution (Article 41 of the IDPA). Since no vaccines or treatments have been developed to date, hospitals are providing antiviral drugs or antibiotics to prevent secondary infections.

2. Companies' countermeasures

(1) In case of individual infection: If an employee is infected during his personal activities, he/she will be quarantined and treated according to the relative infectious disease prevention method, and in case of suspension, there will be certain financial support in the government (Article 41 of the IDPA). In similar cases to this, it has been held as a principle that any absence would be considered unpaid leave because it was attributed to personal fault. However, if an employee is infected during a business trip, this is considered to be a work-related illness under the Industrial Accident Compensation Insurance Act (Article 34 of the Enforcement Decree of the Act).

(2) Shut-downs due to the presence of an infected person: If an infected person caught the infection at the workplace and the workplace is closed in order to prevent spread of the disease, this may not be regarded as attributable to the employer, and may be an exception to the payment of shut-down allowances.

(3) Closed to prevent infection: If an employer shuts down a workplace to prevent the spread of an infectious disease according to the law and the government's instructions, this may be considered an exception to the shut-down allowance. However, in the event of shut-down in order to prevent infection, shut-down allowance shall be paid.

(4) In case of shut-downs due to the lack of raw materials caused by the coronavirus: Shut-down allowances shall be paid. However, in case of a long-term shut-down, which causes enormous disruption to business operations, shut-down allowances may not be paid with the approval of the Labor Relations Commission (Article 46 of the LSA - Paragraph 2).

---

[61] Naver Encyclopedia, Coronavirus Infectious Disease (COVID-19), checked on February 23, 2020: The official name COVID-19 stands for Co Corona, VI Virus, D Disease, and 19 for the first reported year 2019.

사업장 대응지침에서는 코로나바이러스에 대해 제1급 감염병 증후군을 적용하고 있다. 감염병예방법 제2조 (정의)에 따르면, 제1급 감염병이란 치사율이 높거나 집단 발생의 우려가 커서 발생 즉시 신고하여야 하고, 음압격리(특수 격리 병실)와 같은 높은 수준의 격리가 필요한 감염병이다. 따라서 제1급 감염병에 걸린 감염병환자는 감염병관리기관에서 입원치료를 받아야 한다(동법 제41조). 현재까지 치료를 위한 백신이나 치료제가 개발되지 않았기 때문에 병원에서는 바이러스 공격에 버틸 수 있도록 항 바이러스제나 2차 감염 예방을 위한 항생제 투여 등의 치료를 실시하고 있다.

2. 기업의 사례별 대응방안

(1) 감염자 개인의 경우: 근로자가 개인 활동을 하던 중 감염된 경우에는 감염병예방법에 따라 격리되어 치료를 받게 되고 이때 휴업한 경우에는 국가에서 일정한 지원이 되지만(감염증예방법 제41조), 근로자의 본인의 귀책 사유이므로 무급이 원칙이다. 다만, 근로자가 업무상 출장 중에 발생한 감염된 경우에는 업무상 질병으로 산재보험법에 따라 업무상 질병으로 간주된다(산재법 시행령 제34조).

(2) 감염자 발생으로 휴업한 경우: 회사내에서 감염자가 발생하여 확산을 막기 위해 해당 사업장이 휴업하는 경우에는 사용자의 귀책사유라 볼 수 없기 때문에 휴업수당의 지급의 예외사유가 될 수 있다.

(3) 감염을 예방하기 위해 휴업한 경우: 사용자가 법령과 정부의 지시에 따라 감염병의 예방과 확산을 위해 사업장을 폐쇄하고 감염을 예방하는 경우에는 휴업수당 지급의 예외 사유가 될 수 있으나, 단지 감염을 예방하는 차원에서 휴업하는 경우에는 휴업수당을 지급하여야 할 것이다.

(4) 코로나바이러스로 인하여 원자재 부족으로 휴업한 경우: 원자재 부족으로 휴업한 경우에는 휴업수당을 지급하여야 할 것이다. 그러나 장기간 휴업으로 인하여 사업에 막대한 지장을 초래할 경우에는 노동위원회의 승인을 받아 휴업수당을 지급하지 않을 수 있다(근기법 제46조 제2항).

---

61) 네이버 지식백과, 코로나바이러스 감염증(COVID-19), 2020.2.23. 검색: 공식명칭인 COVID-19는 Co Corona, VI Virus, D Disease, 19는 처음 보고된 2019년을 의미한다.

III. Legal Standards of Shut-down Allowances

1. Concept

According to the Labor Standards Act, when a worker is suspended for reasons attributable to the employer, the employer shall be required to pay at least 70% of the average wage (or 100% of the ordinary wage) (Article 46 (1)). However, if it is impossible to continue the business for unavoidable reasons, an amount that is less than the legal shut-down allowance may be paid if this is approved by the Labor Commission (Article 46 (1)). In order to guarantee the effectiveness of the shut-down compensation system, an employer who violates the provisions of shut-down compensation shall be sentenced to imprisonment of not more than three years or fined not more than KRW 30 million (Article 109).

Shut-down allowances are intended to guarantee workers' right to live by providing certain allowances when they are unable to work for reasons not attributable to them. On the other hand, if an employer is forced, for unavoidable reasons, to pay legal shut-down allowances until the business can no longer continue, this will cause excessive burden on the employer and will severely hinder operations, which may result in the insolvency of the company. This is why an exemption for shut-down compensation is stipulated.[62]

'Shut-down' refers to a situation in which a worker is unable to provide work against his/her will despite being willing to provide the work under the employment contract.[63] Civil Act provisions relating to the shut-down of a business provide exemption of employer fault in case of a force majeure beyond the employer's responsibility.[64] However, if an employee fails to receive work due to the employer's fault, it is possible to claim the full amount of wages, and not just the shut-down allowance.[65] In cases like this, the Civil Act provisions have difficulty

---

[62] Lim Jong-Ryul, Labor Law, 17th edition, Park Young-sa, 2019, p. 422; Jung Myung-hyun, Duality of Legal Characteristics for Shut-down Allowance, Justice Magazine (147), Korea Law Institute, April 2015, p. 253.

[63] Supreme Court ruling on Oct. 11, 2012: 2012da12870.

[64] Civil Act: Article 537 (Obligor's Burden to Bear Risk)
If the performance of an obligation of one of the parties to a bilateral contract becomes impossible by any cause for which neither of the parties is responsible, the obligor may not be entitled to counter-performance.

[65] Article 538(Impossibility of Performance due to Cause for Which Obligee is Responsible)
(1) If the performance of an obligation of one of the parties to a bilateral contract becomes impossible by any cause for which the obligee is responsible, the obligor may demand counter-performance. The same applies to cases where performance becomes impossible by any cause for which neither of the parties is responsible in the case of mora creditoris.(2) In the cases of the preceding paragraph if the obligor has received any benefit by being relieved of his own obligation, he shall return such benefit

Ⅲ. 휴업수당의 법적 기준

1. 의의

　근로기준법에서는 사용자의 귀책사유로 휴업하는 경우에는 그 근로자에게 평균임금의 100분의 70% 이상의 수당(또는 통상임금의 100%)을 지급하여야 한다(제46조 제1항). 다만, 부득이한 사유로 사업을 계속하는 것이 불가능하여 노동위원회의 승인을 받은 경우에는 법정휴업수당에 미달하는 수당을 지급할 수 있다고 규정하고 있다(제46조 제1항). 휴업보상제도의 실효성을 보장하기 위하여 휴업보상 지급규정을 위반한 자는 3년 이하의 징역 또는 3천만 원 이하의 벌금에 처한다고 규정하고 있다(제109조).

　휴업수당은 근로자의 귀책사유가 아닌 이유로 근로를 할 수 없게 된 경우에 일정한 수당을 근로자에게 지급하여 근로자의 생존권을 보장하는데 그 취지가 있다. 이와 함께 사용자가 부득이한 사유로 사업계속이 불가능한 경우까지 법정휴업수당 지급을 강제한다면 사용자에게 지나친 부담을 주어 기업의 운영에 막대한 지장을 초래하여 기업의 파산을 촉진하는 결과까지 초래할 수 있다는 점을 고려한 휴업보상에의 감면규정을 두고 있다.[62]

　'휴업'이란 근로자가 근로계약에 따라 근로를 제공할 의사가 있음에도 불구하고 그 의사에 반하여 근로를 제공하지 못하는 경우를 말한다.[63] 휴업과 관련된 민법 조항은 사용자의 귀책사유가 없는 불가항력적인 사항으로 근로를 수령하지 못한 경우에 책임을 면한다고 규정하고 있다.[64] 그러나 사용자의 책임있는 사유로 근로를 이행하지 못한 경우에는 휴업수당이 아니라 사용자에게 임금 전액을 청구할 수 있다고 규정하고 있다.[65] 이 경우 민법 조항은 사용자의 고의나 과실 등을 증명해야 하는 어려움이 있기 때문에 민법상 위험

---

[62] 임종률, 노동법 제17판, 박영사, 2019, 422면; 정명현, 휴업수당의 법적 성질의 이중성, 저스티스 147, 한국법학원, 2015.4. 253면.
[63] 대법원 2012.10.11. 선고 2012다12870 판결.
[64] 민법 제537조【채무자위험부담주의】쌍무계약의 당사자일방의 채무가 당사자쌍방의 책임없는 사유로 이행할 수 없게 된 때에는 채무자는 상대방의 이행을 청구하지 못한다.
[65] 민법 제538조【채권자귀책사유로 인한 이행불능】① 쌍무계약의 당사자일방의 채무가 채권자의 책임있는 사유로 이행할 수 없게 된 때에는 채무자는 상대방의 이행을 청구할 수 있다. 채권자의 수령지체중에 당사자 쌍방의 책임없는 사유로 이행할 수 없게 된 때에도 같다.② 전항의 경우에 채무자는 자기의 채무를 면함으로써 이익을 얻은 때에는 이를 채권자에게 상환하여야 한다.

in proving the employer's intention or negligence, so the Labor Standards Act provides a shut-down allowance system to guarantee the minimum life standards of workers without relying on the Civil Act's risk-bearing principle.[66]

2. Requirements for shut-down allowance

As a requirement for shut-down,
first, there must be fault attributable to the employer. Employer's fault is any reason that may arise within the employer's managerial influence.
Second, the business should not be closed due to force majeure. Force majeure means that the reason for the shut-down of a business should occur from outside and the employer could do nothing to control it. Typical examples would be natural disasters, war, and large regional blackouts.
Third, it is assumed that shut-down (full or partial closure) has taken place.

3. Amount of Suspension Allowances

(1) Full payment of wages

In case of a shut-down due to an employer's intention or negligence, the full wage shall be paid. This includes suspension without legitimate reason, forced leave, and unfair dismissal. In accordance with Article 538 (1) of the Civil Act, the employer shall pay 100% of wages, not shut-down allowances, when workers are suspended due to illegal activity by the employer. However, an interim benefit obtained during the same period may be deducted pursuant to paragraph 2 of Article 538 of the Civil Act.[67]

(2) Shut-down Allowances

In case of shut-down due to an employer's fault, an allowance shall be paid of at least 70% of the average wage. In principle, employer's fault is a management obstacle that occurs within the scope of the employer's power and will include situations such as being closed due to shortage of funds, shortage of raw materials, decrease in order volume, reduction of market and output, shortage of raw materials in subcontracted factories due to the parent company's poor management, or shortage of operations due to insufficient funds.[68] A partial shut-down allowance

---
to the obligee.
[66] Labor Law Case Study Group, Interpretation of the Labor Standards Act (III), 2nd ed. Parkyoungsa, 2020, p. 121.
[67] Supreme Court ruling on June 28, 1991: 90daka25277 (Damage compensation).

2. 휴업수당의 지급요건

휴업의 요건으로
첫째, 사용자의 귀책사유가 있어야 한다. 사용자의 귀책사유는 사용자의 세력권 내에서 발생할 수 있는 모든 사유를 말한다.
둘째, 불가항력으로 인한 휴업이 아니어야 한다. 불가항력이란 휴업의 사유가 외부로부터 발생하여 사용자의 권한 범위 밖에서 발생한 사유를 말한다. 대표적인 사례가 자연재해, 전쟁, 지역의 대규모 정전사태 등이다.
셋째, 휴업을 할 것을 전제로 한다. 휴업은 전면적 휴업도 될 수 있고, 부분적 휴업도 될 수 있다.

3. 휴업수당의 규모

(1) 임금 전액지급

사용자의 자신의 고의나 과실로 인해 휴업하는 경우 임금 전액을 지급해야 한다. 여기에는 정당한 사유없는 대기발령, 강제휴직, 부당해고 등이 해당된다. 이는 민법 제538조 제1항에 의거하여 사용자의 불법행위로 인하여 근로자가 휴업하는 경우의 휴업수당이 아니라 임금 100%를 지급해야 한다. 다만, 민법 제538조의 제2항에 의거하여 중간이익을 공제할 수 있다.[67]

(2) 휴업수당 지급

사용자의 귀책사유로 인하여 휴업하는 경우 평균임금의 70% 이상의 휴업수당을 지급해야 한다. 사용자의 귀책사유란 원칙적으로 사용자의 세력범위 안에서 생긴 경영장애로 자금난, 원자재 부족, 주문량 감소, 시장불황과 생산량 감축, 모회사의 경영난에 따른 하청공장의 자재부족이나 자금난에 의한 조업

---

66) 노동법실무연구회, 근로기준법 주해(III), 제2판, 박영사, 2020, 121면.
67) 대법원 1991.6.28. 선고 90다카25277 판결(손해배상).

shall be paid when only part of the workplace is closed or when working hours are reduced.[69]

(3) Reduction of shut-down allowances

In order to reduce shut-down allowances, an employer may have urgent cause to not continue business operations for unavoidable reasons, and will need to get approval from the Labor Relations Commission (Article 46 (2) of the LSA).[70] This means that if a company expects to go bankrupt, even if the employer is at fault, it may pay less than the legal shut-down allowance if so approved by the Labor Relations Commission.[71]

Conditions for the reduction of shut-down allowance require (i) as a substantial requirement, the inability to continue business operations for unavoidable reasons and (ii) as a procedural requirement, the approval of the Labor Relations Commission. Even if it is impossible to operate the business for unavoidable reasons, it is not possible to exempt or reduce shut-down allowances without obtaining approval from the Labor Commission.[72]

Shut-down allowances can be paid at less than 70% of the average wage, and can even be reduced in full.[73]

(4) Unpaid leave

Employer's fault under Article 46 of the Labor Standards Act refers to managerial obstacles that occur within the scope of the employer's power and includes situations such as financial shortages, shortage of raw materials, and market recession. If it is impossible to continue the business due to force majeure circumstances, this cannot be regarded as the fault of the employer.[74] Force majeure such as natural disasters cannot be seen as employer's fault because it is impossible for the employer to manage and control such occurrences. There is no obligation to pay shut-down allowances, regardless of whether the Labor Relations Commission

---

[68] MOEL Guides: Gungi 68207-106, Sep. 21, 1999; Wage Policy Team - 711, Mar. 29, 2006
[69] MOEL Guides: The Shut-down Allowance System, Labor Standards - 387, Feb. 13, 2000.
[70] MOEL Guide: Gungi 68207-598, Feb. 28, 2000.
[71] MOEL Guides: Standards of the Shut-down Allowance System, Labor Standards Team - 387, Feb. 13, 2009: Approval Process of Labor Commission Decision on Shut-down Allowance (by Employer) ? Submission of Application for Approval of Reduced Shut-down Allowance (to the Labor Relations Commission) ? Confirmation and Review (by related official) ? Deliberation & Resolution (Judgement Committee, within 30 days) ? Notification
[72] Supreme Court ruling on Sep. 17, 1968: 68nu151.
[73] Supreme Court ruling on Nov. 24, 2000: 99doo4280.
[74] MOEL Guides: Labor Standards Team - 802, Feb. 16, 2010

단축 등으로 인한 휴업을 말한다.[68] 사업장의 일부만 휴업하는 경우나 1일 근로시간 중 일부 근로시간을 단축하는 경우에 부분휴업 수당을 지급한다.[69]

(3) 휴업수당의 감액

휴업수당을 감액하여 지급할 수 있는 경우는 사용자의 귀책사유에도 불구하고 부득이한 사유로 사업계속이 불가능하여 노동위원회의 승인을 얻은 경우이다(근기법 제46조제2항).[70] 이는 기업의 도산이 예상될 정도의 피해가 예상될 경우 사용자의 귀책사유가 있다고 하더라도 노동위원회의 승인을 받은 경우 법정 휴업수당에 못 미치는 휴업수당을 지급할 수 있다.[71]

휴업수당 감액요건에는 (i) 실질적 요건으로 부득이한 사유로 사업계속이 불가능할 것을 요하며, (ii) 절차적 요건으로 노동위원회의 승인으로 요한다. 부득이한 사유로 인해 사업계속이 불가능하다 할지라도, 노동위원회로부터 승인을 받지 못해 절차적 요건을 충족하지 못한다면 휴업수당의 지급을 면하거나 감액할 수 없다.[72]

휴업수당 감액수준은 평균임금의 100분의 70 이하의 휴업수당을 지급할 수 있으며, 전액 감액도 가능하다.[73]

(4) 무급휴업

근로기준법 제46조에 의한 '사용자의 귀책사유'는 원칙적으로 사용자의 세력범위 안에서 생긴 경영장애로서 자금난, 원자재 부족, 시장불황 등으로 인한 경우를 말하며 천재지변이나 재난과 같이 사용자에게 책임을 물을 수 없는 불가항력적인 사정으로 사업 계속이 불가능하게 된 경우에는 사용자의 귀책사유로 볼 수 없다.[74] 천재지변 등 불가항력적인 사유는 사용자의 지배관리가 불가능하므로 사용자의 귀책사유로 볼 수 없다. 이때에는 노동위원회의

---

68) 행정해석: 근기 68207-106, 1999.9.21; 임금근로시간정책팀-711, 2006.3.29
69) 고용노동부 행정해석: 휴업수당제도 기준, 근로기준과-387, 2009.2.13.
70) 행정해석: 근기 68207-598, 2000.2.28
71) 고용노동부 행정해석: 휴업수당제도 기준, 근로기준과-387, 2009.2.13: 노동위원회의 승인절차 휴업결정(사용자) → 기준미달 휴업수당 지급승인 신청서 제출(관할 지방노동위원회) → 확인.검토(심사담당) → 심의.의결(심판위원회, 30일 이내) → 통보
72) 대법원 1968.9.17. 선고 68누151 판결.
73) 대법원 200.11.24 선고 99두4280 판결.
74) 행정해석: 근로기준과-802, 2010.2.16;

has approved them.[75]

IV. Application Cases for Shut-down Allowances

1. Full payment

(1) If an employee's (unfair) dismissal was invalidated or canceled, the employee's status as a worker would still be in existence, and it would be considered that the worker's failure to provide work was attributable to the employer. Article 538 (1) of the Civil Act may request the payment of all wages available for the dismissed period.[76]

(2) If suspension of vehicle driving (discontinuance) measures against a worker was found to be unreasonable, in which case the employee was not able to provide work due to the employer's fault, the employer shall pay a shut-down allowance as prescribed by Article 46 of the Labor Standards Act. If, however, the employee is deemed unable to provide work due to intention or negligence of the employer, a claim for the full amount of wages under Article 538 (1) of the Civil Act shall also occur.[77]

2. Payment of Shut-down Allowances

(1) If a contractor was given an order to suspend the operation by the government, if subcontractors also had to shut down their operations (which cannot be translated as force majeure), the subcontractors should pay shut-down allowances to their workers.[78]

(2) If a contractor's removal of hazardous chemicals restricts access to a subcontractor's workers and if they fail to provide work, this is hardly considered to be force majeure beyond the scope of the employer.[79]

---

[75] MOEL Guides: Gungi 68207-598, Feb. 28, 2000
[76] Supreme Court ruling on Dec. 22, 1981: 81da626.
[77] MOEL Guides: Wage/Working Hour Team - 711, Mar. 29, 2006.
[78] Supreme Court ruling Sep. 10, 2019: 2019do9604.
[79] MOEL guides: Labor Standards Team - 3535, May 30, 2018

승인 여부와 관계없이 휴업수당 지급의 의무가 없다.[75]

Ⅳ. 휴업수당의 적용사례

1. 임금전액 지급

(1) 사용자의 부당한 해고처분이 무효이거나 취소된 때에는 그동안 해고 당사자의 근로자 지위는 계속되고 있었던 것이 되고, 근로자가 그간 근로 제공을 하지 못한 것은 사용자의 귀책사유로 인한 것이라 할 것이니 근로자는 민법 제538조제1항에 의하여 계속 근로하였을 경우 받을 수 있는 임금의 전부 지급을 청구할 수 있다.[76]
(2) 사용자의 근로자에 대한 차량승무정지(배차중단) 조치가 부당한 것으로 판명된 경우라면 사용자의 귀책사유로 인해 근로를 제공할 수 없게 된 경우 근로기준법 제46조 소정의 휴업수당을 지급하여야 할 것이나, 사용자의 고의나 과실로 인하여 근로를 제공하지 못한 것으로 인정되는 경우에는 민법 제538조 제1항의 규정에 의한 임금전액에 대한 청구권도 동시에 발생한다.[77]

2. 휴업수당 지급

(1) 원청업체에 대한 작업중지명령으로 인한 하청회사의 휴업은 불가항력이라고 주장할 수 없는 사유로 휴업한 것으로 근로자에게 휴업수당을 지급할 의무가 있다.[78]
(2) 원청업체의 유해화학 물질 제거 작업에 따라 하도급업체 소속 근로자의 출입이 제한되어 근로를 제공하지 못한 경우라면, 이는 사용자의 세력 범위를 벗어난 불가항력적인 사유로 보기 어렵다.[79]

---

[75] 행정해석: 근기 68207-598, 2000.2.28
[76] 대법원 1981.12.22. 선고 81다626 판결.
[77] 행정해석: 임금근로시간정책팀-711, 2006.3.29
[78] 대법원 2019.9.10. 선고 2019도9604 판결
[79] 행정해석: 근로기준정책과-3535, 2018.5.30

3. Reduction of Suspension Allowances

(1) The Bupyeong plant closed for more than three months due to a sharp drop in sales after an incident with contaminated dumplings, and the inventory increased during this period. As a result, managerial difficulties can be understood as about 80 workers were dismissed for business reasons. Unless consumer confidence was restored in the near future, normal operation would be difficult. Therefore, it is possible to reduce the shut-down allowance if it is impossible to continue the business for unavoidable reasons (Incheon LRC 2004 Shut-down 1).

(2) Due to bankruptcy, deficits accumulated even after the company liquidation procedure began, and there was no alternative for normalization as attempts to sell the company were unsuccessful. In this case, unavoidable shut-down is a valid reason for the reduction of shut-down allowances ((Incheon LRC 2000 Shut-down 1).

(3) A situation in which a company goes to the brink of bankruptcy due to an unforeseen fire is considered an unavoidable reason for the employer (NLRC 89 Shutdown 1)).

4. Unpaid leave

(1) An employer is not obliged to pay any shut-down allowance for a period of suspension due to interruption of work by a third party.[80]
(2) Absence or leave of absence due to natural disaster or other similar instances, and disciplinary actions such as suspension from work, temporary suspension of work, illness, etc., shall not be regarded as a case of employer fault and shall not be reason for payment of a shut-down allowance.[81]

V. Conclusion

The leave allowance system guarantees workers' right to survival by providing shut-down allowances in cases where the worker does not provide labor due to fault on the employer's part. At present, the spread of coronavirus infection is causing

---

[80] Guidelines: Labor Standards Team - 2855, June 9, 2004
[81] Lim Jong-Ryul, Labor Law, 17th edition, Park Young-sa, 2019, p. 423

3. 휴업수당의 감액

(1) 만두파동 이후 3개월 이상 회사 매출이 제로에 가까운 급감, 재고량 증가로 부평공장을 폐쇄하였다. 이로 인하여 약 80명의 근로자를 정리한 사실 등의 경영상 어려움이 인정된다. 앞으로도 소비자의 신뢰가 회복되지 않는 한 정상조업이 어려운 사업계속이 불가능한 경우에 해당하므로 휴업수당 감액에 해당된다(인천지노위 04휴업1).

(2) 부도에 따라 회사정리절차가 개시된 이후에도 적자가 누적되고 있고, 경영정상화를 위한 대안이 존재하지 않아 회사매각을 추진하고 있으나 회사매각도 성과를 거두지 못하고 있다. 이 경우에는 부득이한 휴업상태가 휴업수당의 감액 사유에 해당된다 (인천지노위 ○○휴업1).

(3) 원인 미상의 화재발생으로 인한 기업이 부도 직전까지 가는 경영상 긴박한 상태의 도래는 사용자로서도 어쩔 수 없는 불가항력적인 사유로 휴업수당을 감할 수밖에 없는 경우에 해당된다(중노위 89휴업1).

4. 무급휴업

(1) 제3자의 출근방해로 인한 피치못할 휴업기간에 대하여 사용자가 휴업수당을 지급하여야 할 의무는 없다.[80]
(2) 천재지변이나 그 밖에 이에 준하는 사유, 징계처분으로서 정직, 출근정지, 질병 등에 따른 결근이나 휴직은 사용자의 귀책사유로 볼 수 없고 이는 휴업수당 지급사유가 되지 않는다.[81]

V. 결론

휴업수당제도는 사용자의 귀책사유로 근로자가 근로제공이 없는 경우에도 일정한 휴업수당을 지급하여 근로자의 생존권의 보장을 확보하기 위한 제도이다. 현재, 코로나바이러스 감염의 확산으로 인해 기업과 근로자 모두 힘든 시기를

---

[80] 행정해석: 근로기준과-2855, 2004.6.9
[81] 임종률, 노동법 제17판, 박영사, 2019, 423면

hard times for both companies and workers. If a company pays shut-down allowances without any income, it will be difficult to continue to operate in the future. On the other hand, if an employee cannot earn money due to a lack of a shut-down allowance, survival of the worker would also be a serious problem. When faced with a force majeure situation such as this, urgent measures are needed to guarantee employment through the payment of employment insurance funds.

Section 4. Guidelines for calculating working hours

Ⅰ. Introduction

Working hours refer to the actual working hours which the employee provides labor service prescribed by the employment contract under the employer's direction and supervision. Article 50 of the Labor Standards Act regulates that working hours shall not exceed 8 hours per day and 40 hours per week, excluding recess hours. The employer shall additionally pay fifty percent (50%) of the ordinary wages for extended working hours exceeding the legal standard working hours. Working hours are usually implemented within contractual working hours that the employer and the employee have agreed upon, but there have been some disputes in recognizing working hours in cases where the employee conducted work before or after contractual working hours, or in cases of waiting time for work, training hours, traveling hours, company events, etc. So, I would like to clarify the criteria for judging working hours and review concrete examples regarding working hours.

Ⅱ. Criteria for judging working hours

1. Whether working hours are stipulated in the labor contract, rules of employment or collective agreement

The working hours shall be calculated by the total working hours from when the employee starts to provide contractual work to the employer to when the employee finishes his/her work, excluding recess hours. The Labor Standards Act regulates that the employment contract shall consist of the starting and finishing time of

맞고 있다. 기업에서 수입이 없이 휴업수당을 지급하는 경우에는 경영의 어려움에 처할 것이고, 근로자의 입장에서도 무급휴업을 하는 경우에는 생존권의 문제가 발생할 수 있다. 이러한 불가항력적 사태를 맞은 때에는 고용보험 기금지급을 통해 고용을 보장하는 긴급한 조치가 필요하다고 할 수 있겠다.

제4절 근로시간 계산의 원칙

I. 서 론

근로시간이란 근로자가 사용자의 지휘, 감독 아래 근로계약상의 근로를 제공하는 시간, 실 근로시간을 말한다. 근로기준법 제50조에서 근로시간은 휴게시간을 제하고 1일에 8시간 1주일에 40시간을 초과할 수 없다고 규정하고 있다. 이 법정근로시간을 초과하는 근로시간에 대해 통상임금의 50%를 가산하여 지급하여야 한다. 근로시간은 대개 당사자간에 근로하기로 합의한 소정근로시간 이내에 이루어지지만, 근로자가 사업주의 지시에 의해 시업시간 전 또는 종업시간 후에 업무를 수행한 경우, 또는 그 외 대기시간, 교육시간, 출장시간, 행사시간 등에 대해 근로시간 인정여부에 대한 다툼이 생기는 경우가 많다. 이에 대해 근로시간에 대한 판단 기준을 명확히 하고, 그 구체적 사례에 대해 검토해보고자 한다.

II. 근로시간의 판단기준

1. 근로계약,취업규칙, 단체협약 등에 규정되어 있는지 여부

근로시간의 계산은 근로자가 사용자에게 소정의 근로를 제공하기 시작한 시간부터 그 제공을 종료한 시각까지의 총 시간에서 휴게시간을 공제한 시간으로 산출하는데, 근로기준법에서는 시업과 종업시간을 근로계약에 명시토록

work, and the rules of employment shall contain statutory items to be surely included. (Article 17 and 93 of the Labor Standards Act)

2. Whether the employee is under the employer's direction and supervision

Working hours mean the time at which the employee provides labor service described by the employment contract under the employer's direction and supervision. Even though waiting time or recess and sleeping time are times that the employee is not engaged in actual work in the middle of working hours, if those times are not allowed to be used freely by employees, but are, in practice, under the employer's direction and supervision, those times surely belong to working hours. (Supreme court Mar 9, 93 92da22770)

Whether the subsidiary time required in actual working hours belongs to working hours or not shall be judged by whether those times are implemented under the employer's direction and supervision. Such subsidiary times include the time needed to change into the work uniform and gather necessary tools, waiting time, conferences prior to work, shift-changes, wash-up time after finishing the work day, organizing things for the next day's work after finishing the work day, travel time during business trips, etc. (Supreme Court Mar 9, 93, 92da22770)

3. Whether work characteristics under the employment contract are acceptable or not

The type of work described under the employment contract is not limited to the work tasks themselves, but actual working hours shall include those times essentially required to prepare for work and to arrange things after finishing the work day in relation to actual work performance. It is regarded as working hours in cases where those activities besides actual working hours are stipulated as the employee's mandatory duties according to related laws, collective agreements, rules of employment, labor practices, and employment contracts, or in cases where non-implementation charges disadvantage the employees concerned.

III. Concrete Judgment for Working Hours

1. Time worked before the work starts

(1) **In cases where the employee arrives at the workplace earlier than the official starting hour**

Whether the company shall pay wages for working hours when the employee

하고 취업규칙에서 반드시 기재하여야 할 필요적 기재사항으로 정하고 있다.
(근로기준법 제17조, 제93조)

2. 사용자의 지휘, 감독하에 있는지 여부

근로시간이라 함은 사용자의 지휘·감독 아래 근로계약상의 근로를 제공하는 시간을 말하는 것으로, 작업시간 도중에 현실로 작업에 종사하지 않은 대기시간이나 휴식·수면시간이라 하더라도 그것이 휴게시간으로서 근로자에게 자유로운 이용이 보장된 것이 아니고 실질적으로 사용자의 지휘·감독 아래 놓여있는 시간이라면 당연히 근로시간에 포함시켜야 한다. (대판 '93.5.27, 92다24509)

작업복을 갈아 입는 시간, 작업도구 준비시간, 대기시간, 작업 전 회의, 교대시간, 작업 후 목욕시간, 작업종료 후 정돈 시간, 출장 중 이동시간 등 실제 근로에 부속되는 시간이 근로시간 인지 여부도 사용자의 지휘 명령 아래서 이루어지는지에 따라 판단된다. (대판 93.3.9, 92다22770)

3. 근로계약상 업무성이 인정되는지 여부

근로계약에서 정하여진 근로의 종류는 반드시 그 근로자체만을 뜻하지 않고 그 근로에서 실작업에 필요불가결한 준비행위나 작업종료 후 뒷정리를 위한 시간도 실근로시간에 포함된다. 실 근로시간외의 활동으로 법령, 단체협약, 취업규칙, 노사관행 또는 근로계약에서 근로자의 의무로 명백히 정하거나 그 불이행에 대한 일정한 불이익이 과해진 경우에는 근로시간에 포함된다.

III. 근로시간 여부 구체적 판단

1. 시업전 시간

(1) 조기출근한 경우 근로시간
시업시간 이전에 조기 출근토록 하여 시업에 지장이 없도록 하는 것을

comes earlier to the company to ensure normal operations shall be dependent upon the following: 1) If the employee did not come to work earlier than the official starting hour, his wages could be reduced or he might be punished for a violation of service regulations. If this situation does not exist, then the time before the official starting hour does not belong to working hours. (Aug 30, 1988, kungi 01254-13305)

(2) Conferences held before working hours

Conferences held before working hours deal with safety training for underground mine workers, work directions and organization of working groups. These meetings shall be held essentially for the purpose of underground shift work and be implemented under the employer's direction and supervision. So, these meetings shall be included in actual working hours. (Supreme Court, Sep 28, 93, 93da3363)

2. Time worked after the work day finishes

The end of the work day is the time for the employee to be free from the employer's direction and supervision. When the employee continues to be under the employer's direction and supervision after he finishes his regular work time, actual working hours end when the employee is actually free from the employer's direction and supervision. Such examples of the end of the workday not being the end of actual working hours are workplace repairs, examinations, organization and cleaning, conducted after completing work under the employer's direction and supervision. (Supreme Court Mar 9, 93, 92da2270)

3. Waiting time

Recess hours under the Labor Standards Act mean the time that employees can use freely, away from the employer's direction and supervision, regardless of the name given for such times, such as recess hours, waiting time, etc. In this case, unlike the working structure stipulated by the rules of employment, under the employer's implied agreement, the employees work every two hours in repeated practices and off-time employees take recess hours, playing chess or baduk, or watching TV. There is a clear division of waiting time and working hours. The employees cannot go out of the workplace during this waiting time, but they can

근로시간으로 인정하여 임금이 지급되어야 할 것인가 여부는 조기출근을 하지 않을 경우 임금을 감액하거나 복무 위반으로 제재를 가하는 권리의무관계라면 근로시간에 해당될 것이나 그렇지 않다면 근로시간에 해당되지 않는다. (1988.08.30, 근기 01254-13305)

(2) 작업시간 전 취업회의 시간

작업시간 전에 갖는 취업회의 내용인 갱내 근무자에 대한 보안교육이나 작업지시 및 작업조의 편성은 갱내 교대근무를 위한 필요불가결한 것으로서 사용자의 지휘 감독에 의한 구속하에 행해질 수밖에 없으므로 실근로시간에 포함시키는 것이 타당하다. (대판 1993.9.28, 93다3363)

2. 종업후 시간

근로시간이 끝나는 종업시각은 근로자가 사용자의 지휘 감독으로부터 벗어났다고 인정되는 작업종료 시각이다. 그러나 작업이 끝나도 계속하여 사용자의 지휘 감독아래 있을 때는 시업시각의 경우처럼 그 구속으로부터 벗어난 시각이 종업시각이 된다. 사용자의 지휘 감독아래 하는 작업 후 기계 기구의 정비 점검 정돈과 사업장의 청소 등 이에 속한다. (대판 1993.3.9 92다2270)

3. 대기시간

근로기준법상의 휴게시간이란 휴게시간·대기시간 등 명칭여하에 불구하고 근로자가 사용자의 지휘·감독으로부터 벗어나 자유로이 사용할 수 있는 시간을 말한다. 따라서 취업규칙상 근로형태는 아니지만 사업주의 묵시적인 동의하에 관례적으로 근로자들 스스로 2시간 단위로 작업을 하고 작업을 하지 않는 근로자들은 대기실에서 장기, 바둑, TV시청 등을 하는 형태로써, 대기시간과 근무시간의 구분이 명백하고, 근로자가 사전에 대기시간을 알고 있으며, 그 대기시간 중에는 사업장 밖으로 나갈 수는 없지만 사용자의 지휘·감독을 벗어나 자유로이 이용할 수 있다면 이는 휴게시간으로 인정할 수 있다고 판단된다. (2000.10.25, 근기 68207-3298)

use it freely, away from the employer's direction and supervision. In this case, the waiting time shall be recognized as recess hours. (Oct 25, 00, kungi 68207-3298)

In cases where an employee drives a company car as necessary from time to time, just like a regular driver of a company car, if the employee cannot use the waiting time freely, this shall be regarded as working hours, but if such time is free for the employee to use as he/she wishes, it is considered part of recess hours and cannot be included in working hours. (Supreme Court July 28, 92, 92da14007)

4. Education and training time

It is working hours when the employer implements job training during working hours in relation to work, concerning work safety and work efficiency to improve productivity, and it is also working hours when the employer gives compulsory training after working hours or during a holiday. However, it is not working hours when the employee shall attend compulsory individual training like driver's education, regardless of the company's business, or when moral or safety training etc., is recommended to employees, and provided by the nation due to major national policies after working hours or during a holiday. (Sep 29, 88, gungi 01254-14835)

5. Company picnics or events

In cases where the company hosts a picnic party, athletic event, etc., if the employee shall attend the picnic party, athletic event, etc., the participating time shall be deemed as working hours. Conversely, if the employer hosts a picnic party, athletic event, etc. for the purpose of welfare, and if employees are free to participate in the event at their own discretion, it shall not be deemed as working hours even though employees attend such an event. (Jan 10, 89, gungi 01254-554)

If the company hosts a picnic party on a working day according to the company's operation rules, the wages for that day shall be paid accordingly. If the picnic party was held on a holiday, the wages payable on that holiday and ordinary wages to compensate for holiday work (the picnic party) shall be paid. (Jul 12, 79, gungi 1455-7105)

6. Business travel

업무용 자동차 운전자와 같이, 필요할 때마다 간헐적으로 운전업무를 하는 경우 다음 운전업무까지 대기하는 시간은 그 시간을 자유롭게 이용할 수 없는 한 이를 근로시간으로 보는 것이 원칙이나 자유로운 이용이 보장되면 휴게시간으로서 근로시간에 포함되지 않을 수 있다. (대판 1992.7.28, 92다14007)

4. 교육시간

사용자가 근로시간중에 작업안전, 작업능률 등 생산성 향상 즉 업무와 관련하여 실시하는 직무교육과 근로시간 종료후 또는 휴일에 근로자에게 의무적으로 소집하여 실시하는 교육은 근로시간에 포함되어야 할 것이다. 그러나 근로자가 회사와는 관계없는 운전면허증 소지자에 대한 소양교육과 같은 법적 이행 개인의무사항 교육이나 국가기관 등의 시책사업으로 사용자에게 협조를 요구하여 근무시간외 또는 휴일에 회사에서 단체로 근로자에게 의무사항이 아닌 권고사항으로 시행하는 국민정신교육, 안전관계교육 등은 근로시간에 포함된다고 볼 수 없을 것이다. (1988.09.29, 근기 01254-14835)

5. 야유회 등의 행사

일반적으로 사용자가 근로자의 야유회, 체육대회 등의 행사를 행하는 경우, 그 야유회, 체육대회 등의 참가자가 근로자의 의무로서 강제되는 경우에는 그 참가시간은 근로시간으로 보아야 할 것이고, 반대로 이러한 야유회, 체육대회 등을 사용자가 복리후생적인 의미에서 행하고 근로자가 이에 참가하는 여부가 그의 자유에 맡겨진 때에는 근로자가 임의로 이에 참가 하더라도 그 시간은 근로시간이 아니라고 보아야 할 것이다. (1989.1.10, 근기 01254-554)
회사운영방침에 따라 근로하여야 할 날에 야유회를 실시하는 경우라면 임금은 당연히 지급되어야 하며, 유급휴일에 야유회를 실시하는 경우라면 휴일에 당연히 지급되는 임금과 당해 유급휴일의 근로(야유회)에 대한 소정의 통상임금을 지급하면 되는 것이다. (1979.07.12, 근기 1455-7105)

6. 출장

(1) Travel time between employee accommodations and the appointed workplace

In calculating working hours for business travel, travel time to the workplace shall be included in working hours in principle, but when the workplace is on the way to the regular office, such travel time can be excluded from working hours. However, for long-distance business travel, travel time from the company's location to the workplace on business travel shall be included into working hours. (Jun 14, '01, gungi 68207-1909)

(2) When the employee shall engage in business travel at night or during a holiday by order of the employer, such time shall be regarded as night time and holiday work.

In cases where the employee carries out his duty in whole or in part outside the workplace for business travel or for other reasons, the calculation of working hours shall follow Paragraphs 1 and 2, Article 57 of the Labor Standards Act. In consideration of the concept of the same Article, if it is evident that the employee conducts business travel at night or during holidays by order of the employer, the night work and holiday work shall be considered as working hours. However, if the employee only travels to the workplace during the night or holiday, and does not engage in any business, it is hard to deem such travel time as night time work or holiday work. (Aug 5, 02, gungi 68207-2650)

〈Case Study〉
Whether a Managing Director is Considered to hold a Managerial

I. Introduction

In the Seoul office of a foreign company (hereinafter referred to as "the Company") that hired about 300 employees and is engaged in the apparel business, a labor case has occurred due to escalating disputes between directors in April 2015. With two departments of the Company combining into one department, the executive managing director told the managing director that it would be not desirable to have two directors in one department, and told the managing director that she needed to resign from the Company. The managing director (hereinafter referred to as "the Employee") told the Company that she would sue it for violating the Labor Standards Act and would also report additional claims of other employees unless the Company paid her a severance bonus of two years' annual

(1) 출장업무 수행을 위해 이동하는 시간

출장에 있어 통상 필요한 시간을 산정할 경우 출장지로의 이동에 필요한 시간은 근로시간에 포함시키는 것이 원칙이나 출퇴근에 갈음하여 출장지로 출근 또는 출장지에서 퇴근하는 경우는 제외할 수 있을 것이다. 다만, 장거리 출장의 경우 사업장이 소재하는 지역에서 출장지가 소재하는 지역까지의 이동시간은 근로시간에 포함시키는 것이 타당하다고 사료된다. (2001.06.14, 근기 68207-1909)

(2) 사용자의 지시에 의해 야간 또는 휴일에 출장업무상 이동이 명확한 때에는 야간·휴일근로로 볼 수 있다

출장근무 등 사업장 밖에서 근로하는 경우에 있어서의 근로시간 산정에 관하여는 근로기준법 제57조 제1항 및 제2항에서 특례를 규정하고 있는 바, 동조의 취지로 볼 때 사용자의 지시에 의해 야간 또는 휴일에 출장업무를 수행하는 것이 명확한 때에는 야간, 휴일근로로 볼 수 있으나 단순히 야간 또는 휴일에 이동하는 때에는 야간, 휴일근로를 한 것으로 보기 어렵다고 사료된다.(2002.08.05, 근기 68207-2650)

〈노동사건사례〉
외국기업의 상무가 관리감독자 여부 판단

I. 문제의 소재

서울에 사무소를 두고 300여명을 고용하여 의류 사업을 하고 있는 한 외국기업에서, 2015년 4월에 임원간의 갈등이 노동사건으로 확대된 사건이 발생하였다. 부서가 통폐합 되면서 한 부서에 전무와 상무가 같이 근무하게 되었는데, 전무가 상무에게 하나의 부서에 임원 둘이 같이 근무하는 것은 바람직하지 않으니, 퇴사할 것을 권유하였다. 이에 상무(이하, "이 사건의 근로자"라 함)는 회사가 근로기준법을 위반하였다고 주장하면서, 2년치 퇴직 위로금을 주지 않을 경우 회사를 고용노동부에 고소하고, 다른 직원들에 대한

wages. The Company responded that it did not order the Employee to resign, rejected her demand for a severance bonus, and explained that the Company had not violated the Labor Standards Act. Just after that, the Employee began a lawsuit against the Company and visited the Gangnam Labor Office to claim the Company had violated the Labor Standards Act, and had not paid additional allowance for her overtime work.

There is a main item in these accusations: As the Employee's job title as the managing director placed her in the "directors" group, the question is whether or not this high position is included in 'persons to be excluded from the application of working hours, recess and holidays' stipulated by the Labor Standards Act.

II. Overtime Work Allowance for Managerial and Supervisory Positions

1. Current situation

The Employee claimed that she had never received any additional allowance for overtime or holiday work during her service period, and that she was entitled to additional allowances for overtime and holiday work for the past three years. The Employee requested the information of her office PC's "on-and-off" data to check her working time as she had not recorded it in the related documents.

The Company responded that the Employee is not entitled to overtime work allowance or holiday work allowance due to her high position as the managing director, putting her in a managerial and supervisory position according to Article 63 of the LSA.

2. Related law, guideline and judicial ruling regarding overtime work allowance for personnel in managerial and supervisory positions

(1) Regulation of the LSA

Article 63 (Exceptions to Application) of the LSA regulates that the provisions regarding working hours, recess and holiday shall not apply to managerial and supervisory positions.[82]

---

[82] Article 63 (Exceptions to Application) The provisions of this Chapter and Chapter V as to working hours, recess, and holidays shall not apply to workers engaged in any of tasks described in the following subparagraphs:
1. cultivation of arable land, reclamation work, seeding and planting, gathering or picking-up or other agricultural and forestry work;

위반사항도 고발할 것이라 압박하였다. 이에 대해 회사는 이 사건의 근로자에게 퇴직을 권유하지 않았으며, 근로기준법을 위반한 사실도 없다고 하면서 퇴직위로금의 지급을 거부하였다. 그러자 이 사건의 근로자는 회사가 연장근로에 대한 가산임금을 지급하지 않는 등 근로기준법을 위반하였다고 '강남 고용지청'에 회사를 고소하였다.

이 고소내용에 대한 주요 쟁점사항을 살펴보면, 이 사건의 근로자 직급이 임원에 속하는 '상무'로 근로기준법상 '근로시간, 휴게, 휴일의 적용제외자'로 인정받을 수 있는지의 여부이다.

Ⅱ. 관리감독자에 대한 연장근로수당

1. 현 실태

이 사건의 근로자는 근무기간 중 연장근로와 휴일근로를 많이 하였음에도 한 번도 가산임금을 받아본 적이 없다고 주장하면서, 과거 3년간 연장근로수당과 휴일근로수당을 청구하였다. 근로자는 관련된 자료를 기록하고 있지 않기 때문에 '본인 업무용 컴퓨터 사용기록(on-off 자료)'를 요청하였다. 이에 대해 회사는 이 사건의 근로자는 직급상 상무직급으로 회사의 임원에 해당되므로 근로기준법 제63조의 규정에 따른 '관리감독자'로 연장근로, 휴일근로에 대해 적용대상자가 아니라고 판단하여 지급하지 않았다.

2. 관리감독자에 대한 연장근로수당의 법규정, 행정해석, 판례

(1) 근로기준법 규정

현행 근로기준법 제63조(적용제외)에는 관리감독자에 대해서는 근로시간, 휴게와 휴일에 관한 규정을 적용하지 않는다고 규정하고 있다.[82]

---

[82] 제63조【적용의 제외】제4장과 제5장에서 정한 근로시간, 휴게와 휴일에 관한 규정은 다음 각 호의 어느 하나에 해당하는 근로자에 대하여는 적용하지 아니한다.
  1. 토지의 경작·개간, 식물의 재식·재배·채취 사업, 그 밖의 농림 사업
  2. 동물의 사육, 수산 동식물의 채포·양식 사업, 그 밖의 축산, 양잠, 수산 사업
  3. 감시 또는 단속적으로 근로에 종사하는 자로서 사용자가 고용노동부장관의 승인을 받은 자
  4. 대통령령으로 정하는 업무에 종사하는 근로자 (사업의 종류에 관계없이 관리·감독 업무 또는 기밀을 취급하는 업무를 말한다: 시행령 제34조)

(2) Related guideline

'The provisions of Chapter 4 and Chapter 5 as to working hours, recess, and holidays shall not apply to persons engaged in management and supervision' (Article 63 (4ho) of the LSA and Article 34 of its Enforcement Decree). Here, 'persons engaged in management and supervision' refers to those in managerial positions in the decision-making process of working conditions. This position shall be determined collectively in consideration of whether the person participates in deciding labor management or has authority for supervision and control in labor management regardless of his/her formal designation, whether the person's working hours are strictly regulated (such as time to arrive at and leave the workplace), whether the person receives a special allowance due to the position, etc.

Administrative guidelines explain, for those in the position of 'section manager' who are authorized to plan and implement general duties and detailed job assignments for their subordinates, and control their business trips, overtime, and vacations, even though the section manager did not receive a special allowance in accordance with that position, if the section manager has not been strictly regulated in time of arrival at and leaving the workplace, the section manager shall be considered as a person who is in line with the employer in determining working conditions and other forms of labor management (Guideline Kunjung-41, Mar 3, 2011).

(3) Judicial ruling

The Supreme Court (February 28, 1989, 88daka2974) ruled that working hours, recess and holidays stipulated by the Labor Standards Act do not apply to persons in a managerial and supervisory position in terms of deciding subordinates' working conditions, and does not have their times of arrival at and leaving the workplace strictly regulated, and is managing his/her own working hours flexibly. Persons in this position cannot receive additional allowance for overtime work exceeding contractual working hours or holiday work according to the Labor Standards Act.

3. The Employer's countermeasures

---

2. livestock breeding, catch of marine animals and plants, cultivation of marine products or other cattle-breeding, sericulture and fishery business;
3. surveillance or intermittent work, for which the employer has obtained the approval of the Minister of Employment and Labor;
4. any other work prescribed in Presidential Decree. [Implementation Decree (Article 34) - "Work provided for in Presidential Decree" means managerial and supervisory work and work of handling confidential information, irrespective of the type of business.]

(2) 행정해석

'관리·감독업무에 종사하는 근로자(제63조 제4호 및 시행령 제34조)'는 근로기준법 제4장 및 제5장에서 정한 근로시간, 휴게와 휴일에 관한 규정을 적용하지 않는다. 여기서 '관리·감독업무에 종사하는 자'라 함은 근로조건의 결정 기타 노무관리에 있어서 경영자와 일체적인 지위에 있는 자를 말하는 것으로 사업장내 형식적인 직책에 불구하고 노무관리방침의 결정에 참여하거나 노무 관리상의 지휘·감독 권한을 가지고 있는지 여부, 출·퇴근 등에 있어서 엄격한 제한을 받는지 여부, 그 지위에 따른 특별수당을 받고 있는지 여부 등을 종합적으로 검토하여 판단하여야 할 것이다.

행정해석은 회사의 위임전결규정 등의 자료에 의하여 '실장'이 일반 업무에 대한 방침 및 소관업무에 관한 세부계획 수립 및 집행 등에 대한 결정권과 소속 직원에 대한 출장, 연장근로 지시, 휴가 승인 등 노무관리상의 지휘·감독 권한을 가지고 있는 것으로 보여지는 경우 비록 그 지위에 따른 특별수당을 지급 받지 않는다 하더라도 일반 직원과 달리 출·퇴근 등에 있어서 엄격한 제한을 받지 않는 경우라면 전반적으로 근로조건의 결정 기타 노무관리에 있어서 경영자와 일체적인 지위에 있는 자로 볼 수 있다고 해석하고 있다 (2011.03.03. 근정과-41).

(3) 판례

판례는 "부하직원의 근로조건의 결정 기타 노무관리에 있어 경영자의 지위에 있으면서 기업경영상의 필요에 의하여 출·퇴근에 관하여도 엄격한 제한을 받지 아니하고 자기의 근무시간에 관한 융통성을 가지고 있어 회사의 감독, 관리의 지위에 있던 자는 근로기준법에서 정한 근로시간, 휴게와 휴일에 관한 규정이 적용되지 아니한다. 이러한 위치에 있는 자는 평일의 법내 잔업시간은 물론 일요일 근무에 대해서도 근로기준법 소정의 시간외 또는 휴일근무라 하여 같은 근로기준법에 정한 가산금을 지급받을 수는 없다(대법원 1989.02.28. 선고 88다카2974 판결)"고 판시하고 있다.

3. 회사의 대응 및 처리결과

Even though the 'managing director' for the foreign company in this case has a considerably high position, it is not clear whether this high ranking person is working just as a manager, and not a department head which would place her in a managerial and supervisory position.

The Employee in this case is not a department head due to the combination of two departments, but has received the high salary of a director, twice the incentives of other employees, and her time of arrival at and leaving the workplace has not been strictly controlled as it has been for other employees. In consideration of these facts, the Gangnam Labor Office in charge of this case concluded that the Employee in this case is in a managerial and supervisory position and can be excluded from the provisions on working hours, recess and holiday provisions in Article 63 of the Labor Standards Act. In the end, as the Employee recognized that she could not receive a severance bonus from the Company, she withdrew the lawsuit and instead of resigning, took childcare leave.

III. Conclusion

On the point of whether the managing director of a foreign company shall be entitled to an additional allowance for overtime work shall be determined collectively in consideration of not only the official designation of the employee as being in a high position but also the manager's authority, observance of commuting time, and any special allowances assigned to the position.[83] Through this evaluation, companies should prepare measures to avoid having to later deal with matters regarding overtime and holiday work for such a position.

This labor case began with the Employee's demand to receive a severance bonus from the Company by taking advantage of the Company's violation of labor law. When a company has violated labor law and has to settle with certain employees to end labor disputes, other employees will rush to claim compensation from the company as well. In particular, for many foreign companies with registered representative directors working as directors in their home countries, those representative directors have to come to Korea to attend investigation procedures in the Labor Office, which will cause considerable embarrassment for their local Korean branches. In this point, companies need to thoroughly observe labor law to avoid labor disputes with potentially dissatisfied employees and reduce in advance the risk of related damages.

---

[83] Ha, Kaprae,『The Labor Standards Act (27th edition)』Joongan Economy, 2015, page 315.

본 사건에서 외국기업의 '상무'와 같이 상당한 직급을 가지고 있음에도 불구하고, 단지 관리자이지 부서장이 아닌 경우에 관리 감독자인지 여부에 대해 판단을 하기 어려운 경우가 많다.

이 사건의 근로자인 경우에는 부서의 통폐합으로 인해 부서장은 아니지만, 고위의 직급에 임원급의 임금, 일반 근로자의 2배 이상의 인센티브를 받고 있으며, 출퇴근시간에 대해서도 일반근로자와 달리 엄격히 통제 받지 않았다. 이러한 사정을 고려하여 이 사건을 담당한 강남노동지청은 이 사건의 근로자를 근로기준법 제63조에 따른 근로시간, 휴일, 휴게에 대해 예외를 인정받을 수 있는 관리·감독자로서 인정하였다. 결국, 이 사건의 근로자는 퇴직위로금을 받지 못하자, 퇴직하는 대신 고소사건을 취하하고, 육아휴직을 청구하여 휴직하게 되면서 이 사건은 종결되었다.

Ⅲ. 결론

외국기업의 상무가 연장근로에 대한 가산임금을 지급여부에 대한 판단은 직급의 고하(高下)만을 가지고 판단할 것이 아니라 관리자로서의 권한, 출퇴근시간준수 의무, 지급에 따른 특별수당 지급여부 등을 복합적으로 고려하여 판단하여야 할 것이다.[83] 이를 통해 연장근로나 휴일근로에 대해 차후 문제가 발생하지 않도록 하여야 할 것이다.

이와 같이 이 노동사건의 발단은 회사의 노동법 위반사항을 빌미로 근로자가 회사를 압박하여 퇴직위로금을 받기 위해서였다. 회사가 노무관리를 잘못하였을 때나, 회사가 근로자의 요구를 일부 수용하여 합의하는 경우에 다른 직원들이 얼마든지 동일한 노동사건을 제기할 수 있다는 점에서 시사점이 크다고 할 수 있다. 특히, 외국인 회사의 경우에는 등기된 대표이사가 본사의 중역을 맡고 있는 경우에 대표이사가 고소사건 조사에 출석하여 조사를 받아야 하기 때문에 상당한 곤혹을 치르는 경우가 많다. 이러한 점에서 회사는 노동법에 입각한 철저한 노무관리를 통해 잠재적 불만이 있는 근로자에게 합법적으로 대응하여 부당한 손해를 겪는 일이 없도록 해야 하겠다.

---

[83] 하갑래, 『근로기준법(제27판)』, 중앙경제, 2015, 315면.

Section 5. Recess Periods and Designing a Working Hour System

I. Introduction

The purpose of a recess is to restore workers' fatigue and reduce the boredom caused by continual work, thereby enabling them to continue to work feeling refreshed and with a willingness to work.[84] A 'recess period' is the period of time during which a worker is free to rest without being directed or supervised by an employer.[85]

The Labor Standards Act states Working hours per week shall not exceed forty hours excluding recess hours. Working hours per day shall not exceed eight hours excluding recess hours. In calculating working hours, waiting hours the worker spends while under the employer's direction and supervision for work shall be regarded as working hours. (Article 50 of the LSA). The recess period in the Labor Standards Act is excluded from working time, but time waiting for work is determined to be working time, not a recess period. Although the relationship between working time and recess period is clear, there is a vague distinction between 'waiting time' and 'recess period'. In designating working hours, it is possible to secure optimal working hours even within statutory working hours if the proper recess period is used in consideration of the characteristics of the work. In order to design a suitable working time system, the concept of recess periods, and the criteria for distinguishing between 'waiting time' and 'recess period' is explained, along with examples of some working time systems using relevant recess periods.

II. The Concept of a Recess Period and its Practical Use

1. Legal regulations

According to the Labor Standards Act, An employer shall allow a recess period of 30 minutes or more for every 4 working hours and more than 1 hour for every

---

[84] Kaprae Ha, 「The Labor Standards Act」 28th ed., 2016, p 323; Jongyul Lim, 「Labor Act」 17th ed., 2019, p 460.
[85] Government Guide: Bubmoo 811-28682, issued on May 15, 1980.

제5절 휴게시간과 근로시간 설계

I. 문제의 소재

휴게제도는 근로자가 계속해서 근로할 경우 육체적·정신적 피로가 쌓이게 되므로 근로자의 피로를 회복시키고 권태감을 감소시켜 노동력의 재생산과 작업의욕을 확보 유지하는 데 그 목적이 있다.[84] 휴게시간은 근로시간 중간에 사용자의 지휘와 감독을 받지 않고 근로자가 자유로이 휴식을 가지는 시간을 말한다.[85]

근로기준법에서는 1주 간의 근로시간을 휴게시간을 제외하고 40시간을 초과할 수 없고, 1일의 근로시간은 휴게시간을 제외하고 8시간을 초과할 수 없다고 기술하고 있다. 근로를 제공하지는 않지만 작업을 위하여 근로자가 사용자의 지휘와 감독 아래에 있는 대기시간은 근로시간으로 보고 있다(법 제50조). 근로기준법상 휴게시간은 근로시간에서 제외되지만, 근로를 위해 대기하는 시간은 휴게시간이 아니라 근로시간으로 판단하고 있다. 이 경우 근로시간과 휴게시간의 관계가 명확하지만 대기시간과 휴게시간은 구분이 모호한 면이 있다. 근로시간을 설계함에 있어서 업무의 특성을 고려하여 적절한 휴게시간을 잘 이용한다면, 법정근로시간내에서도 최적의 근로시간 확보가 가능하다. 이하에서는 적합한 근로시간제도의 설계를 위하여 휴게시간의 개념, 대기시간과 휴게시간을 구분하는 기준을 이해하고, 휴게시간을 이용한 근로시간제도 사례를 검토해 보고자 한다.

II. 휴게시간의 개념과 사용

1. 법규정

근로기준법에서 근로시간이 4시간인 경우에는 30분 이상, 8시간인 경우에는 1시간 이상의 휴게시간을 근로시간 도중에 주어야 한다(근기법 제54조).

---

[84] 하갑례, 「근로기준법」 제28판, 2016년, 323면; 임종률, 「노동법」 제17판, 2019년, 460면.
[85] 법무 811-28682, 선고일자 : 1980-05-15

8 working hours during working hours (Article 54 of the LSA). Any person who violates the provision of 'recess period' shall be punished by imprisonment of up to two years or by a fine not exceeding twenty million won (Article 110). Working hours per week shall not exceed 40 hours excluding recess hours, and working hours per day shall not exceed 8 hours excluding recess hours, and waiting hours that the worker spends while under the employer's direction and supervision for work shall be regarded as working hours (Article 50).

2. Free use of recess periods

'Recess period' means time which a worker is free to use away from the supervision and command of an employer during working hours.[86] Here, the term 'working hours' refers to the time when a worker provides work in a labor contract under the direction and supervision of an employer. Even if a worker is not actively working (i.e. waiting time, rest time, sleeping time, etc.), if it is a period of time when that free use is not guaranteed to the worker and is actually time under the control and supervision of an employer, this time is included in working hours.[87]

A recess period is part of the working hours from the start to the end of work, so even during a recess period it is unavoidable that a worker may still be subject to a certain level of restriction, such as the command and supervision of an employer to continue to carry out work. In other words, workers can be given free breaks, but at the same time there may be some restricted recess periods, depending on the nature of the work, when it is necessary to maintain continuity of work and efficiently respond to emergency situations. In this case, if workers are free to use the recess period beyond the command and supervision of the employer, even though they are restricted within the workplace or are not allowed to leave the workplace during the break without permission, these limitations, which may be required in order to meet objective criteria recognized in advance, can be accepted as a reasonable limitation as to where and how to use breaks.[88]

3. Scope and use of recess periods

(1) Principle: Article 54 (1) of the Labor Standards Act stipulates that an employer

---

[86] Supreme Court ruling on April 14, 1992: 91da20548.
[87] Supreme Court ruling on November 23, 2006: 2006da41990; Supreme Court ruling on December 5, 2017: 2014da74254.
[88] Government Guide: The Legislative Office 16-0239, issued on August 19, 2016.

이 휴게규정을 위반한 자는 2년 이하의 징역 또는 1천만 원 이하의 벌금에 처한다(법 제110조). 또한 법정근로시간은 휴게시간을 제외하고 주40시간, 1일 8시간으로 제한하고, 작업을 위한 대기시간은 휴게시간이 아닌 근로시간으로 규정하고 있다(법 제50조).

2. 휴게시간의 자유이용

휴게시간이란 근로자가 근로시간 도중에 사용자의 지휘명령으로부터 완전히 벗어나 자유로운 이용이 보장된 시간을 의미한다.[86] 여기서 근로시간이라 함은 근로자가 사용자의 지휘감독 아래 근로계약상의 근로를 제공하는 시간을 말한다. 근로자가 작업시간의 도중에 실제로 작업에 종사하지 않은 대기시간이나 휴식수면시간 등이라 하더라도 그것이 휴게시간으로서 근로자에게 자유로운 이용이 보장된 것이 아니고 실질적으로 사용자의 지휘감독하에 놓여있는 시간이라면 이는 근로시간에 포함된다.[87] 휴게시간은 작업의 시작으로부터 종료 시까지로 제한된 시간 중의 일부이므로, 휴게시간 중이라고 하더라도 다음 작업의 계속을 위하여 사용자의 지휘감독 등 일정 수준의 제약을 받는 것은 부득이하다. 즉, 근로자에게 그 종사하는 업무의 특성에 따라 자유로운 휴게시간을 부여하면서도 업무의 연속성을 유지하고 업무와 관련한 긴급 상황에 효율적으로 대응할 수 있도록 하는 등 최소한의 질서유지를 위하여 휴게시간의 이용에 관한 제한이 이루어질 수 있다. 이 경우 근로자로 하여금 사용자의 지휘감독을 벗어나 휴게시간을 자유롭게 이용할 수 있도록 하고 그 장소를 사업장 안으로 제한하거나 휴게시간에 사업장 밖에 나갈 수 있도록 하면서도 이를 사전에 마련된 객관적 기준에 합치되는 경우에만 허가하는 등의 제한은 휴게시간의 이용 장소와 방법에 관한 합리적인 제한이다.[88]

3. 휴게시간의 범위와 부여방법

(1) 원칙: 근로기준법 제54조 제1항은 사용자는 근로시간이 4시간인 경우에는

---

[86] 대법원 1992.4.14. 선고 91다20548 판결
[87] 대법원 2006.11.23. 선고 2006다41990 판결; 대법원 2017.12.5. 선고 2014다74254 판결
[88] 법제처 16-0239,회시일자 : 2016-08-19

shall provide a recess period of 30 minutes or more in the case of 4 hours of work, or 1 hour or more in the case of 8 hours of work. This is the minimum standard for recess periods that employers must provide for workers who work continuously for specific periods of time.[89] Even if the recess period is provided and given in divided portions distinctive from working hours, as long as such recess periods are reasonable in view of the nature of the work and the working conditions, this cannot be regarded as a violation of the recess regulation.[90]

(2) **Working hours of less than 8 hours:** Employers shall provide 30 minutes or more of recess period during the working hours to workers whose working time is more than 4 hours and less than 8 hours.[91] However, since this is the lowest standard, it is not a problem to provide more recess time.

(3) **Divided recess periods:** The Labor Standards Act does not provide any provision for dividing a recess period into 10 minutes for every hour or 20 minutes for every two hours. A breakdown of subdivided hours may not be admitted, as the purpose of a recess period is to provide rehabilitation from fatigue, promotion of work efficiency, prevention of work accidents, eating time and to meet other socio-cultural requirements.[92]

(4) **Working hours exceeding 8 hours:** In case of overtime work for more than 8 hours per day, a recess period of 30 minutes or more for 4 hours of overtime work and 1 hour or more for 8 hours or more shall be provided pursuant to Article 54 of the Labor Standards Act.[93]

III. Classification of Waiting Time and Recess Period

1 Judgment standard

(1) Working time and recess period

'Working time' refers to the time during which an employee provides work under the direction and supervision of an employer. Any waiting time is under the

---

[89] Government Guide: The Legislative Office 15-0847,issued on December 24, 2015.
[90] Government Guide: Gungi 68207-3307,December 2, 2002.
[91] Government Guide: The Legislative Office 15-0847,issued on December 24, 2015.
[92] Government Guide: Gungi 0125-884, June 25, 1992.
[93] Government Guide: Working condition guide team-722,February 6, 2009.

30분 이상, 8시간인 경우에는 1시간 이상의 휴게시간을 근로시간 도중에 주어야 한다고 규정하고 있다. 이는 문헌상 일정 시간 동안 계속적으로 근로하는 근로자에게 사업주가 부여하여야 하는 휴게시간의 최저기준을 정한 것이다.[89] 근무시간과 명백히 구분하여 휴게시간을 분할하여 부여하더라도 작업의 성질, 근로여건 등에 비추어 사회통념상 합리성이 있고 휴게제도의 취지를 벗어나지 않는 한 이를 법위반으로 보기 어렵다.[90]

(2) **8시간 미만의 근로시간**: 사용자는 근로시간이 4시간 이상 8시간 미만인 근로자에게 30분 이상의 휴게시간을 근로시간 도중에 주어야 한다.[91] 다만, 이는 최저기준이므로 더 많은 시간을 주는 것은 문제가 없다.

(3) **분할부여**: 휴게시간을 분할해 1시간마다 10분, 2시간마다 20분 등과 같이 세분화해 부여할 수 있는지에 대해 근로기준법에는 이에 대한 규정이 없으나 피로회복, 작업능률증진, 재해발생예방, 식사 기타 사회적-문화적 욕구의 실현 등이 휴게의 목적인 만큼 지나치게 세분화된 휴게시간은 인정되지 않을 수 있다.[92]

(4) **8시간을 초과하는 근로시간**: 하루 8시간을 초과하여 연장 근로를 하는 경우, 연장 근로 4시간에 대하여 30분 이상, 8시간 이상 근로시 1시간 이상의 휴게 시간을 근로기준법 제54조에 의거하여 부여할 법적 의무가 있다.[93]

Ⅲ. 대기시간과 휴게시간의 구분

1 판단기준

(1) 근로시간과 휴게시간

근로시간은 근로자가 사용자의 지휘감독 아래 근로계약상의 근로를 제공하는 시간을 말하는 것으로 명칭 여하를 불문하고 근로자가 그 노동력을 사용자의

---

[89] 법제처 15-0847,회시일자 : 2015-12-24
[90] 근기 68207-3307,회시일자 : 2002-12-02
[91] 법제처 15-0847,회시일자 : 2015-12-24
[92] 근기 0125-884, 1992.6.25
[93] 근로조건지도과-722,회시일자 : 2009-02-06

direction and supervision of the employer, and so shall be regarded as working time (Article 53 (3) of the LSA). On the other hand, 'recess period' refers to the time which a worker is free to use away from the command and supervision of an employer during working hours.[94]

(2) Waiting time and recess period

Both 'waiting time' and 'recess period' are common, in terms of occurring during working hours. The difference is that 'waiting time' is the time preparatory to engaging in work as soon as the employer instructs and is therefore under the direction and supervision of the employer. 'Recess period' on the other hand, is time which workers are free to use separate from the direction and supervision of an employer. Therefore, the distinction between the two is determined according to whether the worker can freely use the time available.[95] If the worker can clearly distinguish the recess period before starting work, and can freely use it with no direction or supervision of an employer, it must be regarded as a recess period, but if it is not known when there will be a work-related instruction from the employer while the worker is waiting, the time cannot be considered a recess period, but as working time.[96]

2. Related cases

(1) Drivers for transportation companies

When workers of transportation companies, such as tour bus drivers, go to work and are not sure at what time they will be placed dispatched for work, and freely wait at the workplace, but when workers wait without knowing when they will be requested to work for the employer, such waiting time is not considered a recess period. However if, due to the nature of the work, it is not possible to uniformly set a certain recess period in advance, if the dispatch time of the day is clearly defined so that the distinction between the dispatch time (vehicle operation time)

---

[94] (2016.10) The Guideline of working hours and recess period for surveillance or intermittent work
[95] Seonggil Lee, Recess period in Labor Law, 「Labor Law」April 2004, Vol. 155. Joongang Kyungjae
[96] Government Guide: Gungi 01254-12495,August 5, 1987.

처분 아래에 두고 있는 경우에는 근로시간으로 인정한다. 작업을 위하여 근로자가 사용자의 지휘감독 아래에 있는 대기시간 등은 근로시간으로 본다 (법 제53조제3항). 이에 반해 휴게시간은 근로자가 근로시간의 도중에 사용자의 지휘명령으로부터 완전히 벗어나 자유로운 이용이 보장된 시간을 말한다.[94]

(2) 대기시간과 휴게시간

대기시간과 휴게시간은 모두 출근한 상태에서 근로시간 중간에 부여한다는 공통점이 있다. 그러나 대기시간은 사용자의 지시가 있으면 바로 작업에 종사해야 하는 시간으로서 그 작업상의 지휘감독 하에 놓여져 있다. 반면에 휴게시간은 사용자의 작업상의 지휘감독에서 이탈하여 근로자가 자유로이 이용할 수 있는 시간이다. 따라서 양자의 구별은 그 시간을 근로자가 자유롭게 이용할 수 있는지의 여부에 따라 판단한다.[95] 작업의 진행상황에 따라 근로자가 미리 작업개시 전에 휴게시간을 명백히 구분할 수 있는 상황에 있고, 그 시간 중에 사용자의 지휘감독을 벗어나 자유로이 사용할 수 있다면 휴게시간으로 보아야 할 것이다. 다만 사용자로부터 언제 업무지시가 있을지 불분명한 상태에서 대기하는 시간은 휴게시간으로 볼 수 없고 근로시간으로 본다.[96]

2. 구분사례

(1) 운수회사의 버스기사

관광버스 등의 운수회사의 근로자가 출근시간에 출근하여 퇴근시까지 어느 시간에 배차가 될지 불확실하여 사업장내에서 어느 정도 자유롭게 대기는 하고 있으나 사용자로부터 언제 운행 요구가 있을지 모르는 상태에서 근로자가 대기 중일 경우에는 그 대기중의 시간은 휴게시간이라고는 볼 수 없다. 그러나 업무의 성질상 일정시간의 휴게시간을 미리 일률적으로 정할 수는 없으나 근무전일 혹은 근무당일에 출근과 동시에 당일의 배차시간이 명백히 정하여져서 배차시간(차량운행시간)과 대기시간의 구분이 명백하고, 근로자가 사전에 대기시간을 알고 있으며, 그 대기시간 중에는 사용자의 지휘감독을 벗어나

---
[94] (2016.10) 감시, 단속적 근로자의 근로시간과 휴게시간 구분에 대한 가이드라인
[95] 이승길, 노동법상의 휴게시간, 월간 노동법률, 2004년 4월호, Vol. 155. 중앙경제.
[96] 근기 01254-12495,회시일자 : 1987-08-05

Chapter3-5. Recess Periods and Designing a Working Hour System

and waiting time is clear before work or on the day of work, and if the worker knows the waiting time in advance and if such waiting time is available freely beyond the direction and supervision of the employer, this is a recess period.[97]

(2) Apartment guards

In this instance, apartment guards worked 24 hours from 07:00 to 07:00 the next day, and then rested. Among the 24 hours of work, the recess period consisted of 6 hours, and was divided into 1 hour for lunch, 1 hour for dinner, and 4 hours for night break (from 24:00 to 04:00). They were required to respond immediately if something urgent happened, even if it occurred during the night recess period. Although guards were wearing their work uniforms and took a nap during the night recess period, they were ready to react immediately in case of an emergency, and therefore such night rest periods should be regarded as working time.[98]

(3) Goshiwon (long-stay inn) receptionists

Goshiwon receptionists do not have predetermined times set aside for recess periods. As visitors or new tenants do not have a fixed arrival time, the receptionists must remain in place without leaving the Goshiwon house. The owner provides the necessary work instructions without special time constraints, and receptionists must also fulfill unscheduled instructions. Although the receptionists did not have any special work to do, and although they took long breaks or studied during many of the waiting hours, such time is considered to be a waiting time for work, not a recess period completely free from direction and supervision.[99]

(4) Postal vehicle drivers

Drivers working in the postal logistic service have often taken breaks (such as eating or sleeping) at work, while working every other day. However, these breaks were taken during gaps in time while waiting to provide labor between the time of going to work and leaving work at a specific time. In other words, such periods

---

[97] Government Guide: Bubmoo 811-28682,issued on May 15, 1980.
[98] Supreme Court ruling on December 13, 2017: 2016da243078.
[99] Seoul Central District Court ruling on June 23, 2017: 2017no922.

자유로이 이용할 수 있다면 이는 휴게시간이다.[97]

(2) 아파트 야간 경비원

한 아파트의 경비원들은 아침 7시부터 다음날까지 24시간을 근무하고, 그 다음날은 쉬는 격일제 근무를 해 왔다. 24시간 중 휴게시간은 총 6시간으로 구성됐고 휴게시간은 점심 1시간, 저녁 1시간, 야간휴게시간(자정 12시부터 새벽 4시까지) 4시간으로 구분됐다. 입주민들은 경비원들에게 야간휴게시간에 가수면상태라도 급한 일이 발생하면 즉각 반응 할 것을 서면으로 지시했다. 경비원들이 야간휴게시간에 근무복을 입고 가수면상태로 휴식을 취하면서 급한 일이 발생하면 즉각 반응할 수 있는 상태로 일했다면, 이러한 야간휴게시간은 근로시간으로 본다.[98]

(3) 고시원 총무

고시원 총무들에게는 휴게시간으로 사용할 수 있는 구체적 시간이 미리 정해져 있지 않았다. 방문자나 새로운 세입자가 찾아오는 것은 정해진 시간이 있는 것이 아니므로 고시원을 벗어나지 않고 항상 자리를 지키고 있어야 했다. 고시원 주인은 특별한 시간의 제약이 없이 그때 그때 필요한 업무지시를 하였고, 돌발적인 업무지시를 이행하였다. 비록 고시원 총무들이 특별한 업무가 없어 휴식을 취하거나 공부를 하는 등으로 시간을 보냈다고 하더라도, 그 시간은 고시원 주인의 지휘명령으로부터 완전히 벗어나 자유로운 이용이 보장되는 휴게시간이 아니므로 근로를 위한 대기시간에 해당한다.[99]

(4) 우편운송 차량기사

우편물운송차량의 운전직에 종사하는 직원들은 격일제 근무형태로 근무하는 도중에 수시로 수면이나 식사 등의 휴식을 취하여 왔다. 그러나 이는 어디까지나 일정한 시각에 출근하여 퇴근할 때까지 항상 사업장 내에서 운전업무 등의 노무제공을 위하여 대기하는 상태에서 그 공백시간에 틈틈이 이루어진 것이지 결코 일정한 수면시간이나 휴식시간이 보장되어 있지 않으므로 사업주의 지휘,

---

[97] 법무 811-28682, 선고일자 : 1980-05-15
[98] 대법원 2017.12.13 선고 2016다243078 판결.
[99] 서울중앙지법 2017. 6. 23 선고 2017노922 판결.

(5) Nursing assistants

The labor contract of nursing assistants who worked a three-shift schedule specified a four-hour rest period during the night shift and the availability of a night-time sleeping room. However, in reality they often could not sleep there due to emergency calls from patients at the nursing hospital where they worked. Such periods should be regarded as waiting hours for work.[101]

IV. Recess Periods and Related Working Hour Cases

1. Recess periods in hotel restaurants

In many restaurants, there are times when it is not busy, such as between breakfast and lunch and between lunch and dinner, so the business closes for two to three hours per day. Workers who are preparing for their work are recognized as working, but other workers are allowed to use this time freely to go out or rest. In response to this, the Ministry of Employment and Labor presented this opinion: Article 54 of the Labor Standards Act only specifies the minimum standard of a recess period, but there is no regulation on the longest time. Therefore long recess periods (2-3 hours) exceeding statutory recess periods are acceptable, but unlimited long intervals during working hours are against the original intent of the recess system. In order to view such long breaks as a recess period under the Labor Standards Act, there must be objective reasons that can be generally recognized as necessary and socially valid in view of the nature of the work or the working conditions of the workplace. Such recess period should be decided in advance by collective agreement, employment rules, labor contract, etc., so that employers cannot change or extend it arbitrarily, and workers should be guaranteed to be able to use it free from the provision of labor.[102]

2. Long recess periods at hotels

---

[100] Supreme Court ruling on May 27, 1993: 92da24509.
[101] Supreme Court ruling on September 8, 2016: 2014do8873.
[102] Government Guide: Gungi 01254-1344, August 11, 1992.

감독으로부터 벗어나 자유로운 휴게시간으로 이용한 것이 아니다.[100]

(5) 요양보호사

3교대로 근무하는 요양보호사의 근로계약서에는 야간 근무시간 중 4시간의 휴게시간이 명시돼 있고 잠을 잘 수 있는 야간수면실도 운영했지만 실제로는 요양 대상자가 비상벨을 누르는 경우가 많아 잠을 이루지 못하고 늘 대기상태에 대해 법원은 이들의 당해 야간근무 중 휴게시간은 근로시간으로 본다.[101]

Ⅳ. 휴게시간과 관련한 근로시간제도 사례

1. 호텔식당의 휴게시간

호텔의 일부 식당에서는 조식과 중식 사이, 중식과 석식 사이 등 고객이 오지 않는 시간대가 있어 일시 사업장의 문을 닫고 영업을 중지하는 시간이 보통 하루에 1인당 2~3시간 정도며 이 시간 동안 다음 영업의 준비를 위하여 근무하는 사원은 근무로 인정하나 그 외 사원들에게는 외출·휴게 등을 자유로이 이용할 수 있도록 하고 있다. 이에 대해 고용노동부의 의견: 근로기준법 제54조에서는 휴게시간의 최저기준만을 규정하고 있을 뿐 최장시간에 대한 규제 규정이 없으므로 법정시간 이상 상당히 긴 시간(2~4시간)을 휴게시간으로 부여하는 것은 무방하나 휴게제도의 본래 취지에 어긋난 무제한 인정은 부당하다. 이러한 장시간의 휴식시간을 근로기준법상 휴게시간으로 보기 위해서는 작업의 성질 또는 사업장의 근로조건 등에 비추어 사회통념상 필요하고도 타당성이 있다고 일반적으로 인정될 수 있는 객관적인 사유가 있어야 할 것이며, 이러한 휴게시간은 단체협약, 취업규칙, 근로계약 등에 의하여 미리 정하여져 있어 사용자가 임의변경 하거나 연장할 수 없어야 하고 근로자는 근로의 제공으로부터 완전히 이탈하여 자유로이 이용할 수 있도록 보장되어 있어야 한다.[102]

2. 호텔 휴게시간

---

100) 대법원 1993.5.27 선고 92다24509 판결.
101) 대법원 2016.9.8 선고 2014도8873 판결.
102) 근기 01254-1344,회시일자 : 1992-08-11

A break time system refers to a working hour system that allows workers to rest for a time period longer than the stipulated time of the law by using time when the work load is significantly less or non-existent (In case of hotel business, 14:00 ~ 17:00 break time is usually used). It is difficult to say if it is illegal for an employer to enforce a break time system for workers because the Labor Standards Act specifies only the minimum standard for a recess period with no maximum regulated limits.[103]

3. Middle East construction workers' long recess periods

In the Middle East, it is objectively recognized that workers cannot work outside on construction sites where the temperature rises rapidly during the day. Instead, they work from 06:00 to 10:00, taking recess time from 10:00 to 16:00, and then working from 16:00 to 20:00, according to collective agreements, employment rules or labor contracts. During the recess period, workers are completely free from work-related activities. In such cases, even though the recess period is long, such long intervals between working hours can be recognized as recess periods.[104]

V. Conclusion

Whether a break or waiting time set out in a labor contract falls within 'working hours' or 'recess period' cannot be judged exclusively according to a particular kind of business or type of work. It should be judged based upon considerations such as (i) the terms of the employment contract, the rules of employment, or collective agreement applicable to the workplace, (ii) the work provided by the employee and the specific type of work at the workplace, (iii) the employer's control and supervision of employees during recess hours, (iv) whether there is a freely-available resting place, and (v) other circumstances such as whether or not the worker's actual rest can be interrupted or whether there are situations which allow the employer to direct and supervise workers during recess hours.[105]

---

[103] Government Guide: Inspection 01254-6504,November 28, 1990.
[104] Government Guide: Bubmoo 811-28682,issued on May 15, 1980.
[105] Supreme Court ruling on June 28, 2018: 2013da28926.

브레이크타임제란 근무시간중 작업량이 현저히 적거나 없는 시간을 이용하여 법이 정한 휴식시간 이상의 장시간을 휴식하게 하는 제도를 말한다(호텔업인 경우 보통 14:00~17:00 브레이크타임 적용). 휴게시간의 최저기준만을 명시할 뿐 기타 상한적 규제가 명시된 바 없으므로 사용자가 근로자에게 브레이크타임제를 실시토록 하는 것이 불법이라고 보기에는 곤란하다.[103]

3. 중동 건설근로자의 장시간 휴게시간

중동지방에서는 낮에는 기온이 상승하여 야외에서 작업하는 건설공사현장 근로자들이 작업을 할 수 없는 것이 사회통념상 객관적으로 인정할 수 있으며, 또한 단체협약, 취업규칙 또는 근로계약 등에 매일의 작업시간이 06:00~10:00까지의 작업, 10:00~16:00까지 휴게시간, 16:00~20:00까지 작업시간으로 정하여 작업한 경우, 동 휴게시간 중에는 근로자가 근로행위로부터 완전히 이탈하여 자유로이 활용할 수 있다면 휴게시간이 장시간이라 할지라도 이를 휴게시간으로 인정한다.[104]

V. 결론 (법원의 판례를 인용하면서 이를 결론에 갈음한다)

근로계약에서 정한 휴식시간이나 대기시간이 근로시간에 속하는지 휴게시간에 속하는지는 특정 업종이나 업무의 종류에 따라 일률적으로 판단할 것이 아니다. 이는 (i) 근로계약의 내용이나 해당 사업장에 적용되는 취업규칙과 단체협약의 규정, (ii) 근로자가 제공하는 업무 내용과 해당 사업장의 구체적 업무 방식, (iii) 휴게 중인 근로자에 대한 사용자의 간섭이나 감독 여부, (iv) 자유롭게 이용할 수 있는 휴게 장소의 구비 여부, (v) 그 밖에 근로자의 실질적 휴식이 방해되었다거나 사용자의 지휘감독을 인정할 만한 사정이 있는 지와 그 정도 등 여러 사정을 종합하여 각각의 사안에 따라 구체적으로 판단한다.[105]

---

103) 감독 01254-6504,회시일자 : 1990-11-28
104) 법무 811-28682,선고일자 : 1980-05-15
105) 대법원 2018. 6. 28. 선고 2013다28926 판결

Section 6. Contractual Holidays and Contractual Leave

I. Introduction

An important question every company needs to have an answer to is whether it is required to provide paid off-days on public holidays and paid leave in cases where an employee was absent due to sickness caused by non-occupational activities. In short, if the public holidays are statutory holidays, and if sick leave is statutory leave, the answer is "Yes". In some cases, it is left to the company's discretion, or the requirements of the collective agreement or Rules of Employment. That is, in cases where these days are stipulated as paid off-days according to labor law, they become statutory holidays and statutory leaves. However, if they are not so stipulated, whether to pay or not is the company's decision, upon which they would be considered contractual holidays and contractual leaves. Only Labor Day, public holidays, and the weekly holiday are legally considered statutory holidays. Contractual holidays are those holidays approved by the company. "Statutory leave" refers to annual paid holidays, maternity leave, and paternity leave, etc., while "contractual leave" consists of congratulatory and condolence leave, sick leave, and summer leave, etc. I'd like to look into this in more detail, as well as examples of application.

	Statutory	Contractual
Holiday	Weekly Holidays (Article 55) Public holidays Labor Day (Establishment of Labor Day on May 1st)	Company holidays (e.g. Company foundation day)
Leave	Annual paid leave (Article 60) Maternity/paternity leave (Article 74)	1) Congratulatory/condolence leave; 2) Sick leave; 3) Summer leave
Remarks	1) Obligated by law 2) Wage is paid	1) Based upon collective agreement, Rules of Employment, etc. 2) Issue of payment depends on mutual agreement

제6절 약정휴일 및 약정휴가

I. 들어가며

국가공휴일을 반드시 유급으로 부여하여야 하는 지와 근로자가 업무와 상관없이 발생한 질병이나 부상으로 인해 결근하는 경우에 유급으로 휴가를 부여해야 하는지에 대해 다소 혼란이 생길 수 있다. 이와 관련하여, 국가공휴일이 법정휴일이고 병가가 법정휴가인 경우에는 반드시 해당 근무 일에 또는 해당 기간에 대해 유급으로 휴일 또는 휴가를 부여해야 한다. 그러나 이것이 순전히 회사의 재량사항인 경우에는 사용자의 승인, 단체협약 또는 취업규칙으로 유급이나 무급여부를 결정할 수 있다. 즉, 노동법 상 유급으로 정해진 경우에는 법정휴일과 법정휴가가 되며, 노동법으로 정해지지 않고 회사의 재량에 따라 부여여부가 결정되면 약정휴일, 약정휴가가 된다. 법정휴일에는 주휴일, 국가공휴일, 근로자의 날이 해당되며, 약정휴일은 회사에서 실시하는 모든 휴일이 해당한다. 그리고 법정휴가는 연차유급휴가, 산전산후가, 배우자 출산휴가 등이 있고, 약정휴가에는 경조휴가, 병가, 하계휴가 등이 있다. 이와 관련된 주요내용과 적용 사례를 살펴보고자 한다.

구분	법 정	약 정
휴일	주휴일(근로기준법 제55조) 2) 국가공휴일 3) 근로자의 날 (근로기준법)	기업의 휴일 (회사창립일등)
휴가	1) 연차유급휴가(근로기준법 제60조) 2) 산전·산후휴가(근로기준법 제74조)	1) 경조휴가 2) 병가 3) 하계휴가
특징	1) 법에 근거하여 의무적으로 부여 2) 임금지급(유급)	1) 부여 여부, 부여 조건 등이 단체 협약, 취업규칙 등을 통해 결정됨 2) 임금지급 여부도 결정하는 바에 따름

II. Contractual holidays

1. Concept

Unlike statutory holidays, contractual holidays must be stipulated in the Rules of Employment or collective agreement in order to be legally recognized as paid or unpaid holidays. Statutory holidays shall be granted on particular dates and if work is done on those days, the company shall pay an additional holiday work allowance. Statutory holidays consist of a weekly holiday (Article 55 of the LSA: An employer shall allow a worker on the average one or more paid holidays per week) and Labor Day (Act Concerning Establishment of Labor Day: The day of May 1st shall be proclaimed as Labor Day and is a paid holiday as determined by the National Labor Relations Commission.) However, contractual holidays are determined exclusively by the employer regarding particular dates and whether the holidays are paid or unpaid. If an employee works on a holiday stipulated as paid, the company shall pay an additional overtime allowance.

2. Types of contractual holidays

Corporate holidays refer to paid off-days, such as Company Foundation Day, Labor Union Day, etc., that the company has designated in the collective agreement and the Rules of Employment.

3. Relationship between labor law and contractual holidays

In cases where contractual holidays are settled as paid off-days, employees are exempted from provision of labor, and if employees had to work on contractual holidays like paid public holidays, they are entitled to paid wages (100%), which are already included in monthly wages, and additional holiday work allowance (150%) (Article 56 of the LSA: Additional Allowances).

III. Contractual Leave

1. Concept

Ⅱ. 약정휴일

1. 개념

약정휴일은 법정휴일과 다르게 반드시 취업규칙이나 단체협약으로 정해진 경우에 인정되는 것으로 사용자가 무급휴일 또는 유급휴일로 운용할 수 있다. 법정휴일의 경우에는 해당되는 특정일자에 반드시 휴일을 부여하거나 근로자가 근무할 경우에는 그에 따른 별도의 휴일근로수당을 지급해야 한다. 법정휴일은 「근로기준법」 제55조에 의한 주휴일(사용자는 근로자에게 1주일에 평균 1회 이상의 유급휴일을 주어야 한다)과 「근로자의 날 제정에 관한 법률」에 의한 근로자의날(5월 1일을 근로자의 날로 하고 이 날을 「근로기준법」에 의한 유급휴일로 한다.)이 있다. 그러나, 약정휴일은 날짜지정이나 유급 또는 무급을 전적으로 사용자의 판단에 따른다. 약정휴일이 유급으로 정해진 경우에 약정휴일에 근무한 경우에는 휴일근로수당을 지급해야 한다.

2. 약정휴일의 유형

회사가 정한 회사의 창립일, 노조설립일 등으로 회사가 단체협약이나 취업규칙으로 유급휴일로서 인정하는 경우에 해당된다.

3. 노동법과 약정휴일과의 관계

약정휴일을 유급으로 설정한 경우에는 그 약정휴일에는 근로제공의무가 제외되며, 이 약정휴일에 사용자의 지시에 의해 근로를 제공한 경우에는 근로제공이 없더라도 지급받을 수 있었던 임금(100%)와 휴일근로 가산임금(150%: 근로기준법 제56조: 가산임금)을 추가로 지급해야 한다.

Ⅲ. 약정휴가

1. 개념

Chapter3-6. Contractual Holidays and Contractual Leave

Contractual leave refers to paid vacation, free of labor provision in accordance with employer approval, a collective agreement or the Rules of Employment. Such leaves include congratulatory and condolence leave, sick leave, summer vacation, and other special leave, etc. Contractual leaves are not statutory like annual paid leave, or maternity/paternity leave, but are introduced to maintain traditional Korean values and improve employee well-being, and can be stipulated as paid, partially paid, or unpaid leaves. A company that does not stipulate these contractual leaves is not in violation of the Labor Standards Act.

2. Types of contractual leave

(1) Congratulatory and condolence leave

Many companies provide congratulatory and condolence leaves for wedding and funeral services in accordance with traditional Korean rituals. Although the coverage and number of leaves vary from company to company, these leaves are granted as an addition to annual paid leaves. A maximum of five leave days are given for an employee's wedding as congratulatory leave, a maximum of five days are given as condolence leave in the event of the death of an employee's direct family member, and one day is given for a parent's 60th birthday.

(2) Sick leave

Should an employee be unable to carry out his/her duties due to non-occupational injury or illness, the employee shall use annual paid leave to receive medical treatment and shall bear the medical expenses him/herself as there is no statutory sick leave. Government employees can use up to 60 days per year sick leave according to Article 18 of the Government Employee Service Regulations (Sick Leave). In the private sector, if an employee has used up all his/her annual leave days, he/she may request unpaid leave to take care of illness or injury. If the employee has to continually be absent in order to receive treatment for his/her illness or injury, the company can dismiss the employee for reasons attributable to the employee. Many companies have some restricted types of sick leave, such as follows.

약정휴가는 사용자의 승인, 단체협약이나 취업규칙으로 유급휴가를 제공함으로써 근로제공의무를 면제해주는 휴가로 경조휴가, 병가, 하계휴가, 특별휴가 등이 있다. 약정휴가는 연차유급휴가, 산전산후휴가, 배우자출산휴가와 같이 근로기준법으로 보장된 것이 아니라 한국의 전통적 가치를 존중하고 근로자들의 복지차원에서 도입된 휴가라 할 수 있다. 이러한 약정휴가를 설정해놓지 않았다고 하여 근로기준법을 위반한 것이 아니며, 그 약정휴가에 대해 회사의 재량에 따라 유급, 부분적 유급, 또는 무급으로 설정하여 운용할 수 있다.

2. 약정휴가의 유형

(1) 경조휴가

많은 회사들이 한국의 오래된 관혼상제의 전통에 따라 혼례와 상례에 관련하여 경조휴가를 부여하고 있다. 그 대상범위나 부여일수가 다를 수 있지만, 일반적으로 연차유급휴가와 별개로 추가적으로 유급휴가를 부여한다. 본인 결혼의 경우 5일 이내, 직계가족의 사망시에 5일이내, 부모님의 환갑의 경우 1일을 부여한다.

(2) 병가

근로자가 업무 외에 발생한 개인적 질병이나 부상으로 인하여 직무를 수행할 수 없을 때에는 법정 병가가 인정되지 않고 있기 때문에 본인의 연차유급휴가를 사용하여 요양을 해야 하고 또는 치료비 일체도 근로자 개인이 부담해야 한다. 다만, 공무원인 경우에는 「국가공무원 복무규정」 제18조(병가) 규정에 의해 연60일까지 유급병가를 사용할 수 있다. 따라서 병가규정이 없는 일반 회사의 경우에 근로자는 병가를 신청할 수 없기 때문에 자신에게 주어진 잔여 연차유급휴가를 사용하여 치료를 하여야 하고, 연차유급휴가를 모두 사용한 경우에는 무급휴직을 청구하게 된다. 근로자가 질병 또는 부상 치료를 위해 계속해서 결근하는 경우에는 회사는 근로자의 귀책사유로 인한 통상해고를 할 수 있다. 많은 회사들이 취업규칙에 제한적인 유급 병가규정을 설정하고 있는데 그 유형은 다음과 같다.

Type 1	No regulation for sick leave days. Annual paid leave shall be used instead.
Type 2	"The company may grant unpaid sick leave of up to 90 days per calendar year.
Type 3	"If an employee requires an extended time of absence due to accident or illness unrelated to his/her duties, he/she may request to use paid leave. The period shall not exceed 14 calendar days, provided that the accrued annual leave has been used up already."
Type 4	"In case of a leave of absence due to non-work related injury or illness, 90% of monthly ordinary wage shall be paid for the first month, 70% of monthly ordinary wage for the second month and 50% of monthly ordinary wage for the third to sixth months."

(3) Summer vacation

Summer vacation refers to contractual leave granted of a maximum one week besides annual paid leave during the heat of the summer in order to promote employee morale. This summer leave is used collectively by production companies, while smaller companies generally use annual paid leave days as summer vacation.

3. Relationship between labor law and contractual leave

(1) It is impossible to change the date for congratulatory or condolence leave or to apply for it retroactively (Gungi 68207-1452, Sep 14, 1994)

Congratulatory and condolence leave refers to paid leaves granted on particular days or for a particular period to the corresponding employee in accordance with the collective agreement or Rules of Employment so that the employee can participate in congratulatory or condolence events. It is not possible to change the period of leave nor retroactively apply for them.

(2) Congratulatory and condolence leave not granted during labor strikes (Gungi 68207-883, Dec 15, 1999)

According to the Labor Standards Act (LSA), "holiday" refers to a day when the employee is exempted from the provision of labor for the employer, while "leave" refers to days exempted from the obligation to provide work even though the employer is available to receive the labor service. While contractual

유형1	병가규정없음. 이 경우 연차휴가로 사용하여야 함.
유형2	"회사는 역년으로 90일까지의 병가를 지급할 수 있다. 병가는 무급으로 한다."
유형3	"직원이 업무 외의 사고나 질병으로 장기간 결근해야 할 경우, 연차휴가를 모두 사용하고 휴일을 포함하여 14일을 초과하지 않는 범위 안에서 유급 병가를 신청할 수 있다."
유형4	"개인상병에 의한 휴직일 경우에는 최초1개월: 월 통상급여의 90%; 2개월 차: 월 통상급여의 70%; 3~6개월차: 월 통상급여의 50%를 지급한다."

(3) 하계휴가

하계휴가는 연차유급휴가와 별도로 직원들의 사기진작을 위해 한여름에 1주일이내에서 지급하는 약정휴가제도이다. 주로 제조업체서 집단적으로 사용하고, 소규모 사업장의 경우에는 연차휴가를 대체해서 하계휴가로 사용하기도 한다.

3. 노동법과 약정휴가와의 관계

(1) 경조휴가 시기변경권 불가능 및 소급 불가(근기68207-1452, 1994.09.14)

경조휴가는 노사가 단체협약이나 취업규칙 등으로 경조일의 기념이나 경조사 참여를 보장하기 위해 해당 근로자에게 특정일 또는 특정기간에 유급으로 부여하는 휴가로서 사용자의 휴가시기 변경권행사가 불가능하고 또한 그 기일이 경과하면 휴가 사용목적이 소멸되어 휴가청구권 또한 소멸한다.

(2) 쟁의행위기간 중 경조유급휴가는 발생하지 않음(근기68207-883, 1999.12.15)

근로기준법상 휴일이라 함은 근로자가 사용자에 대하여 근로제공의무가 없는 날을 말하며, 근로기준법상 휴가라 함은 사용자가 근로자의 노무수령을 할 수 있는 상태임에도 사용자가 그날의 근로제공의무를 면제시켜 주는 것을 말한다. 노사간 단체협약 또는 취업규칙에서 정한 이른바 약정휴일

holidays or contractual leaves stipulated by a collective agreement or Rules of Employment are not statutory holidays exempted from work provision according to the Labor Standards Act (LSA), they are to be exempted from work provision on working days due to special agreement between employer and employee. Accordingly, if there is a certain condition where the employer, in reality, could neither receive the employee's labor nor exempt him/her from providing labor, then the contractual holiday or contractual leave cannot occur. However, for those who did not participate in strikes during labor disputes, whether a contractual holiday or contractual leave occurred should be judged according to whether the employer could receive the employee's labor or not.

(3) Calculation of average wages during periods of leave (Retirement Pension Dept-518, Oct 21, 2008)

"Average wages" where an employee came to resign after a period of leave from work that the employee took with approval from the employer due to non-occupational injury, illness or other reason shall be calculated as follows: "average wages" to calculate severance pay refer to the amount calculated by dividing the total amount of wages paid to the relevant employee during three calendar months prior to the date of calculation by the total number of calendar days during those three calendar months (Article 2 of the LSA). If the amount calculated by this method is lower than the ordinary wages of the employee concerned, the amount of the ordinary wages shall be deemed as average wages. In cases where the period of calculating average wages includes the period falling under a period of leave from work with approval from the employer caused by non-occupational injury, illness, or other reason, the period and wages paid for that period shall be deducted respectively from a basis period for the calculation of average wages and the total amount of average wage (Article 2 of Enforcement Decree of the LSA). Therefore, in cases where an employee took a leave of absence for non-occupational injury, illness or other reason in accordance with Article 2 (8) of the Enforcement Decree of the LSA (with approval from the employer), the remaining period and wages excluding the period mentioned above shall be used for the calculation of average wages. If the leave of absence exceeds three months, the first day of the leave of absence shall be the date for calculating average wages based on the previous three months. In any case, if the amount calculated above is lower than the ordinary wages of the employee concerned, the amount of the ordinary wages shall be deemed as average wages.

(4) In cases where change of contractual leave is considered a disadvantageous Rule of Employment (Working Conditions Inspection Team-1774, Mar 25, 2009)

또는 약정휴가의 경우는 근로제공의무가 없는 근로기준법상 휴일과는 달리 근로제공의무가 있는 날임에도 노사간 특약에 의하여 사용자가 근로자의 근로제공의무를 면제시켜 준 것으로 보아야 할 것이다. 따라서 사용자가 사실상 근로자의 노무제공을 수령할 수 없고 사용자의 면제행위도 행사할 수 없는 상태였다면 약정휴일 또는 약정휴가 자체가 발생하지 아니한다. 다만 파업기간중 파업 미참석자의 경우에는 사용자가 근로자의 노무제공을 수령할 수 있는 상태인지의 여부에 따라 판단해야 한다.

(3) **휴직기간의 평균임금 산정방법** (행정해석: 퇴직연금복지과-518, 2008.10.21)
업무 외 부상이나 질병, 그 밖의 사유로 사용자의 승인을 받아 휴업한 후 퇴직하게 된 경우에 평균임금을 다음과 같이 계산한다. 퇴직금산정을 위한 평균임금은 이를 산정하여야 할 사유가 발생한 날 이전 3개월 동안에 그 근로자에게 지급된 임금의 총액을 그 기간의 총일수로 나눈 금액을 말하며 (「근로기준법」 제2조), 이러한 방법으로 산출된 평균임금액이 당해 근로자의 통상임금보다 저액일 경우에는 그 통상임금을 평균임금으로 하도록 정하고 있다. 평균임금 산정기간 중에 업무상외 부상 또는 질병으로 사용자의 승인을 받아 휴업한 경우에는 그 기간과 그 기간에 지불된 임금은 평균임금 산정기준이 되는 기간과 임금의 총액에서 각각 공제하도록 규정하고 있다 (근로기준법시행령 제2조). 따라서 근로자가 업무 외 부상이나 질병, 그 밖의 사유로 사용자의 승인을 받아 휴업한 기간일 경우에는 동기간을 제외한 나머지 일수 및 임금을 대상으로 평균임금으로 산정하여야 하며, 휴직한 기간이 3개월을 초과하여 평균임금 산정기준 기간이 없게 되는 경우에는 휴직한 첫 날을 평균임금산정 사유발생일로 보아 이전 3월간을 대상으로 평균임금을 산정하여야 한다. 아울러, 위와 같은 방법으로 산출된 평균임금액이 당해 근로자의 통상 임금보다 저액일 경우에는 그 통상임금액을 평균임금으로 하여야 한다.

(4) **약정휴가 사용변경은 취업규칙불이익변경** (근로조건지도과-1774, 2009.03.25)
회사에서는 직급, 근속년수에 따라 1년에 5~10일의 '건강휴가'를 부여하고 있고 그 사용시기에 관하여는 별도의 제한을 두고 있지 않았다. 그러나,

A particular company has provided 5 to 10 days of 'health vacation' per year according to rank and length of service, but did not set any restrictions on the time of use. If it were to later decide to allow its use only after annual paid leave is used up, this would be restricting free use of the contractual leave, and so would be acceptable and applicable after consent is received according to the appropriate procedures (Article 94 of the LSA).

IV. Conclusion

Contractual holidays and contractual leaves are only effective if they are regulated by a collective agreement, Rules of Employment or the employment contract. As sick leave is widely accepted by many countries as statutory leave, many foreign employees assume sick leave is statutory in Korea too, but as I have explained earlier, it is considered contractual leave. Accordingly, by taking advantage of these contractual holidays and contractual leaves, healthy medium-sized companies can use these holidays and leaves to improve employee morale, while small companies can use them to adjust their working conditions.

Section 7. Annual Paid Leave and Foreign Workers

I. Introduction

According to Annual Paid Leave (Article 60) of the Labor Standards Act (LSA), employees who work 80% or more a year will be given a 15-day paid leave. For employees who have worked for three years or more, one day's paid leave is added for every two years of employment, up to a total of 25 days. However, in instances where incurred annual leave is not completely used, the employer shall compensate for the unused portion by paying ordinary wages. In Korea, the use rate of paid annual leave is only 50%, and the unused leave is compensated for. This does not fit with the purpose of annual paid leave, which was designed to rehabilitate the exhausted minds and bodies of employees through paid vacation, enabling them to live comfortable lives.

종전에는 '건강휴가'의 사용시기에 대하여 아무런 조건없이 허용하다가 이를 연차유급휴가 소진 이후에만 사용할 수 있도록 변경하는 것은 결과적으로 자유로운 사용이 제약되는 것으로, 이는 불이익한 변경에 해당하고 따라서 소정의 동의절차(근로기준법 제94조제1항)를 거쳐야 유효하게 적용될 수 있다.

Ⅳ. 맺는 말

약정휴일과 약정휴가는 전적으로 단체협약, 취업규칙 또는 근로계약에 규정된 경우에 한해서 사용할 수 있다. 병가의 경우에도 법정휴가로 인정하는 국가가 많은 관계로 외국인 근로자들이 당연히 병가를 받을 수 있다고 생각하지만, 상기한 바와 같이 한국에서는 아직까지 병가는 약정휴가에 해당된다. 따라서 이러한 약정휴일이나 약정휴가를 잘 이해함으로써 중견기업에서는 휴일 및 휴가를 직원들의 사기진작을 위한 방향으로 사용할 수 있고, 소규모 열악한 사업장의 경우에는 사업장 수준에 맞는 근로조건을 설정하는데 사용할 수 있다.

제7절 연차유급휴가

Ⅰ. 문제의 소재

근로기준법의 연차유급휴가(제60조) 규정에 따르면, 1년간 80% 이상 출근한 근로자에게는 15일의 유급휴가가 주어진다. 3년 이상 근로한 근로자에게는 매 2년에 대해 1일의 유급휴가가 가산되고 최대 25일 까지 늘어난다. 하지만 매년 발생한 연차휴가를 다 사용하지 못하는 경우에는 미사용 연차유급휴가에 대해 사용자는 통상임금으로 보상해야 한다. 우리나라는 연차유급휴가 사용률이 50% 정도에 지나지 않고, 미사용휴가에 대해서는 금전보상을 하고 있는데 이는 휴가를 통해 근로를 통해 지친 심신을 회복하고 문화적인 생활을 하도록 하는 연차유급휴가의 취지와 맞지 않다고 할 수 있다.

II. Purpose of Annual Paid Leave and Legal Standards

1. Purpose of annual paid leave

Annual paid leave is intended to provide paid leave (separately from paid weekly holidays) in order to allow workers to realize a healthy and relaxed lifestyle.[106] More specifically, the Constitutional Court stated the purpose of the annual leave: "Rest hours or weekly holidays are primarily for the physiological recovery of workers who have accumulated physical or mental fatigue due to daily or weekly work. Annual paid leave is designed to give workers freedom from work for a period of time and to have the opportunity to engage in social and cultural civic life by providing a voluntary leave period without a loss of wages.[107] As for this, the Supreme Court also explains, "It is the purpose of providing an opportunity for mental and physical recreation and improving cultural life by exempting workers from the obligation to work for a certain period of time."[108] Therefore, the objective of annual leave is to improve the quality of life of workers by adding aspects of cultural life in terms of relaxation from work.[109]

2. Comparison of international and national standards for annual paid leave

The international standard for annual paid leave and the Korean standard as per the Labor Standards Act can be compared by dividing them into ① the number of leave days and requirements for the occurrence, ② method of use, ③ the guarantee of annual paid leave, and ④ compensation for unused leave.

The annual paid leave (Article 60) in the Korean Labor Standards Act prescribes the use of leave in principle, but also specifies compensation for unused days.

① As for the number of leave days and the requirements for the occurrence of annual paid leave, "An employer shall grant 15 days' paid leave to a worker who has registered not less than 80 percent of attendance during one year (Article 1). After the first year of service, an employer shall grant one day's paid leave for each two years of consecutive service in addition to the 15 days' paid leave to a worker who has worked consecutively for 3 years or more. In this case, the total number of leave days including the additional

---

[106] Jongryul Lim, 「Labor Law 」, Park Young Sa, 2016, page 454.
[107] Supreme Court ruling on May 28, 2015. 2013 hunma 619 (The purpose of annual paid leave)
[108] Supreme Court ruling on December 26, 2003. 2011 da 4629 (The purpose of annual paid leave)
[109] Hingyoung Kim, "System improvement for annual paid leave to secure rest", 「Study on Labor Laws」, 2016 Volume 40, Seoul University's Labor Law Society, page 165.

Ⅱ. 연차유급휴가의 취지 및 법정기준

1. 연차유급휴가의 취지

연차휴가는 근로자의 건강하고 문화적인 생활을 실현하기 위하여 유급주휴일과 별도로 유급휴가를 부여하려는 것이다.[106] 좀더 구체적으로 헌법재판소도 연차휴가의 취지를, "휴게시간이나 주휴일은 하루 또는 일주일의 노동으로 육체적·정신적 피로가 누적된 근로자들의 생리적인 회복을 위한 것이 주목적이라면, 연차유급휴가는 임금 삭감 없이 휴가기간을 스스로 결정할 수 있게 함으로써 근로자들이 노동으로부터 일정기간 해방되고 사회적·문화적 시민생활을 영위할 수 있는 기회를 보장하기 위한 것이다."라고 기술하고 있다.[107] 이에 대해 대법원도 "근로자에게 일정 기간 근로의무를 면제함으로써 정신적·육체적 휴양의 기회를 제공하고 문화적 생활의 향상을 기하려는데 그 취지가 있다."라고 설명한다.[108] 따라서 연차휴가에 대한 설명의 공통점은 근로에 대한 휴식의 측면에 문화적 생활의 측면을 덧붙여 근로자의 생활의 질을 향상시키는 것이라 할 수 있다.[109]

2. 연차유급휴가제도

연차유급휴가 제도에 대한 국제기준과 우리나라의 근로기준법상 기준에 대해서는 ① 휴가일수 및 발생요건, ② 사용방법, ③ 연차유급휴가 보장, ④ 미사용 연차휴가에 대한 보상으로 나누어 비교해 볼 수 있다.

우리나라 근로기준법 상의 연차유급휴가(제60조)는 휴가사용을 전제로 하지만, 미사용시 금전보상을 명시하고 있다.

① 휴가일수 및 발생요건을 살펴보면 "1년간 80% 이상 출근 근로자에게 15일의 연차유급휴가를 주어야 한다(제1조). 3년 이상 계속하여 근로한 근로자에게 최초 1년을 초과하는 계속 근로연수 매2년에 대해 1일을 가산한 유급휴가를

---

[106] 임종률, 「노동법」, 박영사, 2016, 454면.
[107] 헌법재판소 2015.5.28. 선고 2013헌마619 결정 (연차휴가의 취지)
[108] 대법원 2003.12.26. 선고 2011다4629 판결 (연차휴가의 취지)
[109] 김홍영, "휴식 보장을 위한 연차휴가의 제도개선론", 「노동법연구」, 2016 상반기 제40호, 서울대노동법연구회, 165면.

leave shall not exceed 25 (Article 4).

② Regarding the use of annual leave, "An employer shall grant paid leave upon request by a worker. However, the leave period concerned may be changed, if granting the leave as requested by the worker might cause serious impediment to the operation of the business (Article 5). Paid leave can be used continuously over a certain day or several days. Here, if a worker requests a leave day by designating a desired date (a claim for a leave), the employer can adjust the date of the leave in consideration of the work.

③ In relation to the guarantee of annual paid leave, the annual paid leave shall be granted as paid off-days on the normal working days of the worker (Article 5). Therefore, annual paid leave shall not be granted on weekly holidays, unpaid holidays, or other paid holidays.

④ Regarding compensation for unused annual leave, "the annual paid leave will expire if not exercised for one year" (Article 7). This means that in the event that an employee fails to use the annual paid leave, the employer shall pay the employee for the unused paid leave.[110]

III. Annual paid leave

1. Guaranteeing annual paid leave

The ILO and the EU's annual paid leave regulations, in principle, prohibit the substitution of unused annual leave for benefits and exempt monetary compensation only at the end of employment.[111] Korea still pays for unused annual paid leave because using annual paid leave is not widely accepted. In order to eliminate this monetary compensation, the principle of promoting the use of annual leave is stipulated in Article 61 of the Labor Standards Act. If a worker fails to use the annual leave despite the measures promoting the use of annual paid leave, the annual leave shall expire and the employer shall be exempted from liability for compensation. In addition, in order to encourage the use of leave, it is encouraged to collectively take paid annual leave through the substitution of paid leave on particular working days (Article 62 of the Labor Standards Act).

---

[110] Supreme Court ruling on December 26, 2013. 2011 da 4629 (Unused annual leave allowance is regarded as wage.)
[111] ILO Convention (No. 132) – Article 5; EU Guide, Number 2003/88/EC – Article 7 (2)

주어야 하고, 최대 25일을 한도로 한다(제4조)."
② 사용방법을 보면 연차휴가는 근로자가 청구한 시기에 유급휴가를 주어야 하지만, 근로자가 청구한 시기에 휴가를 주는 것이 사업 운영에 막대한 지장이 있는 경우에는 그 시기를 변경할 수 있다(제5조). 유급휴가는 특정일 또는 여러 날에 걸쳐 연속적으로 사용할 수 있다. 여기서 근로자는 원하는 날짜를 지정하여 휴가를 청구하면(휴가청구권) 사용자는 업무의 상황을 고려하여 휴가 청구일을 조정할 수 있다(시기변경권).
③ 연차유급휴가 보장과 관련하여 연차유급휴가는 근로자의 근무일에 유급으로 보장해주어야 한다(제5조). 따라서 연차유급휴가는 주휴일이나 무급휴무일, 약정휴일에 부담하여서는 아니 된다.
④ 미사용 연차휴가에 대한 보상과 관련하여 "연차유급휴가는 1년간 행사하지 아니하면 소멸된다. 다만, 사용자의 귀책사유로 사용하지 못한 경우에는 그러하지 아니하다(제7조)." 이는 근로자가 연차유급휴가를 사용하지 못한 경우에 사용자는 연차유급휴가 미사용 수당을 지급해야 한다는 것이다.[110]

Ⅲ. 연차유급휴가 적용

1. 연차유급휴가 보장

ILO나 EU의 연차유급휴가 규정은 미사용 연차휴가에 대한 수당대체를 원칙적으로 금지하고 있고, 고용종료 시에만 예외적으로 금전보상 하도록 하고 있다.[111] 우리나라는 아직 연차유급휴가 사용이 정착되지 않아 미사용 연차유급휴가에 대해 금전보상을 하고 있다. 이러한 금전보상의 폐단을 없애기 위해 연차휴가 사용촉진조치(근로기준법 제61조) 규정을 두고 휴가사용을 원칙으로 하고 있다. 사용자가 휴가사용촉진 조치를 하였음에도 불구하고 연차휴가를 사용하지 못한 경우에는 연차휴가가 소멸되며, 사용자는 이에 대한 보상책임을 면제 받는다. 또한 휴가 사용촉진을 위해 유급휴가의 대체(근로기준법 제62조)를 통해 집단적으로 연차유급휴가를 사용하도록 유도하고 있다.

---

[110] 대법원 2013.12.26. 선고 2011다4629 판결 (미사용 연차유급휴가 수당은 임금이다.)
[111] ILO 제132호 협약 제5조 및 EU지침 2003/88/EC 제7조 제2항.

2. Compensation allowance for unused annual leave

If a worker's employment ends before his or her annual paid leave is used, the worker will be compensated for unused annual paid leave days. The right to use Annual Leave as paid days off is acquired definitely as remuneration for labor when the employee has worked for a one-year period. As soon as the employee acquired the right of Annual Paid Leave, his employment was terminated due to retirement, etc. before using his Annual Paid Leave. In this case, while the right to use Annual Leave requires continuous labor service, this cannot be granted due to retirement. However, the right to request Annual Leave allowance does not require continuous labor service and so shall be compensated as a paid allowance. Accordingly, the employee can request the Annual Leave allowance equivalent to the whole number of Annual Leave days unused up to the employment termination date.[112]

3. Concerning severance pay and compensation for delayed wages

When calculating the severance pay of an employee, the annual paid leave allowance that occurred before the cessation of employment, regardless of whether the employee received compensation for unused annual paid leave days or not, should be included for the amount equivalent to 3/12 based on the average wage calculation.[113] However, this is not the case if there is no unused annual paid leave. For unpaid annual paid leave allowance and benefits, an additional amount of severance pay, to be re-calculated after including compensation allowance for unused annual paid leave, shall be paid.

If a worker's employment ends, an employer shall pay the wages and other money or valuables within 14 days after the cause for such payment has occurred (Article 36 of the LSA). If an employer fails to pay wages and severance pay subject to be paid pursuant to Article 36, delay interest shall be payable within the range of the interest rate prescribed by the Presidential Decree within 40/100 of the number of days delayed from the next day to the payment date (Article 37 of the LSA). Here, the rate determined by the president is "20/100 per year" (Article 17 of the Enforcement Decree of the LSA).

---

[112] Supreme court ruling on May 27, 2005, 2003da 48549, 2003da 4855:

[113] Labor Ministry, "Guidelines for the right to ask for annual paid leave, and paid allowance for unused annual leave", Wage/working hours policy team-2820, September 21, 2006.

2. 연차유급휴가 미사용 수당

연차유급휴가를 사용하기 전에 퇴직하여 근로관계가 종결된 경우에는 미사용 연차유급휴가에 대해 금전보상을 받게 된다. 유급(연차휴가수당)으로 연차휴가를 사용할 권리는 근로자가 1년간 소정의 근로를 마친 대가로 확정적으로 취득하는 것이므로, 근로자가 일단 연차유급휴가권을 취득한 후에 연차유급휴가를 사용하기 전에 퇴직 등의 사유로 근로관계가 종료된 경우, 근로관계의 존속을 전제로 하는 연차휴가를 사용할 권리는 소멸한다 할지라도 근로관계의 존속을 전제로 하지 않는 연차휴가수당을 청구할 권리는 그대로 잔존하는 것이어서, 근로자는 근로관계 종료 시까지 사용하지 못한 연차휴가 일수 전부에 상응하는 연차휴가수당을 사용자에게 청구할 수 있는 것이다.[112]

3. 퇴직금 반영 및 임금지체 보상금

근로자의 퇴직금을 계산할 때 퇴직하기 전에 발생하였던 연차유급휴가수당에 그 수령여부와 상관없이 퇴직 전전년도 출근률에 의하여 퇴직 전년도에 발생한 연차유급휴가수당을 3/12을 퇴직금 산정을 위한 평균임금 산정 기준임금에 포함하여야 한다.[113] 다만, 연차유급휴가를 모두 사용하여 미사용 연차유급휴가수당이 발생하지 않은 경우는 그러하지 않는다. 미사용 연차유급수당 미지급 만큼 퇴직금 계산에 포함하여 계산한 평균임금 차액이 발생하는 퇴직금을 추가적으로 지급해야 한다.

근로자가 퇴직한 경우 퇴직일로부터 14일 이내에 임금 등 일체의 금품을 지급해야 한다(근로기준법 제36조). 사용자가 제36조에 따라 지급하여야 할 임금과 퇴직금을 지급하지 아니한 경우에는 그 다음 날부터 지급하는 날까지의 지연일수에 대해 연 100분의 40 이내에서 대통령령이 정하는 이율의 범위에서 지연이자를 지급해야 한다.(근기법 제37조). 여기서 대통령이 정하는 이율이란 "연 100분의 20"을 말한다(근기법 시행령 제17조).

---

[112] 대법원 2005.05.27. 선고 2003다48549, 2003다48556 판결:
[113] 고용노동부 "연차유급휴가청구권, 수당, 미사용수당과 관련된 지침", 임금근로시간정책팀-2820, 2006.9.21.

Section 7-2. Changes of Judicial Rulings Related to Annual Leave Compensation

Ⅰ. Introduction

The purpose of annual paid leave is to guarantee sufficient paid leave to workers who are exhausted from long-term work so they can recover their physical and mental health and enjoy a cultural life.[114] Monetary compensation is applied only in exceptional cases where annual leave is not available. As Supreme Court rulings have been made based on the purpose of such annual leave, existing rulings are currently being revised to reflect this.

The Supreme Court ruling on October 14, 2021 (2021 da 227100) ruled that the annual leave days for one-year fixed-term workers amounted to 11 days, not 26. Even in the case of retirees, the Supreme Court ruling on June 28, 2018 (2016 da 48297) ruled that, in cases where the calculation period of annual leave is from January 1 to December 31 of each year, if the retirement date is December 31, there was no annual leave allowance owing in the following year. Currently, the Ministry of Employment and Labor stipulates in its annual leave-related guideline "A fixed-term worker with a one-year employment contract must be granted up to 26 days of paid leave allowance when the contract period expires after meeting 80% or more of the attendance rate for one year."[115] This is a combination of 15 days of annual leave granted for employees who have worked 80 percent or more for one year according to Article 60 (1) of the Labor Standards Act, and up to 11 days of accumulated monthly leave for employees who have worked less than one year, according to Article 60 (2). Based on this, front-line labor inspectors penalize employers for violating the Labor Standards Act if the employer does not pay 26 annual leave days.

As a result of these court rulings, the current guidelines of the Ministry of Employment and Labor lose their effect. With this in mind, how is annual leave calculated for fixed-term workers and retirees? In addition to this issue, I would like to examine in detail the standards upon which the Ministry of Employment and Labor decisions were based.

---

[114] Constitutional Court decision on May 28 2015: 2013 Honma 619; Kim Hong-Young, "Theory on System Improvement of Annual Leave for Guaranteed Rest," Labor Law Research, (40), Seoul National University Labor Law Research Society, March 2016, p. 161.

[115] Ministry of Employment and Labor, "'Explanation on Revised Labor Standards Act' on the Expansion of Annual Leave Guarantee for Those who Work for Less Than One Year, etc.", May 2018.

제7-2절 연차휴가 보상과 관련 판례의 변화

Ⅰ. 문제의 소재

연차유급휴가의 목적은 장기간 근로에 지친 근로자에게 충분한 유급휴가를 보장해서 신체적, 정신적 건강을 회복하고 문화적 생활을 가질 수 있도록 하기 위함이다.[114] 금전보상은 휴가를 사용할 수 없는 예외적인 경우에만 적용된다. 최근 이러한 연차휴가의 목적에 충실한 대법원 판례가 일관성 있게 나오면서 기존에 근로의 대가성에 대한 금전보상에 근거한 판례를 수정하고 있다.

2021년 10월 14일 대법원(2021다227100)은 1년 기간제 근로자의 연차휴가수당은 26일이 아니라 11일이라는 판결을 하였다. 기업의 정년 퇴직자의 경우에도 2018년 6월 28일 대법원(2016다48297)은 연차휴가 기산점을 매년 1월 1일부터 12월 31일로 하고 있는 경우, 퇴직일이 12월 31일인 경우 그 다음해에 발생하는 연차휴가수당은 없다고 판시하였다. 현재, 고용노동부는 연차휴가 설명자료에서 "근로계약기간이 1년인 기간제 노동자가 1년간 출근율 80% 이상 충족 후 계약기간 만료 시 미사용수당으로 최대 26일분을 지급해야 한다"고 명시하고 있다.[115] 이는 근로기준법 제60조 제1항에 1년간 80% 이상 개근시 15일의 연차휴가와 제2항에서 1년 미만자에 매 1개월 만근시 발생하는 월차휴가 총 11개를 합친 것이다. 이를 근거로 일선 근로감독관은 사업주가 26일 분의 수당을 지급하지 않는 경우에는 근로기준법 위반으로 사업주를 형사처벌 하고 있다.

따라서 기간제 근로자나 정년퇴직자의 경우 기간만료에 따라 퇴직이 예정돼 있는 경우 발생했던 연차휴가수당은 이번 판례로 그 효력을 상실하게 되었다. 이와 관련하여 퇴직자의 연차휴가의 계산이 어떻게 되는지? 그리고 고용노동부의 연차휴가 발생기준은 어디에 있었는지에 대해 구체적으로 살펴보고자 한다.

---

[114] 헌법재판소 2015.5.28. 2013헌마619 결정; 김홍영, "휴식보장을 위한 연차휴가의 제도개선론", 노동법연구, (40), 서울대학교 노동법 연구회, 2016. 3, 161면.
[115] 고용노동부, "1년 미만 근로 등에 대한 연차휴가 보장 확대 관련 '개정 근로기준법 설명자료'", 2018.5.

II. Judgments of the Supreme Court Rulings in 2018 and 2021

1. A case related to annual leave of retirees[116]

Workers were hired by the Uijeongbu City Facility Management Corporation and retired as street cleaners. In the employment rules it is stipulated that retirement "shall be the last day of December of the year in which the person turns 61." In accordance with the provisions of the collective agreement, 20 days of special paid leave were used for those eligible for mandatory retirement, and the mandatory retirement was on December 31st. The workers said, "The last day of December of the year in which we turned 61 was a special leave period, so the actual retirement date should be considered as January 1 of the following year. The employer is obliged to pay the workers the allowance for the unused annual leave due to their retirement on January 1st, since annual leave was accrued in the year they turned 61 years of age."

Regarding this, the first and second trials agreed to the workers' legal claims, but the Supreme Court ruled "The employment rules set the retirement age as the end of December when they turn 61. The retirement age is reached on December 31, when the person turns 61, and the employment relationship is naturally terminated. Therefore, workers cannot acquire the right to annual leave in return for work in the year in which they turn 61. Therefore, it cannot be seen that their retirement date is postponed to January 1 of the following year."

2. A case related to annual leave of fixed-term workers[117]

A worker used 15 days of annual leave while working as a caregiver at an aged care welfare facility for one year from August 1, 2017 to July 31, 2018. On May 5, 2018, the Ministry of Employment and Labor distributed the guideline for the revised Labor Standards Act as it related to the expansion of the annual leave guarantee for workers with less than one year of employment. The guideline stated "If the contract period of a one-year fixed-term worker expires, an unused annual leave allowance of up to 26 days must be paid."

The worker submitted a complaint to the Chungbu Regional Labor Office stating

---

[116] Supreme Court ruling on June 28, 2018: 2006 da 48297.
[117] Supreme Court ruling on October 14, 2021: 2021 da 227100.

Ⅱ. 2018년과 2021년 대법원의 판단 내용

1. 정년퇴직자의 연차휴가 사례[116]

근로자들은 의정부시 시설관리공단에 고용되어 가로환경미화원으로 근무하다 정년퇴직을 하였다. 사용자의 고용내규에는 정년에 관해 '만 61세가 되는 해의 12월 말일로 한다.'라고 규정하고 있다. 단체협약 규정에 따라 정년퇴직 대상자들은 특별유급휴가 20일을 사용하고, 12월 31일에 정년퇴직을 하였다. 근로자들은 "만 61세가 되는 해의 12월 말일이 특별유급휴가기간으로 근무를 한 것이고 그에 따라 실제 퇴직일은 다음해 1월 1일로 보아야 한다. 만61세가 되는 해에 계속 근로한 것에 대한 연차휴가는 발생했으므로 사용자는 근로자들에게 그 다음에 1월 1일 퇴직으로 사용하지 못한 연차휴가에 대한 수당을 지급할 의무가 있다"고 주장했다.

이에 대해 1심과 2심은 근로자들의 입장을 인용하였으나, 상고심인 대법원은 "사용자의 고용내규는 정년을 만 61세가 되는 12월 말일로 정하고 있다. 만 61세가 되는 12월 31일에 정년에 도달하여 근로관계가 당연히 종료된다. 따라서 근로자가 만61세가 되는 해의 근로에 대한 대가로서의 연차휴가에 관한 권리를 취득할 수 없다."라고 판시하면서 "근로자들이 만 61세가 되는 해의 12월 31일 까지 특별유급휴가를 사용하였다고 하여 이들의 퇴직일이 다음해 1월 1일로 미루어진다고 볼 수 없다"고 판단하였다.

2. 기간제 근로자의 연차휴가 사례[117]

근로자는 2017년 8월 1일부터 2018년 7월 31일까지 1년간 노인요양복지시설에서 요양보호사로 근무하면서 15일의 연차휴가를 사용하였다. 고용노동부는 2018년 5월 "1년 미만 근로자 등에 대한 연차휴가 보장 확대 관련 개정 근로기준법 설명자료를 배포하였는데, 위 자료에서 "1년 기간제 노동자의 계약기간이 만료되는 경우에는 최대 26일분의 연차휴가 미사용수당을 지급

---
[116] 대법원 2018.6.28. 선고 2016다48297 판결.
[117] 대법원 2021.10.14. 선고 2021다227100 판결

that he had not been paid 11 days' annual leave allowance. With the guidance of the labor inspector, the employer paid 717,150 won to the worker as an annual leave allowance for 11 days.

Later, the employer stated that the information that up to 26 days of annual leave would be granted to workers who signed a one-year fixed-term employment contract was incorrect. Since the worker used all the annual leave granted to him, he could not receive annual leave pay. The employer claimed that the worker is obligated to return the overpaid allowance because the employer paid the additional 11 days' annual leave allowance based on the erroneous guidance of the labor inspector.

In response, the lower court (the second trial) recognized the claim of the employer and issued an order for the worker to pay back the overpaid amount. The worker then appealed to the Supreme Court. The Supreme Court ruled "The right to use annual leave or the right to claim annual leave allowance naturally arises when an employee provides work while meeting the attendance rate in the previous year, and is equivalent to the consideration for work for one year in the preceding year, not the year in which the annual leave is to be used. Paid annual leave as stipulated in Article 60 (1) of the Labor Standards Act is granted to workers who have worked at least 80% of one year, and the worker does not use annual leave within one year after acquiring the right to annual leave, or retires before one year has elapsed. In the event that annual leave can no longer be used due to reasons attributable to the employer, the worker can claim an annual leave allowance, which is a wage corresponding to the number of days of annual leave.[118] However, the right to use a 2nd year's annual leave shall be deemed to occur on the day following completion of work for one year of the preceding year, unless otherwise specified. If the employment relationship is terminated due to retirement before then, no annual leave allowance may be claimed as compensation for the right to use annual leave."[119] Therefore, it was determined that workers who signed a one-year fixed-term employment contract were granted up to 11 days of annual leave.

Ⅲ. Existing Standard Precedents on Annual Leave and Guidelines from the Ministry of Employment and Labor

---

[118] Supreme Court ruling on May 17, 2017: 2014 da 232296.
[119] Supreme Court ruling on June 28, 2018: 2006 da 48297.

하여야 함"이라고 기재되어 있었다.

근로자는 중부지방노동청에 11일분의 연차휴가수당을 지급받지 못하였다는 내용의 진정서를 제출하였다. 사용자는 근로감독관의 계도에 따라 근로자에게 11일분의 연차휴가수당으로 717,150원을 지급하였다.

이에 사용자는 1년 기간제 근로계약을 체결한 근로자에게 최대 26일의 연차휴가가 발생한다는 취지의 이 사건 설명자료는 잘못되었고, 근로자가 자신에게 부여된 연차휴가를 모두 사용하여 더 이상 연차휴가수당을 청구할 수 없는데도 사용자가 근로감독관의 잘못된 계도에 따라 11일분의 연차휴가수당을 추가로 지급하였으므로 근로자는 사용자에게 이를 반환할 의무가 있다고 주장한다.

이에 대해 원심(2심)은 사용자의 주장을 인정하여 근로자에게 지급명령을 내렸다. 이에 근로자는 대법원에 상고하였다. 대법원은 "연차휴가를 사용할 권리 또는 연차휴가수당 청구권은 근로자가 전년도에 출근율을 충족하면서 근로를 제공하면 당연히 발생하는 것으로, 연차휴가를 사용할 해당 연도가 아니라 그 전년도 1년간의 근로에 대한 대가에 해당된다. 근로기준법 제60조 제1항이 규정한 유급 연차휴가는 1년간 80퍼센트 이상 출근한 근로자에게 부여되는 것으로, 근로자가 연차휴가에 관한 권리를 취득한 후 1년 이내에 연차휴가를 사용하지 아니하거나 1년이 지나기 전에 퇴직하는 등의 사유로 인하여 더 이상 연차휴가를 사용하지 못하게 될 경우에는 사용자에게 그 연차휴가일수에 상응하는 임금인 연차휴가수당을 청구할 수 있다.[118] 다만, 연차휴가를 사용할 권리는 다른 특별한 정함이 없는 한 그 전년도 1년간 근로를 마친 다음 날 발생한다고 보아야 한다. 그 전에 퇴직으로 근로관계가 종료되는 경우에는 연차휴가를 사용할 권리에 대한 보상으로 연차휴가수당도 청구할 수 없다."고 판단하였다.[119] 따라서 1년 기간제 근로계약을 체결한 근로자에게는 최대 11일의 연차휴가가 부여된다고 보았다.

Ⅲ. 연차휴가에 대한 기존의 기준 판례와 고용노동부의 지침

---

[118] 대법원 2017.5.17. 선고 2014다232296 판결.
[119] 대법원 2018.6.28. 선고 2016다48297 판결.

Chapter3-7. Annual Paid Leave and Foreign Workers

1. Standards for judging annual leave compensation before 2005.

In the case of fixed-term workers or retirees before 2005, if they retire one day before the date of annual leave is granted, no annual leave allowance is paid, even if they have worked full time in the previous year. This is because the purpose of annual leave is to ensure continuous long-term employment through rest.

The Ministry of Employment and Labor makes this clear in the official Q&A guide. "Company A's annual leave period is one year from January 1 to December 31 of the current year, and annual leave compensation is paid for the number of days that annual leave is not taken." In this case, the following is the answer to the question of whether an employee can claim annual leave compensation if the retirement date is December 31. "Annual paid leave occurs according to the attendance rate in the period subject to vacation calculation. Annual paid leave is not granted if there is no day left to use the leave due to the termination of the employment relationship, even if the employee has worked or attended more than 90 percent of the time during the period subject to vacation calculation. There is no meaning in granting annual leave, and so there is no problem related to the payment of annual vacation pay for not using vacation."[120]

2. Annual leave compensation from 2005 to 2018

The Supreme Court ruled that the annual leave as compensation for work should be considered as the nature of compensation for work regardless of whether or not annual leave was available. In accordance with this decision, the Ministry of Employment and Labor also shifted to the position that fixed-term workers should be compensated for 15 days of annual leave, which are the subject of work, even if they retire due to the expiration of the contract period, according to the purpose of this precedent.

The stipulations are as follows: The Supreme Court ruled "The right to use annual leave with annual leave allowance is acquired by an employee as a result of completing a prescribed amount of work for one year. After an employee obtains the right to annual paid leave, if he/she retires before using the annual paid leave, the right to use the annual paid leave is terminated because the right to annual leave is available only during employment. An employee can claim from the

---

[120] MOEL guidelines, July 15, 1999: Gungi 68207-1667.

1. 2005년 이전 연차휴가보상 판단기준

2005년 이전 기간제 근로자나 정년퇴직자의 경우 연차휴가발생시점 하루 전에 퇴직하는 경우 만근 하였더라도 연차휴가수당은 발생하지 않는다. 이는 연차휴가의 목적이 휴식을 통해서 계속적인 장기 고용을 보장하기 위한 것이기 때문이다.

이와 같이 고용노동부는 질의회신에서 이를 명확히 하고 있다. "A사의 연차휴가 개근기간은 매년 1월 1일부터 당해년도 12월 31일까지 1년으로 하고 있으며 연차휴가를 실시하지 못한 일수에 대해서는 매년 휴가보상비를 지급하고 있다. 이 경우 근로자의 정년퇴직일이 12월 31일인 경우 연차휴가보상비를 청구할 수 있는지 여부" 문의에 대해 다음과 같이 답변하고 있다. "연차유급휴가는 휴가 산정대상기간의 출근율에 따라 발생하는 것으로 휴가 산정대상기간 동안 개근 또는 90퍼센트 이상 출근하였다 하더라도 근로관계가 종료되어 휴가를 사용할 날이 하루도 없게 되는 경우에는 연차유급휴가를 부여할 의미가 없고, 휴가를 사용하지 않은데 따른 연차휴가근로수당 지급 문제도 발생하지 않는다."[120]

2. 2005년부터 2018년 연차휴가보상 기준

대법원은 연차휴가의 개념을 근로에 대한 보상으로 연차휴가 사용가능여부와 상관없이 근로에 대한 보상의 성격을 우선하는 판결을 하였다. 이 대법원 판결에 따라 고용노동부도 이러한 대법원의 판례 취지에 근거하여 기간제 근로자가 계약기간 만료로 퇴직하더라도 근로의 대상인 연차휴가 15개에 대해 보상을 해야 한다는 입장으로 전환하게 되었다.

그 내용은 다음과 같다. 대법원 "유급(연차휴가수당)으로 연차휴가를 사용할 권리는 근로자가 1년간 소정의 근로를 마친 대가로 확정적으로 취득하는 것이다. 근로자가 일단 연차유급휴가권을 취득한 후에 연차유급휴가를 사용하기 전에 퇴직의 사유로 근로관계가 종료된 경우, 근로관계의 존속을 전제로 하는 연차휴가를 사용할 권리는 소멸한다. 그러나 근로관계의 존속을 전제로 하지

---
[120] 고용노동부 행정해석, 1999.7.15. 근기 68207-1667.

employer an annual leave allowance equivalent to the number of unused annual leave days until the end of the employment relationship."[121] After this precedent, the Ministry of Employment and Labor held that if one year of full work (the requirement for annual leave) was met, annual leave would occur regardless of the termination of employment, and it obligated compensation for unused annual leave.

3. Compensation for annual leave from 2018 to 2021

The Labor Standards Act9, which was amended by Act No. 15108 on November 28, 2017 and enforced on May 29, 2018, deleted Article 60 (3) which stipulated, "If an employer gives a worker paid leave for the first year of work, 15 days, including the leave under Paragraph 2, and if the employee has already used the leave under Paragraph 2, the number of days of leave used shall be subtracted from 15 days."[122] The reason for this amendment is to delete the rule that, when using paid leave for the first year of work, subtract it from the paid leave of the following year, so that a maximum of 11 days in the first year and 15 days in the second year can be received, respectively. This was designed to prevent annual leave from being reduced in the following year when it is used for the first year.[123]

However, the interpretation of the Ministry of Employment and Labor was different from the standard of precedent.[124] MOEL clarified with "How to pay unused allowance when a contract period expires after a fixed-term worker with a one-year employment contract after the enforcement of the revised law meets 80% or more of the attendance rate for one year." The precedent is that fixed-term workers who have a one-year labor contract have the right to claim 15 days' worth of annual leave compensation at the end of the contract period if the attendance rate for one year is 80% or more.[125] The Ministry of Employment and Labor explained in its administrative guidance: "According to the amendment of the law, paid leave that occurs one day for each month of work in the first year is

---

[121] Supreme Court ruling on May 27, 2005: 2003 da 48549, 48556.
[122] Article 60 (Annual Paid Leave) (1) Every employer shall grant any employee who has worked not less than 80 percent of one year a paid leave of 15 days.
(2) Every employer shall grant any employee who has continuously worked for less than one year or who has worked less than 80 percentage of one year one paid-leave day for each month during which he/she has continuously worked.
[123] Supreme Court ruling on October 14, 2021: 2021 da 227100.
[124] MOEL Guidelines "Guidelines for the revised Labor Standards Act related to the expansion of annual leave for workers less than one year, etc.", May 2018.
[125] Supreme Court ruling on May 27, 2005: 2003 da 48549, 48556.

않는 연차휴가수당을 청구할 권리는 그대로 잔존하는 것이어서, 근로자는 근로관계 종료시까지 사용하지 못한 연차휴가일수 전부에 상응하는 연차휴가수당을 사용자에게 청구할 수 있다."고 판시하고 있다.[121] 이 판례 이후에 고용노동부는 연차휴가발생 요건인 1년 만근이 충족되면 고용의 종료와 무관하게 연차휴가가 발생하고, 미사용 연차휴가에 대해 보상할 의무가 있다고 보았다.

3. 2018년 이후부터 2021년 연차휴가보상

2017년 11월 28일 법률 제15108호로 개정되어 2018년 5월 29일 시행된 근로기준법은 제60조 제3항에 규정되어 있던 "사용자는 근로자의 최초 1년간의 근로에 대하여 유급휴가를 주는 경우에는 제2항에 따른 휴가를 포함하여 15일로 하고, 근로자가 제2항에 따른 휴가를 이미 사용한 경우에는 그 사용한 휴가 일수를 15일에서 뺀다."라는 규정을 삭제하였다.[122] 이와 같이 개정한 이유는 최초 1년간의 근로에 대한 유급휴가를 사용한 경우 이를 다음 해 유급휴가에서 빼는 규정을 삭제하여 1년차에 최대 11일, 2년차에 15일의 유급휴가를 각각 받을 수 있게 하기 위한 것이다. 이는 최초 1년간 연차휴가를 사용한 경우 그 다음 해 연차휴가가 줄어드는 것을 방지하기 위한 것이다.[123]

그러나 이에 대한 고용노동부의 해석은 판례의 기준과 달랐다.[124] 고용노동부는 "개정법 시행 후 근로계약기간이 1년인 기간제노동자가 1년간 출근율 80% 이상 충족 후 계약기간 만료 시 미사용수당 지급방법"을 설명하였다. 판례는 근로계약기간을 1년으로 한 기간제노동자의 1년간의 출근율이 80% 이상이면 계약기간 만료 시 15일분의 연차휴가보상청구권이 발생한다는 입장이다.[125] 고용노동부는 "법 개정에 따라 1년차 때 1개월 개근시 1일씩 발생하는 유급휴가도 별도로 인정되는 만큼, 개정법 시행 이후 1년 기간제노동자의

---

121) 대법원 2005.5.27. 선고 2003다48549, 48556판결.
122) 근로기준법 제60조 제1항과 제2항: ① 사용자는 1년간 80퍼센트 이상 출근한 근로자에게 15일의 유급휴가를 주어야 한다.
② 사용자는 계속하여 근로한 기간이 1년 미만인 근로자 또는 1년간 80퍼센트 미만 출근한 근로자에게 1개월 개근 시 1일의 유급휴가를 주어야 한다.
123) 대법원 2021.10.14. 선고 2021다227100 판결
124) 고용노동부, "1년 미만 근로자 등에 대한 연차휴가 보장 확대 관련 개정 근로기준법 설명자료", 2018. 5.
125) 대법원 2005.5.27. 선고 2003다48549, 48556판결.

recognized separately. After the amendment of the law, when the contract period of one year of fixed-term workers expires, up to 26 days of unused allowance must be paid." Therefore, as compensation for work of less than one year is accrued as 11 days and 15 additional days in return for 1 year of work, a total of 26 annual paid leave days should be guaranteed.

4. After the precedent in 2021

Since the right to use annual leave shall be deemed to arise on the day following completion of work for one year of the preceding year, if the employment relationship is terminated due to retirement, no annual leave allowance may be claimed as compensation for the right to use annual leave.[126] Due to the logic of this precedent, the guideline of the Ministry of Employment and Labor has lost its effect. In the future, this regulation will be applied to all retirees and fixed-term workers with an expiration period of one or two years, so that they do not have the right to claim annual leave allowance.

Ⅳ. Excerpts From the Current Annual Leave and Suggestions for Improvement

Annual paid leave is a paid leave granted to recover bodies and minds which have been exhausted from long-term work and 15 days are granted to workers who have worked more than 80% of the year. In addition, one additional day is added every 3 years, and the maximum granted is up to 25 days. If an employee does not use annual leave within one year after acquiring the right to it, or retires before one year has elapsed, he/she may claim annual leave allowance (a wage equivalent to the number of days of annual leave) from the employer. According to the annual leave regulations of the Labor Standards Act which were changed in 2018, the amount of annual leave accrued for one year is 11 days, with one paid leave day per month. At the end of the first year, 15 days are generated on the premise of continuous service and will be used for one year.

If an employee works for one full year and quits the next day, he can claim 11 annual leave days and 15 annual leave days on the premise of the last full year of work. This may be somewhat of a violation of the principle of equity. There are

---

[126] Supreme Court ruling on October 14, 2021: 2021 da 227100; Supreme Court ruling on June 28, 2018: 2006 da 48297.

계약기간이 만료되는 경우에는 최대 26일분의 미사용수당을 지급하여야 한다."고 행정지도를 하였다. 따라서 근로의 대가로 1년 미만의 기간에 대해서는 11개의 연차유급휴가와 1년의 근로에 대한 대가로 유급휴가 15개가 추가적으로 발생하므로, 총 26개의 연차유급휴가를 보장해주어야 한다는 입장을 견지하고 있다.

4. 2021년 판례이후

연차휴가를 사용할 권리는 그 전년도 1년간의 근로를 마친 다음 날 발생한다고 보아야 하므로 그 전에 퇴직으로 근로관계가 종료한 경우에는 연차휴가를 사용할 권리에 대한 보상으로 연차휴가수당도 청구할 수 없다.[126] 이 판례로 인하여 고용노동부의 행정해석은 효력을 상실하게 되었고, 앞으로 정년퇴직자, 기간제 근로자의 1년이나 2년 기간 만료로 인한 퇴직 등은 모두 이 규정을 적용하여 연차휴가수당 청구권이 발생하지 않게 되었다.

Ⅳ. 현 연차휴가의 내용과 개선방안

연차 유급휴가는 장기간의 근로로 인하여 지친 심신을 회복하기 위해 부여되는 유급휴가로, 1년간 80퍼센트 이상 출근한 근로자에게 15일을 부여한다. 그리고 매 3년마다 1개 씩 추가적으로 가산하여 지급하면서 최종 25일을 한도로 지급된다. 근로자가 연차휴가에 관한 권리를 취득한 후 1년 이내에 연차휴가를 사용하지 않거나 1년이 지나기 전에 퇴직하는 경우에는 사용자에게 그 연차휴가일수에 상당하는 임금인 연차휴가수당을 청구할 수 있다. 2018년에 변경된 근로기준법 연차규정에 따르면, 1년간 발생하는 연차휴가는 매월 만근시 1개의 월차휴가가 발생하여 1년간 11개가 된다. 만 1년되는 시점에 계속근무를 전제로 15개가 추가로 발생하여 1년 동안 사용하게 된다.

근로자가 만1년을 근속하고 그 다음날 그만 두는 경우, 매월 발생하는 연차 11개와 최종 1년 만근을 전제로 발생하는 15개의 휴가수당을 각각 청구할 수 있다. 이는 형평성의 원칙에 위반이 될 수 있다고 본다. 전년도

---

[126] 대법원 2021.10.14. 선고 2021다227100 판결; 대법원 2018.6.28. 선고 2016다48297 판결.

differences in the paid allowance when an employee leaves the company on a specific day, because of annual paid leave that occurs based on the previous year's work. Therefore, it is often the case that a worker has determined his/her resignation date based upon the days of additional annual leave to be granted. As a way to solve this problem, a method of calculating the current annual leave system in proportion to the length of service may be proposed. For example, 11 days are granted for the first year of service, and 15 annual leave days accrued in the second year are guaranteed to be used continuously or in installments. However, if the employee resigns in the middle of the second year, quarterly deductions can be made proportionally. I think this would be helpful in improving the existing method of granting annual leave.

V. Conclusion

I think that the precedent for the retirees in 2018 on annual leave and the precedent for the one-year fixed-term worker are reasonable judgments in line with the purpose of guaranteeing annual leave. I believe that the purpose of annual leave is to guarantee sufficient paid leave to recover bodies and minds exhausted from long-term work, but not as a simple monetary compensation.

Unfortunately however, the fact that the number of days of annual leave varies greatly may violate the principle of equity and may be a reason for workers to adjust their resignation date. Therefore, in improving annual leave, I think it would be better if paid leave were guaranteed in an equitable way in proportion to the length of the relative labor service, regardless of what actual point in time the individual resigns.

Case Study:
Whether Unused Annual Leave should be Compensated

I. Introduction

In the Seoul office of a foreign company (hereinafter referred to as "the Company") that hired about 300 employees and is engaged in the apparel business,

근무를 기준으로 발생하는 연차 유급휴가는 어느 특정한 날에 퇴사할 때 변화가 많다. 따라서 근로자들은 이때를 퇴직시점을 정하는 경우가 많다. 이를 해소하는 방법은 현 연차휴가제도를 근속기간에 비례하여 정산하는 방법이 제시될 수 있다. 예를 들어 근속년수 최초 1년에 대해 11개를 부여하고, 2년차에 발생한 연차휴가 15개에 대해 연속적이거나 분할사용이 가능하도록 보장은 하되, 근로자가 중도에 퇴사한 경우에는 분기별로 그 발생 숫자를 비례해서 공제한다면, 기존의 연차휴가 부여 방식의 개선에 도움이 되지 않을까 생각한다.

V. 결론

연차휴가에 대한 2018년의 정년 퇴직자에 대한 판례와 1년 기간제 근로자에 대한 판례는 연차휴가의 보장 취지에 맞춘 합리적인 판단이라고 본다. 연차휴가의 목적이 장기간의 노동에 지친 심신을 회복하기 위해 충분한 유급휴가를 보장하는 것이지 금전보상의 목적이 되어서는 안된다는 내용에 충실한 것이라 본다.

그러나 아쉽게도 우리나라의 연차휴가가 특정일에 퇴직함에 따라 연차휴가의 발생 일수가 크게 달라지는 점은 형평성의 원칙에 위배될 수 있고, 이는 근로자가 퇴직시점을 결정하는 이유도 될 수 있다. 따라서 앞으로 연차휴가 개선에 있어 어느 시점에 퇴직하더라도 근로의 대가에 대한 형평성 있는 유급휴가의 보장이 이뤄어진다면 더 합리적이지 않을까 생각한다.

〈노동사건사례〉
미사용 연차수당 지급 가능 여부

I. 문제의 소재

서울에 사무소를 두고 300여명을 고용하여 의류 사업을 하고 있는 한 외국 기업에서, 2015년 4월에 임원간의 갈등이 노동사건으로 확대된 사건이 발생

Chapter3-7. Annual Paid Leave and Foreign Workers

a labor case has occurred due to escalating disputes between directors in April 2015. With two departments of the Company combining into one department, the executive managing director told the managing director that it would be not desirable to have two directors in one department, and told the managing director that she needed to resign from the Company. The managing director (hereinafter referred to as "the Employee") told the Company that she would sue it for violating the Labor Standards Act and would also report additional claims of other employees unless the Company paid her a severance bonus of two years' annual wages. The Company responded that it did not order the Employee to resign, rejected her demand for a severance bonus, and explained that the Company had not violated the Labor Standards Act. Just after that, the Employee began a lawsuit against the Company and visited the Gangnam Labor Office to claim the Company had violated the Labor Standards Act, and had not paid annual leave allowance for unused leave.

There is a main item in these accusations: the Company has regulated in the Rules of Employment that it would not compensate for unused annual leave and instead would promote the use of annual leave, which the Company did through individual emails to all personnel. Where the promotion of using annual leave has been done through email, the main point is whether or not the Company must give financial compensation for unused leave.

II. Measures for Promoting the Use of Annual Leave

1. Current situations

The Company regulated in the Rules of Employment that it would not compensate for unused leave, and had informed personnel of the number of available annual leave days in the early part of the year, and sent similar emails again after six months to the Employees to actively promote the use of annual leave. And then in October it notified each individual employee by email that he or she needed to use his/her remaining annual leave days by the end of the year, and if they did not, there would be no financial compensation for unused leave. In reality, the Company has not paid any allowance for unused annual leave so far.

2. Related law and guideline regarding measures for promoting use of annual leave

하였다. 부서가 통폐합 되면서 한 부서에 전무와 상무가 같이 근무하게 되었는데, 전무가 상무에게 하나의 부서에 임원 둘이 같이 근무하는 것은 바람직하지 않으니, 퇴사할 것을 권유하였다. 이에 상무(이하, "이 사건의 근로자"라 함)는 회사가 근로기준법을 위반하였다고 주장하면서, 2년치 퇴직위로금을 주지 않을 경우 회사를 고용노동부에 고소하고, 다른 직원들에 대한 위반사항도 고발할 것이라 압박하였다. 이에 대해 회사는 이 사건의 근로자에게 퇴직을 권유하지 않았으며, 근로기준법을 위반한 사실도 없다고 하면서 퇴직위로금의 지급을 거부하였다. 그러자 이 사건의 근로자는 회사가 미사용 연차휴가에 대한 연차수당을 지급하지 않아 근로기준법을 위반하였다고 '강남고용지청'에 회사를 고소하였다.

이 고소내용에 대한 주요 쟁점사항을 살펴보면, 회사는 취업규칙(연차휴가 사용촉진)을 통해 근로자에게 미사용 연차휴가는 보상하지 않는다고 규정하고 있고, 이메일로 개인별 휴가사용을 적극적으로 권장하였다. 눈여겨볼 사항은 이러한 이메일상 휴가사용촉진조치를 한 경우, 사용자의 금전보상이 면제될 수 있는지 여부이다.

Ⅱ. 연차휴가 사용촉진조치

1. 현 실태

취업규칙에 '연차휴가 사용촉진' 규정을 두어 미사용 연차휴가는 보상을 하지 않는다고 명시하고 있고, 회사는 이메일을 통해 연초에 휴가 일수를 알려주었으며, 6개월이 지난 후에는 잔여일수를 알려주고 휴가사용을 적극 권장하였다. 그리고 매월 10월에는 휴가사용에 대해 개인별로 미사용휴가 일수를 이메일로 알려주었고, 휴가를 사용하지 않을 시에는 금전보상이 없음을 이미 통지하였다. 또한 실제로 휴가사용을 권장하는 등 수차례의 관련 이메일을 발송하였다. 실제로 회사는 미사용 연차휴가에 대한 수당을 한번도 지급한 사례가 없었다.

2. 연차휴가 사용촉진 조치에 대한 법규정과 행정해석

Chapter3-7. Annual Paid Leave and Foreign Workers

(1) Regulation of the Labor Standards Act (LSA)

The current LSA regulates the provision of 'promoting the use of annual paid leave' in relation with 'annual paid leave'.[127]

(2) Related guideline

The 'written document' mentioned in Article 61 of the LSA refers to a paper document. Electronic documents are only possible in exceptional cases where the company has handled every operation by means of electronic documents in the process of its drafting, obtaining approval and implementing through equipped electronic work-processing systems (Guideline Gunjung-1128, Feb. 7, 2012). Accordingly, informing by email in the course of promoting the use of annual leave cannot be regarded as the notification by written document (Guideline Gujung-6488, Nov 1, 2013).

If the employee has submitted a vacation plan with stipulated dates of leave after the employer has promoted the use of annual leave, the stipulated dates of leave shall be regarded as the employee's declaration of intention to use his/her annual leave. Provided, in cases where the employee comes to work on the stipulated date of leave, if the employer received the employee's labor and did not express a rejection of his/her coming in to work, it shall be regarded that the employer has approved the labor service on the expected date of leave, and so the employer shall pay an unused leave allowance (Guideline Limjang-285, Oct 21, 2005).

---

[127] Article 60 (Annual Paid Leave) (1) An employer shall grant 15 days' paid leave to a worker who has registered not less than 80 percent of attendance during one year.
(2) An employer shall grant one day's paid leave per month to a worker whose consecutive service period is shorter than one year or whose attendance is less than 80 percent, if the worker has offered work without absence throughout a month.
(3) In case an employer grants a worker paid leave for the first one year of his/her service, the number of leave days shall be 15 including the leave prescribed in paragraph (2), and if the worker has already used the leave prescribed in paragraph (2), the number of used leave days shall be deducted from the 15 days of leave.
(4) After the first year of service, an employer shall grant one day's paid leave for each two years of consecutive service in addition to the leave prescribed in paragraph (1) to a worker who has worked consecutively for 3 years or more. In this case, the total number of leave days including the additional leave shall not exceed 25.
(7) The leave referred to in paragraphs (1) through (4) shall be forfeited if not used within one year. However, this shall not apply in cases where the worker concerned has been prevented from using the leave due to any cause attributable to the employer.
Article 61 (Promoting the Use of Annual Paid Leave) If a worker's leave has been forfeited for non-use pursuant to Article 60 (7) despite the fact that the employer has taken measures described in any of the following subparagraphs to promote the use of paid leave prescribed in Article 60 (1), (3) and (4), the employer shall have no obligation to compensate the worker for the unused leave, and shall not be deemed to have caused the non-use through reasons attributable to the employer's action(s) under the proviso of Article 60 (7):
1. Within the first 10 days of the six months before unused leave is to be forfeited pursuant to Article 60 (7), an employer shall notify each worker of the number of his/her unused leave days and urge them in writing to decide when they will use the leave and to inform the employer of the decided leave period; and
2. If a worker, despite the urging prescribed in subparagraph (1), has failed to decide when he/she will use whole or part of the unused leave and to inform the employer of the decided leave period within 10 days after they were urged, an employer shall decide when the worker uses the unused leave and notify the worker of the decided leave period in writing no later than 2 months before the unused leave is to be forfeited pursuant to Article 60 (7).

(1) 근로기준법 규정

현행 근로기준법상 연차휴가와 관련해 연차유급휴가의 사용촉진에 대해서는 규정을 두고 있다.[127]

(2) 행정해석

근로기준법 제61조의 서면은 종이로 된 문서를 의미하고 전자문서는 회사가 전자결제체계를 완비해 전자문서로 모든 업무의 기안, 결재, 시행과정을 관리하는 경우에만 예외적으로 가능하다(2012.2.7. 근정과-1128). 이에 연차유급휴가의 사용촉진조치와 관련해 이메일로 통보하는 것이 근로자 개인별로 서면촉구 또는 통보하는 것에 비해 도달 여부의 확인 등이 불명확한 경우 서면으로 촉구 또는 통보로 인정되기 어렵다(2013.11.01 근정과-6488).

휴가사용촉진조치에 의하여 근로자가 휴가사용시기를 정하여 사용자에게 휴가 사용계획서를 제출하였다면 그 지정된 시기에 연차유급휴가의 사용 하겠다는 의사표시로 볼 수 있을 것이므로 휴가를 청구한 것으로 볼 수 있다. 다만, 근로자가 휴가사용시기를 지정하고도 출근한 경우 사용자가 노무수령 거부의 의사표시 없이 근로를 제공받았다면 휴가일 근로를 승낙한 것으로 보아야 하므로 연차유급휴가근로수당을 지급하여야 한다(2005.10.21. 임장팀-285).

---

[127] 제60조【연차 유급휴가】① 사용자는 1년간 80퍼센트 이상 출근한 근로자에게 15일의 유급휴가를 주어야 한다.
② 사용자는 계속하여 근로한 기간이 1년 미만인 근로자 또는 1년간 80퍼센트 근로자에게 1개월 개근 시 1일의 유급휴가를 주어야 한다.
③ 사용자는 근로자의 최초 1년 간의 근로에 대하여 유급휴가를 주는 경우에는 제2항에 따른 휴가를 포함하여 15일로 하고, 근로자가 제2항에 따른 휴가를 이미 사용한 경우에는 그 사용한 휴가 일수를 15일에서 뺀다.
④ 사용자는 3년 이상 계속하여 근로한 근로자에게는 제1항에 따른 휴가에 최초 1년을 초과하는 계속 근로 연수 매 2년에 대하여 1일을 가산한 유급휴가를 주어야 한다. 이 경우 가산휴가를 포함한 총 휴가일수는 25일을 한도로 한다.
⑦ 제1항부터 제4항까지의 규정에 따른 휴가는 1년간 행사하지 아니하면 소멸된다. 다만, 사용자의 귀책사유로 사용하지 못한 경우에는 그러하지 아니하다.
제61조【연차 유급휴가의 사용 촉진】사용자가 유급휴가(제60조제1항·제3항 및 제4항)의 사용을 촉진하기 위하여 다음 각 호의 조치를 하였음에도 불구하고 근로자가 휴가를 사용하지 아니하여 소멸된 경우(제60조제7항: 1년간 휴가청구권의 소멸시효 기간의 경과)에는 사용자는 그 사용하지 아니한 휴가에 대하여 보상할 의무가 없고, 사용자의 귀책사유(제60조제7항 단서)에 해당하지 아니하는 것으로 본다.
첫째. 휴가청구권의 소멸시효기간(제60조제7항 본문)에 따른 기간이 끝나기 6개월 전을 기준으로 10일 이내에 사용자가 근로자별로 사용하지 아니한 휴가 일수를 알려주고, 근로자가 그 사용 시기를 정하여 사용자에게 통보하도록 서면으로 촉구할 것;
둘째. 제1호에 따른 촉구에도 불구하고 근로자가 촉구를 받은 때부터 10일 이내에 사용하지 아니한 휴가의 전부 또는 일부의 사용 시기를 정하여 사용자에게 통보하지 아니하면 휴가청구권의 소멸시효기간(제60조제7항 본문)에 따른 기간이 끝나기 2개월 전까지 사용자가 사용하지 아니한 휴가의 사용 시기를 정하여 근로자에게 서면으로 통보할 것

3. The Employer's countermeasures

The Company has promoted the use of annual leave through email, but has not done so through written documents. Also, the Company did not evidentially reject the provision of the employee's labor when the employee provided work on dates expected to be used as annual leave. Based upon these facts, the employer recognized that it had not taken measures promoting the use of leave as stipulated by the LSA, and then paid unused annual leave allowance for the past three years in the salary payment for June 2015.

III. Conclusion

The labor case herein is a very common case that can occur easily for companies. Regarding promotion of the use of annual leave, it is frequent for companies to take formal measures without assigning annual leave for definite working days to employees and in this way avoid paying allowance for the unused annual leave. That is, companies promote the use of annual leave by informing through email only. In cases where the employees come to work on days designated for annual leave, companies do not pay annual leave allowance for unused annual leave owing to their efforts to promote the use of annual leave. However, as this case shows that the Company did not provide the use of annual leave on the designated days, the fact that employees could not use annual leave was due to reasons attributable to the Employer and the Employer shall pay an unused annual leave allowance.

Section 8. Protection of Motherhood and Minors

Section 8-1. Protection of Motherhood

I. Understanding Motherhood Protection

The Korean government is taking steps to protect motherhood through specific

3. 회사의 대응 및 처리결과

회사는 이메일로 연차휴가 사용촉진조치를 하였지, 근로기준법에 따른 서면에 의한 사용촉진 조치를 하지 않았다. 또한 근로자가 휴가신청을 한 경우에도 불구하고 휴가신청기간에 근로를 제공한 경우에 근로거부 표시를 명확히 하지 않았다. 이러한 사실에 대해 회사는 근로기준법에 정한 휴가사용촉진조치를 하지 않았다는 것을 인정하고, 2015년 6월 급여에서 전 직원의 최근 3년 기간의 미사용 연차휴가수당을 모두 지급하였다.

Ⅲ. 결론

위에서 다루었던 사례는 기업에서 일상적으로 일어날 수 있는 사건이다. 사용자가 연차휴가 사용촉진조치에 대해 형식적 조치 만을 취하고 실질적으로 연차휴가를 부여하지 않으면서도 미사용 연차휴가수당을 지급하지 않는 경우가 많다. 즉, 연차휴가 사용촉진 조치를 이메일로 통보하면서, 휴가일자에 출근하여 근무를 하는 경우에 회사가 휴가사용촉진조치를 다하였기 때문에 미사용 연차수당을 지급하지 않아도 된다고 생각하는 경우가 많다. 하지만, 이러한 경우에 사용자가 휴가를 보장하지 않은 것이라 볼 수 있기 때문에 사용자의 귀책사유로 휴가를 사용하지 못한 것으로 간주하여 미사용 연차휴가수당을 지급해야 한다.

제8절 모성보호와 연소자

제8-1절 모성보호

Ⅰ. 여성보호의 의의

우리나라는 모성과 관련하여 헌법에 의한 명시적 보호규정[128]과 노동법에

provisions stipulated by the Constitution of the Republic of Korea[128] as well as other practical provisions stipulated by various labor laws. Despite these protection laws, the birthrate has decreased to an average of just 0.78 persons per couple as of 2022, and the government has strengthened its efforts in response towards revising labor laws designed to promote workforce participation by women and also increase the birthrate.

II. Protection of Maternal Employees

A maternal employee refers to a woman who is pregnant or is within her first year after childbirth, and is therefore provided special protection under the various laws so designed.

1. Employment in hazardous/dangerous work prohibited

Employers shall not assign maternal employees to mentally and physically hazardous work. In addition, they shall not assign women aged 18 or older who are not pregnant to work that is hazardous to their possible future pregnancy and/or childbirth. Occupations that are prohibited are described in the attached Table 4 of the Presidential Decree(Article 65 of the LSA(Labor Standards Act)).

2. Restrictions on extended work, night work and holiday work

(1) Extended work

Employers shall not place pregnant female employees on overtime duty or flexible work, and, in the event of such a request from the employee, she shall be assigned light duties. Employers shall not permit women for whom less than one year has passed since childbirth to work more than 2 hours in overtime per 8-hour work day, and 6 hours per work week of 40 hours, even if so agreed in a collective agreement(Article 51, 71, 74 of the LSA).

(2) Night work and holiday work (Article 70 of the LSA)

Employers shall not assign maternal employees to work at night(from 10 P.M to

---

[128] Constitution of the Republic of Korea (Article 36, Subparagraph 2): The State shall endeavor to protect mothers.

의한 실천적 보호규정을 두고 엄격하게 모성을 보호하고 있다. 이러한 법률적 보호규정에도 불구하고 출산율이 계속 떨어져 2022년에는 0.78명에까지 하락함에 따라 여성근로를 장려하고 출산율을 높이기 위한 노력이 노동법에 반영되고 있다.

Ⅱ. 임산부 보호

임산부는 임신 중이거나 산후 1년이 지나지 아니한 여성을 말하며, 이 기간 동안 모성보호를 위한 각종 보호 규정을 통해 특별한 보호를 받는다.

1. 유해·위험한 사업에 사용금지

사용자는 임산부를 도덕상 또는 보건 상 유해·위험한 사업에 사용하지 못한다. 특히, 임산부가 아닌 18세 이상의 여성을 보건 상 유해·위험한 사업 중 임신 또는 출산에 관한 기능에 유해·위험한 사업에 사용하지 못한다. 이와 관련 임산부의 금지직종은 근로기준법시행령 별표 4호에 명시하고 있다 (근기법 제65조).

2. 연장근로, 야간근로, 휴일근로의 제한

(1) 연장근로(근로기준법 제51조, 제71조, 제74조)

사용자는 임신 중의 여성 근로자에게 연장근로 및 탄력적 근로를 하게 하여서는 아니 되며, 그 근로자의 요구가 있는 경우에는 쉬운 종류의 근로로 전환하여야 한다. 사용자는 산후 1년이 지나지 아니한 여성에 대하여는 단체협약이 있는 경우라도 1일의 8시간 근무에 2시간, 1주일 40시간 근무에 6시간을 초과하는 연장근로를 시키지 못한다.

(2) 야간근로 및 휴일근로(근기법 제70조)

사용자는 임산부를 야간근로(오후 10시부터 오전 6시까지)와 휴일 근로를

---

128) 헌법 제36조 제2항: 국가는 모성의 보호를 위하여 노력하여야 한다.

6 A.M.) or on holidays. However, exception to such restrictions on night work and holiday work are possible in cases where the employer obtains permission in advance from the Minister of Employment and Labor and ① there is consent from the employee for whom less than one year has passed since childbirth; or ② a pregnant woman makes such a request.

3. Protection leave for maternal employees

(1) Maternity leave

Employers shall grant pregnant female employees 90 days of maternity leave(120 days if a woman is pregnant with two or more babies), to be used before and after childbirth. In such cases, a minimum of 45 days(60 days for multiple babies) shall be allocated after childbirth. At the end of the maternity leave, the employer shall allow the female employee to return to the same work, or other work at the same rate of pay as before the leave. The first 60 days(75 days for multiple babies) of leave shall be paid. The remaining 30 days(or 45 days for multiple babies) qualify for reimbursement of up to 2 million won through employment insurance, provided, that for companies[129] eligible for preferential support, the employee concerned will receive the first 60 days' maternity leave allowance(up to 2 million won per month) from employment insurance. In this case, the employer will pay the amount of the ordinary wage exceeding the government subsidy(Article 74 of the LSA).

Employers shall not dismiss any female employee during a period of temporary interruption of work before or after childbirth as provided herein and within 30 days thereafter. For the purpose of calculating annual paid leave, the maternity leave shall be regarded as attended days. Also, in calculating the average wage for purposes of severance payment, the period of maternity leave and the wage paid during the maternity period shall be deducted from the calculation of average wage required to be included in the period and wage.

---

[129] Preferentially Supported Companies (Article 12 of the Presidential Decree to the LSA)

Type of Industry (Classification Code)	Number of Employees
1. Manufacturing (C);	Up to 500 persons
2. Mining (B); 3. Construction (F); 4. Transportation (H); 5. Publishing, filming, broadcasting, and IT services (J); 6. Facility management and company support services (N); 7. Professional, science and technology services (M); 8. Health and social security insurance services (Q).	Up to 300 persons
9. Wholesale and retail services (G); 10. Hotel and restaurant services (I); 11. Finance and insurance (K); 12. Art, sports, and other leisure-related services (R);	Up to 200 persons
13. Other businesses	Up to 100 persons

근로시키지 못한다. 다만, 예외적으로 사용자가 노동부장관의 인가를 받고, ① 산후 1년이 지나지 아니한 여성의 동의가 있는 경우와 ② 임신 중의 여성이 명시적으로 청구하는 경우에는 야간근로와 휴일근로가 가능하다.

3. 임산부의 보호휴가

(1) 출산휴가

사용자는 임신 중의 여성에게 출산 전과 출산 후를 통하여 90일(한 번에 둘 이상 자녀를 임신한 경우에는 120일)의 출산전후휴가를 주어야 한다. 이 경우 휴가 기간의 배정은 출산 후에 45일(한 번에 둘 이상 자녀를 임신한 경우에는 60일) 이상이 되어야 한다. 사용자는 출산전후휴가 종료 후에는 휴가 전과 동일한 업무 또는 동등한 수준의 임금을 지급하는 직무에 복귀시켜야 한다. 사용자는 출산휴가 중 최초 60일(한 번에 둘 이상 자녀를 임신한 경우에는 75일)은 통상임금을 지급해야 한다. 나머지 30일은 고용보험에서 최대 200만 원까지 통상임금을 보전해 준다. 다만, 우선지원 대상기업[129]은 국가로부터 최초 60일에 대해서도 매월 200만 원까지 지원을 받을 수 있는데, 이 경우에는 정부지원금을 초과하는 통상임금에 대해서만 유급으로 지급하면 된다(근기법 제74조).

출산휴가는 해고 제한에 해당되어 사용자는 근로자가 산전·산후의 여성이 이 법에 따라 휴업한 기간과 그 후 30일 동안은 해고하지 못한다. 연차유급휴가 계산에 있어 출산휴가는 출근한 것으로 본다. 퇴직금 계산을 위한 평균임금 산정에 있어서도 출산휴가 기간과 그 기간 중에 지급된 임금은 평균임금 산정기준이 되는 기간과 임금의 총액에서 **뺀다**.

[129] 우선지원 대상기업의 상시 사용하는 근로자 기준(고용보험법시행령 제12조 관련)

산업분류(분류기호)	상시 근로자 수
1. 제조업(C);	500명 이하
2. 광업(B), 3.건설업(F), 4.운수업(H), 5.출판, 영상, 방송통신 및 정보서비스업(J), 6. 사업시설관리 및 사업지원 서비스업(N), 7.전문, 과학 및 기술 서비스업(M), 8.보건업 및 사회보험 서비스업(Q)	300명 이하
9. 도매 및 소매업(G), 10.숙박 및 음식점업(I), 11.금융 및 보험업(K), 12.예술, 스포츠 및 여가관련 서비스업(R)	200명 이하
13. 그 밖의 업종	100명 이하

<Maternity Leave Benefits>

> * Amount of maternity leave benefits for companies eligible for priority support
> 1) Maximum amount: 6 million won (2 million won per month) in cases where the amount of ordinary wage corresponding to 90 days of maternity leave or miscarriage/stillbirth leave exceeds 6 million won, provided that in cases where the period of payment of maternity leave benefits, etc., is less than 90 days, the amount shall be calculated based on the number of actual leave days; and
> 2) Minimum amount: an amount equivalent to ordinary wage for the period of payment of the maternity leave benefits, etc., calculated using the hourly minimum wage as the hourly ordinary wage of the employee in cases where the hourly ordinary wage of the employee is lower than the hourly minimum wage applied on the beginning date of maternity leave or miscarriage/stillbirth leave in accordance with the Minimum Wage Act

(2) Advance maternity leave

In cases where an employee who is or was recently pregnant requests leave due to a miscarriage or other pregnancy-related reason, the employer shall allow her to take leave at any time prior to the expected due date. In any case, 45 or more continuous days(60 days for multiple babies) shall be provided after childbirth or miscarriage.

Reasons for advance maternity leave are as follows(Article 74 of the LSA).

① In cases where a pregnant employee went through a miscarriage or stillbirth in the past;
② In cases where a pregnant employee is over 40 years of age at the time of the request for maternity leave; and
③ In cases where a pregnant employee submits a medical document issued by a hospital that describes the danger of miscarriage or stillbirth.

(3) Maternity leave for miscarriage or stillbirth

At the request of a female employee who has suffered a miscarriage or stillbirth, the employer shall grant her leave for miscarriage or stillbirth, except where the miscarriage is the result of an artificially-induced abortion. If a female employee who has had a miscarriage or stillbirth asks for maternity leave, she must submit to the employer an application for miscarriage or stillbirth leave, providing the

<출산휴가 급여지원>

> * 출산휴가 급여지원
> 1) 상한액: 출산전후휴가기간 또는 유산·사산휴가기간 90일에 대한 통상임금에 상당하는 금액이 600만 원(월 200만 원)을 초과하는 경우에는 600만 원. 다만, 출산전후휴가 급여등의 지급기간이 90일 미만인 경우에는 일수로 계산한 금액으로 한다.
> 2) 하한액: 출산전후휴가 또는 유산·사산휴가기간 시작일 당시 적용되던 「최저임금법」에 따른 시간 단위에 해당하는 최저임금액 보다 그 근로자의 시간급 통상임금이 낮은 경우에는 시간급 최저임금액을 시간급 통상임금으로 하여 산정된 출산전후휴가 급여등의 지원기간 중 통상임금에 상당하는 금액

(2) 조기출산휴가

사용자는 임신 중인 여성 근로자가 유산의 경험 등 사유로 출산휴가를 청구하는 경우 출산 전 어느 때라도 휴가를 나누어 사용할 수 있도록 하여야 한다. 이 경우 출산 후의 휴가 기간은 연속하여 45일(한 번에 둘 이상 자녀를 임신한 경우에는 60일) 이상이 되어야 한다(근기법 제74조, 시행령 제43조).

여기서 조기 출산휴가의 사유는 다음과 같다.
① 임신한 근로자에게 유산·사산의 경험이 있는 경우
② 임신한 근로자가 출산전후휴가를 청구할 당시 연령이 만 40세 이상인 경우
③ 임신한 근로자가 유산·사산의 위험이 있다는 의료기관의 진단서를 제출한 경우

(3) 유산·사산휴가

사용자는 임신 중인 여성이 유산 또는 사산한 경우로서 그 근로자가 청구하면 유산·사산 휴가를 주어야 한다. 다만, 인공 임신중절 수술에 따른 유산의 경우는 그러하지 아니하다. 이 경우, 유산 또는 사산한 근로자가 유산·사산휴가를 청구하는 경우에는 휴가 청구 사유, 유산·사산 발생일 및

reason for the request for leave, the date of the miscarriage or stillbirth and the pregnancy period, along with a medical certificate issued by a medical organization. In cases of miscarriage or stillbirth, the employer shall pay the ordinary wage for the period given for maternity leave, just as with a normal maternity leave, as follows:

① A pregnancy period of 11 weeks or less: five days from the date of miscarriage or stillbirth;
② A pregnancy period of 12 weeks or more but less than 15 weeks: ten days from the date of miscarriage or stillbirth;
③ A pregnancy period of 16 weeks or more but less than 21 weeks: thirty days from the date of miscarriage or stillbirth;
④ A pregnancy period of 22 weeks or more but less than 27 weeks: sixty days from the date of miscarriage or stillbirth; and
⑤ A pregnancy period of 28 weeks or more: ninety days from the date of miscarriage or stillbirth.

(4) Reduced working hours during the pregnancy period

In cases where a female employee who is pregnant for 12 weeks or less or 36 weeks or more applies for reduced working hours, the employer shall allow it. Provided that the pregnant employee's current working hours are fewer than 8 per day, the employer may reduce her working hours to 6 hours per day. The employer cannot reduce the wage of the employee due to the reduced working hours(Article 74 of the LSA).

(5) Allowing paid time off for prenatal examinations

If a pregnant female employee requests time off from work to receive a regular prenatal health checkup, the employer shall allow her to do so. An employer shall not reduce an employee's wage on the grounds that she took time off for the relevant health checkup. The paid time off allowance for prenatal examinations is as follows:

① one time every two months up to the 7th month of pregnancy;
② one time per month during the 8th and 9th months;
③ one time every two weeks during the 10th month or later(Article 74-2 of the LSA, Article 10 of the Protection of Motherhood Act).

4. Paternity Leave

임신기간 등을 적은 유산·사산휴가 신청서에 의료기관의 진단서를 첨부하여 사용자에게 제출하여야 한다. 사용자는 유산·사산휴가도 출산휴가와 같이 주어진 휴가범위 내에서 통상임금을 지급해야 한다(근기법 제74조, 시행령 제43조).
① 임신기간이 11주 이내인 경우: 유산 또는 사산한 날부터 5일까지
② 임신기간이 12주 이상 15주 이내인 경우: 유산 또는 사산한 날부터 10일까지
③ 임신기간이 16주 이상 21주 이내인 경우: 유산 또는 사산한 날부터 30일까지
④ 임신기간이 22주 이상 27주 이내인 경우: 유산 또는 사산한 날부터 60일까지
⑤ 임신기간이 28주 이상인 경우: 유산 또는 사산한 날부터 90일까지

(4) 임신기간 중 단축근로

사용자는 임신 후 12주 이내 또는 36주 이후에 있는 여성 근로자가 1일 2시간의 근로시간 단축을 신청하는 경우 이를 허용하여야 한다. 다만, 1일 근로시간이 8시간 미만인 근로자에 대하여는 1일 근로시간이 6시간이 되도록 근로시간 단축을 허용할 수 있다. 사용자는 근로시간 단축을 이유로 해당 근로자의 임금을 삭감하여서는 아니 된다(근기법 제74조 제7항, 제8항).

(5) 태아건강 검진시간 보장

사용자는 임신한 여성 근로자가 정기건강진단을 받는데 필요한 시간을 청구하는 경우 이를 허용하여 주어야 한다. 사용자는 건강진단 시간을 이유로 그 근로자의 임금을 삭감하여서는 아니 된다. 정기건강검진 실시기준은
① 임신 7월까지는 매 2월에 1회
② 임신 8월에서 9월까지는 매 1월에 1회
③ 임신 10월 이후에는 매 2주에 1회이다(근기법 제74조의 2, 모자보건법 제10조).

4. 배우자 출산휴가

If an employee requests leave on the grounds of his spouse giving birth, the employer shall grant him paid leave of up to 10 days. The leave may not be requested after a lapse of 90 days from the date when the employee's spouse gave birth(Article 18-2 of the Equal Employment Opportunity and Work-Family Balance Act). Paternity leave will also be usable on two separate periods if desired.

To reduce the burden on SMEs of this extended period of paid leave, the government will pay for 5 days of those paternity leave benefits(100% of normal wage) for SME workers.

5. Nursing hours

A female employee who has an infant under twelve months of age shall be allowed to take paid nursing recesses, twice per day for at least 30 minutes each(Article 75 of the LSA).

III. Childcare Leave and Reduced Working Hours for the Childcare Period

1. Childcare Leave[130]

Employers shall grant childcare leave if an employee asks for it to take care of his/her child(including an adopted child) aged 8 or under who is attending up to the 2nd grade of elementary school. This shall not apply in such cases where an employee has offered continuous services in the business concerned for less than 6 months prior to the scheduled date of childcare leave. An employee who intends to apply for childcare leave shall submit to his/her employer an application with documentation verifying the birth date of the infant to be cared for, not less than 30 days prior to the scheduled start date of leave.

The period of childcare leave shall be one year or less. The childcare leave can be used all at once or at two different times, up to a total period of one year. The period of childcare leave shall be included in the employee's continuous service period. Employers shall not dismiss or give any other unfavorable treatment to a employee on account of taking childcare leave, nor dismiss the employee

---

[130] Article 19 of the Equal Employment Act: Article 10 and 11 of its Presidential Decree, Article 70 of the Employment Insurance Act

사용자는 근로자가 배우자의 출산을 이유로 휴가를 청구하는 경우에 10일의 유급휴가를 주어야 한다. 배우자 출산휴가는 근로자의 배우자가 출산한 날부터 90일이 지나면 청구할 수 없다(고평법 제18조의 2). 배우자 출산휴가는 1회에 한해서 분할하여 사용할 수 있다.

휴가기간 확대에 따른 중소기업의 부담을 덜어주기 위해 정부는 중소기업(우선지원 대상기업) 근로자의 유급 5일분에 대해서는 배우자 출산휴가급여(통상임금의 100%)를 지급한다.

5. 육아시간

생후 1년 미만의 유아를 가진 여성 근로자가 청구하면 1일 2회 각각 30분 이상의 유급 수유 시간을 주어야 한다(근기법 제75조).

Ⅲ. 육아휴직과 육아기 근로시간 단축

1. 육아휴직[130]

사용자는 근로자가 만 8세 이하 또는 초등학교 2학년 이하의 자녀(입양한 자녀를 포함한다)를 양육하기 위하여 육아휴직을 신청하는 경우에 이를 허용하여야 한다. 다만, 육아휴직을 시작하려는 날의 전날까지 해당 사업에서 계속 근로한 기간이 6월 미만인 근로자는 제외된다. 육아휴직을 신청하려는 근로자는 휴직개시예정일의 30일전까지 해당 자녀의 출생 등을 증명할 수 있는 서류를 첨부하여 육아휴직신청서를 사용자에게 제출하여야 한다.

육아휴직의 기간은 1년 이내로 하며, 1회에 1년간 사용하든지 총 사용기간 1년 이내에서 1회에 한하여 분할 사용할 수 있다. 육아휴직 기간은 근속기간에 포함한다. 사용자는 육아휴직을 이유로 해고나 그 밖의 불리한 처우를 하여서는 아니 되며, 육아휴직 기간에는 그 근로자를 해고하지 못한다. 다만, 사업을 계속할 수 없는 경우에는 그러하지 아니하다. 사용자는 육아휴직을

---

[130] 고평법 제19조, 시행령 제10조, 제11조, 고용보험법 제70조

concerned during the childcare-leave period; provided that this shall not apply if the employer is not able to continue operating his/her business. After the end of the childcare leave, the employer shall restore the employee to the same work as before the leave, or any other work paying the same level of wage. In calculating the attendance rate for the annual paid leave, the period of childcare leave shall be included for the contractual working hours, which means that the annual paid leave is granted for the period of actual work. The period of childcare leave for a fixed-term employee or a dispatched employee shall not be included in the employment period or the dispatched period.

2. Reduction of working hours for the childcare period(Article 19 of the Equal Employment Act, Article 73-2 of the Employment Insurance Act):

If an employee eligible to ask for childcare leave requests a reduction of working hours instead of childcare leave, the employer shall grant it. However, the employer is not required to grant it in cases where it is not possible to hire replacement personnel, and where it causes a considerable difficulty for the normal operation of business If the employer does not grant the reduction of working hours for the childcare period, the employer shall notify the employee in writing of the reason for such decision, and have the employee take normal childcare leave or else consult with the employee as to whether to support him/her through other measures. Employers shall not apply unfavorable working conditions to an employee who works reduced working hours for the childcare period on grounds of the working hour reduction, except when applying them in proportion to the usual working hours.

The period of working hour reduction for the childcare period shall be two years or less. If the employer grants a reduction of working hours for the childcare period to the relevant employee, the working hours after reduction shall be a minimum of 15 hours per week but shall not exceed 35 hours per week. Employers shall not dismiss or give any other disadvantageous treatment to the employee on account of the working hour reduction. After the period of working hour reduction is over, the employer shall restore the employee to the original work or to other work paying the same level of wage as before the reduction of working hours.

마친 후에는 휴직 전과 같은 업무 또는 같은 수준의 임금을 지급하는 직무에 복귀시켜야 한다. 연차유급휴가의 개근여부 계산에 있어 육아휴직기간은 소정근로일수계산에서 포함되기 때문에 육아휴직기간에 대해서 연차유급휴가가 발생한다. 기간제 근로자 또는 파견 근로자의 육아휴직 기간은 사용기간 또는 근로자파견기간에 산입하지 아니한다.

2. 육아기 근로시간 단축

사용자는 육아휴직을 신청할 수 있는 근로자가 육아휴직 대신 육아기 근로시간 단축을 신청하는 경우에 이를 허용하여야 한다. 다만, 대체인력 채용이 불가능한 경우, 정상적인 사업 운영에 중대한 지장을 초래하는 경우 등의 경우에는 그러하지 아니하다. 사업주가 육아기 근로시간 단축을 허용하지 아니하는 경우에는 해당 근로자에게 그 사유를 서면으로 통보하고 육아휴직을 사용하게 하거나 그 밖의 조치를 통하여 지원할 수 있는지를 해당 근로자와 협의하여야 한다. 고용보험으로부터 근로자가 수령하는 육아기 근로시간 단축급여는 정상적인 육아휴직 급여를 기준으로 단축된 근로시간에 비례한 금액으로 한다. 사업주는 육아기 근로시간 단축을 하고 있는 근로자에 대하여 근로시간에 비례하여 적용하는 경우 외에는 육아기 근로시간 단축을 이유로 그 근로조건을 불리하게 하여서는 아니 된다(고평법 제19조의 2, 고용보험법 제73조의 2).

육아기 근로시간 단축기간은 2년 이내로 한다. 사용자가 해당 근로자에게 육아기 근로시간 단축을 허용하는 경우 단축 후 근로시간은 주당 15시간 이상이어야 하고 35시간을 넘어서는 아니 된다. 사용자는 육아기 근로시간 단축을 이유로 해당 근로자에게 해고나 그 밖의 불리한 처우를 하여서는 아니 된다. 사용자는 근로자의 육아기 근로시간 단축기간이 끝난 후에 그 근로자를 육아기 근로시간 단축 전과 같은 업무 또는 같은 수준의 임금을 지급하는 직무에 복귀시켜야 한다.

Section 8-2. Korean Labor Law and Working Conditions for Minors

Ⅰ. Introduction

Minors are in the process of growing up as adults, so they are less developed physically and mentally, and receive special protection because they are legally required to go to school.[131] Korea's Constitution (Article 32, Paragraph 5) stipulates that special protection shall be accorded to working minors, and Chapter 5 of the Labor Standards Act specifically describes the working conditions of minors. Minors work as short-term workers, fixed-term workers, and workplace trainees in 24-hour convenience stores, fast food restaurants, and production plants. Therefore, when considering their working conditions, it is necessary to consider the conditions at workplaces with fewer than 5 workers in mind. For field trainees in particular, working conditions vary by whether they are working as students or workers.

All the protections in the Labor Standards Act (LSA) apply to working minors as well as adult workers. This includes the prohibitions against discrimination, forced labor, and violence, restrictions on unfair dismissal and managerial layoffs, and the requirement to issue written employment contracts. However, in workplaces with fewer than 5 employees, dismissal restrictions, shut-down allowances, additional wages for overtime work, and annual paid allowances do not apply.[132]

---

[131] Lim, Jongyul, Labor Law (18th Ed.), Parkyoungsa, 2020, p. 611; Ha, Kapryel, The Labor Standards Act (33rd Ed.), Joongang Economy, 2020, p. 693.

[132] Laws applicable to workplaces ordinarily employing fewer than five people

Division		Applicable articles
Labor Standards Act	Chapter 1. General Provisions	Article 1~Article 13
	Chapter 2. Labor Contract	Article 15, Article 15, Article 17, Article 19 (1), Article 20, Article 20~22, Article 23 (2), Article 26, Article 35~42
	Chapter 3. Wages	Article 43~45, Article 47~49
	Chapter 4. Working Hours and Recess	Article 54, Article 55, Article 63
	Chapter 5. Females and Minors	Article 64, Article 65 (1) & (3) (restricted to pregnant women and minors), Article 66~69, Article 70 (2) & (3), Article 71, Article 72, Article 74
	Chapter 6. Safety & Health	Article 76
	Chapter 8. Accident Compensation	Article 78~92
	Chapter 11. Labor Inspectors, etc.	Article 101~106
	Chapter 12. Penal Provisions	Article 107~116
Minimum Wage Act		All employees
Equal Employment Act		All employees
Industrial Accident		All employees: Companies in certain sectors (including companies in

제8-2절 연소근로자의 근로조건

I. 문제의 소재

연소자는 성인으로 성장하는 과정에 있기 때문에 신체적 정신적으로 미숙하고, 의무교육을 받아야 하기 때문에 특별한 보호의 대상이 된다.[131] 헌법(제32조 제5항)에 연소자의 근로는 특별한 보호를 받아야 한다고 규정하고 있으며, 근로기준법 제5장에서 연소자의 근로조건에 대해 구체적으로 기술하고 있다. 연소근로자는 24시간 편의점, 패스트푸드점, 생산 공장 등에서 단시간 근로자, 기간제 근로자, 현장실습생 등으로 일하고 있다. 따라서 연소근로자의 근로조건을 고려할 때, 연소자, 단시간 근로자, 기간제 근로자, 5인 미만 사업장의 근로조건을 모두 염두에 두고 판단하여야 한다. 특히, 현장실습생의 경우 학생 신분인지 근로자 신분인지에 따라 근로조건이 달라지게 된다.

연소자도 일반근로자와 마찬가지로 근로기준법의 모든 규정이 적용된다. 일반적으로 차별금지, 강제근로의 금지, 폭행의 금지, 근로계약의 서면작성, 부당해고 제한, 정리해고 제한 등에 적용된다. 다만, 5인 미만 사업장의 경우에는 해고제한, 휴업수당, 가산임금, 연차유급수당 등이 적용되지 않는다.[132]

연소근로자의 근로조건을 각 부분별 구체적으로 열거하고 특별한 보호규정을

---

131) 임종률, 노동법(18판), 박영사, 2020, 611면; 하갑레, 근로기준법(33판), 중앙경제, 2020. 693면.
132) 상시 5인 미만의 근로자를 사용하는 사업 또는 사업장에 적용하는 법규정

구 분		적 용 법 규 정
근로기준법	제1장 총칙	제1조부터 제13조까지의 규정
	제2장 근로계약	제15조, 제17조, 제18조, 제19조제1항, 제20조부터 제22조까지의 규정, 제23조제2항, 제26조, 제35조부터 제42조까지의 규정
	제3장 임금	제43조부터 제45조까지의 규정, 제47조부터 제49조까지의 규정
	제4장 근로시간과 휴식	제54조, 제55조, 제63조
	제5장 여성과 소년	제64조, 제65조제1항·제3항(임산부와 18세 미만인 자로 한정한다), 제66조부터 제69조까지의 규정, 제70조제2항·제3항, 제71조, 제72조, 제74조
	제6장 안전과 보건	제76조
	제8장 재해보상	제78조부터 제92조까지의 규정
	제11장 근로감독관	제101조부터 제106조까지의 규정
	제12장 벌칙	제107조부터 제116조까지의 규정
최저임금법		전사업장
남녀고용평등법		전사업장
산업재해보상보험법		전사업장 (단, 5인 미만 농, 임, 어민 등 일부 업종은 제외)
고용보험법		전사업장 (단, 5인 미만 농, 임, 어민 등 일부 업종은 제외)
노동조합 및 노동관계조정법		전사업장

I would like to list the working conditions for minors in detail by sections and special protection regulations together. In addition, I will examine whether trainees are students or workers in legal disputes.

II. Scope of Working Minors and Occupations from which They Are Prohibited

1. Scope of Working Minors

In principle, no person under the age of 15 shall be employed as a worker. However, those 13 to 15 years of age with an employment permit issued by the Minister of Employment and Labor may be so employed, as long as the employment does not interfere with their compulsory education (Article 64 of the LSA and Article 35 of its Enforcement Decree). The employer shall keep in the workplace a certificate proving the family relationships and written consent from their parent or guardian for each working minor under 18 (Article 66).

2. Prohibited Occupations

Under the Labor Standards Act, employers cannot assign pregnant women or those under 18 years of age to work that involves moral or health hazards or danger (Article 65). Prohibited occupations include high-pressure work and diving work, jobs or businesses that prohibit the employment or entry of children under the age of 18, work in prisons and mental hospitals, work in incineration and slaughter, and work dealing with oil.[133] However, they can be employed for gas station refueling service for passenger vehicles.

Employers shall not assign women or minors under the age of 18 to work in mines except where the work is temporarily needed to perform the certain duties such as health, medicine, news reporting, news coverage, etc. (Article 72).[134]

Compensation Insurance Act	agriculture, forestry and fisheries with 4 employees or fewer) are excluded.
Employment Insurance Act	All employees: Companies in certain sectors (including companies in agriculture, forestry and fisheries with 4 employees or fewer) are excluded.

[133] Prohibited occupations include: ① In the 「Rules on Occupational Safety and Health Standards」, high-pressure work and diving work, ② In the 「Construction Equipment Management Act」and 「Road Traffic Act」, etc., driving, and its related works which are prohibited for those younger than 18 years, ③ Jobs or business employment or entry of minors under the age of 18 is prohibited by other laws such as the 「Youth Protection Act」, ④ Jobs in prisons and mental hospitals, ⑤ incineration and slaughter, ⑥ handling fuel tasks (excluding refueling passenger vehicles with gasoline), ⑦ Work related to 2-bromopropane handling or exposure, ⑧ Other tasks designated and publicly announced by the Minister of Employment and Labor after deliberation.

[134] Article 42 (Jobs Permitted for Working Inside Pits) The jobs for which women and those under the age

기술하고, 법적인 쟁점이 되는 현장실습생에 대한 판단기준에 대해 살펴보고자 한다.

Ⅱ. 연소자의 범위와 사용금지 직종

1. 연소근로자의 범위

사용자는 15세 미만인 사람은 근로자로 사용하지 못한다. 다만, 예외적으로 고용노동부장관이 의무교육에 지장이 없다고 판단하여 취직인허증을 발급하는 경우에 한해 13세이상 15세미만자도 근로자로 사용할 수 있다(근기법 제64조, 시행령 제35조). 사용자는 18세 미만인 사람에 대하여는 그 연령을 증명하는 가족관계기록사항에 관한 증명서와 친권자(부모) 또는 후견인(친권자 부재)의 동의서를 사업장에 갖추어 두어야 한다(제66조).

2. 사용금지 직종

근로기준법에서 사용자는 임산부와 18세 미만자를 도덕상 또는 보건상 유해·위험한 사업에 사용하지 못한다(제65조). 금지직종은 고압작업 및 잠수작업, 18세 미만 청소년의 고용이나 출입을 금지하고 있는 직종이나 업종, 교도소와 정신병원에서의 업무, 소각과 도살의 업무, 유류를 취급하는 업무 등이다.[133] 다만, 유류를 취급하는 업무 중 주유업무는 제외한다.

사용자는 여성과 18세 미만인 사람을 갱내(坑內)에서 근로시키지 못한다. 다만, 보건·의료, 보도·취재 등 업무를 수행하기 위하여 일시적으로 필요한 경우에는 그러하지 아니하다.(제72조)[134]

---

[133] 금지직종은 ①「산업안전보건기준에 관한 규칙」고압작업 및 잠수작업, ②「건설기계관리법」, 「도로교통법」등에서 18세 미만인 자에 대하여 운전, 조종면서 취득을 제한하고 있는 직종과 업종의 운전, 조정업무, ③「청소년보호법」등 다른 법률에서 18세 미만 청소년의 고용이나 출입을 금지하고 있는 직종이나 업종, ④ 교도소와 정신병원에서의 업무, ⑤ 소각과 도살의 업무, ⑥ 유류를 취급하는 업무(주유업무는 제외한다), ⑦ 2-브로모프로판을 취급하거나 노출될 수 있는 업무, ⑧ 그 밖에 고용노동부장관이 심의를 거쳐 지정하여 고시하는 업무.

[134] 제42조(갱내근로 허용업무) 법 제72조에 따라 여성과 18세 미만인 자를 일시적으로 갱내에서 근로시킬 수 있는 업무는 다음 각 호와 같다. 1. 보건, 의료 또는 복지 업무.
2. 신문·출판·방송프로그램 제작 등을 위한 보도·취재업무.
3. 학술연구를 위한 조사 업무. 4. 관리·감독 업무.
5. 제1호부터 제4호까지의 규정의 업무와 관련된 분야에서 하는 실습업무

Employers shall not abuse workers in training, workers on probation or any other apprentice whose purpose is to acquire a technical skill, or assign them to domestic work or other work not related to the acquirement of technical skill (Article 77).

Businesses where entry and employment of minors (under the age of 19) is prohibited under the Youth Protection Act (Article 2, Item 5) are:

(1) Businesses where minors are prohibited from entering or working: entertainment and other bars, video rooms, karaoke rooms (businesses with facilities that make it legal for minors to enter are excluded from the entry ban), telephone rooms, dancing academies, dancing rooms, businesses involving speculative behavior, and those involving the handling of sexual devices.

(2) Businesses prohibited from hiring minors: Accommodation, barber shops, bathing businesses in which a massage room is set up or which is divided into private rooms, tobacco retail, toxic product manufacturing, sales and handling, ticket coffee shop, places selling alcohol like soju bars, beer bars, cafes, etc., music record sales, video sales and rental shops, general game rooms, and comic book rental shops.

III. Special Protection of Labor Contracts

Employers seeking to hire minors shall draw up employment contracts for the minors to sign if they so desire in the same position in determining the working conditions (Article 4). In this case, the parents[135] or guardians[136] cannot act on behalf of the minor, but if the employment contract is deemed unfavorable to the minor, they can terminate it later (Article 67). Under the Civil Act, those under the age of 19 cannot engage in legal actions such as signing contracts independently, and so may engage in legal actions only with the consent of a parent or guardian. So, in the Labor Standards Act, those under the age of 18 must submit consent from their parents at the time of employment. However, working minors may independently engage in legal actions such as claiming wages and joining a labor union.

The employer must write and deliver the necessary items in the working minor's

---

of eighteen may be placed temporarily inside a pit under Article 72 of the Act shall be as follows:
1. Jobs for health, medical treatment and welfare;
2. Jobs for the gathering and reporting of news for newspapers, or to publish and produce broadcasting programs;
3. Surveying for the purpose of academic research;
4. Jobs for management and supervision;
5. Practical training work performed in the fields relating to subparagraphs 1 through 4.

[135] Civil Act - Article 909 (Custodian) (1) Parents shall have parental authority over their minor child.
[136] Civil Act - Article 928 (Commencement of Guardianship for Minors)
Where there is no person with parental authority over a minor or where a person with parental authority is unable to exercise all or part of his/her parental authority, a guardian shall be appointed for the minor.

사용자는 양성공, 수습, 그 밖의 명칭을 불문하고 기능의 습득을 목적으로 하는 근로자를 혹사하거나 가사, 그 밖의 기능 습득과 관계없는 업무에 종사시키지 못한다(제77조).

청소년보호법에서 미성년자(19세 미만)에 대해 출입과 고용을 금지하는 업소(청소년 보호법 제2조 5목)는 다음과 같다.
(1) 청소년 출입·고용금지 업소: 유흥주점, 단란주점, 비디오방, 노래방 (청소년의 출입이 허용되는 시설을 갖춘 업소에는 출입만 가능), 전화방, 무도학원업, 무도장업, 사행행위영업, 성기구 취급업소
(2) 청소년 고용금지 업소: 숙박업, 이용업, 목욕장업 중 안마실을 설치하거나 개실로 구획하여 하는 영업, 담배소매업, 유독물 제조·판매·취급업, 티켓다방, 주류판매 목적의 소주방, 호프, 카페 등 형태의 영업, 음반판매업, 비디오물 판매·대여업, 일반게임장, 만화대여업

Ⅲ. 근로계약의 특별보호

연소근로자와 사용자는 근로조건의 결정 시 동등한 지위에서 자유로운 의사에 의하여 근로계약을 작성하여야 한다(제4조). 이 경우 친권자[135]나 후견인[136]이 미성년자의 근로계약을 대리할 수는 없으나, 근로계약이 미성년자에게 불리하다고 인정하는 경우에는 이를 해지할 수 있다(제67조). 민법상 19세 미만인 미성년자는 독자적으로 계약체결 등 법률행위를 할 수 없고, 친권자나 후견인의 동의를 받아 법률행위를 할 수 있다. 노동법에서도 연소근로자는 근로계약시 친권자의 동의서를 제출해야 한다. 그러나 연소근로자는 임금청구, 노동조합 가입 등의 법률행위를 독자적으로 할 수 있다.

사용자는 연소자와 근로계약 체결시 필수 기재사항에 대해 서면으로 작성하여 교부하여야 하고, 근로조건이 변경된 경우 변경된 근로계약서를 교부하여야 한다(제17조). 서면 명시내용은 다음과 같다.
① 임금: 임금의 구성항목, 계산방법, 지급방법.
② 소정근로시간: 연소자의 법정근로시간 내에서 정해져야 한다 (1일 7시간,

---
[135] 민법 제909조(친권자) ①부모는 미성년자인 자의 친권자가 된다.
[136] 민법 제928조(후견인) 미성년자에게 친권자가 없거나 친권자가 친권의 전부 또는 일부를 행사할 수 없는 경우에는 미성년후견인을 두어야 한다.

employment contract, and if working conditions are changed, a revised employment contract must be issued (Article 17). The written contents shall include:

① (Wages) Wage composition, calculation method, and payment method;
② (Contractual working hours) shall be determined within the legal working hours for minors (7 hours per day, 35 hours per week);
③ (Weekly holidays) If workers work more than 15 hours a week, they are entitled to an average of 1 or more paid weekly holidays per week;
④ (Paid Leave) Workplaces with five or more employees must guarantee monthly paid leave and annual paid leave;
⑤ (Place of employment and work to be engaged in).

Ⅳ. Wages

Employers must pay wages directly, in currency, and in full to working minors, at least once a month on a fixed date (Article 43). When working minors quit or the working relationship is terminated due to dismissal, any owed wages, severance pay, and other money shall be paid within 14 days of the termination (Article 36). Employers must not pay wages to the parents of their minor workers (Article 68). If working children are unable to provide work due to reasons attributable to the employer, they shall be paid 70% of their average wage (Article 46). If an emergency situation such as illness or accident occurs and working minors require immediate payment of wages for work performed before the request date in order to cover the related expenses, employers shall pay wages ahead of payday (Article 45).

Wages must be set at minimum wage at least, and cannot be lowered on account of the worker being a minor. However, for unskilled minors who have signed an employment contract for at least one year, the minimum wage may be reduced up to 10% for the probationary first 3 months. However, this is not applicable to simple labor work (Article 5 of the Minimum Wage Act, or "MWA").

If working children quit after continuing to work for one year or more, severance pay equal to the 30 days' average wage per year of continual work shall be paid (MWA, Article 34). However, there is no obligation to pay severance pay if the average working hours are fewer than 15 per week for each 4 week period. If some months the minor works an average of fewer than 15 hours per week and some months the minor works an average of 15 hours or more per week, only the months in which the minor worked an average of 15 hours or more per week are calculated, and severance pay is incurred only when such period is one year or longer (Article 18).

Ⅴ. Special Protection of Working Hours and Rest

1주 35시간 이내).
③ 주휴일: 1주 15시간 이상 근무한 경우에는 1주일에 평균 1일 이상의 유급 주휴일을 주어야 한다.
④ 유급휴가: 5인 이상의 사업장은 월차 유급휴가와 연차 유급휴가를 보장하여야 한다.
⑤ 취업의 장소와 종사하여야 할 업무.

Ⅳ. 임금

사용자는 연소근로자에게 임금을 직접, 통화로, 그 전액을 지급하여야 하고, 매월 1회 이상 일정한 기일을 정하여 지급하여야 한다(제43조). 연소근로자가 퇴직하거나 해고로 인하여 근로관계가 종료된 경우에는 14일 이내에 임금, 퇴직금, 기타의 금품을 지급하여야 한다(제36조). 사용자가 임금을 친권자에게 지급하면 안된다(제68조). 사용자의 귀책사유로 연소근로자가 근로를 제공하지 못한 경우에는 평균임금의 70%의 휴업수당을 지급하여야 한다(제46조). 연소근로자가 질병이나 재해 등의 비상한 상황이 발생해 그 비용을 충당하기 위해 임금지급일 전에 기왕의 근로에 대한 임금을 지급해 줄 것을 요구하면 사용자는 지급해야 한다(제45조).

임금은 최저임금 이상으로 책정되어야 하고, 연소자라는 이유로 최저임금을 저하시킬 수 없다. 다만, 1년 이상의 근로계약을 체결하고 수습 중인 근로자의 경우에는 최저임금의 10%를 감한 범위내에서 정할 수 있다. 그러나 그 업무가 단순 노무업무의 경우에는 해당되지 않는다(최저임금법 제5조).

연소근로자가 1년 이상 계속근무한 후 퇴직하는 경우에는 계속근로년수 1년에 30일분의 평균임금으로 하는 퇴직금을 지급하여야 한다(제34조). 다만, 근로시간이 4주간 평균 1주 근로시간이 15시간 미만인 경우에는 퇴직금 지급의무가 없다. 1주 평균 15시간 미만인 달과 그 이상인 달이 섞여 있는 경우에는 1주 평균 15시간 이상인 달만 계산하여 그 기간이 1년 이상인 경우에 한해 퇴직금이 발생한다(제18조).

Ⅴ. 근로시간과 휴식의 특별보호

The working hours of persons aged 15 to 18 shall not exceed 7 hours per day and 35 hours per week. However, this may be extended by up to 1 hour per day and 5 hours per week if there is agreement between the parties. Since 1 week refers to 7 days including holidays, the longest working hours for working minors shall be 40 hours a week. Therefore, flexible working hours and selective working hours are not applicable to working minors (MWA, Articles 51 and 52).

An employer shall allow a recess period of 30 minutes or more for every 4 working hours and at least 1 hour for every 8 working hours during the work day. During these rest hours, rest should be freely available to working minors (Article 54).

If working minors continue to work for 15 hours or more per week, they are given paid weekly holidays (Article 55). If they have completed their contractual working hours for one week, they are entitled to a weekly leave allowance of one or more days (Article 55). The weekly leave allowance for working minors is determined according to the ratio calculated by the working hours of ordinary workers engaged in the same type of work at the workplace, just as the working conditions for part-time workers (Article 18).[137]

When working minors have worked for more than the contractual working hours, employers must pay overtime allowance amounting to 50% or more of the normal wage, in addition to the normal wage (Article 6 of the Fixed-Term Employment Act).

Employers are not allowed to have those under the age of 18 work from 10 pm to 6 am or on holidays, unless the employer obtains the consent of those under the age of 18 and approval from the Minister of Employment and Labor (Article 70). According to the approval standards of the Ministry of Employment and Labor,[138] if nighttime operations are inevitable for fast food restaurants where many minors work part-time, in consideration of the safety of working children, their health, and protecting their ability to learn during the day, the limit is 12 midnight, unless approval from the Minister of Employment and Labor is gained for special reasons. Here, the term "special reasons" refers to cases where the necessity for night work is accepted and will have no detrimental effect on the health of working minors.

Employers shall give 15 days of annual leave when working minors have attended the workplace for at least 80% of the contracted work hours during one year. Employers shall also provide one day of paid leave for each month to working minors who have

---

[137] For 4 hours a day, 5 days a week, and an hourly wage of 10,000 won, the weekly vacation allowance is calculated according to the proportional principle of short-time workers. (20 hours / 40 hours per week) x 8 hours = 4 hours; 4 hours x 10,000 won = 40,000 won.

[138] Ministry of Employment and Labor Guidelines on approval for minors to engage in night work (Equality Policy Division-July 26, 2004).

15세 이상 18세 미만인 사람의 근로시간은 1일에 7시간, 1주에 35시간을 초과하지 못한다. 다만, 당사자 사이의 합의에 따라 1일에 1시간, 1주에 5시간을 한도로 연장할 수 있다. 1주란 휴일을 포함한 7일을 말하기 때문에 연소근로자가 근로할 수 있는 최장시간은 주40시간이 된다. 따라서 연소근로자에 대해서는 탄력적 근로시간제와 선택적 근로시간제가 적용되지 않는다(제51조, 제52조).

사용자는 연소근로자의 근로시간이 4시간인 경우에는 30분 이상, 8시간인 경우에는 1시간 이상의 휴게시간을 근로시간 중에 주어야 한다. 이 경우 휴게시간은 연소근로자가 자유롭게 이용할 수 있어야 한다(제54조).

연소근로자가 1주 15시간 이상 계속 근무한 경우에는 유급 주휴일을 부여받는다(제55조). 연소근로자가 1주간 소정근로일수를 개근한 경우에는 1일 이상의 주휴수당을 주어야 한다(제55조). 연소자의 주휴수당은 단시간 근로자의 근로조건과 같이 그 사업장의 같은 종류의 업무에 종사하는 통상 근로자의 근로시간을 기준으로 산정한 비율에 따라 결정된다(제18조).[137]

연소근로자가 소정근로시간을 초과하여 근무한 경우에는 통상임금의 100분의 50 이상을 가산한 연장근로수당을 지급하여야 한다(기간제법 제6조).

사용자는 18세 미만자를 오후 10시부터 오전 6시 까지의 시간과 휴일에 근로시키지 못한다. 다만, 사용자가 18세 미만자의 동의와 고용노동부장관의 인가를 받으면 야간시간과 휴일에 근로를 할 수 있다(제70조). 고용노동부의 인가기준에 따르면,[138] 연소자가 다수 아르바이트를 하고 있는 패스트푸드점에 대하여 업종의 특성상 야간 가동(영업)이 불가피 하다고 볼 수 있지만, 연소근로자의 건강보호 및 학습보장, 귀가 등 안전을 고려하여 특별한 사유가 없는 한 오후 12시까지 제한적으로 인가한다. 여기서 "특별한 사유"라 함은 사업주의 야간근로 필요성과 연소근로자의 건강 등에 무리가 없는 경우를 말한다.

사용자는 연소근로자가 1년간 80%퍼센트 이상 출근한 경우에 15일을 연차휴가를 주어야 한다. 사용자는 계속하여 근로한 기간이 1년 미만인 연소근로자

---

[137] 1일 4시간, 1주일에 5일, 시간급 10,000원 인 경우, 주휴수당은 단시간근로자의 비례원칙에 따라 계산된다. (주 20시간 / 40시간) x 8시간 = 4시간; 4시간 x 10,000원 = 40,000원이 된다.
[138] 고용노동부의 연소근로자 야간근로 인가업무 처리지침(평등정책과-2004.7.26)

continued to work for less than one year or those who have attended the workplace for less than 80 percent of the contracted work hours during one year (Article 60).

VI. Coverage by the Four Major Social Insurances

In principle, coverage by the four major social insurances are required for working minors. However, if the on-site trainees are students who are not workers, they are not eligible. For working minors, the four insurances are applied slightly differently.

(1) Industrial Accident Compensation Insurance: Applies the same as for all workplaces using workers. However, on-site trainees who are not workers are exceptionally eligible for compensation from workers' compensation (Article 123 of the Industrial Accident Compensation Insurance Act).

(2) Employment Insurance: Working minors who are employed for 1 day or longer are covered by employment insurance, but short-time workers with fewer than 60 working hours per month are excluded.

(3) National Pension and National Health Insurance: The national pension is mandatory for those aged 18 or over and under 60 who work at a workplace. However, the National Health Insurance applies to all workers working in the workplace, regardless of age. The same applies to daily workers whose employment period is shorter than one month, and short-time workers whose contractual working hours per month are fewer than 60.

VII. Legal Issues related to Working Children

Whether or not the trainees in third grade of vocational high school are workers depends on whether or not they are students. If the main purpose for field training is to develop practical learning abilities to earn high school credits, they cannot be considered workers. However, if on-site trainees are recognized as having a subordinate relationship with the employer, they are considered workers under the Labor Standards Act.

1. Student Status[139]

In accordance with the Industrial Education Promotion Act, 2 + 1 year public

---

[139] MOEL Guidelines: Employment support unemployment benefits-262, Jan. 19, 2011; Kungi 68207-1833, May 4, 2002.

또는 1년간 80퍼센트 미만 출근한 연소근로자에게는 1개월 개근 시 1일의 유급휴가를 주어야 한다(제60조).

Ⅵ. 4대보험 적용

연소근로자에 대해서 4대보험을 원칙적으로 가입해야 한다. 다만, 현장실습생이 근로자가 아닌 학생 신분이면 4대보험 가입대상이 아니다. 연소근로자에 있어 4대 보험별로 조금씩 다르게 적용된다.
(1) 산업재해보상보험: 근로자를 사용하는 모든 사업장에 적용되므로 연소근로자에게도 당연히 적용된다. 다만, 근로자가 아닌 현장실습생은 예외적으로 산재보상의 대상이 된다(산재법 제123조).
(2) 고용보험: 1일 이상 고용된 연소근로자는 고용보험에 가입되지만, 1개월의 소정근로시간이 60시간 미만인 단시간 근로자는 제외된다.
(3) 국민연금과 국민건강보험: 국민연금은 사업장에서 근무하는 18세 이상 60세 미만 자이다. 그러나 국민건강보험은 연령과 상관없이 사업장에서 근로를 하는 모든 근로자에게 적용된다. 가입제외 대상은 동일하게 고용기간이 1개월 미만인 일용근로자, 1개월의 소정근로시간이 60시간 미만인 단시간 근로자이다.

Ⅶ. 연소자 관련 법적 쟁점

직업계고등학교 3학년의 실습생이 근로자인지의 여부는 학생 신분인지 아닌지에 따라 달리 적용되고 있다. 현장실습생의 주 목적이 학점이수 등 실질적 학습능력을 위한 것이면 근로자로 볼 수 없다. 그러나 현장실습생이 사업주와의 사용종속관계가 인정되면 근로기준법상 근로자에 해당된다.

1. 학생 신분인 경우[139]

2 + 1 체제의 공고실습생은 산업교육진흥법에 의거하여 고교 3년 과정중에

---

[139] 행정해석: 고용지원 실업급여과-262, 2011.1.19; 근기 68207-1833, 2002.5.4

high school students take the 3rd year (1 year) course as students during the 3rd year of high school and engaged in industrial field training. A standard agreement is signed between the business, the school, and the students, and the students engage in on-site practice according to the on-site practice plan prepared in consultation with the business and the school. The business is supposed to evaluate trainee performance during on-the-job training according to the standards set by the school and notify the school of the results. Field training is a part of the curriculum in accordance with the Industrial Education Promotion Act and aims to help students acquire the knowledge, skills, and attitudes necessary for them to engage in industry in the future. In this case, it is difficult to see the trainee as a worker who provides work for the purpose of wages.

2. Worker status[140]

Applicants who are expected to graduate are considered workers, if a subordinate relationship is recognized, and the Labor Standards Act is applied. In other words, even if they are trainees who are expected to graduate from high school and their working period is temporary, it cannot be concluded that they are not covered by the Labor Standards Act only for these reasons. In cases where it is recognized that there is a subordinate relationship pursuant to Article 2 of the Labor Standards Act based on the actual relationship between the employer and the trainee regarding the employment contract, the nature and content of work, and whether or not compensation is paid, the Labor Standards Act shall apply to the trainee.

VIII. Conclusion

Working minors are in their mental and physical growth stages, and since education should be given priority, they need special protection beyond that needed by adult workers. Chapter 5 of the Labor Standards Act specifies the details of this special protection. Recently, there have been many cases of industrial accidents involving students in field training, so special caution is required. Because working minors are still developing physically and mentally, they absolutely need special protection. All special protection requirements for working minors are mandatory regulations, and employers will be liable for punishment if these regulations are violated.

---

[140] Supreme Court ruling on June 9, 1987: 86 daka 2920.

3학년(1년) 과정을 학생의 신분으로 산업체현장에서 현장실습을 실시한다. 산업체, 학교, 학생간에 표준협약서를 체결하고, 산업체와 학교측이 협의하여 작성한 현장실습계획에 따라 학생이 현장실습을 실시한다. 산업체에서는 학교측이 정한 기준에 따라 실습생의 현장실습 내용을 평가하여 그 결과를 학교측에 통보하는 것으로 되어 있다. 현장 실습은 산업교육진흥법에 따라 교육과정의 일부로써 공고생이 향후 산업에 종사하는 데 필요한 지식·기술·태도 습득을 목적으로 한다. 이 경우에는 실습생은 임금을 목적으로 근로를 제공하는 근로자로 보기 어렵다.

2. 근로자 신분인 경우[140]

졸업예정 실습생도 사용종속관계가 인정되면 근로자에 해당되고 근로기준법이 적용된다. 즉 고등학교 졸업예정자인 실습생이고 또 그 작업기간이 잠정적인 것이라 할지라도 바로 이러한 사유만으로 근로기준법을 적용받지 않는 근로자라고 단정할 수는 없다. 사업주와 실습생 사이의 채용에 관한 계약내용, 작업의 성질과 내용, 보수의 여부 등 실질적인 관계에 의하여 근로기준법 제2조의 규정에 의한 사용종속관계가 있음이 인정되는 경우에는 그 실습생은 근로기준법의 적용을 받는 근로자에 해당된다.

Ⅷ. 결론

연소근로자는 정신적, 신체적으로 성장단계에 있고, 교육이 우선되어야 하는 시기이므로 성인근로자와는 달리 특별한 보호가 필요하다. 이러한 취지에서 근로기준법 제5장에서 특별보호의 내용을 구체화하고 있다. 최근 현장실습 중인 학생들의 산재가 발생하는 경우가 허다하여 이에 대한 주의가 요구된다. 연소근로자는 아직 성장단계에 있고, 신체적으로나 정신적으로 약한 사람들이기에 특별한 보호가 절실히 필요하다. 연소근로자의 특별보호 요건은 모두 강행규정으로 사업주가 이를 위반시 처벌의 대상이 된다는 사실을 명심하여야 할 것이다.

---

[140] 대법원 1987. 6. 9. 선고 86다카2920 판결.

Section 9. Rules of Employment

Section 9-1. Rules of Employment and the Employer's Legal Responsibilities

I. Introduction

Rules of employment set up an important system so that employers can systematically and uniformly manage their workers in a business or workplace. These rules refer to the employer determining the regulations needed to maintain corporate order and work efficiency at the workplace and the working conditions that will apply to all workers.[141] These rules of employment must be observed by the workers in the process of providing work, and also outline consequences for violating these rules. Working conditions refer to the conditions stipulated in the rules of employment in relation to worker wages, working hours, procedures for dismissal, and other treatment.[142]

Rules of employment can be written and enforced unilaterally by the employer, but once they are written, the employer and employees are bound to them and consequences for breaking those rules will apply to the applicable party, whether worker or employer. Employers cannot unilaterally change working conditions that have already been established. Any unfavorable changes are of no legal effect without the consent of a majority of the workers to whom the changes apply. In addition, the employer has both a legal obligation to prepare and report the rules to the Ministry of Employment and Labor, and a legal obligation to notify the workers of those rules in a public way. This is to ensure that the minimum standards set by the Labor Standards Act apply, through the rules of employment, to workplaces.[143]

I would like to take a detailed look at the legal requirements for rules of employment and how they are applied in practice.

II. Legal Nature of Rules of Employment

---

[141] Supreme Court ruling on Nov. 28, 1997: 97da24511.
[142] Supreme Court ruling on June 23, 1992: 91da19210.
[143] Lee, Seonggil, A Legislative Review of the Employment Rules System, Labor Law Research (8) 69-119, Seoul National University Labor Law Research Society, June 1999, p. 78.

제9절 취업규칙

제9-1절 취업규칙과 사업주의 법적의무

I. 문제의 소재

　사용자가 사업 또는 사업장에서 근로자를 체계적이고 통일적으로 관리할 수 있도록 중요한 시스템을 설정하는 것이 취업규칙이다. 취업규칙은 사용자가 사업장에서 기업의 질서유지와 효율적 업무수행을 위하여 필요한 복무규정과 근로자 전체에 적용될 근로조건을 정한 규정을 말한다.[141] 여기서 복무규율이라고 하면 근로자가 근로를 제공하는 과정에서 지켜야 할 작업질서에 관한 규칙과 이를 위반한 경우에 대한 제재를 말한다. 그리고 근로조건이라고 하면 근로자의 임금, 근로시간, 해고 그 밖에 근로자의 대우에 관하여 정한 조건을 말한다.[142]

　취업규칙은 사용자가 일방적으로 작성하여 시행할 수 있지만, 일단 작성된 규정은 사용자와 근로자가 이에 구속되어 이를 위반한 경우에는 각각 제재가 가해진다. 그리고 사용자는 이미 확정된 근로조건에 대해 일방적으로 변경할 수 없다. 사용자가 취업규칙을 불이익 하게 변경할 때에는 그 적용 근로자의 과반수 동의를 얻어야 법적 효력을 가진다. 또한 사용자는 취업규칙을 작성하여 이를 고용노동부에 신고해야 하는 법적 의무와, 그 내용을 근로자들에게 게시하고 주지시켜야 하는 법적의무를 동시에 가지고 있다. 이렇게 하는 이유는 취업규칙을 통해서 근로기준법이 정한 최저 기준이 사업장에 적용될 수 있도록 하는 입법적 배려라고 할 수 있다.[143] 이러한 취업규칙의 법적의무에는 어떤 내용이 있는 지와 어떻게 실무에서 적용되는지에 대해 구체적으로 살펴보고자 한다.

II. 취업규칙의 법적 성질

---

141) 대법원 1997. 11. 28. 선고 97다24511 판결.
142) 대법원 1992. 6. 23. 선고 91다19210 판결.
143) 이승길, 취업규칙법제에 관한 입법론적 고찰, 노동법 연구(8) 69-119, 서울대학교 노동법연구회, 1999. 6. 78면.

Rules of employment enforce legal regulations that must be observed in the workplace (legal effect), while providing the principle of equal decision-making between labor and management in determining working conditions (contractual effect).[144] The courts have ruled, Rules of employment are written by the employer, based on the employer's corporate management rights, in order to unify the service rules and working conditions of workers at the workplace. This is because the purpose of the Labor Standards Act is to protect and strengthen the position of workers in their reality of subordinate labor relations to protect and improve their basic livelihoods. This compels that rules of employment be drafted and become the legal norm.[145]

Contractual effect refers to the effect that arises from the relationship between the employer and the worker in the employment contract. Although working conditions are stipulated in rules of employment, any unfavorable changes are of no legal effect without the consent of the majority of the target workers (proviso to Article 94 of the Act). This is in accordance with the principle of protecting workers' vested rights and determining equal working conditions (Article 4 of the Act).

Ⅲ. Specific Legal Obligations of the Employer in Relation to the Rules of Employment

Rules of employment are legal obligations that must be prepared by employers who employ at least a certain number of workers. Their specific details and effect are described in the Labor Standards Act.

1. Size of workplaces obligated to draw up rules of employment rules

(1) Legal requirements

Employers who employ 10 or more ordinarily-employed workers must prepare rules of employment and report them to the Minister of Employment and Labor (Article 93 of the Act). It is much more difficult for smaller workplaces to have rules of employment in place, so their preparation is left to the discretion of the

---

[144] Kim, Hyungbae, 「Labor Law」 24th ed., Parkyoungsa, Feb. 2015. p. 297; Lim, Jong-ryul, 「Labor Law」, 24th ed., Parkyoungsa, p. 366.
[145] Supreme Court ruling on July 26, 1977: 77da355.

취업규칙은 사업장에서 준수해야 하는 법규적 규정을 강제하면서도 근로조건의 결정에 있어서는 노사 대등결정원칙을 제공하고 있다. 이는 법규범적 효력과 계약적 효력을 동시에 가지고 있다고 할 수 있다.[144] 판례도 취업규칙은 사용자가 기업경영권을 바탕으로 사업장에 있어서의 근로자의 복무규율이나 근로조건을 획일적이고 통일적으로 정립하기 위하여 작성하는 것이다. 이는 근로기준법이 종속적 노동관계의 현실에서 불평등한 근로자의 입장을 보호하고 강화하여 그들의 기본적 생활을 보호하고 향상시키려는 목적으로 그 작성을 강제하고 이에 법규범성을 부여하고 있다[145]고 설명하고 있다.

계약적 효력은 사용자와 근로자 간의 근로계약 관계에서 발생하는 효력을 말한다. 취업규칙에 정해진 근로조건에 따라 근로자들의 근로조건이 구속되지만, 취업규칙에 정한 근로조건을 불이익 하게 변경할 경우에는 그 대상 근로자 과반수의 동의를 전제로 법적 효력이 발생한다(법 제94조의 단서). 이는 근로자의 기득권 보호, 근로조건 대등결정의 원칙에 따른 것이다 (법 제4조).

Ⅲ. 취업규칙과 관련된 사용자의 구체적 법적의무

취업규칙은 일정규모 이상의 근로자를 고용한 사용자가 의무적으로 작성해야 하는 법적 의무사항이다. 근로기준법은 취업규칙에 관한 구체적 내용과 효력을 기술하고 있다.

1. 취업규칙의 작성의무가 있는 사업장 규모

(1) 법적 요구사항

'상시 10명 이상'의 근로자를 사용하는 사용자는 취업규칙을 작성하여 고용노동부장관에게 신고하여야 한다(법 제93조). 10인 이상의 사업장에 법적의무를 주고 있는 것은 10인 미만의 영세규모의 사업장은 회사의 체계가 갖추어 졌다고 보기 어렵기 때문에 일정규모 이상의 사용자에게 법적의무를 두고 있다. 10인 미만 사업장의 경우에는 취업규칙의 작성이 법적의무가 아닌

---

[144] 김형배, 「노동법」 제24판, 박영사, 2015.2. 297면; 임종률, 「노동법」 제24판, 박영사, 366면.
[145] 대법원 1977. 7. 26. 선고 77다355 판결.

employer and is not a legal obligation.

(2) Practical application

The number of ordinarily-employed workers is determined by dividing the number of total employees by the number of working days in the one month prior to the date of occurrence of the reason for application of the law (the time when it is necessary to determine whether the rules of employment have been drawn up and the duty to report) (Enforcement Decree to the Labor Standards Act, Article 7-2). While employers employing fewer than 10 workers are not obligated to prepare or report establishment of rules of employment, if they are drawn up, all regulations stipulated by law related to those rules apply.[146] Here, employers obliged to prepare and report establishment of rules of employment refer to those who have substantial authority and responsibility for matters that constitute the details of those rules, such as workplace rules and working conditions.[147]

2. Items to be stated in the rules of employment

(1) Legal requirements

Article 93 of the Labor Standards Act lists the items to be written in the rules of employment as it relates to working conditions and employment regulations to be uniformly applied to a business or workplace. Article 93 consists of 13 items and applies to all workers in the relevant business or workplace, and can be divided into mandatory and optional items.

(2) Practical application

Of the matters listed in Article 93 of the Labor Standards Act, rules of employment must stipulate essential working conditions such as wages, working hours, recess hours, and holidays. Since there are no standards required by law in a number of areas related to shift work, family allowance, and others, including these items in rules of employment is optional. However, any wage reductions in the rules of employment (as part of the employer's disciplinary options) are limited

---

[146] Seoul High Court ruling on Sep. 15, 2005: 2004nu23621.
[147] Supreme Court ruling on Dec. 24, 1992: 92do2341.

사업주의 재량에 맡겨져 있다.

(2) 실무적용

상시근로자 수는 법 적용 사유(취업규칙 작성과 신고 의무 적용여부를 판단해야 하는 시점) 발생일 전 1개월 동안 사용한 근로자의 연인원을 가동일수로 나누어 판단한다(시행령 제7조의2). 10인 미만을 고용한 사업주는 취업규칙의 작성과 신고의무는 없으나 일단 작성된 경우에는 법에서 정한 취업규칙에 관한 모든 규정이 적용된다.[146] 여기서 취업규칙을 작성하고 신고해야 할 의무가 있는 사용자는 직장규율이나 근로조건의 결정 등 취업규칙의 내용을 이루는 사항에 관해서 실질적인 권한과 책임을 갖는 자를 의미한다.[147]

2. 취업규칙의 기재사항

(1) 법적 요구사항

작성 내용은 사업 또는 사업장에 통일적으로 적용할 근로조건과 복무규율에 관한 내용으로 근로기준법 제93조에서 취업규칙의 기재사항을 열거하고 있다. 모두 13가지의 사항으로 구성되어 해당 사업 또는 사업장의 근로자 전체에 대해 적용되는 사항으로 필수적 기재사항과 임의적 기재사항으로 구분할 수 있다.

(2) 실무적용

근로기준법 제93조에 열거된 사항 중 임금, 근로시간, 휴게시간, 휴일 등과 같이 근로자 보호를 위하여 지켜야 하는 필수적인 근로조건은 반드시 그 내용을 취업규칙에 기재하여야 한다(필수적 기재사항). 그러나 교대근로, 가족수당 등에 관한 사항 등은 법에서 정한 기준이 없고 그 시행이 강제되는 것이 아니므로 해당 사업 또는 사업장에서 이를 도입하거나 시행하는 경우에만 취업규칙에 기재하여야 할 의무가 있다(임의적 기재사항). 다만, 취업규칙에 감급(減給)의 제재를 정한 경우에는 그 감액의 총액이 1임금지급시기의 10%를

---

146) 서울고등법원 2005. 9. 15. 선고 2004누23621 판결.
147) 대법원 1992. 12. 24. 선고 92도2341 판결.

to no more than 10% of one pay period. Finally, nothing in the rules of employment can be of a lower standard than in the Labor Standards Act or the applicable workplace collective agreement (Articles 95 and 96).

3. Procedures for drafting and changing rules of employment

(1) Legal requirements

The law defines how rules of employment are to be drafted and changed. The employer shall hear the views of the labor union organized by a majority of workers, or if there is no union organized by a majority of workers, the employer shall hear the views of a majority of workers in the relevant business or workplace. However, if the rules of employment are to be changed unfavorably for workers, their consent must be obtained before such change will have any effect (Article 94 of the Act). If the employer does not hear the views of applicable workers or obtain their consent before changing the rules unfavorably, a fine of not more than 5 million won shall be imposed (Article 114 of the Act). This is to protect the principle of equality between labor and management in determining working conditions and to ensure decent working conditions for the workers.

(2) Practical application

In general, if the already-existing working conditions or employment regulations are written into rules of employment, it is sufficient to inform the workers that rules of employment have been created and reflect the already-existing working conditions/employment regulations. When introducing any new regulations into the rules, the views of a majority of the workers must be heard. If there are any changes that will be unfavorable to the workers, the consent of the affected workers must be obtained.

Changes to rules of employment that are considered unfavorable to workers generally include lowering the working conditions or removing the existing rules on working conditions and introducing new rules that are less favorable. There are three categories of criteria for judging whether changes to the rules of employment are disadvantageous. First, if there are multiple changes to the rules, a decision will be made for each individual working condition, but if there is an interactive relationship or linkage between factors that determine one working condition, it shall be decided comprehensively. For example, even if the severance pay rate is adjusted downward, it is not considered a disadvantage if the total amount of severance pay does not

초과할 수 없고 취업규칙의 내용이 근로기준법이나 해당 사업장의 단체협약보다 더 낮아서는 안된다 (법 제95조, 제96조).

3. 취업규칙의 작성과 변경절차

(1) 법적 요구사항

취업규칙을 어떻게 작성할 것인가와 어떻게 변경할 것인지는 법으로 정해져 있다. 사용자는 취업규칙의 작성 또는 변경에 관하여 해당 사업 또는 사업장에 근로자의 과반수로 조직된 노동조합이 있는 경우에는 그 노동조합, 근로자의 과반수로 조직된 노동조합이 없는 경우에는 근로자 과반수의 의견을 들어야 한다. 다만, 취업규칙을 근로자에게 불리하게 변경하는 경우에는 그들의 동의를 받아야 한다(법 제94조). 사용자가 취업규칙 변경과정에서 의견청취 또는 동의를 얻지 않는 경우 500만 원 이하의 벌금에 처한다(법 제114조). 이는 근로조건의 결정에 있어 노사 대등의 원칙을 반영하고 근로자의 근로조건 보호를 위한 것이다.

(2) 실무적용

취업규칙의 작성과 변경 절차에 있어 근로자 과반수의 의견청취인지 그 동의를 받아야 하는지에 대해서는 새로운 취업규칙의 작성인지 아니면 기존 취업규칙의 변경인지에 따라 달라 질 수 있다. 일반적으로 기존의 근로조건 또는 복무규정에 관한 사항을 취업규칙에 기재한 경우에는 근로자들에게 취업규칙의 작성이나 변경에 대해 주지시키는 정도로 충분하다. 취업규칙에 기존에 없던 복무규정을 도입하는 경우에는 근로자의 과반수의 의견을 들어야 한다. 그리고 변경되는 취업규칙이 근로자들에게 불이익한 변경인 경우에는 그 대상 근로자들의 동의를 얻어야 한다.

취업규칙의 불이익한 변경은 기존의 규정을 변경하여 근로조건을 낮추는 것이 일반적이지만, 기존의 근로조건에 관한 규정을 삭제하는 경우, 이전의 근로조건보다 불리한 규정을 신설하는 경우도 포함된다. 취업규칙 불이익 변경의 판단기준은 다음의 세가지로 구분할 수 있다. 첫째, 취업규칙 변경 사항이 여러 개인 경우에는 개별 근로조건별로 판단하되, 하나의 근로조건을

decrease because the number of wage items included in the average wage increases.[148] Second, if a change to the rules of employment is beneficial to some workers and unfavorable to others, it is deemed unfavorable if the benefits resulting from the favorable and unfavorable are mixed with each other.[149] Third, if the change subdivides and materializes the contents conceptually because the existing regulations are unclear or comprehensive, and therefore are intended to resolve controversies in interpretation, it cannot be regarded as a disadvantageous change.[150]

4. Reporting rules of employment

(1) Legal requirements

Employers who regularly employ 10 or more workers must prepare rules of employment and report them to the Minister of Employment and Labor after hearing the views of their affected workers (Articles 93 and 94 of the Act). Before reporting the establishment or changes to the rules of employment, the employer must submit
① the employment rules and
② documents proving that the views of the labor union representing the majority of the workers, or the majority of the workers themselves, have been heard.
If changes to the rules are unfavorable, documents must be submitted proving that consent has been obtained from the labor union representing the majority of workers, or from the majority of workers themselves (Article 15 of the Enforcement Regulation).

(2) Practical application

When a report of establishment of or changes to the rules of employment is received, the labor inspector shall check whether the necessary information pursuant to Article 93 of the Labor Standards Act is included and whether documents have been attached that prove that the views have been heard/consent has been obtained from a labor union representing the majority of workers, or a majority of the workers themselves. After that, a review is made by the labor inspector within 20 days of receiving the report, to ensure the details of the rules of employment do not conflict with relevant laws or regulations or the relevant collective agreement, and that any changes to the rules of employment, without proof of worker consent,

---

[148] Supreme Court ruling on Aug. 28, 1997: 96da1726.
[149] Supreme Court ruling on May 14, 1993: 93da1893.
[150] Supreme Court ruling on Aug. 25, 2011: 2010guhap42263.

결정짓는 여러 요소 사이에 서로 대가관계나 연계성이 있는 경우에는 종합적으로 판단한다. 예를 들어 퇴직금 지급률이 하향 조정되더라도 평균임금에 포함되는 임금 항목이 많아져서 전체적으로 퇴직금액이 감소되지 않는다면 불이익으로 보지 않는다.[148] 둘째, 취업규칙의 내용 변경이 일부 근로자에게는 유리하고, 일부 근로자에게는 불리한 경우와 같이 유불리에 따른 이익이 근로자 상호간에 충돌되는 경우에는 불이익한 변경으로 판단한다.[149] 세번째로 종래의 규정이 불명확하거나 포괄적이어서 그 내용을 개념적으로 세분화하여 구체화하는 차원에서 취업규칙 내용을 변경하는 경우에는 해석상 논란을 해소하기 위한 것으로써 불이익한 변경으로 볼 수 없다.[150]

4. 취업규칙의 신고

(1) 법적 요구 사항

상시 10인 이상의 근로자를 사용하는 사용자는 취업규칙을 작성하고 그에 대한 의견청취를 거친 뒤에 고용노동부장관에게 신고하여야 한다(법 제93조, 제94조). 취업규칙을 신고하거나 변경하려면
① 취업규칙과
② 근로자의 과반수를 대표하는 노동조합 또는 근로자 과반수의의견을 들었음을 증명하는 자료를 첨부하여 제출하여야 한다.
취업규칙을 불이익하게 변경하는 경우에는 과반수 노동조합이나 근로자의 과반수의 동의를 받았음을 증명하는 자료를 제출하여야 한다(시행규칙 제15조).

(2) 실무적용

근로감독관은 취업규칙 신고가 들어온 경우 근로기준법 제93조에 따른 필수 기재사항 포함 여부와 근로자 과반수를 대표하는 노동조합 또는 근로자 과반수 의견이 첨부되어 있는지를 확인한다. 그후 내용 심사를 통해 취업규칙의 내용 법령 저촉 여부, 당해 단체협약 저촉 여부, 변경된 취업규칙의 근로자 불리 여부 등을 심사한다. 근로감독관은 신고 접수 후 20일 이내

---

[148] 대법원 1997. 8. 26. 선고 96다1726 판결.
[149] 대법원 1993. 5. 14. 선고 93다1893 판결.
[150] 대법원 2011. 8. 25. 선고 2010구합42263 판결.

are not unfavorable. If the procedural requirements for the rules of employment are not met, or if the details are in violation of law or collective agreements, a period of up to 25 days shall be given to comply with an order for correction.[151] Here, if the employer submits a "Report on Establishment of/Changes to Rules of Employment" certified by a licensed labor attorney, along with a report of that labor attorney's review of the rules of employment or changes to those rules, an additional examination of the relevant rules by the labor inspector will be waived.[152]

5. Obligation to notify workers of the rules of employment

(1) Legal requirements

Employers must post or retain the rules of employment in a place where workers can read them at any time, and make them widely known to workers (Article 14 of the Act). The rules must not be seen by the workers as merely internal documents of the employer and of no effect. Since rules of employment are the norms within the company as determined by the employer, it is not necessary to follow the method stipulated in Article 14 of the Labor Standards Act for new or changed rules to take effect, but the rules of employment must be made widely known to the workers by any suitable method.[153]

(2) Practical application

The workers must be notified by the employer for the drafted or changed rules of employment to have any effect. Although the method of posting is not described in detail by law, if the right of access is guaranteed so that workers can read them at any time, it can be considered that the duty of disclosure has been fulfilled by the employer, even if the rules are posted on the internal computer network.[154]

6. Representation of a majority of workers

(1) Legal requirements

---

[151] Ministry of Employment and Labor, Regulation No. 48, Guidelines for Examination of Rules of Employment.
[152] Labor Standards Team-8048, Nov. 29, 2007, Guidelines for Waiving Examination of Workplace Rules of Employment upon Confirmation of Examination by Certified Labor Attorney.
[153] Supreme Court ruling on Feb. 12, 2004: 2001da63599.
[154] Supreme Court ruling on June 23, 1992: 92nu4253.

심사한 후, 취업규칙의 절차적 구비요건을 갖추지 못한 경우나 내용이 법령이나 단체협약에 위반 된 경우 25일 이내의 시정기간을 부여하여 변경을 명한다.[151] 여기서 취업규칙 심사 시 사용자가 신고서와 함께 공인노무사의 「취업규칙 작성(변경) 신고 확인보고서」를 제출하는 경우에는 해당 취업규칙에 대한 심사를 면제한다.[152]

5. 취업규칙 주지의무

(1) 법적 요구사항

사용자는 취업규칙을 근로자가 자유롭게 열람할 수 있는 장소에 항상 게시하거나 갖추어 두어 이를 근로자에게 널리 알려야 한다(법 제14조). 주지할 수 없는 취업규칙은 사용자의 내부문서에 불과하고 취업규칙으로써 효력이 없기 때문이다. 취업규칙은 사용자가 정하는 기업 내의 규범이기 때문에 신설 또는 변경된 취업규칙의 효력이 생기기 위해서는 근로기준법 제14조에 정한 방법에 의할 필요는 없지만 적어도 법령의 공포에 준하는 절차로 그것이 새로운 기업 내 규범인 것을 널리 종업원 일반으로 하여금 알게 하는 절차 즉, 어떠한 방법이든지 적당한 방법에 의한 주지가 필요하다.[153]

(2) 실무적용

작성 또는 변경한 취업규칙의 효력이 발생하려면 사용자가 이 내용을 근로자들에게 알려야 한다. 게시방법에 대해 구체적으로 기술하고 있지 않으나, 예를 들면, 근로자가 언제든지 쉽게 열람할 수 있도록 접근권이 보장된다면 사내 전산망에 게시한 경우 주지의무를 이행하였다고 볼 수 있다.[154]

6. 과반수 근로자의 대표

(1) 법적 요구사항

---

151) 고용노동부예규 제48호, 취업규칙 심사요령
152) 근로기준팀-8048, 2007.11.29. 공인노무사 심사확인시 사업장 취업규칙 심사 면제에 관한 지침
153) 대법원 2004. 2. 12. 선고 2001다63599 판결.
154) 대법원 1992. 6. 23. 선고 92누4253 판결.

Chapter3-9. Rules of Employment

When reporting the rules of employment, the views of the labor union shall be heard if there is a labor union organized by a majority of workers in the relevant business or workplace, or the opinion of a majority of workers shall be heard if no such labor union exists. Consent must be obtained from this union, or the majority of workers if no such union exists, if changes are unfavorable (Article 94 of the Act). A majority of workers refers to the majority of the workers who are subject to the change(s) in the rules of employment.[155]

(2) Practical application

1) **When the rules of employment are applied uniformly:** In order to unilaterally make changes to existing working conditions in a way that is unfavorable to workers, consent from the group of workers to whom the previous rules of employment apply must be obtained through a collective decision-making method. In addition, if the changes to the rules are to apply only to a specific group of workers at the time of the change, but application to other groups of workers is expected in the future, consent from all workers expected to be affected now or in the future shall be obtained. In other words, even if only company executives are directly disadvantaged in the immediate changes to the salary system for executives, if the rules shall apply to any general employee in the future through promotion, the consent of a majority of all employeesexecutives and general employeesis required.[156]

2) **When working conditions differ between worker groups and separate employment rules apply:** There are no personnel transfers between worker groups, and workers in the two groups have different working conditions at the time of hiring. Under such circumstances, if the rules of employment are changed for a specific group, the majority of workers is deemed to be the majority of workers in the affected group, not the entire workforce. This would apply, for example, in a workplace where personnel are divided into production and management according to business necessity.[157]

---

[155] Supreme Court ruling on Feb. 29, 2008: 2007da85997.
[156] Supreme Court ruling on May 28, 2009: 2009doo2238.

취업규칙을 신고할 때 해당 사업 또는 사업장에 근로자의 과반수로 조직된 노동조합이 있는 경우에는 그 노동조합, 근로자의 과반수로 조직된 노동조합이 없는 경우에는 근로자의 과반수의 의견을 들어야 한다. 그리고 불이익한 변경인 경우에는 그 동의를 받아야 한다(법 제94조). 그 동의방법은 근로자 과반수로 조직된 노동조합이 있는 경우에는 노동조합의, 그와 같은 노동조합이 없는 경우에는 근로자들의 회의방식에 의한 과반수의 동의가 있어야 하고 여기서 말하는 근로자의 과반수라 함은 기존 취업규칙의 적용을 받는 근로자집단의 과반수를 뜻한다.[155]

(2) 실무적용

1) **취업규칙이 동일하게 적용되는 경우**: 취업규칙의 변경에 의하여 기존 근로조건의 내용을 일방적으로 근로자에게 불이익하게 변경하려면 종전 취업규칙의 적용을 받고 있던 근로자 집단의 집단적 의사결정방법에 의한 동의를 요한다. 그리고 취업규칙의 변경 시점에는 특정 근로자 집단만이 직접적인 적용대상이지만 다른 근로자집단에게도 변경된 취업규칙의 적용이 예상되는 경우에는 해당 집단을 포함한 근로자집단을 기준으로 판단한다. 즉, 간부사원 급여체계 변경은 당장에는 간부사원만이 직접적인 불이익을 받더라도 일반 사원도 승진에 따라 장래에는 변경된 간부사원 급여체계의 적용이 예상되므로 이때는 간부사원과 일반사원을 포함한 전체근로자 과반수의 동의가 필요하다.[156]

2) **근로자집단 간 근로조건이 다르고 각각 별개의 취업규칙을 적용받는 경우**: 근로자집단 사이에 인사이동에 의한 교류가 없고 입사 시부터 별도의 근로조건을 적용받는 근로조건이 이원화 되어 둘 이상의 집단으로 구분되는 상황에서 특정 집단을 대상으로 취업규칙이 변경되는 경우 전체 근로자가 아닌 해당 집단의 근로자를 대상으로 과반수 여부를 판단한다. 예를 들면, 한 사업장에서 경영상 필요에 따라 생산직과 관리직으로 나누어 인사노무관리를 별도로 하고 있는데 이 중 관리직만을 대상으로

---

[155] 대법원 2008. 2. 29. 선고 2007다85997 판결.
[156] 대법원 2009. 5. 28. 선고 2009두2238 판결.

3) **Labor union organized by a majority of workers:** A labor union organized by a majority of workers refers to a union organized by a majority of all workers for whom the existing rules of employment apply, regardless of whether or not they are members of a union: i.e., it does not mean a labor union organized by a majority of only workers eligible to join a labor union. Even if changes are made disadvantageously only towards executives who are not eligible for union membership, if the changed working conditions will likely apply to ordinary workers in the future, consent from the union organized by a majority of workers shall include those for whom the changed working conditions are expected to apply in the future.[158]

IV. Conclusion

Legally requiring that rules of employment be introduced at workplaces ordinarily employing at least 10 workers, and reporting the establishment of rules of employment to the Ministry of Employment and Labor, is designed to ensure at least a minimum standard for working conditions at workplaces and in worker management and supervision. Rules of employment stipulate the employer's regulations for employment and employee working conditions. If the rules of employment are changed in a way unfavorable to the workers, then consent must be obtained from the majority of workers (through the worker representative(s)) or the labor union representing the majority of workers. This measure protects the principle of equality in working conditions by law. Employers need to therefore make systematic efforts to create, through their rules of employment, a workplace culture able to maintain and improve working conditions while establishing a desirable management order.

Section 9-2. Rules of Employment: Relevant Laws, Judicial Rulings, and Administrative Interpretations

I. Legal duty to establish the Rules of Employment

---

157) Supreme Court ruling on Dec. 7, 1990: 90daka19647.
158) Supreme Court ruling on Nov. 12, 2009: 2009da49377.

취업규칙을 변경하는 경우라 할 수 있다.[157]

3) **근로자 과반수로 조직된 노동조합**: 근로자 과반수로 조직된 노동조합은 조합원 자격 유무에 관계 없이 기존 취업규칙의 적용을 받고 있던 전체 근로자 과반수로 조직된 노동조합을 의미한다. 노동조합에 가입할 수 있는 자격을 가진 근로자의 과반수로 조직된 노동조합을 의미하는 것은 아니다. 이는 조합원 자격이 인정되지 않는 간부 직원에게만 불이익하게 변경하는 경우라 하더라도 일반 근로자에게도 장래에 변경된 근로조건의 적용이 예상된다면 변경된 근로조건의 적용이 예상되는 근로자를 포함한 전체 근로자의 과반수로 조직된 노동조합이 동의의 주체가 된다.[158]

Ⅳ. 결론

각 사업장에서 취업규칙을 의무적으로 도입하고 이를 고용노동부에 신고하는 것은 근로자의 최저 근로조건을 각 사업장에서 도입하고 이를 관리 감독하기 위한 노동법적 체계라고 할 수 있다. 즉, 취업규칙은 사용자의 복무규정과 근로자의 근로조건을 명시한 사업장의 준칙이다. 특히, 취업규칙의 내용을 불이익하게 변경하는 경우에는 과반수 근로자 대표나 과반수 노동조합의 동의를 얻도록 되어 있다. 이는 근로조건의 대등원칙을 법으로 보호하기 위한 조치라고 할 수 있다. 따라서 사용자는 취업규칙을 통하여 바람직한 경영 질서를 세우면서도 근로자의 근로조건을 유지 향상 시킬 수 있는 직장문화를 만드는 노력을 체계적으로 하여야 할 것이다.

제9-2절 취업규칙에 관한 법령, 판례 및 행정해석

Ⅰ. 취업규칙의 작성의무

---

[157] 대법원 1990. 12. 7. 선고 90다카19647 판결.
[158] 대법원 2009. 11. 12. 선고 2009다49377 판결.

Article 93 (Preparation and Submission of Rules of Employment)

An employer who regularly employs ten or more employees shall prepare the rules of employment regarding the following matters and report such rules to the Minister of Employment and Labor. The same shall also apply where he/she amends such rules:

1. Matters pertaining to the beginning and ending time of work, recess hours, holidays, leaves, and shifts;
2. Matters pertaining to the determination, calculation and payment method of wages, the period for which wages are calculated, the period for paying wages, and pay raises;
3. Matters pertaining to the methods of calculation and payment of family allowances;
4. Matters pertaining to retirement;
5. Matters pertaining to retirement benefits set under Article 4 of the Act on the Guarantee of Employees' Retirement Benefits, bonuses, and minimum wages;
6. Matters pertaining to the burden of employees' meal allowances, expenses of operational tools or necessities and so forth;
7. Matters pertaining to educational facilities for employees;
8. Matters pertaining to the protection of employees' maternity and work family balance assistance, such as leaves before and after childbirth and child-care leaves;
9. Matters pertaining to safety and health;
9-2. Matters pertaining to the improvement of a workplace environment according to characteristics of employees, such as sex, ages, or physical conditions;
10. Matters pertaining to assistance with respect to occupational and non-occupational accidents;
11. Matters pertaining to the prevention of workplace harassment and the measures to be taken in cases of occurrence of workplace harassment;
12. Matters pertaining to award and punishment;
13. Other matters applicable to all employees within the business or workplace concerned.

1. Concept of the Rules of Employment (Supreme Court Dec. 29, 1997, 77 da 1378)

The employer with the managerial authority shall set up the Rules of Employment and formulate regulations for the employees' service and working

제93조 【취업규칙의 작성·신고】

상시 10명 이상의 근로자를 사용하는 사용자는 다음 각 호의 사항에 관한 취업규칙을 작성하여 고용노동부장관에게 신고하여야 한다. 이를 변경하는 경우에도 또한 같다.

1. 업무의 시작과 종료 시각, 휴게시간, 휴일, 휴가 및 교대 근로에 관한 사항
2. 임금의 결정·계산·지급 방법, 임금의 산정기간·지급시기 및 승급(昇給)에 관한 사항
3. 가족수당의 계산·지급 방법에 관한 사항
4. 퇴직에 관한 사항
5. 「근로자퇴직급여 보장법」제4조에 따라 설정된 퇴직급여, 상여 및 최저임금에 관한 사항
6. 근로자의 식비, 작업 용품 등의 부담에 관한 사항
7. 근로자를 위한 교육시설에 관한 사항
8. 출산전후휴가·육아휴직 등 근로자의 모성 보호 및 일·가정 양립 지원에 관한 사항
9. 안전과 보건에 관한 사항
9의2. 근로자의 성별·연령 또는 신체적 조건 등의 특성에 따른 사업장 환경의 개선에 관한 사항
10. 업무상과 업무 외의 재해부조(災害扶助)에 관한 사항
11. 직장 내 괴롭힘의 예방 및 발생 시 조치 등에 관한 사항
12. 표창과 제재에 관한 사항
13. 그 밖에 해당 사업 또는 사업장의 근로자 전체에 적용될 사항

1. 취업규칙의 의의 (대판 1997.12.29, 77다 1378)

취업규칙은 사용자가 기업경영권에 기하여 사업장에서의 근로자의 복무규율과 근로조건의 기준을 획일적, 통일적으로 정립하기 위하여 작성하는 것

conditions in a uniform and collective manner at the workplace. Under the subordinate labor relations, the Labor Standards Act seeks to protect and strengthen the status of employees in an unequal position. It also aims to secure and improve their fundamental living standards. So, the Rules of Employment shall be established as a compulsory duty for employers and at the same time have the characteristics of a legal benchmark.

2. Function of the Rules of Employment (Supreme Court July 26, 1997, 77 da 355)

Employers are not allowed to revise working conditions by amending the Rules of Employment in a one-sided manner that is unfavorable to the employees. This can violate the spirit behind the protection law under the Labor Standards Act (LSA), the principle of protecting vested right, and Article 3 (Establishment of Working Conditions) of the LSA: The working conditions shall be freely established on the basis of equality, as agreed between workers and their employer.

'Ordinarily hired employees of 10 or more' means an average of 10 or more employees who are subjected to the entire or part of the Labor Standards Act (Dec. 17, 2002, Kungi 68207-3367)

The Rules of Employment refer to unified rules concerning working conditions and service regulations applicable to all employees of the corresponding workplace, regardless of their title. Article 96 of the Labor Standards Act regulates that an employer who ordinarily employs ten or more employees shall prepare the Rules of Employment and report to the labor office. Here, the employer who ordinarily employs ten or more employees means that the number of employees who are subjected to the entire or part of the Labor Standards Act is 10 or more on average. So, the employees under the ordinarily hired employees of 10 or more shall include temporary, regular, daily-rated and outsourced employees.

II. Procedures for Preparation and Amendment of Rules of Employment

Article 94 (Procedures for Preparation and Amendment of Rules of Employment)
① An employer shall, with regard to the preparation or alteration of the rules of employment, hear the opinion of a trade union if there is a trade union comprising the majority of the workers in the business or

으로서, 이는 근로기준법이 종속적 노동관계의 현실에 입각하여 실질적으로 불평등한 근로자의 지위를 보호, 강화하여 그들의 기본적 생활을 보장, 향상시키려는 목적의 일환으로 그 작성을 강제하고 이에 법규범성을 부과한 것이라 할 것이다.

2. 취업규칙의 기능 (대판 1997.7.26, 77다 355)

취업규칙의 변경에 의하여 기존 근로조건의 내용을 사용자가 일방적으로 근로자에게 불이익하게 변경하는 것은 근로기준법의 보호법으로서의 정신과 기득권보호의 원칙 및 근로조건은 근로자와 사용자가 동등한 지위에서 자유의사에 의하여 결정되어야 한다는 근로기준법 제3조의 규정상 허용될 수 없다.

'상시근로자 10인 이상'이라 함은 근로기준법의 전부 또는 일부를 적용 받는 근로자가 상태적으로 보아 10인 이상인 경우를 의미한다 (2002.12.17, 근기 68207-3367)취업규칙이란 그 명칭에 관계없이 당해 사업장의 전 근로자에게 적용되는 근로조건과 복무규율 등에 관한 통일적인 준칙을 말하는 것인 바, 이러한 취업규칙의 작성신고의무는 근로기준법 제96조에 상시 10인 이상의 근로자를 사용하는 사용자로 규정하고 있음. 여기서 「상시 10인 이상의 근로자를 사용하는 사용자」라 함은 동법 동조의 취지로 볼 때, 근로기준법의 전부 또는 일부를 적용 받는 근로자가 상태적으로 보아 10인 이상인 경우를 의미한다고 볼 수 있을 것인 바, 임시직·정규직·일용직·상용직·도급직 근로자 등을 총망라하여 상태적으로 근로자수가 10인 이상인지 여부를 가지고 판단함이 타당하다고 사료됨.

II. 취업규칙의 변경절차

제94조【규칙의 작성, 변경 절차】
① 사용자는 취업규칙의 작성 또는 변경에 관하여 해당 사업 또는 사업장에 근로자의 과반수로 조직된 노동조합이 있는 경우에는 그

> workplace concerned, or otherwise hear the opinion of the majority of the said workers; Provided that in case of amending the rules of employment unfavorable to workers, an employer shall obtain their consent.
> ② When an employer submits the rules of employment pursuant to Article 93, he shall attach a document containing the opinion as referred to in paragraph (1).

1. Authority to amend the Rules of Employment

The employer has full authority concerning the amendment of the Rules of Employment.
If an employer revised the Rules of Employment to the disadvantage of a group of employees without their consent, the revised Rules of Employment is still legally effective. However, current employees whose vested interests are infringed upon shall be subjected to previous Rules of Employment (Dec. 23, 1996, Supreme Court 95 da 32631).

2. Advantageous amendment

If the amendment of the Rules of Employment is neither advantageous nor disadvantageous to the employees, the employer is not obliged to comply with, but only hear the opinions of his/her employees.

3. Disadvantageous amendment

Procedures of disadvantageous amendment for the Rules of Employment (Mau 14, 2004, Supreme Court 2000 da 23185, 23192)

If an employer revises the existing working conditions unfavorably to employees by amending the Rules of Employment, it requires the agreement of the employees who are subjected to previous working conditions or previous Rules of Employment through their collective decision-making method. It cannot be effective to have the amendment of the Rules of Employment without this type of agreement. The method shall require an agreement from the majority of employees in the form of a conference in cases where there is no labor union. The agreement in the form of an employees' conference can be accepted in cases where employees exchange opinion with one another, sum up

> 노동조합, 근로자의 과반수로 조직된 노동조합이 없는 경우에는 근로자의 과반수의 의견을 들어야 한다. 다만, 취업규칙을 근로자에게 불리하게 변경하는 경우에는 그 동의를 받아야 한다.
> ② 사용자는 제93조의 규정에 의하여 취업규칙을 신고할 때에는 제1항의 의견을 기입한 서면을 첨부하여야 한다.

1. 취업규칙의 변경권한

취업규칙의 변경에 관한 권한은 사용자에게 있다.

취업규칙이 근로자집단의 동의없이 근로자에게 불이익하게 변경된 경우에도 법규적 효력을 가진 취업규칙은 변경된 취업규칙이고, 기득이익이 침해되는 기존 근로자에 대해서는 종전 취업규칙이 적용된다 (1996.12.23, 대법 95다32631)

2. 유리한 변경의 경우

유리하거나 불리하지 않은 경우에는 동의를 얻을 의무는 없고 의견청취만 하면 된다.

3. 불이익변경의 경우

취업규칙 불이익 변경의 절차(2004.05.14, 대법 2002다 23185, 23192)
사용자가 취업규칙의 변경에 의하여 기존의 근로조건을 근로자에게 불리하게 변경하려면 종전 근로조건 또는 취업규칙의 적용을 받고 있던 근로자의 집단적 의사결정방법에 의한 동의를 요하고, 이러한 동의를 얻지 못한 취업규칙의 변경은 효력이 없으며, 그 동의의 방법은 노동조합이 없는 경우에는 근로자들의 회의방식에 의한 과반수의 동의를 요하고, 회의방식에 의한 동의라 함은 사업 또는 한 사업장의 기구별 또는 단위 부서별로 사용자측의 개입이나 간섭이 배제된 상태에서 근로자간에 의견을 교환하여 찬반을 집약한 후 이를

the pros and cons, and come up with the result for the organization or unit of the business or workplace without an employer's interference or intervention. Here, an employer's interference or intervention means that the employer pressures employees to accept the agreement in an expressed or implied method that obstructs employees' autonomous and collective decision making. However, if the employer explained about the revised contents of the Rules of Employment and publicized them, it is hard to regard it as the employer's interference or intervention.

If the company revises the wage regulation unfavorably to employees, even though the company went through the resolution process of the Board of Directors, but did not receive consent from employees via a decision-making method, the revised rules are not applicable to employees who were employed before the amendment of the rules (May 26, 2005, Daegu-Kimchun district court 2004 gadan 5538).

In cases where the employer revises the working conditions stipulated in the Rules of Employment unfavorably to employees, he should receive consent by a collective decision-making method from the employees who are subjected to the Rules of Employment. The consent shall be obtained from the labor union if there is one consisting of the majority of employees, and if there is not such a labor union, the consent means an agreement by majority of employees obtained by way of integrating the employees' independent opinion. Accordingly, if there is no consent in the above-mentioned method, the amendment of the Rules of Employment is not effective, and it applies likewise to individual employees who agreed to the revision of the Rules of Employment.

It is not effective in cases where the employer one-sidedly revised existing working conditions unfavorably to employees or applied the Rules of Employment of the new company that succeeded their previous working conditions disadvantageously (Feb. 12, 1998, Seoul District Court 96 Kagap 9363).

In the case where the existing working conditions were succeeded inclusively, existing status under the previous employment contractis succeeded and the employee's working conditions according to previous employment relations are maintained identically in the succeeded company. In order that the employer can one-sidedly revise existing working conditions, or apply the working conditions that the company succeeded unfavorably from previous working conditions, he shall obtain an agreement by a collective decision-making method from the majority of employees who have maintained the status of previous employment contract. Accordingly, without such consent mentioned above, it is not effective in the cases where the employer one-sidedly revised existing working conditions unfavorably to employees or applied

전체적으로 취합하는 방식도 허용된다고 할 것인데, 여기서 사용자측의 개입이나 간섭이라 함은 사용자측이 근로자들의 자율적이고 집단적인 의사결정을 저해할 정도로 명시 또는 묵시적인 방법으로 동의를 강요하는 경우를 의미하고 사용자측이 단지 변경될 취업규칙의 내용을 근로자들에게 설명하고 홍보하는 데 그친 경우에는 사용자측의 부당한 개입이나 간섭이 있었다고 볼 수 없다.

직원들에게 불리한 급여규정을 개정하면서 이사회의 결의를 거쳤을 뿐 직원들의 의사결정방법에 의한 동의를 받지 않은 이상 개정이 있기 전에 근로관계를 맺은 근로자에 대하여는 무효이다(2005.05.26, 대구지법김천지원 2004가단5538)

사용자가 취업규칙에 규정된 근로조건의 내용을 근로자에게 불이익하게 변경하는 경우에는 그 변경이 사회통념상 합리성이 있다고 인정되지 않는 한 취업규칙의 적용을 받고 있던 근로자들의 집단적 의사결정방법에 의한 동의를 얻어야 하고 그 동의는 근로자 과반수로 조직된 노동조합이 있는 경우에는 노동조합의, 노동조합이 없는 경우에는 근로자들의 자주적인 의견의 집약에 의한 과반수의 동의를 의미하는 것으로서 위와 같은 방법에 의한 동의가 없는 한 취업규칙 변경은 효력이 없고, 이는 그러한 취업규칙의 변경에 대하여 개인적으로 동의한 근로자에 대하여도 마찬가지라 할 것이다.

사용자가 일방적으로 종전의 근로조건을 근로자에게 불리하게 변경하거나 종전의 근로조건보다 불이익하게 승계한 법인의 취업규칙을 적용하는 것은 효력이 없다 (1998.02.12, 서울지법 96가합 9363)

근로관계가 포괄적으로 승계되는 경우에는 근로자의 종전의 근로계약상의 지위도 승계되는 것이어서 종전의 근로관계에 따라 근로한 근로자는 승계한 법인에서도 종전의 근로관계와 동일한 근로관계를 유지하게 되고, 사용자가 일방적으로 취업규칙을 변경하거나 종전의 근로관계보다 불이익 하게 승계한 법인의 취업규칙을 적용하기 위하여는 종전의 근로계약상 지위를 유지하던 근로자 집단의 집단적 의사결정방법에 의한 동의 등의 사정이 있어야 하며 이러한 동의 등이 없는 한 사용자가 일방적으로 종전의 근로조건을 근로자에게 불리하게 변경하거나 종전의 근로조건보다 불이익 하게 승계한 법인의 취업

the Rules of Employment of the new company that succeeded their previous working conditions disadvantageously. In this case, employees who are working at a new company that succeeded the previous working conditions are subjected continuously to previous Rules of Employment. (Aug. 26, 1994, Supreme Court 93 da 58714)

4. Standard of judgment for disadvantageous amendment

The Rules of Employment are null and void when their revision results in a clash of advantage and disadvantage among the employees (Jan 23, 1997, Seoul District Court, 96 kagap 54787)

In case where there is a clash of advantage and disadvantage among employees due to the amendment of the Rules of Employment, this revision shall be considered as unfavorable to employees. Accordingly, it would be made null and void as a result of violating Article 95 of the Labor Standards Act if the employer did not receive consent from all the employees or the labor union consisting of the majority of employees.

Ⅲ. The effect of the Rules of Employment

Article 96 (Observance of Collective Agreement)
① Rules of employment shall not conflict with any Act, subordinate statute, or a collective agreement applicable to the business or workplace concerned.
② The Minister of Labor may order the modification of any part of the rules of employment which conflicts with any Act, subordinate statute or the collective agreement.

Article 97 (Effect of Violation)
If a labor contract includes any part of working conditions which does not meet the standards provided in the rules of employment, such part shall be null and void. In this case, the invalidated part shall be governed by the standards provided in the rules of employment.

The difference between the collective agreement and the Rules of Employment (April 25, 1997, Supreme Court 96 nu 5421)
The collective agreement concerns working conditions and other standards on the treatment of employees, and should be in writing and signed by both parties, that is, the employer and the employee representative. Besides, the collective agreement is, in principle, effective only to unionized employees for a limited period of time.

규칙을 적용하는 것은 효력이 없다 할 것이므로 이 경우 종전의 근로조건을 그대로 유지한 채 승계한 법인에서 근무하게 되는 근로자에 대하여는 종전의 취업규칙이 그대로 적용된다(1994.8.26, 대법 93다 58714 참조).

4. 불이익변경여부의 판단기준

근로자 상호간의 유·불리가 충돌되게 개정된 취업규칙은 무효이다 (1997. 01.23, 서울지법 96가합 54787)

취업규칙 변경으로 인해 근로자 상호간의 유·불리가 충돌되는 경우 그와 같은 변경은 근로자에게 불리한 것으로 보아 회사가 전체 근로자 또는 근로자 과반수가 가입한 노동조합으로부터 동의를 못 받았다면 근로기준법 제95조의 위반으로 무효라고 본다.

Ⅲ. 취업규칙의 효력

제96조【단체협약의 준수】
① 취업규칙은 법령이나 해당 사업 또는 사업장에 대하여 적용되는 단체협약과 어긋나서는 아니 된다.
② 노동부장관은 법령이나 단체협약에 어긋나는 취업규칙의 변경을 명할 수 있다.

제97조【위반의 효력】
취업규칙에서 정한 기준에 미달하는 근로조건을 정한 근로계약은 그 부분에 관하여는 무효로 한다. 이 경우 무효로 된 부분은 취업규칙에 정한 기준에 따른다.

단체협약과 취업규칙의 차이 (1997.4.25, 대법 96누5421)

단체협약은 근로조건 기타 근로자의 대우에 관한 기준 등에 관한 사항을 정하는 협정으로서 서면으로 작성하여 노사 쌍방이 서면날인 하여야 하고, 유효기간에 있어서 일정한 제약이 따르며, 원칙적으로 노동조합원 이외의 자에

By contrast, the Rules of Employment are drawn up unilaterally by the employer and contains general rules and regulations on the employees' service and working conditions applicable to all employees at the workplace.

The amendment of the Rules of Employment that infringed the collective agreement is ineffective, regardless of justifiable procedure in the amendment of the Rules of Employment (Mar 18, 2003, Seoul District Court 2002 guhap 31671)

As the Article 99 (1) of the Labor Standards Act regulates that Rules of Employment shall not conflict with any Act, subordinate statute, or a collective agreement applicable to the business or workplace concerned, the amendment of the Rules of Employment that infringed the collective agreement is ineffective, regardless of justifiable procedure in the amendment of the Rules of Employment. Accordingly, it is definitely unfair dismissal if the employer notified the dismissal to the employee on the basis of the regulation of 'retirement age' as stipulated in the ineffective Rules of Employment.

It is not effective if there is no consent of the labor union in the disadvantageous revision of the Rules of Employment to employees (Jan 19, 2001, Seoul Administrative Court, 2000 gu 12156)

It is true that Paju Agricultural Bank received the later approval from 60 out of 64 union members about the amendment of the Rules of Employment, but in the case where there is a workplace with the labor union consisting of more than majority of employees, disadvantageous amendment of the Rules of Employment shall require the approval of the labor union itself, and so approval from individual employees belonging to the labor union cannot replace the labor union's approval. Therefore, as the revision of personnel regulation does not apply to employees, it is unfair for the disciplinary measure, an order to leave one's post and wait for further action, to be based upon this rule.

The revision procedure of the Rules of Employment concerning working conditions after the collective agreement became ineffective (Aug. 26, 2003, Gungi 68207-1087)

Although the collective agreement became ineffective, portions concerning working conditions among contents of void collective agreement have been continuously applied as before. A revision procedure is required as stipulated in Article 97 of the Labor Standards Act, in order to revise the Rules of Employment unfavorably to employees about portions related to working conditions. On the other hand, an employer shall, with regard to the disadvantageous amendment of the Rules of Employment, receive the consent of a labor union if there is a labor union composed of the majority of the workers in the business or workplace concerned, or otherwise obtain the consent of the majority of the said employees. Accordingly, the sole approval of the employee

대하여는 그 규범적 효력이 미치지 아니하는 것이고, 이에 비하여 취업규칙은 사용자가 근로자의 복무규율과 임금 등 당해 사업의 근로자 전체에 적용될 근로조건에 관한 준칙을 규정한 것을 말한다.

단체협약에 반하는 취업규칙의 변경은 절차의 적법 여부에 관계없이 그 효력이 없다 (2003.03.18, 서울행법 2002구합31671)

근로기준법 제99조 제1항은 '취업규칙은 법령 또는 당해 사업 또는 사업장에 대하여 적용되는 단체협약에 반할 수 없다'고 규정되어 있으므로 단체협약에 반하는 취업규칙의 변경은 절차의 적법여부와 관계없이 그 효력이 없다 할 것이어서 결국 무효인 취업규칙에서 정한 정년에 근거하여 참가인에 대하여 한 퇴직통보는 사실상 부당한 해고에 해당한다 할 것이다.

근로자에게 불이익한 취업규칙 변경시 노조의 동의가 없었다면 효력은 인정되지 않는다 (2001.01.18, 서울행법 2000구12156)

파주농조가 인사규정 개정에 대해 노동조합원 64명중 60명의 사후동의를 받은 사실은 인정되나, 근로자 과반수로 조직된 노조가 존재하는 사업장의 경우 근로자에게 불이익한 취업규칙 변경은 노조 자체의 동의를 필요로 하고, 노조에 소속된 개별 근로자들의 동의로써 노조 동의를 대신할 수 없으므로 효력을 인정할 수 없다. 그러므로 인사규정의 개정은 참가인들에게 효력이 없어 이에 근거한 원고의 대기발령 처분도 부당하다

단체협약이 실효된 후 근로조건에 관한 취업규칙의 변경절차 (2003.8.26, 근기 68207-1087)

단체협약이 실효되었음에도 불구하고 실효된 단체협약 내용 중 근로조건에 관한 부분은 실효 이전과 같이 계속 적용하여 온 경우, 이러한 근로조건에 관한 부분은 취업규칙의 개정으로 불이익하게 변경하기 위해서는 근로기준법 제97조에 규정된 변경절차를 거쳐야 할 것임. 한편, 취업규칙을 불이익하게 변경하는 경우에는 당해 사업 또는 사업장에 근로자의 과반수로 조직된 노동조합이 있을 경우에는 그 노동조합, 근로자의 과반수로 조직된 노동조합이 없을 경우에는 근로자 과반수의 동의를 얻어야 하며 근로자대표의 동의만

representative cannot be seen to implement the procedure of disadvantageous revision.

Section 9-3. Possible Cases Changing Working Conditions unfavorably - the Legal Principle of Socially Acceptable Rationality

I. Introduction

With the Aged Employment Promotion Act[159] revised in 2013, along with implementation of the compulsory retirement system starting in 2016, workplaces with seniority-based wage systems are expecting a rapid increase in labor costs. Under these circumstances, it is debatable whether unilateral introduction of a wage peak system by employers seeking to cope with the new labor costs is simply disadvantageous to employees or socially acceptable rationality. For guidance, it is necessary to look at the legal criteria required in labor laws for changing working conditions, which is equivalent to changing the Rules of Employment. With labor issues appearing in this area, I would like to explain appropriate ways to make or change the Rules of Employment, obtain consent for unfavorably-changed rules and the legal principle of socially acceptable rationality.

II. The Rules of Employment: Concept & Making Changes

1. Concept

The Rules of Employment refer to the company regulations that an employer stipulates unilaterally regarding working conditions and service rules. The Labor

---

[159] Act on Prohibition of Age Discrimination in Employment & Aged Employment Promotion, May 22, 2013 Article 19 (Retirement Age)
① When an employer sets a retirement age, he/she shall set it at 60 years of age or older. ② Regardless of Subparagraph ①, in cases where the employer has previously set a retirement age at less than 60 years of age, his/her retirement age policy shall be regarded as having been set at 60 years of age.
Article 19-2 (Changing the Wage system, etc. due to Extension of the Retirement age) ①The employer of a business or workplace who extends the retirement age in accordance with Subparagraph ① of Article 19, and a labor union which is formed by the majority of all workers (or a person representing the majority of all workers) shall take the steps necessary to revise the wage system, etc. according to the conditions pertaining to the business or workplace concerned.
Addenda This Act shall enter into force one year from the date of enforcement of its promulgation. Provided, that the revised rules of Article 19, Paragraph ① and of Article 19-2 shall enter into force in accordance with the following: 1. Businesses or workplaces with 300 or more full-time workers, public institutes in accordance with Article 4 of the Act on the Operation of Public Institutions, local public enterprises and local corporations under Articles 49 and 76 of the Local Public Enterprises Act: effective January 1, 2016;2. Businesses or workplaces with fewer than 300 workers, national and local governments: effective January 1, 2017.

으로는 불이익변경의 절차를 이행한 것으로 볼 수 없다고 사료됨.

제9-3절 근로조건의 변경(사회적 합리성 이론)

Ⅰ. 문제의 소재

2013년에 개정된 「고령자 고용법」에 따라 2016년부터 의무정년제[159]가 시행되면서 연공서열형 임금구조를 갖고 있는 사업장의 경우에는 급격한 인건비 상승이 예상된다. 이에 대응하여 사용자가 일방적으로 임금피크제를 도입할 경우에 이는 근로조건의 불이익이면서도 사회통념상 합리성이 인정될 수 있어 사용자의 일방적 근로조건의 변경이 타당한지에 대해 의문이 있을 수 있다. 이러한 이유로 근로조건의 변경에 대한 노동법적 판단기준을 살펴볼 필요가 있다. 근로조건의 변경은 취업규칙 변경과 관련된다. 이와 관련해 실제로 나타나는 노동법상 주요 쟁점을 중심으로 취업규칙의 작성 및 변경, 불리한 변경시 근로자와의 동의방법 및 사회합리성 법리에 대하여 각각 살펴보고자 한다.

Ⅱ. 취업규칙의 의의 및 변경

1. 취업규칙의 의의

취업규칙은 사용자가 일방적으로 근로조건과 복무규율에 대해 일방적으로 작성하는 회사의 규칙을 말한다. 근로기준법은 취업규칙 작성 및 신고의무(제93조), 취업규칙의 작성방법 및 변경방법(제94조)을 명시하고 있다. 특히

---

[159] 「고용상 연령차별금지 및 고령자고용촉진에 관한 법률」변경 내용(2013.5.22)제19조(정년) ① 사업주는 근로자의 정년을 60세 이상으로 정하여야 한다.② 사업주가 제1항에도 불구하고 근로자의 정년을 60세 미만으로 정한 경우에는 정년을 60세로 정한 것으로 본다.제19조의2(정년연장에 따른 임금체계 개편 등) ① 제19조제1항에 따라 정년을 연장하는 사업 또는 사업장의 사업주와 근로자의 과반수로 조직된 노동조합(과반수를 대표하는 자)은 그 사업 또는 사업장의 여건에 따라 임금체계 개편 등 필요한 조치를 하여야 한다.부칙: 이 법은 공포 후 1년이 경과한 날부터 시행한다. 다만, 제19조, 제19조의2 제1항 및 제2항의 개정규정은 다음 각 호의 구분에 따라 시행한다.1. 상시 300명 이상의 근로자를 사용하는 사업 또는 사업장, 「공공기관의 운영에 관한 법률」제4조에 따른 공공기관, 「지방공기업법」 제49조에 따른 지방공사 및 같은 법 제76조에 따른 지방공단: 2016. 1. 1.2. 상시 300명 미만의 근로자를 사용하는 사업 또는 사업장, 국가 및 지방자치단체: 2017. 1. 1.

Standards Act stipulates the employer's obligations for preparing and filing their rules (Article 93) and ways to compose and change the rules (Article 94). In particular, if a labor contract includes employment conditions which are below the standards stipulated in the Rules of Employment, the nonconforming part of the labor contract is null and void (Article 97). Korean law stipulates that areas in which employment conditions have been invalidated shall be governed by the standards provided for in the Rules of Employment. The Rules of Employment are to put the employer and workers on equal footing, which shows that the employer can compose or revise the rules unilaterally when revising working conditions advantageously, but shall obtain collective consent from the majority of employees when revising them disadvantageously.

2. Making Changes to the Rules of Employment

(1) Advantageous changes

When preparing or revising the Rules of Employment, the employer should, as a rule, consider the views of the majority of employees. For favorable changes to working conditions, it is sufficient that the employer listens to the majority of employees, but there is no obligation to consult with or obtain consent from them.[160] Violations of the duty to consider employee opinions regarding changes to the Rules of Employment are subject to punitive action: the violation does not invalidate the change(s). Considering employee opinions serves as a way of protecting those employees by giving the employer opportunity to reflect their opinions in changes, but the failure to do so does not invalidate those changes.[161]

(2) Disadvantageous changes

When working conditions stipulated in the Rules of Employment are changed disadvantageously, existing employees will continue to work under the previous conditions if their consent was not received for the changes, but new employees hired after revision of the Rules of Employment will be subject to those changes.[162]

1) Changing the Rules of Employment unfavorably

The acceptable methods for receiving employee consent are as follows:
① If there is no labor union composed of the majority of employees, it is necessary to receive consent from the majority of employees by means of allowing them to hold their own conference. Here, 'obtaining consent through a

---

[160] Jongryul Lim, 『Labor Law』, 13th edition, 2015, Parkyoung sa, page 353.
[161] Hyungbae Kim, 『Labor Law』, 24th edition, 2015, Parkyoung sa, page 304.
[162] Supreme Court ruling on June 24, 2011, 2009da58364.

취업규칙에서 정한 기준에 미달하는 근로조건을 정한 근로계약은 무효로 한다라는 규정이 있다(제97조). 이 경우 무효로 된 부분은 취업규칙에서 정한 기준에 따른다고 하여 취업규칙의 규범적 효력을 설명하고 있다. 이러한 취업규칙의 특징은 근로조건의 결정이 노사 당사자의 합의 원칙에 충실하기 위해 유리한 조건은 사용자가 일방적으로 작성하여도 문제가 없지만, 불이익한 변경인 경우에는 근로자의 집단적 동의를 요구하고 있다.

2. 취업규칙의 변경

(1) 취업규칙의 유리한 변경

사용자가 취업규칙을 작성/변경할 때, 근로자의 과반수의 의견을 들어야 된다. 유리한 변경인 경우 근로자 집단의 의견청취로 충분하고 협의/합의할 의무 또는 반대의견을 반영할 의무는 없다.[160] 의견청취 의무의 위반시 취업규칙의 효력에 대해서 의견청취는 단속규정이고 효력규정은 아니다. 의견청취의 목적은 의견반영의 기회를 부여해 근로자를 보호하려는 것으로 근로자의 의견청취를 하지 않아 무효로 볼 수 없기 때문이다.[161]

(2) 취업규칙의 불이익 변경

사용자가 취업규칙에서 정한 근로조건을 근로자에게 불리한 변경시 근로자의 동의가 없다면 그 변경으로 기득이익이 침해되는 기존 근로자에게 효력이 없어 종전 취업규칙의 효력이 그대로 적용되지만, 변경후 변경된 취업규칙에 따른 근로조건을 수용하고 근로관계를 갖게 된 근로자는 당연히 변경된 취업규칙이 적용된다.[162]

1) 불이익 변경방법

동의의 방법은 다음과 같다.
① 과반수를 대표하는 노동조합이 없다면 근로자들의 회의방식에 의한 과반수의 동의가 필요하다. 여기서, '회의방식에 의한 동의'란 사업 또는 한 사업장의

---

160) 임종률, 『노동법』제13판, 2015, 박영사, 353면.
161) 김형배, 『노동법』제24판, 2015년, 박영사, 304면.
162) 대법원 2011.6.24. 선고, 2009다58364 판결.

conference' means that employees get together and exchange their opinions for and against particular issues at the division or department level of a workplace or business, without interference from or participation of the employer, and then gathering their collective opinions for delivery to the employer.[163]

② If there is a labor union composed of the majority of employees, the revised Rules of Employment upon the union's consent to the changes will also be in effect for non-union employees who have not had any input into the agreement.[164]

③ If working conditions are different for production and management divisions, and for regular and non-regular employees, consent shall be received from those groups who will be affected by the revised working conditions. This means the employer does not have to receive consent from the majority of all employees if some of them will not be affected by the changes.[165]

④ At the time the Rules are changed, even though only a certain group of employees will be disadvantageously affected, if the revisions will affect other groups of employees, consent from these other groups shall also be required.[166]

2) Criteria for changed working conditions to be considered disadvantageous

Whether amendment of the Rules of Employment is disadvantageous or not shall be evaluated substantially by considering all factors such as reasons and procedures for the amendment, characteristics of the jobs, and the structure of each regulation of the Rules of Employment. Accordingly, even though one working condition has been revised disadvantageously, if other related factors were changed favorably or other favorable changes were made in return for the disadvantageous change, whether these revisions were disadvantageous or not should be determined after considering all the changes.[167]

Court rulings have showed:

① In cases where regulations on accumulating retirement payments were changed disadvantageously to non-accumulating retirement payments, if employee wages were increased and their working hours shortened, that change will not automatically be considered disadvantageous.[168]

② In cases where a wage regulation in the Rules of Employment was changed disadvantageously for some employees, but advantageously for other employees, such changes shall be considered as disadvantageous.[169]

---

[163] Supreme Court ruling on May 14, 2004, 2002da23185. June 24, 2011, 2009da58364.
[164] Supreme Court ruling on February 29, 2008, 2007da85997.
[165] Supreme Court ruling on December 7, 1990, 90da19647.
[166] Supreme Court ruling on May 28, 2009, 2009du2238.
[167] Supreme Court ruling on January 27, 2004, 2001da42301.
[168] Supreme Court ruling on November 13, 1984, 84daka414.

기구별 또는 단위 부서별로 사용자측의 개입이나 간섭이 배제된 상태에서 근로자간에 의견을 교환해 찬반을 집약한 후 이를 전체적으로 취합하는 방식도 말한다.[163]
② 근로자의 과반수로 구성된 노동조합이 있다면, 그 노동조합의 동의를 얻어 변경된 취업규칙은 개별적 동의절차를 거치지 않은 비조합원에게도 당연히 적용된다.[164]
③ 생산직과 사무직, 정규직과 계약직 등으로 근로조건이 이원화되어 있다면 취업규칙 중 불이익 변경 부분을 적용받고 있는 근로자 집단을 대상으로 동의를 받아야 한다. 즉, 전체 근로자의 과반수의 동의를 받지 않아도 된다.[165]
④ 불이익 변경의 시점에서 특정 근로자 집단만이 불이익을 받게 되더라도 장차 다른 근로자 집단에게도 변경된 취업규칙의 적용이 예상된다면 그러한 근로자 집단까지 포함한 근로자 집단으로부터 동의를 받아야 한다.[166]

2) 불이익 변경의 판단기준

취업규칙의 불이익변경의 여부는 그 변경의 취지와 경위, 해당 사업장의 업무의 성질, 취업규칙 각 규정의 전체적인 체계 등 제반 사정을 종합해 구체적으로 판단해야 한다. 따라서 근로조건을 결정짓는 여러 요소 중 한 요소가 불이익하게 변경되더라도 그와 대가관계나 연계성이 있는 다른 요소가 유리하게 변경되는 경우 이를 종합적으로 고려해야 한다.[167]

이와 관련된 법원판례로는 다음과 같다.
① 누진제 퇴직금지급규정이 근로자에게 불이익한 비누진제로 변경됨과 아울러 임금인상 및 근로시간단축 등 근로자에게 유리한 부분도 포함되어 있다면 그 변경이 근로자에게 일방적으로 불이익한 것이라고 단정할 수 없다.[168]
② 취업규칙의 일부인 급여규정의 변경이 일부의 근로자에게는 유리하고 일부의 근로자에게는 불리한 경우 그러한 변경은 근로자에게 불이익한 것으로 볼 수 있다.[169]

---

163) 대법원 2004.5.14. 선고 2002다23185 판결.
164) 대법원 2008.2.29. 선고 2007다85997 판결.
165) 대법원 1990.12.7. 선고 90다19647 판결.
166) 대법원 2009.5.28. 선고 2009두2238 판결.
167) 대법원 2004.1.27. 선고 2001다42301 판결.
168) 대법원 1984.11.13. 선고, 84다카414 판결.

③ Reducing or abolishing overtime work exceeding legal standard working hours cannot be regarded as a disadvantageous change to the Rules of Employment.[170]

④ In cases where working at night or on holidays in the working shift system, employees used to receive additional allowances. However after changing work shifts to day time only, night and holiday work allowances were no longer available. In this case, the reduced wages cannot be seen as disadvantageous.[171]

III. Disadvantageous Changes to the Rules of Employment and the Legal Principle of Socially Acceptable Rationality

1. Socially Acceptable Rationality

In cases where working conditions in the Rules of Employment were revised disadvantageously, if the Rules of Employment were revised without consent of the employee group, the changed rules will be invalid due to the unilateral nature of the change. However, if the revision of the Rules of Employment can be admitted as socially acceptable rationality, the change(s) may be considered legitimate. There are two opposing opinions regarding this issue: 1) As long as socially acceptable rationality is admitted, employer revisions to the Rules of Employment are effective (theory of affirmative recognition)[172], and 2) Disadvantageous employer revisions of the Rules of Employment are invalid (theory of negative recognition).[173]

The point of dispute is whether, when introducing the extension of mandatory retirement to age 60, the employer can introduce a wage peak system to employees under a seniority-based wage system without their consent. We will review disadvantageous revision of working conditions under the theory of socially acceptable rationality.

2. Criteria for Socially Acceptable Rationality

A judicial ruling regarding criteria for socially acceptable rationality stipulated, It is not permitted to apply disadvantageous working conditions that deprive employees of their existing rights and interests through unilateral establishment or

---

[169] Supreme Court ruling on May 14, 1993, 93da1893.
[170] MOEL Guideline (Kungi 68207-286, March 13, 2003).
[171] MOEL Guideline (Kungi 68207-691, June 11, 2003).
[172] Chulsoo Lee, It is possible for an employer to unilaterally implement a wage peak system!, 『Labor Law』, Jungang Economy, April 2015.
[173] Kaprae Ha, It is impossible for an employer to unilaterally implement a wage peak system!, 『Labor Law』, Jungang Economy, April 2015.

③ 법정근로시간을 초과하는 연장근로의 축소?폐지는 취업규칙의 불이익 변경으로 볼 수 없다.[170]

④ 교대제 근무시 야간근로 및 휴일근로가 발생되어 수당이 지급되나 주간근무로 근무여건이 변경될 경우 야간근로·휴일 근로수당이 발생되지 않게 되어 금전적 손실이 있어도 이를 불이익 처분이라 보기는 어렵다.[171]

Ⅲ. 취업규칙의 불이익 변경과 사회적 합리성 법리

1. 사회적 합리성의 문제

취업규칙의 변경으로 근로조건을 불이익하게 변경한 경우 근로자집단의 동의없이 취업규칙을 변경했다면 근로조건의 일방적 불이익 변경이므로 법적으로 변경효력이 없다. 그러나 이 취업규칙의 변경이 사회적 합리성을 인정받는 경우에는 적법한 취업규칙 변경이 된다. 이와 관련하여 견해의 대립이 있다. 사회적 합리성만 인정된다면 근로자 집단의 동의가 없더라도 사용자가 일방적으로 불이익하게 변경된 취업규칙이 효력을 가진다는 견해(=인정설)[172]와 취업규칙의 불이익은 효력이 없다는 견해(=부정설)[173]이다.

주요 쟁점은 2016년부터 60세 정년제가 시행되는데, 이에 연공형 임금제에서 사용자가 60세 이전에 임금피크제를 근로자 집단의 동의없이 일방적으로 도입할 수 있는지 여부이다. 여기서 근로조건의 불이익 변경을 '사회적 합리성 이론'을 가지고 그 타당성 여부를 살펴본다.

2. 사회적 합리성의 판단기준

판례는 사회적 합리성의 판단기준에 대하여, 사용자가 일방적으로 새로운 취업규칙의 작성변경을 통하여 근로자가 가지고 있는 기득의 권리나 이익을

---

[169] 대법원 1993.5.14. 선고, 93다1893 판결.
[170] 근기 68207-286, 2003.3.13.
[171] 근기 68207-691, 2003.6.11.
[172] 이철수, 임금피크제의 사용자 일방 시행 가능하다!, 『노동법률』, 중앙경제, 2015년 4월.
[173] 하갑래, 임금피크제의 사용자 일방시행 가능하지 않다!†『노동법률』 중앙경제, 2015년4월.

revision of Rules of Employment by the employer. However, in cases where there is sufficient socially acceptable rationality to recognize justification in terms of both necessity and the details of the establishment or revision, even when considering the degree of employee disadvantage, the effectiveness cannot be denied simply because there was no collective consent obtained from employees to whom the previous working conditions or Rules of Employment applied. Whether there is socially acceptable rationality or not shall be evaluated by collectively considering several items such as the degree of disadvantage the employees suffer under the changed Rules of Employment, the degree of employer necessity to change the ROE, efforts to replace or compensate for the changes to the ROE, negotiation situation with the Labor Union, and other general conditions in the domestic business. Provided, as changing the Rules of Employment disadvantageously for employees ignores the provision of the Labor Standards Act requiring their consent, this should be interpreted as necessary only a limited basis under stringent conditions.[174]

3. Review

(1) Theory of affirmative recognition

The following points are used as support in the argument that unilaterally changing working conditions disadvantageously is rational to a degree that is socially acceptable: First, according to Paragraph 1 of Article 19-2 of the Aged Employment Promotion Act, The employer of a business or workplace who extends the retirement age, and a labor union which is formed by the majority of all workers (or a person representing the majority of all workers) shall take the steps necessary to revise the wage system, etc. according to the conditions pertaining to the business or workplace concerned. In a seniority-based wage system, this article can be regarded as necessary, as changing the wage system is unavoidable and socially acceptable rationality. Secondly, Paragraph 2 of Article 19-2 mentions, as the Employment Insurance Act outlines a system for subsidies related to implementation of the wage peak system in accordance with the retirement extension, such a change to working conditions would not be considered disadvantageous because there is no decreased wage in reality. Therefore, introducing a wage peak system along with extended retirement can be regarded socially acceptable rationality because of sufficient follow-up measures. In consideration of these arguments, this theory claims that employers can revise the ROE without consent of the employee group.[175]

---

[174] Supreme Court ruling on January 28, 2010, 2009da32362.

박탈하여 불이익한 근로조건을 부과하는 것은 원칙적으로 허용되지 아니한다. 그러나 당해 취업규칙의 작성 또는 변경이 그 필요성 및 내용의 양면에서 보아 그에 의하여 근로자가 입게 될 불이익의 정도를 고려하더라도 여전히 당해 조항의 법적 규범성을 시인할 수 있을 정도로 사회통념상 합리성이 있다고 인정되는 경우에는 종전 근로조건 또는 취업규칙의 적용을 받고 있던 근로자의 집단적 의사결정방법에 의한 동의가 없다는 이유만으로 그의 적용을 부정할 수는 없다. 여기서 '사회통념상 합리성의 유무'는 취업규칙의 변경에 의하여 근로자가 입게 되는 불이익 정도, 사용자측 변경 필요성의 내용과 정도, 변경 후의 취업규칙 내용의 상당성, 대상조치 등을 포함한 다른 근로조건의 개선상황, 노동조합 등과의 교섭 경위 및 노동조합이나 다른 근로자의 대응, 동종 사항에 관한 국내의 일반적인 상황 등을 종합적으로 고려하여 판단하여야 한다. 다만, 취업규칙을 근로자에게 불리하게 변경하는 경우에는 그 동의를 받도록 한 근로기준법을 사실상 배제하는 것이므로 제한적으로 엄격하게 해석하여야 한다.[174] 라고 판시하고 있다.

3. 검토

(1) 인정설

사회통념상 합리성이 인정된다는 주장은 첫째, 고령자고용법 제19조의2 제1항에 따르면, 정년을 연장하는 사업 또는 사업장의 사업주와 근로자의 근로자대표(과반수 노동조합)는 그 사업 또는 사업장의 여건에 따라 임금체계 개편 등 필요한 조치를 하여야 한다. 라고 요구하고 있다. 이는 연공서열형 임금제에서는 임금제도의 변경이 불가피하다는 사회적 합리성을 인정한 것이라 본다. 둘째, 제19조의 2 제2항에서 고용보험법은 정년연장에 따른 임금피크제의 시행에 대한 지원금제도가 마련되어 시행되고 있기 때문에 사실상 근로자의 임금에 저하가 있을 수 없기 때문에 불이익한 변경이라 볼 수 없다. 따라서 정년제도를 도입하면서 정년 이전에 임금피크제를 도입하는 것은 사회통념상 합리성이 있고, 그 후속조치도 적합하기 때문에 근로자 집단의 동의 없이도 변경이 가능하다는 논리이다.[175]

---

[174] 대법원 2010.1.28. 선고, 2009다32362 판결.

(2) Theory of negative recognition

The following points are used as support in the argument that unilaterally changing working conditions disadvantageously is not rational to a degree that is socially acceptable[176]: Article 19 of the Aged Employment Promotion Act stipulates that introduction of the retirement age extension to 60 years is a normative provision, while Article 19-2 stipulates that the provision on introducing a wage peak system is a suggestive one and not legally binding. The related judicial ruling shows that the theory of socially acceptable rationality shall be strictly limited as this effectively ignores the provision in the Labor Standards Act requiring employee consent.[177]

(3) Our interpretation

In introducing extended retirement, it will not be considered justifiable for an employer to introduce a unilaterally-determined wage peak system to cut wages as this violates the principle of labor and management having decision-making power over working conditions. Provided, if the employer extends retirement age beyond the mandatory retirement age while introducing a wage peak system, this revision can be regarded as socially acceptable rationality as it contains advantages for both labor and management.

Ⅳ. Conclusion

Revision of working conditions is possible at any time the employees and the employer agree. In cases where working conditions are revised advantageously, the employer does not need the consent of the employee group. However, if the revisions are disadvantageous, the employer needs to obtain consent from the employee group before the revision(s) shall be considered legally effective. Unilateral revision by employers violates the principle of labor and management determining working conditions, and shall not be effective due to violating both the contractual characteristics of the Rules of Employment and its normative effect.[178] For this reason, socially acceptable rationality as a theory allowing the employer to revise working conditions unilaterally, shall be evaluated strictly on a case-by-case basis, after considering a fair comparison of the necessity of revising the Rules of Employment and the disadvantage created for affected employees in unfavorable revisions.

---

175) Chulsoo Lee, The wage peak system is possible to be implemented unilaterally by the employer!
176) Gaprye Ha, "The Subject of Consent in Disadvantageous Changes to Employment Rules"
177) Supreme Court ruling on January 28, 2010, 2009da32362.
178) Jung Lee, Whom to get consent for revising the Rules of Employment disadvantageously,『Labor Law』, Jungang Economy, September 2009.

(2) 부정설

사회통념상 합리성이 인정되지 않는다는 주장[176]은 고령자고용법 제19조의 만60세 정년제 도입은 규범적 규정인데 반하여, 제19조의 2는 임금개편 조치에 대한 요구는 아무런 법적 구속력이 없는 훈시규정이라는 점을 지적한다. 또한 이와 관련한 판례[177]는 사회통념상 합리성 이론은 근로기준법의 동의규정을 배제하는 효과를 가지므로 엄격히 해석해야 한다는 논리이다.

(3) 소결

정년연장을 도입하면서 사용자가 법정 정년 내에서 일방적으로 임금피크제도를 도입해 임금을 삭감하는 것은 근로조건의 결정의 노사자치를 무시한 것이라 인정되기 어렵다고 판단한다. 다만, 정년이 법정화된 이상 정년을 추가 연장하는 조건(정년연장형)으로 임금피크제도를 도입한다면, 사용자에게 유리한 점, 근로자에게 유리한 점이 모두 포함되어 있기 때문에 사회적 합리성을 인정할 수 있다.

VI. 결론

근로조건의 변경은 근로자와 사용자가 동의하는 경우에는 언제든지 가능하다. 사용자가 일방적으로 근로조건을 변경하는 경우에 유리한 조건인 경우에는 근로자의 동의가 없더라도 유효한 근로조건의 변경이 되지만, 불이익한 근로조건의 변경은 근로자 집단의 동의를 받아야 유효한 변경이 된다. 사용자가 일방적으로 근로조건을 변경한 것은 근로조건의 결정원칙에 위반되며, 취업규칙의 계약적 성질과 법규범적 효력 자체를 모두 위반함으로 유효한 근로조건의 변경이라 할 수 없다.[178] 이러한 이유로, 사회통념상 합리성이론도 사용자가 일방적으로 근로조건을 변경하는 것이므로 그 적용에 대해서는 취업규칙의 변경의 필요성과 해당 근로자가 입게 되는 불이익과의 비교형량을 한 후, 각 사례별로 엄격하게 판단하여야 할 것이다.

---

175) 이철수, 임금피크제의 사용자 일방시행 가능하다!
176) 하갑례, 취업규칙 불이익 변경시 동의주체
177) 대법원 2010.1.28. 선고, 2009다32362 판결.
178) 이정, 취업규칙 불이익 변경시 동의 주체†『노동법률』, 2009년9월, 중앙경제.

Section 10. Paying Out Retirement Benefits

Section 10-1. The Retirement Pension Plan

I. Introduction

Before December 2005, there were only two types of retirement payments stipulated in the Labor Standards Act: the Statutory Severance Pay Plan to be paid upon resignation and the Interim Severance Pay Plan which could be paid while the employee was still employed. However, in December 2005, the Employee Retirement Benefit Security Act (hereinafter referred to as the ERBS Act) was enacted and introduced something new: the Retirement Pension Plan, which can take the form of either a Severance Pay System or a Retirement Pension Plan. The Retirement Pension Plan is also further broken down into three types: the Defined Benefit Plan, the Defined Contribution Plan and the Individual Retirement Plan. Under these plans and upon retirement, employees can receive gains made from investment of their pension funds, either as a lump sum or monthly pension from an outside financial agency.

The ERBS Act, revised July 26, 2012, strengthened the Retirement Benefit Plan to ensure the retirement benefit is used as income during old age, rather than extra income before retirement. Interim severance payments are now restricted, and one of only seven reasons must exist.[179] The Individual Retirement Plan has also been introduced. In cases where retirement pension holders resign before retirement, opening of an IRP is mandatory, and funds are transferred as a lump sum from the previous employer to either the new employer's pension plan, or an IRP

---

[179] Enforcement Decree (Article 3) of the Employee Retirement Pension Security Act (Reasons for Interim Severance Pay) ① 1. Where an employee who has not owned a house has purchased a house in his/her own name; 2. Where an employee who has not owned a house makes a "key money" deposit (according to Article 303 of the Civil Act) or a security deposit (according to Article 3-2 of the Housing Lease Protection Act) for the purpose of moving into a residence. In this case the employee can only apply for the retirement pension one time during employment in a company or business;
3. Where an employee, employee's spouse according to Article 50 (Paragraph 1) of the Income Tax Act, or his/her dependent family member has received medical care for six months or more;
4. Where an employee has been declared bankrupt under the Debtor Rehabilitation and Bankruptcy Act within five years from the time of providing the retirement reserve as collateral;
5. Where an employee has received a decision for commencement of a rehabilitation proceeding under the Debtor Rehabilitation and Bankruptcy Act within five years from the time of providing the retirement reserve as collateral;
6. Where wages are decreasing due to the Wage Peak System according to rules from Paragraph 1 ~ 3 of Article 28 (1) of the Enforcement Decree of the Employment Insurance Act; and
7. Where other reasons and conditions prescribed by Ordinance of the Ministry of Employment and Labor, such as natural disasters, etc., are met.

제10절 퇴직급여 지급

제10-1절 퇴직연금제도

I. 들어가며

 2005년 12월 이전에는 근로기준법 퇴직금제도(근로자가 퇴사할 할 때 일시금으로 받는 법정퇴직금제도와 근로자가 재직 중에 받을 수 있는 퇴직금 중간정산제도)만 존재하였으나, 2005년 12월 "근로자퇴직급여보장법(근퇴법)"이 제정되면서 퇴직연금제도가 도입되었다. 현행 퇴직급여제도는 퇴직금제도와 퇴직연금제도로 구성된다. 여기서 퇴직연금제도는 확정급여형 퇴직연금제도(DB), 확정기여형 퇴직연금제도(DC), 개인형퇴직연금제도(IRP)로 3가지 형태로 구성된다. 퇴직연금제도는 회사가 근로자의 재직기간 동안 퇴직급여의 지급에 필요한 재원을 외부 금융기관에 적립하면, 근로자가 퇴직할 때 적립된 재원으로부터 연금 또는 일시금의 퇴직급여를 받아 노후생활에 사용할 수 있도록 하는 제도이다.

 2012년 7월 26일 개정된 근퇴법은 근로자의 퇴직급여가 생활자금으로 소모되지 않고 노후에 소득재원으로 사용될 수 있도록 퇴직금 제도를 정비하였으며, 크게 2가지의 특징을 갖는다. 첫째 특징은 퇴직금 중간정산의 엄격한 제한이다. 즉, 퇴직금을 재직 중에 중간정산할 수 있는 사유가 7가지로 한정된다.[179] 둘째 특징은 개인형퇴직연금제도(IRP)를 도입이다. 이 IRP 제도는

---

[179] 근로자퇴직급여보장 시행령 제3조(퇴직금의 중간정산 사유) ①
  1. 무주택자인 근로자가 본인 명의로 주택을 구입하는 경우
  2. 무주택자인 근로자가 주거를 목적으로 「민법」 제303조에 따른 전세금 또는 「주택임대차보호법」 제3조의2에 따른 보증금을 부담하는 경우. 이 경우 근로자가 하나의 사업 또는 사업장에 근로하는 동안 1회로 한정한다.
  3. 근로자, 근로자의 배우자 또는 「소득세법」 제50조제1항에 따른 근로자 또는 근로자의 배우자와 생계를 같이하는 부양가족이 질병 또는 부상으로 6개월 이상 요양을 하는 경우
  4. 퇴직금 중간정산을 신청하는 날부터 역산하여 5년 이내에 근로자가 「채무자 회생 및 파산에 관한 법률」에 따라 파산선고를 받은 경우
  5. 퇴직금 중간정산을 신청하는 날부터 역산하여 5년 이내에 근로자가 「채무자 회생 및 파산에 관한 법률」에 따라 개인회생절차개시 결정을 받은 경우
  6. 「고용보험법 시행령」 제28조제1항제1호부터 제3호까지의 규정에 따른 임금피크제를 실시하여 임금이 줄어드는 경우
  7. 그 밖에 천재지변 등으로 피해를 입는 등 고용노동부장관이 정하여 고시하는 사유와 요건에 해당하는 경우

account. The accumulated retirement benefit in this IRP account will, by law, be kept and managed until the employee is 55.

Hereafter, I would like to look at the differences between the severance pay system and the Retirement Pension Plan, the necessity for the Retirement Pension Plan, and details of the different types of pension plans.

II. Differences between the Severance Pay System and the Retirement Pension Plan

The differences between the Retirement Pension Plan and the Severance Pay System are as follows:

1. Under the Retirement Pension Plan, the company deposits the retirement contributions with an outside financial agency, and the employee receives a retirement benefit from the financial agency upon resignation. Under the Severance Pay System, the employer pays a pre-determined amount in severance pay upon employee resignation.

2. The Defined Benefit Plan is the same as the severance pay system, with the amount calculated in the same way: multiplying the average wage for each of the most recent three months by the years of service. The Defined Contribution Plan requires a deposit of 1/12 of the employee's annual salary every year, with the individual retirement benefit varying according to performance of fund investments.

3. In cases where an employee receives a lump sum from the Retirement Pension Plan, he/she shall receive it into an IRP. However, under the Severance Pay System, the employee can still receive a lump sum as before, as there is no obligation to transfer to an IRP in the Severance Pay System. However, the employee can open an IRP account and receive payment there if he or she wishes.

4. The Retirement Pension Plan guarantees the principal funds contributed, as they are managed by an outside agency. Under the Defined Benefit Plan also, the principal deposited outside is guaranteed. However, the Severance Pay System has a weakness in that should the company go bankrupt, the funds may not be available, since they were deposited within the company.

5. The Retirement Pension Plan requires regular retirement contributions to an outside agency, which can reduce the company's financial burden as it does not have to pay out large amounts upon resignation, contrary to the severance pay system. As the severance pay should be paid in full as a lump sum upon

퇴직연금제도에 가입한 근로자가 중도 퇴직하는 경우 의무적으로 가입하여야 하며, 이직 또는 조기 퇴직으로 인해 수령한 퇴직 일시금은 반드시 IRP계좌로 이전되며, 이 적립된 퇴직급여는 55세까지 의무적으로 보관, 운용할 수 있도록 한 제도이다.

다음에서 퇴직금과 퇴직연금의 차이점, 퇴직연금제도의 도입의 필요성, 퇴직연금 종류별 세부내용에 대해 구체적으로 알아보고자 한다.

Ⅱ. 퇴직금제도와 퇴직연금제도 비교

퇴직금제도와 퇴직연금제도의 차이점을 비교하면 다음과 같다.
1. 먼저 퇴직연금제도는 근무기간 중 일정금액의 퇴직급여를 금융기관에 사외 적립하고, 근로자 퇴직시점에 금융기관이 퇴직급여를 지급하는 방식으로 운영한다. 퇴직금제도에서는 근로자가 퇴직할 때 회사가 산정된 금액의 퇴직급여를 직접 지급한다.
2. DB제도는 퇴직급여 산정방식이나 지급되는 금액 등이 퇴직금제도와 동일하다. 따라서 퇴직금 제도와 DB제도의 경우 퇴직 전 최근 3개월의 평균임금에 근속년수를 곱한 금액이 지급금액이 된다. 반면, DC제도에서는 연간 임금총액의 12분의 1 이상을 매년 적립하고, 가입자 개개인의 운용성과에 따라 퇴직급여 수령액이 달라지게 된다.
3. 지급방법은 퇴직연금제도에서는 퇴직 일시금을 지급받을 경우에 반드시 IRP로 수령해야 한다. 그러나 퇴직금제도에서는 퇴직급여의 IRP 강제이전 의무가 없기 때문에 기존방식처럼 일시금으로 퇴직급여를 지급하면 되고, 원하는 근로자는 별도로 IRP를 개설하여 퇴직급여를 수령할 수도 있다.
4. 퇴직연금제도는 사외적립방식이므로 사외적립된 비율만큼 수급권이 보호되며, DB제도 전액 적립시 지급액 전액에 대하여 수급권이 보호된다. 반면 퇴직금제도의 경우 퇴직급여를 사내에 유보하므로 회사가 도산하면 근로자가 퇴직급여를 못 받을 가능성이 높다.
5. 퇴직연금제도에서는 퇴직급여를 주기적으로 사외에 적립함으로써 비용부담을 분산하고 있어 사용자의 재정부담이 경감되나 퇴직금제도에서는 근로자 퇴직 시 일시에 퇴직금을 지급해야 하므로 회사의 재정부담이

retirement, the company will have a heavier financial burden.

III. Necessity for and Introduction of the Retirement Pension Plan

1. Necessity for the Retirement Pension Plan

From the employee's perspective, the reasons necessitating the Retirement Pension Plan are as follows: Firstly, it is necessary to supplement the social welfare system. Currently, most people depend on the National Pension only. However, this is not enough for necessities. With three levels of social security (National Pension, Retirement Pension, and Individual Pension), the employee will be far better prepared. Secondly, it is necessary to protect the right for employees to secure their retirement benefits. If the company goes bankrupt, the employee will most likely not receive wages of any kind. To ensure benefits do not remain unpaid, companies shall deposit their contributions at an outside financial agency through the Retirement Pension Plan.

From the employer's perspective, the reasons necessitating the Retirement Pension Plan are as follows: Firstly, companies can reduce corporate tax through the Retirement Pension Plan. Only 20% of the retirement benefit reserve each year can be considered business expenses, and each year this percentage will be reduced 5% until 2016, when there will be no tax benefit at all. However, 100% of retirement reserve for the Retirement Pension Plan can be claimed as a tax deduction each year. Secondly, the Defined Benefit Plan aids in reducing company debt, as the retirement pension deposit is deducted from the retirement reserve. The Defined Contribution plan allows the total amount the company has paid into the retirement benefit each fiscal year to be regarded as actual retirement payout, thereby reducing company debt. Thirdly, companies introducing the Retirement Pension Plan can also save from a reduction in wage claim premiums: 50% of the premiums multiplied by the guaranteed rate covered by the Defined Contribution retirement benefit.

2. Introduction of the Retirement Pension Plan

The employer shall establish pension regulations, obtain the consent of the employee representative, and permission from the Ministry of Employment & Labor before introducing the Retirement Pension Plan. Upon employee retirement, the financial agency shall pay out a lump sum or a regular pension from the retirement fund the employer deposited. The retirement pension company (trustee) will be a

가중된다.

Ⅲ. 퇴직연금제도의 필요성 및 도입

1 퇴직연금제도의 필요성

　근로자의 입장에서 퇴직연금이 필요한 이유는 첫째, 사회보장제도의 보충효과를 위해서 필요하다. 현재 노후자금은 국민연금에만 의존하고 있는 경우가 대부분인데, 노후 대비를 국민연금만으로 하기에는 많이 부족하다. 따라서 국민연금, 퇴직연금, 개인연금의 3층 노후보장수단이 필요하다. 둘째, 퇴직금 수급권 보장 차원에서 필요하다. 기업이 도산할 경우에 근로자는 퇴직금을 받을 수 없다. 이를 해결하기 위해서는 퇴직연금제도를 통해 퇴직급여를 사외 금융기관에 안전하게 예치할 필요가 있다.
　사용자 입장에서 퇴직연금이 필요한 이유는 첫째, 법인세 절감 효과를 들 수 있다. 퇴직금제도로 사내적립을 한 경우 2012년 기준으로 적립금 추계액의 20%만 손비로 인정되며, 매5%씩 감소하여 2016년에는 사내적립금에 대한 손비인정이 없어진다. 그러나, 퇴직연금제도는 추계액 범위 내에서 기업 납입금의 100%가 비용으로 인정을 받는다. 둘째, 회사의 부채비율 개선효과가 있다. DB형 제도에 가입하게 되면 퇴직연금예치금을 퇴직급여충당금에서 차감형식으로 표시하여 기업의 부채비율 개선효과가 있고, DC형 제도로 가입했을 경우 당해 회계기간에 회사가 납부한 퇴직연금 부담금 전액을 퇴직급여(비용)으로 인식하므로 기업의 퇴직부채가 소멸되는 효과가 있다. 셋째, 퇴직연금제도를 도입한 기업에 대해서는 임금채권부담금이 일정부분 경감되어 이를 통한 추가적인 비용절감을 할 수 있다. 경감 금액은 부담금의 50%에 퇴직연금제도로 지급 보장되는 비율을 곱한 금액이다.

2. 퇴직연금제도의 도입

　퇴직연금을 도입하기 위해서는 사용자는 근로자 대표의 동의를 얻어 연금 규약을 작성하고 고용노동부의 승인을 받아야 한다. 퇴직연금사업자(금융

financial agency such as a bank, insurance company, or securities firm, and perform operational management and asset management. Operational management includes designing of the retirement pension, operational method of the assets, and administration. Asset management includes such tasks as depositing contributions and paying out retirement benefits, maintaining and managing assets, establishing and managing/operating the account.

Ⅳ. Types of Retirement Pension Plan

1. The Defined Benefit Retirement Plan (DB)

(1) **Concept:** Under the Defined Benefit plan the company deposits 60% or more of the retirement contributions expected for the year to an outside agency, and the financial agency pays 100% of the retirement benefit within its obligation to pay[180]. The Defined Benefit plan is characterized by a prior confirmation of the severance payment. This is calculated in the same way as in the existing Severance Pay System, and is equal to the final month's total wage. Severance pay is calculated by multiplying the average monthly wage (over the final 3 months) before resignation/retirement by the years of service.

(2) **Characteristics:** As the amount of retirement benefit is determined beforehand, plans for the retirement years are possible. As the company contributes to and manages the retirement reserve directly, the employee is free of those responsibilities. One disadvantage is that transferring the retirement deposits to another company is difficult. Depositing additional money or withdrawing money early is not allowed by law, but it is possible to borrow the money as a secured loan, for the following purposes: 1. First-time purchase of a house; 2. Medical treatment for 6 months or longer for the employee or his/her dependents; 3. Decision for commencement of a rehabilitation proceeding; 4. Bankruptcy; or 5. Other reasons and conditions such as natural disasters, etc., prescribed by Ordinance of the Ministry of Employment & Labor. The DB Plan is suitable for companies with job security, low turnover, and who provide high salary increases.

---

[180] The Minimum Reserve is the amount equivalent to 60% of the Standard Mandatory Reserve from July 26, 2012 to the end of 2013. After this period, the Minimum Reserve is to increase 10% every two years, becoming 70% of the Standard Mandatory Reserve from 2014 to the end of 2015, then 80% of the Standard Mandatory Reserve from 2016 to the end of 2017, and the rate stipulated by decree of the Minister of Employment & Labor from 2018 on.

기관)은 근로자 퇴직시 기업이 적립한 퇴직급여를 퇴직근로자에게 일시금 또는 연금으로 지급한다. 퇴직연금사업자는 은행, 보험, 증권사 등의 금융기관이 있으며 운용관리와 자산관리의 업무를 수행한다. 운용관리 업무는 퇴직연금 제도설계, 자산의 운용방법 제시, 행정적 측면의 제도운영이 있고, 자산관리 업무는 부담금 수령 및 퇴직급여 지급, 자산의 보관 및 관리, 계좌의 설정 및 관리, 운용지시를 이행하는 일이다.

Ⅳ. 퇴직연금제도의 종류

1. 확정급여 퇴직연금제도 (DB)

(1) **개념**: DB제도는 회사가 기준책임준비금의 60%이상을 사외 금융기관에 예치하고[180], 금융기관이 지급의무가 있는 범위의 100%를 지급하는 방식이다. 확정급여형은 근로자가 받을 퇴직금이 기존 퇴직금 제도와 동일하게 최종임금 수준에 따라 퇴직금이 결정된다. 퇴직금은 퇴직시의 평균임금에 근속연수를 곱하여 산정하며 이 때 퇴직시의 평균임금은 최종 3개월간의 평균임금입니다.

(2) **특징**: DB제도는 퇴직할 때 받을 급여수준이 확정되었기 때문에 안정적인 노후설계가 가능하며, 부담금 납입과 적립금 운영을 기업이 대신하므로 근로자의 부담이 없는 반면 직장 이동에 따른 연금의 이동성이 원활하지 못하다. 또한 추가납입이나 중도인출은 불가하고 법정 사유에 한해 담보대출만 가능하다. 그 법정사유는 무주택자의 주택구입, 본인 또는 부양가족의 6개월 이상 요양, 파산 선고, 개인회생절차 개시,기타 천재사변 등으로 노동부장관이 인정하는 경우이다. 따라서 DB제도는 기업이 1) 안정적이고 이직율이 낮으며, 2) 임금상승률이 높은 경우에 적합한 제도이다.

---

[180] 사용자의 최소적립금은 2012년 7월 26일부터 2013년 말까지는 기준책임 준비금의 60%에 해당하는 금액이며, 그 후 매 2년마다 10%씩 상승한다. 2014년부터 2015년 말까지는 최소적립금은 70%, 2016년부터 2017년 말까지는 기준책임준비금의 80%, 2018년 이후 부터는 고용노동부령에서 정하는 비율을 적용한다.

Chapter3-10. Paying Out Retirement Benefits

(3) Conditions for eligibility: The employee receives retirement pension or lump sum allowance upon retirement. The retirement pension is eligible for those who are 55 years old or older and have subscribed to it for 10 years or more. In this case, the beneficiary period shall be 5 years or longer. The lump sum payment is paid to those who were not eligible for pension and who want to receive it as a lump sum payment. This lump sum payment means that the retirement benefit is transferred to the IRP account.

2. The Defined Contribution Retirement Plan (DC)

(1) Concept: The level of contribution the employer and employee make is predetermined by pension law, with the employee's final retirement benefit determined by the company's contributions and the employee's investment gains. Investment outcomes are up to the employee and the final payment depends on the performance of his or her investments. The employer deposits 1/12 of the employee's annual salary every year. A retirement payment is deposited every month, like an interim severance payment. Final payout is determined by performance of the employee's investments. The employee's retirement benefit is equal to company contributions and investment returns.

(2) Characteristics: Employees can put additional money into this fund. As the fund is separately managed, it is easy to move it to another company, plus, payout can be higher than the Defined Benefit plan if the investment returns are good. However, management of the retirement funds is at the risk of each employee, who is responsible for choosing appropriate investments. The companies that are more suited to the Defined Contribution plan are 1) Companies with lower salary increases and 2) Companies implementing an annual salary system.

(3) Conditions for eligibility: The employer deposits 1/12 of the employee's annual salary every year. The employee manages the retirement fund, and will receive it as a monthly pension or lump sump payment upon retirement. The retirement pension is eligible for those who are 55 years old or older and have subscribed to for 10 years or more. In this case, the beneficiary period shall be 5 years or longer. The lump sum payment is paid to those who were not eligible for pension or who want to receive it as a lump sum payment. This lump sum payment means that the retirement benefit is transferred to the IRP account.

(3) **수급요건**: 퇴직시에 연금 또는 일시금으로 수령한다. 연금수령은 연금가입자가 55세 이상으로서 가입기간이 10년 이상, 이 경우 연금의 지급기간은 5년 이상이어야 한다. 일시금은 연금수급자격을 갖추지 못했거나 일시금 수령을 원하는 자에 지급하며, 일시금은 IRP계좌로의 전환을 의미한다.

2. 확정기여 퇴직연금제도 (DC)

(1) **개념**: DC제도는 기업의 퇴직급여 부담금 수준을 노사가 사전에 연금규약으로 확정하고 부담금을 납부하는 제도로 근로자의 최종 퇴직급여 수령액은 기업이 부담한 금액과 근로자 개인의 운용수익에 따라 결정된다. 사용자는 가입자의 연간임금총액의 12분의 1에 해당하는 금액을 퇴직급여의 부담금으로 납부하여야 한다. 매년 발생하는 퇴직급여를 개인별로 적립하는 점에서 매년 중간정산을 하는 것과 유사하다. 근로자 개인의 운용 성과에 따라 향후 받을 퇴직급여 수령액이 달라질 수 있으며, 운용결과에 대한 책임은 근로자가 진다. 근로자가 받을 퇴직급여는 기업부담금과 운용수익을 합한 금액입니다.

(2) **특징**: DC 제도는 근로자 추가부담금 납입이 가능하며, 적립금이 개인별로 관리되므로 직장이동시 적립금의 이동성이 편리하며, 운용수익률 예상치가 급여상승률 보다 높을 경우 확정급여형보다 유리하다. 그러나, 적립금 운용을 위한 근로자 각자의 노력이 요구되고, 금융상품 선택과 운용에 따른 위험부담이 있다. DC제도가 적합한 기업은 1) 임금인상률이 낮은 기업, 2) 연봉제를 실시하는 기업 등이다.

(3) **수급요건**: 사용자가 매년 근로자 연간 임금총액의 1/12 이상을 근로자 계좌에 적립하면, 근로자가 직접 적립금을 운용하다가 퇴직 시 연금 또는 일시금의 형태로 받을 수 있다. 연금수령은 연금가입자가 55세 이상으로서 가입기간이 10년 이상, 이 경우 연금의 지급기간은 5년 이상이어야 한다. 일시금은 연금수급자격을 갖추지 못했거나 일시금 수령을 원하는 자에

The Defined Contribution Plan holder can legally withdraw the deposit or borrow the money as a secured loan during employment for the following reasons: 1) First-time purchase of a house; 2) Medical treatment for 6 months or longer for the employee or his/her dependents; 3) Decision for commencement of a rehabilitation proceeding; 4) Bankruptcy; or 5) Other reasons and conditions such as natural disasters, etc., prescribed by Ordinance of the Ministry of Employment & Labor.

3. The Individual Retirement Plan (IRP)

(1) Concept: The Individual Retirement Plan can take the form of a Company IRP or an individual IRP. The Company IRP is a retirement pension plan as described in the Employee Retirement Benefit Security Act and is acceptable as a retirement benefit scheme for companies that employ 9 or fewer employees. It operates in basically the same way as the Defined Contribution plan, but companies do not have to create the pension rules. In cases where the company later employs 10 or more employees, the Defined Contribution plan shall be adopted. The Individual IRP was designed for the employee to be able to manage his or her own retirement benefit until retirement or until receiving it if resignation occurs earlier.

(2) Characteristics/ Conditions for eligibility: Under the Retirement Pension Plan, when the employee resigns or retires, the retirement benefit shall be transferred to an IRP. Upon reaching the age of 55, the employee can receive a regular retirement pension or lump sum payment. The IRP reserve cannot be withdrawn earlier than the required age except for the legal reasons described in Article 2 of the Enforcement Decree of the ERBS Act: Reasons for Offering Right to Receive Benefits as Collateral. However, The Retirement Pension Plan (DB, DC, Company IRP) shall be transferred to the IRP except in the following situations: 1) The subscriber receives payment after age 55 upon retirement; 2) The subscriber returns the borrowed money with wage collateral; 3) The retirement fund is equal to 1.5 million won or less, as stipulated by the Minister of Employment & Labor.

V. Conclusion

Although the Retirement Pension plans were introduced in December 2005, they have not yet been widely used due to the existing severance pay system. However, recent revisions to related law restricts interim severance payment and provides many

지급하며, 일시금은 IRP계좌로의 전환을 의미한다.

DC 제도에 있어 법정 사유에 한하여 적립금 담보대출 또는 중도인출이 가능하다. 그 법정사유는 무주택자의 주택구입, 본인 또는 부양가족의 6개월 이상 요양, 파산 선고, 개인회생절차 개시,기타 천재사변 등으로 노동부장관이 인정하는 경우이다.

3. 개인형퇴직연금제도 (IRP)

(1) **개념**: 개인형 퇴직연금제도는 기업형 IRP제도와 퇴직후의 개인형 IRP제도로 구분할 수 있다. 기업 IRP는 상시 근로자 10인 미만의 사업장인 경우 퇴직급여 제도로 인정된다. 기본적 운용구조는 DC제도와 동일하나, 퇴직연금규약 작성의무가 없다. 향후 근로자가 10인 이상이 될 경우 DC로 전환해야 한다. 개인형 IRP는 근로자가 이직 또는 조기 퇴직 시 수령한 퇴직급여를 은퇴할 때까지 보관, 운용할 수 있도록 한 제도이다.

(2) **특징/수급요건**: 퇴직연금제도에서 퇴직 또는 이직하는 경우에는 퇴직급여를 반드시 개인형 IRP로 이전해야 한다. 이 경우, IRP 적립금은 55세 이후에 연금으로 수령하거나 일시금으로 수령할 수 있다. IRP의 적립금은 자유로이 인출할 수 없으며, 인출을 원하는 경우에는 법정사유(시행령 2조: 담보대출사유)에 해당되어야 한다. 다만, 퇴직연금제도(DB, DC, 기업IRP)에서 퇴직시 개인 IRP로 강제이전이 제외되는 경우는 다음과 같다. (시행령9조) 1) 가입자가 55세 이후에 퇴직하여 급여를 받는 경우; 2) 가입자가 퇴직급여를 담보로 대출받은 금액 등을 상환하기 위한 경우; 3) 퇴직급여액이 노동부장관이 정하는 금액(150만 원) 이하인 경우이다.

V. 맺은 말

2005년 12월 이후 도입된 퇴직연금제도가 기존의 퇴직금제도로 인해서 활성화 되지 못하였다. 그러나 최근 근퇴법 개정으로 인해, 퇴직금의 중간정산을 엄격히 제한하고, 또한 퇴직연금제도에 많은 혜택을 부여하고 있어

incentives to introduce the Retirement Pension plans, incentives which are expected to gradually increase use of the Retirement Pension plans. Retirement benefits have often been used as an additional bonus to normal wages. However, they should be used as retirement benefits to supplement old-age security. Accordingly, these Retirement Pension plans should be encouraged further to help people have the funds they will need, through strategic government support. Employees also need to recognize that the retirement benefit is not money to be spent on pre-retirement costs, but is to be saved as a matter of course to prepare for the golden years.

Section 10-2. Severance Pay: Labor Ministry Guidelines and Judicial Rulings

I. Those Eligible for Severance Pay

Whether to pay severance pay to an employee who was appointed as a company director (Nov. 27, 2001 Wage 68200-814)

In the case where an employee was appointed as company director without terminating employment, the matters related to severance pay shall be evaluated as follows:

① In cases where the director fulfills his duties with the authority of a representative director or execution director commissioned by the company by means of the commercial law and the civil law, and receives a service charge, the director cannot be deemed an employee under the Labor Standards Act. Therefore, his severance pay occurs from the time when he was appointed as director (on the terminated date of employment by the LSA). The extinctive prescription is also calculated from the same date.

② In cases where, despite the director's title, he maintains subordinate employment with the employer and is actually in an employee position, the severance pay occurs from the time when the director resigned from the company. The extinctive prescription is also calculated from the same date.

How to calculate severance pay for a person assigned to regular position from daily worker (Nov 14, 2000, Wage 68207-581)

The consecutive year of employment to calculate the severance pay of an employee

점차적으로 활성화 될 것이라 예상된다. 퇴직급여가 퇴직을 위해서 사용되어야 함에도 불구하고 급여에 덧붙여진 보너스 형태로 사용된 부분이 많았다. 그러나 퇴직금은 그 용어와 같이 근로자의 퇴직을 위해서 노후보장용으로 사용되는 것이 원칙이라 할 수 있다. 따라서 앞으로 퇴직연금제도를 활성화하여 노후자금을 준비할 수 있는 자금확보 수단으로 사용되어야 할 것이다. 이를 위해 퇴직연금제도에 대한 일관적인 정책적 지원과 기업과 근로자들이 퇴직금이 생활자금이 아닌 퇴직연금은 노후보장을 위한 저축이라는 인식의 전환이 필요하다고 하겠다.

제10-2절 퇴직금에 관한 행정해설 및 판례

Ⅰ. 퇴직금 지급 대상자

직원이 임원으로 선임된 경우 퇴직금 지급여부 (2001.11.27, 임금 68200-814)
　재직중인 직원이 근무기간의 단절없이 이사로 선임된 경우에 있어 퇴직금을 둘러싼 법률관계는 아래와 같이 판단하여야 함
① 이사가 상법 및 민법에 의하여 회사의 업무대표권 또는 집행권을 위임받아 업무를 수행하고, 보수를 받는 등 근로기준법상 근로자로 볼 수 없는 경우에는 임원으로 선임된 날(근로기준법상의 근로관계가 종료된 날)을 기준으로 퇴직금 지급청구권이 발생하고, 소멸시효 또한 이날부터 기산됨
② 명칭만 이사일 뿐 사용자와 여전히 고용종속관계를 유지하고 있는 등 사실상 근로기준법상의 근로자에 해당되는 경우에는 이사로서 퇴직한 날을 기준으로 퇴직금 지급청구권이 발생하고, 이날부터 소멸시효가 기산됨

일용직으로 근무하다가 정규직으로 환직된 경우의 퇴직금 산정방법 (2000.11.14, 임금 68207-581)
　동일한 사업장에서 일용직으로 입사하여 근무하다가 정규직으로 임용되어 계속근로한 근로자의 퇴직금 계산을 위한 계속근로년수 판단은 아래와 같이

who joined the company as a daily worker, but was reemployed as a regular employee shall be considered collectively based on the concrete facts as follows:

If a temporary employee quitted his temporary position, the employer accepted it, and he took employment procedures by applying for regular position, his previous labor contract was terminated effectively regardless of new employment. However, if the temporary employee was rehired to regular position while maintaining temporary employment, this is only the transfer to regular position from irregular position and his employment cannot be deemed effectively as terminated status.

When the retired employee was rehired at the identical company, the employer cannot make a special contract not to pay severance pay, which violates a compulsory law and becomes null and void. (Mar 12, 1999, Kungi 68207-584)

When re-hiring a retired employee, the company shall pay severance pay to the employee whose service period has become more than one year after the re-employment. Even though both parties agreed not to pay severance pay, the agreement violates a compulsory law and becomes null and void.

Whether a full-time lecturer at the entrance exam institute is entitled to severance pay (Nov 10, 2006, Seoul District Court 2004 gadan 69638)

If a full-time lecturer registered as individual service provider provided labor service to the employer under substantial employment relations, he/she can receive severance pay. Whether a person belongs to the employee of the Labor Standards Act or not shall be estimated based upon the fact: whether the employee provides labor service to the employer under subordinate relations for the purpose of wages in a business or workplace regardless whatever contract type. Full-time lecturers at the institute attended every day (6 days per week) distinct from other part-time lecturers, received fixed amount of wages, and observed service regulations and personnel regulations such as starting time and finishing time. So, full-time lecturers are employees who provided labor service under subordinate relations.

If a person has continuously maintained daily employment formally as a daily employee, he/she shall be applied to the Labor Standards Act and the employer shall pay severance pay to the daily employee who has served more than one year. (Apr 19, 1996, Seoul District Court 95 kahap 11509)

구체적인 사실관계를 종합적으로 고려하여야 할 것임.

근로자의 자발적인 의사에 따라 일용직 사직의사 표시와 사용자의 사직 수리가 이루어진 이후에 정규직으로의 환직을 위한 시험응시 등 임용절차를 거친 경우라면 이는 정규직 임용여부와는 관계없이 기왕의 일용직에 대한 근로관계는 유효하게 단절된 것으로 볼 수 있을 것이나, 일용직 근로관계를 계속 유지하고 있는 상태에서 정규직으로의 채용이 이루어진 경우라면 이는 일용직에서 정규직으로 환직된 것에 불과한 것이므로 근로관계가 유효하게 단절되었다고는 볼 수 없을 것임.

정년퇴직자가 동일 사업장에 재고용시 퇴직금 부지급은 강행법규 위반으로 무효이다(1999.03.12, 근기 68207-584)

정년퇴직한 근로자를 재고용하는 경우에도 재고용 시점부터 계속 근무한 기간이 1년 이상이면 퇴직금을 지급하여야 하는 바, 당사자간에 이를 지급하지 않기로 합의하였다 하더라도 동 합의는 강행법규 위반으로 무효임.

입시학원 종합반 전임강사가 퇴직시 퇴직금을 받을 수 있는지 여부(2006.11. 10, 서울지법 2004가단69638)

개인사업자로 등재된 입시학원 종합반 전임강사가 실질적인 종속관계로 사용자에게 근로를 제공했다면 퇴직시 퇴직금을 받을 수 있다.근로기준법상 근로자에 해당 되는지 여부는 그 계약형식에 상관없이 실질에 있어 근로자가 사업 또는 사업장에 임금을 목적으로 종속적인 관계에서 사용자에게 근로를 제공했는지 여부에 따라 판단해야 한다. 원고들은 학원에서 재학생반 전임 강사로 다른 시간강사 내지 단과반 강사들과 달리 매일(주 6일) 출근하며 고정적인 월급을 받았던 점, 출퇴근 시간 등 학원 강사들에 대한 복무규정과 인사규정이 시행됐던 점 등에 비추어 종속적인 관계에서 근로를 제공한 근로자로 봄이 상당하다.

형식상 일용근로자로 되어 있다 하더라도 일용관계가 계속되어온 경우, 상용 근로자로 보아 근로기준법을 적용해야 하고 1년 이상 근로한 자에 대하여는 퇴직금을 지급해야 한다(1996.04.19, 서울지법 95가합 11509)

If a person has been a daily worker formally, but maintained daily employment without cessation, he/she shall be considered a regular employee. It is not true that the continuity of employment shall be estimated not by providing 25days or longer on monthly average, but by providing 4 or 5 days to 15 days every month. As daily employees have provided labor service for 4 or 5 days every month without exception, they shall be considered continuous employment and shall be applied to the Labor Standards Act.

Illegal migrant employees are applied to the regulation of severance pay in the Labor Standards Act (Aug 26, 1997, Supreme Court 97 da 18875)
The term "employee" used in Article 14 of the Labor Standards Act means a person, regardless of being engaged in whatever occupation, who offers work to a business or workplace for the purpose of earning wages. In Article 5 of the Act, an employer shall not take discriminatory treatment in relation to the working conditions on the ground of nationality. Foreign migrant employees are applicable to the Labor Standards Act unless there are special occasions. Accordingly, the rules of severance pay stipulated in the Labor Standards Act apply to illegal migrant employees.

II. Consecutive Year of Employment

The consecutive year of employment to calculate severance pay shall be included into total employment period excluding the period of time when the employer ordinarily hires less than five employees. (Jul 20, 2006, Retirement benefit security team-2582)
The severance pay according to Article 4 and 8 of the Employee Retirement Benefit Security Act applies to all businesses or workplaces in which not less than five employees are ordinarily employed. In cases where the company has maintained five or more in the ordinary number of employees for a long period of time, but the number of employees were reduced to less than five employee for a certain period of time, the consecutive year of employment to calculate severance pay shall include the total employment period excluding the period of time when the employer ordinarily hired less than five employees.

The period of disciplinary 'suspension from work' due to the employee's own reason shall be included into the period of continuous employment, which is the

형식상으로는 비록 일용근로자로 되어 있다고 하더라도 일용관계가 중단되지 않고 계속되어 온 경우에는 상용근로자로 보아야 할 것이고, 또한 근로자가 월 평균 25일 이상 근무하여야만 근로관계의 계속성을 인정할 수 있는 것은 아니며, 매월 빠뜨리지 않고 4, 5일 내지 15일 정도씩 계속하여 일해 온 경우에는 근로관계의 계속성이 인정된다 할 것인바, 원고들이 피고회사에서 일용근로자로 근무하는 동안 매월 빠뜨리지 않고 최소한 4, 5일 이상 계속하여 근무해 온 사실을 인정할 수 있으므로 원고들에 대하여도 계속적 근로관계가 인정되어 근로기준법이 적용되어야 할 것이다.

불법체류외국인 근로자에게도 근로기준법상의 퇴직금 규정이 적용된다(1997.08. 26, 대법 97다 18875)

근로기준법 제14조에 근로자라 함은 직업의 종류를 불문하고 사업 또는 사업장에 임금을 목적으로 근로를 제공하는 자를 말한다고 규정하고 있고, 또 같은 법 제5조에 의하면 사용자는 근로자에 대하여 국적을 이유로 근로조건에 대한 차별적 대우를 하지 못한다고 규정하고 있으므로 특별한 사정이 없는 한 외국인 근로자에 대하여도 근로기준법이 적용된다 할 것이다. 따라서 불법체류 외국인 근로자에게도 근로기준법상의 퇴직금 규정이 적용된다.

Ⅱ. 계속근로연수

퇴직금계산을 위한 계속근로년수는 전체 재직기간중에서 상시근로자수가 5인 미만인 기간을 제외한 기간을 합산한 기간으로 해야 한다(2006.07.20, 퇴직급여보장팀-2582)

근로자퇴직급여보장법 제4조 및 제8조의 규정에 의한 퇴직금은 상시 5인 이상의 근로자를 사용하는 사업(장)에 적용되고 있습니다. 사업장에서 상당기간 동안 상시근로자수가 5인 이상을 유지하다가 5인 미만으로 감소되어 상당기간 동안 유지되는 경우 퇴직금계산을 위한 계속근로년수는 전체 재직기간중에서 상시근로자수가 5인 미만인 기간을 제외한 기간을 합산한 기간으로 함을 알려 드립니다.

basic data for calculating severance pay, if a person maintains subsidiary employment relations with his employer. (May 11, 2006, Retirement benefit security team-1596)

According to Article 8 (1) of the Employee Retirement Benefit Security Act, an employer shall pay severance pay equivalent to the average wage for thirty day or more for each one year of continuous employment. The period of continuous employment in this Act means "the period from the establishment of labor contract to its termination". The period in which the employee did not provide labor service, but was under subordinate employment relations with an employer shall be included into the period of continuous employment for calculating severance pay. Accordingly, the period of disciplinary 'suspension from work' due to the employee's own reason shall be included into the period of continuous employment as the basic data for calculating severance pay, if an employee has maintained subsidiary employment relations with his employer.

III. Calculation of Severance Pay

'Suspension period from work' due to the employee's personal reason shall be included to the period for calculating average wages. (Feb 27, 2003, Wages 68207-132)

Average wage to calculate severance pay by Article 19 of the Labor Standards Act means the amount calculated by dividing the total amount of wages paid to a relevant employee during three calendar months immediately before the day on which a cause for calculating his average wages occurred by the total number of calendar days during those three months. When the amount calculated in this method is lower than that of the ordinary wage of the employee concerned, the amount of the ordinary wage shall be deemed his average wages. In cases where the period of calculating average wages includes the period of falling under any of Subparagraph 1 to 8 of Article 2 (1) of Enforcement Decree of the LSA, the period and wages paid for that period shall be deducted respectively from a basis period for the calculation of average wages and the total amount of average wage.

However, the period in which the employee did not provide labor service due to his own reasons such as absence shall not be excluded from a basis period for the calculation of average wages. Accordingly, in cases where the employee did not provide labor service during the basis period to calculate severance pay due to his personal reason like absence, the identical period shall be included into a basis period of average wages and calculated for severance pay.

근로자의 귀책사유로 인한 징계정직기간의 경우 사용종속관계가 유지되고 있다면 퇴직금산정의 기초가 되는 계속근로기간에 포함하는 것이 타당하다(2006.05. 11, 퇴직급여보장팀-1596)

　근로자퇴직급여보장법 제8조제1항에 의하면 퇴직금은 계속근로기간 1년에 대하여 30일분이상의 평균임금을 지급하여야 합니다. 동법에서 계속근로기간이라 함은 『근로계약을 체결하여 해지될 때까지의 기간』을 의미하므로, 실제로 근로를 제공하지 않은 기간이라 하더라도 사용종속관계가 유지되고 있는 기간은 퇴직금 산정을 위한 계속근로년수 산정시 포함하여야 할 것입니다. 따라서 근로자의 귀책사유로 인한 징계정직기간의 경우에도 사용종속관계가 유지되고 있다면 특별한 사정이 없는 한 그 기간은 퇴직금산정의 기초가 되는 계속근로기간에 포함하는 것이 타당할 것입니다.

Ⅲ. 퇴직금액 산정

휴직기간이 근로자 귀책사유에 해당되는 경우 평균임금산정 기준기간에 포함하여 평균임금을 산정하여야 한다(2003.02.27, 임금 68207-132)

　퇴직금산정을 위한 평균임금은 근로기준법 제19조의 규정에 의거 이를 산정하여야 할 사유가 발생한 날 이전 3월간에 지급된 임금총액을 그 기간의 총 일수로 나눈 금액을 말하며, 이러한 방법으로 산출된 평균임금액이 당해 근로자의 통상임금보다 저액일 경우에는 그 통상임금액을 평균임금으로 하도록 정하고 있음.

　평균임금 산정기간 중에 같은 법 시행령 제2조 제1항 제1호 내지 제8호에 해당하는 기간이 있는 경우에는 그 기간과 그 기간 중에 지불된 임금은 평균임금 산정기준이 되는 기간과 임금의 총액에서 각각 공제하도록 규정되어 있음.

　그러나 결근 등 근로자 귀책사유에 의하여 근로를 제공하지 못한 기간은 평균임금 산정기준이 되는 기간에서 공제하도록 규정되어 있지 아니함.

　만일 평균임금 산정기준이 되는 기간에 근로를 제공하지 못한 사유가 결근 등 근로자 귀책사유에 해당되는 경우에는 동기간도 평균임금산정 기준기간에 포함하여 평균임금을 산정하여야 함.

How to include bonuses paid through one year into the amount subject to the calculation of average wages (Feb. 24, 2003, Wages 68207-120)

There are no regulations stipulated in the Labor Laws about the matters concerning payment of bonuses, but bonuses shall be deemed wages as remuneration for work when they are stipulated in the Rules of Employment for payment conditions, amount, and payment period or when they have been paid so habitually to all employees that the employee may have natural expectations to receive bonus as a matter of course. On the other hand, in cases where payment rate of bonuses was established per year-unit and paid for the period exceeding one month, the total amount of bonus paid for a certain month shall not be included into calculation of average wages. The bonuses shall be calculated by dividing the total amount of bonuses paid to a relevant employee during twelve calendar months before the day on which a cause for calculating his average wages occurred by the total number of calendar months, which is 3/12 times the total amount of bonuses paid per year. **In cases where the severance pay regulation has been revised justifiably in the middle of the consecutive work period, the calculation of severance pay shall be applied to the severance pay regulation effective at the time of retirement. The calculation shall not be applied differently by dividing the period before or after the revision of the severance pay regulation.** (Sep 10, 1996, Supreme Court 95 da 15414)

IV. Prohibition of Discriminating System for Severance Pay

Discriminating severance pay between full-time employee and part-time employee violates the principle of prohibition for different application. (Oct 20, 2000, Seoul District Court 2000 Kahap 8606)

Article 34 (2) of the Labor Standards Act prohibits establishment of different severance pay system according to job classification, title, business classification, etc. in one workplace and shall apply one severance pay system. The Company's different application of severance pay between full-time employee and part-time employee violates the principle of prohibition against discrimination. Even though the company hired full-time employees and part-time employees differently and applied them differently in the hiring procedures, job characteristics, promotion/transfer, etc., the discrimination of severance pay shall not be justified with a reasonable cause.

That the company included the amount equivalent to severance pay into the monthly

1년간 지급받은 상여금을 평균임금 대상금품에 산입하는 방법(2003.02.24, 임금 68207-120)

　상여금의 지급 등에 대하여는 노동관계법에 별도 규정되어 있지 아니하나, 취업규칙 등에 지급조건, 금액, 지급시기가 정해져 있거나 전 근로자에게 관례적으로 지급하여 사회통념상 근로자가 당연히 지급 받을 수 있다는 기대를 갖게 되는 경우에는 근로의 대상성을 갖는 임금으로 보고 있음.

　한편 상여금의 지급률을 연간단위로 설정하여 1개월을 넘는 단위로 지급하고 있는 경우에는 이를 지급 받은 그 월의 임금으로 취급하여 일시에 전액을 평균임금에 산입하는 것이 아니며, 평균임금을 산정하여야 할 사유가 발생한 날 이전 12개월의 기간동안에 지급 받은 상여금 전액을 그 기간동안의 근로월수로 분할 계산하여 즉, 3/12을 평균임금산정 기준 임금총액에 산입함.

　계속근무기간의 중간에 퇴직금규정이 유효하게 변경된 경우 퇴직금을 산출함에 있어서는 전체 근무기간에 대하여 퇴직당시에 유효한 퇴직금규정을 적용해야 하는 것이지 퇴직금규정 변경 전후의 기간을 나누어 변경전 근무기간에 대해 변경전의 규정을 적용할 것은 아니다(1996.09.10, 대법 95다 15414)

Ⅳ. 퇴직금 차등제도 금지

정규직직원과 시간제직원에 대해 차등의 퇴직금제도를 두어 차별하는 것은 차등금지원칙에 위반된다(2000.10.20, 서울지법 2000가합8606)

　근로기준법 제34조 제2항은 하나의 사업 내에서 직종, 직위, 업종 등에 따라 차등의 퇴직금제도를 두는 것을 금지하고 하나의 퇴직금제도를 적용하도록 하는 것인 바, 피고회사가 정규직직원과 시간제직원에 대해 차등의 퇴직금제도를 두어 차별하는 것은 위 차등금지원칙에 위반하는 것이라고 보아야 할 것이고, 정규직직원과 시간제직원 사이에 피고회사 주장과 같은 채용절차, 근로의 성격, 승급·전보조치의 유무 등에서 차이가 있다고 하더라도 이것이 위와 같은 차별을 정당화할 합리적인 이유가 된다고 할 수 없다.

외국인 조종사에 대하여는 월급여 속에 퇴직금 상당액을 포함시켜 지급하기로

wage for foreign pilots was the establishment of a different application between foreign employees and native employees. (Mar 27, 1998, Supreme Court 97 da 19725) If the company agreed to include the amount equivalent to severance pay into the monthly wage for foreign pilots, it means that the company will not pay severance pay in time of retirement for foreign pilots. This is a different system of severance pay, prohibited by Article 28 (2) of the previous Labor Standards Act, compared to the native pilots who receive severance pay when quitting job. Therefore, foreign pilots can apply for severance pay by the Rules of Employment applying to majority of employees.

If there are two different applications at severance pay: the Rules of Employment regulating a cumulative severance pay system for native employees and individual employment contracts regulating a singular severance pay system for foreign workers, this violates the regulation to prohibit different application of severance pay. (Nov 28, 1997, Supreme Court 97 da 24511)

In case where employment relation of employees has been inclusively succeeded through business transfer or corporate merger, if a severance pay regulation before succession is inferior to the severance pay regulation after succession, the employer cannot apply the severance pay regulation after succession without obtaining consent by a collective decision-making method of the majority of employees. (Dec 26, 1995, Supreme Court 95 da 41659)

V. How to Pay Severance Pay

In case where reason to reduce severance pay occurred after payment of interim severance pay, such as abolition of a cumulative severance pay system, the company shall apply to the reduced severance pay system: it calculates both amounts of previously paid interim severance pay and final severance pay and may pay severance pay after deducting the amount already paid. (Apr 8, 2004, Wage policy team-1173)

According to Article 34 (1) of the Labor Standards Act, the liability of an employer's severance pay occurs when the employment was terminated. However, by Article 34 (3) of the LSA, an employer may, upon a request of an employee,

한 것은 내국인 근로자와의 사이에 차등제도를 설정한 것이다(1998.03.27, 대법 97다 19725)

　외국인 조종사에 대하여는 월급여 속에 퇴직금 상당액을 포함시켜 지급하기로 합의하였다고 하더라도, 이는 결국 외국인 조종사에 대하여는 퇴직시에 퇴직금을 지급하지 않는다는 것이므로, 퇴직시에 퇴직금을 지급받는 내국인 근로자와의 사이에 구 근로기준법 제28조 제2항이 금지하는 차등제도를 설정한 것이라 할 것이고, 따라서 원고는 피고에 대하여 최다수 근로자에 대한 퇴직금제도임이 기록상 분명한 피고의 취업규칙에 따른 퇴직금을 청구할 수 있다.

　퇴직금 지급에 관하여 누진제를 적용하도록 규정한 국내 직원에 대한 취업규칙과 달리 해외 기능공에 대해서는 개별 근로계약에 의해 단수제를 적용한 경우, 퇴직금차등제도 금지 규정에 위반된다(1997.11.28, 대법 97다 24511)

　영업양도나 기업합병 등에 의하여 근로계약 관계가 포괄적으로 승계된 경우에 근로자의 종전 근로계약상의 지위도 그대로 승계되는 것이므로, 승계 후의 퇴직금규정이 승계 전의 퇴직금규정보다 근로자에게 불리하다면 근로기준법 제95조 제1항 소정의 당해 근로자집단의 집단적인 의사결정 방법에 의한 동의 없이는 승계 후의 퇴직금규정을 적용할 수 없다(1995.12.26, 대법 95다41659)

V. 퇴직금 지급방법

중간정산 후 퇴직금 감액사유가 발생한 경우(퇴직금 누진제 폐지) 퇴직금 감액규정을 적용하여 중간정산 퇴직금액과 최종 퇴직금액을 산정하고 이미 지급된 금액을 공제하여 퇴직금을 지급할 수 있다(2004.04.08, 임금정책과 -1173)

　근로기준법 제34조 제1항의 규정에 의하여 사용자의 퇴직금 지급의무는 근로계약이 종료된 때에 발생하는 것임. 다만, 동조 제3항에 의하여 근로자의 요구가 있는 때에는 근로자가 퇴직하기 전에 당해 근로자가 계속 근로한

even before his retirement, pay severance pay calculated on the basis of consecutive years of employment. Interim severance pay does not have different characteristics from normal severance pay. In case where reason to reduce severance pay occurred after payment of interim severance pay, the company shall apply to the reduced severance pay system and calculate previously paid interim severance pay and final amount of severance pay, and then the company may pay severance pay (refund of overcharged severance pay) after deducting the amount it already paid in the interim severance pay. (Supreme court 2001 da 54977, May 16, 2003)

Is it possible to pay interim severance pay for entire employees with the consent obtained from the majority of employees? (Feb 20, 2002, Wages 68200-111)

According to Article 34 (3) of the Labor Standards Act, an employer may, upon a request of an employee, even before his retirement, pay a severance pay calculated on the basis of consecutive years of employment. In this case, the number of consecutive years of employment for the calculation of a severance pay after such advance payment shall be reckoned anew from the moment of the latest adjustment of balances. Although this interim severance pay was established previously for the relevant regulation or criteria of the interim severance pay in the collective bargaining agreement or rules of employment, it shall require individual employees' concrete demands before its implementation.

Accordingly, with consent from more than 50% of total employees, the employer cannot satisfy the requirements needed for interim severance pay.

Even though the company has paid some amount as severance pay in the wages paid every month, it cannot be accepted as payment of severance pay. (Mar 11, 2005, Supreme court 2005 do 467)

The severance pay stipulated in Article 34 (1) of the Labor Standards Act occurs on the condition of termination of employment relations, and, in principle, it will not occur during the middle of the labor contract. If the employer agreed with the employee on payment of certain amount of money as name of severance pay inside wages paid every month, this cannot be valid as payment of severance pay stipulated in Article 34 (1) of the Labor Standards Act.

기간에 대한 퇴직금을 미리 정산하여 지급할 수 있으나, 중간정산 퇴직금이라고 하여 퇴직금과 별도의 성격을 갖는 것은 아니므로, 달리 볼 특별한 사정이 없는 한 퇴직금 중간정산이 있은 후에 퇴직급여규정에 정하고 있는 퇴직금 감액사유가 발생한 경우에는 이미 중간정산된 부분에 대하여도 퇴직급여 규정상의 감액규정이 적용되는 것이고, 사용자로서는 중간정산된 근로기간과 그 후의 근로시간에 대하여 각각 위 감액규정을 적용하여 중간정산 퇴직금액과 최종 퇴직금액을 산정하고 여기에서 이미 지급된 금액을 공제하고 퇴직금을 지급(초과지급의 경우에는 환수) 할 수 있다고 사료됨(대법 2001다54977, 2003.5.16. 참조).

퇴직금 중간정산을 집단적 동의를 받아 시행할 수 있는지(2002.02.20, 임금 68200-111)

　근로기준법 제34조제3항의 규정에 의거 사용자는 근로자의 요구가 있는 경우에는 근로자가 퇴직하기 전에 당해 근로자가 계속근로한 기간에 대한 퇴직금을 미리 정산하여 지급할 수 있으며, 이 경우 미리 정산하여 지급한 후의 퇴직금 산정을 위한 계속근로년수는 정산시점부터 새로이 기산하도록 정하고 있음.

　이러한 퇴직금 중간정산은 단체협약이나 취업규칙 등에 퇴직금 중간정산을 실시할 수 있는 근거나 기준을 정하고 있는 경우에도 개별 근로자의 구체적 요구가 있어야만 시행할 수 있는 것임.

　따라서, 전 근로자의 50%이상의 동의만으로는 퇴직금 중간정산의 요건을 적법하게 갖추었다고 볼 수는 없을 것임.

근로관계가 계속되는 동안 매월 지급되는 임금 속에 퇴직금이라는 명목의 금원을 지급하였다고 하여도 퇴직금 지급으로서의 효력은 없다(2005.03.11, 대법 2005도 467)

　근로기준법 제34조 제1항에서 규정한 퇴직금이란 퇴직이라는 근로관계의 종료를 요건으로 하여 비로소 발생하는 것으로 근로계약이 존속하는 동안에는 원칙으로 퇴직금 지급의무는 발생할 여지가 없는 것이므로 사용자와 근로자들 사이에 매월 지급받는 임금 속에 퇴직금이란 명목으로 일정한 금원을 지급

It is null and void due to violation of the Labor Standards Act if an employee made a special contract to give up a right of requesting severance pay or not to make a civil suit. (Aug 23, 2002, Supreme court 2001 da 41568)

Severance pay is the remuneration characteristic of differed wages to be paid in return for continuous employment to the employee who retires after serving a certain period of time. The concrete right to request severance pay occurs on the condition of the fact, termination of continuous employment. It is null and void due to violation of the Labor Standards Act, compulsory regulation, if an employee previously made a special contract that the employee would give up a right of requesting severance pay in the time of retirement or would not make a civil suit.

Section 11. Korean labor law: Criteria for Determining Whether Workplace Harassment Has Occurred

I. Introduction

The Workplace Anti-Bullying Act was enacted in January 2019 and came into effect in July of the same year. Three incidents contributed to enactment of this law. The first case is known as the nut rage incident involving an executive of Korean Air in 2014. Vice President Cho 00, a daughter of Korean Air's owners, exploded in rage that her Macadamia nuts were served in a bag, not on a plate, verbally abusing the flight attendant and the chief flight attendant and forcing both to kneel and apologize to her. Ms. Cho then ordered the planeheading for a runway at New York's John F. Kennedy Airport to fly to Seoulto return to the boarding gate where she ordered the chief flight attendant to get out. Then the plane departed.[181] In 2019, Korean Air was ordered by the court to pay 70 million won to former chief flight attendant Park 00, for the personnel disadvantages received as a result of the incident.[182] The second case involves a nurse who killed herself, leaving a suicide note that said, "Workplace harassment makes it difficult to work." In March 2019, the Labor Welfare Corporation's Disease Judgment

---

[181] Moon, Kangboon, Is this workplace harassment? 2020. Gadian, p. 34.
[182] Seoul High Court ruling on Nov. 5, 2019.

하기로 약정하고 사용자가 이를 지급하였다고 하여도 그것은 근로기준법 제34조 제1항에서 정하는 퇴직금 지급으로서의 효력은 없다.

퇴직금청구권을 포기하거나 민사소송을 제기하지 않겠다는 부제소특약은 근로기준법에 위반되어 무효이다(2002.08.23, 대법 2001다41568)

   퇴직금은 사용자가 일정기간을 계속하여 근로하고 퇴직하는 근로자에게 그 계속근로에 대한 대가로서 지급하는 후불적 임금의 성질을 띤 금원으로서 구체적인 퇴직금청구권은 계속근로가 끝나는 퇴직이라는 사실을 요건으로 하여 발생되는 것인 바, 최종 퇴직시 발생하는 퇴직금청구권을 사전에 포기하거나 사전에 그에 관한 민사상 소송을 제기하지 않겠다는 부제소특약을 하는 것은 강행법규인 근로기준법에 위반되어 무효이다.

제11절 직장 내 괴롭힘 예방

I. 문제의 소재

   직장내 괴롭힘 방지법이 2019년 1월에 제정되어 동년 7월부터 시행되었다. 직장내 괴롭힘 방지법 제정에 결정적인 계기가 되었던 3가지의 관련된 사건이 사회적 이슈가 되었다. 첫 번째 사건은 2014년, 대항한공의 '땅콩 회항' 사건이다. 대한항공 소유주 일가인 조○○ 부사장이 마카다미아(Macadamia) 땅콩을 봉지 채 서비스한 것을 문제 삼아 승무원에게 폭언을 하고 사무장을 불러 무릎을 꿇리고 빌도록 했는데, 그래도 화가 안 풀려 뉴욕공항에서 서울로 향하던 항공기를 돌려 사무장을 내려놓은 뒤 출발한 사건이다.[181] 2019년 이 사건으로 인사상 불이익을 받은 박○○ 전 사무장에게 대한항공이 7000만원 배상을 해야 한다는 판결이 나왔다[182] 두 번째 사건은 2018년 2월 서울아산병원의 신입 간호사가 태움(병원 내 집단 괴롭힘) 때문에 일하기 힘들다는

---
181) 문강분, 이것도 직장내 괴롭힘 인가요? 2020. 가디언, 34면.
182) 서울고등법원 2019.11.5.선고 2019나2004517 판결.

Committee recognized the incident as an industrial accident caused by workplace harassment. In the third case, at the end of 2018, a video surfaced of Yang 00, chairman of WeDisk, a start-up IT company, calling in an ex-employee and brutally assaulting in the office. Yang is currently in prison for this and illegal business activities.[183]

Until recently, investigation and treatment of workplace harassment has been entirely up to companies.[184] There were only two related rules when the Workplace Anti-Bullying Act was enacted. First, rules of employment had to include procedures for dealing with workplace harassment and for remedy. Second, employers were to be punished if they disadvantage those who report harassment in the workplace. The procedures for handling reports of bullying were entirely up to the employer, which did little to actually resolve the problem. Accordingly, in April 2021, the following five employer obligations were added in amendments to the relevant laws. Employers are now obligated to:

1) Prohibit bullying in the workplace,
2) Conduct objective investigations of reported bullying incidents in the workplace,
3) Take appropriate actions to protect alleged victims,
4) Establish and carry out disciplinary action in response to bullying in the workplace, and
5) Comply with confidentiality requirements related to harassment investigations in the workplace, with fines levied for negligence.

When determining whether bullying has occurred in the workplace, the criteria are somewhat complex given the blur between the employer's discretionary personnel rights and the employee's personal rights. I will take a look at the related details and criteria for judgement herein.

II. Responsibilities of the Employer

The Workplace Harassment Prevention Act was introduced in January 2009 as a revision to the Labor Standards Act. At that time the purpose of the legislation was to prevent workplace harassment and to suggest voluntary measures to prevent recurrence by rationally handling harassment incidents within the company. The definition of workplace harassment and the employer's obligations to deal with it were stipulated through the introduction of Chapter 76-2 of the Labor Standards Act. In Article 93 of the Labor Standards Act "⑪ Matters concerning the

---

[183] Moon, Kangboon, Is this workplace harassment? 2020. Gadian, pp. 35-36.
[184] Shin, Kwonchul, Legal Concepts and Criteria for Determining the Occurrence of Bullying in the Workplace, Labor Law (69), Korean Labor Law Association, Mar. 2019, p. 228.

유서를 남기고 자살한 사건이다. 이 사건에 대해 2019년 3월 근로복지공단의 질병판정위원회는 직장내 괴롭힘으로 인해 발생한 산업재해로 인정하였다. 세 번째 사건은 2018년 말 신생 IT 기업 위디스크의 양○○ 회장이 퇴사한 직원을 불러 사무실에서 무차별 폭행을 하는 동영상이 공개된 사건이다. 그는 현재 이 사건과 더불어 불법 기업활동으로 법정 구속되어 형을 살고 있다.[183]

직장내 괴롭힘에 대한 조사와 처리는 전적으로 회사에 맡겨져 있다.[184] 이 법 제정 시에는 관련 규칙이 두 가지만 있었다. 첫째 직장내 괴롭힘에 대한 내용과 구제절차를 취업규칙의 필수기재 사항으로 하였고, 둘째 직장내 괴롭힘을 신고한 자에게 불이익을 주는 경우 해당 사업주를 처벌하도록 하는 내용이었다. 이러한 취업규칙에 근거하여 괴롭힘 사건을 처리하는 방식은 사업주에게 전적으로 맡겨 놓았기 때문에 실질적 문제해결이 되지 못했다. 이에 2021년 4월 관련법 개정을 통해, 사용자의 실질적인 직장내 괴롭힘에 대한 국가적 관여를 강제하면서 다음의 5가지 사항을 추가하였다.
(i) 사업주의 직장내 괴롭힘 금지의무,
(ii) 직장내 괴롭힘 사건에 대해 객관적 조사 실시의무,
(iii) 피해근로자에 대한 적절한 보호조치의무,
(iv) 직장내 괴롭힘 행위자에 대한 필요한 징계조치,
(v) 직장내 괴롭힘 조사와 관련된 내용에 대해 비밀준수 의무 등 신설조항과 과태료 조항의 도입이다.

직장내 괴롭힘을 판단하면서 사용자의 재량적 인사권과 근로자의 인격권 사이에서 직장내 괴롭힘 판단기준에 대해 다소 애매모호한 점이 많아 다음에서는 이와 관련된 내용과 판단기준에 대해 구체적으로 살펴보고자 한다.

Ⅱ. 사업주의 책임

직장 내 괴롭힘 방지법은 근로기준법의 개정으로 2009년 1월에 도입되었다. 당시 입법의 목적은 직장 내 괴롭힘 문제를 예방하고 괴롭힘 사건 발생시 회사 내에서 합리적으로 처리하여 재발방지를 막기위한 자율적인 조치였다. 근로

---

[183] 문강분, 위 출판물, 35-36면.
[184] 신권철, 직장 내 괴롭힘의 법적 개념과 요건, 노동법학(69), 한국노동법학회, 2019.3. 228면.

prevention of workplace harassment and measures to be taken in case of occurrence" were introduced as essential items in the rules of employment. There was a penalty provision only for cases where the employer disadvantageously treated a worker or victim who reported the fact of harassment. After examining the effectiveness of prevention of workplace harassment for the previous two years, this law was found to be not effective, as the procedures and methods of dealing with workplace harassment were left entirely to the discretion of the employer.[185]

In order to correct this, in April 2021, the Workplace Harassment Prevention Act was reinforced with provisions to punish employers who violate their duty to take measures when workplace harassment occurs. A new regulation was established to impose a fine of up to 10 million won in cases where an employer or relative family member is a perpetrator of workplace harassment (Article 116 of the LSA). In particular, Article 76-3 of the Labor Standards Act specifically describes the employer's obligations in case of harassment, with provisions for fines in cases of non-compliance. In an instance of workplace harassment,

① there must be objective investigation to confirm the facts,
② protective measures on behalf of the victim must be established if the issue is recognized as harassment,
③ necessary disciplinary measures against offenders must be taken, and
④ there is a prohibition of adverse treatment to prevent secondary damage, along with an obligation to maintain confidentiality. Practical measures for these steps are suggested.

1. Obligation of objective investigation

When a report of workplace harassment is received by or recognized by the employer, a duty of objective investigation is imposed on the employer (Article 76-3 of the LSA, Paragraph 2). This is a mandatory rule that imposes a fine for negligence when violated. The purpose here is to prevent the employer from conducting biased research.[186]

2. Obligation to take appropriate measures for victims when workplace harassment is confirmed

---

[185] Lee Sang-gon, A Study on Improvements to the Workplace Harassment Law, Ajou Graduate School Ph.D. thesis, August 2020. Page 116.
[186] Ministry of Employment and Labor, March 24, 2021 press release, Seven amendment bills including the Wage Bond Guarantee Act passed by the National Assembly plenary session

기준법 제76장의2 도입으로 직장 내 괴롭힘의 정의와 사용자의 직장 내 처리 의무를 명시하였고, 동법 제93조에 취업규칙의 필수적 기재사항에 직장 내 괴롭힘의 예방 및 발생 시 조치 등에 관한 사항을 도입하였다. 예외적으로 사용자가 직장 내 괴롭힘 발생 사실을 신고한 근로자나 피해근로자에게 불이익 처우를 할 경우에 한해서만 벌칙 규정을 두고 있었다. 지난 2년 동안 직장 내 괴롭힘 방지 효과를 검토할 때, 이에 대한 처리절차와 처리방식이 전적으로 사업주의 재량에 맡겨져 있다 보니, 법의 실효성이 없었다.[185] 이러한 문제를 해결하기 위하여 2021년 4월 직장 내 괴롭힘 발생시 조치의무를 위반한 사업주를 처벌하는 조항을 갖춘 직장 내 괴롭힘 방지법이 보강되었다. 그 내용은 사업주나 사업주의 친족 근로자가 직장 내 괴롭힘의 가해자가 된 경우 1000만 원 까지 과태료 부과 규정이 신설되었다(근기법 제116조). 특히, 근로기준법 제76조3에 각 괴롭힘 발생시 사업주의 의무를 구체적으로 기술하고, 불이행 시 과태료 규정이 적용된다. 앞으로 직장 내 괴롭힘 발생시
① 사실확인을 위한 객관적 조사,
② 괴롭힘으로 인정될 경우 피해근로자 보호조치,
③ 행위자에 대한 필요한 징계조치, 그리고
④ 제2차 피해를 예방하기 위한 불리한 처우 금지조치와 비밀유지 의무에 대한 현실적 조치를 제시하고 있다.

1. 객관적 조사의무

직장 내 괴롭힘이 사용자에게 접수되거나 이를 인지한 경우 사용자에게 객관적인 조사의무를 부과하고 있다(근기법 제76조의3, 제2항). 이는 위반시 과태료 처분이 있는 의무규정이다. 그 목적은 사용자가 편향적인 조사를 하지 않도록 하기 위함이다.[186]

2. 직장 내 괴롭힘 확인시 피해자를 위한 적절한 조치의무

---

[185] 이상곤, 직장 내 괴롭힘 법제의 개선방안 연구, 아주대학원 박사학위 논문, 2020.8. 116면.
[186] 고용노동부, 2021. 3. 24. 보도자료, 임금채권보장법 등 7개 개정 법률안 국회 본회의 통과

In the provision of fines for negligence of workplace harassment, Chapter 76-3, paragraph 4 stipulates that if it is necessary to protect the victim when workplace harassment is confirmed, for orders changing the place of work, change of job, and paid leave to the victim, etc., appropriate measures should be taken.

3. Obligation to prohibit unfavorable treatment

Employers shall not dismiss or give other unfavorable treatment to workers, victims, etc. who have reported the occurrence of workplace harassment (Article 76-3 of the LSA, paragraph 6). Violation of this rule is punishable by imprisonment for not more than 3 years or a fine not exceeding 30 million won. Paragraph 6 of Article 14 of the Equal Employment Act prohibits unfavorable punishment for workers or victims who report sexual harassment in the workplace, and describes possible prohibition in detail as follows below. This also applies to workplace harassment.[187]

1. Dismissal, removal from office, discharge or any other disadvantageous treatment corresponding to the loss of status;
2. Inappropriate personnel actions, such as disciplinary punishment, suspension from office, salary reduction, demotion, or restrictions on promotion;
3. Failure to assign duties, reassignment of duties, or any other personnel actions against the wishes of the relevant person;
4. Discrimination in performance evaluations or peer reviews, or differential payment of wages, bonuses, etc. following such discrimination;
5. Restrictions on opportunities of education and training for the development and improvement of vocational skills;
6. Engagement in any act of causing mental or physical harm, such as group bullying, assault, or verbal abuse, or neglect of an occurrence of such act;
7. Any other disadvantageous treatment against the employee who reports the occurrence of sexual harassment or the harassed employee, etc.

4. Confidentiality Obligation

The Act stipulates that a person who has investigated the occurrence of

---

[187] Lee, Jaehyun, Establishment of a system for countermeasures against workplace harassment and improvement of organizational culture, Labor Law Forum, No. 34, Nov. 2021, page 239.

직장 내 괴롭힘의 과태료 규정에 있어 제76조의 3에 있어 제4항은 직장 내 괴롭힘이 확인된 경우 피해 근로자를 보호하기 위하여 필요한 경우 해당 피해 근로자 등에 대하여 근무장소의 변경, 배치전환, 유급휴가의 명령 등 적절한 조치를 하여야 한다 고 규정하고 있다.

3. 불리한 처우 금지의무

사용자는 직장 내 괴롭힘 발생사실을 신고한 근로자 및 피해근로자 등에게 해고나 그 밖의 불리한 처우를 하여서는 아니된다(제76조의3, 제6항). 이 규정을 위반할 경우에는 3년이하의 징역 또는 3천만 원 이하의 벌금에 처한다고 규정하고 있다. 남녀고용평등법 제14조의 제6항은 직장 내 성희롱 발생 사실에 대해 신고한 근로자나 피해근로자에게 불리한 처벌을 금지하는 내용을 규정하면서, 그 금지 규정의 내용을 다음과 같이 구체적으로 기술하고 있다. 이 규정은 직장 내 괴롭힘에서도 동일하게 적용된다.[187]

1. 파면, 해임, 해고, 그 밖에 신분상실에 해당하는 불이익 조치
2. 징계, 정직, 감봉, 강등, 승진 제한 등 부당한 인사조치
3. 직무 미부여, 직무 재배치, 그 밖에 본인의 의사에 반하는 인사조치
4. 성과평가 또는 동료평가 등에서 차별이나 그에 따른 임금 또는 상여금 등의 차별지급
5. 직업능력 개발 및 향상을 위한 교육훈련 기회의 제한
6. 집단 따돌림, 폭행 또는 폭언 등 정신적·신체적 손상을 가져오는 행위를 하거나 그 행위의 발생을 방치하는 행위
7. 그 밖에 신고를 한 근로자 및 피해근로자등의 의사에 반하는 불리한 처우

4. 비밀준수의무

---

[187] 이재현, 직장 내 괴롭힘 대응조치 체계구축과 조직문화의 개선, 노동법포럼, 제34호, 2021.11. 239면.

workplace harassment, a person who has received a report on the investigation, and a person who has participated in any other investigation process shall not divulge the information learned in the course of the investigation to other persons against the will of the victim, etc. (Article 76-3 of the LSA, paragraph 6). In the case of sexual harassment at work and related incidents, it was judged that the person carrying out the investigation had the obligation to compensate for non-compliance with the duty of confidentiality. This is in consideration of the fact that, if the person conducting the investigation does not comply with confidentiality, there is a high probability of secondary damage, which may lead to the victim being unable to even report sexual harassment.[188]

<Obligation of employer to take action for workplace harassment (Article 76-3 of the LSA)>

Contents	Penalty
1: Anyone can report if anyone becomes aware of workplace harassment	None
2: When an employer receives a report or recognizes that workplace harassment has occurred, an objective investigation must be conducted without delay to confirm the facts. A fine of not more than 5 million won for non-compliance.	Not more than 5mil. KRW
3: The employer shall take appropriate measures to protect the victim or the alleged victim during the investigation period.	None
4: When workplace harassment is confirmed, the employer shall take appropriate measures upon the request of the victim.	Not more than 5mil. KRW
5: When it is confirmed that workplace harassment has occurred, the employer must take necessary measures against the offender without delay. In this case, the opinion of the injured worker must be heard before taking any measures such as disciplinary action.	Not more than 5mil. KRW

---

[188] Seoul High Court ruling on December 18, 2015: 2015na2003264.

사용자는 직장 내 괴롭힘 발생 사실을 조사한 사람, 조사 내용을 보고받은 사람 및 그 밖의 조사 과정에 참여한 사람은 해당 조사 과정에서 알게 된 비밀을 피해근로자 등의 의사에 반하여 다른 사람들에게 누설하여서는 아니된다고 규정하고 있다(제76의3, 제6항). 직장 내 성희롱 사건과 관련 판례에서도 조사업무 수행자가 비밀유지를 의무를 지키지 않는 것에 대해 손해배상 의무를 진다고 판단하였다. 이는 조사업무를 수행하는 사람이 비밀준수를 하지 않을 경우 상당한 수준의 2차 피해가 발생할 개연성이 있고, 이는 피해근로자가 성희롱을 신고조차 못하게 하는 것으로 이어질 수 있다는 점을 염두에 둔 것이다.[188]

<직장 내 괴롭힘 발생시 사용자의 조치의무 (근기법 제76조의3)>

내 용	벌칙조항
1항: 누구든지 직장 내 괴롭힘 발생 사실을 알게 된 경우 사용자에게 신고 가능	없음
2항: 사용자는 신고를 접수하거나 직장 내 괴롭힘 발생 사실을 인지한 경우 지체없이 사실확인을 위한 객관적 조사를 실시해야 함.	500만 원 이하의 과태료
3항: 사용자는 조사 기간 동안 피해자 또는 피해 주장 근로자를 보호하기 위하여 적절한 조치를 하여야 함.	없음.
4항: 사용자는 직장 내 괴롭힘 발생 사실이 확인된 때에는 피해근로자가 요청하면 적절한 조치를 하여야 함.	500만 원 이하의 과태료
5항: 사용자는 직장 내 괴롭힘 발생 사실이 확인된 때에는 지체없이 행위자에 대하여 필요한 조치를 해야 함. 이 경우 징계 등의 조치를 하기 전에 피해 근로자의 의견을 들어야 함.	500만 원 이하의 과태료

---

[188] 서울고등법원 2015. 12. 18. 선고 2015나2003264 판결.

6: Article 6: Employers shall not dismiss or otherwise adversely treat workers or victims who report workplace harassment.	Imprisonment for less than 3 years or up to 30mil. KRW
7: A person who has investigated the occurrence of workplace harassment, a person who has received a report on the investigation, and any other person who has participated in the investigation process shall not divulge the information learned during the investigation process to others against the will of the victim.	Not more than 5mil. KRW

III. Factors in Determining Whether Workplace Harassment Has Occurred

1. Concept of workplace harassment

The Labor Standards Act (Article 76-2) prohibits harassment in the workplace, which is defined as an act of inflicting physical or mental pain on other workers or worsening the working environment through an abuse of the superior position of the employer or relationships in the workplace. There are four components to workplace harassment:

(i) Defined target: employer or employee,
(ii) Abuse of position: Using position or work relationship against the target,
(iii) Repeated actions towards the target, or assigning of tasks, unnecessary for performance of contracted work: Actions beyond the appropriate scope of work,
(iv) Infringements of human rights and/or degradation of the working environment: Any action that causes physical or mental pain or worsens the working environment.

All four factors above must be met for an incident to qualify as workplace harassment.

2. Explanation of the factors in harassment[189]

(1) Defined target: Employer or employee

---

[189] Ministry of Employment and Labor, Manual for Judgment and Prevention of Harassment in the Workplace, 2019, pp. 24-27.

6항: 사용자는 직장 내 괴롭힘 발생 사실을 신고한 근로자 및 피해근로자에게 해고나 그 밖의 불리한 처우를 해서는 아니됨.	3년이하 징역/ 3천만 이하 벌금
7항: 직장 내 괴롭힘 발생 사실을 조사한 사람, 조사내용을 보고받은 사람, 그 밖에 조사과정에 참여한 사람은 조사과정에서 알게 된 비밀을 피해근로자의 의사에 반하여 다른 사람에게 누설하여서는 아니됨.	500만 원 이하의 과태료

Ⅲ. 직장내 괴롭힘의 판단요소

1. 직장내 괴롭힘의 개념

근로기준법(제76조의2)는 직장 내 괴롭힘을 금지하고 있다. 직장 내 괴롭힘을 사용자 또는 근로자는 직장에서의 지위 또는 관계 등의 우위를 이용하여 업무상 적정범위를 넘어 다른 근로자에게 신체적·정신적 고통을 주거나 근무환경을 악화시키는 행위로 규정하고 있다. 직장 내 괴롭힘의 구성요소는 다음의 4가지이다.

(i) 주체: 사용자 또는 근로자,
(ii) 지위의 활용: 직장에서의 지위나 관계 등에서의 우위,
(iii) 업무일탈: 업무의 적정범위 이상의 행위,
(iv) 인적, 환경적 침해행위: 근로자에게 신체적, 정신적 고통을 주거나 근무환경을 악화시키는 행위.

위의 4가지 요소를 모두 충족해야만 직장내 괴롭힘에 해당한다.

2. 괴롭힘의 판단요소[189]

(1) 주체: 사용자 또는 근로자

---
[189] 고용노동부, 직장내 괴롭힘 판단 및 예방 대응 매뉴얼, 2019. 24-27면.

The Labor Standards Act (Article 2 (2)), defines an employer as someone in charge of managing the business, or a person who acts on behalf of the employer with respect to matters related to workers. Someone in charge of managing the business does not have to be the business owner but is in charge of general business management, and refers to someone who represents a business externally after comprehensive delegation from the business owner for all or part of the business management. Anyone who acts on matters related to workers for the business owner is delegated authority from the business owner or the person in charge of business management and is involved in making personnel decisions, such as hiring and dismissal of those within their own realm of responsibility, and directing and supervising the workers on the job, and working conditions. It also refers to someone who can decide and execute matters related to working conditions. Relatives of the employer are included in the scope of employer with revision of the Labor Standards Act in 2021 (Article 116). Employer includes those with an advantage over other workers, such as via position or work relationship.

In the worker dispatch relationship, according to the Act on the Protection, etc., of Dispatched Workers, a bullying agent in the workplace can also include an employer who directly supervises and directs the work of a dispatched worker.

(2) Abuse of position: Using position or work relationship, etc., against the target

Harassment in the workplace mainly occurs in places where there is a strong organizational culture or authoritarian hierarchy. It occurs mainly in the form of actions by people with superior social or economic status using their power and superior status against those less socially privileged.[190]

A superior relationship refers to one in which it is likely to be difficult for those in lower positions to resist any bullying behavior. An abuse of position refers to an offender using their superiority against someone in a command-and-control relationship, or even if it is not a direct command-order relationship, it is to use the higher position or rank system. Workplace harassment does not occur unless it involves the abuse of superiority in position or relationship.

(3) Repeated actions towards the target, or assigning of tasks, unnecessary for performance of contracted work: Actions beyond the appropriate scope of work

Actions that are inappropriate and recognized as exceeding the scope of work can

---

[190] Lee, Soo-Yeon, The Concept of Workplace Harassment and Judgment Criteria, Ewha Gender Law 10(2), Ewha Womans University Gender Law Research Institute, Aug. 2018, p. 119.

직장 내 괴롭힘에서 금지의 주체는 사용자와 근로자이다. 근로기준법 (제2조제2항)에서 사용자라고 하면 사업주 또는 사업 경영 담당자, 그 밖에 근로자에 관한 사항에 대하여 사업주를 위하여 행위 하는 자를 말한다. 사업경영담당자는 사업주가 아니면서 사업경영 일반을 책임지는 자로서, 사업주로부터 사업 경영의 전부 또는 일부에 대해 포괄적인 위임을 받고 대외적으로 사업을 대표하거나 대리하는 자를 말한다. 근로자에 관한 사항에 대해 사업주를 위하여 행위하는 자는 사업주 또는 사업경영 담당자로부터 권한을 위임받아 자신의 책임 아래 근로자 채용, 해고 등 인사처분을 할 수 있고, 직무상 근로자의 업무를 지휘, 감독하며 근로조건에 관한 사항을 결정하고 집행할 수 있는 자를 말한다. 특히, 2021년 근로기준법 개정을 통해서 사용자의 범위에 사용자의 친족도 포함하였다(제116조). 여기서 금지의 주체인 근로자라고 하면 다른 근로자에 대해 직장에서의 지위나 관계 등의 우위를 가진 자를 말한다.

근로자파견관계에서는 파견법에 따라 파견 중인 근로자의 경우 직접 업무를 감독하고 지시하는 사용사업주도 직장 내 괴롭힘 행위자로 인정된다.

(2) 지위의 활용: 직장에서의 지위나 관계 등에서의 우위

직장내 괴롭힘은 조직문화나 권위주의적 위계질서가 강한 곳에서 주로 발생한다. 이는 사회적 경제적으로 우월한 지위에 있는 사람들이 사회적 약자를 대상으로 권력형, 우월적 지위를 이용한 행위의 형태로 주로 발생한다.[190]

우위성이라고 하면 피해자가 괴롭힘 행위에 대해 저항 또는 거절이 어려울 가능성이 높은 관계를 의미한다. 지위의 우위는 괴롭힘 행위자가 지휘명령 관계에서 상위에 있거나 직접적인 지휘명령 관계가 아니어도 직위, 직급체계상 상위에 있음을 이용하는 것이다. 관계의 우위는 행위자가 피해자와의 관계에서 우위에 있는지는 특정 요소에 대해 사업장 내에서 통상적으로 이루어지는 평가를 바탕으로 판단한다. 따라서 직장에서의 지위나 관계 등의 우위를 이용한 것이 아니라면 직장 내 괴롭힘에 해당되지 않는다.

(3) 업무일탈: 업무의 적정범위 이상의 행위

업무의 적정범위를 넘는 것으로 인정되는 행위는 다음의 7가지로 분류할

---
[190] 이수연, 직장 괴롭힘의 개념과 판단기준에 관한 판례법리, 이화젠더법학 10(2), 이화여자대학교 젠더법학연구소, 2018.8. 119면.

be classified into the following seven categories.
1) Violence and intimidation: Actions that involve direct physical force or the threat of physical force, such as directly or indirectly inflicting violence on an object.
2) Verbal behavior, such as violent, abusive language or gossip: If it is determined that gossip is spread to a third party, such as in an open place, to damage the victim's reputation, it is beyond the appropriate scope for work. In particular, continuous and repetitive verbal abuse or abusive language can seriously harm the victim's personal rights and cause mental pain, so engaging in it constitutes an act beyond the appropriate scope for work.
3) Orders to perform tasks related to assistance with non-work affairs: These are orders that exceed the appropriate scope of work and beyond what is considered normally acceptable in human relations. Examples include continuous and repetitive instructions to run personal errands related to daily life.
4) Bullying and exclusion: Intentional disregard and exclusion in the process of performing work are acts that are beyond the appropriate scope of work and beyond the social norm. Examples include intentionally not providing important information related to work or excluding someone entitled to participation in the decision-making process without justifiable reason, forcing someone to move or leave the department without good reason, discriminating against someone in training, promotion, rewards, or routine benefits without good reason, etc.
5) Repetitive instructions for work unrelated to the employment contract: If instructions are given to an employee repeatedly to do work that is unrelated to that specified at the time the labor contract was signed, and if a justifiable reason is not recognized, it amounts to an act beyond the appropriate scope for work. Examples including menial tasks only when an employee was hired for specific other tasks, or giving the employee little work without justifiable reason.
6) Assigning an excessive amount of work: If the action is judged to be inappropriate, such as not allowing even the minimum amount of time physically necessary for the task, without unavoidable reasons, it is beyond the appropriate scope of work.
7) Interfering with smooth business performance: Actions that interfere with smooth business performance, such as not providing essential equipment (computers, telephones, etc.) necessary for business, or blocking access to the Internet or

수 있다.
1) 폭행 및 협박 행위: 신체에 직접 폭력을 가하거나 물건에 폭력을 가하는 등 직, 간접의 물리적 힘을 행사하는 폭행이나 협박행위는 업무상 적정범위를 넘은 행위이다.
2) 폭언, 욕설, 험담 등 언어적 행위: 공개된 장소에서 이루어지는 등 제3자에게 전파되어 피해자의 명예를 훼손할 정도인 것으로 판단되면 업무상 적정범위를 넘은 행위이다. 특히, 지속 반복적인 폭언이나 욕설은 피해자의 인격권을 심각하게 해치고 정신적인 고통을 유발할 수 있으므로 업무상 적정범위를 넘는 행위이다.
3) 사적 용무 지시: 개인적인 심부름을 반복적으로 시키는 등 인간관계에서 용인될 수 있는 부탁의 수준을 넘어 행해지는 것은 업무상 적정범위를 넘은 행위이다. 예)사적인 심부름 등 개인적인 일상생활과 관련된 일을 하도록 지속적, 반복적으로 지시하는 것
4) 집단 따돌림과 배제시킴: 업무수행 과정에서의 의도적 무시와 배제는 사회통념을 벗어난 업무상 적정 범위를 넘어선 행위이다. 예) 정당한 사유없이 업무와 관련된 중요한 정보제공이나 의사결정 과정에서 배제시키는 것. 정당한 이유없이 부서이동 또는 퇴사를 강요하는 것. 정당한 이유없이 훈련, 승진, 보상, 일상적인 대우 등에서 차별하는 것 등.
5) 업무와 무관한 일을 반복 지시: 근로계약 체결 시 명시했던 업무와 무관한 일을 근로자의 의사에 반하여 지시하는 행위가 반복되고 그 지시에 정당한 사유가 인정되지 않는다면 업무상 적정범위를 넘어선 행위이다. 예)근로계약서 등에 명시되어 있지 않은 허드렛일만 시키거나 일을 거의 주지 않는 것.
6) 과도한 업무 부여: 업무상 불가피한 사정이 없음에도 불구하고 해당업무 수행에 대해 물리적으로 필요한 최소한의 시간 마저도 허락하지 않는 등 그 행위가 타당하지 않은 것으로 판단되면 업무상 적정 범위를 넘어선 행위이다.
7) 원활한 업무수행을 방해하는 행위: 업무에 필요한 주요 비품(컴퓨터, 전화 등)을 제공하지 않거나, 인터넷 사내 인트라넷 접속을 차단하는 등 원활한 업무수행을 방해하는 행위는 사회 통념을 벗어난 행위로서 업무상 적정

company intranet, are beyond social norms and inappropriate for business.

(4) Infringements of human rights and/or degradation of the working environment

This refers to actions of an employer or a worker that inflict physical or mental pain on another worker through harassment in the workplace or worsening the working environment. It can be said that the working environment has been degraded if an employer intentionally moves certain workers to work in front of the washroom, embarrassing them or creating an environment in which workers cannot perform their duties properly. Intention of the offender is not a prerequisite to determining that actions directly cause physical or mental pain or worsen the working environment.

IV. Criteria for Determining Workplace Harassment

1. Conflict between the employer's right to order work and the employee's personal rights

In determining whether or not bullying has occurred in the workplace, there are cases in which the employer's right to order work and the employee's personal rights are in conflict. In labor disputes, an employer's exercise of personnel rights in a way that violates the employee's personal rights is often viewed as illegal under the Civil Act.

The employer's right to command work is one of the personnel rights, which is an authority unique to the employer and necessary to maintain and establish corporate order. The courts have ruled that employers have considerable discretion in determining the extent of personnel management necessary for business, as they are responsible for personnel.[191] In contrast, the Constitutional Court argues that the right to work includes not only the right to a place to work but also the right to a reasonable environment in which to work, with the latter a basic right to protect against infringement on human dignity. It has ruled that this right includes the right to demand a healthy working environment, fair compensation for work, and guarantee of reasonable working conditions.[192]

Here, in determining the appropriate scope of work, it is necessary to determine whether the employer's right to order the work or the worker's personal rights should take precedence. In this case, it is necessary to determine whether or not it

---

[191] Supreme Court ruling on July 22, 2003: 2002do7225, and many similar rulings.
[192] Constitutional Court decision on Nov. 28, 2002: 2001hunba50; Constitution Court decision on Aug. 30, 2007: 2004hunma670.

범위를 넘어선 행위이다.

(4) 인적, 환경적 침해행위

사용자나 근로자가 다른 근로자에게 직장내 괴롭힘을 통해 근로자에게 신체적, 정신적 고통을 주거나 근무환경을 악화시키는 행위이다. 사업주가 의도적으로 특정 근로자를 화장실 앞으로 업무자리를 옮겨 창피를 주거나 근로자가 제대로 된 업무를 수행할 수 없는 환경을 조성하는 경우 근무환경을 악화시켰다고 볼 수 있다. 행위자의 의도가 없었더라도 그 행위로 인해 신체적, 정신적 고통을 느꼈거나 근무환경이 예전보다 나빠졌다면 인정될 수 있다.

Ⅳ. 직장내 괴롭힘의 판단기준

1. 사용자의 업무지시권과 근로자의 인격권과 충돌

직장내 괴롭힘 여부를 판단함에 있어서 사용자의 업무지시권과 근로자의 인격권이 충돌되는 경우가 있다. 노동분쟁에서 사용자의 인사권 행사가 근로자의 인격권을 침해한 경우에는 민법상의 불법행위로 구성되는 경우가 많다.

사용자의 업무지시권은 인사권으로 기업질서의 유지와 확립을 위해 사용자가 가지는 고유한 권한이다. 사용자의 인사명령에 대해 법원은 인사권자인 사용자의 권한에 속하므로 업무상 필요한 범위에서는 상당한 재량을 가진다고 한다.[191] 이에 반해, 헌법재판소는 근로의 권리가 일할 자리에 관한 권리 뿐만 아니라 일할 환경에 관한 권리도 함께 내포하고 있고, 후자는 인간의 존엄성에 대한 침해를 방어하기 위한 자유권적 기본권의 성격도 갖고 있어 건강한 작업환경, 일에 대한 정당한 보수, 합리적인 근로조건의 보장 등을 요구할 수 있는 권리 등을 포함한다고 밝히고 있다.[192]

여기서 업무의 적정범위에 대한 판단에 있어 사용자의 업무 지시권을 우위에 두어야 하는지 아니면 근로자의 인격권 보호를 우위에 두어야 하는지를 판단해야 한다. 이 경우 업무상 적정범위는 '이익형량[193]'을 통해서 위법성 여부가

---
[191] 대법원 2003.7.22. 선고 2002도7225 판결 등. 다수
[192] 헌법재판소 2002. 11. 28. 선고 2001헌바50 결정; 헌법재판소 2007. 8. 30. 선고 2004헌마670 결정.
[193] 네이버 국어사전: 서로충돌하는기본권의법익을비교하고판단하여결정하는일.

is illegal to determine certain work as falling within the appropriate scope for a job through an evaluation of conflicting fundamental rights.[193] Of the requirements for determining whether an action constitutes workplace harassment, whether or not it departs from the appropriate scope of work needs to be determined so that conflicts over the basic rights of the employer and employee can be harmoniously resolved.[194] This is determined in the light of sound common sense and practices of the social community, and whether there is rationality or substantiality in common social concepts, etc., which shall be judged individually and in relationship to each other.[195] However, since the problem of workplace harassment arises on the premise of an imbalance of opwer and infringes on the personal rights of workers, an evaluation of conflicting fundamental rights is required from the perspective of the victim, and should focus more on the protection of personal rights.[196]

2. Criteria for determining whether workplace harassment has occurred

The factors and criteria suggested by the court can be used to determine whether workplace harassment has occurred. This shall be decided by considering and evaluating the following collectively:

① the relationship between the offender and victim,

② the motive and intention of the act,

③ the timing, place, and situation,

④ the details of the victim's explicit or presumed reaction,

⑤ the content and extent of the act, and

⑥ the repetition or continuity of the act.[197] Simply put, it is possible for an employer to infringe on human and personal rights or worsen the employment environment with position (power relations), related work (work relations), or other actions unwanted by the receiving party that are outside the scope of the relevant work (harassment, abusive language, etc.).[198]

The employer is the exerciser of authority, while the employee has voluntarily

---

[193] Naver Korean dictionary: An evaluation to compare and judge the legal interests of conflicting fundamental rights.

[194] Lee, Sang-Gon, A Study on Improvement of the Law on Bullying in the Workplace, PhD Thesis, Graduate School of Ajou University, Aug 2020, pp. 163-164.

[195] Supreme Court ruling on Feb. 10, 1998: 95da39533: Whether the employer is liable for compensation for harassment in the workplace.

[196] Lee, Sang-Gon, A Study on Improvement of the Law on Bullying in the Workplace, PhD Thesis, Graduate School of Ajou University, Aug. 2020, p. 165.

[197] Supreme Court ruling on Feb. 10, 1998: 95da39533.

[198] Kim, Elim, Gender Equality and Law, Korea National Open University Press and Culture Center, 2013, p. 242.

판단되어야 한다.[194] 직장내 괴롭힘의 성립요건 중 '업무상 적정범위 일탈' 여부는 사용자와 근로자의 기본권이 상호 조화적으로 해결될 수 있도록 목적에 부합하는 이익형량이 요구된다. 즉, 두 기본권이 충돌할 경우 어느 기본권을 우위에 두어야 하는지의 여부는 사회공동체의 건전한 상식과 관행에 비추어 볼 때 용인될 수 있는 정도의 것인지, 사회통념상 합리성이 없거나 상당성 결여 여부 등을 종합하여 개별적, 상대적으로 판단해야 할 것이다.[195] 다만, 직장내 괴롭힘의 문제는 힘의 불균형을 전제로 하여 발생되고 근로자의 인격권을 침해한다는 점에서, 인격권 보호에 주안점을 두고 피해근로자의 관점에서 다소 상향된 이익형량이 요구된다.[196]

2. 직장내 괴롭힘의 판단기준

법원이 제시한 직장내 성희롱의 위법성 판단요소와 기준을 살펴보면 직장내 괴롭힘 여부를 판단하는 기준으로 삼을 수 있을 것이다. 괴롭힘 행위인지의 여부는
① 위법행위와 관련한 행위자와 피해자의 관계,
② 행위의 동기와 의도,
③ 시기와 장소 및 상황,
④ 피해자의 명시적 또는 추정적 반응의 내용,
⑤ 행위의 내용과 정도,
⑥ 행위의 반복성이나 지속성 등을 종합하여 노동인격의 침해여부를 가려야 할 것이다.[197]

이를 단순히 정리하면, 사용자가 지위를 이용하여(권력관계), 업무와 관련하여(업무관련성), 상대방이 원하지 않는 행동(괴롭힘, 언동 등)을 함으로써, 인권 및 인격권을 침해하거나 고용환경을 악화시키는지 여부를 판단하는 것이다.[198]

직장내 괴롭힘의 판단에 있어 행위자인 사용자는 권한 행사자로서 외관을

---
194) 이상곤, 직장내 괴롭힘 법제의 개선방안 연구, 아주대학교 대학원 박사학위 논문, 2020. 8. 163-164면.
195) 대법원 1998.2.10. 선고 95다39533 판결: 직장 내에서 성희롱 관련 사용자의 배상책임 여부.
196) 이상곤, 직장내 괴롭힘 법제의 개선방안 연구, 위의 논문, 165면.
197) 대법원 1998.2.10. 선고 95다39533 판결
198) 김엘림, 남녀평등과 법, 한국방송통신대학교 출판문화원, 2013, 242면.

consented to perform subordinate duties. Therefore, it is not easy to distinguish if harassment has occurred or if the employee is simply unhappy with work duties.[199] Nevertheless, if the above criteria are individually reviewed and judged comprehensively, it is believed that clarity will emerge in each individual case as to whether or not workplace harassment has occurred.

V. Conclusion

The Workplace Anti-Bullying Act, introduced in July 2019, is a major influence on reducing the existing patriarchal authoritarian culture in the workplace and guaranteeing the personal rights of workers. Nevertheless, if resolving workplace harassment is left up to companies, there will be no effective results any time an employer deals with bullying half-heartedly. Amendment to the Workplace Anti-Bullying Act in April 2021 includes provisions to punish employers for engaging in or failing to take the appropriate action for workplace harassment, and obligate employers to conduct an objective investigation if they become aware of workplace harassment. This amendment is particularly helpful to workers. In the future, when harassment occurs in the workplace, the Ministry of Employment and Labor will thoroughly review the incident and actively intervene and punish any employers who fail to take appropriate action, which will work to drastically reduce recurrence. Actions to prevent workplace harassment and provide practical remedies when it does happen can be expected to occur at the same time.

Section 12. Minimum Wage Act

I. Introduction

The minimum wage system is the nation intervening in the decision-making process between employer and employee, designed to protect employees earning low wages

---

[199] Shin, Kwonchul, Legal Concepts and Criteria for Determining the Occurrence of Bullying in the Workplace, p. 243.

갖추고 있고, 피해자인 근로자는 근로의무의 수행원으로서 자발적 동의에 의해 이루어진다. 따라서 이를 구분하기는 쉽지 않다.[199] 그럼에도 불구하고 위의 기준을 가지고 개별적으로 검토하여 종합적으로 판단한다면 직장내 괴롭힘 여부 판단에 있어 개별 사안별로 분명한 기준이 나올 것이라고 본다.

V. 결론

2019년 7월 도입된 직장내 괴롭힘 방지법은 직장내에서 기존의 가부장적 권위주의적 조직 문화를 개선하고 근로자들의 인격권 보장에 큰 역할을 하였다. 그럼에도 불구하고 회사의 자율에 맡겨져 노사간 스스로 문제해결을 시도하면서, 사용자가 실질적으로 직장내 괴롭힘 사건에 있어 큰 열의가 없을 경우에는 실효적 효과를 가져올 수가 없었다. 그래서 이번 2021년 4월에 새롭게 도입된 직장내 괴롭힘 방지법에서는 사용자가 직장내 괴롭힘 행위자인 경우 처벌을 할 수 있는 조항이 신설되었고, 사용자가 직장내 괴롭힘을 인지한 경우 객관적 조사를 하여야 할 의무조항이 도입되어 실질적으로 근로자에게 도움이 된다는 것에 그 의미가 있다. 앞으로 직장내 괴롭힘 사건 발생시 고용노동부에서는 적극적 개입을 통해 사용자가 사건을 철저히 조사하여 관련자를 처벌하게 할 것이고, 이로 인해 차후 사건 재발을 방지할 수 있는 획기적인 변화를 가져올 것이다. 이를 통해 직장내 괴롭힘 사건에 대한 실질적 구제조치와 예방조치가 동시에 이루어질 수 있을 것이라 기대한다.

제12절 최저임금법

I. 최저임금의 이해

최저임금제란 국가가 노사간의 임금결정과정에 개입하여 임금의 최저수준을 정하고, 사용자에게 이 수준 이상의 임금을 지급하도록 법으로 강제함으로써

---
[199] 신권철, 직장 내 괴롭힘의 법적 개념과 요건, 위의 논문, 243-244면.

by stipulating and legally requiring employers to pay minimum wage levels or higher. The minimum wage is determined on August 5th every year by the Minimum Wage Council, composed of 9 representatives from each of the following groups: labor, management and government. The minimum wage they determine is effective from January 1 to December 31 the following year. The minimum wage mainly influences small and medium-sized companies who employ low-income workers such as guards, janitors, migrant workers, etc., and this directly affects the process of making decisions on salary. Here, I would like to explain the employer's duties related to minimum wages, methods of application, and examples of application.

II. Minimum Wage and Employer Obligations

1. Obligation to give notice

When the minimum wage is announced, the employer shall inform employees of 1) The minimum wage rate, 2) Scope of wages excluded from application of minimum wage, and 3) Effective date. This notice must be posted in places where it can easily be seen by employees, or through other appropriate methods.

2. Obligation to pay minimum wage

An employer shall pay the minimum wage in full to employees covered by the minimum wage rules. If a labor contract between an employer and employee provides for a wage that is less than the minimum wage rate, such provision shall be null and void and the invalidated provision shall be regarded as stipulating that the same wage as the minimum wage rate shall be paid.

3. Joint liability for contractor

In the event that a project is carried out under contract, if the contractee has paid his/her employees wages lower than the minimum wage rate for reasons for which the contractor is liable, the contractor, along with the contractee, shall take joint liability. The reasons a contractor will be considered liable are
1) A contractor's act of determining unit labor costs lower than the minimum wage rate at the time of the signing of the contract; and

저임금 근로자를 보호하는 제도이다. 최저임금은 각 9인씩의 노·사·공익 대표로 구성(총 27인)된 최저임금위원회에서 매년 8월 5일 까지 결정하고, 다음 연도 1월 1일부터 12월 31일까지 적용된다. 최저임금은 주로 저임금 근로자를 사용하는 중소기업 사업장에 많은 영향을 가져오며, 저임금 근로자인 경비원, 청소원, 외국인 노동자 등의 임금결정에 직접적인 결과를 가져온다. 다음은 이러한 최저임금제와 관련된 사업주의 의무와 적용방법 및 그리고 실제 적용실례를 설명하고자 한다.

Ⅱ. 최저임금과 관련 사업주 의무

1. 사용자의 주지의무

사용자는 최저임금이 고시되면 1) 최저임금액, 2) 최저임금에 산입하지 않는 임금의 범위, 3) 효력발생일 등에 관하여 근로자들이 쉽게 볼 수 있는 장소에 게시하거나 그 외의 적당한 방법으로 근로자에게 주지시켜야 한다.

2. 최저임금의 지급의무

사용자는 최저임금의 적용을 받는 근로자에 대하여 최저임금액 이상을 지급하여야 한다. 최저임금액에 미달하는 임금을 정한 근로계약은 그 부분에 한하여 이를 무효로 하며, 무효로 된 부분은 최저임금액과 동일한 임금을 지급하기로 한 것으로 간주된다.

3. 도급사업자의 연대책임

도급으로 사업을 행하는 경우 수급인이 도급인의 책임 있는 사유로 근로자에게 최저임금액에 미달하는 임금을 지급한 때에는 도급인은 해당 수급인과 연대하여 책임을 진다. 그 책임 있는 사유의 범위는
1) 도급인이 도급계약의 체결 당시 인건비 단가를 최저임금액에 미치지 못하는 금액으로 결정하는 행위,

2) A contractor's act of lowering unit labor costs to below the minimum wage rate in the middle of the contract period.

4. Penal provisions for violation of the minimum wage level

(1) Imprisonment of up to three years or a fine not exceeding 20 million won
- paying lower than the minimum wage rate
- lowering the previous wages on grounds of the minimum wage, according to the 'Minimum Wage Act'
- failure to pay the required supplement allowance if reduced contractual working hours result in reduced wages

(2) Fine not exceeding one million won
- failure to inform employees of the minimum wages announced by decision of the Minister of Labor

III. Application of the Minimum Wage

1. The employer's obligations

The minimum wage system guarantees the minimum amount of hourly wage for employees. An employer can pay more than the minimum wage, and an employment contract stipulating a wage which is less than the minimum wage shall be invalid only for that part, and any wage that was paid at less than the minimum wage must be paid additionally. In cases of violation of this, the employer shall be punished by imprisonment for up to three years or a fine not exceeding KRW 20 million (Articles 6 and 28 of the Minimum Wage Act). In addition, when a minimum wage is announced, the employer shall inform employees of 1) the new minimum wage rate, 2) the scope of wages excluded from application of minimum wage, and 3) the effective date. This notice must be posted in places where it can be easily seen by all employees, or through other appropriate methods. In case of violation of this, the employer shall be punished by a fine of up to KRW one million (Article 11 and Article 31 of the Act). Exceptions to the application of the minimum wage are: ① persons who are in a probationary period and who are within 3 months of the day of probation (except for employment contracts of less than one year) and ② surveillance or intermittent

2) 도급인이 도급계약 기간 중 인건비 단가를 최저임금액에 미치지 못하는 금액으로 결정하는 행위

4. 최저임금법 위반의 벌칙

(1) 3년 이하의 징역 또는 2천만 이하의 벌금
- 근로자에 대하여 최저임금액 이상의 임금을 지급하지 아니한 경우
- '최저임금법'에 의한 최저임금을 이유로 종전의 임금수준을 저하시키는 경우
- 근로시간 단축에 따른 임금보전을 행하지 않는 경우

(2) 100만 원 이하의 과태료
- 노동부장관이 결정 고시한 최저임금액 등을 근로자에게 주지시키지 않은 경우

Ⅲ. 최저임금의 적용

1. 사업주의 의무

최저임금은 근로자에 대하여 임금의 최저수준을 보장하는 제도이므로 사용자는 최저임금액 이상을 지급하여야 하고, 최저임금액에 미달하는 임금을 정한 근로계약은 그 부분에 한하여 무효로 하며, 무효로 된 부분에 있어 최저임금액과의 차액의 임금을 추가적으로 지급하여야 한다. 이를 위반한 경우 3년 이하의 징역 또는 2천만 원 이하의 벌금에 처한다(최임법 제6조, 28조). 또한 사용자는 최저임금이 고시되면 최저임금액, 최저임금에 산입하지 않는 임금의 범위, 효력발생일 등에 관하여 근로자들이 쉽게 볼 수 있는 장소에 게시하거나 그 외의 적당한 방법으로 근로자에게 주지시켜야 한다. 이를 위반한 경우 100만 원 이하의 과태료를 부과된다(최임법 제11조, 31조). 최저임금의 적용에 예외는 ① 수습기간 중에 있는 자로서 수습 사용한 날부터 3개월 이내인 자(단, 1년 미만 기간 근로계약은 제외)와 ② 고용노동부장관의

work approved by the Minister of Employment and Labor.[200]

2. Criteria for determining violation of minimum wage

To determine whether the wages paid by a workplace are less than the minimum wage, ① the total wages included in the minimum wage from the wages paid monthly, ② will be divided by the monthly contractual working hours, and then hourly minimum wage will be calculated, ③ and then the amount will be compared with the minimum wage.[201]
The scope of wages to be included in calculation of minimum wage according to the Minimum Wage Act includes 1) wages or allowances to be paid according to wage items stipulated in a collective agreement, the Rules of Employment, and/or an employment contract, or repeated regular payments; and 2) wages or allowances to be paid periodically or in a lump sum once or more every month for contractual labor according to previously agreed-upon payment conditions and payment rate (Article 2 of Enforcement Regulation of the Act (Table 2).
Wages excluded from minimum wage rules are as follows (Table 1 of the Act):

(1) Wages, other than those paid regularly once or more every month

① Diligence allowances paid for superior attendance over periods exceeding one month;
② Long-service allowances paid for continuous work over periods exceeding one month;
③ Incentives, efficiency allowances, or bonuses presented for various reasons over periods exceeding one month; and
④ Other allowances paid temporarily or incidentally, such as marriage allowances, winter fuel allowances, kimchi allowances, exercise subsidies, etc., and which have no fixed payment date or are irregularly paid, even though payment conditions were determined in advance.

(2) Wages, other than those paid for contractual working hours or contractual working days

① Annual or monthly paid allowances, work allowance on paid leave, work

---

[200] If workers engaged in surveillance and intermittent work have not obtained approval from the Minister of Employment and Labor under subparagraph 3 of Article 63 of the Labor Standards Act, the minimum wage in accordance with Article 5 (1) of the Minimum Wage Act will be applied (Supreme Court ruling on June 11, 2015 2003 da 38695).
[201] Supreme Court ruling on June 29, 2007 2004 da 48836 (Calculation of minimum wage).

승인을 받은 감시 또는 단속적 근로에 종사 하는 자이다.[200]

2. 최저임금의 위반여부 판단기준

사업장에서 지급하는 임금이 최저임금 위반인지 여부를 판단하기 위해서는 ① 월 단위로 지급받는 임금에서 최저임금에 포함되는 임금 총액을, ② 월 소정근로시간으로 나누어 시간당 임금으로 환산해, ③ 고시된 최저임금과 비교하여야 한다.[201]

최저임금 산정 시 포함되는 임금 범위는 ① 단체협약·취업규칙 또는 근로계약에 임금항목으로서 지급근거가 명시되어 있거나 관례에 따라 지급하는 임금 또는 수당 ② 미리 정해진 지급조건과 지급률에 따라 소정근로에 대하여 매월 1회 이상 정기적·일률적으로 지급하는 임금 또는 수당이다(최임법 시행규칙 제2조 별표2).

최저임금에 산입되지 않는 임금의 범위(최임법 시행규칙 제2조 별표1)는 다음과 같다.

(1) 매월 1회 이상 정기적으로 지급하는 임금 외의 임금:
① 1월을 초과하는 기간의 출근성적에 의하여 지급하는 정근수당,
② 1월을 초과하는 일정기간의 계속근무에 대하여 지급하는 근속수당,
③ 1월을 초과하는 기간에 걸친 사유에 의하여 산정하는 장려수당, 능률수당 또는 상여금,
④ 기타 결혼수당, 월동수당, 김장수당, 체력단련비 등 임시 또는 돌발적인 사유에 따라 지급하거나, 지급조건이 사전에 정하여진 경우에도 그 사유 발생일이 확정되지 아니하거나 불규칙적인 임금·수당이 이에 해당된다.

(2) 소정의 근로시간 또는 소정의 근로일에 대하여 지급하는 임금외의 임금:
① 연·월차휴가 근로수당, 유급휴가 근로수당, 유급휴일 근로수당,

---

[200] 고용노동부승인을 받지 않은 감시단속적 근로자에 대하여는 최저임금법 제5조제1항에 따른 최저임금액이 적용된다(대법원 2015. 6. 11. 선고 2013다38695 판결)
[201] 대법원 2007. 6. 29. 선고 2004다48836판결 (최저임금 계산)

allowance on paid holidays;

② Wages and additional allowances for extended work or holiday work;

③ Additional allowances for night work;

④ Day & night-duty allowances; and

⑤ Wages not admitted to be paid for a contractual working day, regardless of how such payments are termed.

(3) Other wages deemed inappropriate to be included in the minimum wage:
Actual or similar expenses to support employee welfare such as meals, dormitory accommodation or other housing, company shuttle buses, etc.

3. Hourly wage calculation for the minimum wage

The minimum wage shall be determined in units of hours, days, weeks, or months. When determining the minimum wage in units of days, weeks or months, the hourly wage should also be indicated. The hourly wage determined for a month shall be the monthly amount divided by the number of contractual working hours in one month. In order to calculate the hourly wage of the monthly wage, the amount of the wage divided by the number of working hours per month becomes the hourly minimum wage (Article 5 of the Act, Article 5 of the Enforcement Decree). The prescribed working time of one month includes paid weekly holiday allowances (Article 55 of the Labor Standards Act) and paid allowances on off-days according to a collective agreement. The related court ruling and administrative interpretations are as follows:

(1) Court ruling

The court ruling for the contractual working hours per month is that "Article 5 of the Enforcement Decree of the Minimum Wage Act stipulates that the wages paid on a weekly or monthly basis shall be wages divided by the number of contractual working hours per week or month. The so-called "weekly holiday allowance", which is a wage for a paid holiday, is a wage that is regularly paid at least once a month for given work. Therefore, this regularly paid weekly holiday allowance should be included in the wage calculation."[202] In a sample case of 40 hours per week, the contractual working hours for the month is 209, including the

---
[202] Supreme Court ruling on January 11, 2007, 2006 da 64245 (Case related to minimum wage)

② 연장시간 근로, 휴일근로에 대한 임금 및 가산임금,
③ 야간근로에 대한 가산임금,
④ 일·숙직수당,
⑤ 기타 명칭여하에 관계없이 소정근로에 대하여 지급하는 임금이라고 인정할 수 없는 임금이 이에 해당된다.

(3) 기타 최저임금액에 산입하는 것이 적당하지 아니한 임금:
식사, 기숙사, 주택제공, 통근차 운행 등 현물이나 이와 유사한 형태로 지급되는 급여 등 근로자의 복리후생을 위한 성질의 것이 이에 해당된다.

3. 최저임금 시간급 계산

최저임금액은 시간·일(日)·주(週) 또는 월(月)을 단위로 하여 정한다. 이 경우 일·주 또는 월을 단위로 하여 최저임금액을 정할 때에는 시간급으로도 표시하여야 한다. 월(月) 단위로 정해진 임금은 그 금액을 1개월의 소정근로 시간 수로 나눈 금액으로 한다. 월 임금의 최저임금을 계산하기 위해서는 월 단위의 최저임금에 포함되는 임금을 1개월의 소정근로시간 수로 나눈 금액이 시간급 최저임금이 된다(최임법 제5조, 시행령 제5조). 1개월의 소정근로시간은 유급주휴수당(근기법 제55조)과 단체협약 등에서 유급으로 처리된 유급수당도 포함한다. 관련한 판례와 행정해석은 다음과 같다.

(1) 판례
1개월의 소정근로시간 수에 대해 판례는 "최저임금법 시행령 제5조는 주 단위 또는 월 단위로 지급된 임금에 대하여 '1주 또는 월의 소정근로시간 수'로 나눈 금액을 시간에 대한 임금으로 하도록 규정하고 있는바, 주급제 혹은 월급제에서 지급되는 유급휴일에 대한 임금인 이른바 주휴수당은 소정의 근로에 대해 매월 1회 이상 정기적으로 지급되는 임금이라 할 것이어서 비교 대상 임금을 산정함에 있어 주휴수당을 가산하여야 한다"고 판시하고 있다.[202] 이 경우 주40시간의 경우 주휴수당을 포함하여 월의 소정근로시간은

---
[202] 대법원 2007. 1. 11. 선고 2006다64245 판결 (최저임금 관련 사건)

weekly holiday allowance.

(2) Labor Ministry guideline

According to Article 5-2 of the Minimum Wage Act and Article 5 of the Enforcement Decree of the same Act regarding wages for application of the minimum wage, the monthly wage prescribed for a monthly period shall be the wage divided by the number of contractual working hours per month. In a workplace that conducts a 40-hour workweek each month, 'if 8 hours of Saturday work are treated as paid working hours' even though there is no work duty provided on this Saturday, the number of hours worked in a month for the application of the minimum wage is calculated as 243 hours including paid weekly holiday allowance [{40 hours + 8 hours (Saturday paid work) + 8 hours (paid weekly holiday)} x 365/7 ÷ 12 ≒ 243 hours].[203]

Ⅳ. Practical Applications of the Minimum Wage

1. Quarterly incentives, meal charge and vehicle maintenance expenses

(1) Quarterly incentives shall not be considered as part of the minimum wage.
(2) The "meal charge (food expenses)" is paid regularly and uniformly to all employees on a monthly basis in accordance with the collective agreement and the rules of employment, and so it is decided to include these in the ordinary wages in the Rules of Employment. So, the meal charge is included as wages for the application of the minimum wage (it is applied gradually from January 1, 2019). A "vehicle management fee" is paid to the driving worker at least once a month in accordance with predetermined payment conditions, and is understood as a duty or service allowance for the specific worker, and can therefore be included as wages for the application of the minimum wage.[204]

2. Bonuses and sales bonuses

(1) Bonuses calculated on a yearly basis and regular bonuses

---

[203] MOEL guideline on August 21, 2004, Wage Policy-3074; December 21, 2009, Labor Standards-5970
[204] MOEL guideline on December 15, 2010 Wage welfare-2356

209시간이 된다.

(2) 행정해석

최저임금의 적용을 위한 임금의 환산방법에 대하여 「최저임금법」 제5조의2 및 같은 법 시행령 제5조의 규정에 의하면 월 단위로 정하여진 임금에 대하여는 그 금액을 1월의 소정근로시간수로 나눈 금액을 시간에 대한 임금으로 환산하고 있다. 1주 40시간제를 실시하는 사업장에서 당초 근로제공 의무가 없는 '토요일의 8시간을 유급처리하는 경우'에 최저임금 적용을 위한 1월의 환산 근로시간수는 매주 유급처리되는 8시간을 합하여 월 243시간[{40시간+8시간(토요일 유급처리분) + 8시간 (유급 주휴)} × 365/7÷12 ≒ 243시간]을 적용한다.[203]

Ⅳ. 구체적 최저임금 적용 사례

1. 분기성과급, 식대, 차량관리비

(1) 분기성과급은 최저임금 산입을 위한 임금에 포함되지 않는다.
(2) "식비(식대)"는 단체협약 및 취업규칙에 따라 전 근로자에게 매월 정기적·일률적으로 지급하면서 취업규칙에서 통상임금으로 포함하기로 정하였다면 최저임금에 산입되는 임금이다.(2019.1.1 부터 점진적으로 시행) "차량관리비"는 운전근로자에 한하여 미리 정하여진 지급조건에 따라 일률적으로 매월 1회 이상 정기적으로 지급하고 있다면 이는 특정 업무 종사자에 대한 직무수당 또는 운행수당 등의 성격으로 이해되므로 최저임금 산입을 위한 임금에 포함된다.[204]

2. 상여금 및 판매수당(생산고)

(1) 1년 단위 산정 상여금, 정기상여금

---

[203] 행정해석 임금정책과-3074 (2004. 8. 21); 2009. 12. 28. 근로기준과-5970.
[204] 행정해석 2010. 12. 15. 임금복지과-2356

In cases where a bonus is paid equally each month, after it is calculated and fixed for the yearly period, this monthly bonus is included in the minimum wage.

(2) Sales bonus (based on results)

The sales bonus, for which the monthly amount varies according to the sales results of the individual salesperson, is equivalent to a wage, in accordance with the sales incentive bonus set forth in Article 5 (2) of the Enforcement Decree of the Minimum Wage Act. Therefore, Article 5-2 of the Minimum Wage Act stipulates that the sum of the monthly sales bonus divided by the total number of working hours per month and the monthly salary divided by the number of working hours per month shall be included in the minimum wage.[205]

In cases where a health trainer carries out individual fitness training work for a member, if the trainer receives an additional tuition fee according to a predetermined payment condition and payment rate, such fee can be considered to be equivalent to a sales bonus and included in the minimum wage. Such sales bonus is calculated into hourly wage after it is divided by monthly contractual working hours; the wage determined in monthly units, such as the basic wage, is also divided by monthly contractual working hours. The sum of both wages should be evaluated to determine whether it exceeds the minimum wage.[206]

3. Welfare benefits

(1) It is reasonable that a treatment improvement fee corresponding to money for welfare, such as an allowance which helps to improve the life of an employee is money which does not count in the minimum wage.[207]
(2) Even if a "welfare allowance" is included in regular wages, if it is explicitly stated in the collective agreement that it is a subsidy for living expenses or a benefit for welfare, according to Table 1 of Article 2 of the Enforcement Rule of the Minimum Wage Act, it shall be seen as a wage not included in the wage for the application of the minimum wage in terms of welfare benefits.[208]

---

[205] MOEL guideline on February 14, 2004 Wage Policy-501; April 3, 1990 Wage 32240-4770; October 2, 2005 Wage Policy-801; June 20, 2003 Wage 68200-471
[206] MOEL guideline on October 2, 2015 Labor Standards-4782
[207] MOEL guideline on February 7, 2014 Labor Improvement-659
[208] MOEL guideline on May 17, 1989 Wage 32240-7146

상여금의 산정기간이 연간 단위로 계산하여 월로 분할하여 균등하게 지급되는 경우에는 최저임금에 포함된다.

(2) 판매수당(실적에 의한 수당)

영업사원의 판매실적에 따라 매월 금액이 달라지는 판매수당은 「최저임금법 시행령」 제5조제2항에서 정하고 있는 생산고에 따른 임금에 해당된다 할 것이므로 「최저임금법」 제5조의2 및 「최저임금법 시행령」 제5조제3항에 의거 당해 월 총근로시간수로 나눈 금액과 월 기본급을 월 소정근로시간수로 나눈 금액을 합산한 후 당해 연도 최저임금과 비교하여 위반 여부를 판단해야 한다.[205]

헬스 트레이너가 회원별 개인수업(PT) 업무를 맡아 수행할 경우 미리 정하여진 지급조건과 지급률에 따라 추가적으로 수업료를 지급받고 있다면 이는 최저임금에 산입되는 생산고 임금에 해당된다고 볼 수 있으므로, 수업료는 총 근로시간으로 나눠 시간당 임금으로 환산한 뒤, 기본급 등 월단위로 정하여진 임금을 소정근로시간(유급으로 지급되는 주휴수당 등 포함)으로 나누어 환산한 시간당 임금과 합산하여 시간급 최저임금 미달 여부를 판단하여 한다.[206]

3. 복리후생 수당

(1) 근로자의 생활을 보조하는 수당 등 복리후생을 위한 금품에 해당하는 처우개선비는 최저임금에 산입하지 않는 임금으로 봄이 타당하다.[207]
(2) "복지수당"이 비록 통상임금에 포함되어 지급되고 있다 하더라도 단체협약 등에 명백하게 생계비보조 또는 복리후생적인 성격의 수당임을 명시하고 있다고 한다면 이는 최저임금법시행규칙 제2조 별표 1에서 규정하고 있는 복리후생적인 수당으로 보아 최저임금의 적용을 위한 임금에 산입하지 아니하는 임금으로 보아야 한다.[208]

---

[205] 행정해석 2004.2.14. 임금정책과-501; 1990.4.3. 임금32240-4770; 2005. 10. 2. 임금정책과-801; 2003. 6. 20, 임금 68200-471
[206] 행정해석 2015.10.2.). 근로기준정책과-4782)
[207] 행정해석, 2014. 2. 7. 근로개선정책과-659
[208] 행정해석 1989. 5. 17. 임금 32240-7146

4. Differences from ordinary wages[209]

Item	Ordinary wage	Minimum wage
Definition/ Purpose	Ordinary wages means hourly wages, daily wages, weekly wages, monthly wages, or contract wages which are determined to be paid periodically or in lump sum to a worker for his/her prescribed work or whole work (Article 6 of the Enforcement Decree of the Labor Standards Act Enforcement Decree).	The purpose of this Act is to stabilize workers' lives and improve the quality of the labor force by guaranteeing a minimum level of wages (Article 1 of the Minimum Wage Act).
Calculation method	Calculated into hourly wage rate (Monthly ordinary wage ÷ monthly contractual working hours).	Calculated into hourly wage rate (Monthly minimum wage ÷ monthly contractual working hours).
Legal enforcement	No legal enforcement.	Legal enforcement, with cases of violation being invalid.
Usage	Wages determined to be paid in advance; used for paid leave allowances.	Wages actually paid; used for guaranteeing employees' livelihood.
(i) Regular meal charge	Included in ordinary wage.	Included in the minimum wage.
(ii) Performance bonus	1) Fixed bonuses are included in ordinary wages. 2) Performance bonuses are recognized as ordinary wages to the extent that they are guaranteed to a minimum. 3) Sales bonuses are excluded.	1) Annual bonus payments are excluded. 2) Monthly bonuses are included in the minimum wage. 3) Monthly performance bonuses are included in the minimum wage. 4) Sales bonuses are included in the minimum wage.
(iii) Welfare allowance	Regular, uniform, and fixed welfare allowances are included.	Monthly regular, uniform, and fixed welfare allowances are included.

---

[209] Supreme Court ruling on January 11, 2007 2006 da 64245; MOEL guideline on June 29, 2006 Wage and working hours 1539; MOEL guideline on December 20, 2006 Wage and working hours 3848

4. 통상임금과의 차이[209]

구분	통상임금	최저임금
목적	근로자에게 정기적이고 일률적으로 소정근로 또는 총근로에 대하여 지급하기로 정한 시간급 금액, 일급 금액, 주급 금액, 월급 금액 또는 도급 금액을 말한다 (근기법 시행령 제6조).	근로자에 대하여 임금의 최저수준을 보장하여 근로자의 생활안정과 노동력의 질적 향상을 꾀함을 목적으로 한다(최임법 제1조).
계산방법	시간급으로 계산(월 통상임금 ÷ 월 소정근로시간)	시간급으로 계산 (월 최저임금 ÷ 월 소정근로시간)
법적강제 여부	법적강제 없음	법적 강제 및 위반시 무효
사용용도	사전적 임금으로 유급수당 계산근거	사후적 임금으로 근로자의 생활보장
(i) 정기식대	통상임금 포함	최저임금 포함
(ii) 성과급	1) 고정상여금은 통상임금에 포함 2) 성과상여금은 최저한도로 보장되는 한도 내에서 통상임금 인정 3) 판매수당 미포함	1) 연단위 산정하여 매월 지급하는 상여금 제외됨. 2) 매월 산정단위 상여금 최저임금 포함, 3) 매월 단위 성과상여금 최저임금 포함 4) 생산고(판매수당)에 따른 임금 포함
(iii) 복지수당	정기적 일률적 고정적 복지수당 포함	월 단위 정기적 일률적 복지수당 포함

---

[209] 대법원 2007.01.11. 선고 2006다64245 판결; 행정해석 2006. 6. 29, 임금근로시간정책팀-1539; 2006. 12. 20. 임금근로시간정책팀-3848

Section 13. Prevention of Sexual Harassment in the Workplace

I. Understanding Sexual Harassment in the Workplace[210]

1. Definition of "sexual harassment in the workplace"

The Equal Employment Act defines sexual harassment in the workplace as any act of an employer, superior, or employee using their position in the workplace or work-related relationship to cause another employee to feel sexual humiliation or disgust due to sexual advances or demands, or to inflict disadvantageous employment conditions and consequences on them for refusing such advances or demands (Article 2-2).

2. Requirements for establishing that sexual harassment in the workplace has occurred

To be recognized as "sexual harassment" as defined by the National Human Rights Commission Act, the requisites in below Table must be met, regarding the perpetrator and the victim, the context, the means, the harm, and the behavior.

Requisites for Establishing that Sexual Harassment in the Workplace Has Occurred (according to the Equal Employment Act)

Perpetrator	Employer, superior, or employee
Victim	Employee
Occurrence	Using one's position in the workplace or work relationship
Means	Sexual language or gestures
Behaviors	• Behaviors that cause the victim to feel sexual humiliation or hatred • Behaviors that result in the victim suffering disadvantageous employment conditions or treatment due to refusing to comply with sexual advances or demands

---

[210] El-lim Kim, Bongsoo Jung, Manual on Bullying and Sexual Harassment in the Workplace, June 2023, K-labor press, pp. 33-41.

제13절 직장 내 성희롱 예방

Ⅰ. 직장 내 성희롱 이해하기[210]

1. '직장 내 성희롱'의 개념 정의

「남녀고용평등법」은 '직장 내 성희롱'을 "사업주·상급자 또는 근로자가 직장 내의 지위를 이용하거나 업무와 관련하여 다른 근로자에게 성적 언동 등으로 성적 굴욕감 또는 혐오감을 느끼게 하거나 성적 언동 또는 그 밖의 요구 등에 따르지 아니하였다는 이유로 근로조건 및 고용에서 불이익을 주는 것"(제2조제2호)으로 정의하고 있다.

2. '직장 내 성희롱'의 성립요건

어떠한 언동이 「남녀고용평등법」에 말하는 '직장 내 성희롱'이 되려면 다음 표에서 정리한 당사자(행위자와 상대방), 경위, 수단, 피해와 행태의 요건을 갖추어야 한다.

「남녀고용평등법」의 '직장 내 성희롱' 성립요건

행위자	사업주, 상급자 또는 근로자
상대방	근로자
경 위	직장 내의 지위를 이용하여 또는 업무와 관련하여
수 단	성적 언동 등
행 태	■ 상대방에게 성적 굴욕감 또는 혐오감을 느끼게 하는 행위 ■ 상대방이 성적 언동 또는 그 밖의 성적 요구에 따르지 아니하였다는 이유로 근로조건 및 고용에서 불이익을 주는 행위

---

[210] 김엘림, 정봉수, 「직장 내 괴롭힘과 성희롱 예방 매뉴얼」, 2023. 6. 강남노무법인, 33-41면.

Chapter3-13. Prevention of Sexual Harassment in the Workplace

1) Parties involved

According to the Labor Standards Act, "employer" refers to "a business owner, a person responsible for management of a business, or a person who works on behalf of a business owner with respect to matters relating to workers" (Article 2 (1) 2). However, the Equal Employment Act defines a perpetrator of sexual harassment in the workplace as "an employer, superior, or employee" instead of using only the term "employer." Here, "superior" refers to an individual in a higher position than the victim, whether or not they assist the employer with management authority and responsibilities.

Meanwhile, again according to the Labor Standards Act, the term "employee" refers to "any person who provides labor to a business or workplace for the purpose of receiving wages, regardless of the type of occupation" (Article 2 (1) 1). However, the Equal Employment Act defines the receiver (victim) of sexual harassment in the workplace as "an employee," which refers to "any person employed by an employer or any person who intends to be employed" (Article 2-4).

2) Circumstances

This law defines the circumstances of sexual harassment in the workplace as "using one's position in the workplace or engaging in work-related actions." Therefore, work-relatedness is an essential factor in deeming whether sexual harassment has occurred in the workplace. Unwanted sexual behaviors that occur in places related to work, such as on business trips or at social gatherings, dinners, or a residence belonging to one of the parties, are all recognized as sexual harassment in the workplace.

3) Means

This law defines sexual harassment in the workplace as involving "sexual language and behaviors," which in turn refer to physical relations between a man and woman or physical, linguistic and visual behaviors in relation to the male or female physical appearance.

As summarized in below Table, the Enforcement Decree to this law classifies "sexual language and behaviors" as "physical acts," "verbal acts," "visual acts," or

1) 당사자

「근로기준법」에서 '사용자'란 "사업주 또는 사업 경영 담당자, 그 밖에 근로자에 관한 사항에 대하여 사업주를 위하여 행위하는 자"(제2조제1항제2호)를 말한다.

「남녀고용평등법」은 직장 내 성희롱의 행위자를 '사용자'로 하지 않고 '사업주와 상급자, 근로자'로 하고 있다. 여기서 '상급자'란 사용자뿐 아니라 사용자의 경영상의 권한과 책무를 지지 아니하더라도 피해자보다 상위의 직급에 있는 사람을 말한다.

한편, 「근로기준법」에서 '근로자'란 "직업의 종류와 관계없이 임금을 목적으로 사업이나 사업장에 근로를 제공하는 사람"(제2조제1항제1호)을 말한다. 「남녀고용평등법」은 직장 내 성희롱의 상대방(피해자)을 "다른 근로자"로 규정하고 있는데 이 법에서 '근로자'란 "사업주에게 고용된 사람과 취업할 의사를 가진 사람"(제2조제4호)을 말한다. 그러므로 모집·채용과정에서 사업주·상급자 또는 근로자가 지위를 이용하거나 업무와 관련하여 구직자에게 성적 굴욕감 또는 혐오감을 느끼게 하는 성적 언동을 하는 경우도 직장 내 성희롱에 해당된다.

2) 경위

이 법은 직장 내 성희롱의 경위를 "직장 내의 지위를 이용하거나 업무와 관련하여"라고 규정하고 있다. 그러므로 업무관련성은 직장 내 성희롱의 요건이 된다. 사업장 내 뿐 아니라 출장지, 야유회, 회식 장소, 당사자의 거주지도 업무와 관련되는 행위가 이루어지거나 업무가 수행되는 경우에는 직장 내 성희롱의 발생 장소로 인정된다.

3) 수단

이 법은 직장 내 성희롱의 수단을 "성적 언동 등으로"라고 규정하고 있다. '성적 언동'이란 성적 성질을 가지는, 성적 의미가 내포된 말과 행동을 말하는데 성적 요구도 포함된다.

이 법의 시행규칙 [별표1]은 <표>에서 정리한 바와 같이 직장 내 성희롱에 해당하는 성적 언동을 '육체적 행위', '언어적 행위' '시각적 행위' '그 밖에

"other language or behavior recognized as causing sexual humiliation or disgust according to social norms."

Examples of "Sexual Language and Behaviors" according to the Enforcement Decree to the Equal Employment Act

Physical Behaviors	• Physical contact such as kissing, hugging from in front or behind • Touching private parts of the body, like the breast, backside, etc. • Behaviors such as forcing a massage or caressing
Verbal Behaviors	• Saying a filthy joke or speaking lustful and indecent words, including in telephone conversations • Likening appearance to sexual things • Asking about sexual relationships or facts, or intentionally distributing information of a sexual nature • Forcing or requesting sexual relations • Forcing a woman to sit close and fill glasses at a dinner meeting, etc.
Visual Behaviors	• Putting up or displaying lustful photos, pictures, drawings, etc., including distribution by email or fax • Intentionally exposing or touching one's own physical parts in a sexual manner
Other language or behavior which makes other workers feel sexually humiliated or offended as a socially accepted notion.	

4) Behaviors

This law defines sexual harassment behaviors in the workplace as "actions that cause the other person to feel sexual humiliation or aversion" and "taking disadvantageous actions regarding the employee's working conditions or employment because they did not comply with sexual advances or other sexual demands."

사회통념상 성적 굴욕감 또는 혐오감을 느끼게 하는 것으로 인정되는 언어나 행동'로 구분하여 예시하고 있다.

「남녀고용평등법 시행규칙」의 '성적 언동' 예시

육체적 행위	■ 입맞춤, 포옹 또는 뒤에서 껴안는 등의 신체적 접촉행위 ■ 가슴·엉덩이 등 특정 신체부위를 만지는 행위 ■ 안마나 애무를 강요하는 행위
언어적 행위	■ 음란한 농담을 하거나 음탕하고 상스러운 이야기를 하는 행위 (전화통화를 포함한다) ■ 외모에 대한 성적인 비유나 평가를 하는 행위 ■ 성적인 사실 관계를 묻거나 성적인 내용의 정보를 의도적으로 퍼뜨리는 행위 ■ 성적인 관계를 강요하거나 회유하는 행위 ■ 회식자리 등에서 무리하게 옆에 앉혀 술을 따르도록 강요하는 행위
시각적 행위	■ 음란한 사진·그림·낙서·출판물 등을 게시하거나 보여 주는 행위(컴퓨터통신이나 팩시밀리 등을 이용하는 경우를 포함한다) ■ 성과 관련된 자신의 특정 신체부위를 고의적으로 노출하거나 만지는 행위
그 밖에 사회통념상 성적 굴욕감 또는 혐오감을 느끼게 하는 것으로 인정되는 언어나 행동	

4) 행태

이 법은 직장 내 성희롱의 행태를 "상대방에게 성적 굴욕감 또는 혐오감을 느끼게 하는 행위"와 "상대방이 성적 언동 또는 그 밖의 성적 요구에 따르지 아니하였다는 이유로 근로조건 및 고용에서 불이익을 주는 행위"로 규정하고 있다.

Attached Form 11 of the Enforcement Decree to this law provides behavioral examples of sexual harassment in the workplace, such as "unfair treatment in employment such as failure to hire, demotion, promotion denial, job transfer, suspension, leave of absence, or termination."

3. Criteria for determining whether sexual harassment in the workplace has occurred

In the "Note" to Attached Form 1 of the Enforcement Decree to this law, there is a standard for evaluating whether or not sexual harassment has occurred in the workplace, stating that "when determining whether sexual harassment has occurred in the workplace, the subjective circumstances of the victim should be taken into account."

It also considers "how a reasonable person would evaluate and respond to behavior that would be problematic from the victim's perspective according to social norms, and ultimately assessing whether such behavior creates a threatening or hostile work environment that impairs work efficiency."

4. Use of the concept of "sexual harassment in the workplace"

The "Equal Employment Act " aims to guarantee equal opportunities and treatment for men and women in employment, promote maternity protection and women's employment, and support the reconciliation of work and family life in order to improve the quality of life for all citizens in accordance with the equality principles of the "Constitution of the Republic of Korea" (Article 1). This law includes provisions on the prohibition and prevention of workplace sexual harassment in Chapter 2, Section 2 (Prohibition and Prevention of Workplace Sexual Harassment) of the "Guarantee of Equal Opportunities and Treatment between Men and Women in Employment." Therefore, the concept of "workplace sexual harassment" in this law refers to actions that employers, superiors, and employees must not engage in and the measures that employers must take to ensure equal opportunities and treatment between men and women.

5. Scope of application of regulations regarding 'workplace sexual harassment'

The law also stipulates the actions that employers must take to ensure equal opportunities and treatment for men and women and applies to all businesses or workplaces (hereinafter referred to as "businesses") that employ workers (Article 4). However, the entire law does not apply to businesses consisting solely of close relatives living together or domestic workers (Article 2 of the Enforcement Decree).

이 법의 시행규칙은 [별표 1]에서 직장 내 성희롱의 행태 중 "고용에서 불이익을 주는 것"에 대하여 "채용탈락, 감봉, 승진탈락, 전직(轉職), 정직(停職), 휴직, 해고 등과 같이 채용 또는 근로조건을 일방적으로 불리하게 하는 것"으로 예시하고 있다.

3. '직장 내 성희롱'의 판단기준

이 법의 시행규칙은 [별표 1]의 '비고'에서 "직장 내 성희롱 여부를 판단하는 때에는 피해자의 주관적 사정을 고려하되, 사회통념상 합리적인 사람이 피해자의 입장이라면 문제가 되는 행동에 대하여 어떻게 판단하고 대응하였을 것인가를 함께 고려하여야 하며, 결과적으로 위협적·적대적인 고용환경을 형성하여 업무능률을 떨어뜨리게 되는지를 검토하여야 한다."라고 판단기준을 제시하고 있다.

4. '직장 내 성희롱' 개념의 용도

「남녀고용평등법」은 "「대한민국헌법」의 평등이념에 따라 고용에서 남녀의 평등한 기회와 대우를 보장하고 모성 보호와 여성 고용을 촉진하여 남녀고용 평등을 실현함과 아울러 근로자의 일과 가정의 양립을 지원함으로써 모든 국민의 삶의 질 향상에 이바지하는 것을 목적으로 한다."(제1조).

이 법은 직장 내 성희롱의 금지와 예방 등에 관한 규정들을 [제2장 고용에서 남녀의 평등한 기회보장 및 대우등]의 제2절(직장 내 성희롱의 금지 및 예방)에 편성하고 있다. 그러므로 이 법의 '직장 내 성희롱' 개념은 남녀의 평등한 기회 및 대우를 보장하기 위하여 사업주, 상급자, 근로자가 해서는 아니되는 행위와 사업주가 해야 할 조치를 규정한 것이다.

5. '직장 내 성희롱' 관련 규정의 적용범위

이 법은 근로자를 사용하는 모든 사업 또는 사업장(이하 "사업"이라 한다)에 적용한다(제4조). 다만, 동거하는 친족만으로 이루어지는 사업과 가사사용인에 대하여는 법의 전부를 적용하지 아니한다(시행령 제2조).

II. Characteristics of Sexual Harassment and Its Relationship to Workplace Harassment, Sexual Assault, and Gender Discrimination

Sexual harassment encompasses elements of work-relatedness, power dynamics, violence, and discrimination. In this regard, sexual harassment shares similarities and differences with workplace bullying, sexual violence, and gender discrimination.

1. Work-relevance of sexual harassment and its relationship with workplace harassment

Sexual harassment is connected to sexual behavior related to work or the use of position. Such behavior is mainly directed towards individuals in a vulnerable position by those with authority and higher positions. For example, if sexual harassment occurs in a regular workplace, the employer or a superior is often the perpetrator. In a university, it might be a professor. Therefore, sexual harassment is both relevant to power and work.

2. Relationship between sexual harassment and workplace harassment

(1) Definition of workplace harassment and "gap-jil" ("power harassment")

As mentioned in Chapter 1, when the Labor Standards Actwas revised on January 15, 2019, regulations were added to prevent workplace harassment and to handle victims' grievances. According to this law, "workplace bullying" refers to "behavior by an employer or employee who uses their superior position or relationship in the workplace to cause physical or mental pain to other employees beyond the reasonable scope of work or to worsen the working environment" (Article 76-2 (1)).

Meanwhile, government departments jointly announced "Guidelines for Eradicating Workplace Harassment in the Public Sector" on February 18, 2019. These guidelines define "power harassment" as "unfair demands or treatment imposed on another person by someone who holds a superior position in social or economic relationships, or who exercises practical influence derived from that position."

(2) Similarities and differences between sexual harassment and workplace harassment

Sexual harassment, workplace harassment, gap-jil(power harassment), and unfair acts such as using one's superior position to inflict physical and mental pain on

Ⅱ. 성희롱의 특성과 직장 내 괴롭힘·성폭력·성차별과의 관계

성희롱은 업무관련성과 권력성, 폭력성, 차별성을 가진다. 이 점에서 성희롱은 직장 내 괴롭힘, 성폭력, 성차별과 공통점과 차이점을 가진다.

1. 성희롱의 업무관련성과 '직장 내 괴롭힘'과의 관계

성희롱은 업무와 관련하거나 지위를 이용하여 행한 성적 언동을 기본요건으로 한다. 그런데 이러한 언동은 주로 권한이 많고 지위가 높은 사람이 취약한 지위를 가지는 사람을 대상으로 하여 많이 행해진다. 예를 들면, 일반 사업장에서는 사업주와 사용자 또는 상급자가, 대학에서는 교수가 행위자가 되는 경우가 많다. 그리하여 성희롱은 업무관련성과 권력성을 가진다.

2. 성희롱과 '직장 내 괴롭힘'과의 관계

(1) '직장 내 괴롭힘', '갑질'의 의의
「근로기준법」은 2019년 1월 15일에 개정될 때, '직장 내 괴롭힘'을 방지하고 피해자의 고충을 처리하는 규정들을 신설하였다. 이 법에서 '직장 내 괴롭힘'이란 "사용자 또는 근로자가 직장에서의 지위 또는 관계 등의 우위를 이용하여 업무상 적정범위를 넘어 다른 근로자에게 신체적·정신적 고통을 주거나 근무환경을 악화시키는 행위"(제76조의2제1항)를 말한다.

한편, 정부 관계부처는 합동으로 2019년 2월 18일, 「공공분야 갑질 근절을 위한 가이드라인」을 발표하였다. 이 가이드라인은 '갑질'을 "사회·경제적 관계에서 우월적 지위에 있는 사람이 권한을 남용하거나, 우월적 지위에서 비롯되는 사실상의 영향력을 행사하여 상대방에게 행하는 부당한 요구나 처우"라고 정의하였다.

(2) 성희롱과 '직장 내 괴롭힘'의 공통점과 차이점
성희롱은 주로 우월적 지위를 가진 사람들이 비교적 취약한 지위에 있는 사람들을 대상으로 인권침해와 업무상의 피해를 주는 점에서 '직장 내 괴롭힘',

other civil servants all involve harassment and human rights violations. They also cause work-related harm to relatively vulnerable individuals targeted by those in superior positions.

However, those in superior positions are not the only ones who might sexually harass someone else. A colleague or student can also be guilty of this. It also differs from workplace harassment because sexual behavior is the constituent requisite.

3. Its relationship with sexual assault

(1) Relationship between sexual harassment, sexual assault, and other sexual crimes

"Sexual assault" (violence) is a term commonly used internationally to refer to unwanted sexual behavior that involves violent acts that violate a victim's physical and psychological well-being, as well as their right to sexual self-determination. "Sexual crimes" refer to acts of sexual assault that are punished by the state because they are severely damaging.

However, in South Korea, sexual assault and sexual crimes are considered the same behavior. The Sexual Assault Prevention Act defines sexual assault as "an act that corresponds to the crime specified in Article 2 (1) of the Act on Special Cases Concerning the Punishment Etc. of Sexual Crimes." However, Article 2 (1) of the same Act only lists the types of sexual crimes without giving a solid definition of sexual assault. It also designates various sexual crimes specified in the Criminal Act and new sexual crimes added in Chapter 2 (Article 3-15) of this law as sexual assault crimes. These sexual crimes include offenses related to rape, molestation, adultery, obscenity, invasion of privacy in multi-use places for sexual purposes, and illegal filming.

(2) Comparing sexual harassment and sexual assault

Sexual harassment and sexual assaults or sexual crimes share the common characteristic of involving the use of sexually oriented behavior that goes against the will of the other party. Also, it has a violent nature that causes physical and mental harm to the victim, violating their personality and sexual self-determination. They are also both considered a form of "violence against women" under the UN Declaration on the Elimination of Violence against Women and South Korea's

'갑질', '우월적 지위 등을 이용하여 다른 공무원 등에게 신체적·정신적 고통을 주는 등의 부당행위'와 공통점을 가진다.

그런데 한편, 성희롱은 우월적 지위를 이용한 사람들에 의해서만 발생하는 것은 아니며 동료 근로자나 학생에 의해서도 발생할 수 있는 점, 성적 언동을 성립요건으로 하는 점, 특정 성에게 편중되어 발생하는 점에서 '직장 내 괴롭힘'과 차이가 있다.

3. '성폭력' 과의 관계

(1) 성희롱과 '성폭력' 및 '성폭력범죄' 와의 관계

'성폭력'이란 국제적으로 널리 사용되고 있는 'sexual violence', 'sexual assault'를 지칭하는 용어다. 상대방이 원하지 아니한 성적 언동을 수반하는 모든 폭력행위로서 피해자에게 심신의 피해와 인격권과 성적 자기결정권을 침해하는 행위를 말한다. '성폭력범죄'란 성폭력 중에서 죄질이 나쁘고 피해가 심해 국가가 형벌로 처벌하는 행위를 말한다.

그런데 우리나라 법은 성폭력과 성폭력범죄를 같은 행위로 보고 있다. 즉 「성폭력방지 및 피해자 보호 등에 관한 법률」(약칭: 성폭력방지법)은 '성폭력'을 "「성폭력범죄의 처벌 등에 관한 특례법」(약칭: 성폭력처벌법) 제2조제1항에 규정된 죄에 해당하는 행위"라고 규정하고 있다. 「성폭력처벌법」제2조제1항은 성폭력의 개념을 정의하지 않고, 성폭력범죄에 해당되는 범죄를 열거하고 있다. 「성폭력처벌법」은 「형법」에 규정된 다양한 성범죄와 이 법 제2장(제3조~제15조)에서 새로이 추가한 성범죄를 모두 성폭력범죄로 규정하고 있다. 이러한 성폭력범죄의 행태는 다양한데 강간 관련죄, 추행 관련죄, 간음 관련죄, 음란 관련죄, 다중이용장소의 성적 목적 침입 관련죄, 불법 촬영·반포 관련죄의 6개의 유형으로 구분할 수 있다.

(2) 성희롱과 '성폭력' 의 공통점과 차이점

성희롱과 성폭력·성폭력범죄는 상대방의 의사에 반하는 성적 언동을 수단으로 하는 폭력성을 가지는 점, 피해자에게 신체적·정신적 피해를 주고 인격권과 성적 자기결정권을 침해하는 행위인 점, UN의「여성폭력철폐선언」과

Framework Act on the Prevention of Violence against Women, since women are the most common victims.

However, sexual harassment differs from sexual assault as it requires a work-related or hierarchical relationship as basic criteria for determining whether it has occurred. In contrast, sexual assault, including sexual crimes specified in Article 303 of the Criminal Act (Sexual Intercourse by Abuse of Occupational Authority) and Article 10 of the Punishment Act for Sexual Assault (Sexual Molestation Committed by Force or Coercion), requires the existence of a power relationship, but not necessarily a work-related one. Additionally, not all sexual assault or sexual crimes require work-related or hierarchical relationships as basic criteria. Furthermore, while all sexual assault or sexual crimes are subject to criminal punishment under current law, not all cases of sexual harassment are subject to criminal punishment. However, if the behavior/conduct of sexual harassment meets the standard for sexual assault or sexual crime, the perpetrator shall be subject to criminal punishment.

Ⅲ. Sexual Harassment Case, and Procedures for Handling a Sexual Harassment Case

1. Summary (Introduction)[211]

Incidents of sexual harassment occurred in a Korean branch office (hereinafter referred to as "the Company") of a foreign company. The female employee victimized by the sexual harassment (hereinafter, "the victim-employee") submitted a petition to the National Human Rights Commission over the incidents. The victim-employee then informed the company of the petition she had submitted, and details within her statement to the Human Rights Commission. From this, the Company investigated the senior sales manager concerned (hereinafter, "Offender A"), estimated that his actions were sexual harassment, and then took appropriate disciplinary action against him. Shortly after, the Human Rights Commission transferred this case to the Gangnam Labor Office of the Ministry of Employment and Labor. On June 16, 2011, the Company received a written notice from the Labor Inspector in charge of sexual harassment cases, that there would be an investigative hearing. The Labor Inspector also informed the Company that there were two more alleged offenders that the victim-employee had not mentioned to the Company. After being informed of the additional alleged sexual harassment, the Company investigated the sales director (hereinafter, "Offender B") and the country manager (hereinafter, "Offender C"), and

---

[211] A sexual harassment petition case at GangNam Labor Office from Apr to Jun 2011

우리나라 「여성폭력방지기본법」이 정의한 '여성폭력'의 일종으로서 주로 여성이 피해자가 되는 점에서 공통점을 가진다.

그런데 성희롱은 업무와 관련하거나 지위를 이용하여 이루어지는 업무관련성을 기본요건으로 하는 점에서 이를 기본요건으로 하지 않는 성폭력과 구별된다. 성폭력범죄 중 「형법」의 제303조(업무상 위력 등에 의한 간음)와 「성폭력처벌법」제10조(업무상 위력 등에 의한 추행 등)가 규정한 성폭력범죄는 업무관련성을 구성요건으로 하지만 모든 성폭력, 성폭력범죄가 업무관련성을 기본요건으로 하지 않는다. 또한 현행법상 모든 성폭력범죄는 형사처벌의 대상이 되지만, 모든 성희롱이 형사처벌의 대상이 되는 것은 아니라는 점에서도 차이가 있다. 그러나 성희롱의 행위 행태가 성폭력범죄에 해당되는 경우에는 행위자는 형사처벌을 받게 된다.

Ⅲ. 성희롱사건 소개와 관련 처리 절차 설명

1. 사건개요 (서론)[211]

모 외국계 회사의 국내지사 (이하 "회사"라 함)에서 직장내 성희롱 사건이 발생하였고, 2011.5.23. 성희롱 피해를 당한 여직원(이하 '피해자'라함)은 국가인권위원회에 진정서를 제출하였다. 또한 피해자는 본 사건과 관련하여 진정서를 제출한 사실과 그 내용을 회사에 통보하였다. 이에 회사는 해당 영업부장 (이하 "가해자 A")과 피해자를 조사한 후, 성희롱 여부를 판단하여 가해자 A에게 적절한 징계조치를 하였다. 그런데, 국가인권위원회는 본 사건을 관할 노동사무소인 고용노동부 서울강남지청으로 이관하였고, 2011.6.16. 본 성희롱 진정사건에 담당 근로감독관으로부터 출석요구를 통지 받았고, 여기에 피해자가 진술하지 않았던, 추가적으로 2명의 성희롱 가해자가 있다는 사실을 확인하였다. 이러한 추가적인 성희롱 사실을 통보 받은 회사는 영업이사(이하 "가해자 B")와 지사장(이하 "가해자 C")에 대해 조사하였으며 피해자의 진술서도 받아 성희롱 여부를 판단한 후, 가해자 B와 C에 대해 적절한 징계조치를 하였다. 2011. 6.28. 상기 노동사무소에 출석한 회사는 회사가 취한 법령에

---
[211] 2011. 4월 ~ 6월 간 고용노동부 서울강남지청 진정사건

after evaluation, determined their behaviors were also sexual harassment, based upon their statements and the victim's, and took appropriate disciplinary actions against Offenders B and C. On June 28, 2011, the Company attended the investigative hearing at the Labor Office and explained the measures that it had taken appropriately according to related law. The Labor Inspector in charge agreed that the Company had taken the proper actions and closed the petition. However, the Labor Inspector discovered that the Company had not given any education to its employees to prevent sexual harassment at work in 2008 and 2009, but had started only in 2010. For this non-fulfillment of the Company's legal duty to provide education on sexual harassment prevention, the Company was fined 2 million won.

According to the 'Equal Employment and Work-Home Balance Assistance Act,' sexual harassment at work refers to "a situation where a person's superior or colleague harasses him/her with sexually-charged behavior or language," and it is the employer who is responsible to prevent sexual harassment at work and take appropriate measures if such harassment occurs. I would like to review the appropriate measures taken by the Company.

2. Details of the Sexual Harassment Case at Work

(1) Sexual Harassment by Offender A

On April 27, 2011, during a team-building event at a company workshop with all employees (about 30), the victim-employee had to do something as a penalty in a game. The penalty was that she had to write her name with her backside. Before doing so, she told everybody that they couldn't take any video with their cameras or cell phones. The sales manager (Offender A) took a video of her with his cell phone secretly, saved it and forgot about it. On May 19, 2011, at a company dinner, Offender A remembered the video he had secretly recorded, and showed the video to his colleagues in turn. The conversation among those employees was sexually humiliating for the victim-employee, and included such expressions as "It would be fun to show this as a highlight at a Sales Kick-Off event," and "Since we can't see her face, send her ID picture to me with the video." The victim-employee demanded Offender A to delete the video, but Offender A did not do so. At this, the victim-employee informed the personnel team of her displeasure and requested a formal apology from him. Offender A would not offer a formal apology, and simply showed his displeasure at her informing the personnel team.

(2) Sexual Harassment by Offender B

On May 19, 2011, at the same company dinner, Offender B wandered around, pouring traditional wine for his colleagues. When he came to the victim-employee's

따른 적절한 조치 내용을 설명하였고, 또한 담당 근로감독관도 회사의 조치에 대해 긍정적으로 수긍하였다. 다만, 직전 3년간의 직장내 성희롱예방교육 실시 여부를 확인한 결과, 회사는 작년도에는 교육을 실시하였으나 2008년과 2009년에 대해 직장내 성희롱예방 교육을 실시하지 않아 200만 원의 과태료 처분을 받고 납부하면서, 본 사건은 종결되었다.

'남녀고용평등과 일,가정 양립지원에 관한 법률'에 따르면 직장내 성희롱은 직장 내에서 상급자나 직장동료가 다른 동료를 성적 언동 등으로 괴롭히는 것이기 때문에 사업주에게 직장내 성희롱 예방의무를 부여하고, 성희롱 발생시 적절한 조치를 취할 것을 요구하고 있다. 그러면 본 사건과 관련하여 회사가 취한 적절한 조치사항에 대해 구체적으로 살펴보도록 하겠다.

2. 직장내 성희롱 사건 내용

(1) 가해자 A의 성희롱

2011.4.27. 회사의 전 직원 (30여명)이 참석한 워크숍에서 피해자는 엉덩이로 이름쓰기 하는 벌칙에 걸렸다. 피해자는 엉덩이로 이름을 쓰기 전에 카메라 및 핸드폰 촬영을 하지 말라고 당부하였다. 영업부장인 가해자 A는 몰래 핸드폰으로 촬영하였고, 그것을 자신의 핸드폰에 저장해 둔 채 잊고 지냈다. 2011. 5.19. 가해자 A는 회사의 전체회식에서 회사의 워크숍에서 피해자 몰래 촬영한 핸드폰 동영상을 남자직원들과 돌려보면서, "Sales Kick Off 때 하이라이트로 틀면 재미있겠다.", "얼굴이 돌아서서 잘 안보이니 증명사진 붙여서 보내라." 등 피해자에게 성적수치심을 일으키는 대화가 오갔다. 피해자는 그 자리에서 가해자 A에게 그 동영상의 삭제를 요구했지만, 가해자 A는 아무런 조치를 취하지 않았다. 이에 피해자는 인사부에 불쾌함을 알리면서 가해자 A가 정식으로 사과해야 한다고 통보했다. 이에 가해자 A는 정식 사과도 하지 않고 인사부에 통지한 것에 대해 불쾌함을 표시했다.

(2) 가해자 B의 성희롱

2011. 5.19. 직원전체 회식자리에서 가해자 B는 직원들에게 전통주를 한 잔씩 직원들에게 따라 주면서 피해자가 앉은 자리로 오면서 "이 대리가

seat, he said to her, "Ms. Lee, you sat in my seat. You must like me" and sat beside her. He then said, "Shall we have a love shot?" The victim-employee was humiliated as he was suggesting that she was a "bar hostess" (a position which sometimes involves sexual behavior). The victim-employee very obviously did not like his suggestion, saying "That is a very dangerous thing to say." To which Offender B replied, "I'm not dangerous."

On March 29, 2011, at a company dinner, all the employees went to a Singing Room after dinner. There, while the victim-employee was singing a song by Sym Subong at someone's request, Offender B approached the victim-employee with a gesture in blue dancing, but the victim-employee avoided looking at him. After the song was finished, she sang another song by Ju Hyunme, which talked about a 'confession of love' many times. When she returned to her seat, Offender B said to her, "You were talking to me. That story was about me, right?"

On February 11, 2011, at a company dinner, Offender B approached the victim-employee and said, "Let's hug each other!" It was hard for the victim-employee to refuse in front of all her colleagues, so she patted his shoulder from a distance. The victim-employee began to wonder seriously how she could continue working with her manager (Offender B) who, without hesitation, had shown sexually-charged behavior and caused this humiliation to a married employee at a company dinner with their colleagues.

(3) Sexual Harassment by Offender C

On March 29, 2011, the victim-employee was trying to get out of the company dinner because she was humiliated by Offender B's sexual behavior, but after giving it more thought, she went to the country manager (Offender C) to say 'good-bye'. When she said to him, "I have to go home early," Offender C offered his hand to shake hers. Shortly after they shook, Offender C said goodbye again, wanted to shake hands again, and attempted to kiss her hand. Surprised, the victim-employee took her hand back quickly, but some of her fingers touched Offender C's lips. The victim-employee was very embarrassed, shocked, and humiliated.

3. Company Recognition of Sexual Harassment and Handling Procedures

(1) Employer procedures in dealing with sexual harassment complaints

내 자리 앉았네. 나를 좋아하나 보다."라고 말하며 옆에 앉아 "러브샷 한번 할까?"라고 말하는 것에 대해 피해자는 술집접대부로 여기는 것 같아서 수치심을 느꼈고, 그 자리에서 "위험한 행동입니다."라고 거부의사를 표시하였다. 이에 가해자 B는 "나는 안 위험한데?"라고 말했다.

2011. 3.29. 직원전체 회식자리에서 2차로 노래방에 가게 되었다. 피해자가 심수봉씨의 노래를 요청하여 불렀는데, 가해자 B는 '블루스춤'을 추는 시늉을 하며 피해자에게 다가왔고 피해자는 이를 외면하였다. 노래가 끝나자 직원들이 앵콜 요청이 있어 주현미의 노래를 불렀고 그 가사에 '사랑고백' 관련된 단어가 많이 포함되어 있었다. 피해자가 노래를 마치고 자리로 돌아오는데, 가해자 B는 "나한테 하는 얘기지? 내 이야기지?"하는 식으로 이야기를 했다.

2011.2.11. 회사의 전체 회식자리에서 가해자 B는 피해자에게 "허그 한번 하자."고 다가왔다. 피해자는 전 직원들이 있는 자리에서 거절하는 것이 어려웠고, 대신 최대한 어깨를 두드리는 수준에서 마무리했다. 피해자는 다른 직원들이 있는 회식자리에서 결혼까지 한 유부녀에게 이런 수치심을 유발하는 행동을 스스럼없이 하는 직원이 상급자로 있는 회사를 다녀야 하는지 고민이 빠졌다.

(3) 가해자 C의 성희롱

2011. 3.29. 회식자리에서 가해자 B에게 성희롱을 당한 것에 기분이 좋지 않아 서둘러 그 자리를 빠져 나오려고 하였으나, 지사장 (가해자 C)에게 인사라도 하고 가야 할 것 같아서 가해자 C에게로 갔다. "먼저 들어가야 할 것 같다."고 인사를 하자 가해자 C는 악수를 청했고, 이에 악수에 응했다. 그런 후 바로 가해자 C는 피해자에게 다시 한 번 인사를 하고 악수를 청하면서 자신의 입술을 피해자의 손에 갖다 대려 하였다. 피해자는 놀라서 손을 급히 빼려 했는데 그 순간 자신의 손가락 일부가 가해자 C의 입술에 닿게 되었다. 이에 피해자는 너무 당황하였고 어이가 없고 수치스러움을 느꼈다.

3. 회사의 사건인지 및 처리 절차

(1) 사업주의 직장내 성희롱문제 처리절차

Chapter3-13. Prevention of Sexual Harassment in the Workplace

Upon receiving a complaint of sexual harassment, the employer will conduct interviews, investigate the facts, implement appropriate measures such as disciplinary punishment, etc. and then inform the victim-employee.

- **1st Stage: Receipt of the sexual harassment complaint (HR or Labor Department)**
- **2nd Stage: Interview and investigation**

    Upon receiving the complaint, the person-in-charge is to quickly set up an interview and begin a thorough investigation. If necessary, the investigator can hear the defendant's testimony instead by organizing a face-to-face meeting between him/her and the victim.

    The person-in-charge shall weigh the collected information obtained during the investigation. As soon as the person-in-charge reaches a final conclusion, it shall be reported to the employer.

- **3rd Stage: Confirmation and disciplinary measures**

    If it is confirmed that sexual harassment has occurred, the employer shall take appropriate action against the offender, such as a transfer to another department or position, warning, reprimand, work suspension, or dismissal, etc.

- **4th Stage: Report of the results**

    Upon closing the investigation, the company shall notify the victim and the offender of the results.

- **5th Stage: Preventative action**

    The employer shall pay special attention to the victim-employee after the closure of the sexual harassment case to prevent further sexual harassment of that employee.

(2) The Company's handling of the above cases of sexual harassment

When it recognized the victim-employee's accusations regarding sexual harassment, the Company immediately requested statements from the victim-employee and the alleged offenders. As the country manager (Offender C) was involved in this case, the Company used a labor attorney to interview the victim-employee and the alleged offenders and receive their statements, to ensure fair conclusions. After receiving their statements and witness accounts, the Company determined the related behaviors were sexual harassment according to the criteria

직장내 성희롱 관련 내용이 접수되면 사업주는 당사자 상담과 조사를 통하여 사실관계를 확인하고, 징계 등 적절한 조치와 함께 처리 결과를 피해 근로자에게 통보하는 순서로 처리한다.

- 1단계 : 성희롱 접수 (인사부서, 노무부서)
- 2단계 : 상담과 조사:

  사건 접수를 하면 피해자와 성희롱 용의자에게 신속하게 성희롱 사건 전모를 듣고 공정하고 세심하게 조사한다. 필요한 경우에는 피해자의 입장을 성희롱 용의자와의 대면 대신 증인의 증언을 통해 들을 수 있다. 담당자는 조사 과정에서 취득한 개인정보를 양자의 사생활 보호 측면에서 비밀로 지켜야 한다. 공식 조사된 결과가 직장내 성희롱이라고 판단하면 담당자는 사업주에 보고한다.

- 3단계 : 확인과 징계절차:

  사업주는 성희롱 사실이 확인되면 성희롱 행위자에 대해 부서 이동, 경고, 견책, 전직, 대기발령, 정직, 해고 등의 적절한 조치를 취해야 한다.

- 4단계 : 결과 통지:

  조사를 종결할 때에는 피해자와 성희롱 행위자 모두에게 조사 결과를 통지한다.

- 5단계 : 사후 재발 방지:

  사업주는 성희롱 사건에 대한 조치 후에도 향후 피해 근로자에 대한 성희롱 문제가 재발하지 않도록 관심을 가져야 한다.

(2) 회사의 성희롱 사건처리

회사가 성희롱 사건에 대해 인지하였을 때, 지체 없이 피해자와 가해자들의 진술서를 확보하였다. 이 과정에서 가해자 C(지사장)가 관련되어 있어서, 공정한 판단을 위해 외부의 공인노무사를 통해 피해자, 그리고 가해자들과 상담한 후 진술서를 받았다. 회사는 이 진술서와 당시 목격자들의 의견을 들어

for evaluating whether certain behavior is sexual harassment at work. In this process, the Company handled the investigations quickly and confidentially, in order to protect the alleged offenders and the victim-employee at the same time. The alleged offenders resisted this investigation, saying they did not intend to harass her sexually. However, the Company explained to them seriously of the criteria for determining the existence of sexual harassment, "In evaluating whether certain behavior is sexual harassment or not, the victim's subjective conditions must be considered. As a socially accepted idea, how a reasonable person evaluates or copes with a situation against the particular controversial behaviors involved must also be considered in the victim's case." The Company concluded that the three men's behaviors were sexual harassment and they were disciplined in accordance with the level of their violations. After this, the Company invited an external expert, (a labor attorney), and implemented training for all employees towards preventing sexual harassment at work. The Company also strove to prevent the reoccurrence of any sexual harassment by posting a notification on the bulletin board, detailing ways to prevent any further sexual harassment in the work environment.

The Company held a Disciplinary Action Committee composed of three members designated by the Company in accordance with the disciplinary regulations in the Rules of Employment, and took disciplinary action after reviewing the disciplinary details. There are five types of discipline: 1) written warning, 2) wage reduction, 3) suspension from work, 4) recommended resignation, and 5) dismissal. The Company decided the level of discipline according to the level of violation as follows.

Offender A:
   ① 10% wage reduction from one month's salary;
   ② Suspension of promotion for six months;
   ③ Official apology to the victim in front of company directors

Offender B:
   ① Written warning;
   ② 2.5% wage reduction from one month's salary (July)

Offender C: Written warning

4. Conclusion

These cases of sexual harassment at work were related to environmental sexual harassment, and the employees recognized that their behavior at company dinners could be interpreted as sexual harassment even if they didn't think much about it. These cases brought some educational benefit to the Company as well as the employees realized that their unintentional behavior could be interpreted as sexual harassment because the criteria for determining sexual harassment is partly judged from the victim's perspective,

성희롱 여부에 대해 직장내 성희롱 판단기준에 따라 판단하였다. 또한 이 과정에서 피해자와 가해자들을 보호하기 위해 보안을 유지하면서 사건처리를 신속하게 진행하였다. 가해자 A, B, C는 자신들이 특정한 의도를 가진 성희롱이 아니었다고 반발하였다. 그러나 회사는 이들에게 성희롱 판단의 기준은 "피해자의 주관적 사정을 고려하되, 사회 통념상 합리적인 사람이 피해자의 입장이라면 문제가 되는 행동에 대하여 어떻게 판단하고 대응하였을 것인가를 함께 고려하여야 한다."라는 기준으로 판단한다고 설명을 해주었다. 회사는 가해자 A, B, C의 행위가 모두 성희롱에 해당된다는 결론을 내리고, 그 위반 정도에 따라 징계조치를 하였다. 또한 외부전문가인 공인노무사를 통해 회사 전체직원들에게 직장내 성희롱예방 교육을 실시하였으며, 직원들 간에 이와 같은 환경형 성희롱이 더 이상 확산되지 않도록 직원 전체에 대해 '공고물' 게시함으로써 성희롱 재발방지를 위해 노력하였다.

회사는 취업규칙의 징계규정에 따라 회사가 지명하는 3인으로 징계위원회를 구성하고, 징계내용을 심의한 후 징계조치를 취했다. 회사의 징계의 종류는 1) 서면견책, 2) 감봉, 3) 정직, 4) 권고사직, 5) 해고의 5가지가 있고, 회사는 위반정도에 따라 다음과 같이 징계 수위를 결정하였다.

가. 가해자 A의 경우:
    ① 1개월 감봉 – 월급의 10%;
    ② 6개월간 진급연기;
    ③ 회사 경영진 앞에서 피해자에게 공식사과
나. 가해자 B의 경우:
    ① 서면견책;
    ② 1개월 감봉 – 7월 평균임금의 2.5%
다. 가해자 C의 경우: 서면견책

4. 결론

이번 직장내 성희롱 사건은 환경형 성희롱으로서 회사 영업부 직원들이 회식자리에서 일상적으로 대수롭지 않게 생각하고 한 행동들이 성희롱이 될 수 있다는 사실을 인식하게 한 교육적인 효과가 있었다. 이 사건으로 말미암아

rather than the offender's intention. In addition, this case contributes to the building of healthy relationships between employees. The Company was able to protect the victim from being further humiliated, through appropriate measures against sexual harassment. The Company also took appropriate action to prevent a repeat of sexual harassment by determining acceptable discipline for the offenders, carrying that discipline out, and providing education to prevent sexual harassment of other employees.

Due to the victim-employee's complaint of sexual harassment to the Labor Office, the Company was investigated to determine whether or not it had followed the employer procedures for handling sexual harassment complaints. The Labor Office found that the Company had carried out its duties as employer very well according to the Equal Employment Act, except for one, which was skipping its obligation for two years before setting up sexual harassment education last year. As already mentioned, the Company was fined 2 million won for two occurrences of failing to provide education to prevent sexual harassment. Beyond this, the victim-employee's petition to the Labor Office was concluded without any further penalty or demand.

Section 14. Equal Treatment: Criteria for Judgment & Related Cases

I. Introduction

Recently, one of the most noticeable court rulings is one where the court ruled as discrimination by social status in a case where the employer made up a particular group of only non-fixed employees recently transferred and treated them unequally to their regular employee counterparts. This verdict has increased public interest in matters related to equal treatment. The Constitution of the Republic of Korea (Article 11-①) stipulates, †..there shall be no discrimination in political, economic, social or cultural life on account of sex, religion or social status. In aligning with this, the Labor Standards Act contains a provision on equal treatment which includes the additional item of 'nationality', stipulating, No employer shall discriminate against employees on the basis of gender, or give discriminatory treatment in relation to working conditions on the basis of nationality, religion or social status. Other provisions on equal treatment are gradually being introduced in other Acts as social need arises to do so, regarding irregular employment status,

회사는 물론 회사의 모든 직원들에게도 '성희롱 판단기준이 가해자의 입장이 아닌 피해자의 관점에서 판단하기 때문'에 가해자의 의도와 관계없이 성희롱이 될 수 있다는 사실을 인식하도록 해 주었다. 아울러 이 사건은 직원들의 건전한 대인관계 형성에도 기여하였다고 할 수 있다.

회사는 성희롱 사건에 대한 적절한 조치를 통해, 피해자에게 더 이상의 피해가 발생하지 않도록 보호할 수 있었고, 또한 성희롱 가해자들에게 수긍할 수 있는 징계 수위를 결정·부과하였고 성희롱에 대한 예방교육을 통해 성희롱 사건이 재차 발생하지 않도록 적절한 조치를 이행하였다.

회사는 이번 성희롱 사건을 통해 성희롱 관련 사업주의 이행 의무 사항에 대하여 관할 노동사무소의 조사를 받았다. 그 결과로 근로감독관은 회사가 최근 3년 동안 (금년 제외) 성희롱 예방교육을 2번 누락한 것에 대한 200만원의 과태료를 부과하였으며, 그 밖에 사항에 대해서는 회사가 남녀고용평등법에 의한 사업주의 의무를 모두 이행하였으므로 별도의 명령이나 제재 없이 이번 성희롱사건을 종결하였다.

제14절 균등처우의 판단기준과 관련사례

I. 문제의 소재

최근 화제가 된 판결이 무기계약직으로 전환된 근로자들에게 일반 정규직과 다른 별도의 직군을 만들어 차별을 한 사안에서, 이를 사회적 신분에 따른 차별이라 판결하였다. 이 판결로 인하여 균등처우에 대한 관심이 높아지고 있다. 우리나라 헌법 제11조 1항은 … 누구든지 성별·종교 또는 사회적 신분에 의하여 … 모든 영역에서 차별을 아니한다라고 규정하고 있다. 이와 관련하여 근로기준법도 균등처우 규정을 두고 '국적'을 추가하여 성별, 국적, 신앙과 사회적 신분을 이유로 근로조건에 대한 차별적 처우를 하지 못한다라고 규정하고 있다. 근로기준법 외에도 사회적 변화에 따른 차별금지 조항이 계속해서 추가되어 현재는 비정규직, 연령, 장애인, 외국인 등에 대한 차별금지 규정을

age, disability, and foreign workers, etc.

There are two principles the Court uses in identifying the criteria for determining whether discriminative treatment, which it defines as the same thing treated in a different way, or different things treated in the same way, is justifiable or not. First, in order for a situation/action to be considered discriminative treatment, the primary requisite is that the employees claiming discrimination should be basically in the same working group with the target comparison employees.[212] Second, even though the employees claiming discrimination and the target comparison employees are working in the same workplace and at the same kind of job, if the employer discriminates in their working conditions based upon reasonable criteria in consideration of the detail and type of work and other conditions, this discrimination can be considered justifiable.[213] In this article, I would like to review the criteria for judgment of whether discriminative treatment is justifiable or not, and related cases.

II. Gender Discrimination

1. Criteria for judgment

Gender discrimination is prohibited under Article 11(1) of the Constitution, with a more detailed explanation given in Article 32(4): Special protection shall be accorded to working women, and they shall not be subjected to unjust discrimination in terms of employment, wages and working conditions. Article 6 of the Labor Standards Act prohibits gender discrimination and includes penalties for violations. In particular, the Equal Employment Act enacted in 1987 defines gender discrimination (Article 2) as follows:

First, the term discrimination means that an employer applies different hiring and working conditions to employees, or takes other disadvantageous measures against them without justifiable reason on account of gender, marriage, status within the family, and whether or not they are pregnant or have had a child, etc.

Second, it is discrimination even if an employer applies the same hiring or working conditions, but the number of one gender to whom the conditions apply is considerably less than that of the opposite gender, thus causing a disadvantageous result to the opposite gender. This reflects the fact that indirect discrimination due to corporate culture can be deemed as gender discrimination.

Third, provided that this shall not apply to cases involving any of the following

---

[212] Supreme Court ruling on October 29, 2015: 2013da1051.
[213] Supreme Court ruling on February 26, 2002: 2000da39064

개별 법률로써 도입하고 있다.
 그러면 차별금지에 대한 판단기준을 어떻게 보아야 하는가? 에 있어 법원은 차별적 처우란 '같은 것을 다르게, 다른 것을 같게 취급하는 것'이라 정의하면서 다음의 두 가지 원칙을 제시하고 있다. 첫째, 차별적 처우에 해당하기 위해서는 우선 그 전제로써 차별을 받았다고 주장하는 사람과 그가 비교대상자로 지목하는 사람이 본질적으로 동일한 업무집단에 속해 있어야 한다.[212] 둘째, 같은 사업장에서 같은 직종에 근무하는 근로자 집단이라고 하더라도 근로의 내용, 근무형태 등 제반 여건을 고려하여 합리적인 기준을 정하여 차별하는 경우에는 정당한 차별로 인정하고 있다.[213] 이와 관련된 판단기준과 관련 사례를 다음과 같이 살펴보고자 한다.

II. 성별

1. 판단기준

 성차별금지는 헌법 제11조 1항에 명시되어 있으며, 헌법 제32조 4항에서 여자의 근로는 특별한 보호를 받으며, 고용·임금 및 근로조건에 있어서 부당한 차별을 받지 아니한다고 구체적으로 기술하고 있다. 이를 현실적으로 반영하는 근로기준법 제6조에서는 성차별을 금지하고, 위반한 자에 대해 벌칙조항을 두고 있다. 특히 1987년에 제정된 남녀고용평등법에서는 성차별(제2조)을 아래와 같이 규정하고 있다.
 첫째, '차별'이란 사업주가 근로자에게 성별, 혼인, 가족 안에서의 지위, 임신 또는 출산 등의 사유로 합리적인 이유 없이 채용 또는 근로의 조건을 다르게 하거나 그 밖의 불리한 조치를 하는 경우이다.
 둘째, 사업주가 채용조건이나 근로조건은 동일하게 적용하더라도 그 조건을 충족할 수 있는 남성 또는 여성이 다른 한 성(性)에 비하여 현저히 적고 그에 따라 특정 성에게 불리한 결과를 초래하며 그 조건이 정당한 것임을 증명할 수 없는 경우를 포함한다. 즉, 기업문화에서 간접적인 차별도 성차별로 인정

---
[212] 대법원 2015. 10. 29. 선고 2013다1051 판결
[213] 대법원 2002. 2. 26. 선고 2000다39063 판결

Chapter3-14. Equal Treatment: Criteria for Judgment & Related Cases

items:

① Where a specific gender is inevitably required in view of the nature of the duties;

② Where measures are taken to protect maternity, such as during pregnancy, childbirth or breastfeeding by female employees, etc.; or

③ Other cases where affirmative action measures are taken under this Act or other Acts. These exceptions are designed to avoid any reverse discrimination.[214]

2. Details of gender discrimination

Concrete provisions regarding gender discrimination in the Equal Employment Act can be summarized as follows:

① An employer shall not discriminate on grounds of gender in recruitment and hiring of employees. When recruiting and hiring female employees, an employer shall not present nor demand certain physical conditions, such as appearance, height, weight, etc., and marital status not required for performance of the relevant duties (Article 7).

② An employer shall provide equal pay for work of equal value in the same business. The criteria for work of equal value shall be skills, efforts, responsibility and working conditions, etc. required to perform the work (Article 8). 'Work of equal value' in judicial rulings means the same work when comparing men and women in the corresponding workplace and nearly the same work in practical terms, or the work of basically the same value as evaluated through objective job evaluations in spite of slightly different jobs. Whether the work is of equal value or not shall be estimated in comprehensive consideration of technology, working conditions, education, career, working period, etc.[215]

③ An employer shall not discriminate on grounds of gender in providing benefits, such as money, goods or loans, etc., in order to compensate his/her employees aside from wages (Article 9).

④ An employer shall not discriminate on grounds of gender in education, assignment and promotion of his/her workers (Article 10).

⑤ An employer shall not discriminate on grounds of gender in retirement age or whether certain workers are dismissed or designated to retire. No employer shall make a labor contract that stipulates marriage, pregnancy or childbirth of

---

[214] Jongryul Lim, 「Labor Law」, 14th edition, 2016. Parkyoungsa, p. 374.
[215] Supreme Court ruling on March 14, 2003: 2002do3883; Supreme Court ruling on March 14, 2013: 2010da101011.

할 수 있다.

셋째, 차별에 대한 예외로서
① 직무의 성격에 비추어 특정 성이 불가피하게 요구되는 경우,
② 여성 근로자의 임신·출산·수유 등 모성보호를 위한 조치를 하는 경우,
③ 그 밖에 이 법 또는 다른 법률에 따라 적극적 고용개선조치를 하는 경우를 두고 있다.

이는 다른 성에 대한 역차별 문제를 사전에 배제하기 위한 것이다.[214]

2. 성차별금지의 내용

남녀고용평등법에서 성차별에 관한 구체적인 규정은 다음과 같이 요약된다.
① 모집과 채용에서 차별을 금지하고(제7조), 특히 사업주가 여성 근로자의 모집과 채용에서 그 직무에 필요하지 아니한 용모, 키, 체중 등의 신체적 조건, 미혼 조건 등을 제시하거나 요구 하여서는 아니 된다.
② 임금에서 동일한 사업 내의 동일 가치 노동에 대하여는 동일한 임금을 지급하여야 한다(제8조). 동일 가치 노동의 기준은 직무 수행에서 요구되는 기술, 노력, 책임 및 작업 조건 등으로 한다. 여기서 판례가 말하는 '동일 가치 노동'이란 해당 사업내의 서로 비교되는 남녀의 노동이 동일하거나 실질적으로 거의 같은 성질의 노동 또는 그 직무가 다소 다르더라도 객관적인 직무평가 등을 통하여 본질적으로 동일한 가치가 있다고 인정되는 노동에 해당하는 것을 말하고 동일 가치의 노동인지 여부는 직무 수행에서 요구되는 기술, 작업 조건, 학력·경력·근속기간 등의 기준을 종합적으로 고려하여 판단하여야 한다.[215]
③ 임금 외의 금품으로 근로자의 생활을 보조하기 위한 금품의 지급 또는 자금의 융자 등 복리후생에서 남녀를 차별 하여서는 아니 된다(제9조).
④ 교육·배치 및 승진에서 남녀를 차별 하여서는 아니 된다(제10조).
⑤ 정년·퇴직 및 해고에서 남녀의 차별을 하여서는 아니 된다. 특히 여성 근로자의 혼인, 임신 또는 출산을 퇴직 사유로 예정하는 근로계약을 체결

---

[214] 임종률, 「노동법」, 제14판, 2016. 박영사, 374면.
[215] 대법원 2003. 3. 14. 선고 2002도3883 판결; 대법원 2013. 3. 14. 선고 2010다101011 판결

female workers as grounds for resignation (Article 11).

III. Discrimination Based on Nationality

1. Criteria for Judgment

Nationality refers to the status according to the Nationality Act, and discrimination can exist for certain employees such as foreigners without Korean nationality, overseas Koreans, and illegal migrant workers, etc. Recently, discrimination due to nationality has caused significant social issues due to the increased number of foreign workers. Article 22 of the Foreign Workers Employment Act enacted in August 2003 stipulates, No employer shall discriminate or unfairly treat any person on the grounds that he/she is a foreign worker. However, this article does not include any penal provisions and only applies to non-professional workers in relation to the employment permit system. Accordingly, the prohibition of discrimination based on nationality follows Article 6 of the Labor Standards Act that No employer shall give discriminatory treatment in relation to the working conditions on the basis of nationality, and the penal provisions therein. However, justifiable discrimination is allowed, with the related Labor Ministry Guidelines explaining, Determining whether discrimination based on nationality exists or not shall require consideration of all related items collectively: whether the discrimination in working conditions was only based on nationality or not; other entire factors regarding the working conditions such as wages and working hours; and in addition, whether discrimination exists that exceeds reasonable criteria for the work.[216]

2. Related cases

There are many cases related to discrimination due to nationality.
① A Constitutional Court ruling in 2007, in which it stipulated, Even though industrial trainees with a trainee's contract provided labor service under the employer's direction and supervision, they then received wages. In actual relations, as only foreign industrial trainees were excluded from the application of major labor laws without justifiable reason, we find this unreasonable. The fact that industrial trainees are excluded from some parts of the Labor

---

[216] Labor Ministry Guideline: May 25, 1994, Gungi 68207-585.

하여서는 아니 된다(제11조).

Ⅲ. 국적

1. 판단기준

　국적은 국적법상 지위를 말하며, 대한민국의 국적을 소유하지 않은 외국인 근로자, 해외동포, 불법체류자 등을 대상으로 한 차별이 발생할 수 있다. 최근에 외국인근로자가 증가하면서 국적에 의한 차별이 주요 사회적 이슈가 되고 있다. 2003년도 8월에 제정된 '외국인근로자고용법'에서 사용자는 외국인 근로자라는 이유로 부당하게 차별하여 처우 하여서는 아니 된다라고 규정하고 있지만(제22조), 이에 대해 처벌규정이 없고, 적용범위도 고용허가제와 관련된 비전문직 외국인 근로자에게만 적용되어 한계가 있다. 따라서 국적에 의한 차별은 근로기준법 제6조 … 국적을 이유로 근로조건에 대한 차별적 처우를 하지 못한다는 규정과 위반 시 관련 벌칙규정에 따른다고 할 수 있다. 다만, 차별에 합리적인 이유가 있는 경우에는 그 예외가 인정된다. 관련 행정해석은 국적을 이유로 근로조건을 차별하는 것에 해당하는지의 판단은 근로조건에 대한 차별이 단순히 국적만을 이유로 한 것인지 여부와 차별의 대상인 근로조건에 대하여 임금, 근로시간 등 근로자 대우에 관한 일체의 요소를 전반적으로 고려하여 합리적인 기준에서 벗어난 차별이 있었는지 여부 등을 종합적으로 판단하여야 한다는 입장이다.[216]

2. 차별 사례

　국적에 의한 차별의 사례로
① 헌법재판소는 산업연수생이 연수라는 명목 하에 사업주의 지시·감독을 받으면서 사실상 노무를 제공하고 수당 명목의 금품을 수령하는 등 실질적인 근로관계에 있는 경우에는, 근로기준법이 보장한 근로기준 중 주요사항을 외국인 산업연수생에 대하여만 적용되지 않도록 하는 것은 합리적인

---

[216] 행정해석 1994. 5. 25. 근지 68207-585.

Standards Act, unlike ordinary employees, is arbitrary discrimination.[217]

② Supreme Court ruling in 1995: Foreign worker A from Thailand, who came to Korea under a trainee working visa, was seriously injured while working beyond the permitted sojourn period. Foreign worker A applied for compensation from the Employee Welfare Corporation for medical treatment, but was rejected by the Corporation as foreign worker A was an illegal migrant worker working illegally. However, the Supreme Court ruled that even though illegal employment is clearly an act warranting punishment, the work already provided is actual performance that makes the worker subject to the protection of labor law. Accordingly, illegal foreign workers may apply for and receive Industrial Accident Compensation Insurance.[218]

③ Supreme Court ruling in 2015: Some illegal foreign workers living in Seoul and Gyeonggi Province submitted a report of their establishment of a labor union to the Seoul Regional Labor Office on May 3, 2005, but their application was rejected due to their illegal status. Even in the courts there have been disputes on whether a labor union of illegal foreign workers is permissible or not, but the Supreme Court ruled on June 25, 2015 that it was.[219]

Ⅳ. Religious Discrimination

1. Criteria for judgment

The Labor Standards Act regulates that no employer shall give discriminatory treatment in relation to working conditions on the basis of religion, which includes specific religions, religious beliefs, world view, socialist creed, or political line of a particular political party, etc.[220] However, with the exception of purpose-based companies organized to carry out business directly connected to specific ideas, it is not deemed a violation if there is discrimination regarding an employee whose behavior is in conflict with the purpose of the company he or she works for.

2. Related cases

---

[217] Constitutional Court (Industrial trainee system): August 30, 2007 2004hnma670.
[218] Supreme Court ruling: September 15, 1995: 94nu12067 (Rejection for application of occupational injury)
[219] Supreme Court ruling on June 25, 2015: 2007do4995 (Rejection of labor union's report of establishment)
[220] Hyungbae Kim, 「Labor Law」, 24th edition, 2015, Parkyoungsa, p. 239.

근거를 찾기 어렵다고 하여 근로기준법을 일부 적용하지 않는 것은 위헌이라고 판단하였다.[217]

② A는 태국국적 외국인으로 산업연수 체류자격으로 입국하였으나, 체류기간을 초과하여 불법체류자로 근무하던 중에 부상을 입었다. A는 요양신청을 하였으나 공단은 A가 불법 취업한 외국인이라는 이유로 산재불승인을 하였다. 그러나 대법원은 불법체류는 단속의 대상임을 명백히 하고 있으나, 이미 제공된 사실적 행위의 노동에 대해서는 노동법의 보호가 있어야 한다는 취지에서 불법체류자도 산재보험이 적용된다고 판결하였다.[218]

③ 서울과 경기도의 불법체류자로 구성된 외국인근로자들이 2005년 5월 3일 서울지방노동청에 노동조합 설립신고를 제출하였으나 불법체류자라는 이유로 거부당하였다. 이 노동조합 인정여부에 대해 장기간 법원에서 다툼이 있었으나 2015년 6월 25일 결국 대법원 합의체 판결에서 불법체류자들로 구성된 노동조합의 설립을 인정하였다.[219]

IV. 신앙

1. 판단기준

근로기준법은 신앙을 이유로 근로조건에 대한 차별적 처우를 하지 못한다고 규정하고 있다. 신앙을 이유로 한 차별은 특정의 종교, 종교적 신념, 정치적 세계관, 사회주의적 신조, 특정정당의 정치노선 등을 이유로 해당 근로자를 차별하는 것이다.[220] 다만, 특정의 사상과 직접적으로 연결된 목적으로 수행하는 사업인 경향사업에 있어서는 그 사업목적에 반하여 행동하는 경우에는 차별적 처우를 허용하고 있다.

2. 차별 사례

---

[217] 헌법소원 사건(산업연수생제도): 2007. 8. 30, 헌재 2004헌마670
[218] 대법원 1995. 9. 15. 선고 94누12067 판결 (요양불승인처분취소)
[219] 대법원 2015. 6. 25. 선고 2007두4995 전원합의체 판결(노동조합설립신고서 반려처분취소)
[220] 김형배, 「노동법」, 제24판, 2015. 박영사, 239면.

① In 2005, the Constitutional Court ruled as justifiable dismissal in cases where the employee behaved in violation of the purpose of his/her employing company. Whether there is justifiable reason or not when an employer intends to dismiss an employee shall be considered concretely for each individual case. Such general reasons are that the employee's violations should be serious enough to make it very difficult to maintain continuous employment relations with the employer, which means that the employer cannot expect any further work from the employee concerned due to the serious violation. Justifiable reasons for dismissal include: in cases where the employee's work performance was seriously inferior to his/her occupational abilities; in cases where the employee cannot work due to some illness; and, exclusively for purpose-based companies organized to carry out business directly connected to specific ideas, in cases where the employee disagrees with the purpose of his/her employing company; and others.[221]

② In 1994, the Supreme Court ruled that an employee's behavior that violates the purpose of his/her employing company is deemed a justifiable reason for dismissal. Even though the employee's real estate speculation, which was the reason for disciplinary dismissal, seemed like some minor misconduct in his personal life, in comprehensive consideration of the purpose of his employer, the Urban Development Corporation, which was established to create for citizens housing security and improve welfare through residential land development and supply, housing construction, etc., and the work scope of the employee engaged in real estate-related compensation, this real estate speculation by the employee could cause very negative effects of the social evaluation for the Urban Development Corporation.[222]

V. Social Status

1. Criteria for judgment

'Social status' which is a position formed over a considerable time and part of social evaluation refers to a social position that one cannot adjust through one's intention or performance.[223] A judicial ruling on June 19, 2016 explained, Social status is a position formed over a long time in society and part of social evaluation, and refers to the social classification that a specific group of employees cannot adjust through their intention or performance.[224]

---

221) Constitutional Court decision on March 31, 2005: 2003hunba12 (Justifiable reasons for dismissal).
222) Supreme Court ruling on December 13, 1994: 93nu23275 (ruling related to a purpose-based company)
223) Jongryul Lim, p. 376; Hyungbae Kim, p. 240; Kaprae Ha, 「The Labor Standards Act」28th edition, Joongang Economy, p. 79.

관련 사례로 헌법재판소는 경향사업에 저촉되는 경우를 정당한 해고의 사유로 인정하고 있다. ① 사용자가 근로자를 해고함에 있어서 정당한 이유의 유무는 개별적 사안에 따라 구체적으로 결정될 일이지만 그 일반적 내용은 해당 근로자와 사용자 사이의 근로관계를 계속 유지할 수 없을 정도의 이유, 즉 해당 근로자와의 근로관계의 유지를 사용자에게 더 이상 기대할 수 없을 정도의 것이 되어야 하는 것이다. 여기에는 업무에 대한 적성에 흠이 있거나 직무능력이 부족한 경우, 계약상의 노무급부를 곤란하게 하는 질병, … 특정 신조나 사상과 밀접히 연관된 소위 경향사업(傾向事業)에 있어서 근로자가 이러한 경향성을 상실한 경우 등이 일반적으로 이러한 정당한 이유에 해당하는 것으로 인정되고 있다.[221]

대법원도 경향사업에 반하는 근로자의 행위에 대해 정당한 해고로 인정하고 있다. ② 근로자에 대한 징계사유인 부동산투기행위가 근로자의 사생활에서의 비행에 불과하다고 할지라도, 택지의 개발과 공급, 주택의 건설 등을 통하여 시민의 주거생활의 안정과 복지향상을 목적으로 설립한 도시개발공사의 설립 목적, 부동산보상 관련업무를 담당하는 근로자의 업무내용 등의 여러 사정을 종합적으로 고려하면, 도시개발공사 소속 근로자의 부동산투기행위는 객관적으로 그 공사의 사회적 평가에 심히 중대한 악영향을 미치는 것으로 평가될 수 있는 경우라고 할 것이다.[222]

V. 사회적 신분

1. 판단기준

'사회적 신분'이란 상당한 기간이 지나면서 형성된 지위로서 사회적 평가가 수반되고, 자신의 의사나 능력으로 피할 수 없는 사회적 위치를 말한다.[223] 판례는 사회적 신분이란 사회에서 장기간 점하는 지위로서 일정한 사회적 평가를 수반하는 것으로서, 사업장 내에서 근로자 자신의 의사나 능력발휘에 의해서 회피할 수 없는 사회적 분류를 말한다[224]고 판시하고 있다.

---
221) 헌법재판소 2005. 3. 31. 결정, 헌재2003헌바12 선고(해고에 대한 정당한 이유의 해석).
222) 대법원 1994. 12. 13. 선고 93누23275 (경향사업 관련 판결)
223) 임종률, 376면; 김형배, 240면; 하갑례, 「근로기준법」 제28판, 2016, 중앙경제, 79면.

2. Related cases

Recently, there has been some headline news on a judicial ruling regarding a case of discrimination owing to social status. The employees concerned were transferred to non-fixed term employment and then placed in their own group after being hired for temporary positions. Unlike regular employees, the workers in this group were not eligible for title promotions. Different salary regulations were applied, and they were also ineligible for housing or family allowances, or meal expenses. The employees concerned took legal action for the unpaid allowances, stating that this discrimination was null and void due to it being a violation of equal treatment according to Article 6 of the Labor Standards Act. The court ruled, Besides job, the type of work and position can be part of social status if they require social evaluation or are social classifications that an employee cannot change through intention or performance. The court judged that being part of a group of workers with non-fixed employment status was part of social status, adding, With the exception of salary regulations, the same rules of employment and personnel regulations apply to non-fixed term employees. The quantity, quality and difficulty of their work and their contribution to the company were not less than their regular employee counterparts, so this discrimination amounts to a violation of Article 6 of the Labor Standards Act.

VI. Conclusion

The Labor Standards Act contains a penal provision for discrimination on the basis of gender, nationality, religion or social status, and an employee can seek an order for correction of such discrimination through a petition or making a claim with the Employment Labor Ministry. Hereby, the employee can also retroactively claim that lower wages were paid in a discriminatory manner. On the other hand, a particularly notable point in the prohibition of discrimination on the basis of gender is that an employer shall not discriminate on such grounds in recruitment and hiring of employees. Also, it can be deemed as indirect discrimination when an equal number of men and woman are employed at entry level, but this is not the case at the managerial level. The provision against discrimination on the basis of nationality has become a social issue due to the increased number of foreign employees, while regarding discrimination on the basis of religion, more cases have been related to purposed-based companies rather than against particular religions. Finally, in discrimination on the basis of social status, the courts recently ruled

---

[224] Seoul Southern Court ruling on June 19, 2016: 2015kahap3505.

2. 차별 사례

최근에 사회적 신분으로 인한 차별사건에 대한 판결이 나와 화제가 되고 있다. 그 내용은 다음과 같다. 해당 근로자들은 계약직 근로자로 입사해 업무직(무기계약직) 근로자로 전환이 됐다. 이들은 회사에서 일반직 근로자들과 달리 직급 승진도 적용 받지 못했다. 또 일반직 근로자들과 보수규정도 다르게 적용 받으며 주택수당, 가족수당, 식대 등 수당도 지급받지 못했다. 이에 근로자들은 이러한 차별은 근로기준법 제6조의 균등처우규정을 위반해 차별적 대우는 무효'라며 수당 지급을 청구했다. 이에 법원은 직업 뿐 아니라 사업장 내의 직종, 직위도 사회적 평가를 수반하거나, 근로자 스스로의 의사나 능력으로 벗어날 수 없는 사회적 분류라면 사회적 신분이라 할 수 있다고 판단하며 무기계약직을 '사회적 신분'으로 판단했다. 법원은 보수규정만 달리 적용하고 있을 뿐, 무기계약직 근로자와 일반직 근로자들은 동일한 취업규칙, 인사규정을 적용 받고 있으며, … 업무의 양과 질, 난이도나 회사에 대한 기여도가 무기계약직 근로자가 적다고 보기 어려운 점 등을 들어 … 근로기준법 제6조를 위반했다고 판단했다.

VI. 결론

근로기준법에서 언급한 성별, 국적, 신앙, 사회적 신분에 의한 차별은 벌칙 규정이 있고, 근로자는 고용노동부에 진정이나 고소를 통해 차별시정을 구할 수 있다. 근로자는 차별에 의한 불이익으로 인해 발생한 임금손실에 대해 소급해서 청구가 가능하다. 한편, 성별에 대한 차별금지에서 특히 주목해야 할 점은 모집과 채용단계에서도 차별금지 규정이 적용된다는 것이다. 또한 간접차별로 인해서 입사할 때 동일한 직급의 남녀사원 숫자가 고위 직책에서는 여성이 극소수를 차지하는 경우에는 간접 차별로 간주될 수 있다. 국적에 있어서도 차별금지조항은 근래 외국인의 증가로 인하여 사회적 이슈가 되고 있으며, 신앙을 이유로 한 차별에 있어서는 특정 종교 보다는 경향사업과 관련한 사례가 다수 발생하고 있다. 마지막으로, 사회적 신분을 이유로 한

---

224) 서울남부지법 2016. 6. 10. 선고 2014가합3505 판결(사회적 신분과 관련 판결).

discrimination exists against social status when an employer sets up a certain working group only for those with non-fixed employment status.

Section 15. The Discrimination Correction System concerning Non-regular Employees[225]

I. The Discrimination Correction System

The discrimination correction system is based on guidelines newly introduced in the "Act concerning Protection, etc. for Short-term and Part-time Employee" (hereinafter called "Short-term Employee Act") and the "Act concerning Protection, etc. for Dispatched Employees" (hereinafter called "Employee Dispatch Act"), which together are referred to as the "Non-regular Employee Protection Act". The discrimination correction system is designed to prohibit disadvantageous treatment (without justification) regarding wages and other working conditions of non-regular employees (a short-term, part-time, or dispatched employee) in comparison with target employees (a term-less contract employee, ordinary employee, or directly hired employee). The discriminative treatment can be rectified through the remedy process of the Labor Relations Commission.

The discrimination prohibition system for non-regular employees does not mean that the employer shall treat all working conditions of non-regular employees the same as working conditions of regular employees, however, the employer is prohibited from disadvantageous treatment without justification. That is, the employer is allowed to discriminate if there is a justifiable reason based on productivity, job skill, etc.

II. The Discrimination Correction System for a Short-term and Part-time Employee

1. Applicant for discrimination correction

The applicant for discrimination correction who can be protected from an employer's discriminative treatment shall be an employee of the Labor Standards Act and shall also be short-term employees or part-time employees.

---

[225] Administrative Guidelines, June 2007, Since then, it has been updated.

차별에 있어서 최근 판례와 같이 비정규직을 무기계약직으로 전환하면서 별도의 직종을 두어 차별하는 경우에도 사회적 신분에 의한 차별에 해당된다.

제15절 비정규직 근로자에 대한 차별시정제도[225]

Ⅰ. 차별시정제도

차별시정제도는 "기간제 및 단시간근로자 보호 등에 관한 법률"(이하 '기간제법'이라 함)과 "파견근로자보호 등에 관한 법률"(이하 '파견법'이라 함)(이하 '비정규직보호법'으로 통칭함)에서 새로이 도입된 제도이다. 차별시정제도는 사용자가 비정규직근로자(기간제, 단시간, 파견근로자)를 비교대상 근로자(무기계약근로자, 통상근로자, 직접고용근로자)에 비하여 임금 그 밖의 근로조건 등에 있어서 합리적인 이유 없이 불리하게 처우하는 것을 금지하는 제도이며, 차별적 처우에 대해서는 노동위원회를 통해 시정 절차를 마련하고 있다.

비정규직근로자에 대한 차별금지제도는 비정규직근로자의 모든 근로조건을 정규직근로자의 근로조건과 동일하게 대우하라는 것은 아니며, 합리적 이유 없이 불리하게 처우하는 것을 금지하는 것이다. 즉, 생산성, 숙련도 차이 등 합리적 이유가 있는 경우에는 비정규직근로자에 대하여 차등 대우하는 것이 허용된다.

Ⅱ. 기간제, 단시간근로자에 대한 차별시정제도

1. 차별시정신청권자

사용자의 차별처우로부터 보호를 받을 수 있는 차별시정신청권자는 근로기준법상의 근로자이어야 하며, 근로자 중에서도 기간제근로자 및 단시간근로자이어야 한다.

---

[225] 노동부지침, 2007년 6월, 이후 계속 수정 보완된 최신자료임.

2. Estimating time for the status of short-term and part-time employees

The time to estimate the status of short-term and part-time employees is not the time of filing an application for discrimination correction, but the time the employer engaged in the discriminative behavior.

3. The scope of 'wages and other working conditions' in prohibiting discrimination

The scope of 'wages and other working conditions' deals with ① working conditions regulated in the Labor Standards Act and working conditions stipulated in the Collective Bargaining Agreement, Rules of Employment and/or Labor Contract. Therefore, the scope includes not only wages, but also working hours, holidays, leave, safety, health and industrial accident compensation.

4. Target employee for comparison

The judgment of discrimination for short-term and part-time employees shall require the existence of target employees for comparison. The target employees do not only play a role as comparison criteria to estimate disadvantageous treatment, but also play a role as the basis and criteria for the Discrimination Correction Committee to determine parameters of the correction order. In comparison with short-term employee, the target employees shall be term-less contract employees engaged in the same or similar job in the business or workplace (Article 8(1) of the Short-term Employee Act). In comparison with part-time employee, the target employees shall be ordinary employees who were engaged in the same or similar job in the business or workplace (Article 8(2) of the Short-term Employee Act).
The 'same or similar job' means the job that is similar in job classification, duties, and job specification. That is, it will be considered synthetically based on the possibility of substitution within each group of employees.

5. Disadvantageous treatment

Disadvantageous treatment means that short-term and part-time employees receive low treatment in wages and other working conditions in comparison with target

2. 기간제, 단시간근로자 지위의 존재시점

기간제, 단시간근로자 인정여부에 대한 판단은 차별시정 신청 당시가 아니라 사용자에 의한 차별처우가 있었던 때를 기준으로 한다.

3. 차별처우 금지영역으로서 '임금 그 밖의 근로조건 등'의 범위

'임금 그 밖의 근로조건 등'의 범위는 ① 근로기준법이 규율하는 근로조건과 ② 단체협약, 취업규칙 또는 근로계약 등에 의한 근로조건으로서, 근로관계에서 발생하는 임금을 비롯하여 근로시간, 휴일, 휴가, 안전, 보건 및 재해보상 등이 포함될 것이다.

4. 비교대상 근로자

기간제, 단시간근로자에 대한 차별판단을 위해서는 이들 주체와 비교할 수 있는 다른 대상이 존재하여야 한다. 비교대상근로자는 불리한 처우가 있었는지 여부를 판단하는 비교기준으로서의 역할뿐만 아니라 시정명령의 내용을 결정하는 근거 및 기준으로서의 역할도 수행하게 된다. 기간제근로자의 비교대상 근로자는 ① 당해 사업 또는 사업장에서 ② 동종 또는 유사한 업무에 종사하는 ③ 기간의 정함이 없는 근로계약을 체결한 근로자(기간제법 제8조제1항)가 된다.
단시간근로자의 비교대상근로자는 ① 당 해 사업 또는 사업장의 ② 동종 또는 유사한 업무에 종사하는 ③ 통상근로자(기간제법 제8조제2항)가 된다. '동종 또는 유사한 업무'란 직종, 직무 및 작업내용이 동일성, 유사성을 가진 업무를 말한다. 즉, 업무성격의 유사성, 업무에 있어서 각 근로자의 집단의 상호대체가능성 등을 종합 고려하여 판단하여야 할 것이다.

5. 불리한 처우

불리한 처우란 기간제, 단시간근로자가 비교대상근로자에 비하여 임금 그 밖의 근로조건 등에 있어서 낮은 대우를 받는 것을 의미한다. 불리한

employees. In judging whether or not there is disadvantageous treatment, it is a principle that detailed items relating to wages and working conditions paid to short-term and part-time employees shall be compared with detailed items paid to target employees.

As disputes occur, comparable wages and working hours shall be categorized and compared as follows: ① In cases where some aspect of wages and working conditions are better for target employees, but other aspects are lower; and ② in cases where short-term and part-time employees are treated disadvantageously in comparison with target employees on particular wages and working conditions; and (3) in cases where the employer provides other purpose-based wages and working conditions. In this case, payment in accordance with actual provision of labor service (overtime, nighttime, holiday work allowance, etc.) shall be exempted from the scope of comparison.

In cases where it is hard or impossible to compare detailed items or categories because of the inclusive wage system or annual salary system, the wages and working conditions of target employees shall be compared and estimated overall.

As part-time employees' wages are determined based upon hourly wages, it is required to calculate ordinary employees' wages into hourly wages to confirm whether or not there is disadvantageous treatment. In this case, the comparison basis shall be hourly wages calculated based upon ordinary wages per contractual working hours.

6. Justifiable reason

1) Concept of justifiable reason

If there is a justifiable reason that the employer treats short-term and part-time employees disadvantageously in comparison with target employees, disadvantageous treatment can be justifiable and will not be considered discriminatory.

2) Short-term employee and employment period

When the employer applied wages and other working conditions in proportion to the employment period for short-term employees and this resulted in disadvantageous treatment, it can be accepted as justifiable.

처우의 여부를 판단함에 있어서 기간제, 단시간근로자에게 지급되는 임금 및 근로조건의 세부지급항목이 존재하는 경우 이에 상응하는 비교대상근로자의 세부지급항목과 비교하여 판단하는 것이 원칙이다.

세부지급항목별 비교가 현실적으로 ① 임금 및 근로조건에 있어서 특정 부분은 비교대상근로자보다 높은 반면 다른 특정 부분은 낮은 경우, ② 기간제, 단시간근로자가 특정 임금 및 근로조건에 대해 비교대상근로자에 비하여 불리한 처우를 받았다고 주장하는 반면, 사용자는 그 특정 임금 및 근로조건에 대신하여 다른 명목의 임금 및 근로조건을 제공하였음을 주장하여 다투는 경우에는, 비교 가능한 임금 및 근로조건을 하나의 범주로 묶어 비교, 판단할 수 있을 것이다. 이 경우 실제로 제공된 근로에 따라 지급되는 급부(연장, 야간, 휴일 근로수당 등)는 비교범주에서 제외된다.

포괄산정임금제 또는 연봉제로 산정하여 세부지급항목별 또는 범주화에 의한 비교가 곤란하거나 불가능한 경우에는 비교대상근로자의 임금 및 근로조건을 전체적으로 비교, 판단할 수 있을 것이다.

단시간근로자는 시간급 임금으로 정해지기 때문에 불리한 처우가 있는지를 확인하기 위해서는 통상근로자의 임금을 시간급 임금으로 환산하여야 한다. 이 경우 소정근로시간에 대하여 통상적으로 지급하는 임금을 기준으로 산정된 시간급을 원칙으로 한다.

6. 합리적 이유

1) 합리적 이유의 의의
사용자가 기간제, 단시간근로자를 비교대상근로자에 비하여 불리하게 처우함에 합리적 이유가 있다면 당해 불리한 처우는 정당화되고 차별처우에 해당하지 않게 된다.

2) 기간제근로자와 취업기간
사용자가 기간제근로자에 대하여 취업기간에 따라 임금 그 밖의 근로조건을 비례적으로 적용한 결과, 비교대상 근로자에 비해 불리한 처우가 발생하는 경우 합리적 이유가 인정될 수 있을 것이다.

3) Part-time employee and principle of protection by time proportion

Working conditions of part-time employees shall be determined on the basis of a relative ratio computed by comparing the work hours of part-time employees with those of full-time employees engaged in the same kind of work at the pertinent workplace, which is an application of the proportional time principle (Article 18(1) of the Labor Standards Act). Accordingly, it is justifiable to apply wages and divisible working conditions in proportion to time.

4) Disadvantageous treatment in accordance with short-term employment

The difference in wage and working conditions in accordance with characteristics of short-term employment, such as employment type (e.g., short-term employee), can be regarded as justifiable. It will also be considered as justifiable when the employer excludes short-term employees from wages and working conditions paid based on long-term employment and/or continuous service, such as long-term service allowance and compensational special bonus for those who retiring after long-term employment.

5) Disadvantageous treatment due to employment condition and criteria

If an employer discriminates against an employee justifiably on account of different employment factors (such as career, certification of qualification, etc.), the disadvantageous treatment can be justifiable when such factors determine wages, etc.

6) Disadvantageous treatment based on employment methods and procedures

Even though employment methods and procedures (open employment/closed employment, written test/interview, etc.) are different, if shot-term and part-time employees provide labor service with the same conditions as target employees, then disadvantageous treatment is not justifiable solely because of different employment methods and procedures. However, if the employer applies employment methods and procedures differently in order to reflect different work performance ability, it can be utilized as indirect evidence to confirm differences in work performance ability.

7) Difference in the job scope

As the job scope is directly related to quality and quantity of work and

3) 단시간근로자와 시간비례보호의 원칙

단시간근로자의 근로조건은 그 사업(장)의 동종 또는 유사한 업무에 종사하는 통상근로자의 근로시간을 기준으로 산정한 비율에 따라 결정되는, 이른바 시간비례의 원칙이 적용된다(근로기준법 제18조제1항). 따라서 임금 및 분할가능한 근로조건을 시간비례에 따라 적용하는 경우 합리적인 이유가 인정될 것이다.

4) 기간제근로자라는 단기고용의 특성에 따른 불리한 처우

기간제근로라는 고용형태, 즉 단기고용이라는 특성에 따른 임금 및 근로조건 등에서 차이는 합리적 이유가 있는 것으로 본다. 또한 장기고용 및 계속 근로를 전제로 지급하는 임금 및 근로조건, 예컨대 장기근속수당, 장기근속 퇴직자에 대한 공로보상적 특별지급금품 등에서 기간제근로자를 배제하는 것은 합리적 이유가 있는 것으로 볼 수 있을 것이다.

5) 채용 조건, 기준에 불리한 처우의 근거를 두는 경우

사용자가 불리한 처우를 정당화하는 합리적 이유로서 채용 조건, 기준(경력 및 자격증 등의 요건)이 다름을 주장하는 경우, 채용 조건, 기준이 당해 사업장의 임금결정요소라면 이 범위 내에서 불리한 처우는 정당화될 수 있을 것이다.

6) 채용 방법, 절차에 불리한 처우의 근거를 두는 경우

채용방법, 절차는 다르나(공개채용/비공개채용, 필기시험/면접 등), 기간제, 단시간근로자가 비교대상근로자와 동일한 조건 및 내용의 근로를 제공하는 경우 채용 방법, 절차가 다르다는 사정만으로는 불리한 처우를 정당화하는 합리적 이유가 될 수 없다. 다만, 사용자가 상이한 업무수행능력을 반영하기 위해 채용 방법, 절차를 달리 한 것이라면 이는 업무수행능력 차이를 뒷받침하는 간접적인 증거로 활용될 수 있을 것이다.

7) 업무의 범위가 다른 경우

업무범위는 근로의 양, 질과 직결되고 임금결정의 중요한 요소가 되므로

becomes an important factor in determining wages, target employees shall be selected carefully in consideration of differences in job scope. Disadvantageous treatment in wages and working conditions due to differences in the job scope can be regarded as justifiable.

8) **Difference in authority and responsibility related to job**

It can be justifiable to discriminate based on wages in accordance with the level of authority and responsibility. If the employer pays allowances (position allowance, title allowance, etc.) corresponding to the level of authority and responsibility, even though the level of authority and responsibility were not reflected in determining wages, it can be justifiable to exclude such allowances for short-term and part-time employees who do not have such authority and responsibility.

9) **Low labor productivity**

If the reason short-term and part-time employees' labor productivity is low is because of previous experience and/or prejudice and not the result of their service, then discriminatory practice is not justifiable. However, it is justifiable if the employer discriminates on wages according to a wage system based on low labor productivity in comparison with target employees.

10) **Disadvantageous treatment in accordance with decision factors for wages and working conditions**

It can be regarded as justifiable when the employer considers relevant factors (duty, ability, skill, technology, qualification, career, education background, service year, responsibility, achievement, performance, etc.) of labor service in determining wages and pays discriminative wages in accordance with such differences.

11) **Legal allowances**

Legal allowances, which are allowances to be paid by law, are additional allowances (Article 56 of the LSA) for overtime, nighttime and holiday work, annual paid leave allowance (Article 60(5) of the LSA), etc.

업무범위의 차이를 엄격하게 고려하여 비교대상근로자를 선정하여야 하며, 업무범위의 차이로 인한 임금 및 근로조건 등에서 불리한 처우는 합리적인 이유 가 있는 것으로 볼 수 있다.

8) 업무의 권한, 책임 등이 다른 경우

권한, 책임의 정도에 따라 임금에 차이를 두는 것도 합리적 이유로 인정될 수 있다. 권한, 책임의 정도를 임금결정에는 반영하지 않더라도 그에 상응하는 대가를 별도의 수당명목(직책수당, 직급수당 등)으로 지급하는 경우, 만약 기간제, 단시간근로자가 이러한 권한과 책임을 갖고 있지 않다면 당해 기간제, 단시간근로자를 수당 지급대상에서 제외하여도 합리적 이유가 인정될 수 있을 것이다.

9) 노동생산성이 낮은 경우

기간제, 단시간근로자의 노동생산성이 낮다는 것이 직접적인 근로의 결과에서 확인된 것이 아니라 선험적 평가 및 편견에 의한 것이라면 이는 합리적인 이유로 인정될 수 없다. 그렇지만 실제 업무수행 결과인 근로의 질과 비교대상근로자에 비해 낮음을 이유로 임금체계에 따라 차등을 두었다면 이는 합리적 이유로서 인정될 수 있을 것이다.

10) 임금 및 근로조건의 결정요소에 따른 불리한 처우

임금을 결정함에 있어 근로제공에 관련된 요소들(직무, 능력, 기능, 기술, 자격, 경력, 학력, 근속년수, 책임, 업적, 실적 등) 중 어떠한 요소에 따라 결정되는지를 확인하고 그 요소의 차이로 인하여 불리한 임금을 받는 경우는 합리적 이유가 있다고 볼 수 있다.

11) 법정수당의 경우

법정수당은 법에 의해 지급할 의무가 있는 수당으로 연장, 야간, 휴일근로 가산수당(근로기준법 제56조), 연차유급휴가수당(근로기준법 제60조제5항)등이 있다.

III. The Discrimination Correction System for a Dispatched Employee

1. Characteristics

A using employer as well as a sending employer is prohibited from discriminative behavior under the Employee Dispatch Act. Even though the discrimination correction system for dispatched employees is regulated identically to the discrimination prohibition for short-term and part-time employees, the system is different in content and interpretation because of the characteristics of dispatch employment.

In terms of both the legislative consideration of the discrimination prohibition system in the Employee Dispatch Act and the special characteristics of dispatch employment, the scope of prohibition shall be limited to 'wages and other working conditions' established in accordance with the dispatched employees' labor provisions and entry to the workplace.

The using employer and sending employer are both considered parties to prohibit discriminative behaviors and, therefore, will share the responsibility of implementing any correction order, including fines levied for failure to implement the correction order.

2. Applicant for discrimination correction

1) Dispatched employee as an applicant for discrimination correction

The term "dispatched employee" means a person who is subject to employee dispatch as a person employed by a sending employer (Article 2(5) of the Employee Dispatch Act). Regardless of the form of contract, if the employee is a dispatched employee in reality, then he/she can be an applicant for discrimination correction.

2) Illegally dispatched employee as an applicant for discrimination correction

Under the Employee Dispatch Act, an illegal dispatch occurs when the employer:
① violates the permitted jobs of a dispatched employee;
② violates the length of dispatch period, and
③ operates a non-licensed dispatch business.

Ⅲ. 파견근로자에 대한 차별시정제도

1. 특징

파견법에서 차별행위 금지주체로 근로계약 체결당사자인 파견사업주뿐만 아니라 사용사업주까지 규정한 것은 입법정책적 고려에서 도입된 것이다. 따라서 파견근로자에 대한 차별시정제도는 기간제, 단시간근로자에 대한 차별금지와 동일한 형식으로 규정되어 있다 하더라도 고용관계와 사용관계가 분리된 파견근로의 특성에 비추어 실질적으로는 내용상 및 해석상 차이가 있을 수 있다.

파견법상 차별금지제도의 입법정책적 측면과 고용관계 및 사용관계로 분리되는 파견근로의 특수성을 감안할 때 차별처우 금지영역은 파견근로자의 근로제공 및 사업장 편입에 따른 형성되는 '임금 그 밖의 근로조건 등'이 될 것이다.

사용사업주와 파견사업주 양자는 각각 사용자 책임영역에 따라 차별행위 금지주체일 뿐만 아니라 시정명령을 받는 주체 및 확정된 시정명령 불이행시 과태료 납부책임의 주체가 된다.

2. 차별시정신청권자

1) 차별시정신청권자로서의 파견근로자
"파견근로자"라 함은 파견사업주가 고용한 근로자로서 근로자파견의 대상이 되는자이다(파견법 제2조제5호). 계약의 형식과 상관없이 실질이 파견근로자이면 차별시정의 신청권자가 될 수 있다.

2) 불법파견시 파견근로자도 차별시정신청권자임
파견법상 불법파견은
① 파견대상 업무를 위반하거나,
② 파견기간을 위반하거나,
③ 무허가 파견을 행하는 경우에 발생한다.

3. Subjects prohibiting discriminative treatment: sending employer and using employer

The Employee Dispatch Act (Article 21(1)) states that "A sending employer and a using employer shall not treat a dispatched employee in a discriminatory manner on account of them being a dispatched employee." Accordingly, the persons responsible for prohibiting discriminatory behavior are the sending employer and the using employer. In addition, they will become the employer concerned for correcting discrimination. According to Article 34 of the Employee Dispatch Act, a sending employer is responsible for wages, annual paid leave, etc. as per the Labor Standards Act, while a using employer is responsible for working hours and recess, use of leave, etc.

4. The prohibition scope of discriminative treatment

In regards to discriminatory treatment, the dispatched employees' 'wages and other working conditions' are analyzed differently from that of short-term and part-time employees, because the dispatched employee has particular characteristics of employment. Working conditions established in relation to the dispatched employee's labor provision and entry to the using employer's workplace shall not be discriminatory, and a sending employer and a using employer shall not discriminate against the dispatched employee by treating them less favorably than employees the using employer hired directly. However, such things like family allowance paid to directly hired employees, are not related to working conditions established by labor provisions and entry to workplace. Accordingly, such things are not prohibited.

5. Target employee in comparison

The dispatched employee's target employee for estimating discrimination shall be "an employee engaged in the same or similar job in a using employer's workplace" (Article 21(1) of the Dispatch Employee Act).

6. Disadvantageous treatment and justifiable reason

1) Basic principle

3. 차별처우 금지주체 : 파견사업주와 사용사업주

파견법에서는 "파견사업주와 사용사업주는 파견근로자임을 이유로 … 차별적 처우를 하여서는 아니된다"(제21조제1항)고 규정하고 있다. 따라서 차별행위의 금지의무자는 파견사업주와 사용사업주이며, 각각 사용자 책임영역에 따라 차별시정의 피신청인이 될 수 있다. 파견법 제34조의 규정에 따라 근로기준법상의 임금, 연차유급휴가 등에 관한 사항은 파견사업주가, 근로시간과 휴게, 휴일의 부여 등은 사용사업주가 사용자로서 책임을 지게 된다.

4. 차별처우 금지영역

차별처우 금지영역으로서 '임금 그 밖의 근로조건 등'의 범위는 파견근로자의 경우 고용관계와 사용관계(지휘명령관계)가 분리되는 고용형태의 특수성으로 인하여 차별처우 금지영역의 범위가 기간제, 단시간 근로자와는 다르다. 파견근로자로서의 근로제공 및 사용사업주의 사업장에의 편입에 따라 형성되는 근로조건은 차별처우 금지영역에 해당되며, 파견사업주 및 사용사업주는 사용사업주가 직접 고용한 근로자와 차별해서는 아니된다. 근로제공 및 사업장 편입에 따른 근로조건이 아닌 나머지 부분(예 : 직접 고용한 근로자신분에 기하여 지급되는 가족수당 등)은 임금 그 밖의 근로조건 등(제2조제7호)에 포함된다고 볼 수 없을 것이므로 차별처우가 금지되는 영역에 해당되지 않을 것이다.

5. 비교대상근로자

차별판단을 위한 파견근로자의 비교대상근로자는 "사용사업주의 사업내의 동종 또는 유사한 업무를 수행하는 근로자"이다(파견법 제21조제1항)

6. 불리한 처우와 합리적 이유

1) 기본원칙

Whether there is disadvantageous treatment or not and whether such treatment is justifiable or not shall be estimated by considering the dispatch employment characteristics. Even though there is disadvantageous treatment, it can be justifiable if the reason is attributable to the type of dispatch employment (e.g., exclusion of promotion opportunity).

2) Wages of a dispatched employee

If a dispatched employee is subject to disadvantageous treatment in regard to wages, as the responsible person for the payment of wages is the sending employer, the dispatched employee can apply for a correction against the sending employer. In this case, when the amount that a dispatched employee received from the sending employer is less than the amount paid to the employee (target employee in comparison) engaged in the same or similar job, it is be discrimination.

3) Other working conditions of a dispatched employee

"Other working conditions" of a dispatched employee shall include items related to working conditions in accordance with "① labor provision of a dispatched employee" and ② "entry to a using employer's workplace".

IV. Discrimination Correcting Procedures

In cases where a short-term employee, part-time employee, or dispatched employee is subject to discriminative treatment, the employee can make a correction application to the Labor Relations Commission within six months from the occurrence date of the discriminative treatment (or the last day in case of continuing discriminative treatment) (Article 9(1) of the Short-term Employee Act, Article 21(2) of the Employee Dispatch Act).

In regards to the penal provision, it shall not be applied to the discriminative behavior itself. If the employer does not implement the correction order after the Labor Relations Commission has found discriminative treatment, the Minister of Labor can level a fine of up to 100 million won against the employer. Also, the Minister of Labor can order the employer to implement the correction order, and if the employer does not follow the order without a justifiable reason, he can be fined up to 5 million won.

파견근로자에 대한 불리한 처우의 유무와 합리적인 이유의 유무는 파견근로의 특성을 고려하여 판단하게 된다. 설사 불리한 처우가 있는 경우에도 그 원인이 파견근로라는 고용형태의 속성으로 인한 경우에는 합리적 이유가 있는 것으로 볼 수 있다(예 : 승진기회의 배제 등).

2) 파견근로자의 임금

파견근로자가 임금에 있어서 불리한 처우를 받고 있는 경우 임금지급에 대한 사용자 책임은 파견사업주가 지므로 파견사업주를 피신청인으로 하여 차별적 임금의 시정을 신청할 수 있다. 이 경우 파견근로자가 파견사업주로부터 지급받은 임금이 '사용사업주가 직접 고용한 사용사업주 사업내의 동종 또는 유사 업무 수행 근로자(비교대상근로자)'에게 지급한 임금에 비해 적다면 차별의 문제가 제기될 수 있다.

3) 파견근로자의 그 밖의 근로조건 등

파견근로자의 "그 밖의 근로조건 등"에서 "① 파견근로자로서의 근로제공" 및 "② 사용사업주의 사업장에의 편입"에 따른 근로조건과 관련된 사항이 포함될 것이다.

Ⅳ. 차별시정절차

기간제근로자, 단시간근로자 및 파견근로자가 차별적 처우를 받은 경우에는 동차별적 처우가 있은 날(계속되는 차별적 처우는 그 종료일)부터 6월 이내에 노동위원회에 그 시정을 신청할 수 있다(기간제법 제9조제1항, 판견법 제21조제2항).

차별적 처우를 한 경우 차별행위 그 자체에 대해서는 벌칙이 부과되지 않는다. 차별적 처우로 판정한 노동위원회의 시정명령이 확정된 후에도 사용자가 정당한 이유없이 이행하지 않을 경우 노동부장관이 사용자에게 1억원 이하의 과태료를 부과하게 된다. 또한 노동부장관은 확정된 시정명령에 대하여 사용자에게 이행상황을 제출할 것을 요구할 수 있으며, 정당한 이유없이 이행상황 제출요구에 불응하는 경우 500만 원 이하의 과태료를 부과한다.

Section 16. Labor-Management Council

1. Concept

The purpose of this Act is to maintain order in industry, and contribute to development of the national economy by promoting the common interests of labor and management through joint participation and cooperation. This Act concerning the Promotion of Worker Participation and Cooperation (hereby, called the Worker Participation Act) provides for a consulting organization, known as the labor-management council (hereinafter also referred to as the Council).
All businesses that ordinarily hire more than 30 persons shall establish a Council. The number of employees hired ordinarily shall meet the standards of Article 14 of the Labor Standards Act, with the exception of the business owner, business representative, and all who are working in favor of the employer.
The unit for its establishment shall be a unit of business or a workplace that is given the authority to outline working conditions. For two different working places for one company, a separate workplace can be established for each. The Council of the Worker Participation Act shall not affect collective bargaining of the labor union, or other union activities.

1) **Employers who have 30 employees or more shall establish a labor-management council in the main office and are permitted to establish a labor-management council in the workplace.**[226]
   According to the Labor-Management Council Act (hereinafter the LMC Act), a labor-management council shall be established in a unit of the business or workplace where there are at least 30 normal employees, so that the employer shall promote employee welfare and healthy development of a business and workplace. The number of employees related to the establishment of the labor-management council shall be estimated on the basis of each business or workplace. In cases where there are fewer than 30 employees in one workplace, the employer does not have to establish a labor-management council. In accordance with Article 4(2) of the LMC Act and Article 2(2) of the Enforcement Decree, where the total number of workers engaged in one business is 30 or more, even if the workers in one business are dispersed in different regions, a labor-management council shall be established at the principal office, and each workplace can also establish a labor-management council.

---

[226] MOEL Guidelines Hyupryeok 68210-409, on Nov. 20, 2003.

제16절 노사협의회 설치와 운영

1. 노사협의회 제도의 의의

　회사와 근로자 쌍방이 참여와 협력을 통하여 상호 공동 이익을 증진함으로써 산업평화를 도모할 목적으로 '근로자참여 및 협력증진에 관한 법률'(이하 '근참법') 에 의거하여 구성하는 협의 기구를 노사협의회라고 한다.

　상시 근로자가 30인 이상인 사업장은 반드시 노사협의회를 설치해야 한다. 상시근로자 수는 근로기준법 제14조(근로자의 정의)의 근로자 총인원에서 사업주, 경영담당자, 사용자를 위하여 행위하는 자를 제외하여 산정한다.

　설치 단위는 근로조건 결정권이 있는 사업 또는 사업장 단위로 설치하되, 하나의 사업에 지역을 달리하는 사업장이 있을 경우에는 해당 사업장 단위로 설치할 수 있다. 노사협의회가 설치되어 있더라도 노동조합의 단체교섭, 기타 모든 활동은 이 법에 의하여 영향을 받지 않는다.

1) **전체 근로자 수가 30인 이상일 경우 그 주된 사무소에 노사협의회를 설치하여야 하고 그 사업장에 대하여도 노사협의회를 설치할 수 있다.**[226]

　　현행 근참법 상의 노사협의회는 근로조건이 있는 상시 30인 이상의 근로자를 사용하는 사업 또는 사업장 단위로 설치하여 당해 사업 또는 사업장의 근로자 복지증진과 기업의 건전한 발전을 도모하는 협의기구로 노사협의회의 설치와 관련된 근로자 수는 노사협의회 설치 단위인 각 사업 또는 사업장별로 판단되어야 할 것인 바, 사업장의 근로자 수가 30인 미만인 경우 해당 사업장에 노사협의회 설치 의무가 없다고 할 것이다. 근참법 제4조 제2항 및 동법 시행령 제2조 제2항에 따라 하나의 사업에 당해 근로자가 지역별로 분산되어 있더라도 전체 근로자 수가 30인 이상일 경우에는 그 주된 사무소에 노사협의회를 설치하여야 하고, 그 사업장에 대하여도 노사협의회를 설치할 수 있다.

2) **영리를 목적으로 하지 않는 사업 또는 사업장이라 해서 노사협의회 설치 대상에서 제외되는 것은 아니다.**

---

[226] 행정해석: 협력 68210-409, 2003.11.20

2) **Non-profit businesses or workplaces are not exempt from the duty to establish a labor-management council.**[227]

A labor-management council shall be established in each business or workplace ordinarily employing 30 employees or more, which is vested with the right to decide working conditions. A non-profit business or workplace is not exempt from the duty to establish a labor-management council.

3) **In cases where one business consists of several workplaces in different regions, the employer shall establish an overall labor-management council combining several workplaces.**[228]

In cases where one business consists of several workplaces in different regions, the employer shall establish an overall labor-management council combining several workplaces (including the headquarters). Accordingly, in cases where workplaces are in Seoul, Jinju, and Daegu, the employer shall establish and operate an overall labor-management council combining the three workplaces. The representative director shall attend the combined labor-management council meetings and the employee members shall be composed of members representing each of the three workplaces. On the other hand, the employer does not have to establish and operate a labor-management council in each workplace, but, if possible, it is recommended. In this case, the labor-management council in each workplace can be held with the attendance of the top-level managers (plant manager, etc.) and employee members from that workplace.

4) **In cases where the company has been divided into two entities, a labor-management council shall be established and operated for each.**[229]

According to the LMC Act, the labor-management council is different from a labor union. A labor union is organized for the purpose of maintaining and improving working conditions and enhancing economic and social status. However, the labor-management council is a consulting organization for the promotion of employee welfare and healthy development of the workplace, and shall be established in each business or workplace ordinarily employing at least 30 employees, which is vested with the right to decide working conditions.

2. Composition of the Council

The Council shall be made up of an equal number of members representing the

---

[227] MOEL Guidelines: Nosa 68107-151, on June 18, 1997.
[228] MOEL Guidelines: Nosa 32271-1633, on Feb. 3, 1987.
[229] MOEL Guidelines: Nosa Hyupryeok Team-3072, on Dec. 2, 2004.

노사협의회는 근로조건 결정권이 있는 상시 30인 이상 근로자를 사용하는 모든 사업 또는 사업장에 설치하도록 되어 있으며 영리를 목적으로 하지 않는 사업 또는 사업장이라 해서 설치대상에서 제외되지는 않는다.[227]

3) **하나의 사업이 지역을 달리하는 여러 개의 사업장으로 구성되어 있는 경우 각 사업장을 통합하는 통합 노사협의회는 반드시 설치되어야 한다.[228]**

　　하나의 사업이 지역을 달리하는 여러 개의 사업장으로 구성되어 있는 경우 각 사업장(본사 포함)을 통합하는 통합 노사협의회는 반드시 설치되어야 한다. 따라서 서울과 진주, 대구에 사업장이 있는 경우 3곳을 통합한 통합 노사협의회가 설치·운영되어야 하며, 통합 노사협의회 회의 시 대표이사는 반드시 참석하여야 하며, 근로자위원도 3개 사업장을 대표하는 위원으로 구성되어야 함. 반면에 각 사업장단위로 노사협의회를 설치·운영하여야 하는 것은 아니나 가급적 설치·운영토록 권장하고 있다. 이 경우 당해 사업장의 최고책임자(공장장 등)와 당해 사업장 근로자위원이 사업장 노사협의회에 참석하면 된다.

4) **회사가 2개의 법인으로 분할된 경우에 별도의 노사협의회 설치·운영하여야 한다.[229]**

　　'근로자참여 및 협력증진에 관한 법률'(이하 '근참법')상 노사협의회는 근로조건 유지·개선 및 근로자의 사회적·경제적 지위향상을 목적으로 하는 노동조합과는 달리 근로자와 사용자가 참여와 협력을 통해 근로자 복지증진과 기업의 건전한 발전을 도모하는 협의기구로 근로조건 결정권이 있는 상시 30인 이상 근로자를 사용하는 사업 또는 사업장 단위로 설치하여야 한다.

2. 노사협의회의 구성

　　노사협의회는 근로자와 사용자를 대표하는 동수의 위원으로 구성하되,

---

[227] 행정해석: 노사 68107-151, 1997.06.18
[228] 행정해석: 노사 32271-1633, 1987.02.03
[229] 행정해석: 노사협력복지과-3072, 2004.12.02

employer and the employees, the number of which shall be at least three but fewer than ten.

While members representing employees shall be elected by the employees, labor union representatives or those recommended by a labor union shall be the employee representative in cases where the labor union is formed by a majority of employees. Employee members of a business or workplace where such a labor union consisting of a majority of employees fails to organize shall be elected by direct and secret vote. If this is deemed impossible due to certain characteristics of the business or workplace, employees may elect their representatives in proportion to the number of employees in different departments. Then, the representative shall be elected by direct and secret vote with majority participation of the voters. However, members representing employers shall be representatives of the business or workplace concerned or the persons designated by such representatives.

The tenure of membership shall be three years until renewal. A representative shall continue to perform his duties until a successor is elected even if the term of office has expired. Members shall not work exclusively for the Council, but shall be compensated for their services to the Council, which exists to maintain the neutrality of members' status and to make certain of work efficiency and impartiality. However, the time spent by the members to attend meetings of the Council shall be regarded as hours devoted to work. The employer shall not take disadvantageous action against the members' interests in relation to the performance of their duties as members of the Council.

1) **The members of the labor-management council representing employees in a unit of a plant where there is no labor union or employee representative shall be elected in a direct and secret vote by the employees.**[230]

    Article 6 of the LMC Act stipulates that, while members representing employees shall be elected by employees, labor union representatives or those recommended by a labor union shall be the employee members in cases where the labor union is formed by a majority of employees. The employee members shall be employees in the corresponding business or workplace and the majority of employees shall be estimated in a unit of the corresponding business or workplace. Accordingly, in establishing a labor-management council in a unit of the workplace, the employee members shall be recommended by the labor union in cases where the labor union is formed by a majority of employees. If the union is formed by less than a majority of employees, the employee members shall be elected by direct and secret vote by the employees.

---

[230] MOEL Guidelines: Nosa Hyupryeok Team-102, on Feb. 6, 2004..

위원 수는 각 3인 이상 10인 이내로 한다.

근로자의 과반수로 조직된 노동조합이 있는 경우 근로자를 대표하는 위원 즉 근로자위원은 노동조합의 대표자가 당연직으로 참가하게 되고, 기타 위원은 노동조합에서 위촉하는 자로 한다. 그 외의 경우 근로자위원은 근로자의 직접·비밀·무기명투표로 선출함이 원칙이나, 사업(장)의 특수성으로 부득이할 때는 작업부서별로 근로자 수에 비례하여 선거인단을 선출하여 이들 과반수의 직접·비밀·무기명투표로 근로자위원을 선출할 수도 있다. 한편, 사용자위원은 당해 사업장의 대표자가 당연직이 되고 기타 위원은 그 대표자가 위촉한다. 위원의 임기는 3년으로 하되 연임할 수 있도록 하고, 임기가 만료되더라도 후임자가 선출될 때까지는 계속 그 직무를 담당하도록 하여 협의회 운영의 연속성을 꾀하고 있다. 위원의 신분상 중립과 업무수행상의 효율과 공정성을 확보하기 위해 협의회 위원은 비상임·무보수로 하되, 협의회 출석에 소요되는 시간에 대하여는 이를 근로한 것으로 본다. 그리고 사용자는 협의회 위원으로서의 직무수행과 관련해서 근로자위원을 불이익처분을 해서는 아니 된다.

1) **노동조합(지부) 또는 근로자대표가 없는 공장 단위의 행정해석: 노사협의회 근로자위원은 근로자들의 직접·비밀·무기명 투표에 의해 선출하여야한다.**[230]

　　근참법 제6조에 의하면 노사협의회 근로자위원은 '근로자가 선출하되, 근로자의 과반수로 조직된 노동조합(과반수 노조)이 있는 경우에는 노동조합의 대표자와 그 노동조합이 위촉하는 자로 한다.'고 규정하고 있는바, 이때 근로자위원은 당해 사업 또는 사업장 소속 근로자이어야 하고 과반수 노조여부는 당해 사업 또는 사업장 단위로 판단되어야 할 것이다. 따라서 사업장 단위 노사협의회 설치 시 당해 사업장에 소속 근로자의 과반수로 조직된 노동조합이 있는 경우에는 당해 노동조합에서 근로자위원을 위촉할 수 있으나 그렇지 않은 경우에는 근로자들의 직접·비밀·무기명 투표에 의해 근로자위원을 선출하여야 할 것이다.

---

[230] 행정해석: 노사협력과-102, 2004.02.06

2) Employer behavior that may affect the election of employee members directly or indirectly shall be prohibited.[231]

① According to Article 6(2) of the LMC Act and Article 3 of its Enforcement Decree, the employee members shall be elected by a free choice of all employees in cases where there is no labor union representing a majority of employees. This means that employees shall voluntarily compose an election administration commission that can implement the registration of candidates and manage the election.

In this regard, Article 10(1) of the LMC Act stipulates that, No employer shall intervene in or interfere with an election of the employee members. This means that the employer shall not take any action directly or indirectly to influence the result of the election.

The employer shall not only be prohibited from actions designed to influence winning or losing of election for a particular candidate, but shall also not influence decision-making about general matters related to the election of an employee commission, like the establishment or activities of an election administration commission. Article 11 of the LMC Act stipulates an order of correction for these violations.

② The employer of the LMC Act is the identical employer stipulated in Article 15 of the Labor Standards Act in accordance with Article 3(3) of the LMC Act: The employer means a business owner, or a person responsible for management of a business or a person who acts on behalf of a business owner with respect to matters relating to workers. The term, a person who acts on behalf of a business owner with respect to matters relating to workers means a person given by the employer a certain range of responsibilities and authority for the determination of working conditions like personnel, wages, welfare, and labor management, and command and supervision for implementation of labor service. This shall not be estimated by a formal job title, such as Section Manager or Senior Manager, but shall be estimated in an individual and concrete manner on the basis of job characteristics and actual work performance.

3) Although the representative of a labor union was dismissed and filed a dismissal case, he cannot maintain his status as employee member because he is not an employee under the Labor Standards Act due to his dismissal.[232]

---

[231] MOEL Guidelines: Nosa Team-239, on Jan. 30, 2004.
[232] MOEL Guidelines: Nosa 68107-5, on Jan. 6, 1998.

2) 근로자위원 선출에 직·간접적으로 영향을 미칠 수 있는 일체의 사용자 행위는 금지된다[231]

① 현행 '근로자참여 및 협력증진에 관한 법률'(이하 '근참법') 제6조 제2항 및 동법 시행령 제3조에 따라 근로자의 과반수로 구성된 노동조합이 존재하지 않는 경우 노사협의회 근로자위원은 전체 근로자의 자유의사에 의하여 선출되어야 할 것으로 근로자들에 의해 자주적으로 구성된 선거관리위원회 등의 주관 하에 후보자등록 및 투표실시 등이 이루어져야 할 것이다. 이와 관련하여 근참법 제10조 제1항은 "사용자는 근로자위원의 선출에 개입하거나 방해해서는 안 된다"고 규정함으로써 근로자위원 선출결과 등에 직·간접적으로 영향을 미칠 수 있는 일체의 사용자 행위를 금지하고 있는바, 입후보 방해·제한 등 특정 근로자의 당선 내지 낙선을 목적으로 하는 행위뿐만 아니라 선거관리위원회의 구성·활동 등 근로자위원 선출절차에 관련한 제반사항에 대한 의사결정에 영향을 미치는 행위까지도 금지된다 할 것으로 근참법 제11조는 이러한 행위에 대한 시정명령을 규정하고 있다.

② 근참법상 사용자는 근참법 제3조 제3호 규정에 의거 근로기준법 제15조의 규정에 의한 사용자로 "사업주 또는 사업경영담당자 기타 근로자에 관한 사항에 대하여 사업주를 위하여 행위하는 자"를 의미한다. 이때 '기타 근로자에 관한 사항에 대하여 사업주를 위하여 행위하는 자'라 함은 인사·급여·후생·노무관리 등 근로조건의 결정 또는 근로의 실시에 관한 지휘명령 내지 감독과 관련한 일정한 책임과 권한이 사업주에 의하여 주어진 자를 말하는 바, 과장·부장 등의 형식적인 직명에 의거 판단할 것이 아니라 여타 근로자에 대한 지휘감독권(업무지시권), 징계·인사권, 복무·근태관리 등 업무성격과 근무실태 등을 토대로 개별·구체적으로 판단되어야 할 것이다.

3) 노조대표자가 해고의 효력을 다투고 있다 하더라도 해고로 인하여 근로기준법상 근로자로서 인정이 되지 않는다면 근로자위원의 자격을 유지한다고 볼 수 없다.[232]

---

[231] 정해석: 노사협력과-239, 2004.01.30

The term Employee in Article 2 of the LMC Act is defined in accordance with the Labor Standards Act. A representative in a labor union that was formed by a majority of employees can become an employee member under Article 6 of the Act and he/she must become an employee under the Labor Standards Act. Accordingly, although a representative of a labor union was dismissed and filed a dismissal case, he/she cannot maintain his status as employee member because he/she is not an employee under the Labor Standards Act due to his/her dismissal.

4) A union officer of an upper level labor union cannot become an employee member of the labor-management council.[233]

The labor-management council is a conversational organization between labor and management, involving only employees and employers in the corresponding workplace. This does not only apply to a compulsory labor-management council under Article 4(1) of the LMC Act, but also to an arbitrary labor-management council under Article 4(2) of the LMC Act. Accordingly, the employee members in the labor-management council established per workplace shall consist of only employees engaged in that workplace, so a union officer of an upper level labor union cannot become a member.

3. Operation of the Council

(1) Council bylaws

A Council shall establish bylaws governing its organization and operations and shall submit a report on them to the Minister of Employment and Labor within fifteen days from the date of establishment. Any amendment thereto shall also be submitted to the Minister of Employment and Labor within fifteen days (Article 18 of the LMC Act).

Where the bylaws of the Council are made or modified, they shall be passed by decision of the Council. The bylaws of the Council shall contain such matters as listed in the following:

① Number of members;

---

[233] MOEL Guidelines: Nosa 68107-277, on Oct. 22, 1997.

'근로자참여 및 협력증진에 관한 법률' 제2조의 「근로자」는 근로기준법에 의한 근로자로 정의되어 있는바, 같은 법 제6조의 근로자위원이 될 수 있는 근로자 과반수로 조직된 노동조합의 대표자 역시 근로기준법상 근로자라야 할 것이다. 따라서 당해 노조대표자가 해고된 경우에는 부당노동행위로 인한 해고의 효력을 다투고 있다 하더라도 근로기준법상 근로자로서 인정이 되지 않는다면 근로자위원의 자격을 유지한다고는 볼 수 없을 것이다.

4) 본조 간부는 사업장별 행정해석: 노사협의회의 근로자위원이 될 수 없다.[233]

노사협의회는 당해 사업장의 노사 간 대화기구로서 당해 사업장의 근로자와 사용자만이 그 주체가 될 수 있으며, 이는 '근로자참여 및 협력증진에 관한 법률' 제4조 제1항에 의한 의무설치 노사협의회 뿐 아니라 같은 법 제4조 제2항에 의한 임의설치 노사협의회에도 적용된다 할 것이다. 따라서 사업장별로 설치된 노사협의회의 근로자위원은 그 사업장 소속 근로자들만으로 구성되어야 하므로 본조 간부는 근로자위원이 될 수 없다 할 것이다.

3. 노사협의회의 운영

(1) 노사협의회 규정

노사협의회는 그 조직과 운영에 관한 규정을 제정하고 이를 협의회의 설치일로부터 15일 이내에 고용노동부장관에게 제출하여야 하며, 이 규정을 변경한 때에도 15일 이내에 고용노동부장관에게 제출해야 한다(근참법 제18조).

협의회 규정은 노사협의회의 운영을 위한 자치규범으로 그 제정이나 변경은 노사협의회의 의결을 거쳐야 한다. 협의회 규정에는 다음과 같은 필요적 기재 사항이 포함되어야 한다.
① 노사협의회의 위원 수

---

[232] 행정해석: 노사 68107-5, 1998.01.06
[233] 행정해석: 노사 68107-277, 1997.10.22

② Matters relating to the procedures for election of employee members and registration of candidates;
③ Matters relating to the qualification of employer members;
④ Matters concerning hours regarded as hours worked by Council members;
⑤ Matters concerning the calling of meetings, sessions and operation, etc. of the Council;
⑥ Matters relating to the method of and procedures for voluntary arbitration; and
⑦ Matters relating to the number of grievance-handling members and to the handling of grievances, etc.

(2) Meetings

In general, the Council shall hold meetings once every three months, but it can hold additional meetings if deemed necessary. The chairman shall call for and preside over the meetings of the Council. If the representative of either labor or management requests a meeting to be held, specifying the purpose of the meeting in writing, the chairman shall call for a meeting of the Council. The chairman shall notify each member of the date, time, place, agenda, etc. of the meeting seven days prior to the meeting.

Meetings shall open in the presence of a majority of employee members and employer members respectively, and a resolution shall be passed by a vote of more than two-thirds of all members present. Council meetings shall be open to the public; however, they may be closed to the public upon resolution of the Council. The minutes shall include the signatures and seals of all attending members and shall be preserved for three years from the date drawn.

4. Council Functions

The function of the Council is to promote employee interests and contribute to managerial rationalizations by consulting about specific items between labor and management.

(1) Matters subject to consultation

Matters subject to consultation are mainly focused on production and personnel & labor management, and those matters discussed at the meetings of the Council are as follows:
1. Productivity improvement and gain sharing;
2. Recruitment, placement, education and training of workers;
3. Handling of worker grievances;

② 근로자위원의 선출절차 및 후보등록에 관한 사항
③ 사용자위원의 자격에 관한 사항
④ 협의회 위원이 근로한 것으로 보는 시간에 관한 사항
⑤ 협의회의 회의 소집, 회기(會期), 그밖에 협의회의 운영에 관한 사항
⑥ 임의중재의 방법·절차 등에 관한 사항
⑦ 고충처리위원 수 및 고충처리에 관한 사항

(2) 회의

노사협의회는 3개월마다 정기적으로 회의를 개최하여야 하고 필요할 때는 임시회의를 개최한다. 회의는 의장이 소집하거나 노사 어느 한 쪽의 대표자가 회의의 목적사항을 문서로 명시하여 회의의 소집을 요구함으로써 개최된다. 의장은 회의개최 7일 전에 회의일시·장소·의제 등을 각 위원에게 통보해야 한다.

회의는 근로자위원과 사용자위원의 각 과반수의 출석으로 개최하고 출석위원 3분의 2 이상의 찬성으로 의결한다. 협의회의 회의는 협의회 의결로 공개하지 않는 경우를 제외하고는 공개회의를 원칙으로 한다.

노사협의회는 회의의 결과를 기록하여 출석위원 전원이 서명·날인한 회의록을 사업장에 비치하여야 하며, 이를 3년간 보존하여야 한다.

4. 노사협의회의 임무

노사협의회의 임무는 노사 간에 일정한 사항을 협의함으로써 근로자의 이익을 증진시키는 한편 경영의 합리화를 꾀하는 데 있다고 하겠다.

(1) 협의사항

협의사항은 대개 생산이나 인사·노무관리에 관한 사항이다. 노사협의회에서의 협의사항은 다음과 같다.
1. 생산성 향상과 성과 배분
2. 근로자의 채용·배치 및 교육훈련
3. 근로자의 고충처리

4. Improvement of occupational safety and health and other aspects of the work environment and promotion of worker health;
5. Improvement of personnel and labor management systems;
6. General rules for employment adjustment, such as assignment and transfer, retraining and dismissal of workers for managerial or technological reasons, etc.;
7. Administration of working hours and recess hours;
8. Improvement of wage payment methods, wage structure, wage system, etc.;
9. Introduction of new machines and technologies or improvement of work processes;
10. Establishment or revision of rules of employment;
11. Establishment of employee stock ownership plans and other support for the creation of worker wealth;
12. Matters concerning rewards given to workers for their work-related inventions, etc.;
13. Promotion of worker welfare;
14. Installation of employee surveillance equipment within a workplace; and
15. Matters concerning the maternity protection of female workers and support for reconciliation between work and family life.
16. Matters concerning the prevention of workplace sexual harassment and sexual harassment by customers, in accordance with Article 2, Paragraph 2 of the Act on the Equal Employment and Support for Work-Family Reconciliation
17. Other matters related to labor-management cooperation

(2) Matters subject to Council resolution

The employer shall seek a resolution from the Council on each of the following:
1. Establishment of basic plans for the education and training and skills development of workers;
2. Setting up and management of welfare facilities;
3. Establishment of an employee welfare fund;
4. Matters not resolved by the grievance handling committee;
5. Establishment of various labor-management cooperative committees.

Matters subject to Council resolution are regulated under the LMC Act to promote the common interests of labor and management through participation and cooperation to prevent the employer from implementing them on the basis of his/her sole judgment.

Meetings shall open in the presence of a majority of worker members and employer members, and resolutions shall be passed by a vote of at least two-thirds of all members present. The matters decided by the Council shall be publicized immediately through company broadcasting, bulletin boards, posting notices and other pertinent

4. 안전, 보건, 그 밖의 작업환경 개선과 근로자의 건강증진
5. 인사·노무관리의 제도 개선
6. 경영상 또는 기술상의 사정으로 인한 인력의 배치전환·재훈련·해고 등 고용조정의 일반원칙
7. 작업과 휴게 시간의 운용
8. 임금의 지불방법·체계·구조 등의 제도 개선
9. 신기계·기술의 도입 또는 작업 공정의 개선
10. 작업 수칙의 제정 또는 개정
11. 종업원지주제(從業員持株制)와 그밖에 근로자의 재산형성에 관한 지원
12. 직무 발명 등과 관련하여 해당 근로자에 대한 보상에 관한 사항
13. 근로자의 복지증진
14. 사업장 내 근로자 감시 설비의 설치
15. 여성 근로자의 모성보호 및 일과 가정생활의 양립을 지원하기 위한 사항
16. '남녀고용평등과 일·가정 양립 지원에 관한 법률' 제2조제2호에 따른 직장 내 성희롱 및 고객 등에 의한 성희롱 예방에 관한 사항
17. 그 밖의 노사협조에 관한 사항

(2) 의결사항

사용자가 노사협의회의 의결을 거쳐야 하는 사항은 다음과 같다.
1. 근로자의 교육훈련 및 능력개발 기본계획의 수립
2. 복지시설의 설치와 관리
3. 사내근로복지기금의 설치
4. 고충처리위원회에서 의결되지 아니한 사항
5. 각종 노사공동위원회의 설치

이처럼 의결사항을 법정화한 것은 사용자가 일방적으로 시행할 수 없도록 하여 근로자의 참여와 협력을 증진시키려는 취지이다.

의결은 근로자위원과 사용자위원 각 과반수의 출석으로 개최한 회의에서 출석위원 3분의 2 이상의 찬성이 있어야 가능하다. 노사협의회에서 의결된 사항은 사내방송·사내보·게시 기타 적절한 방법으로 신속하게 전체 근로자에게 공지시키도록 하는 한편, 의결된 사항을 성실하게 이행할 의무를 노사

methods. The two parties shall be equally responsible for implementing them.

(3) Matters to be reported

The employer shall report and explain in good faith at a regular meeting the following:

1. Matters concerning overall management plans and results;
2. Matters concerning quarterly production plans and results;
3. Matters concerning manpower plans; and
4. Economic and financial conditions of the enterprise.

If the employer regularly reports and explains the above matters, a mutual trust in information sharing builds easily between labor and management. Thus, the employer shall report and explain matters faithfully and formally. In cases where the employer fails to give reports or an explanation, employee members may request relevant documents, and the employer shall respond in good faith to such requests. If the employer does not submit the appropriate data, he/she may be liable under penalty clauses.

1) The concrete realm of matters subject to consultation and matters subject to the Council's resolutions[234]

Matters subject to consultation in accordance with Article 20 of the LMC Act are items to promote the common interests of labor and management, which shall be suggested by one or both parties for consultation and be dealt with by the Council. The concrete realm of matters subject to consultations shall be determined by voluntary discretion of labor and management on the basis of general principles and criteria. Accordingly, the employer shall not have a duty to go through prior consultation with the Council for individual items, such as employment of specific individuals, nor need to issue the council's resolutions (in accordance with Article 21 of the LMC Act), even though some items for consultation were suggested by either labor, management, or both. The realm of employee training and skill development plans among the matters subject to Council resolution shall be standard plans for yearly training hours, major training items, etc. in general job training, cultural education, and other training related to the employee's skills training, but does not have to include concrete

---

[234] MOEL Guidelines: Nosa 68107-41, on Feb. 14, 1998.

모두에게 부과하고 있다.

(3) 보고사항
사용자는 다음 사항을 노사협의회에 성실하게 보고하고 설명하여야 한다.
1. 경영계획 전반 및 실적에 관한 사항
2. 분기별 생산계획과 실적에 관한 사항
3. 인력계획에 관한 사항
4. 기업의 경제적·재정적 상황

사용자는 이러한 사항에 대하여 정기적으로 보고하고 설명한다면 정보공유에 의해 노사 간에 신뢰가 형성될 것인데, 여기서 사용자가 보고사항을 진지하고 성실한 자세로 보고·설명하는 것이 매우 중요하다. 사용자가 보고·설명을 행하지 아니하는 경우에는 근로자위원은 자료의 제출을 요구할 수 있고, 사용자는 이에 성실히 응하여야 한다. 정당한 이유 없이 자료제출의무를 이행하지 않을 경우 벌칙이 부과된다.

1) 행정해석: 노사협의회 협의사항 및 의결사항의 구체적 범위[234]

'근로자참여 및 협력증진에 관한 법률' 제20조에 의한 협의사항은 노사 공동이익의 증진을 위하여 노사협의회에서 협의해야 할 사항으로서 노사 일방 또는 쌍방이 협의안건을 제시함으로써 협의회의 협의의제로 다루어지게 되는 것이므로 각 협의사항의 구체적인 범위는 일반적인 원칙·기준 등을 중심으로 노사가 자율적으로 결정할 사항인 것이다. 따라서 개별근로자 채용과 같은 개별사안에 대하여 사용자가 반드시 노사협의회의 사전협의를 거쳐야 할 의무를 지는 것은 아니며 노사일방 또는 쌍방의 협의안건 제시에 의해 협의하는 경우에도 동법 제21조에 의한 의결사항과는 달리 반드시 의결을 얻어야만 사용자가 이를 시행할 수 있는 것은 아니다. '근로자참여 및 협력증진에 관한 법률' 제21조에 의한 의결사항 중 "근로자의 교육훈련 및 능력개발 기본계획"의 범위는 사용자가 행하는 직업훈련, 교양교육, 기타 근로자의 능력개발을 위한 일체의 교육훈련으로 연간 교육훈련시간, 주요 교육훈련내용 등 "기본계획"이며, 구체적인

---
[234] 행정해석: 노사 68107-41, 1998.02.14

implementation plans.

2) **The concrete realm of matters subject to consultation shall be determined voluntarily by labor and management. The consultation does not require a precondition for agreement and industrial actions are not allowed in the event of non-agreement.**[235]

According to the LMC Act, the concrete realm of matters subject to consultation shall be determined voluntarily by labor and management, but consultation from the Council does not mean its agreement is a precondition and industrial actions are not allowed if there is no agreement from the Council. In cases where Council agreement has been reached (and a resolution passed to that effect) on matters subject to consultation in accordance with Article 20(2) of the LMC Act, both employees and employer shall enforce these matters in good faith in accordance with Article 24 of the LMC Act. If the employer does not implement matters determined by the Council, he/she may be punished under Article 31 of the LMC Act.

3) **On matters subject to consultation, it is enough for labor and management to consult sincerely. The employer does not have to reach agreement with labor or follow the decisions made.**[236]

According to Article 20 of the LMC Act, on matters subject to consultation, it is enough for labor and management to consult sincerely. The employer does not have to reach agreement with labor or follow the decisions made. Accordingly, if matters concerning institutional improvement for personnel management are consulted on sincerely, this is enough even though the employer does not follow Council resolutions or agreements.

4) **Whether Council resolutions concerning working condition are as effective as that of the collective bargaining agreement**[237]

The purpose of the LMC Act is to promote the common interests of labor and management through their joint participation and cooperation. The LMC Act shall also require establishment of a labor-management council to be able to consult or determine matters concerning personnel and management, excluding matters concerning wages and working conditions subject to collective bargaining. Accordingly, it is taken for granted that matters concerning wages and working conditions shall be determined through collective bargaining. However, if both parties agreed on wages and working conditions in a

---

[235] MOEL Guidelines: Hyupryeok 68210-303, on Aug. 2, 2003.
[236] MOEL Guidelines: Nosa 68010-235, on July 9, 2001.
[237] MOEL Guidelines: Nosa 68107-356, on Dec. 1, 1998.

실시계획까지는 포함되지 않는다.

2) **협의사항의 구체적인 협의범위는 노사에 의해 자율적으로 결정되고, 협의는 합의를 전제하지 않으며, 합의되지 않음을 이유로 한 쟁의행위는 허용되지 않는다**[235]

근참법상 협의사항의 구체적인 협의범위는 노사에 의해 자율적으로 결정되어진다 할 것이나 근참법상 협의회의 협의는 합의를 전제하지 않으며, 합의되지 않음을 이유로 한 쟁의행위가 허용되지 않는다는 점에서 쟁의행위가 인정되는 노동조합의 임금협상과는 차이가 존재한다 할 것이다. 또한, 근참법 제20조 제2항에 의거 협의사항을 의결한 경우 같은 법 제24조에 따라 근로자와 사용자는 의결된 사항을 성실히 이행하여야 하며, 정당한 사유 없이 이행하지 않는 경우 법 제31조에 의한 벌칙이 부과된다 할 것이다.

3) **협의사항은 노사가 성실히 협의하는 것으로 충분하며, 반드시 노사합의 또는 결정에 이르러야 하는 것은 아니다**[236]

'근로자참여 및 협력증진에 관한 법률' 제20조에서 정한 협의사항은 노사가 성실히 협의하는 것으로 충분하며, 반드시 노사합의 또는 결정에 이르러야 함을 강제하고 있지는 않다. 따라서 "인사·노무관리의 제도개선"에 관한 사항을 노사협의회에 상정하여 성실히 협의하였다면, 그에 대한 의결 또는 합의 유무와 상관없이 그 효력을 동법에 의해 부인할 수 없을 것으로 사료된다.

4) **근로조건에 대한 노사협의회 합의사항이 단체협약과 동일한 효력을 갖는지 여부**[237]

'근로자참여 및 협력증진에 관한 법률'(이하 '법') 제정취지는 노사 쌍방의 참여와 협력을 통해 노사공동의 이익을 증진하고자 하는 것이며 법에 노사협의회라는 기구를 두어 단체교섭 대상사항인 임금 등 근로조건을 제외한 인사·경영에 관한 근로조건에 관한 사항은 당연히 단체협약을 통해 결정되어야 할 것이며 노사 간 단체협약을 체결할 목적으로 노사

---

[235] 행정해석: 협력 68210-303, 2003.08.02
[236] 행정해석: 노사 68010-235, 2001.07.09
[237] 행정해석: 노사 68107-356, 1998.12.01

labor-management council in order to conclude a collective agreement, the Council meeting shall be regarded as part of collective bargaining.

5) Consultation regarding the number of full-time union officers in a labor-management council is not among the 'matters subject to consultation with the labor-management council'.[238]

Article 20 of the LMC Act regulates matters to be consulted on by the labor-management council. As paragraph 14 (other matters as to cooperation between workers and employers) of Article 20 includes consultable matters other than those stated, the realm of matters shall be estimated individually and concretely, but shall be limited to matters within the purpose and intent of the LMC Act. Accordingly, in accordance with Article 24 of the Trade Union Act, matters related to full-time union officers are matters concerning labor union activities, and consulting on the number of full-time union officers in the labor-management council is not among the 'matters subject to consultation with the labor-management council' and does not correspond to the purpose and intent of the LMC Act.

6) In establishing employee training plans and skill development, seeking a resolution from the labor-management council is required, but this does not mean that a Council resolution is necessary whenever the company implements training and education.[239]

Article 20 and Article 21 of the LMC Act stipulates matters subject to consultation and matters subject to Council resolutions. The matters subject to Council resolutions shall be items that the employer shall consult and determine in the labor-management council in advance, which is distinct from matters subject to consultation not necessarily requiring resolution. Article 21 of the LMC Act requires the employer to seek labor-management council resolution in establishing employee training plans and skill development, but this does not mean that it is necessary to seek Council resolution whenever the company implements training and education. The employer shall sincerely implement the items decided by the Council or else will be fined 10 million won or less. However, there is no penal provision in the LMC Act when the company does not take issue on matters subject to a Council resolution.

---

[238] MOEL Guidelines: Nosa-1401, on June 29, 2004.
[239] MOEL Guidelines: Nosa 68010-222, on June 23, 2001.

협의회에서 임금 등 근로조건에 관하여 합의를 하였다면 단체교섭으로 보아야 할 것이다.

5) 노조 전임자의 수에 대해 행정해석: 노사협의회에서 협의하는 것은 '행정해석: 노사협의회에서 협의할 사항'으로 볼 수 없다.[238]

근참법 제20조는 노사협의회에서 협의하여야 할 사항을 규정하고 있는바, 동조 제1항 제14호의 '기타 노사협조에 관한 사항'은 본조에 적시된 사항들 외에도 필요한 사항을 협의할 수 있음을 규정한 것으로 그 범위는 사안에 따라 개별·구체적으로 판단되어야 할 것이나 기본적으로 근참법의 목적과 취지에 벗어나지 않은 사항으로 한정된다고 할 것이다. 따라서 '노동조합 및 노동관계조정법' 제24조에 의거 노조 전임자는 노동조합 활동에 관한 사항으로 노조 전임자의 수에 대해 노사협의회에서 협의하는 것은 근참법의 목적과 취지에 부합하지 않는 것으로 '노사협의회에서 협의할 사항'으로 볼 수 없다 할 것이다.

6) 근로자의 교육훈련 및 능력개발 기본계획의 수립 시 노사협의회의 의결을 거치도록 하는 것이지 교육이나 훈련을 실시할 때마다 의결을 거쳐야 하는 것은 아니다.[239]

'근로자참여 및 협력증진에 관한 법률' 제20조 및 제21조는 노사협의회에의 협의사항 및 의결사항을 규정하고 있는바, 의결사항이라 함은 사용자가 사전에 노사협의회에서 의논하여 결정해야 하는 사항으로서 반드시 의결을 필요로 하지 않는 협의사항과 구별된다. '근로자참여 및 협력증진에 관한 법률' 제21조는 근로자의 교육훈련 및 능력개발 기본계획을 수립할 경우에 노사협의회의 의결을 거치도록 하는 것이지 교육이나 훈련을 실시하는 그때마다 의결을 거쳐야 하는 것은 아니다. 협의회에서 의결된 사항은 성실히 이행되어야 하며 그렇지 아니한 경우에는 1,000만 원 이하의 벌금이 부과될 수가 있으며, 의결사항에 대해 의결을 거치지 아니하는 것에 대한 제재규정은 마련되어 있지 않다.

---

[238] 정해석: 협력-1401, 2004.06.29
[239] 행정해석: 노사 68010-222, 2001.06.23

7) **Although a matter concerning wages was agreed on by a labor-management council, the decision cannot be effective in accordance with the LMC Act. However, if the matter was concluded as part of a collective bargaining process, it is effective as a collective agreement.**[240]

In estimating the content of the Council's meeting minutes, a certain meeting did not deal with matters subject to consultation stipulated by Article 20 of the LMC Act, but rather dealt with collective bargaining items. Accordingly, the items agreed upon are not effective according to LMC Act. However, if the agreement was concluded as a collective agreement relating to wages, it is effective as a collective agreement.

8) **Employee members of the Council do not have authority to agree to unfavorable changes to working conditions on behalf of other employees.**[241]

The labor-management council system is designed to maintain order in the industry by promoting the common interests of labor and management through joint participation and cooperation, which is distinct in purpose from a labor union. Although the company stipulates matters concerning working conditions in the matters subject to consultation, employee members of the Council who were elected by the employees do not have authority to agree to unfavorable changes to working conditions on behalf of other employees.

9) **It is null and void for a labor-management council to agree that the service period for overseas assignments will be exempted from calculation of the total service period.**[242]

The consecutive service period to calculate severance pay shall be a period from the first service date to the last day of service. Through mutual agreement in a Council, the service years of employees assigned overseas is regarded as a period included in calculations for interim severance pay and their severance pay will be calculated from the time after the adjustment period of severance pay. Even though the agreement is as effective as a collective agreement, the

---

[240] MOEL Guidelines: Nosa 32271-6506, on Apr. 17, 1986.
[241] Seoul Administrative Court ruling on Dec. 13, 2002 Guhap12519.
[242] Supreme Court ruling on July 25, 1997, 96Da22174.

7) **임금에 관련된 사항을 행정해석: 노사협의회에서 합의하였더라도 행정해석: 노사협의회법상 효력이 인정되지 않으나 임금협약으로 체결되었다면 단체협약으로서의 효력을 갖는다.**[240]

노사협의회 회의록으로 판단컨대 노사협의회는 노사협의회법 제20조에 명시되어 있는 협의사항이 아닌 단체교섭 사항을 다루었으므로 이 노사협의회에서 합의된 사항이 노사협의회법상의 효력을 발생한다고는 볼 수 없으나, 임금협약이 체결되었다면 노동조합법상 단체협약으로서의 효력을 갖는다고 볼 것이다.

8) **노사협의회의 근로자위원들에게 근로조건 불이익 변경에 관해 근로자를 대신해 동의할 권한이 있지 않다.**[241]

노사협의회는 근로자와 사용자 쌍방이 이해와 협조를 통하여 노사공동의 이익을 증진함으로써 산업평화를 도모할 것을 목적으로 하는 제도로서 노동조합과 그 제도의 취지가 다르므로 비록 회사가 근로조건에 관한 사항을 그 협의사항으로 규정하고 있다 하더라도 근로자들이 노사협의회를 구성하는 근로자위원들을 선출함에 있어 그들에게 근로조건을 불이익하게 변경함에 있어서 근로자들을 대신하여 동의를 할 권한까지 포괄적으로 위임한 것으로 볼 수 없다.

9) **해외파견 근로자들에 대하여 근속기간의 통산에 따른 이익을 사전에 포기하도록 하는 내용의 노사협의회 합의는 무효이다.**[242]

퇴직금 산정의 기초가 되는 계속근로연수는 최초 입사일 부터 최종 퇴직일까지 통산하여야 할 것인 바, 만일 중간퇴직이 무효로 인정된다면, 노사협의회에 따른 합의에 의하여 해외파견 근로자들의 퇴직금중간정산의 효력을 인정하고 최종 퇴직 시에는 중간퇴직금정산일 이후의 기간에 대해서만 퇴직금을 계산하기로 한 것은, 결국 최종 퇴직 시 발생하는 퇴직금 청구권의 일부를 사전에 포기하게 하는 것으로서 그와 같은 합의 사항이 단체협약과 동일한 효력이 있다고 하더라도 강행법규인 근로기준

---

[240] 행정해석: 노사 32271-6506, 1986.04.17
[241] 행정법원 2002.12.13 선고 2002구합12519 판결.
[242] 대법원 1997.07.25 선고 96다22174 판결.

agreement violates law the Labor Standards Act and is therefore null and void.

5. Grievance Handling

Grievances refer to individual complaints or difficulties concerning employees' working environment or working conditions. A grievance is a complaint from an individual employee, which is different from industrial disputes related to collective complaints. Compulsory procedures are established to prevent individual employee complaints from enlarging into collective complaints. They also contribute to building mutual reliability in the process of handling such grievances.

(1) Grievance handling representatives

All businesses or workplaces that ordinarily hire 30 employees or more shall have a grievance handling representatives to hear and handle workers' grievances. There shall be a maximum of three grievance handling representatives, representing labor and management, who shall be elected from the Council members by the Council in a business or a workplace where a Council is established, and shall be appointed by the employer in a business or a workplace where no Council is established. Tenure, status and treatment of grievance handling representatives are the same as those of the labor-management council.

(2) Procedures for grievance handling

If a worker has a grievance, he/she may report it to a grievance handling representative verbally or in writing. In this case, the grievance handling representative who receives such a report shall handle it without delay. When a worker takes a grievance to the grievance handling representative, he/she shall be informed of the measures taken and results thereof within ten days by the grievance handling representative. The grievance handling representative shall draw up and keep a ledger relating to the receipt and handling of grievances and keep it for one year.

법에 위반되어 무효이다.

5. 고충처리

고충이라 함은 근로자의 근로환경이나 근로조건에 관한 개별적인 불만이나 애로를 가리킨다. 고충은 개별 근로자가 가지는 불만이라는 점에서 집단성을 띠는 노동쟁의와 구별된다. 이처럼 고충처리절차의 설치를 의무화한 취지는 근로자 개인의 고충이라 하더라도 불만이 누적되면 분쟁화 될 가능성이 있으므로 이것을 미연에 방지하고, 또한, 고충처리 과정에서 노사 간의 신뢰가 조성되기를 기대하는 것이라 할 수 있다.

(1) 고충처리위원

상시 30인 이상의 근로자를 사용하는 모든 사업(장)에는 고충처리위원을 두도록 하고 있는데, 이들은 근로자의 고충을 청취하고 이를 처리하는 기능을 한다. 위원의 수는 3인 이내로 하되, 노사협의회 설치 사업장에서는 협의회가 그 위원 가운데 고충처리위원을 선임하고, 노사협의회가 없는 사업장인 경우에는 사용자가 고충처리위원을 위촉토록 한다. 고충처리위원의 임기·신분·처우는 노사협의회 위원에 관한 것과 동일하다.

(2) 고충처리절차

고충처리는 근로자가 고충을 고충처리위원에게 구두 또는 서면으로 신고함으로써 개시된다. 고충을 청취한 고충처리위원은 지체 없이 이를 처리하여야 하고, 접수한 날로부터 10일 이내에 조치사항 기타 처리결과를 당해 근로자에게 통보하여야 한다. 고충처리위원은 고충사항의 접수 및 그 처리에 관한 대장을 작성·비치하고 이를 1년간 보존하여야 한다.

⟨Appendix⟩ Introduction to the 'Labor Inspection Checklist' in the 'Labor Law App'

KangNam Labor Law Firm has added a "Labor Inspection Checklist" feature to the mobile Labor Law App, allowing users to check and evaluate compliance with labor relations laws online. When accessing the Labor Law App, users can navigate to the "Labor Inspection Checklist," which contains the same content as the "Self-Diagnosis Checklist for Compliance with Labor Relations Laws" used by the Ministry of Employment and Labor. Through this app's "Labor Inspection Checklist," HR managers can assess whether their company is properly complying with labor relations laws and receive a clearly organized report in writing on areas that need improvement.

We hope that the readers of this book will make extensive use of the "Labor Inspection Checklist" in the Labor Law App to evaluate their company's compliance with labor relations laws and effectively address any deficiencies.

⟨Introduction to the 'Labor Inspection Checklist' in the Labor Law App⟩

Welcome to the Self-Assessment Checklist for Labor Inspections. Labor inspectors visit workplaces on a regular basis to inspect whether companies are complying with the legal requirements of the Labor Standards Act. If violations are found during the inspection, companies are either penalized or issued correction orders. Therefore, properly preparing for a labor inspection has become essential for HR and labor managers.

What follows is a self-assessment checklist for you to accurately determine whether your company is in compliance with the Labor Standards Act. It involves 140 questions in a total of 16 areas. Specific explanations about how to prepare against violations being identified during the labor inspection will be of considerable help.

We estimate you will need about 30 minutes to answer the 140 questions in 16 areas. You will mark your answers as Compliant, Incomplete, or Non-compliant. The results can be emailed to you directly or you can print them out.

〈부록〉
'노동법 앱'의 '근로감독 체크리스트 소개

강남노무법인은 모바일 노동법 앱에 '근로감독 체크리스트' 기능을 추가하여 온라인으로 노사관계법령 준수 여부를 확인하고 평가하고 있다. 노동법 앱에 접속하면 고용노동부가 사용하고 있는 '근로감독 자가진단'과 동일한 내용의 '근로감독 체크리스트'에 접속할 수 있다. 이 앱의 '근로감독 체크리스트'를 통해서 회사의 인사담당자는 회사가 노동관계법령을 제대로 준수하고 있는지 여부를 판단할 수 있고, 개선해야 할 부분에 대해서는 일목요연하게 정리된 내용을 서면으로 받아 볼 수 있다.

이 책의 독자들이 노동법 앱의 '근로감독 체크리스트'를 많이 이용하여 회사의 노동관계법령의 준수 여부를 평가하고 부족한 부분을 개선하는데 많이 활용했으면 한다.

〈'근로감독 체크리스트' 안내 글〉

근로감독 자기진단 체크리스트에 찾아 주셔서 감사드립니다. 근로감독은 근로감독관이 주기적으로 기업을 방문하여 근로기준법 준수 여부를 감독하는 것입니다. 근로감독관이 사업장을 점검하면서 위반된 사항을 발견 시에는 시정지시 또는 처벌을 하고 있습니다. 따라서 근로감독에 대비한 기업체의 준비는 인사 노무 담당자들의 필수 업무가 되고 있습니다.

여기 자기진단 체크리스트 총 16개의 분야에 대해 135개의 질문을 통해서 기업의 근로기준법 준비 여부를 정확히 파악할 수 있습니다. 또한 위반된 내용에 대해 구체적인 준비 내용을 설명해 줌으로써 실제 근로감독 준비를 제대로 갖추도록 도와드리고 있습니다.

16개 분야 135문제를 답하는데 약 30분 정도 소요가 됩니다. 여러분들이 해당 질문에 대한 답변을 준수, 미흡, 미준수로 표시하고 있습니다. 그 결과물은 여러분들이 직접 이메일로 받거나 출력하실 수 있습니다.

Chapter2. Checklist for Labor Inspections

❶ Written Statement of Working Conditions

❷ Preservation of Employee Registers and Contract Documents

❸ Payment of Various Money and Goods such as Wages

❹ Violation of limits on working hours and overtime

❺ Granting recess hours

❻ Paid holidays

❼ Annual paid leave

❽ Children and Maternity Protection

❾ Rules of Employment

❿ Payment of retirement benefits

⓫ Prevention of workplace harassment

⓬ Observation of minimum wage

⓭ Prevention of sexual harassment in the workplace

⓮ Prohibition of Sex Discrimination in Employment

⓯ Prohibition of discrimination against non-regular workers

⓰ Establishment of labor-management council

If the results of your self-assessment show a lot of Incomplete or Non-compliant issues, we highly recommend contacting us at Kangnam Labor Law Firm for consultation on properly rectifying the situation.

I hope you find your self-assessment useful and informative.

❶ 근로조건 서면명시
❷ 근로자 명부 및 계약서류 보존
❸ 임금 등 각종 금품 지급
❹ 근로시간 및 연장근로 한도 위반
❺ 휴게시간 부여
❻ 유급휴일 부여
❼ 연차유급휴가 부여
❽ 연소자와 모성보호
❾ 취업규칙
❿ 퇴직급여 지급
⓫ 직장 내 괴롭힘 예방
⓬ 최저임금 준수
⓭ 직장 내 성희롱 예방
⓮ 고용상 성차별 금지
⓯ 비정규직 차별 금지
⓰ 노사협의회 설치

여기서 진단결과가 평균적으로 미흡이나 미준수 내용이 많게 되면, 강남노무법인에 노무 컨설팅을 의뢰하시여 제대로 준비하시는 것을 적극 권장해 드립니다.

그럼, 유익한 근로감독 자기진단이 되시길 바랍니다.

Labor Inspection Manual
근로감독 매뉴얼

발 행 일 : 2024년 8월 10일 초판발행

지 은 이 : 정봉수, 안태욱

펴 낸 이 : 정 봉 수

펴 낸 곳 : 강남노무법인 출판부 (K-Labor Press)

편집·디자인 : 정 영 철

주   소 : 서울시 강남구 대치동 테헤란로 406 A-1501 (대치동, 샹제리제센터)

전   화 : 02-539-0098

팩   스 : 02-539-4167

홈페이지 : www.k-labor.com

출판등록 : 강남, 바00177

I S B N : 979-11-85290-29-4

정   가 : 30,000원

■ 이 책자는 저작권법에 따라 보호받는 저작물이므로 무단전재와 복제를 금합니다.